Austin Phelps, Lowell Mason

The New Sabbath Hymn and tune Book for the Service of Song in the House of the Lord

Austin Phelps, Lowell Mason

The New Sabbath Hymn and tune Book for the Service of Song in the House of the Lord

ISBN/EAN: 9783743325258

Manufactured in Europe, USA, Canada, Australia, Japa

Cover: Foto ©Lupo / pixelio.de

Manufactured and distributed by brebook publishing software (www.brebook.com)

Austin Phelps, Lowell Mason

The New Sabbath Hymn and tune Book for the Service of Song in the House of the Lord

THE NEW SABBATH HYMN AND TUNE BOOK,

FOR

THE SERVICE OF SONG IN THE HOUSE OF THE LORD.

~~~~~~~~~~

PUBLISHED BY
HAMERSLEY & CO.,
PUBLISHERS, BOOKSELLERS, IMPORTERS, STATIONERS,
HARTFORD:

PREFACE TO THE NEW SABBATH HYMN AND TUNE BOOK.

The New Sabbath Hymn and Tune Book differs from the earlier edition only in its tunes. In these, changes have been made in two respects—alterations of tunes have in several cases been discarded and the more familiar forms restored; and many tunes which the present state of the popular taste demands have been substituted for such as are contained in the original edition. Both editions will henceforth be published. Those who desire the edition containing the above changes should be careful to order "The New Sabbath Hymn and Tune Book; those who wish for the earlier edition should order "The Sabbath Hymn and Tune Book."

Attention is asked to the Preface of the first edition.

Experience and observation have confirmed the confidence of the musical editor in the principles there set forth, and followed in the selections of that edition, respecting the true theory of congregational singing, and the character of the tunes best adapted to its culture. He still confidently believes that the best results can be attained only where a congregation are willing to confine themselves to very simple forms of rhythm and melody.

That the Christian public, to a considerable extent, approve a book constructed on those principles, is sufficiently indicated by a sale of the Sabbath Hymn and Tune Book much larger than that of any other book of the kind.

Yet there are many who do not accept these principles, but who desire a wider latitude in the selection of tunes. They regard, as the true test of selection, the degree in which any tune has the favorable testimony of the popular taste. From this class of worshipers the request has frequently come that a new edition of the Sabbath Hymn and Tune Book should be prepared.

As the former edition will continue to be published, unaltered, the editors have felt themselves at liberty to meet the want above indicated. Such is the design of the present volume.

In the selection of its tunes the attempt has been carefully made to collect those which have been widely popular and attractive, and therefore have been used extensively in congregational singing.

The aim has been to make this collection choice and complete. Persons in different parts of the country have been consulted. Thanks are due to many who have contributed the results of their experience to this work.

As the fruit of such inquiry, the present edition is presented, with confidence that it will meet the wishes of those who desire tunes which are familiar in general use in the churches, and approved by the popular taste.

Several popular hymns have become associated with peculiar tunes which are not adapted to any other hymns. These will be found in the Appendix; the same hymns being also in the body of the book, in connection with other tunes.

September, 1864.

Entered, according to Act of Congress, in the year 1859, by
MASON BROTHERS,
In the Clerk's Office of the District Court for the Southern District of New York.

Entered, according to Act of Congress, in the year 1866, by
MASON BROTHERS,
In the Clerk's Office of the District Court for the Southern District of New York.

PREFACE TO THE SABBATH HYMN AND TUNE BOOK.

It is the purpose of this work to furnish suitable tunes for the hymns in "THE SABBATH HYMN BOOK," and to bring the hymns and tunes together, so that both may be easily seen at the same opening of the volume. The tunes are designed to meet the capacity and wants of congregations, though it is hoped they will be found to possess interest and appropriateness for choirs. Every hymn contained in the SABBATH HYMN BOOK will be found here, and in connection with each hymn, or at the same opening of the book, one or more appropriate tunes. All the tunes are also published in a separate volume, entitled the SABBATH TUNE BOOK. The series therefore consists of three volumes:—

THE SABBATH HYMN BOOK, containing Hymns alone.
THE SABBATH HYMN AND TUNE BOOK, containing Hymns and Tunes.
THE SABBATH TUNE BOOK, containing Tunes alone.

Two principal methods have prevailed, to a greater or less degree, in the Service of Song in Christian worship; that of the *whole Congregation*, and that of a *select Choir*. The Congregational was the primitive method, and the only one known in the earlier history of the Church. The method of singing by a choir came into the Church at a later period, with wealth, power, and worldly greatness, and it has been her attendant rather in temporal prosperity, than in poverty and adversity.

At the time of the Reformation, Congregational Singing had become extinct, and the more artistic manner of Choirs, consisting mostly of an inferior order of the clergy, singing in a language unknown to the people, had taken its place. Luther, Calvin, Knox, and others, took early measures to rescue the singing service in public worship from the hands of the clergy, and to reinstate it as an exercise for the people. As the abuses of the Romish church had led to the rejection of chanting (the primitive form of Church Song) the Psalms were translated, or hymns were written in a stanzaic form, and adapted to a simple but dignified form of melody, with special reference to the capabilities of the people. The union of the whole assembly in the exercise was regarded as essential. Other liturgical forms were rejected; but this new one of a metrical Psalmody, for the people's simultaneous utterance of praise and prayer, was received with great favor, and almost universally practiced. It was no attempt on the part of the Reformers to introduce an artistic manner of song, but, on the contrary, a very plain one, a "highway" of Psalmody, in which "the wayfaring man, though a fool, should not err."

The Congregational method, thus restored to the churches, was brought to this country by the Protestant Fathers. It continued to be their only method for about a century and a half. It is not surprising that during this period, amidst the deprivations which the new settlements experienced, attention to song should have been neglected, nor that, neglected by generation after generation, the ability for it should have been well nigh lost. In the early part of the last century the very low condition of the singing in public worship began to attract the attention of some of the friends of religion, and measures were taken by a few of the leading clergymen and others for reform. Hitherto all the singing in the American churches had been unisonous, the melody only having been sung; but in 1720 a book of tunes, in three parts, "Cantus," "Medius" and "Basus," was published by Rev. Thomas Walter. The harmonizing of the tunes in parts undoubtedly grew out of the fact that the more elaborate service of choirs had always taken that form both in the Lutheran and the English church. In the Protestant churches of Europe generally, metrical Psalmody continues to this day to be sung, as it was originally, in unison, and it is at least doubtful whether parts in harmony for the choir and unison for the congregation, would not still be the best arrangement for Church Song. This new arrangement of tunes in parts led to the formation of choirs. At first, they were introduced only as helps to Congregational Singing, but this gradually yielded, as it had done before, and the new method advanced with sure and steady progress, until toward the close of the last century it had become the almost exclusive method of Church Song.

And now, within ten or fifteen years, Congregational singing is again attracting attention, and many persons, especially those who look for a higher religious power in Psalmody, are turning to it, as a remedy for the evils which have grown out of the exclusive method of choirs, and as promising to restore to the Church the almost lost religious aid of song. It is to be regretted that some, in their zeal for Congregational singing, have supposed it necessary to set their faces against choirs, and have even gone so far as to reject the services of such associations. The fact that choirs have, in a great degree, failed to present a method of song truly religious in its influence, is not to be attributed wholly to them; but probably quite as much to those clergymen and people who have mistaken a mere musical excitement for the "quickening and raising up of the affections to God."

PREFACE.

That it is unsafe to depend exclusively upon choirs, is abundantly proved in the history of the Church. The great danger of such a dependence is, that the whole service will degenerate into a mere attempt at musical display. Nor is it safe to trust to the Congregational method alone, for without constant care, the singing will then be very liable to fall into neglect, and become uninteresting, ineffective, and even wearisome. Let the two methods exist together, strengthening one another. Congregational Singing can not be dispensed with by those who seek for the religious influence of Church song; and choirs may do much to promote the true service of Psalmody, by their guidance and encouragement of universal song. Whenever it is practicable, then, let the people who are desirous of Congregational singing avail themselves of the advantages to be derived from such choirs as, formed from among themselves, and disposed to exert a religious influence in the singing exercises, will enlist the sympathy and cooperation of all the people.

But that the present efforts for Congregational Singing, or that any efforts for the improvement of the Service of Song be in any satisfactory degree successful, we regard it as essential that both methods be *practically understood*—at least by those who guide this service—since any attempt to build up the one on the basis of the other must, necessarily, in a great degree fail. Those who seek for Congregational Singing on the principles of Choir Singing, will probably soon give it up as impracticable, and return again to the Choir Singing as the only available method.

The Congregational is *nature's* method of praise. It is, in a great degree, independent of art culture, being indeed above art. It is adapted alike to the voices of the young and the old, of the uncultivated and of the cultivated. It engages all in the simultaneous exercise of the same emotions, furnishes something for every one to do, admits of no listeners, and thus excludes that bane of all true worship, criticism. As individual voices are lost in the chorus of the many, one is naturally led to feel his own insignificance. The essential feature of Chorus Singing, the blending of voices, by which the impurity of individual tones is neutralized, and dissonance harmonized, and in which consists in a great degree its strength and its beauty, is obtained almost without effort when many voices, (even fifty or a hundred,) join in one melody. It is adapted to awaken within us ideas of greatness. It belongs to the sublime in tone; the sublime in nature rather than in art. It may be compared to the mountains, which owe their majesty, not to their fertile soil, nor to any elaboration of architectural skill, but to that Power which commanded the light to shine out of darkness, and brought up from the depths the rough and diversified materials in which consists the "strength of the hills." The mountains are not more necessary to fit the earth to be the habitation of man than is this great method of song to the highest development of that religious life which is perfected through Psalmody.

Choir Singing is the method of *art*; and although for the common purposes of Church Song no very high degree of artistic attainment is required, yet, that Choir Singing which is worthy of the name, must be the result of the proper training of a suitable number of persons who have a more than ordinary portion of intuitive musical ability. It belongs to the beautiful. It depends upon flowing melody, with measure symmetrical, in such soft, elegant, and delicate style as to awaken delight. It may be regarded as one of Zion's "beautiful garments," so that in the proper union of the two methods, it may be said of the Service of Song, "strength and beauty are in the sanctuary."

That we may, if possible, throw still further light upon a subject which we consider of vital importance to the success of Church Song, we will mention some conditions which are indispensable to Choir Singing, but not to Congregational Singing.

1. It is not indispensable, though it is desirable, in order to qualify one to take a part in Congregational Singing, that one should be able to read written music. Let properly conducted singing schools be maintained, and let all be encouraged to attend them; and especially let all children receive, while they are yet young, appropriate vocal training, and be practically taught the elements both of music and notation. And let all be encouraged, whether they have learned any thing of singing or not, to join vocally in the Psalmody *as a religious exercise*, regarding it as their duty and privilege.

2. Purity of tone is not indispensable, though it is desirable, to qualify one to unite in Congregational Singing. Although one's tone may be of a nasal or guttural quality, he is not to be denied the privilege of singing his Maker's praises in the congregation of the people. Yet it may often be the duty of others to exercise forbearance, and to do whatever circumstances allow for the removal of the cause of offense by suitable attempts at cultivation. And it is possible that there may be cases where it may be the duty of one to engage only mentally in the exercise, if thereby one may cease to give pain to another.

3. It is not indispensable, though it is desirable, that one should be able to sing in perfect tune, in order that he may join the Congregational Psalmody. There are very few persons whose intonation is not more or less faulty, but although one may not sing, individually, in tune, there is a "sympathy in sounds" by which, when a multitude sing together, dissonance is resolved, and voices are drawn into unison.

4. It is not indispensable, though it is desirable, that one should be able to appreciate the divisions of time, or, as it is more commonly expressed, to *keep time*, in order to engage in Congregational Singing. If such a natural, easy movement is taken as is alone well adapted to the singing of a promiscuous assembly, there will be no difficulty in *keeping together*, and however feeble may be one's perception of a regular movement, he may safely trust his voice with the voices of the many.

PREFACE.

5. It is not indispensable, though it is desirable, in order to unite in Congregational Singing, that one's articulation or pronunciation should be exactly right. The words are, indeed, of the utmost importance, the indispensable part of a hymnal service, and although we may join devotionally in the act of worship in song, even when we do not know the particular subject of the hymn, as where the service is in a foreign language, yet we can not be in union with the assembly in definite thought and emotion unless we are in possession of the words. Still, no one should be excluded from Congregational Singing on account of an inaccurate articulation, whether this arise from a natural defect in the organs of speech, or from want of proper culture.

6. Artistic application of the laws of accent, emphasis, and general expression, is not indispensable, though it is important, to qualify one to join in Congregational Singing. There should indeed be appropriate expression; but this in one method is quite a different thing from what it is in the other. The expression of the mountain is not more unlike that of the valley, than the legitimate expression of Congregational Singing is unlike that of Choir Song. Let the singing be habitually regarded as a truly religious act; let the people, old and young, be led to engage in it as such; let this one point be taught and guarded from the pulpit; let God be sought habitually and found in the Psalm, and it will not lack a suitable expression; one consisting not so much in the mechanical observance of piano, forte, crescendo, diminuendo, or any dynamic notation, as in the more legitimate conditions of a good tonal utterance. Let the mouth speak "out of the abundance of the heart," and it will be likely to be done with much more propriety than any utterance, however perfect, which arises from the mere observance of rules of art.

As two principal *methods of singing* have prevailed in the service of the Christian Church, so three distinct *forms of song* have arisen; THE CHANT, THE ANTHEM, THE METRICAL TUNE.

The CHANT is supposed to have been the primitive form of Church Song; the same in which the Saviour himself engaged, when, after he had instituted the Sacrament of the Lord's Supper, he sung a hymn with his disciples, before he went out into the Mount of Olives. In its simple state it consists in the intoned recitation, or cantilated delivery of the words of the Psalm, being the nearest approach to an impassioned and dignified reading, which a retained pitch, or the absence of inflection will allow. In chanting, the Psalms may be sung in the very words of the sacred Scriptures, the highest form of lyric poetry; metrical arrangement being unnecessary. The Chant is adapted to a clear enunciation of the words, and thus tends to make music subordinate to thought, and song to religious worship. It is totally dissimilar to all the forms of secular music, and seems to preclude the very idea of display. It leaves the mind open to the full impression of the sacred text, and is most favorable to a heartfelt expression. It furnishes the most simple form in which many voices may unite in a simultaneous utterance of words, and hence, is admirably adapted to the Congregational method, to which it properly belongs. Children easily acquire it, and take great delight in it; and it is a most interesting form of worship in Sabbath Schools, as we have tested by long experience.

These remarks, however, are applicable to Chanting in its primitive use, and not to such a hurried, "confused and disorderly chattering of the words," or to such a "careless, irreverent manner, without a spark of feeling," as, an English writer observes, is often heard in cathedrals; or to such abuses as have grown out of the modern double and florid chants, and from which Chanting has well nigh ceased to be regarded as belonging to the Congregational method.

The word ANTHEM is supposed to be derived from the same Greek root as is *antiphony*, which signifies the alternate or responsive manner of singing said to have been introduced into the Western churches by Ambrose, in the fourth century. Choir singing probably had its origin in antiphonal singing, and hence come Anthems. This form was retained by the English church at the time of the Reformation, though generally rejected elsewhere. In its primitive use it was exclusively by choirs, yet in a simple form it is quite practicable in Congregational Singing, and may be made a feature of much interest and usefulness.

The METRICAL TUNE is that form which, although known to a limited extent in earlier times, came into general use in public worship, at the time of the Reformation, and has ever since been retained in the Protestant, and in a portion of the Romish church. It was the musical form of the restored method of song, in which the people were the actors, and consisted in a simple melody, which, being within the compass of all voices, was sung in unison by the congregation. In the German and other churches on the continent of Europe, the original character of Congregational Tunes and of Congregational Singing still continues, and almost universally prevails to this day. But in England the influence of choirs soon led to the introduction of the different vocal parts, which, although at first not intended for the people, were gradually introduced into Congregational Singing, though seldom, if ever, in such proportion as to produce any thing like symmetrical harmony.

THE SABBATH HYMN AND TUNE BOOK is designed as a Manual for Congregational Singing. In regard to the principles which have guided its editors in the selection of hymns, the reader is referred to the Preface to THE SABBATH HYMN BOOK. In setting the hymns to music, we have valued musical art, only so far as it might be made to contribute to the *religious* purpose in view. Music is employed as a means and not as an end. Our constant object has therefore been to provide for the best *religious expression of the* words.

The aim has been to secure tunes of not merely negative, but of positive merit—tunes possessing such salient points as are at once marked and relevant, with such agreeableness of melody, and individuality of character as shall cause them to be apprehended, **quickly** learned, easily sung, **always remembered**. Tunes free from all such difficulties as would **render** them impracticable to the musically unlearned, and possessing such peculiar excellences **as will** render them attractive **to all**. Nor has it been forgotten that the tunes, generally, **are** to be sung not only in the larger assembly of public worship (to which some of them more properly belong), but **also** in social worship, where, often without much musical ability, **Christians pray** to God, and "admonish **one another in psalms and hymns and spiritual songs**."

It is evident that in preparing a book **like** the present the most obvious musical material is to be found in the *well-known tunes* which are commonly used. It was an important object to secure as complete a collection of these as possible. A circular letter of inquiry was therefore addressed to clergymen and those having charge of church music in various parts of the country. Lists of tunes actually in use were thus obtained, all of which were carefully compared and collated, and from them an index was formed, showing what tunes are most used, and what is the degree of their popularity. This index has been employed as a guide in selecting tunes. As many of these tunes are copyright property, it may be well to add that the editors have been able to insert every tune which they desired, a privilege not often enjoyed by the compilers of similar works. Yet notwithstanding all our care and facilities it is quite probable that some persons will miss in this collection tunes which are to them favorites. There are tunes which have become popular in certain localities, but which are not so generally known or of such intrinsic merit, as to claim a place in a collection like this. In the nature of things it is probable that hardly **any** man will find in any such book, every tune which he would be glad to have inserted.

We have, of course, felt obliged sometimes **to** sacrifice our own taste to what has appeared to be a public demand, and to admit tunes which **we regard as** having structural defects as tunes for Congregational Singing.

The *repetition* of well-known and **most** useful tunes **is** a new feature in **this** book. There are a few tunes which are very widely known and constantly used. If one of these be presented in but one place, it can be in connection with but few hymns, and therefore will not be frequently sung. Such tunes are repeated in this volume, **some** of them several times, and each of them is therefore in connection with a large number of hymns.

The SABBATH HYMN AND TUNE BOOK contains many *New Tunes*, or such, be **they old or new**, as are not generally known in our churches. These are needed not merely for the **sake of variety**, though this might be a sufficient reason for their introduction. There are hymns **of new meters** which must be supplied with Tunes; and there are in some hymns of the more usual **meters**, peculiarities of stanzaic form, which, in singing, require tunes of corresponding rhythmic **or melodic** structure. There are also hymns presenting such new experiences of Christian life, as can **hardly** find an appropriate musical expression in any of the older melodies. That the new tunes **open a** wider field of musical expression, we believe will be readily granted, as new hymns to **new tunes** become familiar in religious worship. We should be very sorry to have the *good* old tunes superseded—the Old Hundredths and the Dundees should be retained, often sung, and handed down, well known and familiar, from generation to generation; but yet there is not only room, but a real demand, for tunes which are **new**. This department **of our** work has been enriched by selections from a very wide range of tunes of all denominations **of** Christians, in different ages and countries. The new tunes have different degrees of merit, yet **all of them** may contribute to the appropriateness and variety of worship in song.

The large supply of *Double Tunes* may be regarded as a new feature **in** our work. The importance of Double tunes consists in the fact that such hymns as contain six or more stanzas, often take up too much time when sung through, and that a time six times repeated may, to those persons whose minds are not intensely fixed upon the hymn service, become 'tiresome. Almost all these Double tunes are intended to move quickly, and when properly sung, will be to some extent a remedy for that slow manner of singing which Dr. Watts condemned, and will prevent the necessity for that frequent abridgment of hymns which weakens the religious effect of the singing exercise.

The SABBATH HYMN AND TUNE BOOK provides an increased **number of** *Minor Tunes*. **The necessity** for these, which have been of late much neglected, arises **out of man's emotional nature. If** there are seasons of sunshine in Christian life, there are also those **of clouds and darkness**. As, on the one hand, there is in every high religious experience a fullness **of joy which can find a suitable utterance** only in the most jubilant strains which musical genius **has ever conceived, so, on the** other, there is a heart-felt sorrow so deep **as** to be far beyond the **expression of any** but the more tender accents, the wailings (it may be) of minor strains. But without going to extremes, it may in truth be said of the Major and Minor in music, that the common experiences of Christian life seem to require, perhaps equally, the animating and invigorating strains of the one, and the tenderly sympathizing and plaintive influences of the other. The educational power of music must be much abridged, if it be confined to the Major mode. Still, as some choirs and congregations are unaccustomed to Minor tunes, they will generally find, opposite to the Minor, and at the same opening of the book, a tune in the Major mode, applicable in some degree to the same hymns which can be most appropriately sung with the Minor tune.

PREFACE. vii

In our adaptation of Minor tunes to hymns, we have not been unmindful of the fact that the propriety of this depends not only upon the emotional character of the words, but also upon times and seasons, and we have sometimes followed the beautiful example of the Episcopal church, which, in the time of her lenten fastings, sings her jubilant canticles in plaintive Minor strains.

The rhythmic form, which is regarded as, in general, the best for metrical tunes, especially for such as are designed for the simultaneous song of many people, is that which, with the exception of the initial and terminal of each line or couplet, consists mostly in tones of equal length. Examples of tunes in this form are on pages 17, 18, 19, 20, 22, 26, 27. "This," says Rev. Mr. Havergal of Worcester, England, "is generally the old form, the traditional form, and the only one which all singers feel to be natural." In this form the older tunes were formerly printed, both in England and in this country, so that in reprinting "The Old Hundredth," "Dundee," and other tunes, as we have done in this work, we do not *alter them from but restore them to* the original. After much observation and practical experience we are fully persuaded that this form furnishes the best movement for metrical Psalms and Hymns. The longer initials and terminals enable all the people to begin and to close **the** line together, and also afford a moment for rest at the end of each line, while the intermediate **shorter** tones are most favorable to the simultaneous utterance of each word and syllable as with **one voice**. But the greatest advantage, perhaps, is that it enables a choir or congregation to sing **together in a** quicker movement than any other, yet is **at** the same time conducive to that simple **strength and** dignity which should ever characterize **the** union of many voices in sacred song.

That we may not be mistaken as to what we mean by quicker movement, we will add that "The Old Hundredth" has been often sung so slowly as to occupy a minute and a half, or even more, in its performance, whereas we suppose, that if sung in its original time, it would not take more than from forty to fifty seconds. The time of this tune, and indeed of all tunes in this rhythmic form, may be learned by using a pendulum of from thirty-five to forty-five inches in length, each beat of which will give the time of one of the intermediate or shorter tones. We do not mean that all these tunes are to be sung, or that any one tune is always to be sung in exactly the same time; there will naturally be a slight variation, depending upon the hymn, and the circumstances of the occasion. We deem it important, however, to remark that there should never be any apparent change of time, during the singing of a hymn; but one movement should be preserved throughout all the stanzas, however they may appear to differ.

A second rhythmic form, one which has become very popular **within the last** twenty-five or thirty years, consists of tones mostly of two lengths, as before, but in alternate groups of two. The tunes Hebron, Denfield, Downs, Boylston, afford specimens of this rhythm. A pendulum of from thirty to forty inches will give the time for the shorter tones in these tunes. It is most important in this class of tunes, that every approach to *staccato* in the short tones be carefully avoided; on the contrary, they should usually be sung quite *legato*, and sustained to their full length. On the other hand, the longer tones must not be too long. Indeed, there may be a little accommodation between the two, **so** that the shorter tones may be, as it were, a little longer, and the longer tones a little shorter, than the exact time indicated by the notes, but this must be done without breaking up a proper distinction between the two, or disturbing the general choriambic character.

A third rhythmic form consists of tones of two lengths as before, but mostly in groups of four. The tunes Uxbridge and Olden illustrate this form. A pendulum of from thirty to thirty-six inches will give the time. The remark in **respect to** the accommodation between the tones of different lengths applies also to this rhythm.

A fourth class includes tunes **in** which the longer and shorter tones regularly alternate; Ortonville, Ray, Rayford, Anley, and many other tunes belong to this class. A pendulum, from sixteen to twenty-four inches, will give the time of quarter notes in these tunes. A somewhat modified form of this general rhythmic structure may be seen in the tunes Becker, Albon, Ware, Albec, and others. These tunes, on account of the prevalence of the shorter tones, require a somewhat slower movement, as indicated by a pendulum of from twenty to twenty-six inches. Again, another modification of the form may be found in such tunes as Bethany and Glyn, which, because of the prevalence of the longer tones, require a somewhat quicker movement, as of a pendulum of ten or twelve inches in length.

Each of the foregoing classes, with slight exceptions, is adapted to a syllabic utterance, or the singing of a single tone to each syllable. The last is, perhaps, somewhat less adapted to Congregational Singing.

A fifth rhythmic form includes tunes in equal (double or quadruple) measure, embracing a greater variety in the length of tones, brought together with less regard to the symmetrical relation of length, and containing syncopes, suspensions, etc. See Duke Street, Federal Street, Lanesboro', Ernan, Hamburg, Lyte, Ward, Dedham, Medfield.

Tunes in unequal (triple or sextuple) measure, but in other respects similar to class five, may be **brought together** as the last rhythmic class which we need to present. Illustrative of this class, **are Howard, St.** Martins, Rothwell, Abridge, Mendon, All Saints, Thatcher. A pendulum of from **twenty-five to thirty** inches will indicate the time of the quarter notes in the last two varieties.

There may be a few tunes which can hardly be assigned to either of the above classes, but in regard to all, whatever may be the movement, sufficient time must always be taken to speak the **words with propriety, for nothing** merely musical can justify a movement, be it quick or slow, **which shall interfere with an** appropriate delivery of the words.

The *Adaptation of Tunes to Hymns* is a department of our labor upon which most careful con-

PREFACE.

sideration has been bestowed, in the belief that it is of great importance to the usefulness of religious song. This has, indeed, been by far the most difficult department of labor in the preparation of this volume. A good hymn may be sung to a good tune, and the two together form an unsatisfactory whole. One may prove a detriment rather than an assistance to the other. The mere metrical fitness of one for the other, though necessary, is a simple, and the very lowest consideration. The music must be suitable to express the emotion which the words describe or imply. A first question then is, what is the emotional condition which the hymn supposes? A second question is, what strains will best assist the expression of this emotion? Is the hymn one of worship, or is it merely didactic, hortatory, or descriptive? Does it imply direct or immediate homage, or only that which is indirect or mediate? These questions have been minutely considered at every step.

Our experience has led us to reject all such aids to musical expression as the marginal marks found in some books of psalmody. We are satisfied of the injurious effects of such notation. It encourages, almost necessitates, a dramatic spirit in singing, which is wholly at variance with the spirit of worship.

Careful attention has also been given to such peculiarities of rhythmical and poetical structure as are found in some of the hymns. Instances may be cited in hymns 8, 292, 298, 339, 357, 471, 556, 718, 1004, 1092, 1267, and many others.

It has been supposed that it would be interesting, where it could be done without detriment in other respects, to set the old versions of the Psalms to corresponding old tunes sung also in early times. Instances in which this has been done are in hymns 13, 31, 32, 46, 49, 65, 220, 230, 243, 336.

There will generally be found at each opening of the book two tunes, either of which is adapted to all the hymns upon the two pages. Commonly one of these is a well-known tune; and the other, one which is less familiar, or entirely new. This arrangement has also enabled us, where we have felt compelled, in deference to its popularity, to insert a tune which we can not regard as free from serious defects, to give in connection with the same hymns a tune of better structure. Care has also been taken to preserve, as far as possible, established associations between hymns and tunes.

The hymns in this book are not arranged in numerical order as in the Sabbath Hymn Book. From the plan of the work, it was impossible that this should be done without sacrificing the proper adaptation of tunes to hymns. Yet it was deemed of great importance, for convenience in using the two books in the same congregation, that the hymns should be numbered alike in both books. It is supposed that the clergyman will always find it most convenient to use "The Sabbath Hymn Book" in selecting his hymns, because of its topical arrangement. When both books are used in the same congregation, it being understood that in the announcement of the page, reference is always made to "The Sabbath Hymn and Tune Book," the hymn may be given out thus: "71st Hymn; 42d page." Those who have only the *Hymn Book* will then turn immediately to the *hymn* by its number, while those who have the *Hymn and Tune Book*, will find it with equal ease by the page.

The *Chants* contained in THE SABBATH HYMN AND TUNE BOOK, are mostly those of the best English composers, and the few new ones are upon the same primitive Anglican model.

A new feature, at least in this country, in a book for Congregational singing, is the introduction of short, easy *Anthems*. The words of these are mostly from the Psalms, and are peculiarly appropriate to the various occasions of public worship. The music is easy, and quite practicable to congregations which are willing to make a little effort to learn it. They will be found useful for choirs as well as congregations.

The Anthem, No. 14, may derive some interest from the fact that it has been supposed to be an ancient Hebrew melody, and substantially the same as was used in the Temple worship.

Two of the Indexes in this volume refer to the number of the hymns, and not to the pages. The pages will be easily ascertained by reference to the table on page II. It was found that the attempt to include in each case in these indexes a references to the *page*, as well as the *number* of the hymn, besides occupying a very large amount of space, would confuse the mind, and be inconvenient in many respects.

As we have already remarked, Congregational singing may be led by a Choir. It may be led by a Precentor; yet he, if he is truly interested in his work, and if he sustain a proper relation to the congregation, would almost immediately gather around him a few aiding voices. In either case the accompaniment of an Organ, Organ Harmonium, or Melodeon, will be important. The choir, who lead, must be content to sing in a plain, simple manner, without any attempt at artistic effect. They should avoid every thing which tends to confuse the congregation or to discourage the general participation in the song; and they should furnish a full volume of sound with which the people can readily unite. It is better that all should sing the melody, at least until the congregation become very thoroughly acquainted with it, and, under all circumstances, it is important that this part should be well sustained by men's voices. The singing of the four different parts is in fact singing four different tunes, and this causes confusion to those who have made little musical proficiency. These remarks may apply, also, in part at least, to the manner of playing the organ, which should have for its constant object the assisting of the people, all the people, in their song, and should avoid every thing having a tendency to mislead or confuse them.

Tunes should be used with which the congregation are familiar. New tunes may be introduced, one at a time, with more or less frequency, according to the facility with which the people learn them. The same tunes should be frequently repeated, since familiarity with the tune is necessary to any high degree of religious influence in the singing exercise. It is not an uncommon thing, in the German congregations, to hear the same tune to two hymns during the same service.

PREFACE.

It is important that *every one* in the congregation make, and continue, the effort to unite in the singing. If a man utter no sound which can be heard even by the person at his side, a good example, at least, is set which may encourage some one else to sing who would otherwise remain silent.

It is desirable that those who can do so should sing heartily, with open mouth and full voice, and not in the smothered, uncertain manner, which is too common, and affords poor encouragement and assistance to others.

The advantage of occasional meetings for singing need hardly be alluded to. We have reference now, not to the usual singing school, the object of which is to teach those who attend to read music, though it is most desirable that such should be encouraged, but to gatherings of all the people for the purpose of learning the tunes chiefly by rote. These should not degenerate into mere *singing*, but should be *religious* meetings. Let the hymns be sung through, and this with meaning. Success in Congregational Singing can not be expected without effort. There must be a willingness on the part of the people to make and persevere in this effort.

Finally, each one should make the song his own, assuming the words as real expressions of the inward sense of his own soul. Even although they may not always be strictly applicable to one's circumstances, yet sympathizing with others, we should surely in this universal and delightful Song Service, rejoice with those who rejoice, and weep with those who weep. An esteemed writer, already quoted, in speaking of the old tunes, says: "If we would have these old tunes to perfection, we must attain more of the old-fashioned piety with which they were formerly sung." If music be substituted for religion, and singing for devotion, the best tune and the best voices will neither increase religion, nor aid devotion. Unless Congregational Singing rest upon a religious foundation, it will be like the house built upon the sand. Unless it be conducted as a religious duty and privilege, it will fail to secure its legitimate ends. But where it is attempted and pursued in a right spirit and with proper efforts, there is no danger from the want of artistic culture.

"We now offer 'The Sabbath Hymn and Tune Book' to the churches, invoking the blessing of the Great Head of the Church upon our labors, that they may meet the wants of devout worshipers, and especially that they may be found conducive to the spirituality of 'The Service of Song in the House of the Lord.'"

LOWELL MASON,
EDWARDS A. PARK,
AUSTIN PHELPS.

ANDOVER, MASS., March, 1859.

INDEX TO PAGES OF HYMNS.

HYMN		PAGE	HYMN		PAGE	HYMN		PAGE
1	...Judson............	358	55	..Newton............	136	108	..Lyte..............	106
2	...Montgomery........	176	56	.Zuinger, translated		109	..Watts.............	48
3	..Sarah J. Hale......	383		by Merrick........	36	110	..Ogilvie............	47
4	..Miss. Williams...370, 452		57	.Wm. Mason.........	227	111	..Watts.............	48
5	..Tate—Brady........	319	58	.Cotterill............	24	112	..Watts.............	65
6	..Watts..............	277	59	..Watts..............	44	113	..Montgomery.......	107
7	....	66	60	..Mrs. Barbauld.....	34	114	....	24
8	...J. Wesley†.........	146	61	..Stennett...........	288	115	..Sir R. Grant......	58
9	...Mrs. Steele........	388	62	..Watts..............	241	116	..Oliver.............	59
10	..Heber..............	147	63	....	144	117	..Smart..............	86
11	..Watts..............	20	64	..Mrs. Brown........	214	118	..Watts.............	26
12	..Lyte...............	22	65	..Ken................	49	119	..Addison..........	90, 453
13	..Milton†............	18	66	..Mrs. Steele........	114	120	..Watts.............	15
14	..Watts..............	52	67	..Watts..............	358	121	..Watts.............	46
15	..Watts..............	53	68	..Keble..............	42	122	..Turner............	271
16	..Watts..............	111	69	..Edmeston..........	234	123	..Watts.............	86
17	..Tate—Brady........	68	70	....	392	124	..Sternhold.........	80
18	..Lyte...............	38	71	..Watts..............	43	125	..Conder............	57
19	..Watts..............	50	72	..C. Wesley..........	340	126	....	19
20	..Watts..............	38	73	..Watts..............	303	127	..Doddridge.........	358
21	..Watts..............	43	74	..Montgomery.......	20	128	....	65
22	..Stennett...........	22	75	..Edmeston..........	280	129	..Blacklock.........	30
23	..Watts..............	34	76	..S. F. Smith........	202	130	..H. K. White......	76
24	..G Burder..........	387	77	..Brown.............	307	131	..H. K. White......	76
25	..Montgomery.......	282	78	....	273	132	..Watts.............	18
26	..Watts..............	46	79	..Montgomery.......	376	133	..Mrs. Steele.......	86
27	..Watts..............	26	80	....	358	134	..Watts.............	240
28	..Tate—Brady........	142	81	....	28	135	..Watts.............	274
29	..Montgomery.......	32	82	..Kelly..............	376	136	..Watts.............	307
30	....	53	83	..Tate—Brady........	79	137	....	51
31	..Sternhold—Hopkins.	17	84	..Newton............	358	138	..Conder............	280
32	..Tate—Brady........	17	85	..Palmer............	387	139	..Thomson..........	68
33	..Watts..............	53	86	..Burder............	407	140	..Madam Guyon.....	388
34	..Watts..............	17	87	..Hart...............	49	141	..Watts.............	181
35	..Montgomery.......	78	88	....	294	142	..Watts.............	274
36	..Watts..............	374	89	..Watts..............	293	143	..Tate—Brady.......	76
37	....	53	90	..Montgomery†......	62	144	..Watts.............	337
38	..Watts..............	72	91	..Newton............	363	145	..Watts.............	31
39	..Goode.............	400	92	....	172	146	..Watts.............	290
40	..Tate—Brady........	26	93	..Newton............	387	147	..Watts.............	69
41	..Mrs. Barbauld†....	274	94	..Gibbons............	380	148	..Gibbons...........	73
42	..Cowper............	292	95	..E. T. Fitch........	182	149	....	322
43	..Watts..............	38	96	....	30	150	....	124
44	..Watts..............	54	97	....	41	151	..Bowring...........	193
45	..Watts..............	42	98	..Conder............	66	152	....	72
46	..Old Latin Hymn...	115	99	..Fawcett............	84	153	..J. Young..........	62
47	..Sir R. Grant......	363	100	..Watts..............	30	154	..Watts.............	48
48	..Ken................	49	101	....	172	155	..Needham..........	307
49	..J. Wesley..........	22	102	..Watts..............	33	156	..Tate—Brady.......	70
50	..Bowring...........	269	103	..Watts..............	30	157	..Watts.............	48
51	..Hawkesworth......	389	104	..Montgomery.......	150	158	..Mrs. Steele.......	69
52	..Tate—Brady........	19	105	..Merrick...........	150	159	..Watts.............	75
53	..Watts..............	22	106	....	372	160	..Tate—Brady.......	49
54	..Hayward...........	24	107	..Watts..............	68	161	..Watts.............	336

HYMN		PAGE	HYMN		PAGE	HYMN		PAGE
162	.. Watts............	176	230	.. Tate—Brady......	178	298	.. Stennett...........	224
163	.. Watts............	43	231	.. Montgomery.......	126	299	.. Watts.............	130
164	.. Watts............	388	232	.. Watts............	358	300	.. Cowper...........	38
165	.. Watts............	75	233	....	231	301	.. Cowper...........	96
166	.. Watts............	64	234	.. Mrs. Steele.......	336	302	....	141
167	.. Wrangham........	19	235	.. Watts............	301	303	.. Watts.............	313
168	.. Watts............	40	236	.. Cowper...........	80	304	....	333
169	.. Watts............	214	237	.. Palmer...........	241	305	.. Watts.............	289
170	.. Tate—Brady......	44	238	.. Watts............	103	306	.. Stennett...........	376
171	.. Watts............	383	239	.. Conder...........	209	307	....	129
172	....	359	240	....	142	308	.. Beddome..........	98
173	....	28	241	.. Beddome..........	103	309	.. Watts.............	117
174	.. Watts............	389	242	.. Hervey...........	191	310	.. Watts.............	337
175	....	31	243	....	178	311	.. Mrs. Steele.......	303
176	.. Doddridge........	133	244	....	100	312	.. Watts.............	98
177	.. Tate—Brady......	73	245	....	81	313	....	174
178	.. Watts............	116	246	.. Watts............	38	314	.. Bonar............	227
179	.. Watts............	65	247	.. C. Wesley.........	178	315	.. Bonar............	311
180	.. Kirkham..........	270	248	.. Watts............	87	316	.. Watts.............	293
181	.. Tate—Brady......	86	249	....	193	317	.. Bowring...........	178
182	.. Needham.........	75	250	.. Doddridge........	63	318	.. C. Wesley.........	62
183	.. Watts............	117	251	.. Watts............	87	319	.. Kelly.............	93
184	.. Watts............	80	252	.. Watts............	92	320	....	302
185	.. E. Scott..........	336	253	.. C. Wesley.........	217	321	....	101
186	.. Fawcett..........	359	254	.. Watts............	304	322	....	124
187	.. Watts............	70	255	.. Watts............	108	323	.. Mrs. Steele.......	210
188	.. Watts............	41	256	.. Wardlaw.........	200	324	.. Watts.............	104
189	.. Watts............	83	257	.. Lyte.............	296	325	.. Watts.............	87
190	.. March............	197	258	.. Watts............	116	326	....	387
191	....	78	259	.. Lyte.............	44	327	.. Mrs. Steele.......	34
192	.. Watts............	90	260	.. C. Wesley.........	348	328	.. S. Stennett........	105
193	.. Watts............	163	261	.. Langford.........	28	329	.. Reed.............	198
194	.. Watts............	138	262	.. Watts............	200	330	.. Haweis...........	379
195	....	68	263	.. Martin Luther.....	114	331	.. Hammond........	196
196	.. Alford............	19	264	.. Bonar............	260	332	.. Stennett...........	40
197	.. Watts............	298	265	.. Robinson.........	103	333	.. Cennick..........	54
198	....	241	266	.. Heber............	79	334	.. Dinney...........	54
199	.. Watts............	76	267	....	200	335	....	123
200	....	408	268	.. Tate.............	112	336	.. Gregory,tr.by Palmer	115
201	.. Mrs. Steele.......	210	269	.. Cawood...........	218	337	.. Watts.............	201
202	.. Addison..........	312	270	.. C. Wesley.........	291	338	.. Watts.............	112
203	.. Mrs. Steele.......	130	271	....	111	339	.. Montgomery.......	74
204	.. Heginbotham.....	92	272	.. Sears............	221	340	....	144
205	.. Heginbotham.....	220	273	....	62	341	....	144
206	.. Merrick...........	202	274	.. Doddridge........	117	342	.. Watts.............	376
207	.. Bowring..........	356	275	.. Watts............	91	343	....	40
208	.. Latrobe..........	324	276	.. Bowring........391	457	344	.. Oliver............	59
209	....	52	277	.. Watts............	200	345	.. Kingsbury.........	40
210	.. Lyte.............	94	278	.. From the German.	29	346	....	27
211	.. Addison..........	370	279	....	132	347	.. Shirley............	42
212	.. Mrs. Steele.......	371	280	.. Watts............	184	348	.. Watts.............	168
213	.. Logan............	309	281	.. Enfield...........	380	349	.. C. Wesley.........	58
214	.. Heginbotham.....	139	282	....	108	350	.. Watts.............	81
215	.. Anna L. Waring...	280	283	.. A. C. Coxe.......	146	351	.. Watts.............	60
216	.. Doddridge........	350	284	....	302	352	.. Watts.............	98
217	.. Watts............	160	285	.. Bache............	114	353	.. Old Latin Hymn...	135
218	.. Tate—Brady......	371	286	.. Beddome..........	286	354	.. Cudworth.........	127
219	.. Addison..........	300	287	.. Watts............	170	355	.. Kelly.............	371
220	....	313	288	.. Cowper...........	371	356	.. Doddridge........	135
221	.. Watts............	83	289	.. Milman...........	146	357	....	110
222	....	370	290	.. Montgomery.......	103	358	.. Watts.............	229
223	.. Watts............	32	291	.. Hart.............	163	359	.. Doddridge........	138
224	.. Montgomery......	72	292	.. Tappan...........	214	360	.. Collyer...........	166
225	.. Watts............	91	293	.. Suggested by Gerhard	336	361	....	123
226	.. Montgomery......	384	294	....	148	362	.. C. Wesley.........	64
227	.. Sandys...........	28	295	....	234	363	.. Tate—Brady......	201
228	.. Milton*..........	126	296	....	393	364	.. Montgomery.......	65
229	.. Tate—Brady......	199	297	.. Francis...........	294	365	....	124

INDEX TO PAGES OF HYMNS.

HYMN		PAGE	HYMN		PAGE	HYMN		PAGE
366	..Bathurst	124	434		140	501	..Watts	293
367	..Conder	226	435	..Mrs. Steele	95	502	..C. Wesley	216
368	..C. Wesley	94	436	..Mrs. Steele	142	503		118
369		73	437		292	504		184
370		120	438	..Newton	192	505		108
371	..Bakewell	218	439		95	506		118
372	..S. M. Waring	242	440	..Watts	25	507		118
373		352	441	..Newton	116	508	.Watts	384
374	..Mrs. Steele	230	442	..Newton	203	509	..Mrs. Steele	170
375	..Mrs. Steele	230	443	..Hebert	351	510	..Doddridge	252
376	..Kelly	63	444	..Bonar	160	511		123, 454
377	..Kelly	372	445	..Doane	38	512	..W. B. Collyert	364
378	..Watts	27	446	..Bonar	118	513		260
379	..Duncan	113	447	..Reed	148	514	..Mrs. Barbauld	203
380	..Kelly	166	448	..Montgomery	176	515		310
381	..Doddridge	87	449	..Heber	206	516	..Dobell	272
382		166	450		260	517	..Allent	295
383	..Mrs. Steele	94	451	..Latin Hymn tr. by		518	..Hartt	295
384	..Bonar	301		Palmer	354	519		140
385	..Watts	92	452	..Hart	272	520	..Haweis	106
386	..Kelly	392	453	..Beddome	168	521	..Thornby	152
387	..Lyte	201	454	..Browne	135	522	..Knox	323
388	..Newton	304	455	..Watts	364	523		199
389		228	456		351	524	..Boden	278
390		112	457	..Reed	66	525	..Bowring	114
391	..C. Wesley	63	458		67	526		340
392	..Montgomery	126	459	..Mrs. Steele	184	527		367
393	..Pope†	57	460		108	528	..Nevin	386
394		84	461	..C. Wesley	344	529		39
395	..Heginbotham	142	462	..Watts	187	530		318
396		202	463	..T. Scott	135	531	..Mrs. Steele	225
397		203	464	..Montgomery	346	532		352
398		386	465	..Watts	276	533		119
399	..Bickersteth	234	466	..Lyte	156	534		162
400		407	467		123	535		330
401		23	468		81	536	..Reed	294
402	..C. Wesley	102	469	..Bonar	21	537	..T. Scott	150
403	..Mrs. Steele	252	470	..Bonar	408	538	..Collyer	188
404	..Zinzendorf	350	471		318	539	..C. Wesley	260
405	..Bonar	184	472	..Montgomery	363	540	..Doddridge†	336
406		105	473		82	541	..Gregg	164
407	..Kelly	301	474		145	542	..Th. Hastings	243
408	..C. Wesley	368	475		137	543	..Fawcett	320
409	..C. Wesley	368	476		145	544		164
410		368	477	..Watts	63	545	..C. Wesley	246
411	..Mrs. Steele	196	478	..Watts	281	546	..S. F. Smith	260
412	..Sir R. Grant	309	479	..Watts	91	547	..Doddridge	404
413	..Raffles	290	480	..Sir R. Grant	92	548	..Watts	255
414	..Newton	264	481	..Watts	330	549	..Mrs. Steele	275
415	..Macduff	167	482	..Watts	330	550		314
416		202	483	..Cowper	34	551	..Bonar	194
417	..Cowper	304	484	..Watts	88	552	..Watts	182
418	..Bonar	284	485	..Mrs. Steele	63	553		140
419	..Nevin	193	486	..Watts	19	554	..Newton	348
420	..Mrs. Steele	182	487	..Watts	228	555	..Watts	236
421	..Bonar	192	488	..Fawcett	214	556	..From the German	318
422		56	489	..Watts	364	557	..Watts	275
423	..Heber	351	490	..Watts	182	558	..Jones	148
424	..Watts	214, 455	491		390	559	..Charlotte Elliott	352
425	..Toplady	572	492	..Watts	344	560	..Stennett	174
426		219	493	..Watts	275	561	..Turner	363
427		242	494	..Watts	380	562	..Watts	174
428	..H. K. White	122	495	..C. Wesley	348	563	..C. Wesley	340
429	..Fawcett	94	496	..Montgomery	340	564	..J. Wesley	225
430		56	497	..Dwight	213	565	..Bonar	170
431	..Medley	122, 454	498	..Watts	344	566	..Watts	135
432	..Doddridge	339	499	..Watts	286	567	..Cowper	286
433	..Medley	57	500	..Watts	390	568	..Newton	174

INDEX TO PAGES OF HYMNS.

HYMN		PAGE	HYMN		PAGE	HYMN		PAGE
569		243	637	..Mrs. Steele	290	704	..C. Wesley	216
570		235	638		232	705	..C. Wesley	128
571	..Watts	248	639	..Sir R. Grant	369	706	..Bernard	121
572		331	640		392	707		339
573	..Heber	370	641		132	708	..Cowper	405
574	..C. Wesley	378	642	..Lyte	281	709	..Cowper	150
575	..Raffles	278	643	..Watts	69	710	..J. Wesley	66
576	..C. Wesley	250	644	..Watts	228	711		247
577	..C. Wesley	338	645	..Watts	331	712	..Heginbotham	251
578	..C. Wesley	360	646	..From the German	165	713		212
579	..Stennett	250	647	..Madame Guyon	397	714	..M'Cheyne	373
580	..Watts	291	648	..Robinson	173	715	..M'Cheyne	371
581	..C. Wesley	213	649	..From the French	218	716	..Bonar	93
582	..Mrs. Steele	168	650	..Watts	77	717	..Bonar	170
583	..Watts	175	651	..Ryland	238	718	..S. F. Smith	318
584		344	652	..Montgomery	185	719	..Macduff	93
585	..Morrison	143	653	..Moir	179	720		354
586		235	654	..Tate—Brady	95	721	..Toplady	101
587	..Watts	175	655	..Watts	343	722	..Palmer	355
588	..C. Wesley	67	656		298	723	..Raffles	147
589	..Newton	261	657	..Ryland	66	724	..Watts	213
590	..Doddridge	404	658		175	725	..Toplady	340
591	..Watts	250	659	..Lyte	235	726	..C. Wesley	196
592	..Raffles	408	660		149	727	..C. Wesley	240
593	..C. Wesley	236	661		334	728	..C. Wesley	360
594	..Watts	345	662	..C. Wesley	217	729	..Bathurst	102
595	..Watts	345	663		265	730		196
596	..Watts	345	664	..C. Wesley	185	731	..Palmer	102
597		328	665	..Mrs. Steele	149	732	..Mrs. Steele	206
598	..Merrick	337	666		406	733	..Newton	237
599	..Montgomery	286	667	..Mrs. Steele	343	734	..Montgomery	404
600	..Watts	250	668	..Mrs. Steele	55	735	..Cennick	60
601	..Watts	240	669	..Tate—Brady	77	736	..Doddridge	149
602	..Newton	306	670	..Cowper	405	737		263
603		349	671	..Tate—Brady	299	738		134
604	..C. Wesley	403	672		110	739	..T. Scott	288
605		115	673		180	740	..Sir R. Grant	247
606		254	674	..Watts	55	741		247
607	..Beddome	298	675	..Gerhard	160	742		362
608	..Mrs. Steele	329	676	..Gerhard	161	743	..J. Wesley	168
609	..Doddridge	54	677	..Montgomery	219	744	..C. Wesley	206
610		129	678		185	745		362
611	..Browne	251	679		285	746	..Bonar	379
612	..J. Taylor	260	680	..Toplady	382	747	..Bonar	154
613	..Tate—Brady	251	681	..Swain	374	748	..Bonar	342
614	..Hillhouse	165	682	..Cotton	128	749		304
615	..Collyer	240	683	..J. Wesley	204	750	..Mrs. Steele	141
616	..Mrs. Steele	175	684	..Watts	96	751	..Watts	171
617	..Newton	329	685	..Xavier	154	752		141
618	..Watts	342	686	..Bernard translated by Palmer	185	753		161
619	..Watts	336				754	..Watts	125
620	..Mrs. Steele	251	687	..Bernard	129	755	..Newton	280
621	..Newton	343	688	..G. Duffield, jr	100	756	..Watts	248
622	..C. Wesley	341	689	..Palmer	338	757		256
623	..Bonar	261	690	..Watts	130	758		384
624	..Conder	246	691		325	759	..Hastings	234
625		287	692		332	760		217
626	..Mrs. Steele	229	693	..Montgomery	390	761		129
627	..Cowper	190	694		140	762	..Lyte	331
628	..Kelly	230	695	..Newton	232	763	..Baxter	154
629	..Watts	281	696		338	764	..Nevin	101
630	..Mrs. Steele	342	697		120	765	..Bernard	303
631	..C. Wesley	216	698	..Doddridge	220	766		237
632	..Newton	246	699		197	767		224
633	..Mrs. Torrey	254	700	..Heginbotham	143	768	..C. Wesley	134
634	..C. Wesley	294	701	..Toplady	206	769	..C. Wesley	161
635	..C. Wesley	364	702	..Mrs. Steele	186	770	..Milman	232
636	..Heath	107	703	..C. Wesley	36	771		353

HYMN		PAGE	HYMN		PAGE	HYMN		PAGE
772	..J. Taylor............	295	840	..Watts...............	410	908	....	403
773	 223,	458	841	..From the German...	409	909	..Newton...........	127
774	..Gallaudet...........	343	842	....	180	910	..Berridge.........	409
775	..Watts...............	98	843	..Rifles............	224	911	....	207
776	....	409	844	..Charlotte Elliott..	358	912	....	207
777	....	404	845	..Stowell...........	289	913	..Cowper...........	132
778	....	237	846	..Mrs. Steele.......	191	914	..Watts............	206
779	..Wreford............	339	847	....	143	915	..Watts............	272
780	..Cowper.............	197	848	..Beddome...........	287	916	..C. Wesley........	272
781	..Conder.............	319	849	..Greek Hymn........	389	917	....	217
782	....	270	850	..Watts.............	365	918	..G. Smith.........	273
783	..Medley.............	212	851	..Watts.............	132	919	....	166
784	....	222	852	....	105	920	....	109
785	....	184	853	..Cowper............	248	921	..Watts............	277
786	..Doddridge..........	253	854	..Newton............	130	922	..Lyte.............	151
787	..C. Wesley..........	206	855	..Logan.............	319	923	..Watts............	293
788	..Reed...............	324	856	..Montgomery........	326	924	..Barton...........	55
789	....	108	857	..Fawcett...........	194	925	..Bonar............	265
790	..Doddridge†.........	176	858	..Watts.............	221	926	..Mrs. Steele......	191
791	....	121	859	..Swain.............	158	927	..Cowper...........	332
792	....	100	860	..Watts.............	46	928	..Bonar............	205
793	....	100	861	..Watts.............	252	929	..Charlotte Elliott..	123
794	..S. F. Smith........	155	862	..Lyte..............	267	930	....	71
795	....	155	863	..Watts.............	134	931	..Doddridge........	333
796	..J. B. Monsell......	263	864	..Mrs. Barbauld.....	280	932	..Darby............	256
797	..Watts..............	35	865	....	365	933	..Ann W. Hall......	245
798	..Gregg..............	56	866	..Watts.............	248	934	..Green............	333
799	..Fellowes...........	44	867	....	363	935	..Watts............	280
800	..Kirkham............	155	868	..Montgomery........	204	936	..Benjamin Schmolk.	264
801	..G. N. Allen........	158	869	..C. Wesley.........	149	937	..Conder...........	257
802	..Kelly..............	205	870	..C. Wesley.........	211	938	....	351
803	..C. Wesley..........	334	871	..C. Wesley.........	211	939	....	329
804	..Furness............	265	872	..Robinson..........	199	940	..Mrs. Hemans......	509
805	..Mrs. Barbauld......	158	873	..Doddridge.........	211	941	..Lyte.............	163
806	....	241	874	..J. Taylor.........	369	942	....	279
807	..Bonar..............	232	875	..Mrs. Barbauld.....	171	943	..Edmeston.........	155
808	..Bernard............	136	876	..G. Herbert........	324	944	..Tate—Brady.......	229
809	..Bernard............	121	877	....	250	945	....	253
810	..Watts..............	380	878	..Bonar.............	57	946	....	276
811	..Watts..............	293	879	..Bonar.............	57	947	..Montgomery.......	129
812	..Mrs. Rowe..........	109	880	..Doddridge.........	85	948	..Bryant...........	277
813	..Montgomery.........	410	881	..Montgomery........	397	949	..Cowper...........	377
814	..Whittier...........	143	882	..Watts.............	45	950	..Bonar............	164
815	..Watts..............	60	883	..Watts.............	211	951	..Logan............	321
816	..Watts..............	288	884	..Montgomery........	394	952	..Moore............	153
817	..Watts..............	236	885	..Watts.............	47	953	..Kelly............	405
818	..Newton†............	207	886	..Watts.............	248	954	..Watts............	320
819	..C. Wesley..........	410	887	..Watts.............	77	955	..Watts............	213
820	..Watts..............	238	888	....	186	956	..Watts............	75
821	..Watts..............	186	889	..Watts.............	74	957	....	136
822	..Oberlin............	225	890	..Watts.............	74	958	..Logan............	296
823	..J. Wesley..........	245	891	..W. Gaskell........	283	959	....	220
824	..Watts..............	86	892	....	374	960	..Kent.............	194
825	..Watts..............	45	893	....	106	961	..Doddridge........	43
826	..Watts..............	229	894	....	208	962	..Tate—Brady.......	305
827	..Montgomery.........	228	895	..Medley............	156	963	....	133
828	....	169	896	....	283	964	..Cowper...........	172
829	..Mrs. Cotterill.....	134	897	..Collyer...........	402	965	..Toplady..........	103
830	....	141	898	..C. Wesley.........	375	966	..Miss Grant.......	172
831	..Montgomery.........	334	899	..From the German...	47	967	..Miss Grant.......	84
832	..Doddridge..........	164	900	..Montgomery........	139	968	..Watts............	33
833	..Windham............	150	901	..Mrs. Barbauld.....	74	969	..Toplady..........	171
834	..Beddome............	410	902	..Duffield..........	394	970	..Heginbotham......	104
835	....	67	903	....	158	971	..Doddridge........	113
836	..Wesley.............	67	904	....	265	972	..Cowper...........	373
837	..Palmer.............	164	905	..Miss E. Fletcher..	221	973	....	157
838	....	261	906	..Bonar.............	266	974	..Watts............	333
839	..Mrs. Steele........	225	907	....	252	975	..Heginbotham......	231

HYMN		PAGE	HYMN		PAGE	HYMN		PAGE
976		215	1044	..Guest............	409	1111	..J. S. Dwight......	401
977	..From the German..	222	1045	..Doddridge........	411	1112	..Heber............	257
978	..From the German..	266	1046	....	411	1113	..Walter Scott.....	71
979	..Watts............	158	1047	..Watts............	411	1114	....	301
980	....	392	1048	....	406	1115	..L. Bacon.........	54
981	....	283	1049	..C. Wesley........	361	1116	..Tate—Brady.......	45
982	....	271	1050	..Montgomery.......	329	1117	....	194
983	..Mrs. Steele......	115	1051	..Thomas Aquinas,		1118	..Mrs. Steele......	233
984	..Montgomery.......	212		tr. by Palmer..	208	1119	....	302
985	..Heber............	378	1052	..Conder...........	101	1120	..S. F. Smith......	401
986	....	277	1053	..Stennett.........	183	1121	....	505
987	..Bonar............	264	1054	....	183	1122	..Doddridge........	103
988	..Richter..........	292	1055	..Watts............	233	1123	..Watts............	71
989	..Sarah F. Adams...	244	1056	..Noel.............	316	1124	....	277
990	....	173	1057	..Watts............	316	1125	..Watts............	82
991	....	285	1058	..Montgomery.......	71	1126	....	229
992	....	384	1059	..Beddome..........	169	1127	..Williams.........	509
993	....	306	1060	..Doddridge........	383	1128	....	51
994	..Montgomery.......	163	1061	..Doddridge........	381	1129	..Watts............	304
995	..C. Wesley........	186	1062	..Watts............	50	1130	..L. Bacon.........	167
996	..C. Wesley........	186	1063	....	82	1131	....	151
997	..C. Wesley........	193	1064	..Montgomery.......	169	1132	..Heber............	355
998	....	252	1065	..Doddridge........	165	1133	..Lyte.............	305
999	....	346	1066	..Beddome..........	183	1134	..Montgomery.......	210
1000	..Watts............	346	1067	..Davies...........	135	1135	..Watts............	247
1001	..Mrs. Steele......	191	1068	..Davies...........	169	1136	....	305
1002	..Watts............	223	1069	..Montgomery.......	287	1137	....	378
1003	..Zinzendorf.......	319	1070	..Montgomery.......	381	1138	....	499
1004	..Bonar............	130	1071	....	85	1139	..S. F. Smith......	46
1005	..Watts............	240	1072	..Montgomery.......	376	1140	..Gaskell..........	411
1006	..M'Cheyne.........	271	1073	..Bryant...........	45	1141	..Mrs. Sigourney...	411
1007	..Kelly............	163	1074	....	193	1142	..Mrs. Barbauld....	127
1008	..Watts............	240	1075	..Watts............	125	1143	..Conder...........	167
1009	..Daviest..........	147	1076	..Montgomery.......	29	1144	..Washburn.........	253
1010	..Palmer...........	345	1077	..Faber............	398	1145	..Watts............	204
1011	..Wingrove.........	85	1078	....	159	1146	..Palmer...........	29
1012	..Watts............	329	1079	....	159	1147	..Bowne............	273
1013	..Watts............	326	1080	..Watts............	398	1148	..Morrison.........	399
1014	..Doddridge........	375	1081	....	394	1149	..Watts............	112
1015	..Newton...........	2.5	1082	....	318	1150	..Watts............	125
1016	..Watts............	35	1083	..Jane Taylor......	399	1151	..Doddridge........	43
1017	..Dwight...........	223	1084	..Cle. Alexandrinus.	354	1152	..Moore............	205
1018	..Watts............	61	1085	....	71	1153	..W. B. C. Peabody.	159
1019	..Bonar............	366	1086	....	445	1154	....	37
1020	..Tate—Brady.......	405	1087	....	39	1155	..Montgomery.......	401
1021	..Watts............	212	1088	159,	458	1156	..Doddridge........	51
1022	..From the German..	393	1089	..Heber............	104	1157	..Watts............	233
1023	..Newton...........	219	1090	..Watts............	125	1158	..Doddridge........	201
1024	..Doddridge........	56	1091	....	193	1159	..Newton.......330,	450
1025	..Watts............	23	1092	..G. Clayton.......	110	1160	..Beddome..........	341
1026	..Watts............	61	1093	....	335	1161	..C. Wesley........	397
1027	..Watts............	50	1094	....	190	1162	..Mrs. Steele......	357
1028	..Watts............	35	1095	....	239	1163	..Watts............	129
1029	..Watts............	61	1096	..Boden............	239	1164	..Watts............	305
1030	....	79	1097	....	326	1165	..Watts............	316
1031	..Kelly............	209	1098	....	329	1166	..Watts............	315
1032	..Bonar............	385	1099	....	369	1167	..J. Burton........	261
1033	..Doddridge........	198	1100	..Crosswell........	187	1168	....	188
1034	..Watts............	73	1101	..Doddridge........	187	1169	....	314
1035	..Logan............	113	1102	..Francis..........	218	1170	..Watts............	29
1036	..Watts............	61	1103	....	133	1171	..Beddome..........	316
1037	..L. Bacon.........	61	1104	..Caroline Seward..	82	1172	..Watts............	305
1038	..A. C. Coxe.......	346	1105	..Voke.............	83	1173	....	321
1039	..Montgomery.......	181	1106	....	215	1174	....	321
1040	..S. F. Smith......	402	1107	..G. Burgess.......	231	1175	..Dale.............	157
1041	....	325	1108	....	263	1176	..Muhlenberg...328,	456
1042	....	391	1109	..Heber............	152	1177	..Malan............	188
1043	....	410	1110	....	83	1178	....	314

INDEX TO PAGES OF HYMNS.

HYMN		PAGE	HYMN		PAGE	HYMN		PAGE
1179		369	1217		365	1255	..Tappan	55
1180	..Mrs. Steele	317	1218	..Heber	153	1256	.C. Wesley	267
1181	..From the German	147	1219	..Doddridge	312	1257	..Watts	267
1182	..Charlotte Elliott	310	1220	..Bonar	366	1258	..Mrs. Steele	231
1183	..Hill	377	1221	..From a Welsh Hymn	407	1259		245
1184		235	1222	..From a Welsh Hymn	407	1260	..Watts	215
1185	..Collyer	321	1223	.Kelly	305	1261		189
1186	..Logan	254	1224	..T. R. Taylor	244	1262	..H. C. von Schwirn-	
1187	..Montgomery	255	1225		131		itz	284
1188		189	1226	..Bonar	173	1263	..Palmer	222
1189	..Pope	412	1227		377	1264		151
1190	..Doddridge	326	1228		262	1265	..Mrs. Steele	267
1191	.Watts	116	1229	..Watts	381	1266	.Watts	297
1192	..Mrs. Barbauld	308	1230		357	1267	..Hebert	146
1193	..Mrs. Barbauld	308	1231		97	1268	..Kelly	127
1194	..Watts	308	1232	.Lyte	99	1269	..Bonar	382
1195	..Mrs. Mackay	305	1233	..Watts	239	1270	..Bonar	195
1196		317	1234	..Stennett	296	1271	..Bonar	315
1197	..Palmer	321	1235	..Watts	21	1272	.Watts	89
1198	..Montgomery	322	1236	..Mrs. Steele	296	1273		347
1199	..W. B. C. Peabody	327	1237	..Montgomery	382	1274	..Watts	99
1200	..Watts	292	1238	.Cennick	361	1275		347
1201	..Mrs. Steele	317	1239	..Noel	239	1276	..H. K. White	313
1202	..Mrs. Hemans	355	1240		327	1277		205
1203	..Notker	279	1241	..Bonar	97	1278	..Watts	291
1204	..Mrs. Gilbert	279	1242	.Gibbons	93	1279	..C. Wesley	299
1205	..Heber	306	1243		381	1280	..Addison†	291
1206	.Dale	153	1244	..Bonar	324	1281		362
1207	..Montgomery	314	1245	..Watts	97	1282	..Von Celano	83
1208	..Mrs. Hemans	267	1246	..Needham	346	1283	..Walter Scott, from	
1209	..S. F. Smith	310	1247		99		Von Celano	254
1210	..Watts	312	1248	..Montgomery	282	1284	..Martin Luther	403
1211		177	1249	..Raffles†	282	1285	..Watts	70
1212	.Watts	317	1250		297	1286		209
1213	.Collyer	310	1251	..Watts	347	1287	..Newton	294
1214	..Montgomery	256	1252	.Watts	385	1288	..Doddridge	299
1215	..Mrs. Gilbert	324	1253	..Doddridge	276	1289		255
1216		303	1254	..Doddridge†	276	1290	..From the German	403

NEW SABBATH HYMN AND TUNE BOOK.

THE OLD HUNDREDTH. L. M.

31. *Old version of the One Hundredth Psalm.*

1 ALL people that on earth do dwell,
  Sing to the Lord with cheerful voice;
  Him serve with fear, his praise forth tell,
  Come ye before him and rejoice.

2 The Lord, ye know, is God indeed,
  Without our aid he did us make;
  We are his flock, he doth us feed,
  And for his sheep he doth us take.

3 Oh, enter, then, his gates with praise;
  Approach with joy his courts unto;
  Praise, laud, and bless his name always,
  For it is seemly so to do.

4 For why? the Lord our God is good,
  His mercy is for ever sure;
  His truth at all times firmly stood,
  And shall from age to age endure.

32. *"Glad homage."*—Psalm 100.

1 WITH one consent, let all the earth,
  To God their cheerful voices raise;
  Glad homage pay, with awful mirth,
  And sing before him songs of praise.

2 Oh, enter ye his temple gate,
  Thence to his courts devoutly press:
  And still your grateful hymns repeat,
  And still his name with praises bless.

3 For he's the Lord, supremely good,
  His mercy is for ever sure;
  His truth, which always firmly stood,
  To endless ages shall endure.

34. *"Enter into His gates with thanksgiving."* Psalm 100.

1 YE nations round the earth, rejoice
  Before the Lord, your sovereign King;
  Serve him with cheerful heart and voice,
  With all your tongues his glory sing.

2 The Lord is God; 't is he alone
  Doth life, and breath, and being give:
  We are his work, and not our own;
  The sheep that on his pastures live.

3 Enter his gates with songs of joy,
  With praises to his courts repair;
  And make it your divine employ
  To pay your thanks and honors there.

4 The Lord is good, the Lord is kind,
  Great is his grace, his mercy sure;
  And the whole race of man shall find
  His truth from age to age endure.

DOXOLOGY.

To Father, Son, and Holy Ghost,
  The God whom earth and heaven adore,
Be glory as it was of old,
  Is now, and shall be evermore!

CHRISTMAS (OLD.) C. M. DOUBLE.

13. *An old Version of the Eighty-fourth Psalm.*

1 How lovely are thy dwellings fair,
   O Lord of hosts! how dear
   The pleasant tabernacles are,
   Where thou dost dwell so near!
2 My soul doth long, and, fainting, sigh
   Thy courts, O Lord, to see;
   My heart and flesh aloud do cry,
   O living God, for thee!
3 Happy, who in thy house reside,
   Where thee they ever praise;
   Happy, whose strength in thee doth bide,
   And in their hearts thy ways.
4 They journey on from strength to strength
   With joy and gladsome cheer,
   Till all before our God at length
   In Zion do appear.
5 For God the Lord, both sun and shield,
   Gives grace and glory bright;
   No good from them shall be withheld,
   Whose ways are just and right.
6 Lord God of hosts, who reign'st on high!
   That man is truly blest
   Who doth on thee alone rely,
   In thee alone doth rest.

132. *"Who, in the heaven, can be compared unto the Lord?"*—Psalm 89.

1 With reverence let the saints appear,
   And bow before the Lord;
   His high commands with reverence hear,
   And tremble at his word.
2 Great God! how high thy glories rise!
   How bright thine armies shine!
   Where is the power with thee that vies,
   Or truth compared to thine!
3 The northern pole, and southern, rest
   On thy supporting hand;

   Darkness and day, from east to west,
   Move round at thy command.
4 Thy words the raging winds control,
   And rule the boisterous deep;
   Thou mak'st the sleeping billows roll,
   The rolling billows sleep.
5 Heaven, earth, and air, and sea are thine,
   And the dark world of hell,
   How did thine arm in vengeance shine,
   When Egypt durst rebel!
6 Justice and judgment are thy throne,
   Yet wondrous is thy grace;
   While truth and mercy joined in one,
   Invite us near thy face.

196. *"In this will I be confident."*—Psalm 46.

1 God is our refuge and our strength,
   When trouble's hour is near;
   A very present help is he;
   Therefore we will not fear.
2 Although the pillars of the earth
   Shall clean removéd be,
   The very mountains carried forth,
   And cast into the sea;
3 Although the waters rage and swell,
   So that the earth shall shake:
   Yea, and the solid mountain roots
   Shall with the tempest quake;—
4 There is a river that makes glad
   The city of our God,—
   The tabernacle's holy place
   Of the Most High's abode.
5 The Lord is in the midst of her;
   Removed she shall not be,
   Because the Lord our God himself
   Shall help us speedily.
6 The Lord our strength and refuge is,
   When trouble's hour is near;
   A very present help is he;
   Therefore we will not fear.

CHRISTMAS (Handel's). C. M.

52. *"Be Thou exalted, O God, above the Heavens."*—Psalm 57.

1 O God, my heart is fully bent
  To magnify thy name;
  My tongue, with cheerful songs of praise,
  Shall celebrate thy fame.

2 Awake, my lute, nor thou, my harp,
  Thy warbling notes delay;
  While I, with early hymns of joy,
  Prevent the dawning day.

3 To all the listening tribes, O Lord,
  Thy wonders I will tell;
  And to those nations sing thy praise
  That round about us dwell;—

4 Because thy mercy's boundless height
  The highest heaven transcends,
  And far beyond th' aspiring clouds
  Thy faithful truth extends.

5 Be thou, O God, exalted high
  Above the starry frame,
  And let the world, with one consent,
  Confess thy glorious name.

126. *"The Lord sitteth King for ever."*
  Psalm 29.

1 Ye hosts of heaven, ye mighty ones,
  Ascribe, with one accord,
  The strength, the power, the majesty,
  To your almighty Lord.

2 Give glory to his holy name,
  And honor him alone;
  In beauty meet of holiness
  Approach his lofty throne.

3 Jehovah's voice of majesty
  Is on the waters wide;
  The God of glory thundereth,
  And on the seas doth ride.

4 Jehovah sits upon the floods,
  And tempests rage in vain

Jehovah sits as Sovereign King,
  And evermore shall reign.

167. *Eternity of God's Mercy.*—Psalm 136.

1 Oh, praise the Lord! for he is good;
  In him we rest obtain:
  His mercy has through ages stood,
  And ever shall remain.

2 Let all the people of the Lord
  His praises spread around;
  Let them his grace and love record,
  Who have salvation found.

3 Now let the east in him rejoice,
  The west its tribute bring,
  The north and south lift up their voice
  In honor of their King.

4 Oh, praise the Lord! for he is good;
  In him we rest obtain:
  His mercy has through ages stood,
  And ever shall remain.

486. *"Oh, how I love thy Law!"*—Psalm 119.

1 Oh, how I love thy holy law!
  'Tis daily my delight;
  And thence my meditations draw
  Divine advice by night.

2 My waking eyes prevent the day
  To meditate thy word;
  My soul with longing melts away
  To hear thy gospel, Lord.

3 How doth thy word my heart engage!
  How well employ my tongue!
  And in my tiresome pilgrimage
  Yields me a heavenly song.

4 When nature sinks, and spirits droop,
  Thy promises of grace
  Are pillars to support my hope,
  And there I write thy praise.

GROVE. L. M. DOUBLE.

11. *"Thou, Lord, hast made me glad through Thy work."*—Psalm 92.

1 SWEET is the work, my God, my King,
   To praise thy name, give thanks, and sing;
   To show thy love by morning light,
   And talk of all thy truth at night.
2 Sweet is the day of sacred rest;
   No mortal cares shall seize my breast:
   Oh, may my heart in tune be found,
   Like David's harp of solemn sound.

3 My heart shall triumph in my Lord,
   And bless his works, and bless his word;
   Thy works of grace, how bright they shine!
   How deep thy counsels, how divine!
4 Fools never raise their thoughts so high;
   Like brutes they live, like brutes they die;
   Like grass they flourish, till thy breath
   Blast them in everlasting death.

5 But I shall share a glorious part,
   When grace hath well refined my heart,
   And fresh supplies of joy are shed,
   Like holy oil, to cheer my head.
6 Then shall I see, and hear, and know
   All I desired or wished below;
   And every power find sweet employ
   In that eternal world of joy.

74. *"I heard the voice of a great multitude."*

1 MILLIONS within thy courts have met,
   Millions, this day, before thee bowed;
   Their faces Zion-ward were set,
   Vows with their lips to thee they vowed.
2 Soon as the light of morning broke
   O'er island, continent, or deep,
   Thy far-spread family awoke,
   Sabbath, all round the world, to keep.

3 From east to west, the sun surveyed,
   From north to south, adoring throngs;
   And still, when evening stretched her shade,
   The stars came out to hear their songs.
4 Not angel-trumpets sound more clear,
   Not elders' harps, nor seraphs' lays,
   Yield sweeter music to thine ear,
   Than humble prayer and thankful praise.

5 And not a prayer, a tear, a sigh,
   Hath failed this day some suit to gain;
   To those in trouble, thou wert nigh:
   Not one hath sought thy face in vain.
6 Yet one prayer more!—and be it one,
   In which both heaven and earth accord:
   Fulfill thy promise to thy Son;
   Let all that breathe call Jesus LORD!

ROCKINGHAM. L. M.

469. *Praise to the Trinity.*

1 Praises to him who built the hills;
Praises to him the stream who fills;
Praises to him who lights each star
That sparkles in the blue afar.

2 Praises to him who wakes the morn,
And bids it glow with beams new-born;
Who draws the shadows of the night,
Like curtains, o'er our wearied sight.

3 Praises to him whose love has given,
In Christ his Son, the life of heaven;
Who for our darkness, gives us light,
And turns to day our deepest night.

4 Praises to him in grace who came
To bear our woe and sin and shame;
Who lived to die, who died to rise,
The God-accepted sacrifice.

5 Praises to him the chain who broke,
Opened the prison, burst the yoke,
Sent forth the captives glad and free,
Heirs of an endless liberty.

6 Praises to him who sheds abroad
Within our hearts the love of God,—
The Spirit of all truth and peace,
The source of joy and holiness.

7 To Father, Son, and Spirit, now
The hands we lift, the knee we bow;
To God Jehovah thus we raise
The ransomed sinner's song of **praise!**

1235. *"Willing rather to be absent from the body."*

1 Descend from heaven, immortal Dove!
Stoop down and take us on thy wings;
And mount, and bear us far above
The reach of these inferior things,—

2 Beyond, beyond this lower sky,
Up where eternal ages roll,
Where solid pleasures never die,
And fruits immortal feast the soul.

3 Oh for a sight, a pleasing sight,
Of our Almighty Father's throne!
There sits our Saviour, crowned with light,
Clothed in a body like our own.

4 Adoring saints around him stand,
And thrones and powers before him fall:
The God shines gracious through the Man,
And sheds sweet glories on them all.

5 Oh! what amazing joys they feel,
While to their golden harps they sing,
And sit on every heavenly hill,
And spread the triumph of their King!

6 When shall the day, dear Lord, appear,
That I shall mount to dwell above;
And stand and bow among them there,
And view thy face, and sing, and love!

Doxology.

Eternal Father! throned above,
Thou Fountain of redeeming love!
Eternal Word! who left thy throne
For man's rebellion to atone;
Eternal Spirit, who dost give
That grace whereby our spirits live;
Thou God of our salvation, be
Eternal praises paid to thee!

FIELD. S. M.

12. "*It is a good thing to give thanks unto the Lord.*"—Psalm 92.

1 Sweet is the work, O Lord,
  Thy glorious acts to sing,
To praise thy name, and hear thy word,
  And grateful offerings bring.

2 Sweet, at the dawning light,
  Thy boundless love to tell:
And when approach the shades of night,
  Still on the theme to dwell.

3 Sweet, on this day of rest,
  To join in heart and voice
With those who love and serve thee best,
  And in thy name rejoice.

4 To songs of praise and joy,
  Be every Sabbath given,
That such may be our blest employ
  Eternally in heaven.

22. "*The place where Thine honor dwelleth.*"

1 How charming is the place
  Where my Redeemer, God,
Unvails the beauties of his face,
  And sheds his love abroad!

2 Here, on the mercy-seat,
  With radiant glories crowned,
Our joyful eyes behold him sit,
  And smile on all around.

3 To him our prayers and cries
  Our humble souls present;
He listens to our broken sighs,
  And grants us every want.

4 Give me, O Lord, a place
  Within thy blest abode,
Among the children of thy grace,
  The servants of my God.

49. *Christ the Day-star.*

1 We lift our hearts to thee,
  Thou Day-star from on high:
The sun itself is but thy shade,
  Yet cheers both earth and sky.

2 Oh, let thy rising beams
  Dispel the shades of night;
And let the glories of thy love,
  Come like the morning light!

3 How beauteous nature now!
  How dark and sad before!—
With joy we view the pleasing change,
  And nature's God adore.

4 May we this life improve,
  To mourn for errors past;
And live this short, revolving day
  As if it were our last.

53. "*Welcome, sweet day of rest.*"

1 Welcome, sweet day of rest,
  That saw the Lord arise,
Welcome to this reviving breast,
  And these rejoicing eyes!

2 The King himself comes near,
  And feasts his saints to-day;
Here may we sit, and see him here,
  And love, and praise, and pray.

3 One day, amid the place
  Where my dear Lord hath been,
Is sweeter than ten thousand days
  Within the tents of sin.

4 My willing soul would stay
  In such a frame as this,
And sit and sing herself away
  To everlasting bliss.

OLMUTZ. S. M.

401. *"He shall gather the Lambs with His arm."*

1 To praise our Shepherd's care,
　His wisdom, love and might,
Your loudest, loftiest songs prepare,
　And bid the world unite.

2 Supremely good and great,
　He tends his blood-bought fold:
He stoops, though throned in highest state,
　The feeblest to uphold.

3 He hears their softest plaint;
　He sees them when they roam;
And if his meanest lamb should faint,
　His bosom bears it home.

4 Kind Shepherd of the sheep!
　A weary flock are we;
And snares and foes are nigh; but keep
　The lambs who look to thee.

5 And if through death's dark vale
　Our feet should early tread,
Oh, may we reach thy fold, and hail
　The love which us hath led!

1025. *"The mountain of His Holiness."* Psalm 48.

1 GREAT is the Lord our God,
　And let his praise be great;
He makes his churches his abode,
　His most delightful seat.

2 These temples of his grace—
　How beautiful they stand!
The honors of our native place,
　And bulwarks of our land.

3 In Zion God is known,
　A refuge in distress;
How bright has his salvation shone
　Through all her palaces!

4 Oft have our fathers told,
　Our eyes have often seen,
How well our God secures the fold
　Where his own sheep have been.

5 In every new distress,
　We'll to his house repair,
We'll think upon his wondrous grace,
　And seek deliverance there.

LABAN. S. M.

MURRAY. H. M.

54. *"Welcome, delightful morn."*

1 WELCOME, delightful morn,
  Thou day of sacred rest!
  I hail thy kind return;—
  Lord, make these moments blest:
From the low train | I soar to reach
Of mortal toys, | Immortal joys.

2 Now may the King descend
  And fill his throne of grace;
  Thy scepter, Lord, extend,
  While saints address thy face:
Let sinners feel | And learn to know
Thy quickening word, | And fear the Lord.

3 Descend, celestial Dove,
  With all thy quickening powers;
  Disclose a Saviour's love,
  And bless the sacred hours:
Then shall my soul | Nor Sabbaths be
New life obtain, | Enjoyed in vain.

58. *"The day that God hath blessed."*

1 AWAKE, ye saints, awake!
  And hail this sacred day;
  In loftiest songs of praise
  Your joyful homage pay:
Come bless the day that God hath blest,
The type of heaven's eternal rest.

2 On this auspicious morn
  The Lord of life arose;
  He burst the bars of death,
  And vanquished all our foes;
And now he pleads our cause above,
And reaps the fruit of all his love.

3 All hail, triumphant Lord!
  Heaven with hosannas rings,
And earth in humbler strains,
  Thy praise responsive sings:
Worthy the Lamb that once was slain,
Thro' endless years to live and reign.

114. *"Praise the Lord from the earth."*

1 ANGELS, assist to sing
  The honors of your God;
  Touch every tuneful string,
  And sound his name abroad:
Come, pour the trembling notes along,
And swell the grand, immortal song.

2 And ye of meaner birth,
  Your joyful voices raise;
  All ye who dwell on earth,
  Your great Creator praise;
Let loud hosannas joyful rise,
Roll round the earth and pierce the skies.

3 Let day and dusky night,
  In solemn order, join
  His praises to recite,
  And speak his power divine:
Let every hill, and every vale,
Re-echo with the sacred tale.

4 Ye winds and raging seas,
  With wild tempestuous roar
  Resound, in mightier lays,
  His name from shore to shore:
Ye thunders, spread his name abroad;
Ye lightnings, flash before your God.

5 Let every creature sing
  The honors of our God;
  Touch every tuneful string,
  And spread his praise abroad:
Come, pour your trembling notes along,
And swell the universal song.

LENOX. P. M.

120. *Adoration of the Creator.*—Psalm 148.

1 YE tribes of Adam, join
  With heaven, and earth, and seas,
And offer notes divine
  To your Creator's praise:
Ye holy throng | In worlds of light,
Of angels bright, | Begin the song.

2 Thou sun, with dazzling rays,
  And moon, that rul'st the night,
Shine to your Maker's praise,
  With stars of twinkling light:
His power declare, | And clouds that fly
Ye floods on high, | In empty air.

3 The shining worlds above
  In glorious order stand;
Or in swift courses move
  By his supreme command:
He spake the word, | From nothing came,
And all their frame | To praise the Lord!

4 Ye vapors, hail, and snow,
  Praise ye th' almighty Lord;
And stormy winds that blow
  To execute his word:
When lightnings shine, | Let earth adore
Or thunders roar, | His hand divine

5 Let all the nations fear
  The God that rules above;
He brings his people near,
  And makes them taste his love:
While earth and sky | His saints shall raise
Attempt his praise, | His honors high.

440. *"Chosen of God and precious."*

1 JOIN all the glorious names
  Of wisdom, love, and power,
That ever mortals knew,
  That angels ever bore:
All are too mean to speak his worth,
Too mean to set my Saviour forth.

2 Great Prophet of our God!
  My tongue would bless thy name;
By thee the joyful news
  Of our salvation came:
The joyful news of sins forgiven,
Of hell subdued, and peace with heaven.

3 Jesus, our great High Priest,
  Offered his blood and died;
My guilty conscience seeks
  No sacrifice beside:
His powerful blood did once atone,
And now it pleads before the throne.

4 O thou almighty Lord!
  My Conqueror and my King!
Thy scepter and thy sword,
  Thy reigning grace I sing:
Thine is the power, behold, I sit,
In willing bonds beneath thy feet.

DOXOLOGY.
To God the Father's throne
  Your highest honors raise;
Glory to God the Son,
  To God the Spirit praise.
With all our powers, eternal King!
Thy name we sing, while faith adores.

LANSING. C. M. DOUBLE.

27. *"Peace be within thee."*—Psalm 122.

1 How did my heart rejoice to hear
  My friends devoutly say:
 "In Zion let us all appear,
  And keep the solemn day."
2 I love her gates, I love the road;
  The church, adorned with grace,
 Stands like a palace, built for God,
  To show his milder face.
3 Up to her courts, with joys unknown,
  The holy tribes repair,
 The Son of David holds his throne,
  And sits in judgment there.
4 He hears our praises and complaints;
  And, while his awful voice
 Divides the sinners from the saints,
  We tremble and rejoice.
5 Peace be within this sacred place,
  And joy a constant guest!
 With holy gifts and heavenly grace
  Be her attendants blest!
6 My soul shall pray for Zion still,
  While life or breath remains;
 There my best friends, my kindred, dwell;
  There God, my Saviour, reigns.

40. *"Say unto God, How terrible art Thou in Thy works."*—Psalm 66.

1 Let all the lands, with shouts of joy,
  To God their voices raise:
 Sing psalms in honor of his name,
  And spread his glorious praise.
2 And let them say, "How dreadful, Lord,
  In all thy works art thou!
 To thy great power thy stubborn foes
  Shall all be forced to bow."
3 "Through all the earth, the nations round
  Shall thee, their God, confess;
 And with glad hymns, their awful dread
  Of thy great name express."
4 Oh, come, behold the works of God!
  And then with me you'll own
 That he to all the sons of men
  Hath wondrous judgments shown.
5 Let all the lands, with shouts of joy,
  To God their voices raise;
 Sing psalms in honor of his name,
  And spread his glorious praise.

118. *"A God doing Wonders."*

1 I sing th' almighty power of God,
  That made the mountains rise,
 That spread the flowing seas abroad,
  And built the lofty skies.
2 I sing the wisdom that ordained
  The sun to rule the day;
 The moon shines full at his command,
  And all the stars obey.
3 I sing the goodness of the Lord,
  That filled the earth with food;
 He formed the creatures with his word,
  And then pronounced them good.
4 Lord, how thy wonders are displayed,
  Where'er I turn mine eye;
 If I survey the ground I tread,
  Or gaze upon the sky!
5 There's not a plant or flower below,
  But makes thy glories known;
 And clouds arise, and tempests blow,
  By order from thy throne.
6 Creatures that borrow life from thee
  Are subject to thy care;
 There's not a place where we can flee,
  But God is present there.

STEPHENS. C. M.

885. *"Am I a soldier of the Cross?"*

1 Am I a soldier of the cross,
   A follower of the Lamb!
And shall I fear to own his cause,
   Or blush to speak his name?

2 Must I be carried to the skies
   On flowery beds of ease,
While others fought to win the prize,
   And sailed through bloody seas?

3 Are there no foes for me to face?
   Must I not stem the flood?
Is this vile world a friend to grace,
   To help me on to God?

4 Sure I must fight, if I would reign:
   Increase my courage, Lord!
I'll bear the toil, endure the pain,
   Supported by thy word.

5 Thy saints, in all this glorious war,
   Shall conquer, though they die;
They view the triumph from afar,
   And seize it with their eye.

6 When that illustrious day shall rise,
   And all thine armies shine
In robes of victory through the skies,
   The glory shall be thine.

346. *Hosanna to the name of Christ.*

1 Now joyful strains we lift on high,
   Amid the faithful throng
Of those who Jesus magnify
   In sweet and holy song.

2 We render thanks, and bless the Lord,
   Who died our souls to save;
Through whom to heavenly peace restored,
   We fear no more the grave.

3 With saints, who all triumphantly
   In paradise record,

O'er sin and death, the victory,
   We strike the silver chord.

4 With angel-hosts that dwell above,
   And weave their golden lays
Around the throne of truth and love,
   We glad hosannas raise.

5 We celebrate the glorious name
   Of earth's Redeemer King;
Our tongues aloud his power proclaim,
   In heart his grace we sing.

378. *Christ's Entrance upon His Kingdom.*

1 Oh, for a shout of sacred joy
   To God, the sovereign King!
Let every land their tongues employ,
   And hymns of triumph sing.

2 Jesus, our God, ascends on high;
   His heavenly guards around
Attend him rising through the sky,
   With trumpets' joyful sound.

3 While angels shout and praise their King,
   Let mortals learn their strains;
Let all the earth his honor sing:
   O'er all the earth he reigns.

4 Rehearse his praise with awe profound
   Let knowledge lead the song;
Nor mock him with a solemn sound
   Upon a thoughtless tongue.

5 Oh, for a shout of sacred joy
   To God, the sovereign King!
Let every land their tongues employ,
   And hymns of triumph sing.

DOXOLOGY.

To Father, Son, and Holy Ghost,
   One God, whom we adore,
Be glory as it was, is now,
   And shall be evermore!

HENDON. 7s.

81. *"Within the vail."*

1 To thy temple I repair;
Lord, I love to worship there,
When within the vail I meet
Thee before the mercy seat.

2 While thy glorious praise is sung,
Touch my lips, unloose my tongue;
That my joyful soul may bless
Thee, the Lord, my Righteousness.

3 While the prayers of saints ascend,
God of love! to mine attend:
Hear me, for thy Spirit pleads;
Hear, for Jesus intercedes.

4 While I hearken to thy law,
Fill my soul with humble awe,
Till thy gospel bring to me
Life and immortality.

5 From thine house when I return,
May my heart within me burn;
And at evening let me say,
"I have walked with God to-day."

173. *Wonders of God's Condescension.*
Psalm 113.

1 HALLELUJAH! raise, oh, raise
To our God the song of praise:
All his servants join to sing,
God, our Saviour and our King.

2 Blessèd be for evermore
That dread name which we adore:
O'er all nations, God alone,
Higher than the heavens his throne.

3 Yet to view the heavens he bends;
Yea, to earth he condescends;
Passing by the rich and great,
For the low and desolate.

4 He can raise the poor to stand
With the princes of the land;
Wealth upon the needy shower;
Set the lowliest high in power.

5 He the broken spirit cheers,
Turns to joy the mourner's tears;
Such the wonders of his ways:
Praise his name, for ever praise.

227. *A Song of Joy in God's Providence.*

1 Thou, who dwell'st enthroned above;
Thou, in whom we live and move;
Thou, who art most great, most high—
God from all eternity!

2 Oh, how sweet, how excellent
When all tongues and hearts consent,
Grateful hearts, and joyful tongues,
Hymning thee in tuneful songs!

3 When the morning paints the skies,
When the stars of evening rise,
We thy praises will record,
Sovereign Ruler, mighty Lord!

4 Decks the spring with flowers the field?
Harvest rich doth autumn yield?
Giver of all good below,
Lord, from thee these blessings flow.

5 Sovereign Ruler! mighty Lord!
We thy praises will record:
Giver of these blessings, we
Pour the grateful song to thee.

261. *"The Heavenly theme."*

1 Now begin the heavenly theme,
Sing aloud of Jesus' name;
Ye, who his salvation prove,
Triumph in redeeming love.

NUREMBURG. 7s.

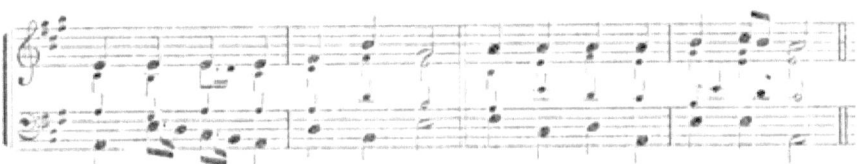

2 Mourning souls, dry up your tears,
  Banish all your guilty fears:
  See your guilt and curse remove,
  Canceled by redeeming love.

3 Welcome, all by sin oppressed,
  Welcome to his sacred rest;
  Nothing brought him from above,
  Nothing but redeeming love.

4 Hither, then, your music bring,
  Strike aloud each joyful string:
  Mortals, join the hosts above,
  Join to praise redeeming love!

278. *Response to the Song of the Angels.*
     Luke 2.

1 Hail the night, all hail the morn,
  When the Prince of Peace was born!
  When, amid the wakeful fold,
  Tidings good the angel told.

2 Now our solemn chant we raise
  Duly to the Saviour's praise;
  Now with carol hymns we bless
  Christ the Lord, our Righteousness.

3 While resounds the joyful cry,
  "Glory be to God on high,
  Peace on earth, good will to men!"
  Gladly we respond, "Amen!"

4 Thus we greet this holy day,
  Pouring forth our festive lay;
  Thus we tell, with saintly mirth,
  Of Immanuel's wondrous birth.

5 We in perfect peace would live,
  We to God would glory give:
  Lauding, with the heavenly host,
  Father, Son, and Holy Ghost.

1076. *Children's Praise to the Trinity.*

1 Glory to the Father give,
  God, in whom we move and live!
  Children's prayers he deigns to hear;
  Children's songs delight his ear.

2 Glory to the Son we bring,
  Christ our Prophet, Priest, and King!
  Children! raise your sweetest strain
  To the Lamb, for he was slain.

3 Glory to the Holy Ghost!
  Be this day a Pentecost;
  Children's minds may he inspire,—
  Touch their tongues with holy fire.

4 Glory in the highest be
  To the blessed Trinity!
  For the gospel from above,
  For the word that "God is love."

1146. *Thanksgiving for a Revival of Religion.*

1 Fount of everlasting love!
    Rich thy streams of mercy are—
  Flowing purely from above,
    Beauty marks their course afar.

2 Lo! thy church, thy garden now
    Blooms beneath the heavenly shower,
  Sinners feel, and melt, and bow—
    Mild, yet mighty, is thy power.

3 God of grace, before thy throne
    Here our warmest thanks we bring;
  Thine the glory, thine alone:
    Loudest praise to thee we sing.

4 Hear, oh, hear, our grateful song;
    Let thy Spirit still descend;
  Roll the tide of grace along,
    Widening, deepening to the end.

THE OLD HUNDREDTH. L. M.

96. *An ancient Hymn of Praise to God.*

1 THEE we adore, eternal Lord!
   We praise thy name with one accord;
   Thy saints, who here thy goodness see,
   Through all the world do worship thee.

2 To thee aloud all angels cry,
   The heavens and all the powers on high:
   Thee, holy, holy, holy King,
   Lord God of hosts, they ever sing.

3 Th' apostles join the glorious throng;
   The prophets swell th' immortal song:
   The martyrs' noble army raise
   Eternal anthems to thy praise.

4 From day to day, O Lord, do we
   Highly exalt and honor thee!
   Thy name we worship and adore,
   World without end, for evermore!

5 Vouchsafe, O Lord, we humbly pray,
   To keep us safe from sin this day:
   Have mercy, Lord! we trust in thee;
   Oh, let us ne'er confounded be!

100. *God exalted.*—Psalm 57.

1 BE thou exalted, O my God!
   Above the heavens where angels dwell;
   Thy power on earth be known abroad,
   And land to land thy wonders tell.

2 My heart is fixed; my song shall raise
   Immortal honors to thy name:
   Awake, my tongue, to sound his praise,
   My tongue, the glory of my frame.

3 High o'er the earth his mercy reigns,
   And reaches to the utmost sky;
   His truth to endless years remains,
   When lower worlds dissolve and die.

4 Be thou exalted, O my God!
   Above the heavens where angels dwell;
   Thy power on earth be known abroad,
   And land to land thy wonders tell.

103. *Brief Call to Praise, from* Psalm 117.

1 FROM all that dwell below the skies,
   Let the Creator's praise arise;
   Let the Redeemer's name be sung,
   Through every land, by every tongue.

2 Eternal are thy mercies, Lord;
   Eternal truth attends thy word;
   Thy praise shall sound from shore to shore,
   Till suns shall rise and set no more!

129. *The Glory of God.*

1 COME, O my soul! in sacred lays,
   Attempt thy great Creator's praise:
   But, oh, what tongue can speak his fame!
   What mortal verse can reach the theme!

2 Enthroned amid the radiant spheres,
   He glory, like a garment wears;
   To form a robe of light divine,
   Ten thousand suns around him shine.

3 In all our Maker's grand designs,
   Almighty power, with wisdom, shines;
   His works, thro' all this wondrous frame,
   Declare the glory of his name.

4 Raised on devotion's lofty wing,
   Do thou, my soul, his glories sing;
   And let his praise employ thy tongue,
   Till listening worlds shall join the song!

DOXOLOGY.

PRAISE God, from whom all blessings flow!
Praise him, all creatures here below!
Praise him above, ye heavenly host!
Praise Father, Son, and Holy Ghost!

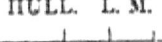

145. *"Thou art from everlasting."*
Psalm 93.

1 JEHOVAH reigns! He dwells in light,
Girded with majesty and might;
The world, created by his hands,
Still on its firm foundation stands.

2 But ere this spacious world was made,
Or had its first foundation laid,
Thy throne eternal ages stood,
Thyself the ever-living God.

3 Like floods the angry nations rise,
And aim their rage against the skies:
Vain floods, that aim their rage so high!
At thy rebuke the billows die.

4 For ever shall thy throne endure:
Thy promise stand for ever sure;
And everlasting holiness
Becomes the dwelling of thy grace.

175. *"O God, Most hidden, and Most manifest!"*

1 WHAT secret place, what distant star,
Is like, dread Lord, to thine abode?
Why dwellest thou from us so far?
We yearn for thee, thou living God!

2 And will the hidden God appear?
We hail thee in the living Word;
Thy heavenly Majesty draws near,
In Christ, our brother and our Lord.

3 In vain we seek for thine abode;
And wilt thou ever to us come?
The Holy Ghost, the mighty God,
Now makes our souls his blessed home.

4 O Glory that no eye can bear!
O Presence bright, our inward Guest!
O Farthest off! O Ever near!
Most hidden and Most manifest!

1115. *"So didst Thou lead Thy people."*

1 O GOD, beneath thy guiding hand,
Our exiled fathers crossed the sea;
And when they trod the wint'ry strand,
With prayer and psalm they worshiped thee.

2 Thou heard'st, well pleased, the song, the prayer:
Thy blessing came; and still its power
Shall onward through all ages bear
The memory of that holy hour.

3 Laws, freedom, truth, and faith in God
Came with those exiles o'er the waves;
And where their pilgrim feet have trod,
The God they trusted guards their graves.

4 And here thy name, O God of love,
Their children's children shall adore,
Till these eternal hills remove,
And spring adorns the earth no more.

1156. *"Still we are guarded by our God."*

1 GREAT GOD! we sing that mighty hand,
By which supported still we stand;
The opening year thy mercy shows;
That mercy crowns it till it close.

2 By day, by night, at home, abroad,
Still we are guarded by our God;
By his incessant bounty fed,
By his unerring counsel led.

3 With grateful hearts the past we own;
The future, all to us unknown,
We to thy guardian care commit,
And peaceful leave before thy feet.

4 In scenes exalted or depressed,
Be thou our joy, and thou our rest;
Thy goodness all our hopes shall raise,
Adored through all our changing days.

BREMEN. S. M. Double.

29. *"The city of our God."*—Psalm 122.

1 Glad was my heart to hear
  My old companions say:
"Come, in the house of God appear,
  For 't is a holy day."
2 Our willing feet shall stand
  Within the temple-door,
While young and old, in many a band,
  Shall throng the sacred floor.

3 Thither the tribes repair,
  Where all are wont to meet,
And joyful in the house of prayer
  Bend at the mercy-seat.
4 Pray for Jerusalem,
  The city of our God:
The Lord from heaven be kind to them
  That love the dear abode.

5 Within these walls may peace
  And harmony be found!
Zion! in all thy palaces,
  Prosperity abound!
6 For friends and brethren dear,
  Our prayer shall never cease;
Oft as they meet for worship here,
  God send his people peace!

223. *"Bless the Lord, O my soul."*
Psalm 103.

1 Oh, bless the Lord, my soul!
  Let all within me join,
And aid my tongue to bless his name,
  Whose favors are divine.

2 Oh, bless the Lord, my soul!
  Nor let his mercies lie
Forgotten in unthankfulness,
  And without praises die.

3 'T is he forgives thy sins;
  'T is he relieves thy pain;
'T is he that heals thy sicknesses,
  And makes thee young again.
4 He crowns thy life with love,
  When ransomed from the grave;
He who redeemed my soul from hell,
  Hath sovereign power to save.

5 He fills the poor with good:
  He gives the sufferers rest:
The Lord hath judgments for the proud,
  And justice for th' oppressed.
6 His wondrous works and ways
  He made by Moses known;
But sent the world his truth and grace
  By his belovéd Son.

224. *"And all that is within me bless His holy name."*—Psalm 103.

1 Oh, bless the Lord, my soul!
  His grace to thee proclaim;
And all that is within me join
  To bless his holy name.
2 Oh, bless the Lord, my soul!
  His mercies bear in mind;
Forget not all his benefits:
  The Lord to thee is kind.

ST. THOMAS. S. M.

3 He will not always chide :
   He will with patience wait :
His wrath is ever slow to rise,
   And ready to abate.
4 He pardons all thy sins,
   Prolongs thy feeble breath ;
He healeth thy **infirmities**,
   And ransoms **thee from death**.
5 He clothes thee with his **love**,
   Upholds thee with **his truth** ;
Then, like the eagle, **he renews**
   The **vigor** of thy youth.
6 Then **bless** his holy name,
   Whose grace hath made thee whole ;
Whose loving kindness crowns thy days :
   Oh, bless the Lord, my soul !

246. " *To the only wise God, our Saviour.*"
   Jude 24, 25.
1 To God, the only wise,
   Our Saviour and our King,
Let all the saints below the skies
   Their humble praises bring.

2 'T is his almighty love,
   His counsel and his care,
Preserves us safe from sin and death,
   And every hurtful snare.

3 He will present our souls,
   Unblemished and complete,
Before the glory of his face,
   With joys divinely **great**.

4 Then all the chosen seed
   Shall meet around the throne,
Shall bless the conduct of his grace
   And make his wonders known.

5 To our Redeemer, God,
   Wisdom and power belong,
Immortal crowns of majesty,
   And everlasting song.

968. " *Rejoicing in hope.*"
1 COME, we who love the Lord,
   And let our joys be known ;
Join in a song of sweet accord,
   And thus surround the throne.

2 Let those refuse to sing
   Who never knew our God ;
But favorites of the heavenly King
   May speak their joys abroad.

3 The men of grace have found
   Glory begun below ;
Celestial fruits on earthly ground
   From faith and hope may grow.

4 The hill of Zion yields
   A thousand sacred sweets
Before we reach the heavenly fields,
   Or walk the golden streets.

5 Then let our songs abound,
   And every tear be dry ;
We 're marching through Immanuel's ground
   To fairer worlds on high.

102. *Brief Ascription of Praise, from*
   Psalm 117.
1 THY name, almighty Lord,
   Shall sound through distant lands ;
Great is thy grace, and sure thy word ;
   Thy truth for ever stands.

2 Far be thine honor spread,
   And long thy praise endure,
Till morning light and evening shade
   Shall be exchanged no more.

DOXOLOGY.
To God, the Father, Son,
   And Spirit, glory be,
As was, and is, and shall remain
   Through all eternity !

HOWARD. C. M.

23. *"This is the day which the Lord hath made."*—Psalm 118.

1 This is the day the Lord hath made;
 He calls the hours his own:
 Let heaven rejoice, let earth be glad,
 And praise surround the throne.

2 To-day he rose, and left the dead,
 And Satan's empire fell;
 To-day the saints his triumph spread,
 And all his wonders tell.

3 Hosanna to th' anointed King,
 To David's holy Son:
 Help us, O Lord! descend and bring
 Salvation from thy throne.

4 Blest be the Lord who comes to men
 With messages of grace;
 Who comes in God his Father's name,
 To save our sinful race.

5 Hosanna in the highest strains
 The church on earth can raise;
 The highest heavens, in which he reigns,
 Shall give him nobler praise.

60. *"Come, see the place where the Lord lay."*

1 Again the Lord of life and light
 Awakes the kindling ray,
 Unseals the eyelids of the morn,
 And pours refulgent day.

2 Oh, what a night was that which **wrapt**
 A guilty world in gloom!
 Oh, what a Sun, which broke this **day**,
 Triumphant from the tomb!

3 This day be grateful homage paid,
 And loud hosannas sung;
 Let gladness dwell in every heart,
 And praise on every tongue.

4 Ten thousand thousand lips shall join
 To hail this happy morn,
 Which scatters blessings from its wings
 On nations yet unborn.

327. *"The unsearchable riches of Christ."*

1 To our Redeemer's glorious name
 Awake the sacred song;
 Oh, may his love—immortal flame!—
 Tune every heart and tongue.

2 His love, what mortal thought can reach!
 What mortal tongue display!
 Imagination's utmost stretch
 In wonder dies away.

3 Dear Lord, while we, **adoring, pay**
 Our humble thanks **to thee,**
 May every heart with **rapture say,**
 "The Saviour died **for me!"**

4 Oh, may the sweet, the blissful **theme,**
 Fill every heart and tongue!
 Till strangers love thy charming **name,**
 And join the sacred song.

483. *The Bible the Light of the World.*

1 A glory gilds the sacred **page,**
 Majestic, like the sun:
 It gives a light to every age;
 It gives, but borrows none.

2 The hand that gave it still supplies
 The gracious light and heat:
 Its truths upon the nations rise;
 They rise, but never set.

3 Let everlasting thanks be thine
 For such a bright display,
 As makes a world of darkness shine
 With beams of heavenly day.

4 My soul rejoices to pursue
 The steps of him I love,
 Till glory breaks upon my view
 In brighter worlds above!

CHRISTMAS (Handel's). C. M.

797. *"I'm not ashamed to own my Lord."—*
2 Tim. 1: 12.

1 I'M not ashamed to own my Lord,
  Or to defend his cause;
  Maintain the honor of his word,
  The glory of his cross.

2 Jesus, my God!—I know his **name**—
  His name is all my trust;
  Nor will he put my soul to shame,
  Nor let my hope be lost.

3 Firm as his throne **his promise stands,**
  And he can well **secure**
  What I've committed to **his hands,**
  Till the decisive hour.

4 Then will he own my worthless name
  Before his Father's face,
  And in the new Jerusalem
  Appoint my soul a place.

880.   *The Heavenly Race.*

1 AWAKE, my soul! stretch every **nerve,**
  And press with vigor on;
  A heavenly race demands thy **zeal,**
  A bright, immortal crown.

2 A cloud of witnesses around
  Hold thee in full survey;
  Forget the steps already trod,
  And onward urge thy way.

3 'Tis God's all animating voice,
  That calls thee from on high;
  'Tis his own hand presents the prize
  To thine aspiring **eye,—**

4 That prize with peerless glories **bright,**
  Which shall new luster boast,
  When victor's wreaths **and** monarch's
     gems
  Shall blend in common dust.

5 Blest Saviour, introduced by thee,
  Have I my race begun;

  And, crowned with victory, at thy feet
  I'll lay my honors down.

1016. *" **Blessed** is he whose transgression is
          forgiven."*

1 SALVATION! oh, the joyful sound!
  'T is pleasure to our ears;
  A sovereign balm for every wound,
  A cordial for our fears.

2 Buried in sorrow and in sin,
  At hell's dark door we lay;
  But **we** arise by grace divine,
  To see a heavenly day.

3 Salvation! let the echo fly
  The spacious earth around,
  While all the armies of the sky
  Conspire **to** raise the sound.

1028. *" Salvation will God appoint for walls
          and bulwarks."—Isaiah 26: 1—6.*

1 How honored is the sacred place,
  Where we adoring stand—
  Zion! the glory of the earth,
  And beauty of the land!

2 Bulwarks of mighty grace defend
  The city where we dwell;
  The walls, of strong salvation made,
  Defy th' assaults of hell.

3 Lift up the everlasting gates,
  The doors wide open fling;
  Enter, ye nations that obey
  The statutes of our King.

4 Here shall you taste unmingled joys,
  And live in perfect peace;
  You who have **known** Jehovah's name,
  And ventured on his grace.

5 Trust in the Lord; for ever trust,
  And banish all your fears:
  Strength in the Lord Jehovah dwells,
  Eternal as his years.

GRETNA. C. P. M.

56. *"Our feet shall stand within thy gates, O Jerusalem."*—Psalm 122.

1 THE festal morn, my God, is come,
  That calls me to thy sacred dome,
    Thy presence to adore:
  My feet the summons shall attend,
  With willing steps thy courts ascend,
    And tread the hallowed floor.

2 With holy joy I hail the day
  That warns my thirsting soul away
    To dwell among the blest!
  For, lo! my great Redeemer's power
  Unfolds the everlasting door,
    And leads me to his rest!

3 Hither, from earth's remotest end,
  Lo! the redeemed of God ascend,
    Their tribute hither bring:
  Here, crowned with everlasting joy,
  In hymns of praise their tongues employ,
    And hail th' immortal King.

117. *There is a God.*

1 I SING of God,—the world he made,
  The glorious light, the soothing shade;
    Dale, plain, and grove, and hill;
  The wide and fathomless abyss,
  Where nature joys in secret bliss,
    And wisdom hides her skill.

2 "Tell them, I AM," Jehovah said:
  The listening earth did hear in dread;
    And, smitten to the heart,
  At once, above, beneath, around,
  All nature, without voice or sound,
    Replied, "O LORD, THOU ART!"

703. *The Fullness of Christ's Love.*

1 O LOVE divine, how sweet thou art!
  When shall I find my willing heart
    All taken up by thee?
  I thirst, I faint, I die to prove
  The greatness of redeeming love,—
    The love of Christ to me.

2 Stronger his love than death or hell:
  No mortal can its riches tell,
    Nor first-born sons of light:
  In vain they long its depths to see;
  They can not reach the mystery,—
    The length, the breadth, the height.

3 God only knows the love of God;
  Oh that it now were shed abroad
    In this poor, stony heart!
  For love I sigh, for love I pine;
  This only portion, Lord, be mine—
    Be mine this better part.

4 Oh that I could for ever sit
  In transport at my Saviour's feet!
    Be this my happy choice;
  My only care, delight, and bliss,
  My joy, my heaven on earth, be this,
    To hear my Saviour's voice.

DOXOLOGY.

To Father, Son, and Holy Ghost,
The God, whom heaven's triumphant host
  And saints on earth adore,
Be glory as in ages past,
Is now, and shall for ever last,
  When time shall be no more!

ARIEL. C. P. M.

433. "*The unsearchable riches of Christ.*"

1 Oh, could I speak the matchless worth,
    Oh, could I sound the glories forth
        Which in my Saviour shine!
    I'd soar, and touch the heavenly strings,
    And vie with Gabriel, while he sings,
        In notes almost divine.

2 I'd sing the precious blood he spilt,
    My ransom from the dreadful guilt
        Of sin and wrath divine.
    I'd sing his glorious righteousness,
    In which all perfect, heavenly dress,
        My soul shall ever shine.

3 I'd sing the characters he bears,
    And all the forms of love he wears,
        Exalted on his throne.
    In loftiest songs of sweetest praise,
    I would to everlasting days
        Make all his glories known.

4 Well, the delightful day will come
    When my dear Lord will bring me home,
        And I shall see his face;
    Then with my Saviour, Brother, Friend,
    A blest eternity I'll spend,
        Triumphant in his grace.

1154. "*The earth is full of Thy riches.*"

1 Thy mighty working, mighty God!
    Wakes all my powers; I look abroad,
        And can no longer rest;
    I, too, must sing when all things sing,
    And from my heart the praises ring
        The Highest loveth best.

2 If thou, in thy great love to us,
    Wilt scatter joy and beauty thus
        O'er this poor earth of ours;
    What nobler glories shall be given
    Hereafter in thy shining heaven,
        Set round with golden **towers**!

3 What thrilling joy, when on our sight
    Christ's garden beams in cloudless light
        Where all the air is sweet;
    Still laden with th' unwearied hymn
    From all the thousand seraphim
        Who God's high praise repeat!

4 Oh, were I there! oh that I now
    Before thy throne, my God, could bow,
        And bear my heavenly palm!
    Then, like the angels, would I raise
    My voice, and sing thine endless praise
        In many a sweet-toned psalm.

ALPHEUS. C. M.

18. *"Peace be within thy walls."*—Psalm 122.

1 WITH joy we hail the sacred day
 Which God hath called his own;
 With joy the summons we obey
 To worship at his throne.

2 Thy chosen temple, Lord, how fair!
 Where willing votaries throng
 To breathe the humble, fervent prayer,
 And pour the choral song.

3 Spirit of grace! Oh, deign to dwell
 Within thy church below;
 Make her in holiness excel,
 With pure devotion glow.

4 Let peace within her walls be found;
 Let all her sons unite
 To spread, with grateful zeal, around
 Her clear and shining light.

5 Great God, we hail the sacred day
 Which thou hast called thine own:
 With joy the summons we obey
 To worship at thy throne.

20. *"One thing have I desired of the Lord."*
 Psalm 27.

1 THE Lord of glory is my light,
 And my salvation, too;
 God is my strength, nor will I fear
 What all my foes can do.

2 One privilege my heart desires;
 Oh, grant me an abode
 Among the churches of thy saints,
 The temples of my God!

3 There shall I offer my requests,
 And see thy beauty still;
 Shall hear thy messages of love,
 And there inquire thy will.

4 When troubles rise, and storms appear,
 There may his children hide;
 God has a strong pavilion, where
 He makes my soul abide.

5 Now shall my head be lifted high
 Above my foes around;
 And songs of joy and victory
 Within thy temple sound.

43. *"My voice shalt Thou hear in the morning."*—Psalm 5.

1 LORD! in the morning thou shalt hear
 My voice ascending high;
 To thee will I direct my prayer,
 To thee lift up mine eye;

2 Up to the hills where Christ is gone,
 To plead for all his saints,
 Presenting at his Father's throne
 Our songs and our complaints.

3 Thou art a God before whose sight
 The wicked shall not stand;
 Sinners shall ne'er be thy delight,
 Nor dwell at thy right hand.

4 But to thy house will I resort,
 To taste thy mercies there;
 I will frequent thy holy court,
 And worship in thy fear.

5 Oh, may thy Spirit guide my feet
 In ways of righteousness!
 Make every path of duty straight,
 And plain before my face.

445. *"The Way, and the Truth, and the Life."*—John 14: 6.

1 THOU art the Way: to thee alone
 From sin and death we flee;
 And he who would the Father seek,
 Must seek him, Lord, by thee.

DEDHAM. C. M.

2 Thou art the Truth : thy word alone
   True wisdom can impart ;
 Thou only canst instruct the mind,
   And purify the heart.

3 Thou art the Life : the rending tomb
   Proclaims thy conquering arm ,
 And those who put their trust in thee
   Nor death nor hell shall harm.

4 Thou art the Way, the Truth, the Life :
   Grant us to know that Way ;
 That Truth to keep, that Life to win,
   Which leads to endless day.

529.   " Come to the Ark."—Gen. 7: 1.

1 COME to the ark, come to the ark ;
   To Jesus come away ;
 The pestilence walks forth by night,
   The arrow flies by day.

2 Come to the ark : the waters rise,
   The seas their billows rear ;
 While darkness gathers o'er the skies,
   Behold a refuge near !

3 Come to the ark, all, all that weep
   Beneath the sense of sin :
 Without, deep calleth unto deep,
   But all is peace within.

4 Come to the ark, ere yet the flood
   Your lingering steps oppose ;
 Come, for the door, which open stood,
   Is now about to close.

924.   " Walk in the light."—1 John 1 : 7.

1 WALK in the light ! so shalt thou know
   That fellowship of love
 His Spirit only can bestow,
   Who reigns in light above.

2 Walk in the light ! and thou shalt own
   Thy darkness passed away,
 Because that light on thee hath shone
   In which is perfect day.

3 Walk in the light ! and ev'n the tomb
   No fearful shade shall wear
 Glory shall chase away its gloom,
   For Christ hath conquered there !

4 Walk in the light ! and thine shall be
   A path, though thorny, bright ;
 For God, by grace, shall dwell in thee,
   And God himself is light !

1087.   The happy Home.

1 HAPPY the home, when God is there,
   And love fills every breast ;
 Where one their wish, and one their
       prayer,
   And one their heavenly rest.

2 Happy the home where Jesus' name
   Is sweet to every ear ,
 Where children early lisp his fame,
   And parents hold him dear.

3 Happy the home where prayer is heard,
   And praise is wont to rise ;
 Where parents love the sacred word,
   And live but for the skies.

4 Lord ! let us in our homes agree,
   This blessèd peace to gain ;
 Unite our hearts in love to thee,
   And love to all will reign.

DOXOLOGY.

LET God the Father, and the Son,
   And Spirit, be adored,
 Where there are works to make him
       known,
   Or saints to love the Lord !

HADDAM. H. M.

168. *"Oh, give thanks unto the God of gods."*
Psalm 136.

1 GIVE thanks to God most high,
　　The universal Lord,
　　The sovereign King of kings;
　　And be his name adored:
Thy mercy, Lord, │ And ever sure
Shall still endure; │ Abides thy word.

2 How mighty is his hand!
　　What wonders hath he done!
　　He formed the **earth** and seas,
　　And spread the heavens alone:
His power and grace │ And let his name
Are still the same; │ Have endless praise.

3 He saw the nations lie
　　All perishing in sin;
　　And pitied the sad state
　　The ruined world was in:
Thy mercy, Lord, │ And ever sure
Shall still endure; │ Abides thy word.

4 He sent his only Son
　　To save us from our woe,
　　From Satan, sin, and death,
　　And every hurtful foe:
His power and grace │ And let his name
Are still the same; │ Have endless praise.

5 Give thanks aloud to God,
　　To God, the heavenly King;
　　And let the spacious earth
　　His works and glories sing:
Thy mercy, Lord, │ And ever sure
Shall still endure; │ Abides thy word.

343. *Response to the "New Song."*
Rev. 5.

1 SHALL hymns of grateful love
　　Thro' heaven's high arches ring,
　　And all the hosts above
　　Their songs of triumph sing;
And shall not we take up the strain,
And send the echo back again?

2 Shall they adore the Lord,
　　Who bought them with his blood,
　　And all the love record
　　That led them home to God;
And shall not we take up the strain,
And send the echo back again?

3 Oh, spread the joyful sound!
　　The Saviour's love proclaim;
　　And publish all around
　　Salvation through his name:
Till all the world take up the strain,
And send the echo back again!

332. *"The Debt of Love."*

1 COME, every pious heart
　　That loves the Saviour's name,
　　Your noblest powers exert
　　To celebrate his fame:
Tell all above, and all below,
The debt of love to him you owe.

2 He left his starry crown,
　　And laid his robes aside;
　　On wings of love came down,
　　And wept, and bled, and died!
What he endured, oh, who can tell?
To save our souls from death and hell!

FLEET STREET. H. M.

3 From the dark grave he rose,
  The mansion of the dead;
  And thence his mighty foes
  In glorious triumph led:
Up thro' the sky the Conqueror rode,
And reigns on high, the Saviour-God.

4 From thence he'll quickly come—
  His chariot will not stay—
  And bear our spirits home
  To realms of endless day:
There shall we see his lovely face,
And ever be in his embrace.

97. *"Holy, holy, holy. Lord God Almighty."*
Rev. 15: 3, 4.

1 O HOLY, holy Lord,
    Creation's sovereign King,
  Thy majesty adored,
    Let all thy creatures sing:
Who wast, and art, | Nor time shall see
And art to be; | Thy sway depart.

2 Great are thy works of praise,
    O God of boundless might!
  All just and true thy ways,
    Thou King of saints in light!
Let all above, | Conspire to show
And all below, | Thy power and love.

3 Who shall not fear thee, Lord!
    And magnify thy name?
  Thy judgments sent abroad
    Thy holiness proclaim:
Nations shall throng | And thee adore,
From every shore, | In holy song.

4 While all the powers on high
    Their swelling chorus raise,
  Let earth and man reply,
    And echo back thy praise:
Thy glory own, | God ever blest,
First, last, and best, | And God alone!

188. *"He is clothed with majesty."*
Psalm 93.

1 THE Lord Jehovah reigns;
    His throne is built on high;
  The garments he assumes
    Are light and majesty:
His glories shine with beams so bright,
No mortal eye can bear the sight.

2 The thunders of his hand
    Keep the wide world in awe;
  His wrath and justice stand
    To guard his holy law;
And where his love resolves to bless,
His truth confirms and seals the grace.

3 Through all his ancient works
    Surprising wisdom shines,
  Confounds the powers of hell,
    And breaks their curs'd designs:
Strong is his arm, and shall fulfill
His great decrees, his sovereign will.

4 And can this mighty King
    Of glory condescend?
  And will he write his name,
    "My Father and my Friend?"
I love his name; I love his word:
Join, all my powers, and praise the Lord

HEBRON. L. M.

21. *Communion with Christ in Worship.*

1 FAR from my thoughts, vain world, be-
    gone!
  Let my religious hours alone!
  Fain would mine eyes my Saviour see;
  I wait a visit, Lord, from thee.

2 My heart grows warm with holy fire,
  And kindles with a pure desire:
  Come, my dear Jesus! from above,
  And feed my soul with heavenly love.

3 Blest Saviour! what delicious fare,
  How sweet thine entertainments are!
  Never did angels taste, above,
  Redeeming grace and dying love.

4 Hail, great Immanuel, all divine!
  In thee thy Father's glories shine:
  Thou brightest, sweetest, fairest One
  That eyes have seen, or angels known!

45.* *"Thou art my God."*—Psalm 63.

1 GREAT God, indulge my humble claim;
    Thou art my hope, my joy, my rest;
  The glories that compose thy name
    Stand all engaged to make me blest.

2 Thou great and good, thou just and wise,
    Thou art my Father and my God;
  And I am thine, by sacred ties—
    Thy son, thy servant bought with blood.

3 With heart and eyes, and lifted hands,
    For thee I long, to thee I look;
  As travelers, in thirsty lands,
    Pant for the cooling water brook.

4 With early feet I love t' appear
    Among thy saints, and seek thy face;
  Oft have I seen thy glory there,
    And felt the power of sovereign grace.

5 I'll lift my hands, I'll raise my voice,
    While I have breath to pray or praise;
  This work shall make my heart rejoice,
    And cheer the remnant of my days.

68. *"Abide with us."*

1 SUN of my soul! thou Saviour dear,
  It is not night if thou be near:
  Oh, may no earth-born cloud arise
  To hide thee from thy servant's eyes!

2 When soft the dews of kindly sleep
  My wearied eyelids gently steep,
  Be my last thought,—how sweet to rest
  For ever on my Saviour's breast!

3 Abide with me from morn till eve,
  For without thee I can not live;
  Abide with me when night is nigh,
  For without thee I dare not die.

4 Be near to bless me when I wake,
  Ere through the world my way I take;
  Abide with me till in thy love
  I lose myself in heaven above.

71.* *"I will both lay me down in peace and
    sleep."*

1 THUS far the Lord has led me on;
    Thus far his power prolongs my days;
  And every evening shall make known
    Some fresh memorial of his grace.

2 Much of my time has run to waste,
    And I, perhaps, am near my home;
  But he forgives my follies past;
    He gives me strength for days to come.

3 I lay my body down to sleep;
    Peace is the pillow for my head;
  While well-appointed angels keep
    Their watchful stations round my bed.

4 Faith in thy name forbids my fear;
    Oh, may thy presence ne'er depart!
  And in the morning make me hear
    The love and kindness of thy heart.

5 Thus, when the night of death shall come,
    My flesh shall rest beneath the ground,
  And wait thy voice to rouse my tomb,
    With sweet salvation in the sound.

* When sung to ARNON, commence the fifth stanza with the second part of the tune.

MALVERN. L. M.

163. *"So great is His mercy."*—Psalm 103.

1 The Lord! how **wondrous are his ways!**
How firm his **truth!** how **large his grace!**
He takes his mercy for his throne,
And thence he makes his glories known.

2 Not half so high his power hath spread
The starry heavens above our head,
As his rich love exceeds our praise,
Exceeds the highest hopes we raise.

3 Not half so far has nature **placed**
The rising morning **from the west,**
As his forgiving grace **removes**
The daily guilt of those **he loves.**

4 How slowly doth his **wrath arise!**
On swifter wings salvation **flies:**
Or, if he lets his anger burn,
How soon his frowns **to pity turn!**

5 His everlasting love is sure
To all his saints, and shall endure;
From age to age his truth shall reign,
Nor children's children hope in vain.

961. *"While I live will I praise the Lord."*
Psalm 146.

1 God of my life! through all my days
My grateful **powers** shall sound **thy praise;**
The song shall wake with opening light,
And warble to the silent night.

2 When anxious care would break my rest,
And grief would tear my throbbing breast,
Thy tuneful praises raised on high,
Shall check the murmur and the sigh.

3 When death **o'er** nature shall prevail,
And all my powers of language fail,
Joy through my swimming eyes shall break,
And mean the thanks I can not speak.

4 But, oh! when that last conflict's o'er,
And I am chained to flesh no more,
With what glad accents shall I rise
To join the music of the skies!

1151. *Love of God seen in the Seasons.*

1 Our Helper, God! we bless thy name,
The same thy power, thy grace the same;
The tokens of thy loving care
Open and crown and close the year.

2 Amid ten thousand snares we stand,
Supported by thy guardian hand;
And see, when we survey our ways,
Ten thousand monuments of praise.

3 Thus far thine arm hath led us on;
Thus far we make thy mercy known;
And, while we tread this desert land,
New mercies shall new songs demand.

4 Our grateful souls on Jordan's shore
Shall raise one sacred pillar more;
Then bear, in thy bright courts above,
Inscriptions of immortal love.

DOXOLOGY.

Praise God, from whom all blessings flow!
Praise him, all creatures here below!
Praise him above, ye heavenly host!
Praise Father, Son, and Holy Ghost!

PALMER. C. M.

59. *The Day of Christ's Resurrection.*

1 BLEST morning! whose young dawning rays
Beheld our rising God;
That saw him triumph o'er the dust,
And leave his dark abode.

2 In the cold prison of a tomb
The great Redeemer lay,
Till the revolving skies had brought
The third, th' appointed day.

3 Hell and the grave unite their force
To hold our God, in vain;
The sleeping Conqueror arose,
And burst their feeble chain.

4 To thy great name, almighty Lord,
These sacred hours we pay;
And loud hosannas shall proclaim
The triumph of the day.

5 Salvation and immortal praise
To our victorious King!
Let heaven, and earth, and rocks, and seas,
With glad hosannas ring.

170. *Condescension of God.*—Psalm 8.

1 O THOU, to whom all creatures bow
Within this earthly frame,
Through all the world, how great art thou!
How glorious is thy name!

2 When heaven, thy beauteous work on high,
Employs my wondering sight;
The moon that nightly rules the sky,
With stars of feebler light;—

3 Lord, what is man, that thou shouldst deign
To bear him in thy mind!
Or what his race, that thou shouldst prove
To them so wondrous kind!

4 O thou, to whom all creatures bow,
Within this earthly frame,
Through all the world, how great art thou!
How glorious is thy name!

259. *"Lo! I come."*—Psalm 40.

1 O LORD, how infinite thy love!
How wondrous are thy ways!
Let earth beneath, and heaven above,
Combine to sing thy praise.

2 Man in immortal beauty shone,
Thy noblest work below;
Too soon by sin made heir alone
To death and endless woe.

3 Then, "Lo! I come," the Saviour said;
Oh, be his name adored,
Who, with his blood, our ransom paid,
And life and bliss restored!

4 O Lord, how infinite thy love!
How wondrous are thy ways!
Let earth beneath, and heaven above,
Combine to sing thy praise.

799. *"I am not ashamed of the gospel of Christ."*

1 DEAR Lord, and will thy pardoning love
Embrace a wretch so vile?
Wilt thou my load of guilt remove,
And bless me with thy smile?

2 Hast thou the cross for me endured,
And suffered all my shame?
And shall I be ashamed, O Lord,
To own thy precious name?

3 No, Lord, I'm not ashamed of thee,
Nor of thy cross and death:
Oh, do not be ashamed of me,
When I resign my breath!

4 Be thou my Shield, be thou my Sun;
Oh, guide me all my days;

ST. MARTINS. C. M.

And let my feet with joy run on
In thy delightful ways.

825. *"And I will praise Thy name for ever and ever."*—Psalm 145.

1 LONG as I live, I'll bless thy name,
My King, my God of love;
My work and joy shall be the same
In the bright world above.

2 Great is the Lord, his power unknown,
Oh, let his praise be great!
I'll sing the honors of thy throne;
Thy works of grace repeat.

3 Thy grace shall dwell upon my tongue;
And while my lips rejoice,
The men who hear my sacred song,
Shall join their cheerful voice.

4 Fathers to sons shall teach thy name,
And children learn thy ways:
Ages to come thy truth proclaim,
And nations sound thy praise.

882. *"Neither shall any man pluck them out of my hand."*—John 10: 28.

1 FIRM as the earth thy Gospel stands,
My Lord, my Hope, my Trust!
If I am found in Jesus' hands,
My soul can ne'er be lost.

2 His honor is engaged to save
The meanest of his sheep;
All whom his heavenly Father gave
His hands securely keep.

3 Nor death nor hell shall e'er remove
His favorites from his breast;
Safe in the bosom of his love
They must for ever rest.

1073. *"Thou and the ark of Thy strength."*

1 O THOU whose own vast temple stands,
Built over earth and sea,

Accept the walls that human hands
Have raised to worship thee!

2 Lord, from thine inmost glory send,
Within these courts to bide,
The peace that dwelleth without end
Serenely by thy side!

3 May erring minds that worship here
Be taught the better way;
And they who mourn, and they who fear,
Be strengthened as they pray.

4 May faith grow firm, and love grow warm,
And pure devotion rise,
While round these hallowed walls the storm
Of earth-born passion dies.

1116. *"Our fathers have told us."*—Psalm 44.

1 O LORD, our fathers oft have told,
In our attentive ears,
Thy wonders in their days performed,
And elder times than theirs.

2 For, not their courage, nor their sword
To them salvation gave;
Nor strength that from unequal force
Their fainting troops could save.

3 But thy right hand and powerful arm,
Whose succor they implored;
Thy presence with the chosen race,
Who thy great name adored.

4 As thee, their God, our fathers owned,
Thou art our sovereign King:
Oh, therefore, as thou didst to them,
To us deliverance bring!

5 To thee the triumph we ascribe,
From whom the conquest came;
In God we will rejoice all day,
And ever bless thy name.

DALSTON. S. P. M.

26. *"Let us go into the house of the Lord."*
Psalm 122.

1 How pleased and blest was I
 To hear the people cry,
"Come, let us seek our God to-day!"
 Yes, with a cheerful zeal
 We haste to Zion's hill,
And there our vows and honors pay.

2 Zion, thrice happy place,
 Adorned with wondrous grace,
And walls of strength embrace thee round!
 In thee our tribes appear
 To pray, and praise, and hear
The sacred Gospel's joyful sound.

3 May peace attend thy gate,
 And joy within thee wait
To bless the soul of every guest:
 The man who seeks thy peace,
 And wishes thine increase,
A thousand blessings on him rest!

4 My tongue repeats her vows,
 "Peace to this sacred house!"
For here my friends and kindred dwell;
 And since my glorious God
 Makes thee his blest abode,
My soul shall ever love thee well.

121. *"Jehovah reigns."*

1 THE Lord Jehovah reigns,
 And royal state maintains,
His head with awful glories crowned;
 Arrayed in robes of light,
 Begirt with sovereign might,
And rays of majesty around.

2 Upheld by thy commands,
 The world securely stands,
And skies and stars obey thy word:
 Thy throne was fixed on high
 Before the starry sky:
Eternal is thy kingdom, Lord!

3 Let floods and nations rage,
 And all their powers engage;
Let swelling tides assault the sky:
 The terrors of thy frown
 Shall beat their madness down:
Thy throne for ever stands on high.

4 Thy promises are true;
 Thy grace is ever new;
There fixed, thy church shall ne'er remove:
 Thy saints, with holy fear,
 Shall in thy courts appear,
And sing thine everlasting love.

860. *Christian Concord.*—Psalm 133.

1 How pleasant 'tis to see
 Kindred and friends agree;—
Each in his proper station move,
 And each fulfill his part,
 With sympathizing heart,
In all the cares of life and love!

2 Like fruitful showers of rain,
 That water all the plain,
Descending from the neighboring hills,
 Such streams of pleasure roll
 Through every friendly soul,
Where love, like heavenly dew, distills.

GANGES. C. P. M.

110. "*Praise ye Him, all His hosts.*"
Psalm 148.

1 BEGIN, my soul, th' exalted lay;
Let each enraptured thought obey,
  And praise th' Almighty's name:
Lo! heaven and earth, and seas and skies,
In one melodious concert rise,
  To swell th' inspiring theme.

2 Ye angels, catch the thrilling sound,
While all th' adoring throngs around
  His boundless mercy sing:
Let every listening saint above
Wake all the tuneful soul of love,
  And touch the sweetest string.

3 Let every element rejoice;
Ye thunders, burst with awful voice
  To him who bids you roll:
His praise in softer notes declare,
Each whispering breeze of yielding air,
  And breathe it to the soul.

Wake, all ye soaring throngs, and sing;
Ye feathered warblers of the spring,
  Harmonious anthems raise
To him who shaped your finer mold,
Who tipped your glittering wings with
    gold,
  And tuned your voice to praise.

5 Let man, by nobler passions swayed,
Let man, in God's own image made,
  His breath in praise employ;

Spread wide his Maker's name around,
While heaven's broad arch rings back
    the sound,—
  The song of holy joy!

899. *Battle-Song of the Reformation.*

1 FEAR not, O little flock, the foe
Who madly seeks your overthrow;
  Dread not his rage and power:
What tho' your courage sometimes
    faints!
This seeming triumph o'er God's saints
  Lasts but a little hour.

2 Fear not! be strong! your cause belongs
To him who can avenge your wrongs;
  Leave all to him, your Lord:
Though hidden yet from mortal eyes,
Salvation shall for you arise,
  He girdeth on his sword!

3 As sure as God's own promise stands,
Not earth, nor hell, with all their bands,
  Against us shall prevail:
The Lord shall mock them from his
    throne;
God is with us, we are his own;
  Our vict'ry can not fail!

4 Amen! Lord Jesus, grant our prayer!
Great Captain! now thine arm make bare,
  Thy church with strength defend:
So shall all saints and martyrs raise
A joyful chorus to thy praise,
  Through ages without end!

MIGDOL. L. M.

109. *"To-day, if ye will hear His voice."*
Psalm 95.

1 COME, let our voices join to raise
A sacred song of solemn praise:
God is a sovereign King; rehearse
His honors in exalted verse.

2 Come, let our souls address the Lord,
Who framed our natures with his word:
He is our Shepherd, we the sheep
His mercy chose, his pastures keep.

3 Come, let us hear his voice to-day;
The counsels of his love obey;
Nor let our hardened hearts renew
The sins and plagues that Israel knew.

4 Seize the kind promise while it waits,
And march to Zion's heavenly gates;
Believe, and take the promised rest;
Obey, and be for ever blest.

111. *"While I live will I praise the Lord."*
Psalm 146.

1 PRAISE ye the Lord! my heart shall join
In work so pleasant, so divine:
My days of praise shall ne'er be passed,
While life, and thought, and being last.

2 Happy the man, whose hopes rely
On Israel's God: he made the sky,
And earth, and seas, with all their train;
And none shall find his promise vain.

3 His truth for ever stands secure;
He saves th' oppressed, he feeds the poor;
He helps the stranger in distress,
The widow and the fatherless.

4 He loves his saints, he knows them well,
But turns the wicked down to hell:
Thy God, O Zion, ever reigns;
Praise him in everlasting strains.

154. *"Oh, that men would praise the Lord
for His goodness!"* — Psalm 107.

1 GIVE thanks to God; he reigns above;
Kind are his thoughts, his name is love:
His mercy ages past have known,
And ages long to come shall own.

2 Let the redeemed of the Lord
The wonders of his grace record;
Israel, the nation, whom he chose,
And rescued from their mighty foes.

3 He feeds and clothes us all the way,
He guides our footsteps lest we stray;
He guards us with a powerful hand,
And brings us to the heavenly land.

4 Oh, let the saints with joy record
The truth and goodness of the Lord!
How great his works! how kind his ways!
Let every tongue pronounce his praise.

157. *Providence and Grace of God.*
Psalm 36.

1 HIGH in the heavens, eternal God!
Thy goodness in full glory shines;
Thy truth shall break thro' every cloud
That vails and darkens thy designs.

2 For ever firm thy justice stands,
As mountains their foundations keep;
Wise are the wonders of thy hands;
Thy judgments are a mighty deep.

3 My God, how excellent thy grace!
Whence all our hope and comfort
springs;
The sons of Adam, in distress,
Fly to the shadow of thy wings.

4 From the provisions of thy house
We shall be fed with sweet repast;
There, mercy, like a river, flows,
And brings salvation to our taste.

5 Life, like a fountain, rich and free,
Springs from the presence of my Lord;
And in thy light our souls shall see
The glories promised in thy word.

TALLIS' EVENING HYMN. L. M.

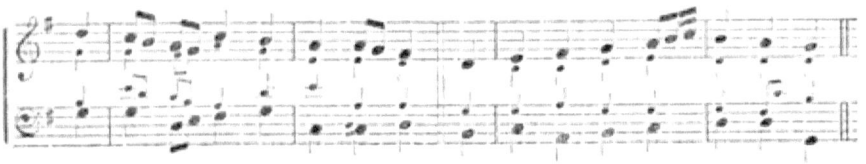

48. *The Morning Sacrifice.*

1 Awake, my soul, and with the sun
  Thy daily stage of duty run;
  Shake off dull sloth, and joyful rise
  To pay thy morning sacrifice.

2 Awake, lift up thyself, my heart,
  And with the angels bear thy part,
  Who all night long unwearied sing
  High praises to th' eternal King.

3 Glory to thee, who safe hast kept,
  And hast refreshed me while I slept;
  Grant, Lord, when I from death shall wake,
  I may of endless life partake.

4 Lord, I my vows to thee renew;
  Scatter my sins as morning dew;
  Guard my first springs of thought and will,
  And with thyself my spirit fill.

5 Direct, control, suggest, this day,
  All I design, or do, or say;
  That all my powers, with all their might,
  In thy sole glory may unite.

65. "*Hide me under the shadow of Thy wings.*"

1 Glory to thee, my God, this night,
  For all the blessings of the light;
  Keep me, oh, keep me, King of kings,
  Beneath the shadow of thy wings.

2 Forgive me, Lord! thro' thy dear Son,
  The ill which I this day have done;
  That with the world, myself, and thee,
  I, ere I sleep, at peace may be.

3 Teach me to live that I may dread
  The grave as little as my bed;
  Teach me to die, that so I may
  Rise glorious at thy judgment day.

4 Be thou my guardian while I sleep,
  Thy watchful station near me keep;
  My heart with love celestial fill,
  And guard me from th' approach of ill.

5 Lord, let my soul for ever share
  The bliss of thy paternal care!
  'Tis heaven on earth, 'tis heaven above,
  To see thy face, and sing thy love.

6 Praise God, from whom all blessings flow;
  Praise him, all creatures here below;
  Praise him above, ye heavenly host;
  Praise Father, Son, and Holy Ghost.

87. "*Bid us all depart in peace.*"

1 Dismiss us with thy blessing, Lord;
  Help us to feed upon thy word;
  All that has been amiss, forgive,
  And let thy truth within us live.

2 Though we are guilty, thou art good;
  Wash all our works in Jesus' blood;
  Give every burdened soul release,
  And bid us all depart in peace.

160. "*Slow to anger, and plenteous in mercy.*"—Psalm 103.

1 My soul, inspired with sacred love,
  God's holy name for ever bless!
  Of all his favors mindful prove,
  And still thy grateful thanks express.

2 The Lord abounds with tender love,
  And unexampled acts of grace;
  His wakened wrath doth slowly move,
  His willing mercy flies apace.

3 As high as heaven its arch extends
  Above this little spot of clay,
  So much his boundless grace transcends
  The best obedience we can pay.

4 As far as 't is from east to west,
  So far has he our sins removed,
  Who, with a father's tender breast,
  Has such as fear him always loved.

5 Let every creature join to bless
  The mighty Lord! and thou, my heart,
  With grateful joy thy thanks express,
  And in this concert bear thy part.

KANE. S. M. DOUBLE.

CLOSE.

D.S.

19. *"Beautiful for situation, the joy of the whole earth."*—Psalm 48.

1 FAR as thy name is known,
  The world declares thy praise;
Thy saints, O Lord, before thy throne,
  Their songs of honor raise.

2 With joy thy people stand
  On Zion's chosen hill,
Proclaim the wonders of thy hand,
  And counsels of thy will.

3 Let strangers walk around
  The city where we dwell,
Compass and view thine holy ground,
  And mark the building well—

4 The order of thy house,
  The worship of thy court,
The cheerful songs, the solemn vows;
  And make a fair report.

5 How decent, and how wise!
  How glorious to behold!
Beyond the pomp that charms the eyes,
  And rites adorned with gold.

6 The God we worship now
  Will guide us till we die;
Will be our God, while here below,
  And ours above the sky.

1062. *"How beautiful upon the mountains."*
Isaiah 52: 7.

1 How beauteous are their feet
  Who stand on Zion's hill!
Who bring salvation on their tongues,
  And words of peace reveal.

2 How charming is their voice!
  How sweet the tidings are!—
"Zion, behold thy Saviour King!
  He reigns and triumphs here."

3 How happy are our ears,
  That hear this joyful sound,
Which kings and prophets waited for,
  And sought, but never found!

4 How blessed are our eyes,
  That see this heavenly light!
Prophets and kings desired it long,
  But died without the sight.

5 The watchmen join their voice,
  And tuneful notes employ;
Jerusalem breaks forth in songs,
  And deserts learn the joy.

6 The Lord makes bare his arm
  Through all the earth abroad:
Let every nation now behold
  Their Saviour and their God.

1027. *"The Head-stone of the corner."*
Psalm 118.

1 SEE what a living stone
  The builders did refuse!
Yet God hath built his church thereon,
  In spite of envious Jews.

2 The scribe and angry priest
  Reject thine only Son;
Yet on this rock shall Zion rest,
  As the chief corner-stone.

3 The work, O Lord, is thine,
  And wondrous in our eyes:
This day declares it all divine;
  This day did Jesus rise.

4 This is the glorious day
  That our Redeemer made:
Let us rejoice, and sing, and pray;
  Let all the church be glad.

5 Hosanna to the King,
  Of David's royal blood!
Bless him, ye saints! he comes to bring
  Salvation from your God.

6 We bless thine holy word,
  Which all this grace displays,
And offer on thine altar, Lord,
  Our sacrifice of praise.

BADEA. S. M.

137. *God present everywhere.*

1 God of almighty power,
　How glorious are thy ways!
Angels thy majesty adore,
　All creatures speak thy praise.

2 Wherever earth is fair,
　Or brighter worlds extend,
Almighty Sovereign! thou art there,
　Creation's Lord and Friend.

3 And where the stars are not,
　Nor sun hath ever shone,
Beyond the flight of human thought,
　There thou art God alone.

4 Heaven is thy glorious throne,
　Earth does thy footstool seem;
But souls redeemed thou lov'st to own
　Thy richer diadem.

5 And, while they bless thy name,
　Hell trembles at thy rod:
Earth, heaven, and hell, thy power proclaim;
　All things proclaim thee God!

1128. *"Thou shalt arise, and have mercy upon Zion."*

1 O Lord our God! arise;
　The cause of truth maintain;
And wide o'er all the peopled world
　Extend her blessèd reign.

2 Thou Prince of life! arise,
　Nor let thy glory cease;
Far spread the conquests of thy grace,
　And bless the earth with peace.

3 Thou Holy Ghost! arise,
　Extend thy healing wing,
And o'er a dark and ruined world
　Let light and order spring.

4 O all ye nations! rise,—
　To God, the Saviour, sing;
From shore to shore, from earth to heaven
　Let echoing anthems ring!

DOXOLOGY.

The Father and the Son
　And Spirit we adore;
We praise, we bless, we worship thee,
　Both now and evermore!

GOLDEN HILL. S. M.

PARK STREET. L. M.

209. *"I will love Thee, O Lord, my strength."*
Psalm 18.

1 THEE will I love, O God, and own
My strength is in thine arm alone.
Jehovah is my rock, my tower,
My Saviour in the darkest hour;
My God, my strength, my confidence,
My buckler, helm, and high defense;
On him I call, and bless his name;
Ne'er shall my hope be put to shame.

2 With forms of death on every side,
Beset with foes, my courage died;
Hell compassed me with horrors dread,
The snares of death were round me spread;
In my distress to God I prayed,
I called upon my God for aid;
He heard my cry; it reached his throne:
Thee will I love, O God, alone.

3 Blest are the saints, who sit on high,
Around thy throne above the sky;
Thy brightest glories shine above,
And all their work is praise and love.

4 Blest are the souls, who find a place
Within the temple of thy grace;
There they behold thy gentler rays,
And seek thy face, and learn thy praise.

5 Blest are the men whose hearts are set
To find the way to Zion's gate;
God is their strength; and thro' the road
They lean upon their helper, God.

6 Cheerful they walk with growing strength,
Till all shall meet in heaven at length;
Till all before thy face appear,
And join in nobler worship there.

14. *"Blessed are they that dwell in Thy house."*—Psalm 84.

1 How pleasant, how divinely fair,
O Lord of hosts, thy dwellings are!
With long desire my spirit faints,
To meet th' assemblies of thy saints.

2 My flesh would rest in thine abode;
My panting heart cries out for God:
My God! my King! why should I be
So far from all my joys and thee!

15. *Joy in the House of God.*—Psalm 84.

1 GREAT God, attend, while Zion sings
The joy that from thy presence springs;
To spend one day with thee on earth,
Exceeds a thousand days of mirth.

2 Might I enjoy the meanest place
Within thy house, O God of grace,
Not tents of ease, nor thrones of power
Should tempt my feet to leave thy door.

DUKE STREET. L. M.

3 God is our sun—he makes our day;
  God is our shield—he guards our way
  From all th' assaults of hell and sin,
  From foes without and foes within.

4 All needful grace will God bestow,
  And crown that grace with glory, too;
  He gives us all things, and withholds
  No real good from upright souls.

5 O God, our King, whose sovereign sway
  The glorious host of heaven obey;
  Display thy grace, exert thy power,
  Till all on earth thy name adore!

36. *"Who is this King of glory?"*—Psalm 24.

1 Oh, hallowed is the land and blest,
  Where Christ, the Ruler, is confessed!
  Oh, happy hearts and happy homes,
  To whom the great Redeemer comes!

2 Lift up your heads, ye mighty gates!
  Behold, the King of glory waits;
  The King of kings is drawing near;
  The Saviour of the world is here.

3 Fling wide the portals of your heart:
  Make it a temple set apart
  From earthly use for heaven's employ,
  Adorned with prayer, and love, and joy.

4 Redeemer, come! I open wide
  My soul to thee; here, Lord, abide!
  Thankful and glad my song I raise,
  And give to thee a life of praise.

33. *"Before Jehovah's awful throne."*
  Psalm 100.

1 Before Jehovah's awful throne,
  Ye nations, bow with sacred joy:
  Know that the Lord is God alone;
  He can create, and he destroy.

2 His sovereign power, without our aid,
  Made us of clay, and formed us men;
  And when, like wandering sheep, we strayed,
  He brought us to his fold again.

3 We are his people, we his care,
  Our souls, and all our mortal frame:
  What lasting honors shall we rear,
  Almighty Maker, to thy name?

4 We'll crowd thy gates with thankful songs,
  High as the heaven our voices raise;
  And earth, with her ten thousand tongues,
  Shall fill thy courts with sounding praise.

5 Wide as the world is thy command,
  Vast as eternity thy love;
  Firm as a rock thy truth shall stand,
  When rolling years shall cease to move.

37. *"Oh, sing unto the Lord a new song."*
  Psalm 96.

1 Unto the Lord, unto the Lord,
  Oh, sing a new and joyful song!
  Declare his glory, tell abroad
  The wonders that to him belong.

2 For he is great, for he is great;
  Above all gods his throne is raised;
  He reigns in majesty and state,
  In strength and beauty is he praised.

3 Give to the Lord, give to the Lord
  The glory due unto his name;
  Enter his courts with sweet accord;
  In songs of joy his grace proclaim.

4 For lo! he comes, for lo! he comes
  To judge the earth in truth and love:
  His saints in triumph leave their tombs,
  And shout his praise in heaven above.

LANESBORO'. C. M.

The third line of each stanza is repeated.

44. *"Early will I seek Thee."*—Psalm 63.

1 EARLY, my God! without delay,
  I haste to seek thy face;
  My thirsty spirit faints away,
  Without thy cheering grace.

2 So pilgrims on the scorching sand,
  Beneath a burning sky,
  Long for a cooling stream at hand,
  And they must drink or die.

3 I've seen thy glory and thy power
  Through all thy temple shine:
  My God! repeat that heavenly hour,
  That vision so divine.

4 Nor life itself, with all its joys,
  Can my best passions move,
  Or raise so high my cheerful voice,
  As thy forgiving love.

5 Thus, till my last expiring day,
  I'll bless my God and King;
  Thus will I lift my hands to pray,
  And tune my lips to sing.

333. *"Thou dear Redeemer, dying Lamb."*

1 THOU dear Redeemer, dying Lamb,
  I love to hear of thee;
  No music's like thy charming name,
  Nor half so sweet can be.

2 Oh, may I ever hear thy voice
  In mercy to me speak;
  In thee, my Priest, will I rejoice,
  And thy salvation seek.

3 My Jesus shall be still my theme,
  While on this earth I stay;
  I'll sing my Jesus' lovely name,
  When all things else decay.

4 When I appear in yonder cloud,
  With all his favored throng,
  Then will I sing more sweet, more loud,
  And Christ shall be my song.

334. *" The Lamb is the light thereof."*

1 O THOU, who art enrobed with light,
  How pure the soul must be,
  When, placed within thy searching sight,
  It shrinks not, but with calm delight
  Can live and look on thee!

2 Lord, how can I, whose native sphere
  Is dark, whose mind is dim,
  Before thy radiant light appear,
  And on my naked spirit bear
  Thine uncreated beam?

3 Is there a way for man to rise
  To that sublime abode?
  Thine off'ring and thy sacrifice,
  Thy pains, and groans, and tears, and cries,
  Thy death, O Lamb of God!—

4 These, these prepare us for the sight
  Of majesty above;
  The sons of ignorance and night
  Can dwell in the eternal Light,
  Through the eternal Love.

609. *"Be of good cheer; thy sins be forgiven thee."*—Matt. 9:2.

1 My Saviour, let me hear thy voice
  Pronounce the word of peace,
  And all my warmest powers shall join
  To celebrate thy grace.

2 With gentle smiles call me thy child,
  And speak my sins forgiven:
  The accents mild shall charm my ear,
  Like the sweet harps of heaven.

HARDY. C. M.

The third line of each stanza is repeated.

3 Cheerful, where'er thy hand shall lead,
  The darkest path I'll tread;
  Cheerful I'll quit these mortal shores,
  And mingle with the dead.

4 When dreadful guilt is done away,
  No other fears we know:
  That hand which scatters pardons down,
  Shall crowns of life bestow.

668. "*Dear Refuge of my weary soul.*"

1 DEAR Refuge of my weary soul,
  On thee, when sorrows rise—
  On thee, when waves of trouble roll,
  My fainting hope relies.

2 To thee I tell each rising grief,
  For thou alone canst heal;
  Thy word can bring a sweet relief
  For every pain I feel.

3 Hast thou not bid me seek thy face?
  And shall I seek in vain?
  And can the ear of sovereign grace
  Be deaf when I complain?

4 No: still the ear of sovereign grace
  Attends the mourner's prayer;
  Oh, may I ever find access
  To breathe my sorrows there!

5 Thy mercy-seat is open still;
  Here let my soul retreat,
  With humble hope attend thy will,
  And wait beneath thy feet.

674. "*Wait, I say, on the Lord.*"—Psalm 27.

1 SOON as I heard my Father say,
  "Ye children, seek my grace,"
  My heart replied, without delay,
  "I'll seek my Father's face."

2 Let not thy face be hid from me,
  Nor frown my soul away;
  God of my life! I fly to thee
  In each distressing day.

3 Should friends and kindred, near and dear,
  Leave me to want, or die:
  My God would make my life his care,
  And all my need supply.

4 My fainting flesh had died with grief,
  Had not my soul believed
  To see thy grace provide relief;
  Nor was my hope deceived.

5 Wait on the Lord, ye trembling saints,
  And keep your courage up;
  He'll raise your spirit when it faints,
  And far exceed your hope.

1255. *Home for the Weary.*

1 THERE is an hour of peaceful rest,
  To mourning wanderers given;
  There is a tear for souls distressed,
  A balm for every wounded breast:
  'T is found above—in heaven.

2 There is a home for weary souls,
  By sin and sorrow driven,—
  When toss'd on life's tempestuous shoals,
  Where storms arise, and ocean rolls,
  And all is drear—but heaven.

3 There faith lifts up her cheerful eye
  To brighter prospects given;
  And views the tempest passing by,
  The evening shadows quickly fly,
  And all serene—in heaven.

4 There fragrant flowers immortal bloom,
  And joys supreme are given;
  There rays divine disperse the gloom;
  Beyond the confines of the tomb
  Appears the dawn of heaven!

MENDON. L. M.

422. *"The Rock of my strength."*

1 Rejoice, ye saints, rejoice and praise
The blessings of redeeming grace!
Jesus, your everlasting tower,
Stands firm against the tempest's power.

2 He is a refuge ever nigh;
His love endures as mountains high;
His name's a rock, which winds above,
And waves below, can never move.

3 While all things change, he changes not;
He ne'er forgets, though oft forgot;
His love will ever be the same;
His word, enduring as his name.

4 Rejoice, ye saints, rejoice and praise
The blessings of this wondrous grace!
Jesus, your everlasting tower,
Can bear, unmoved, the tempest's power.

430. *"He hath done all things well."*
Mark 7: 37.

1 Now, in a song of grateful praise,
To my dear Lord my voice I'll raise;
With all his saints I'll join to tell
That Jesus hath done all things well.

2 Wisdom, and power, and love divine,
In all his works, unrivaled, shine,
And force the wondering world to tell
That he alone did all things well.

3 Howe'er mysterious are his ways,
Or dark and sorrowful my days;
And though my spirit oft rebel,
I know he still doth all things well.

4 And when I stand before his throne,
And all his ways are fully known,
This note in sweetest strains shall swell,
That Jesus hath done all things well.

798. *"Ashamed of Jesus!"*

1 Jesus! and shall it ever be,
A mortal man ashamed of thee?
Ashamed of thee, whom angels praise,
Whose glories shine thro' endless days?

2 Ashamed of Jesus! sooner far
Let evening blush to own a star:
He sheds the beams of light divine
O'er this benighted soul of mine.

3 Ashamed of Jesus! that dear Friend
On whom my hopes of heaven depend!
No: when I blush, be this my shame,
That I no more revere his name.

4 Ashamed of Jesus! yes, I may,
When I've no guilt to wash away;
No tear to wipe, no good to crave,
No fears to quell, no soul to save.

5 Till then—nor is my boasting vain—
Till then I boast a Saviour slain!
And, oh, may this my glory be,
That Christ is not ashamed of me!

1024. *"Awake, awake! put on thy strength, O Zion."*—Isaiah 52: 1.

1 Triumphant Zion! lift thy head
From dust and darkness and the dead;
Though humbled long, awake at length,
And gird thee with thy Saviour's strength.

2 Put all thy beauteous garments on,
And let thy various charms be known:
Then decked in robes of righteousness,
The world thy glories shall confess.

3 No more shall foes unclean invade,
And fill thy hallowed walls with dread;
No more shall hell's insulting host
Their vict'ry and thy sorrows boast.

4 God, from on high thy groans will hear;
His hand thy ruins shall repair;
Nor will thy watchful Monarch cease
To guard thee in eternal peace.

ROTHWELL. L. M.

125. *"The Lord God omnipotent reigneth."*
Rev. 19: 6.

1 The Lord is King! lift up thy voice,
 O earth, and all ye heavens, rejoice!
 From world to world the joy shall ring:
 "The Lord omnipotent is King!"

2 The Lord is King! who then shall dare
 Resist his will, distrust his care?
 Holy and true are all his ways:
 Let every creature speak his praise.

3 The Lord is King! exalt your strains;
 Ye saints, your God, your Father, reigns;
 One Lord one empire all secures:
 He reigns, and life and death are yours.

4 Oh, when his wisdom can mistake,
 His might decay, his love forsake,
 Then may his children cease to sing,
 "The Lord omnipotent is King!"

393. *Reign of the Messiah.*—Isaiah 60.

1 Rise, crowned with light; great Salem, rise!
 Exalt thy head, and lift thine eyes;
 See a long race thy courts adorn,
 Of sons and daughters yet unborn.

2 See nations at thy gates attend,
 And lowly in thy temple bend;
 See crowds on every side arise,
 Eager to mount above the skies.

3 See heaven its portals wide display,
 And pour on thee a flood of day!
 Thy day shall shine for ever bright,
 For God himself shall be thy light.

4 What though the skies in smoke decay,
 Rocks fall, and mountains melt away!
 Fixed is his word, his power remains:
 Thy glorious King, Messiah, reigns!

878. *"Go, labor on."*

1 Go, labor on; spend and be spent,—
 Thy joy to do the Father's will:
 It is the way the Master went;
 Should not the servant tread it still?

2 Go, labor on; 't is not for naught;
 Thine earthly loss is heavenly gain;
 Men heed thee, love thee, praise thee not;
 The Master praises,—what are men?

3 Go, labor on; enough, while here,
 If he shall praise thee, if he deign
 Thy willing heart to mark and cheer:
 No toil for him shall be in vain.

4 Toil on, and in thy toil rejoice;
 For toil comes rest, for exile home;
 Soon shalt thou hear the Bridegroom's voice,
 The midnight peal: "Behold, I come!"

879. *"Go, labor on."*

1 Go, labor on; your hands are weak,
 Your knees are faint, your soul cast down;
 Yet falter not; the prize you seek
 Is near,—a kingdom and a crown!

2 Go, labor on, while it is day;
 The world's dark night is hastening on;
 Speed, speed thy work,—cast sloth away!
 It is not thus that souls are won.

3 Men die in darkness at your side,
 Without a hope to cheer the tomb;
 Take up the torch and wave it wide—
 The torch that lights time's thickest gloom.

4 Toil on,—faint not,—keep watch and pray;
 Be wise the erring soul to win;
 Go forth into the world's highway;
 Compel the wanderer to come in.

LYONS. 10s & 11s. Or 5s & 6s.

115. *"Who is like unto the Lord our God?"*

1 Oh, worship the King, all-glorious above;
  Oh, gratefully sing his power and his love!
  Our Shield and Defender, the Ancient of Days,
  Pavilioned in splendor, and girded with praise.

2 Oh, tell of his might, oh, sing of his grace,
  Whose robe is the light, whose canopy, space!
  His chariots of wrath the deep thunder-clouds form,
  And dark is his path on the wings of the storm.

3 Thy bountiful care what tongue can recite?
  It breathes in the air, it shines in the light,
  It streams from the hills, it descends to the plains,
  And sweetly distills in the dew and the rains.

4 Frail children of dust, and feeble as frail,
  In thee do we trust, nor find thee to fail;
  Thy mercies how tender! how firm to the end!
  Our Maker, Defender, Redeemer, and Friend.

349. *"Salvation to our God."*

1 Ye servants of God,
    Your Master proclaim,
  And publish abroad
    His wonderful name:
  The name, all victorious,
    Of Jesus extol;
  His kingdom is glorious,
    And rules over all.

2 God ruleth on high,
    Almighty to save;
  And still he is nigh,
    His presence we have:
  The great congregation
    His triumph shall sing,
  Ascribing salvation
    To Jesus, our King.

3 "Salvation to God,
    Who sits on the throne,"
  Let all cry aloud,
    And honor the Son:
  Our Saviour's high praises
    The angels proclaim,—
  Fall down on their faces,
    And worship the Lamb.

4. Then let us adore,
    And give him his right—
  All glory and power,
    And wisdom and might;
  All honor and blessing,
    With angels above,
  And thanks never ceasing,
    And infinite love!

NOEL. 6s, 8s & 4s.

116. *Praise the God of Abraham.*

1 THE God of Abrah'm praise,
  Who reigns enthroned above:
Ancient of everlasting days,
  And God of love:
JEHOVAH, great I AM!
  By earth and heaven confessed:
I bow and bless the sacred name,
  For ever blest.

2 The God of Abrah'm praise,
  At whose supreme command
From earth I rise, and seek the joys
  At his right hand:
I all on earth forsake,
  Its wisdom, fame, and power;
And him my only portion make,
  My shield and tower.

3 He by himself hath sworn;
  I on his oath depend;
I shall on eagles' wings upborne
  To heaven ascend:
I shall behold his face,
  I shall his power adore,
And sing the wonders of his grace
  For evermore.

344. *The Vision of Christ's Glory.*

1 THE goodly land I see,
  With peace and plenty blest;
A land of sacred liberty,
  And endless rest:
There milk and honey flow,
  And oil and wine abound;
And trees of life for ever grow
  With mercy crowned.

2 There dwells the Lord, our King,
  The Lord, our righteousness:
Triumphant o'er the world and sin,
  The Prince of Peace,
On Zion's sacred height,
  His kingdom still maintains,
And glorious, with his saints in light,
  For ever reigns.

3 Before the Saviour's face
  The ransomed nations bow,
O'erwhelmed at his almighty grace,
  For ever new:
He shows his prints of love;
  They kindle to a flame,
And sound, through all the worlds above,
  "The slaughtered Lamb!"

4 The whole triumphant host
  Give thanks to God on high:
"Hail, Father, Son, and Holy Ghost!"
  They ever cry.
Hail, Abrah'm's God and mine!
  (I join the heavenly lays)
All might and majesty are thine,
  And endless praise!

DUANE STREET. L. M.

351. *"The joy that was set before Him."*

1 Now for a tune of lofty praise
To great Jehovah's equal Son!
Awake, my voice, in heavenly lays;
Tell the loud wonders he hath done.

2 Sing how he left the worlds of light,
And the bright robes he wore above;
How swift and joyful was his flight
On wings of everlasting love.

3 Deep in the shades of gloomy death,
Th' almighty Captive prisoner lay;
Th' almighty Captive left the earth,
And rose to everlasting day.

4 Lift up your eyes, ye sons of light,—
Up to his throne of shining grace;
See what immortal glories sit
Round the sweet beauties of his face!

5 Among a thousand harps and songs,
Jesus, the God, exalted reigns:
His sacred name fills all their tongues,
And echoes thro' the heavenly plains.

735. *Christ the Way to God.*

1 Jesus, my All, to heaven is gone—
He whom I fix my hopes upon;
His track I see, and I'll pursue
The narrow way, till him I view.

2 The way the holy prophets went,
The way that leads from banishment,
The King's highway of holiness,
I'll go, for all his paths are peace.

3 This is the way I long had sought,
And mourned because I found it not;
Till late I heard my Saviour say,
"Come hither, soul; I am the way."

4 Lo! glad I come; and thou, blest Lamb!
Wilt take me, guilty as I am:
Nothing but sin I thee can give;
Nothing but love shall I receive.

5 Now will I tell to sinners round
How dear a Saviour I have found:
I'll point to thy redeeming blood,
And say, "Behold the way to God!"

815. *"I send the joys of earth away."*

1 I send the joys of earth away;
Away, ye tempters of the mind,
False as the smooth, deceitful sea,
And empty as the whistling wind!

2 Your streams were floating me along,
Down to the gulf of black despair;
And while I listened to your song,
Your streams had ev'n convey'd me there.

3 Lord! I adore thy matchless grace,
Which warned me of that dark abyss,
Which drew me from those treacherous seas,
And bade me seek superior bliss.

4 Now to the shining realms above
I stretch my hands and glance my eyes;
Oh for the pinions of a dove
To bear me to the upper skies!

5 There, from the bosom of my God,
Oceans of endless pleasure roll;
There would I fix my last abode,
And drown the sorrows of my soul!

DOXOLOGY.

Glory to thee, O God, most high!.
Father, we praise thy majesty!
The Son, the Spirit, we adore,
One Godhead, blest for evermore!

MENDON. L. M.

1018. *"The Lord hath chosen Jacob unto Himself."—Psalm 135.*

1 Praise ye the Lord; exalt his name,
While in his holy courts ye wait,—
Ye saints, who to his house belong,
Or stand attending at his gate.

2 Praise ye the Lord! the Lord is good!
To praise his name is sweet employ;
Israel he chose of old, and still
His church is his peculiar joy.

3 The Lord himself will judge his saints:
He treats his servants as his friends;
And, when he hears their sore complaints,
Repents the sorrows that he sends.

4 Bless him, all ye who taste his love!
People and priests, exalt his name:
Among his saints he ever dwells;
His church is his Jerusalem.

1026. *"The Stone which the builders refused."—Psalm 118.*

1 Lo! what a glorious corner-stone
The Jewish builders did refuse!
But God has built his church thereon,
In spite of envy and the Jews.

2 Great God! the work is all divine,
The joy and wonder of our eyes!
This is the day that proves it thine,—
The day that saw our Saviour rise.

3 Sinners, rejoice! and saints, be glad!
Hosanna! let his name be blest;
A thousand honors on his head,
With peace, and light, and glory, rest!

1029. *"God is in the midst of her; she shall not be moved."*

1 Happy the church, thou sacred place,
The seat of thy Creator's grace!
Thine holy courts are his abode,
Thou earthly palace of our God!

2 Thy walls are strength, and at thy gates
A guard of heavenly warriors waits;
Nor shall thy deep foundations move,
Fixed on his counsels and his love.

3 Thy foes in vain designs engage;
Against thy throne in vain they rage:
Like rising waves, with angry roar,
That dash and die upon the shore.

4 God is our shield, and God our sun;
Swift as the fleeting moments run,
On us he sheds new beams of grace,
And we reflect his brightest praise.

1036. *"Unto Thee shall all flesh come." Psalm 65.*

1 The praise of Zion waits for thee,
Great God! and praise becomes thy house;
There shall thy saints thy glory see,
And there perform thy public vows.

2 O thou whose mercy bends the skies,
To save when humble sinners pray!
All lands to thee shall lift their eyes,
And grateful isles of every sea.

3 Soon shall the flocking nations run
To Zion's hill, and own their Lord;
The rising and the setting sun
Shall see the Saviour's name adored.

1037. *"The Lord shall be thine everlasting light."*

1 Though now the nations sit beneath
The darkness of o'erspreading death,
God will arise with light divine,
On Zion's holy towers to shine.

2 That light shall glance on distant lands,
And heathen tribes, in joyful bands,
Come with exulting haste to prove
The power and greatness of his love.

3 Lord, spread the triumphs of thy grace;
Let truth, and righteousness, and peace,
In mild and lovely forms, display
The glories of the latter day.

FLEET STREET. H. M.

153. *"God so loved the world."*

1 Oh, for a shout of joy,
  High as the theme we sing!
To this divine employ
  Your hearts and voices bring:
Sound, sound, through all the earth abroad,
The love, th' eternal love, of God.

2 Unnumbered myriads stand,
  Of seraphs bright and fair;
Or bow at his right hand,
  And pay their homage there:
But strive in vain, with loudest chord,
To sound the wondrous love of God.

3 Though earth and hell assail,
  And doubts and fears arise,
The weakest shall prevail,
  And grasp the heavenly prize;
And through an endless age record
The love, th' unchanging love, of God.

4 Oh, for a shout of joy,
  High as the theme we sing!
To this divine employ
  Your hearts and voices bring:
Sound, sound, through all the earth abroad,
The love, th' eternal love, of God.

273. *"Good tidings of great joy."*—Luke 2.

1 Hark! hark! the notes of joy
  Roll o'er the heavenly plains,
And seraphs find employ
  For their sublimest strains:
Some new delight in heaven is known;
Loud sound the harps around the throne.

2 Hark! hark! the sound draws nigh,—
  The joyful host descends;
Jesus forsakes the sky,
  To earth his footsteps bend:
He comes to bless our fallen race;
He comes with messages of grace.

3 Bear, bear the tidings round!
  Let every mortal know
What love in God is found,
  What pity he can show:
Ye winds that blow, ye waves that roll,
Bear the glad news from pole to pole.

4 Strike, strike the harps again,
  To great Immanuel's name!
Arise, ye sons of men,
  And all his grace proclaim:
Angels and men, wake every string,
'Tis God the Saviour's praise we sing.

318. *Joy in Christ.*

1 Jesus!—harmonious name!
  It charms the hosts above;
They evermore proclaim,
  And wonder at his love:
'Tis all their happiness to gaze,
'Tis heaven to see our Jesus' face.

2 His name the sinner hears,
  And is from sin set free;
'Tis music in his ears,
  'Tis life and victory:
New songs do now his lips employ,
And bounds his gladdened heart with joy.

3 Oh, unexampled love!
  Oh, all-redeeming grace!
How swiftly didst thou move
  To save a fallen race!
What shall I do to make it known,
What thou for all mankind hast done?

ZEBULON. H. M.

4 Oh, for a trumpet voice,
  On all the world to call,
  To bid their hearts rejoice
  In him who died for all!
For all, my Lord was crucified;
For all, my Saviour bled and died.

376. *"A great High Priest, that is passed into the heavens."—Heb. 4: 14.*

1 TH' atoning work is **done**,
    The victim's blood is **shed**,
  And Jesus now is gone
    His people's cause to plead:
He stands in heaven their great High Priest,
And bears their names upon his breast.

2 No temple made with hands
    His place of service is;
  In heaven itself he stands,
    A heavenly priesthood his:
In him the shadows of the law
Are all fulfilled, and now withdraw.

3 And though awhile he be
    Hid from the eyes of men,
  His people look to see
    Their great High Priest again:
In brightest glory he will come,
And take his waiting people home.

391. *"Rejoice, the Lord is King!"*

1 REJOICE! the Lord is King;
    Your Lord and King adore;
  Mortals, give thanks and sing,
    And triumph evermore!
Lift up your hearts, lift up your voice;
Rejoice!—again I say, rejoice!

2 Jesus, the Saviour, reigns,
    The God of truth and love;
  When he had purged **our stains**,
    He took **his** seat above:
Lift up your hearts, lift up your voice;
Rejoice!—again I say, rejoice!

3 His **kingdom can** not fail;
    He rules o'er earth and heaven;
  The keys of death and hell
    Are to our Jesus given:
Lift up your hearts, lift up your voice;
Rejoice!—again I say, rejoice!

4 Rejoice in glorious hope:
    Jesus, the Judge, shall come,
  And take his servants up
    To their eternal home:
We soon shall hear th' archangel's voice;
The trump of God shall sound, Rejoice!

477. *Adoration of the Trinity.*

1 I GIVE immortal praise
    To God the Father's love,
  For all my comforts here,
    And better hopes above:
He sent his own eternal Son
To die for sins that man had done.

2 To God the Son belongs
    Immortal glory, too;
  Who bought us with his blood
    From everlasting woe:
And now he lives, and now he reigns,
And sees the fruit of all his pains.

3 To God the Spirit's name
    Immortal worship give,
  Whose new creating power
    Makes dying sinners live:
His work completes the great design,
And fills the soul with joy divine.

4 Almighty God, to thee
    Be endless honors done;
  The undivided Three,
    And the mysterious One:
Where reason fails, with all her powers,
There faith prevails, and love adores,

GROVE. L. M. DOUBLE.

166. "*His mercy endureth for ever.*"
Psalm 136.

1 GIVE to our God immortal praise;
  Mercy and truth are all his ways:
  Wonders of grace to God belong;
  Repeat his mercies in your song.
2 Give to the Lord of lords renown,
  The King of kings with glory crown:
  His mercies ever shall endure,
  When lords and kings are known no more.

3 He built the earth, he spread the sky,
  And fixed the starry lights on high:
  Wonders of grace to God belong;
  Repeat his mercies in your song.
4 He fills the sun with morning light,
  He bids the moon direct the night:
  His mercies ever shall endure,
  When suns and moons shall shine no
    more.

5 He sent his Son with power to save
  From guilt, and darkness, and the grave;
  Wonders of grace to God belong;
  Repeat his mercies in your song.
6 Through this vain world he guides our
    feet,
  And leads us to his heavenly seat:
  His mercies ever shall endure,
  When this vain world shall be no more.

362. *The King of Glory.*—Psalm 24.

1 OUR Lord is risen from the dead,
  Our Jesus is gone up on high;
  The powers of hell are captive led,
  Dragged to the portals of the sky.
2 There his triumphal chariot waits,
  And angels chant the solemn lay:
  Lift up your heads, ye heavenly gates!
  Ye everlasting doors, give way!

3 Loose all your bars of massy light,
  And wide unfold th' ethereal scene:
  He claims these mansions as his right;
  Receive the King of glory in.
4 Who is the King of glory—who?
  The Lord who all our foes o'ercame;
  Who sin, and death, and hell o'erthrew;
  And Jesus is the Conqueror's name.

5 Lo! his triumphant chariot waits,
  And angels chant the solemn lay;
  Lift up your heads, ye heavenly gates!
  Ye everlasting doors give way!
6 Who is the King of glory—who?
  The Lord, of boundless power pos-
    sessed;
  The King of saints and angels, too,
  God over all, for ever blessed.

ROCKINGHAM. L. M.

112. *"Loud Hallelujahs to the Lord."*
Psalm 148.

1 LOUD hallelujahs to the Lord,
  From distant worlds where creatures dwell!
Let heaven begin the solemn word,
  And sound it dreadful down to hell.

2 Wide as his **vast** dominion lies,
  Make the Creator's name be known;
Loud as his thunder, shout his praise,
  And sound it lofty as his throne.

3 Jehovah—'t is a glorious word!
  Oh, may it dwell on every tongue!
But saints who best have known the Lord,
  Are bound to raise the noblest **song**.

4 Speak of the wonders of that **love**
  Which Gabriel plays **on** every **chord**:
From all below, and all above,
  Loud hallelujahs to the Lord!

128. *"O Lord, my God, Thou art **very** great."*—Psalm 104.

1 GREAT is the Lord! **what** tongue can frame
  An honor equal to his name?
How awful are his glorious ways!
  The Lord is dreadful in his praise.

2 The world's foundations by his hand
  Were laid, and shall for ever stand;
The swelling billows know their bound,
  While to his praise they roll around.

3 Vast are thy works, almighty Lord!
  All nature rests upon thy word;
And clouds, and storms, and fire **obey**
  Thy wise and all-controlling **sway**.

4 Thy glory, **fearless of decline**,
  Thy glory, **Lord, shall ever shine**;
Thy praise shall still our breath employ,
  Till we shall **rise to endless joy**.

179. *God a faithful Creator.*

1 PRAISE, everlasting praise be paid
  To him who earth's foundations laid:
Praise to the God whose strong decrees
  Sway the creation as he please.

2 Praise to the goodness of the Lord,
  Who rules his people by his word;
And there, as strong as his decrees,
  Reveals his kindest promises.

3 Oh, for a strong, a lasting faith,
  To credit what th' Almighty saith!
T' embrace the message of his Son,
  And call **the** joys of heaven **our** own.

4 **Then**, should **the earth's** foundations shake,
  And all the wheels of nature break,
Our steady souls shall fear no more
  Than solid rocks when billows roar.

364. *"The Lord of hosts, He is the **King of Glory**."*—Psalm 24.

1 LIFT up your heads, ye gates! and wide
  Your everlasting doors display:
Ye angel-guards, like flames divide,
  And give the King of glory way.

2 Who is the King of glory?—He,
  The Lord, omnipotent to save;
Whose own right arm, in victory,
  Led captive Death, and spoiled **the** grave.

3 Lift up your heads, ye gates! and high
  Your everlasting portals heave;
Welcome the King of glory nigh:
  Him **must the** heaven of heavens receive.

4 Who is **the** King of glory—who?
  The Lord of hosts; behold his name:
The kingdom, power, and honor due,
  Yield him, ye saints, with glad acclaim!

WINFIELD. 7s.

7. *"Holy, holy, holy is the Lord of Hosts."*

1 Holy, holy, holy Lord,
  Be thy glorious name adored!
  Lord, thy mercies never fail;
  Hail, celestial Goodness, hail!

2 Though unworthy, Lord, thine ear,
  Deign our humble songs to hear;
  Purer praise we hope to bring,
  When around thy throne we sing.

3 While on earth ordained to stay,
  Guide our footsteps in thy way,
  Till we come to dwell with thee,
  Till we all thy glory see.

4 Then with angel harps again
  We will wake a nobler strain;
  There, in joyful songs of praise,
  Our triumphant voices raise.

98. *"Hallowed be Thy name."*

1 Holy, holy, holy Lord,
  In the highest heavens adored,
  Author of all nature's frame,—
  Father, hallowed be thy name.

2 Though estranged from thee in heart,
  Doubtless thou our Father art;
  From thy hand our spirits came:
  Father, hallowed be thy name.

  Born anew, oh, may we feel
  Filial love, the Spirit's seal!
  Cleansed from guilt, redeemed from
    shame!
  Father, hallowed be thy name.

4 When in want, or when in wealth,
  Joy or sorrow, pain or health,
  Still our prayer shall be the same:
  Father, hallowed be thy name.

657. *"My times are in Thy hand."*
    Psalm 81.

1 Sovereign Ruler of the skies,
  Ever gracious, ever wise!
  All my times are in thy hand;
  All events at thy command.

2 Times of sickness, times of health,
  Times of penury and wealth,—
  All must come, and last, and end,
  As shall please my heavenly Friend.

3 O thou gracious, wise and just!
  In thy hands my life I trust;
  Have I somewhat dearer still?—
  I resign it to thy will.

4 Thee at all times will I bless;
  Having thee, I all possess:
  Ne'er can I bereaved be,
  While I do not part with thee.

710. *"As Thou art, so let us be."*

1 Holy Lamb, who thee receive,
  Who in thee begin to live,
  Day and night they cry to thee,
  "As thou art, so let us be!"

2 Gladly would we now be clean;
  Cleanse us, Lord, from every sin;
  Fix, oh, fix our wavering mind!
  To thy cross our spirit bind.

3 Dust and ashes though we be,
  Full of sin and misery,
  Thine we are, thou Son of God:
  Take the purchase of thy blood!

457. *"Holy Spirit, all Divine."*

1 Holy Ghost, with light divine,
  Shine upon this heart of mine!
  Chase the shades of night away,
  Turn my darkness into day.

ROSEFIELD. 7s.

2 Holy Ghost, with power divine,
Cleanse this guilty heart of mine;
Long hath sin, without control,
Held dominion o'er my soul.

3 Holy Ghost, with joy divine,
Cheer this saddened heart of mine:
Bid my many woes **depart,**
Heal my wounded, **bleeding heart!**

4 Holy Spirit, all Divine!
Dwell within this heart of mine;
Cast down **every** idol-throne;
Reign supreme, and reign alone!

458. *"It is God that worketh in you."*

1 HOLY GHOST, thou Source of light!
   We invoke thy kindling ray;
   Dawn upon our spirits' night,
   Turn our darkness into day.

2 To the anxious soul impart
   Hope, all other hopes above;
   Stir the dull and hardened heart
   With a longing and a love.

3 Give the struggling peace for strife,
   Give the doubting light for gloom;
   Speed the living into life,
   Warn the dying of their doom.

4 Work in all, in all renew,
   Day by day, the life divine;
   All our wills to thee subdue,
   All our hearts **to** thee incline.

588. *Poor in Spirit.*

1 WHEN, my Saviour, shall I be
   Perfectly resigned to thee?
   Poor and vile in my own eyes,
   Only in thy wisdom wise?

2 Only thee content to **know,**
   Ignorant of all below?
   Only guided by thy light?
   Only mighty in thy might?

3 Fully in my life express
   All the heights of holiness;
   Sweetly let my **spirit prove**
   All the depths **of humble love.**

835. *Having all in having Christ.*

1 JESUS, take me for **thine own;**
   To thy will my **spirit frame;**
   Thou shalt reign, and thou alone,
   Over all I have **and am.**

2 Making **thus the** Lord my choice,
   I have nothing more to choose,
   But to listen to thy voice,
   And my will in thine to **lose.**

3 Then, whatever may betide,
   I shall safe and happy be,
   Still content and satisfied;—
   Having all in having thee. .

836. *"None but Christ."*

1 JESUS, all-atoning Lamb,
   Thine and only thine I am:
   Take my body, spirit, soul;
   Only thou possess the whole.

2 **Thou my** one thing needful **be;**
   Let me ever cleave to thee;
   Let me choose the better part:
   Let me give thee all my heart.

3 Whom have I on earth below?
   Thee, and only thee, I know:
   Whom have I in heaven but thee?
   Thou art all in all to me.

HOLBEIN. C. M.

17. *"My heart and my flesh crieth out for the living God."—Psalm 84.*

1 O God of hosts, the mighty Lord,
    How lovely is the place,
  Where, in thy glory, we behold
    The brightness of thy face!

2 My longing soul faints with desire
    To view thy blest abode;
  My panting heart and flesh cry out
    For thee, the living God.

3 Thrice happy they, whose choice has thee
    Their sure protection made;
  Who long to tread the sacred ways
    Which to thy dwelling lead.

4 For God, who is our sun and shield,
    Will grace and glory give;
  And no good thing will he withhold
    From them that justly live.

5 O Lord of hosts, my King, my God!
    How highly blest are they,
  Who in thy temple always dwell,
    And there thy praise display!

195. *"I will lift up mine eyes unto the hills."* Psalm 121.

1 Up to the hills I lift mine eyes,
    There all my hope is laid;
  The Lord, who built the earth and skies—
    From him will come mine aid.

2 Thy foot unmoved he ever keeps,
    And all thy ways will guard;
  He slumbers not, and never sleeps—
    Thy keeper is the Lord.

3 The Lord, thy keeper, shades thy way,
    Preserves thee in his sight;
  Nor shall the sun smite thee by day,
    Nor shall the moon by night.

4 The Lord preserves thy soul from sin,
    From evils great and sore—
  Thy going out and coming in,
    Now and for evermore.

485. *Delight in the Scriptures.*

1 Father of mercies, in thy word
    What endless glory shines!
  For ever be thy name adored
    For these celestial lines.

2 Here my Redeemer's welcome voice
    Spreads heavenly peace around;
  And life and everlasting joys
    Attend the blissful sound.

3 Oh, may these heavenly pages be
    My ever dear delight;
  And still new beauties may I see,
    And still increasing light!

4 Divine Instructor, gracious Lord,
    Be thou for ever near;
  Teach me to love thy sacred word,
    And view my Saviour there.

139. *"How precious also are thy thoughts unto me, O God."—Psalm 139.*

1 Jehovah, God! thy gracious power
    On every hand we see;
  Oh, may the blessings of each hour
    Lead all our thoughts to thee!

2 If, on the wings of morn, we speed
    To earth's remotest bound,
  Thy hand will there our footsteps lead,
    Thy love our path surround.

3 Thy power is in the ocean deeps,
    And reaches to the skies;
  Thine eye of mercy never sleeps,
    Thy goodness never dies.

4 From morn till noon—till latest eve,
    Thy hand, O God, we see;
  And all the blessings we receive,
    Proceed alone from thee.

ABRIDGE. C. M.

5 In all the varying scenes of time,
   On thee our hopes depend;
   Through every age, in every clime,
   Our Father, and our Friend.

147. *"The memory of Thy great goodness."*
    Psalm 145.

1 SWEET is the memory of thy grace,
    My God, my heavenly King;
  Let age to age thy righteousness
    In sounds of glory sing.

2 God reigns on high; but ne'er confines
    His goodness to the skies:
  Thro' the whole earth his bounty shines,
    And every want supplies.

3 With longing eyes thy creatures wait
    On thee for daily food;
  Thy liberal hand provides their meat,
    And fills their mouth with good.

4 How kind are thy compassions, Lord!
    How slow thine anger moves!
  But soon he sends his pardoning word
    To cheer the souls he loves.

5 Sweet is the memory of thy grace,
    My God, my heavenly King;
  Let age to age thy righteousness
    In sounds of glory sing.

158. *Wonders of God's* **Grace.**

1 ETERNAL Power! Almighty God!
    Who can approach thy throne!
  Accessless light is thine abode,
    To angel eyes unknown.

2 Before the radiance of thine eye,
    The heavens no longer shine;
  And all the glories of the sky
    Are but the shade of thine.

3 Great God! and wilt thou condescend
    To cast a look below?

  To this vile world thy notice bend—
    These seats of sin and woe?

4 How strange! how wondrous is thy love!
    With trembling we adore:
  Not all th' exalted minds above
    Its wonders can explore.

5 While golden harps and angel tongues
    Resound immortal lays,
  Great God! permit our humble songs
    To rise and speak thy praise.

643. *"There is none like unto the Lord our God!"*

1 My God, my Portion, and my Love,
    My everlasting All,
  I've none but thee in heaven above,
    Or on this earthly ball.

2 To thee I owe my wealth and friends,
    My health, and safe abode;
  Thanks to thy name for meaner things,
    But they are not my God.

3 How vain a toy is glittering wealth,
    If once compared with thee!
  Or what 's my safety or my health,
    Or all my friends to me?

4 Were I possessor of the earth,
    And called the stars my own,
  Without thy graces and thyself,
    I were a wretch undone.

5 Let others stretch their arms like seas,
    And grasp in all the shore;
  Grant me the visits of thy face,
    And I desire no more.

DOXOLOGY.

To Father, Son, and Holy Ghost,
  One God, whom we adore,
Be glory as it was, is now,
  And shall be evermore!

HULL. L. M.

83. *"Let us worship and bow down."*
Psalm 95.

1 OH, come, loud anthems let us sing,
  Loud thanks to our almighty King!
  For we our voices high should raise,
  When our salvation's Rock we praise.

2 Into his presence let us haste,
  To thank him for his favors past;
  To him address in joyful songs
  The praise that to his name belongs.

3 Oh, let us to his courts repair,
  And bow with adoration there!
  Down on our knees, devoutly, all
  Before the Lord, our Maker, fall.

156. *"The Lord reigneth: let the earth rejoice."*—Psalm 97.

1 JEHOVAH reigns; let all the earth
  In his just government rejoice;
  Let all the isles, with sacred mirth,
  In his applause unite their voice.

2 Darkness and clouds of awful shade
  His dazzling glory shroud in state;
  Justice and truth his guards are made,
  And, fixed by his pavilion, wait.

3 Rejoice, ye righteous, in the Lord;
  Memorials of his holiness
  Deep in your faithful breasts record,
  And with your thankful tongues confess.

187. *The Majesty of Jehovah.*—Psalm 68.

1 KINGDOMS and thrones to God belong;
  Crown him, ye nations, in your song!
  His wondrous name and power rehearse;
  His honors shall enrich your verse.

2 He rides and thunders through the sky;
  His name, Jehovah, sounds on high:
  Praise him aloud, ye sons of grace;
  Ye saints, rejoice before his face.

3 God is our shield, our joy, our rest;
  God is our King, proclaim him blest;
  When terrors rise, when nations faint,
  He is the strength of every saint.

1123. *"He shall come down like rain upon the mown grass."*—Psalm 72.

1 GREAT God, whose universal sway
  The known and unknown worlds obey,
  Now give the kingdom to thy Son,
  Extend his power, exalt his throne.

2 As rain on meadows newly mown,
  So shall he send his influence down;
  His grace on fainting souls distills,
  Like heavenly dew on thirsty hills.

3 The heathen lands, that lie beneath
  The shades of overspreading death,
  Revive at his first dawning light,
  And deserts blossom at the sight.

4 The saints shall flourish in his days,
  Dressed in the robes of joy and praise:
  Peace, like a river, from his throne
  Shall flow to nations yet unknown.

1285. *"Justice and judgment are the habitation of thy throne."*—Psalm 97.

1 HE reigns! the Lord, the Saviour reigns!
  Sing to his name in lofty strains;
  Let the whole earth in songs rejoice,
  And in his praise exalt their voice!

2 Deep are his counsels, and unknown;
  But grace and truth support his throne;
  Tho' gloomy clouds his ways surround,
  Justice is their eternal ground.

3 In robes of judgment, lo! he comes,—
  Shakes the wide earth, and cleaves the tombs;
  Before him burns devouring fire!
  The mountains melt, the seas retire!

4 His enemies, with sore dismay,
  Fly from the sight, and shun the day:
  Then lift your heads, ye saints, on high,
  And sing, for your redemption's nigh!

ROCKINGHAM. L. M.

930. *"Welcome to me the darkest night."*

1 WELCOME to me the darkest night,
  If there the Saviour's presence bright
  Beam forth upon the soul dismayed,
  And say, "'T is I: be not afraid!"

2 Welcome the fiercest waves that roll
  Their deepening floods to whelm my soul,
  If he rebuke the storm of ill,
  And bid the tempest, "Peace, be still!"

3 Welcome the thorniest path, if there
  The print-marks of his feet appear;
  If in his footsteps we may tread,
  And follow where our Lord hath led.

4 I will not ask what else is mine,
  If thou, O Lord, account me thine;
  For what but joy can be my lot,
  If God, my God, reject me not?

1058. *Prayer for an Assembly of Ministers.*

1 POUR out thy Spirit from on high;
    Lord, thine assembled servants bless;
  Graces and gifts to each supply,
    And clothe thy priests with righteousness.

2 Within thy temple, where we stand
    To teach the truth, not ours, but thine,
  May we, like stars in thy right hand,
    The angels of the churches, shine!

3 Wisdom, and zeal, and faith impart,
    Firmness with meekness from above,
  To bear thy people on our heart,
    And love the souls whom thou dost love.

4 To watch and pray, and never faint;
    By day and night strict guard to keep,
  To warn the sinner, cheer the saint,
    Nourish thy lambs, and feed thy sheep;

5 Then, when our work is finished here,
    In humble hope our charge resign:

When the chief Shepherd shall appear,
  O God, may they and we be thine!

1085. *"Thy little flock in safety keep."*

1 JESUS, thou Shepherd of the sheep,
  Thy "little flock" in safety keep;
  These lambs within thine arms now take,
  Nor let them e'er thy fold forsake.

2 Secure them from the scorching beam,
  And lead them to the living stream;
  In verdant pastures let them lie,
  And watch them with a shepherd's eye!

3 Oh, teach them to discern thy voice,
  And in its sacred sound rejoice!
  From strangers may they ever flee,
  And know no other guide but thee.

4 Lord, bring thy sheep that wander yet,
  And let their number be complete;
  Then let the flock from earth remove,
  And reach the heavenly fold above.

1113. *A Pillar of Cloud by Day, and of Fire by Night.*—Ex. 13: 21.

1 WHEN Israel, of the Lord beloved,
  Out from the land of bondage came,
  Her fathers' God before her moved,
  An awful guide, in smoke and flame.

2 By day, along th' astonished lands,
  The cloudy pillar glided slow;
  By night, Arabia's crimsoned sands
  Returned the fiery column's glow.

3 Thus present still, though now unseen,
    O Lord, when shines the prosperous day,
  Be thoughts of thee a cloudy screen
    To temper the deceitful ray!

4 And, oh! when gathers on our path,
    In shade and storm, the frequent night,
  Be thou long suffering, slow to wrath,
    A burning and a shining light.

LANSING. C. M. DOUBLE.

38. *"The Lord is a great God, and a great King."*—Psalm 95.

1 SING to the Lord Jehovah's **name**,
  And in his strength rejoice :
  When his salvation is our theme,
  Exalted be our voice.
2 With thanks approach his awful sight,
  And psalms of honor sing :
  The Lord's a God of boundless **might**,
  The whole creation's King.
3 Let princes hear, **let** angels know
  How mean their natures seem,—
  Those gods on high, and gods below,
  When once compared with him.
4 Earth, with its caverns dark and deep,
  Lies in his spacious **hand** ;
  He fixed the seas **what bounds to keep**,
  And where the hills must stand.
5 **Come,** and with humble souls adore ;
  Come, kneel before his face :
  Oh, may the **creatures** of his **power**
  Be children **of his** grace !
6 Now is the time ; he bends his **ear,**
  And waits for your request :
  Come, lest he rouse his wrath, and swear,
  " Ye shall **not see** my rest."

152. *"Oh, magnify the Lord with me !"*
  Psalm 34.

1 I'LL bless the Lord, I'll bless the Lord,
  In all his wondrous ways ,
  My soul his mercies shall record,
  My tongue shall chant his praise.
2 From dawn to eve, with heart, with voice,
  His goodness I'll proclaim,
  Till all that hear me shall rejoice
  In his redeeming name.
3 Oh, magnify the Lord with me !
  His power, his goodness, prove ;
  How blest his sway ! oh, taste and see
  How vast, how kind his love !

4 Beset with darkness, pressed with **cares,**
  To him, in grief, I cried ;
  His mercy listened to my prayers,
  His hand my wants supplied.
5 With angel hosts encamped around,
  To guard them from their foes,
  What peace, what glory, have they found,
  Who in his name repose !
6 Oh, magnify the Lord with me !
  His might, his mercies, prove ;
  How blest his sway ! oh, taste and **see**
  How vast, how kind, his love !

1034. *"The time to favor her, yea, the set time, is come."*—Psalm 102.

1 LET Zion **and her sons** rejoice—
  Behold the promised hour !
  Her God hath heard her mourning voice,
  And comes t' exalt his power.
2 Her dust and ruins that remain
  Are precious in our eyes ;
  Those ruins shall be built again,
  And all that dust shall rise.
3 The Lord will raise Jerusalem,
  And stand in glory there ;
  Nations shall bow before his name,
  And kings attend with fear.
4 He sits a sovereign on his throne,
  With pity in his eyes ;
  He hears the dying prisoners' groan,
  And sees their sighs arise.
5 He frees the soul condemned to death,
  Nor, when his saints complain,
  Shall it be said that praying breath
  Was ever spent in vain.
6 This shall be known when we are dead,
  And left on long record,
  That nations yet unborn may read,
  And trust and praise the Lord.

NEW YORK TUNE. C. M.

148. *"His tender mercies are over all His works."*

1 THY goodness, Lord, our souls confess;
   Thy goodness we adore :
   A spring, whose blessings never fail,
   A sea without a shore !

2 Sun, moon, and stars, thy love attest
   In every golden ray ;
   Love draws the curtains of the night,
   And love brings back the day.

3 Thy bounty every season crowns
   With all the bliss it yields ;
   With joyful clusters loads the vines,
   With strengthening grain the fields.

4 But chiefly thy compassion, Lord,
   Is in the gospel seen ;
   There, like a sun, thy mercy shines,
   Without a cloud between.

5 There pardon, peace, and holy joy,
   Through Jesus' name are given ;
   He on the cross was lifted high,
   That we might reign in heaven.

177. *"He is God, the faithful God."*
   Psalm 33.

1 LET all the just, to God with joy
   Their cheerful voices raise ;
   For well the righteous it becomes
   To sing glad songs of praise.

2 For, faithful is the word of God ;
   His works with truth abound ;
   He justice loves, and all the earth
   Is with his goodness crowned.

3 Whate'er the mighty Lord decrees,
   Shall stand for ever sure ;
   The settled purpose of his heart
   To ages shall endure.

4 Our soul on God with patience waits;
   Our help and shield is he :
   Then, Lord, let still our hearts rejoice,
   Because we trust in thee.

5 The riches of thy mercy, Lord,
   Do thou to us extend ;
   Since we, for all we want or wish,
   On thee alone depend.

369. *"I know that my Redeemer liveth."*
   Job 19: 25.

1 I KNOW that my Redeemer lives ;
   He lives who once was dead :
   To me in grief he comfort gives ;
   With peace he crowns my head.

2 He lives triumphant o'er the grave,
   At God's right hand on high,
   My ransomed soul to keep and save,
   To bless and glorify.

3 He lives to fill my breast with love,
   With joy my heart to feed ;
   He lives to plead for me above,
   To succor me in need.

4 He lives that I may also live,
   And now his grace proclaim ;
   He lives that I may honor give
   To his most holy name.

5 Let strains of heavenly music rise,
   While all their anthem sing
   To Christ, my precious sacrifice,
   And ever-living King.

DOXOLOGY.

To Father, Son, and Holy Ghost,
One God whom we adore,
Be glory as it was, is now,
And shall be evermore !

PARK STREET. L. M.

339. *The Song of Songs.*—Rev. 5.

1 Come, let us sing the song of songs—
  The saints in heaven began the strain—
  The homage which to Christ belongs:
  "Worthy the Lamb, for he was slain!"

2 Slain to redeem us by his blood,
  To cleanse from every sinful stain,
  And make us kings and priests to God—
  "Worthy the Lamb, for he was slain!"

3 To him who suffered on the tree,
  Our souls, at his soul's price, to gain,
  Blessing, and praise, and glory be:
  "Worthy the Lamb, for he was slain!"

4 To him, enthroned by filial right,
  All power in heaven and earth proclaim,
  Honor, and majesty, and might:
  "Worthy the Lamb, for he was slain!"

5 Long as we live, and when we die,
  And while in heaven with him we reign;
  This song our song of songs shall be:
  "Worthy the Lamb, for he was slain!"

889. *"Stand up, my soul, shake off thy fears."*

1 Stand up, my soul! shake off thy fears,
  And gird the gospel armor on;
  March to the gates of endless joy,
  Where Jesus, thy great Captain's gone.

2 Hell and thy sins resist thy course;
  But hell and sin are vanquished foes:
  Thy Jesus nailed them to the cross,
  And sung the triumph when he rose.

3 Then let my soul march boldly on;
  Press forward to the heavenly gate:
  There peace and joy eternal reign, [wait,
  And glitt'ring robes for conquerors

4 There shall I wear a starry crown,
  And triumph in almighty grace,
  While all the armies of the skies
  Join in my glorious Leader's praise.

890. *"They shall mount up with wings as eagles."*—Isaiah 40: 31.

1 Awake, our souls! away our fears!
  Let every trembling thought be gone;
  Awake, and run the heavenly race,
  And put a cheerful courage on!

2 True, 't is a strait and thorny road,
  And mortal spirits tire and faint;
  But they forget the mighty God,
  Who feeds the strength of every saint—

3 The mighty God, whose matchless power
  Is ever new and ever young,
  And firm endures, while endless years
  Their everlasting circles run.

4 From thee, the overflowing spring,
  Our souls shall drink a fresh supply;
  While such as trust their native strength
  Shall melt away, and droop, and die.

5 Swift as an eagle cuts the air
  We 'll mount aloft to thine abode;
  On wings of love our souls shall fly,
  Nor tire amid the heavenly road!

901. *"Stand therefore—taking the shield of faith."*

1 Awake, my soul! lift up thine eyes;
  See where thy foes against thee rise,
  In long array, a numerous host;
  Awake, my soul, or thou art lost!

2 Thou tread'st upon enchanted ground;
  Perils and snares beset thee round;
  Beware of all; guard every part;
  But most, the traitor in thy heart.

3 Come then, my soul! now learn to wield
  The weight of thine immortal shield;
  Put on the armor, from above,
  Of heavenly truth, and heavenly love.

4 The terror and the charm repel,
  And powers of earth, and powers of hell;
  The Man of Calvary triumphed here:
  Why should his faithful followers fear?

NEW SABBATH HYMN AND TUNE BOOK. 75

ERFURT. L. M.

159. *"Bless the Lord, O my soul."*
Psalm 103.

1 BLESS, O my soul! the living God;
Call home thy thoughts that rove abroad:
Let all the powers within me join
In work and worship so divine.

2 Bless, O my soul! the **God** of grace,
His favors claim thy highest praise;
Why should the wonders he hath wrought
Be lost in silence, and forgot?

3 'T is he, my soul, that sent his Son
To die for crimes which thou hast done;
He owns the ransom, and forgives
The hourly follies of our lives.

4 Let every land his power **confess**;
Let all the earth adore his **grace**;
My heart and **tongue** with **rapture join**
In work and **worship so divine**.

165. *Glory of the Grace of God.*

1 Now to the Lord **a noble song**:
Awake, my soul! awake, my **tongue**!
Hosanna to th' eternal Name,
And all his boundless love proclaim!

2 See where it shines in Jesus' face,
The brightest image of his grace:
God, in the person of his Son,
Has all his mightiest works outdone.

3 Grace!—'t is a sweet, a charming **theme**;
My thoughts rejoice at Jesus' name;
Ye angels, dwell upon the sound;
Ye heavens, reflect it to the ground!

4 Oh, may I live to reach the place
Where he unvails his lovely face!
Where I his beauties shall behold,
And sing his name to harps of gold!

182. *"God only wise."*

1 AWAKE, my tongue, thy tribute bring
To him who gave thee power to sing;
Praise him, who has all praise above,
The source of wisdom and of love.

2 How vast his knowledge! how profound!
A depth where all our tho'ts are drown'd!
The stars he numbers, and their names
He **gives to all those** heavenly flames.

3 Through each bright world above, behold
Ten thousand thousand charms unfold;
Earth, air, and mighty **seas combine**,
To speak his wisdom **all divine**.

4 But in redemption, oh, what grace!
Its **wonders**, oh, what thought can trace!
Here **wisdom** shines for ever bright;
Praise him, my soul, with sweet delight.

956. *"I will praise Thee with my whole heart."*—Psalm 138.

1 WITH all my powers of heart and tongue,
I 'll praise my Maker in my song;
Angels shall hear the notes I raise,
Approve the **song**, and join the praise.

2 **To God I** cried when troubles rose;
He heard me, and subdued my foes;
He did my rising fears control,
And strength diffused thro' all my soul.

3 Amid a thousand snares, I stand
Upheld and guarded by thy hand;
Thy **words** my fainting soul revive,
And **keep my dying** faith alive.

4 I 'll sing thy truth and mercy, Lord,
I 'll sing the wonders of thy word;
Not all thy **works** and names below
So much thy power and glory show.

DUNDEE. C. M.

130. *"Our God is full of might."*

1 THE Lord our God is full of **might**,
  The winds obey his will;
  He speaks, and, in his heavenly height,
  The rolling sun stands still.

2 Rebel, ye waves, and o'er the land
  With threatening aspect roar:
  The Lord uplifts his awful hand,
  And chains you to the shore.

3 Howl, winds of night, your force combine;
  Without his high behest
  Ye shall not, in the mountain-pine,
  Disturb the sparrow's nest.

4 His voice sublime is heard afar,
  In distant peals it dies;
  He yokes the whirlwind to his car,
  And sweeps the howling skies.

5 Ye nations, bend—in reverence bend;
  Ye monarchs, wait his nod,
  And bid the choral song ascend
  To celebrate our God.

131. *The Lord of All.*

1 THE Lord our God is Lord of all;
  His station who can find!
  I hear him in the waterfall;
  I hear him in the wind.

2 If in the gloom of night I shroud,
  His face I can not fly;
  I see him in the evening cloud,
  And in the morning sky.

3 He lives, he reigns in every land,
  From winter's polar snows,
  To where, across the burning sand,
  The blasting meteor glows.

4 He smiles, we live; he frowns, we die;
  We hang upon his word;
  He rears his mighty arm on high,
  We fall before his sword.

5 He bids his gales the fields deform;
  Then, when his thunders cease,
  He paints his rainbow on the storm,
  And lulls the winds to peace.

143. *Eternity of God.*—Psalm 102.

1 THROUGH endless years, thou art the same,
  O thou eternal God!
  Ages to come shall know thy name,
  And tell thy works abroad.

2 The strong foundations of the earth
  Of old by thee were laid;
  By thee the beauteous arch of heaven
  With matchless skill was made.

3 Soon shall this goodly frame of things,
  Formed by thy powerful hand,
  Be, like a vesture, laid aside,
  And changed at thy command.

4 But thy perfections all divine,
  Eternal as thy days,
  Through everlasting ages shine,
  With undiminished rays.

5 Our children's children, still thy care,
  Shall own their fathers' God;
  To latest times thy favor share,
  And spread thy praise abroad.

199. *God a Refuge in Temptation.*
  Psalm 55.

1 O GOD, my Refuge, hear my cries!
  Behold my flowing tears;
  For earth and hell my hurt devise,
  And triumph in my fears.

2 Oh, were I like some gentle dove,
  Soon would I stretch my wings,
  And fly, and make a long remove
  From all these restless things!

TALLIS. C. M.

3 God shall preserve my soul from fear,
  Or shield me when afraid;
  Ten thousand angels must appear,
  If he command their aid.

4 By morning light I'll seek his face,
  At noon repeat my cry;
  The night shall hear me ask his grace,
  Nor will he long deny.

5 I cast my burdens on the Lord,
  The Lord sustains them all;
  My courage rests upon his word
  That saints shall never fall.

650. *"I was brought low, and He helped me."*
  Psalm 116.

1 I LOVE the Lord; he heard my cries,
  And pitied every groan.
  Long as I live, when troubles rise,
  I'll hasten to his throne.

2 I love the Lord; he bowed his ear,
  And chased my grief away;
  Oh, let my heart no more despair,
  While I have breath to pray!

3 The Lord beheld me sore distressed,
  He bade my pains remove;
  Return, my soul, to God, thy rest,
  For thou hast known his love!

4 My God hath saved my soul from death,
  And dried my falling tears;
  Now to his praise I'll spend my breath,
  And my remaining years.

669. *Unchanging Trust.*—Psalm 18.

1 No change of time shall ever shock
  My trust, O Lord, in thee;
  For thou hast always been my Rock,
  A sure defense to me.

2 Thou, my deliverer art, O God;
  My trust is in thy power;
  Thou art my shield from foes abroad,
  My safeguard, and my tower.

3 To thee will I address my prayer,
  To whom all praise I owe;
  So shall I, by thy watchful care,
  Be saved from every foe.

4 Then let Jehovah be adored,
  On whom my hopes depend;
  For who, except the mighty Lord,
  His people can defend?

887. *"Why sayest thou, 'My way is hid from the Lord?'"*—Isaiah 40 : 27-31.

1 WHENCE do our mournful thoughts arise,
  And where's our courage fled?
  Has restless sin, or raging hell,
  Struck all our comforts dead?

2 Have we forgot th' almighty Name
  That formed the earth and sea?
  And can an all-creating arm
  Grow weary or decay?

3 Treasures of everlasting might
  In our Jehovah dwell;
  He gives the conquest to the weak,
  And treads their foes to hell.

4 Mere mortal power shall fade and die,
  And youthful vigor cease;
  But we who wait upon the Lord
  Shall feel our strength increase.

5 The saints shall mount on eagles' wings,
  And taste the promised bliss,
  Till their unwearied feet arrive,
  Where perfect pleasure is.

DOXOLOGY.

To Father, Son, and Holy Ghost,
  One God, whom we adore,
Be glory as it was, is now,
  And shall be evermore!

ORD. 11s & 8s.

35.   "*Make a joyful noise unto the Lord, all ye lands.*"—Psalm 100.

1 Be joyful in God, all ye lands of the earth;
Oh, serve him with gladness and fear:
Exult in his presence with music and mirth,
With love and devotion draw near.

2 The Lord he is God, and Jehovah alone,
Creator, and Ruler o'er all;
And we are his people, his scepter we own,—
His sheep, and we follow his call.

3 Oh, enter his gates with thanksgiving and song;
Your vows in his temple proclaim:
His praise with melodious accordance prolong,
And bless his adorable name.

4 For good is the Lord, ever gracious and good,
And we are the work of his hand;
His mercy and truth from eternity stood,
And shall to eternity stand.

SIVAN. 11s & 8s.

191.   "*The Lord is great.*"

1 The Lord is great! ye hosts of heaven, adore him;
And ye, who tread this earthly ball,
In holy songs rejoice aloud before him,
And shout his praise who made you all.

2 The Lord is great! his majesty, how glorious!
Resound his praise from shore to shore;
O'er sin, and death, and hell, now made victorious,
He rules and reigns for evermore.

3 The Lord is great! his mercy, how abounding!
Ye angels, strike your golden chords,
O, praise our God, with voice and harp resounding,
The King of kings, and Lord of lords!

FOLSOM. 11s & 10s.

266. *The Star in the East.*

1 BRIGHTEST and best of the sons of the morning!
  Dawn on our darkness, and lend us thine aid;
  Star of the East, the horizon adorning,
  Guide where our Infant Redeemer is laid.

2 Cold on his cradle the dew-drops are shining;
  Low lies his head with the beasts of the stall:
  Angels adore him, in slumber reclining,
  Maker, and Monarch, and Saviour of all!

3 Say, shall we yield him, in costly devotion,
  Odors of Edom, and offerings divine?
  Gems of the mountain, and pearls of the ocean,
  Myrrh from the forest, or gold from the mine?

4 Vainly we offer each ample oblation,
  Vainly with gold would his favors secure:
  Richer, by far, is the heart's adoration;
  Dearer to God are the prayers of the poor.

5 Brightest and best of the sons of the morning!
  Dawn on our darkness, and lend us thine aid;
  Star of the East, the horizon adorning,
  Guide where our Infant Redeemer is laid.

1030.* " *Arise, shine, for thy light is come.*"

1 DAUGHTER of Zion! awake from thy sadness:
  Awake, for thy foes shall oppress thee no more;
  Bright o'er thy hills dawns the day-star of gladness;
  Arise! for the night of thy sorrow is o'er.

2 Strong were thy foes, but the arm that subdued them,
  And scattered their legions, was mightier far;
  They fled, like the chaff, from the scourge that pursued them;
  For vain were their steeds and their chariots of war!

3 Daughter of Zion! the Power that hath saved thee,
  Extolled with the harp and the timbrel should be:
  Shout! for the foe is destroyed that enslaved thee,
  Th' oppressor is vanquished, and Zion is free!

* Omit the tie for this hymn.

AVON. C. M.

124. *"He bowed the heavens, also, and came down."—Psalm 18.*

1 The Lord descended from above,
  And bowed the heavens most high;
  And underneath his feet he cast
  The darkness of the sky.

2 On cherub and on cherubim,
  Full royally, he rode;
  And on the wings of mighty winds
  Came flying all abroad.

3 He sat serene upon the floods,
  Their fury to restrain;
  And he, as Sovereign, Lord, and King,
  For evermore shall reign.

4 The Lord will give his people strength,
  Whereby they shall increase;
  And he will bless his chosen flock
  With everlasting peace.

5 Give glory to his awful name,
  And honor him alone;
  Give worship to his majesty
  Upon his holy throne.

184. *"Canst thou, by searching, find out God?"*

1 How wondrous great, how glorious bright
  Must our Creator be,
  Who dwells amid the dazzling light
  Of an eternal day!

2 Our soaring spirits upward rise,
  Toward the celestial throne:
  Fain would we see the blessèd Three,
  And the almighty One.

3 Our reason stretches all its wings,
  And climbs above the skies;
  But still, how far beneath thy feet
  Our groveling reason lies!

4 Lord, here we bend our humble souls,
  In awe and love adore;
  For the weak pinions of our mind
  Can stretch a thought no more.

5 Thy glories infinitely rise
  Above our laboring tongue;
  In vain the highest seraph tries
  To form an equal song.

6 In humble notes our faith adores
  The great, mysterious King;
  While angels strain their nobler powers,
  And sweep th' immortal string.

236. *"God moves in a mysterious way."*

1 God moves in a mysterious way
  His wonders to perform;
  He plants his footsteps in the sea,
  And rides upon the storm.

2 Deep in unfathomable mines
  Of never-failing skill,
  He treasures up his bright designs,
  And works his sovereign will.

3 Ye fearful saints, fresh courage take:
  The clouds ye so much dread
  Are big with mercy, and shall break
  In blessings on your head.

4 Judge not the Lord by feeble sense,
  But trust him for his grace:
  Behind a frowning providence
  He hides a smiling face.

5 His purposes will ripen fast,
  Unfolding every hour;
  The bud may have a bitter taste,
  But sweet will be the flower.

6 Blind unbelief is sure to err,
  And scan his work in vain;
  God is his own interpreter,
  And he will make it plain.

PHUVAH. C. M.

245. *"Unto Him that loved us."*
Rev. 1: 5-8.

1 To him who loved the souls of men,
  And washed us in his blood,
  To royal honors raised our head,
  And made us priests to God;—

2 To him let every tongue be praise,
  And every heart be love;
  All grateful honors paid on earth,
  And nobler songs above!

3 Behold, on flying clouds he comes!
  His saints shall bless the day;
  While they that pierced him sadly mourn
  In anguish and dismay.

4 Thou art the First, and thou the Last;
  Time centers all in thee,—
  Th' almighty God, who was, and is,
  And evermore shall be.

350. *God revealed in the Atonement.*

1 FATHER, how wide thy glory shines!
  How high thy wonders rise!
  Known through the earth by thousand signs,
  By thousand through the skies.

2 Those mighty orbs proclaim thy power,
  Their motions speak thy skill;
  And on the wings of every hour
  We read thy patience still.

3 But when we view thy strange design
  To save rebellious worms,
  Where vengeance and compassion join
  In their divinest forms,—

4 Here the whole Deity is known;
  Nor dares a creature guess
  Which of the glories brightest shone,
  The justice, or the grace.

5 Now the full glories of the Lamb
  Adorn the heavenly plains;
  Bright seraphs learn Immanuel's name,
  And try their choicest strains.

6 Oh, may I bear some humble part
  In that immortal song!
  Wonder and joy shall tune my heart
  And love command my tongue.

468. *An ancient Hymn to the Trinity.*

1 To God be glory, peace on earth,
  To all mankind good will;
  We bless, we praise, we worship thee,
  And glorify thee still;

2 And thanks for thy great glory give,
  That fills our souls with light:
  O Lord, our heavenly King, the God
  And Father of all might!

3 And thou, begotten Son of God,
  Before all time begun;
  O Jesus Christ, thou Lamb of God,
  The Father's only Son;

4 Thou who the sins of all the world
  Dost fully take away,
  Have mercy, Saviour of mankind,
  And hear us when we pray!

5 O thou, who sitt'st at God's right hand,
  Upon the Father's throne,
  Have mercy on us, thou, O Christ,
  Who art the Holy One!

6 Thou, only with the Holy Ghost
  Whom earth and heaven adore,
  In glory of the Father art
  Most high for evermore!

THE OLD HUNDREDTH. L. M.

90. *Pastoral Benediction.*

1 Now may the Lord our Shepherd lead
  To living streams his little flock;
 May he in flowery pastures feed,
  Shade us at noon beneath the rock!

2 Now may we hear our Shepherd's voice,
  And gladly answer to his call;
 Now may our hearts for him rejoice,
  Who knows, and names, and loves us all.

3 When the Chief Shepherd shall appear,
  And small and great before him stand,
 Oh, be the flock assembling here
  Found with the sheep on his right hand.

347. *Brief Call to praise Christ.*

1 Worthy the Lamb of boundless sway,
  In earth and heaven the Lord of all:
 Let all the powers of earth obey,
  And low before his footstool fall.

2 Higher, still higher, swell the strain:
  Creation's voice the note prolong!
 Jesus, the Lamb, shall ever reign:
  Let hallelujahs crown the song!

473. *"Thy wondrous Name."*

1 Great One in Three, great Three in One!
  Thy wondrous name we sound abroad;
 Prostrate we fall before thy throne,
  O holy, holy, holy Lord!

2 Thee, Holy Father, we confess;
  Thee, Holy Saviour, we adore;
 And thee, O Holy Ghost, we bless
  And praise and worship evermore.

3 Thou art by heaven and earth adored
  Thy universe is full of thee,
 O holy, holy, holy Lord!
  Great Three in One, great One in Three!

1063. *"Who is for you a faithful minister of Christ."—Col. 1: 7.*

1 With heavenly power, O Lord, defend
  Him whom we now to thee commend;
 Thy faithful messenger secure,
  And make him to the end endure.

2 Gird him with all-sufficient grace;
  Direct his feet in paths of peace;
 Thy truth and faithfulness fulfill,
  And arm him to obey thy will.

1104. *"To let the oppressed go free, and break every yoke."*

1 Lord, when thine ancient people cried,
  Oppressed and bound by Egypt's king,
 Thou didst Arabia's sea divide,
  And forth thy fainting Israel bring.

2 Lo! in these latter days, our land
  Groans with the anguish of the slave!
 Lord God of hosts! stretch forth thy hand,
  Not shortened that it can not save.

3 Roll back the swelling tide of sin,—
  The lust of gain, the lust of power;
 The day of freedom usher in:
  How long delays th' appointed hour?

4 As thou of old to Miriam's hand
  The thrilling timbrel didst restore,
 And to her joyful song the land
  Echoed from desert to the shore,—

5 Oh, let thy smitten ones again
  Take up the chorus of the free:
 "Praise ye the Lord! his power proclaim,
  For he hath conquered gloriously!

1125. *"All kings shall fall down before Him."*

1 Let the seventh angel sound on high;
  Let shouts be heard through all the sky:
 Kings of the earth, with glad accord,
  Give up your kingdom to the Lord.

2 Almighty God! thy power assume,
  Who wast, and art, and art to come;
 Jesus, the Lamb, who once was slain,
  For ever live,—for ever reign!

DUKE STREET. L. M.

189. *The Glory of Jehovah.*—Psalm 97.
1 JEHOVAH reigns; his throne is high,
   His robes are light and majesty;
   His glory shines with beams so **bright**,
   No mortal can sustain the sight.

2 His terrors keep the world in awe;
   His justice guards his holy law;
   His love reveals a smiling face;
   His truth and promise seal **the grace**.

3 Thro' all his works what wisdom **shines!**
   He baffles Satan's deep designs;
   His power is sovereign to fulfill
   The noblest counsels of his will.

4 And will this glorious **Lord descend**
   To be my Father **and my Friend?**
   Then let my songs with **angels join,**
   Heaven is secure, **if God is mine.**

250. *"The same yesterday, and to-day, and for ever."*—Heb. 13: 8.
1 WITH transport, Lord, our souls proclaim
   Th' immortal honor of thy name;
   Assembled round **our Saviour's throne,**
   We make his **ceaseless glories** known.

2 Through all revolving ages, **he**
   The same hath been, the same shall be;
   Immortal radiance gilds his head,
   While stars and suns wax old and fade.

3 The same his power his flock to guard;
   The same his bounty to reward;
   The same his faithfulness and love
   To saints on earth, and saints above.

4 Let nature change, **and sink, and die,**
   Jesus shall raise his **chosen high,**
   And fix them near his **steadfast throne,**
   In glory changeless as his **own.**

1105. *"I, the Lord, will hasten it in his time."*
1 HASTEN, O Lord, that happy time,
   That dear, expected, blessed day!

When men of every **race and** clime
   The Saviour's precepts shall obey.

2 In one sweet symphony of praise,
   Gentile and Jew shall then unite;
   And all the wrongs that man has wrought
   Sink in th' abyss of endless night.

3 Then Afric's long enslaved sons
   Shall join with Europe's polished race,
   To celebrate, in different tongues,
   The glories **of** redeeming grace;

4 **From east to west, from north to south,**
   Immanuel's **kingdom shall extend;**
   And every man, in every face,
   Shall meet a brother and a friend.

1110. *Prayer for general Peace.*
1 THY footsteps, Lord, with joy we trace,
   And mark the conquests of thy grace;
   Complete the work thou hast begun,
   And let thy will on earth be done.

2 Oh, show thyself the **Prince** of peace;
   Command the din of war to cease;
   Oh, bid contending nations rest,
   And let thy love rule every breast!

3 Then peace returns with balmy wing;
   Glad plenty laughs, the valleys sing;
   Reviving commerce lifts her head,
   And want and woe and hate have fled.

4 Thou good and wise, and righteous Lord,
   All move subservient to thy word;
   Oh, soon let every nation prove
   The perfect joy of Christian love!

DOXOLOGY.

PRAISE God, from whom all blessings flow!
Praise him, all creatures here below!
Praise him above, ye heavenly host!
Praise Father, Son, and Holy Ghost!

HARWELL. 8s & 7s. DOUBLE.

99. *Praise to Jehovah.*

1 PRAISE to thee, thou great Creator!
  Praise to thee from every tongue:
Join, my soul, with every creature,
  Join the universal song.
2 Father, Source of all compassion,
  Pure, unbounded grace is thine:
Hail the God of our salvation!
  Praise him for his love divine.

3 For ten thousand blessings given,
  For the hope of future joy,
Sound his praise thro' earth and heaven,
  Sound Jehovah's praise on high.
4 Joyfully on earth adore him,
  Till in heaven our song we raise;
There, enraptured, fall before him,
  Lost in wonder, love, and praise.

394. *"The Desire of all nations."*

1 COME, thou long-expected Jesus,
  Born to set thy people free;
From our fears and sins release us,
  Let us find our rest in thee.
2 Israel's strength and consolation,
  Hope of all the earth thou art;
Dear desire of every nation,
  Joy of every longing heart.

3 Born, thy people to deliver;
  Born a child, and yet a king;
Born to reign in us for ever,
  Now thy gracious kingdom bring.
4 By thine own eternal Spirit,
  Rule in all our hearts alone;
By thine all-sufficient merit,
  Raise us to thy glorious throne.

967. *"From grace to glory."*

1 KNOW, my soul, thy full salvation;
  Rise o'er sin, and fear, and care;
Joy to find in every station
  Something still to do or bear.
Think what Spirit dwells within thee;
  Think what Father's smiles are thine;
Think that Jesus died to win thee;
  Child of heaven, canst thou repine?

2 Haste thee on from grace to glory,
  Armed by faith, and winged by prayer,
Heaven's eternal day before thee—
  God's own hand shall guide thee there.
Soon shall close thine earthly mission,
  Soon shall pass thy pilgrim days;

GREENVILLE. 8s & 7s. DOUBLE.

Hope shall change to glad fruition,
  Faith to sight, and prayer to praise.

1011. *"I am a miracle of Grace."*

1 Hail, my ever blessed Jesus!
    Only thee I wish to sing;
  To my soul thy name is precious,
    Thou my Prophet, Priest, and King;
  Oh, what mercy flows from heaven!
  Oh, what joy and happiness!
  Love I much? I've much forgiven—
    I'm a miracle of grace!

2 Once with Adam's race in ruin,
    Unconcerned in sin I lay;
  Swift destruction still pursuing,
    Till my Saviour passed that way:
  Witness all ye hosts of heaven,
  My Redeemer's tenderness;
  Love I much? I've much forgiven—
    I'm a miracle of grace!

3 Shout, ye bright, angelic choir!
    Praise the Lamb enthroned above!
  While, astonished, I admire
    God's free grace and boundless love:
  That blest moment I received him
  Filled my soul with joy and peace;
  Love I much? I've much forgiven—
    I'm a miracle of grace!

1071. *"And David said, 'Blessed be Thou.'"*
  1 Chron. 29: 10–23.

1 Blest be thou, O God of Israel!
    Thou, our Father and our Lord!
  Majesty is thine for ever;
    Ever be thy name adored.
2 Thine, O Lord, are power and greatness;
    Glory, victory, are thine own;
  All is thine in earth and heaven,
    Over all thy boundless throne.

3 Riches come of thee, and honor;
    Power and might to thee belong;
  Thine it is to make us prosper,
    Only thine to make us strong.
4 Lord, our God, for these, thy bounties,
    Hymns of gratitude we raise;
  To thy name, for ever glorious,
    Ever we address our praise.

DOXOLOGY.

Praise the God of our salvation,
  Praise the Father's boundless love;
Praise the Lamb, our expiation;
  Praise the Spirit from above;
Praise the Fountain of salvation
Him by whom our spirits live
Undivided adoration
  To the one Jehovah give!

UXBRIDGE. L. M.

123. *"The Lord sitteth upon the flood."*
Psalm 29.

1 Give to the Lord, ye sons of fame,
Give to the Lord renown and power:
Ascribe new honors to his name,
And his eternal might adore.

2 The Lord proclaims his power aloud,
O'er all the ocean and the land;
His voice divides the watery cloud,
And lightnings blaze at his command.

3 The Lord sits Sovereign on the flood;
The Thunderer reigns for ever King;
But makes his church his blest abode
Where we his awful glories sing.

4 In gentler language, there the Lord
The counsels of his grace imparts:
Amid the raging storm, his word
Speaks peace and courage to our hearts.

133. *God All-powerful.*

1 The Lord, the God of glory, reigns,
In robes of majesty arrayed;
His rule omnipotence sustains,
And guides the worlds his hands have made.

2 Ere rolling worlds began to move,
Or ere the heavens were spread abroad,
Thine awful throne was fixed above;
From everlasting thou art God.

3 The swelling floods tumultuous rise,
Aloud the angry tempests roar;
Lift their proud billows to the skies,
And foam, and lash the trembling shore.

4 The Lord, the mighty God, on high,
Controls the fiercely raging seas;
He speaks:—and noise and tempest fly,
The waves sink down in gentle peace.

5 Thy sovereign laws are ever sure,
Eternal purity is thine;

And, Lord, thy people shall be pure,
And in thy blest resemblance shine.

181. *"Who can show forth all His praise?"*
Psalm 106.

1 Oh render thanks to God above,
The fountain of eternal love;
Whose mercy firm, through ages past,
Hath stood, and shall for ever last.

2 Who can his mighty deeds express—
Not only vast, but numberless!
What mortal eloquence can raise
His tribute of immortal praise!

3 Extend to me that favor, Lord,
Thou to thy chosen dost afford;
When thou return'st to set them free,
Let thy salvation visit me.

4 Oh, render thanks to God above,
The fountain of eternal love;
His mercy firm, through ages past,
Hath stood, and shall for ever last.

824. *"Every day will I bless Thee."*
Psalm 145.

1 My God, my King, thy various praise
Shall fill the remnant of my days;
Thy grace employ my humble tongue,
Till death and glory raise the song.

2 The wings of every hour shall bear
Some thankful tribute to thine ear;
And every setting sun shall see
New works of duty done for thee.

3 Let distant times and nations raise
The long succession of thy praise;
And unborn ages make my song
The joy and triumph of their tongue.

4 But who can speak thy wondrous deeds?
Thy greatness all our thoughts exceeds;
Vast and unsearchable thy ways!
Vast and immortal be thy praise!

WIMBORNE. L. M.

248. *"Equal with God."*—Phil. 2: 6.

1 Bright King of glory! dreadful God!
Our spirits bow before thy seat;
To thee we lift an humble thought,
And worship at thine awful feet!

2 A thousand seraphs, strong and bright,
Stand round the glorious Deity;
But who, among the sons of light,
Pretends comparison with thee?

3 Yet there is one, of human frame,
Jesus, arrayed in flesh and blood,
Thinks it no robbery to claim
A full equality with God.

4 Then, let the name of Christ, our King,
With equal honors be adored:
His praise let every angel sing,
And all the nations own him Lord.

251. *"Go, worship at Immanuel's feet."*

1 Go, worship at Immanuel's feet;
See in his face what wonders meet:
Earth is too narrow to express
His worth, his glory, or his grace.

2 Nor earth, nor seas, nor sun, nor stars,
Nor heaven his full resemblance bears:
His beauties we can never trace,
Till we behold him face to face.

3 Oh, let me climb those higher skies,
Where storms and darkness never rise:
There he displays his power abroad,
And shines, and reigns, th' incarnate God!

325. *"Unto Him that loved us."*
    Rev. 1: 5–7.

1 Now to the Lord, who makes us know
The wonders of his dying love,
Be humble honors paid below,
And strains of nobler praise above!

2 'T was he who cleansed our foulest sins,
And washed us in his precious blood;
'T is he who makes us priests and kings,
And brings us rebels near to God.

3 To Jesus, our atoning Priest,
To Jesus, our eternal King,
Be everlasting power confessed!
Let every tongue his glory sing.

4 Behold! on flying clouds he comes,
And every eye shall see him move;
Tho' with our sins we pierced him once,
He now displays his pardoning love.

5 The unbelieving world shall wail,
While we rejoice to see the day:
Come, Lord, nor let thy promise fail,
Nor let thy chariot long delay.

381. *"The Prince of Life."*

1 Hail to the Prince of life and peace,
Who holds the keys of death and hell!
The spacious world unseen is his,
And sovereign power becomes him well.

2 In shame and anguish once he died;
But now he lives for evermore:
Bow down, ye saints, around his seat,
And, all ye angel-bands, adore.

3 So live for ever, glorious Lord,
To crush thy foes and guard thy friends;
While all thy chosen tribes rejoice
That thy dominion never ends.

4 Worthy thy hand to hold the keys,
Guided by wisdom and by love;
Worthy to rule o'er mortal life,
O'er worlds below, and worlds above.

5 For ever reign, victorious King!
Wide thro' the earth thy name be known;
And call my longing soul to sing
Sublimer anthems near thy throne.

NASHVILLE. L. P. M.

107. *"Worship the Lord in the beauty of holiness."*—Psalm 96.

1 Let all the earth their voices raise,
To sing the choicest psalm of praise;
  To sing and bless Jehovah's name:
  His glory let the heathen know;
  His wonders to the nations show;
And all his saving works proclaim.

2 He framed the globe, he built the sky
He made the shining worlds on high,
  And reigns complete in glory there:
  His beams are majesty and light;
  His beauties, how divinely bright!
His temple, how divinely fair!

3 Come the great day, the glorious hour,
When earth shall feel his saving power,
  And barb'rous nations fear his name!
  Then shall the race of man confess
  The beauty of his holiness,
And in his courts his grace proclaim.

221 *Everlasting Praise to Jehovah.*
Psalm 146.

1 I'll praise my Maker with my breath;
And when my voice is lost in death,
  Praise shall employ my nobler powers:
  My days of praise shall ne'er be past,
  While life, and thought, and being last,
Or immortality endures.

2 Happy the man whose hopes rely
On Israel's God; he made the sky,
  And earth, and seas, with all their train:
  His truth for ever stands secure
  He saves th' oppressed, he feeds the poor:
And none shall find his promise vain.

3 The Lord hath eyes to give the blind,
The Lord supports the sinking mind;
  He sends the lab'ring conscience peace,
  He helps the stranger in distress,
  The widow and the fatherless,
And grants the prisoner sweet release.

4 He loves his saints, he knows them well,
But turns the wicked down to hell:
  Thy God, O Zion, ever reigns!
  Let every tongue, let every age,
  In this exalted work engage:
Praise him in everlasting strains.

5 I'll praise him while he lends me breath;
And when my voice is lost in death,
  Praise shall employ my nobler powers;
  My days of praise shall ne'er be past,
  While life, and thought, and being last,
Or immortality endures.

484. *"More to be desired than gold."*
Psalm 19.

1 I love the volume of thy word;
What light and joy those leaves afford
  To souls benighted and distressed!
  Thy precepts guide my doubtful way,
  Thy fear forbids my feet to stray,
Thy promise leads my heart to rest.

2 Thy threatenings wake my slumbering eyes,
And warn me where my danger lies;
  But 'tis thy blessed gospel, Lord,
  That makes my guilty conscience clean,
  Converts my soul, subdues my sin,
And gives a free, but large reward.

NEWCOURT. L. P. M.

5 Who knows the errors of his thoughts?
My God, forgive my secret faults,
And from presumptuous sins restrain:
Accept my poor attempts of praise,
That I have read thy book of grace,
And book of nature not in vain.

1272. *"Shall he deliver his soul?"*
Psalm 89.

1 THINK, mighty God, on feeble man,
How few his hours, how short his span!
Short from the cradle to the grave:
Who can secure his vital breath
Against the bold demands of death,
With skill to fly, or power to save?

2 Lord, shall it be for ever said,
The race of man was only made
For sickness, sorrow, and the dust?
Are not thy servants, day by day,
Sent to their graves, and turned to clay?
Lord, where's thy kindness to the just?

3 Hast thou not promised to thy Son,
And all his seed, a heavenly crown?
But flesh and sense indulge despair:
For ever blessed be the Lord,
That Faith can read his holy word,
And find a resurrection there.

4 For ever blessed be the Lord,
Who gives his saints a long reward
For all their toil, reproach, and pain:
Let all below, and all above
Join to proclaim thy wondrous love,
And each repeat his loud Amen!

1282. *"The righteous judgment of God."*
(A Hymn of the Thirteenth Century.)

1 THE last loud trumpet's wondrous sound
Shall wake the nations under ground:
Where, then, my God, shall I be found,—

2 When all shall stand before thy throne,
When thou shalt make their sentence known,
And all thy righteous judgment own!

3 Thou, who for sinners felt such pain,
Whose precious blood the cross did stain,
Who did for us its curse sustain,—

4 By all that man's redemption cost,
Let not my trembling soul be lost,
In storms of guilty terror tossed!

5 Give me in that dread day a place
Among thy chosen, faithful race,
The sons of God, and heirs of grace.

6 Trembling before thy throne I bend;
My God, my Father, and my Friend,
Do not forsake me in the end!

DOXOLOGY.

Now to the great and sacred Three,
The Father, Son, and Spirit, be
Eternal praise and glory given,—
Through all the worlds where God is known,
By all the angels near the throne,
And all the saints in earth and heaven!

GROVE. L. M. Double.

119. *"The hand that made us is Divine."*

1 THE spacious firmament on high,
    With all the blue ethereal sky,
    And spangled heavens, a shining frame,
    Their great Original proclaim.

2 Th' unwearied sun, from day to day,
    Does his Creator's power display,
    And publishes to every land
    The work of an Almighty hand.

3 Soon as the evening shades prevail,
    The moon takes up the wondrous tale,
    And nightly to the listening earth
    Repeats the story of her birth;

4 While all the stars that round her burn,
    And all the planets in their turn,
    Confirm the tidings as they roll,
    And spread the truth from pole to pole.

5 What though, in solemn silence all
    Move round this dark, terrestrial ball?
    What though no real voice nor sound
    Amid their radiant orbs be found?

6 In reason's ear they all rejoice,
    And utter forth a glorious voice;
    For ever singing as they shine,
    "The hand that made us is Divine."

192. *God our Refuge.*—Psalm 46.

1 GOD is the refuge of his saints,
    When storms of sharp distress invade;
    Ere we can offer our complaints,
    Behold him present with his aid.

2 Let mountains from their seats be hurled
    Down to the deep, and buried there,
    Convulsions shake the solid world;
    Our faith shall never yield to fear.

3 Loud may the troubled ocean roar;
    In sacred peace our souls abide;
    While every nation, every shore,
    Trembles and dreads the swelling tide.

4 There is a stream, whose gentle flow
    Supplies the city of our God,
    Life, love, and joy, still gliding through,
    And watering our divine abode.

5 That sacred stream, thine holy word,
    Our grief allays, our fear controls;
    Sweet peace thy promises afford,
    And give new strength to fainting
        souls.

6 Zion enjoys her Monarch's love,
    Secure against a threatening hour;
    Nor can her firm foundations move,
    Built on his truth and armed with
        power.

UXBRIDGE. L. M.

225. *"Up to the hills I lift mine eyes."*
Psalm 121

1 Up to the hills I lift mine eyes,
  Th' eternal hills beyond the skies;
  Thence all her help my soul derives,
  There my almighty Refuge lives.

2 He lives—the everlasting God
  That built the world, that spread the flood;
  The heavens with all their hosts he made,
  And the dark regions of the dead.

3 He guides our feet, he guards our way;
  His morning smiles bless all the day;
  He spreads the evening vail, and keeps
  The silent hours, while Israel sleeps.

4 Israel, a name divinely blest,
  May rise secure, securely rest;
  Thy holy Guardian's wakeful eyes
  Admit no slumber, nor surprise.

5 No sun shall smite thy head by day;
  Nor the pale moon with sickly ray
  Shall blast thy couch; no baleful star
  Dart his malignant fire so far.

6 Should earth and hell with malice burn,
  Still thou shalt go, and still return,
  Safe in the Lord; his heavenly care
  Defends thy life from every snare.

7 On thee foul spirits have no power;
  And, in thy last departing hour,
  Angels, that trace the airy road,
  Shall bear thee homeward to thy God.

275. *"He so loved the world."*—John 16: 17.

1 Not to condemn the sons of men,
  Did Christ, the Son of God, appear;
  No weapons in his hands are seen,
  No flaming sword nor thunder there.

2 Such was the pity of our God,
  He loved the race of man so well,
  He sent his Son to bear our load
  Of sins, and save our souls from hell.

3 Sinners, believe the Saviour's word;
  Trust in his mighty name, and live:
  A thousand joys his lips afford,
  His hands a thousand blessings give.

479. *The Works and the Word of God.*
Psalm 19.

1 The heavens declare thy glory, Lord;
  In every star thy wisdom shines;
  But when our eyes behold thy word,
  We read thy name in fairer lines.

2 The rolling sun, the changing light,
  And night, and day, thy power confess;
  But the blest volume thou hast writ,
  Reveals thy justice and thy grace.

3 Sun, moon, and stars convey thy praise
  Round the whole earth, and never stand;
  So when thy truth began its race,
  It touched and glanced on every land.

4 Nor shall thy spreading gospel rest,
  Till thro' the world thy truth hath run;
  Till Christ hath all the nations blest
  That see the light, or feel the sun.

5 Great Sun of Righteousness, arise!
  Bless the dark world with heavenly light;
  Thy gospel makes the simple wise,
  Thy laws are pure, thy judgments right.

6 Thy noblest wonders here we view
  In souls renewed, and sins forgiven;
  Lord, cleanse my sins, my soul renew,
  And make thy word my guide to heaven.

EFFINGHAM. L. M.

204. *All Things the Gift of God.*

1 Great God! let all my tuneful powers
    Awake, and sing thy mighty name:
Thy hand revolves my circling hours—
    Thy hand, from whence my being came.

2 Seasons and moons, still rolling round
    In beauteous order, speak thy praise;
And years, with smiling mercy crowned,
    To thee successive honors raise.

3 My life, my health, my friends I owe,
    All to thy vast, unbounded love;
Ten thousand precious gifts below,
    And hope of nobler joys above.

4 Thus will I sing till nature cease,
    Till sense and language are no more;
And, after death, thy boundless grace,
    Through everlasting years adore.

252. *"Thy throne, O God, is for ever and ever."—Psalm 45.*

1 Now be my heart inspired to sing
    The glories of my Saviour King:
Jesus, the Lord, how heavenly fair
    His form! how bright his beauties are!

2 O'er all the sons of human race
    He shines with a superior grace;
Love from his lips divinely flows,
    And blessings all his state compose.

3 Thy throne, O God, for ever stands!
    Grace is the scepter in thy hands:
Thy laws and works are just and right;
    Justice and grace are thy delight.

4 God, thine own God, has richly shed
    His oil of gladness on thy head;
And with his sacred Spirit blest
    His first-born Son above the rest.

385. *Worship of Christ upon His Throne.*

1 Jesus, thou everlasting King!
    Accept the tribute which we bring;
Accept the well-deserved renown,
    And wear our praises as thy crown.

2 Let every act of worship be
    Like our espousals, Lord, to thee—
Like that dear hour, when from above
    We first received thy pledge of love.

3 The gladness of that happy day,
    Our hearts would wish it long to stay,
Nor let our faith forsake its hold,
    Nor comfort sink, nor love grow cold.

4 Let every moment, as it flies,
    Increase thy praise, improve our joys,
Till we are raised to sing thy name,
    At the great supper of the Lamb.

480. *"The Word of our God shall stand for ever."*

1 The starry firmament on high,
    And all the glories of the sky,
Yet shine not to thy praise, O Lord,
    So brightly as thy written word.

2 The hopes that holy word supplies,
    Its truths divine, and precepts wise,
In each a heavenly beam I see,
    And every beam conducts to thee.

3 Almighty Lord, the sun shall fail,
    The moon forget her nightly tale,
And deepest silence hush on high
    The radiant chorus of the sky;

4 But fixed for everlasting years,
    Unmoved, amid the wreck of spheres,
Thy word shall shine in cloudless day,
    When heaven and earth have passed away.

WELLS. L. M.

319. *Power of the Cross.*

1 WE sing the praise of him who died,
  Of him who died upon the cross:
  The sinner's hope let men deride;
  For this we count the world as loss.

2 The cross!—it takes our guilt away;
  It holds the fainting spirit up;
  It cheers with hope the gloomy day,
  And sweetens every bitter cup.

3 It makes the coward spirit brave,
  And nerves the feeble arm for fight;
  It takes the terror from the grave,
  And gilds the bed of death with light:

4 The balm of life, the cure of woe,
  The measure and the pledge of love;
  The sinner's refuge here below,
  The angel's theme in heaven above!

716. *It was for me.*

1 JESUS, whom angel-hosts adore,
  Became a man of griefs for me;
  In love, though rich, becoming poor,
  That I thro' him enriched might be.

2 Though Lord of all, above, below,
  He went to Olivet for me;
  There drank my cup of wrath and woe,
  When bleeding in Gethsemane.

3 The ever-blessed Son of God
  Went up to Calvary for me;
  There paid my debt, there bore my load,
  In his own body on the tree.

4 Jesus, whose dwelling is the skies,
  Went down into the grave for me;
  There overcame my enemies,
  There won the glorious victory.

5 'T is finished all: the vail is rent,
  The welcome sure, the access free;—
  Now then, we leave our banishment,
  O Father, to return to thee!

719. *"And that Rock was Christ."*
  1 Cor. 10: 4.

1 ETERNAL Rock! to thee I flee;
  In thy rent fissures would I hide;
  No rill of mercy flows to me
  But issues from thy wounded side.

2 Earth's fondest hopes, and brightest
    dreams,
  Are fitful, fugitive, and vain;
  The best of its polluted streams
  I only drink to thirst again.

3 Forgiveness, peace, salvation, heaven,
  Jesus, I owe alone to thee—
  The Rock whose clefts for me were
    riven,
  The smitten One of Calvary!

1242. *"And dying is but going home."*

1 Now let our souls, on wings sublime,
  Rise from the vanities of time,
  Draw back the parting vale, and see
  The glories of eternity.

2 Born by a new, celestial birth,
  Why should we grovel here on earth?
  Why grasp at vain and fleeting toys,
  So near to heaven's eternal joys?

3 Shall aught beguile us on the road,
  While we are walking back to God?
  For strangers into life we come,
  And dying is but going home.

4 Welcome, sweet hour of full discharge,
  That sets our longing souls at large,
  Unbinds our chains, breaks up our cell,
  And gives us with our God to dwell.

5 To dwell with God, to feel his love,
  Is the full heaven enjoyed above;
  And the sweet expectation now
  Is the young dawn of heaven below

BRADFORD. C. M.

210. *A Psalm of Praise for God's Care.*
Psalm 89.

1 THE mercies of my God and King
  My tongue shall still pursue:
Oh, happy they who, while they sing
  Those mercies, share them, too!

2 As bright and lasting as the sun,
  As lofty as the sky,
From age to age thy word shall run,
  And chance and change defy.

3 The covenant of the King of kings
  Shall stand for ever sure;
Beneath the shadow of thy wings
  Thy saints repose secure.

4 Thine is the earth, and thine the skies,
  Created at thy will;
The waves at thy command arise,
  At thy command are still.

5 In earth below, in heaven above,
  Who, who is, Lord, like thee?
Oh, spread the gospel of thy love
  Till all thy glories see!

368. *The living Saviour faithful to His Friends.*

1 I KNOW that my Redeemer lives,
  And ever prays for me;
A token of his love he gives,
  A pledge of liberty.

2 I find him lifting up my head;
  He brings salvation near;
His presence makes me free, indeed
  And he will soon appear.

3 He wills that I should holy be:
  What can withstand his will?
The counsel of his grace in me
  He surely shall fulfill.

4 Jesus, I hang upon thy word;
  I steadfastly believe
Thou wilt return, and claim me, Lord,
  And to thyself receive.

5 When God is mine, and I am his,
  Of paradise possessed,
I taste unutterable bliss,
  And everlasting rest.

383. *Redemption finished.*

1 TRIUMPHANT, Christ ascends on high,
  The glorious work complete;
Sin, death, and hell, low vanquished lie,
  Beneath his awful feet.

2 There, with eternal glory crowned,
  The Lord, the Conqueror, reigns;
His praise the heavenly choirs resound
  In their immortal strains.

3 Amid the splendors of his throne,
  Unchanging love appears;
The names he purchased for his own,
  Still on his heart he bears.

4 Oh, the rich depths of love divine!
  Of bliss a boundless store!
Dear Saviour, let me call thee mine;
  I can not wish for more.

5 On thee alone my hope relies;
  Beneath thy cross I fall,—
My Lord, my life, my sacrifice,
  My Saviour, and my all!

429. *Infinite Worth of Christ.*

1 INFINITE excellence is thine,
  Thou glorious Prince of grace!
Thy uncreated beauties shine
  With never-fading rays.

2 Sinners, from earth's remotest end,
  Come bending at thy feet;
To thee their prayers and songs ascend,
  In thee their wishes meet.

3 Millions of happy spirits live
  On thine exhaustless store;
From thee they all their bliss receive,
  And still thou givest more.

BARBY. C. M.

4 Thou art their triumph and their joy;
   They find their all in thee:
   Thy glories will their tongues employ,
   Through all eternity.

435. "*The Chiefest among ten thousand.*"

1 Come, heavenly Love, inspire my song
   With thine immortal flame,
   And teach my heart, and teach my tongue
   The Saviour's lovely name.

2 The Saviour!—oh, what endless charms
   Dwell in that blissful sound!
   Its influence every fear disarms,
   And spreads delight around.

3 Wrapped in the gloom of dark despair,
   We helpless, hopeless lay;
   But sovereign mercy reached us there,
   And smiled despair away.

4 Th' Almighty Former of the skies
   Stoops to our vile abode;
   While angels view with wondering eyes
   And hail th' incarnate God.

5 Incarnate God!—now to thine arms
   I yield my captive soul;
   Oh, let thine all-subduing charms
   My inmost powers control!

439. "*Ye are complete in Him.*"—Col. 2: 10.

1 I've found the pearl of greatest price;
   My heart doth sing for joy;
   And sing I must, for Christ is mine—
   Christ shall my song employ.

2 Christ is my Prophet, Priest, and King;
   My Prophet full of light;
   My great High Priest before the throne;
   My King of heavenly might.

3 For he, indeed, is Lord of lords,
   And he the King of kings;
   He is the Sun of Righteousness,
   With healing in his wings.

4 Christ is my Peace: he died for me,
   For me he gave his blood;
   And, as my wondrous sacrifice,
   Offered himself to God.

5 Christ Jesus is my All in All,
   My comfort and my love;
   My life below, and he shall be
   My joy and crown above.

654. "*When shall I come and appear before God?*"—Psalm 42.

1 As pants the hart for cooling streams
   When heated in the chase;
   So longs my soul, O God, for thee,
   And thy refreshing grace.

2 For thee, my God, the living God,
   My thirsty soul doth pine;
   Oh! when shall I behold thy face,
   Thou Majesty divine?

3 Why restless, why cast down, my soul?
   Trust God; and he'll employ
   His aid for thee, and change these sighs
   To thankful hymns of joy.

4 Why restless, why cast down, my soul?
   Hope still; and thou shalt sing
   The praise of him who is thy God,
   Thy health's eternal spring.

DOXOLOGY.

Let God the Father, and the Son,
   And Spirit, be adored,
Where there are works to make him known,
   Or saints to love the Lord!

COWPER. C. M.

300. *"There is a fountain filled with blood."*
(Original Form.)

1 There is a fountain filled with blood,
    Drawn from Immanuel's veins;
  And sinners, plunged beneath that flood,
    Lose all their guilty stains.

2 The dying thief rejoiced to see
    That fountain in his day;
  And there have I, as vile as he,
    Washed all my sins away.

3 Dear, dying Lamb! thy precious blood
    Shall never lose its power,
  Till all the ransomed church of God
    Be saved, to sin no more.

4 E'er since, by faith, I saw the stream
    Thy flowing wounds supply,
  Redeeming love has been my theme,
    And shall be till I die.

5 Then, in a nobler, sweeter song,
    I'll sing thy power to save,
  When this poor, lisping, stammering
      tongue
    Lies silent in the grave.

6 Lord, I believe thou hast prepared
    (Unworthy though I be)
  For me a blood-bought, free reward,
    A golden harp for me!

7 'T is strung and tuned for endless years;
    And formed by power divine,
  To sound in God the Father's ears
    No other name but thine.

301. *"There is a fountain filled with blood."*
(Abridged Form.)

1 There is a fountain filled with blood,
    Drawn from Immanuel's veins;
  And sinners, plunged beneath that flood,
    Lose all their guilty stains.

2 The dying thief rejoiced to see
    That fountain in his day;
  And there may I, though vile as he,
    Wash all my sins away.

3 Dear, dying Lamb! thy precious blood
    Shall never lose its power,
  Till all the ransomed church of God
    Are saved, to sin no more.

4 Since first, by faith, I saw the stream
    Thy flowing wounds supply,
  Redeeming love has been my theme,
    And shall be, till I die."

5 And when this feeble, stammering tongue
    Lies silent in the grave,
  Then, in a nobler, sweeter song,
    I'll sing thy power to save.

684. *Trustful Christian victorious.*

1 My God! the spring of all my joys,
    The life of my delights,
  The glory of my brightest days,
    And comfort of my nights!

2 In darkest shades if he appear,
    My dawning is begun;
  He is my soul's sweet morning star,
    And he my rising sun.

3 The opening heavens around me shine
    With beams of sacred bliss,
  While Jesus shows his heart is mine,
    And whispers, I am his!

4 My soul would leave this heavy clay
    At that transporting word,
  Run up with joy the shining way,
    T' embrace my dearest Lord.

5 Fearless of hell, and ghastly death,
    I'd break through every foe;
  The wings of love and arms of faith
    Should bear me conqueror through.

BARTOW. C. M.

1231. *The New Jerusalem.*

1 JERUSALEM! my happy home!
   Name ever dear to me!
  When shall my labors have an end,
   In joy, and peace, and thee?

2 Oh, when, thou city of my God,
   Shall I thy courts ascend,
  Where evermore the angels sing,
   Where Sabbaths have no end?

3 There happier bowers, than Eden's
    bloom,
   Nor sin nor sorrow know;
  Blest seats! through rude and stormy
    scenes,
   I onward press to you.

4 Why should I shrink at pain and woe?
   Or feel at death dismay?
  I've Canaan's goodly land in view,
   And realms of endless day.

5 Jerusalem, my glorious home!
   My soul still pants for thee;
  Then shall my labors have an end,
   When I thy joys shall see.

1241. *"Come, crown and throne; come, robe and palm."*

1 THESE are the crowns that we shall wear,
   When all thy saints are crowned;
  These are the palms that we shall bear
   On yonder holy ground.

2 These are the robes, unsoiled and white,
   Which we shall then put on,
  When, foremost 'mong the sons of light,
   We sit on yonder throne.

3 That is the city of the saints,
   Where we so soon shall stand,
  When we shall strike these desert-tents,
   And quit this desert-land.

4 Then welcome toil, and care, and pain!
   And welcome sorrow, too!
  All toil is rest, all grief is gain,
   With such a prize in view.

5 Come, crown and throne; come, robe
    and palm;
   Burst forth, glad stream of peace!
  Come, holy city of the Lamb!
   Rise, Sun of righteousness!

1245. *The Cloud of Witnesses.*

1 GIVE me the wings of faith, to rise
   Within the vail, and see
  The saints above—how great their joys,
   How bright their glories be!

2 Once they were mourning here below,
   And wet their couch with tears;
  They wrestled hard, as we do now,
   With sins, and doubts, and fears.

3 I ask them whence their victory came;
   They, with united breath,
  Ascribe their conquest to the Lamb,
   Their triumph to his death.

4 They marked the footsteps that he trod,
   His zeal inspired their breast;
  And following their incarnate God,
   Possess the promised rest.

5 Our glorious Leader claims our praise
   For his own pattern given,
  While the long cloud of witnesses
   Show the same path to heaven.

DOXOLOGY.

LET God the Father, and the Son,
   And Spirit, be adored,
  Where there are works to make him
    known,
   Or saints to love the Lord!

HAVERHILL. S. M.

308. *"None other name under Heaven."*

1 God's holy law, transgressed,
    Speaks nothing but despair;
  Burdened with guilt, with grief oppressed,
    We find no comfort there.

2 Not all our groans and tears,
    Nor works which we have done,
  Nor vows, nor promises, nor prayers,
    Can e'er for sin atone.

3 Relief alone is found
    In Jesus' precious blood:
  'T is this that heals the mortal wound,
    And reconciles to God.

4 High lifted on the cross,
    The spotless victim dies:
  This is salvation's only source,
    Hence all our hopes arise.

312. *"In Christ Jesus."*—1 Cor. 1 : 30.

1 How heavy is the night
    That hangs upon our eyes,
  Till Christ, with his reviving light,
    Upon our souls arise!

2 Our guilty spirits dread
    To meet the wrath of Heaven;
  But in his righteousness arrayed,
    We see our sins forgiven.

3 Unholy and impure
    Are all our thoughts and ways:
  His hands infected nature cure,
    With sanctifying grace.

4 The powers of hell agree
    To hold our souls in vain:
  He sets the sons of bondage free,
    And breaks the accursed chain.

5 Lord, we adore thy ways,
    To bring us near to God,—
  Thy sovereign power, thy healing grace,
    And thine atoning blood.

352. *The Fifty-third Chapter of Isaiah.*

1 Like sheep we went astray,
    And broke the fold of God;
  Each wandering in a different way,
    But all the downward road.

2 How dreadful was the hour,
    When God our wanderings laid,
  And did at once his vengeance pour
    Upon the Shepherd's head!

3 How glorious was the grace,
    When Christ sustained the stroke!
  His life and blood the Shepherd pays,
    A ransom for the flock!

4 But God shall raise his head
    O'er all the sons of men;
  And make him see a numerous seed,
    To recompense his pain.

5 "I'll give him," saith the Lord,
    "A portion with the strong;
  He shall possess a large reward,
    And hold his honors long."

775. *"Mine eyes are ever toward the Lord."*
    Psalm 25.

1 Mine eyes and my desire
    Are ever to the Lord;
  I love to plead his promises,
    And rest upon his word.

2 Lord, turn thee to my soul;
    Bring thy salvation near:
  When will thy hand release my feet
    From sin's destructive snare?

3 When shall the sovereign grace
    Of my forgiving God
  Restore me from those dangerous ways
    My wandering feet have trod?

BADEA. S. M.

4 Oh, keep my soul from death,
   Nor put my hope to shame !
For I have placed my only trust
   In my Redeemer's name.

5 With humble faith I wait
   To see thy face again :
Of Israel it shall ne'er be said,
   He sought the Lord in vain.

1232. *"How shall we sing the Lord's song in a strange land ?"—Psalm 137.*

1 FAR from my heavenly home,
   Far from my Father's breast,
Fainting, I cry, "Blest Spirit, come,
   And speed me to my rest !"

2 Upon the willows long
   My harp has silent hung ;
How should I sing a cheerful song,
   Till thou inspire my tongue ?

3 My spirit homeward turns,
   And fain would thither flee ;
My heart, O Zion, droops and yearns,
   When I remember thee.

4 To thee, to thee I press—
   A dark and toilsome road :
When shall I pass the wilderness,
   And reach the saints' abode ?

5 God of my life, be near ;
   On thee my hopes I cast :
Oh, guide me through the desert here,
   And bring me home at last !

1247. *Thanks for all Saints.*

1 For all thy saints, O God,
   Who strove in Christ to live,
Who followed him, obeyed, adored,
   Our grateful hymn receive.

2 For all thy saints, O God,
   Accept our thankful cry,
Who counted Christ their great reward,
   And yearned for him to die.

3 They all, in life and death,
   With him, their Lord, in view,
Learned from thy Holy Spirit's breath
   To suffer and to do.

4 For this, thy name we bless,
   And humbly pray that we
May follow them in holiness,
   And live and die in thee.

1274. *"This mortal shall put on immortality."*

1 AND must this body die ?
   This mortal frame decay ?
And must these active limbs of mine
   Lie moldering in the clay ?

2 God, my Redeemer, lives
   And ever from the skies
Looks down and watches all my dust,
   Till he shall bid it rise.

3 Arrayed in glorious grace
   Shall these vile bodies shine,
And every shape, and every face
   Look heavenly and divine.

4 These lively hopes we owe
   To Jesus' dying love ;
We would adore his grace below,
   And sing his power above.

5 Dear Lord ! accept the praise
   Of these our humble songs,
Till tunes of nobler sound we raise
   With our immortal tongues.

DOXOLOGY.

To God, the Father, Son,
   And Spirit, glory be,
As was, and is, and shall remain
   Through all eternity.

TOPLADY. 7s. 6 LINES.

244. *Jesus.—I am.—The Word.*

1 JESUS, hail! thou great I AM!
High and holy is thy name:
Angel-harps resound thy praise;
Saints adore thy saving grace:
Every creature bows the knee
Worshiping thy majesty.

2 Hail, thou everlasting Lord!
"God with us!" incarnate Word!
Glory of thy church thou art,
Life and light of every heart:
Angels, saints, below, above,
Join to praise thy boundless love.

519. *The Peace of Christ.*

1 YE who in these courts are found,
Listening to the joyful sound,—
Lost and helpless, as ye are,
Sons of sorrow, sin, and care,—
Glorify the King of kings,
Take the peace the gospel brings.

2 Turn to Christ your longing eyes,
View his bleeding sacrifice;
See, in him, your sins forgiven,
Pardon, holiness, and heaven:
Glorify the King of kings,
Take the peace the gospel brings.

DOXOLOGY.

PRAISE the name of God most high;
Praise him, all below the sky;
Praise him, all ye heavenly host—
Father, Son, and Holy Ghost!
As through countless ages past,
Evermore his praise shall last.

520. *Welcome!*

1 FROM the cross uplifted high,
Where the Saviour deigns to die,
What melodious sounds we hear,
Bursting on the ravished ear!—
"Love's redeeming work is done;
Come and welcome, sinner, come!

2 "Spread for thee, the festal board
See with richest dainties stored;
To thy Father's bosom pressed,
Yet again a child confessed,
Never from his house to roam:
Come and welcome, sinner, come!

3 "Soon the days of life shall end;
Lo, I come, your Saviour, Friend!
Safe your spirits to convey
To the realms of endless day,
Up to my eternal home:
Come and welcome, sinner, come!"

688. *"Only Thee."*

1 BLESSED Saviour! thee I love,
All my other joys above;
All my hopes in thee abide,
Thou my hope, and naught beside:
Ever let my glory be
Only, only, only thee.

2 Once again beside the cross,
All my gain I count but loss;
Earthly pleasures fade away,—
Clouds they are that hide my day;
Hence, vain shadows! let me see
Jesus crucified for me.

LORAINE. 7s. 6 LINES.

3 From beneath that thorny crown
Trickle drops of cleansing down:
Pardon from thy pierced hand
Now I take while here I stand;
Only then I live to thee,
When thy wounded side I see.

4 Blesséd Saviour! thine am I,
Thine to live, and thine to die;
Height, or depth, or earthly power
Ne'er shall hide my Saviour more;
Ever shall my glory be
Only, only, only thee!

721. "*Rock of Ages.*"—1 Cor. 10: 4.

1 Rock of Ages! cleft for me,
Let me hide myself in thee!
Let the water and the blood,
From thy riven side that flowed,
Be of sin the double cure—
Cleanse me from its guilt and power.

2 Could my zeal no respite know,
Could my tears for ever flow—
All for sin could not atone:
Thou must save, and thou alone!
Nothing in my hand I bring;
Simply to thy cross I cling.

3 While I draw this fleeting breath,
When my eyelids close in death,
When I soar to worlds unknown,
See thee on thy judgment throne,—
Rock of Ages! cleft for me,
Let me hide myself in thee!

764. *Blessedness of Trust in Christ.*

1 Saviour! happy would I be,
If I could but trust in thee;
Trust thy wisdom me to guide;
Trust thy goodness to provide;
Trust thy saving love and power;
Trust thee every day and hour:

2 Trust thee as the only light
In the darkest hour of night;
Trust in sickness, trust in health;
Trust in poverty and wealth;
Trust in joy, and trust in grief;
Trust thy promise for relief:

3 Trust thy blood to cleanse my soul;
Trust thy grace to make me whole;
Trust thee living, dying, too;
Trust thee all my journey through;
Trust thee till my feet shall be
Planted on the crystal sea!

1052. "*My flesh is meat, indeed.*"

1 Bread of heaven! on thee I feed,
For thy flesh is meat, indeed;
Ever may my soul be fed
With this true and living Bread;
Day by day with strength supplied
Through the life of him who died.

2 Vine of heaven! thy blood supplies
This blest cup of sacrifice;
'Tis thy wounds my healing give;
To thy cross I look, and live;
Thou, my Life, oh, let me be
Rooted, grafted, built on thee!

DOXOLOGY.

Blessing, honor, glory, might,
And dominion infinite,
To the Father of our Lord,
To the Spirit and the Word:
As it was all worlds before,
Is, and shall be evermore.

BAIRD. L. M.

321.* *The Man of Sorrows.*—Isaiah 53.

1 Despised is the Man of grief,
Rejected, and denied belief
By them whose sorrows he hath worn—
For whom he bears the bitter scorn,
The shameful robe, the scourge, the thorn!

2 All we, like sheep, have gone astray,
And turned aside from wisdom's way;
But he the path of death hath trod,
And humbly kissed affliction's rod,
To lead our stricken souls to God.

3 Oh, let us cast each vice away,
Beneath the cross each passion lay;
With contrite heart and weeping eye,
Behold the Saviour lifted high,
And every sin and folly fly!

402. *Longing to follow Christ.*

1 O thou, to whose all-searching sight
The darkness shineth as the light,
Search, prove my heart; it pants for thee;
Oh, burst these bonds and set it free!

2 Wash out its stains, refine its dross;
Nail my affections to the cross;
Hallow each thought; let all within
Be clean as thou, my Lord, art clean.

3 While in this darksome wild I stray,
Be thou my light, be thou my way;
No foes, no danger will I fear,
While thou, Almighty God, art near.

4 When rising floods my soul o'erflow,
When sinks my heart in waves of woe,
Jesus, thy timely aid impart,
And raise my head, and cheer my heart.

5 Saviour, where'er thy steps I see,
Dauntless, untired, I follow thee;
Oh, let thy hand support me still,
And lead me to thy holy hill!

* Repeat the third line of the tune for this hymn.

729. *"A bruised reed shall he not break."*

1 Before thy cross, my dying Lord,
I cast my soul, and trust thy love;
Oh, here thy saving power afford,
And seal my pardon from above!

2 No threatening foes shall drive me hence,
Helpless and fainting I draw near;
Resolved (for 't is my last defense),
If I must die, to perish here.

3 But, Saviour! for thy mercy's sake,
Relieve the anguish of my heart;
The bruiséd reed thou wilt not break,
Nor bid the contrite soul depart.

4 Washed in thy blood, I shall be pure;
Cheered by thy smile, shall feel no shame;
Saved by thy love, I stand secure,
And triumph in a Saviour's name!

731. *The Liberty of Faith.*

1 Before thy throne with tearful eyes,
My gracious Lord, I humbly fall;
To thee my weary spirit flies,
For thy forgiving love I call.

2 How free thy mercy overflows,
When sinners on thy grace rely!
Thy tender love no limit knows;
Oh, save me—justly doomed to die!

3 Yes! thou wilt save; my soul is free!
The gloom of sin is fled away;
My tongue breaks forth in praise to thee,
And all my powers thy word obey.

4 Hence, while I wrestle with my foes,—
The world, the flesh, the hosts of hell,—
Sustain thou me till conflicts close,
Then endless songs my thanks shall tell.

IOSCO. L. M.

238. *Sovereignty of God in Conversion.*

1 MAY not the sovereign Lord on high
  Dispense his favors as he will;
  Choose some to life, while others die,
  And yet be just and gracious still?

2 Shall man reply against the Lord,
  And call his Maker's ways unjust,
  The thunder of whose dreadful word
  Can crush a thousand worlds to dust?

3 But, O my soul! if truth so bright
  Should dazzle and confound thy sight,
  Yet still his written will obey,
  And wait the great decisive day.

4 Then shall he make his justice known,
  And the whole world, before his throne,
  With joy or terror, shall confess
  The glory of his righteousness.

241. *"Be still, and know that I am God."*

1 WAIT, O my soul, thy Maker's will!
  Tumultuous passions, all be still;
  Nor let a murmuring thought arise:
  His ways are just, his counsels wise.

2 He in the thickest darkness dwells,
  Performs his work, the cause conceals;
  And, though his footsteps are unknown,
  Judgment and truth support his throne.

3 In heaven, and earth, and air, and seas,
  He executes his firm decrees;
  And by his saints it stands confessed,
  That what he does is ever best.

4 Wait, then, my soul, submissive wait,
  With reverence bow before his seat;
  And, 'mid the terrors of his rod,
  Trust in a wise and gracious God.

1117. *"Oh, spare our guilty country, spare."*

1 ON thee, O Lord our God, we call,
  Before thy throne devoutly fall;
  Oh, whither should the helpless fly?
  To whom but thee direct their cry?

2 Lord, we repent, we weep, we mourn,
  To our forsaken God we turn;
  Oh, spare our guilty country, spare
  The church thine hand hath planted here!

3 We plead thy grace, indulgent God!
  We plead thy Son's atoning blood;
  We plead thy gracious promises;
  And are they unavailing pleas?

4 These pleas, presented at thy throne,
  Have brought ten thousand blessings down
  On guilty lands in helpless woe:
  Let them prevail to save us, too.

1122. *"Look down, O God, with pitying eye."*

1 INDULGENT Sovereign of the skies,
  And wilt thou bow thy gracious ear?
  While feeble mortals raise their cries,
  Wilt thou, the great Jehovah, hear?

2 How shall thy servants give thee rest,
  Till Zion's moldering walls thou raise;
  Till thine own power shall stand confess'd,
  And make Jerusalem a praise?

3 Look down, O God, with pitying eye,
  And view the desolation round;
  See what wide realms in darkness lie,
  And hurl their idols to the ground.

4 Loud let the gospel trumpet blow,
  And call the nations from afar;
  Let all the isles their Saviour know,
  And earth's remotest ends draw near.

RAYFORD. C. M. DOUBLE.

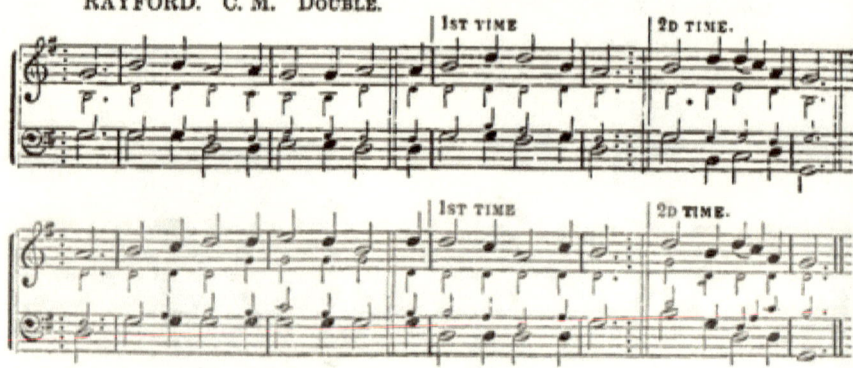

324. *"Thy Righteousness, even Thine only."*
Psalm 71.

1 My Saviour! my almighty Friend!
  When I begin thy praise,
Where will the growing numbers end,
  The numbers of thy grace?

2 Thou art my everlasting trust;
  Thy goodness I adore:
And since I knew thy graces first,
  I speak thy glories more.

3 My feet shall travel all the length
  Of the celestial road;
And march, with courage in thy strength,
  To see my Father, God.

4 When I am filled with sore distress
  For some surprising sin,
I'll plead thy perfect righteousness,
  And mention none but thine.

5 How will my lips rejoice to tell
  The victories of my King!
My soul, redeemed from sin and hell,
  Shall thy salvation sing.

6 Awake, awake, my tuneful powers!
  With this delightful song
I'll entertain the darkest hours,
  Nor think the season long.

970. *"Your sorrow shall be turned into joy."*

1 Come, humble souls—ye mourners, come,
  And wipe away your tears:
Adieu to all your sad complaints,
  Your sorrows and your fears.

2 Come, shout aloud the Father's grace,
  The Saviour's dying love;
Soon shall you join the glorious theme
  In loftier strains above.

3 God, the eternal, mighty God,
  To dearer names descends:
Calls you his treasure, and his joy,
  His children, and his friends.

4 My Father, God! and may these lips
  Pronounce a name so dear?
Not thus could heaven's sweet harmony
  Delight my listening ear.

5 For ever let my grateful heart
  His boundless grace adore,
Which gives ten thousand blessings now,
  And bids me hope for more.

6 Transporting hope!—still on my soul
  With radiant glories shine,
Till thou thyself art lost in joys
  Immortal and divine.

1089. *The Godly Child.*

1 By cool Siloam's shady rill
  How fair the lily grows!
How sweet the breath, beneath the hill,
  Of Sharon's dewy rose!

2 Lo! such the child, whose early feet
  The paths of peace have trod,
Whose secret heart, with influence sweet,
  Is upward drawn to God.

3 By cool Siloam's shady rill
  The lily must decay;
The rose that blooms beneath the hill,
  Must shortly fade away.

4 And soon, too soon, the wint'ry hour
  Of man's maturer age
Will shake the soul with sorrow's power,
  And stormy passion's rage.

5 O thou, whose infant feet were found
  Within thy Father's shrine,
Whose years, with changeless virtue crowned,
  Were all alike divine,—

6 Dependent on thy bounteous breath,
  We seek thy grace alone,
In childhood, manhood, age, and death,
  To keep us still thine own.

ORTONVILLE. C. M.

328. *"This is my Friend."*—Cant. 5: 10-16.

1 MAJESTIC sweetness sits enthroned
  Upon the Saviour's brow;
  His head with radiant glories crowned,
  His lips with grace o'erflow.

2 No mortal can with him compare,
  Among the sons of men;
  Fairer is he than all the fair
  That fill the heavenly train.

3 He saw me plunged in deep distress,
  He flew to my relief;
  For me he bore the shameful cross,
  And carried all my grief.

4 To him I owe my life and breath,
  And all the joys I have;
  He makes me triumph over death,
  He saves me from the grave.

5 To heaven, the place of his abode,
  He brings my weary feet;
  Shows me the glories of my God,
  And makes my joy complete.

6 Since from his bounty I receive
  Such proofs of love divine,
  Had I a thousand hearts to give,
  Lord! they should all be thine.

406.   *Our Saviour.*

1 WE 'LL sing the power of him who died
  His people to redeem;
  He is our Saviour, true and tried,
  And he shall be our theme.

2 For he is precious in the sight
  Of all who know his voice:
  'T was he who brought us to the light,
  And taught us to rejoice.

3 From worldly snares, and Satan's wile,
  He guards us by his power;
  And keeps us safe from force and guile
  In every trying hour.

4 And till his ransomed people come,
  His house above to fill,
  'T is he who safely guides them home,
  Beyond the reach of ill.

5 Then let us ever make our boast
  Of him, and him alone,
  Who came from heaven to seek the lost,
  And bring us to his throne.

852.   *The Power of Man in Prayer.*

1 THERE is an eye that never sleeps
  Beneath the wing of night;
  There is an ear that never shuts,
  When sink the beams of light.

2 There is an arm that never tires,
  When human strength gives way;
  There is a love that never fails,
  When earthly loves decay.

3 That eye is fixed on seraph throngs;
  That arm upholds the sky;
  That ear is filled with angel songs;
  That love is throned on high.

4 But there's a power which man can wield
  When mortal aid is vain,
  That eye, that arm, that love to reach,
  That listening ear to gain.

5 That power is prayer, which soars on high,
  Through Jesus, to the throne;
  And moves the hand which moves the world,
  To bring salvation down!

DOXOLOGY.

LET God the Father, and the Son,
  And Spirit, be adored,
  Where there are works to make him known,
  Or saints to love the Lord!

RAYNER. S. M. DOUBLE.

255. *Love of God in the Gift of Christ.*

1 RAISE your triumphant songs
  To an immortal tune;
Wide let the earth resound the deeds
  Celestial grace has done.

2 Sing how eternal love
  Its chief Belovéd chose,
And bade him raise our wretched race
  From their abyss of woes.

3 His hand no thunder bears;
  No terror clothes his brow:
No bolts to drive our guilty souls
  To fiercer flames below.

4 'T was mercy filled the throne,
  And wrath stood silent by,
When Christ was sent with pardons down
  To rebels doomed to die.

5 Now, sinners, dry your tears;
  Let hopeless sorrow cease:
Bow to the scepter of his love,
  And take the offered peace.

6 Lord, we obey thy call;
  We lay an humble claim
To the salvation thou hast brought,
  And love and praise thy name.

331. *"The Song of the Lamb."*
Rev. 15: 3, 4.

1 AWAKE, and sing the song
  Of Moses and the Lamb!
Wake, every heart, and every tongue,
  To praise the Saviour's name!

2 Sing of his dying love;
  Sing of his rising power:
Sing how he intercedes above
  For those whose sins he bore.

3 Sing, till we feel our hearts
  Ascending with our tongues;
Sing, till the love of sin departs,
  And grace inspires our songs.

4 Sing on your heavenly way,
  Ye ransomed sinners, sing!
Sing on, rejoicing every day
  In Christ, th' exalted King.

5 Soon shall we hear him say,
  "Ye blessèd children, come!"
Soon will he call us hence away
  To our eternal home.

6 Soon shall our raptured tongue
  His endless praise proclaim,
And sweeter voices tune the song
  Of Moses and the Lamb.

893. *"Endure hardness, as a good soldier of Jesus Christ."*

1 ARISE, ye saints, arise!
  The Lord our Leader is;
The foe before his banner flies,
  For victory is his.

2 Lead on, almighty Lord,
  Lead on to victory!
Encouraged by the bright reward,
  With joy we 'll follow thee.

3 We 'll follow thee, our Guide,
  Our Saviour and our King;
We 'll follow thee, through grace supplied
  From heaven's eternal spring.

4 We hope to see the day
  When all our toils shall cease;
When we shall cast our arms away,
  And dwell in endless peace.

5 This hope supports us here,
  It makes our burdens light;
'T will serve our drooping hearts to cheer,
  Till faith shall end in sight.

6 Till, of the prize possessed,
  We hear of war no more;
And oh, sweet thought! for ever rest
  On yonder peaceful shore.

LABAN. S. M.

636. *"Watch and pray."*

1 My soul! be on thy guard;
   Ten thousand foes arise;
   The hosts of sin are pressing hard
   To draw thee from the skies.

2 Oh, watch, and fight, and pray!
   The battle ne'er give o'er;
   Renew it boldly every day,
   And help divine implore.

3 Ne'er think the victory won,
   Nor once at ease sit down;
   Thy arduous work will not be done
   Till thou obtain thy crown.

4 Fight on, my soul, till death
   Shall bring thee to thy God!
   He'll take thee, at thy parting breath
   Up to his blest abode.

113. *"Bless the Lord, your God, for ever and ever."*—Neh. 9: 5.

1 STAND up, and bless the Lord,
   Ye people of his choice;
   Stand up, and bless the Lord your God,
   With heart, and soul, and voice.

2 Though high above all praise,
   Above all blessing high,
   Who would not fear his holy name,
   And laud, and magnify?

3 Oh, for the living flame
   From his own altar brought,
   To touch our lips, our souls inspire,
   And wing to heaven our thought!

4 God is our strength and song,
   And his salvation ours;
   Then be his love in Christ proclaimed
   With all our ransomed powers.

5 Stand up, and bless the Lord;
   The Lord your God adore;
   Stand up, and bless his glorious name,
   Henceforth, for evermore!

DOXOLOGY.

To God, the Father, Son,
And Spirit, glory be,
As was, and is, and shall remain
Through all eternity!

WATCHMAN. S. M.

PRESTON. C. M.

282. *"He reviled not again."*

1 What grace, O Lord, and beauty shone
    Around thy steps below;
  What patient love was seen in all
    Thy life and death of woe.

2 For, ever on thy burdened heart
    A weight of sorrow hung;
  Yet no ungentle, murmuring word
    Escaped thy silent tongue.

3 Thy foes might hate, despise, revile,
    Thy friends unfaithful prove;
  Unwearied in forgiveness still,
    Thy heart could only love.

4 Oh, give us hearts to love like thee!
    Like thee, O Lord, to grieve
  Far more for others' sins than all
    The wrongs that we receive.

5 One with thyself, may every eye,
    In us, thy brethren, see
  The gentleness and grace that spring
    From union, Lord! with thee,

460. *The Holy Spirit our Friend.*

1 Lord, am I precious in thy sight?
    Lord, wouldst thou have me thine?
  May it be given me to delight
    The Majesty divine?

2 Lord, dost thou sweetly urge and press
    My soul thy Heaven to win?
  Lord, dost thou love my holiness?
    Lord, dost thou hate my sin?

3 O Holy Spirit! dost thou mourn
    When I from thee depart?
  Dost thou rejoice when I return,
    And give thee back my heart?

4 O happy Heaven! where thine embrace
    I never more shall leave,
  Nor ever cast away thy grace,
    Nor once thy Spirit grieve.

5 Oh, let me, Lord, each grace possess
    That makes thy heaven more bright,
  And bring the humble holiness
    That gives my God delight!

505. *"I will give you rest."*—Matt. 11 . 28–30.

1 Come unto me, all ye who mourn,
    With guilt and fear oppressed;
  Resign to me the willing heart,
    And I will give you rest.

2 Take up my yoke, and learn of me
    A meek and lowly mind;
  And thus your weary, troubled souls
    Repose and peace shall find.

3 For light and gentle is my yoke:
    The burden I impose
  Shall ease the heart which groaned before
    Beneath a load of woes.

789. *One with Christ.*

1 Lord Jesus, are we one with thee?
    O height, O depth of love!
  With thee we died upon the tree;
    In thee we live above.

2 Such was thy grace, that for our sake
    Thou didst from heaven come down,
  Our mortal flesh and blood partake,
    In all our misery one.

3 Our sins, our guilt, in love divine,
    Were borne on earth by thee;
  The gall, the curse, the wrath were thine
    To set thy members free.

4 Ascended now in glory bright,
    Still one with us thou art;
  Nor life, nor death, nor depth, nor height,
    Thy saints and thee can part.

5 Soon, soon shall come that glorious day,
    When, seated on thy throne,
  Thou shalt to wondering worlds display
    That thou with us art one!

DENFIELD. C. M.

792. *"When He shall appear we shall be like Him."*

1 Oh! mean may seem this house of clay,
  Yet 't was the Lord's abode;
  Our feet may mourn this thorny way,
  Yet here Immanuel trod.

2 This fleshly robe the Lord did wear;
  This watch the Lord did keep;
  These burdens sore the Lord did bear;
  These tears the Lord did weep!

3 Our very frailty brings **us near**
  Unto the Lord **of** heaven;
  To every grief, **to every tear,**
  Such glory strange is given.

4 But not this fleshly robe alone
  Shall link us, Lord, to thee;
  Nor always in the tear and groan
  Shall the dear kindred be.

5 We shall be reckoned for thine own,
  Because thy heaven we share;
  Because we sing around thy throne,
  And thy bright raiment wear.

793. *"Who died for us that we should live with Him."*

1 Thou, to our woe who down didst come,
  Who one with us wouldst be,
  Wilt lift us to thy heavenly home,
  Wilt make us one with thee.

2 Our earthly garments thou hast worn,
  And we thy robes shall wear!
  Our mortal burdens thou hast borne,
  And we thy bliss **may** bear.

3 Oh, mighty grace! our life to live,
  To make our earth divine;
  Oh, mighty grace! thy heaven to give,
  And lift our life to thine!

4 Oh, strange the gifts and marvelous,
  By thee received and given!
  Thou tookest woe and death from us,
  And we receive thy heaven!

812. *"God, my exceeding Joy."*

1 To thee, O God, my prayer **ascends,**
  But not for golden stores;
  Nor covet I the brightest gems
  That shine on eastern shores;

2 Nor that deluding, empty joy,
  Men call a mighty name;
  Nor greatness, with its pride and state,
  My restless thoughts inflame;

3 Nor pleasure's fascinating charms
  My fond desires allure;
  But nobler things than **these from thee**
  My wishes would **secure.**

4 **The** faith and hope **of** things unseen
  My best affections move—
  Thy light, thy favor, and thy smiles,
  Thine everlasting love.

5 **These** are the blessings I desire:
  Lord, be these blessings mine;
  And all the glories of the world
  I cheerfully resign.

920. *Prayer for a pure Heart.*

1 O LORD, our carnal mind control,
  And make us pure within;
  Purge more and more our inmost soul
  From willful thoughts of sin.

2 Let not the world with spot or soil
  Our secret heart defile;
  Nor Satan round our spirit coil
  His chain of fraud and guile.

3 Be ours the blessed lot of those
  Who every **evil flee;**
  Whose holy **converse** clearly shows
  Communion **full** with thee;—

4 **That** when thou shalt in might appear,
  We may thy grace declare,
  And thence through heaven's eternal year
  Thy glorious kingdom share.

ZEBULON. H. M.

357. *"Thou hast led Captivity captive."*

1 The happy morn is come;
  Triumphant o'er the grave,
  The Saviour leaves the tomb,
  Almighty now to save:
Captivity is captive led,
For Jesus liveth, who was dead.

2 Who now accuseth them,
  For whom the Surety died?
  Or who shall those condemn,
  Whom God hath justified?
Captivity is captive led,
For Jesus liveth, who was dead.

3 The ransom Christ hath paid—
  The glorious work is done;
  On him our help is laid,
  By him our victory won:
Captivity is captive led,
For Jesus liveth, who was dead.

4 All hail, triumphant Lord!
  The resurrection, thou;
  All hail, incarnate Lord!
  Before thy throne we bow:
Captivity is captive led,
For Jesus liveth, who was dead.

672. *Safety in trusting God.*—Psalm 125

1 Their hearts shall not be moved
  Who in the Lord confide,
  But, firm as Zion's hill,
  They ever shall abide:
As mountains shield Jerusalem,
The Lord shall be a shield to them.

2 His blessing on them rests,
  Like freshening dew from heaven;
And succor from his throne
  In all their need is given:
Omnipotence shall guard them well,
And peace remain on Israel.

3 One like the Son of God
  Is walking at their side,
  When by the fervid flame
  And fiery furnace tried;
And 't is enough that he is near,
To strengthen them in every fear.

1092. *"The Saviour calls: Oh, hear His voice."*

1 From yon delusive scene,
  Where death and ruin smile,
  Beneath a treacherous mien,
  The sinner to beguile,
The Saviour calls: Oh, hear his voice,
And make his love your early choice!

2 Down from the realms of light,
  To this dark world of woe,
  He came with speedy flight,
  Redemption to bestow:
The Saviour calls: Oh, hear his voice,
And make his love your only choice.

3 With pardon in his hands,
  And purity and joy,
  How sweet are his commands!
  His bliss without alloy:
The Saviour calls: Oh, hear his voice,
And make his love your happy choice.

4 Through life your guard and guide,
  In death your strength and stay,
  He'll keep you near his side,
  Nor ever turn away:
The Saviour calls: Oh, hear his voice,
And make his love your lasting choice!

SWAINE. H. M.

16. "*A day in Thy courts.*"—Psalm 84.

1 LORD of the worlds above,
    How pleasant and how fair
  The dwellings of thy love,
    Thine earthly temples are!
To thine abode | With warm desires,
My heart aspires, | To see my God.

2 Oh, happy souls that pray
    Where God appoints to hear!
  Oh, happy men that pay
    Their constant service there!
They praise thee still; | Who love the way
And happy they | To Zion's hill.

3 They go from strength to strength,
    Through this dark vale of tears,
  Till each arrives at length,
    Till each in heaven appears.
Oh, glorious seat, | Shall thither bring
When God our King | Our willing feet!

4 The Lord his people loves;
    His hand no good withholds
  From those his heart approves,
    From pure and upright souls.
Thrice happy he, | Whose spirit trusts
O God of hosts, | Alone in thee!

271. "*Glory to God—Good will to men.*"
    Luke 2.

1 HARK! what celestial sounds,
    What music fills the air!
  Soft warbling to the morn,
    It strikes the ravished ear:
Now all is still; | In tuneful notes,
Now wild it floats | Loud, sweet, and shrill.

2 Th' angelic hosts descend,
    With harmony divine;
  See how from heaven they bend,
    And in full chorus join:
"Fear not," say they, | Jesus, your King,
"Great joy we bring" | Is born to-day.

3 "He comes, your souls to save
    From death's eternal gloom;
  To realms of bliss and light
    He lifts you from the tomb."
Your voices raise, | Your songs unite
With sons of light; | Of endless praise.

4 "Glory to God on high!
    Ye mortals, spread the sound,
  And let your raptures fly
    To earth's remotest bound:
For peace on earth, | To man is given,
From God in heaven, | At Jesus' birth."

CHRISTMAS (OLD.) C. M. DOUBLE.

268. *The Watch of the Shepherds.*—Luke 2.

1 WHILE shepherds watched their flocks by night,
All seated on the ground;
The angel of the Lord came down,
And glory shone around.
2 "Fear not," said he (for mighty dread
Had seized their troubled mind),
"Glad tidings of great joy I bring
To you and all mankind.
3 "To you, in David's town, this day,
Is born of David's line,
The Saviour, who is Christ, the Lord,
And this shall be the sign:
4 "The heavenly Babe you there shall find,
To human view displayed,
All meanly wrapped in swathing bands,
And in a manger laid."
5 Thus spake the seraph; and forthwith
Appeared a shining throng
Of angels, praising God, and thus
Addressed their joyful song:
6 "All glory be to God on high,
And to the earth be peace;
Good-will, henceforth, from heaven to men
Begin, and never cease!"

338. "*The voice of many angels.*"—Rev. 5.

1 COME, let us join our cheerful songs
With angels round the throne;
Ten thousand thousand are their tongues,
But all their joys are one.
2 "Worthy the Lamb that died," they cry,
"To be exalted thus!"
"Worthy the Lamb!" our lips reply,
"For he was slain for us."
3 Jesus is worthy to receive
Honor and power divine;
And blessings more than we can give,
Be, Lord, for ever thine!

4 Let all that dwell above the sky,
And air, and earth, and seas,
Conspire to lift thy glories high,
And speak thine endless praise.
5 The whole creation join in one,
To bless the sacred name
Of him who sits upon the throne,
And to adore the Lamb!

390. "*Hosanna to the Son of David.*"
Matt. 21: 9.

1 HOSANNA! be our cheerful song
To Christ our Saviour King;
His praise, to whom we all belong,
Let all unite to sing.
2 Hosanna! here in joyful bands,
Let old and young proclaim;
And hail, with voices, hearts, and hands,
The Son of David's name.
3 Hosanna! sound from hill to hill,
And spread from plain to plain;
While louder, sweeter, clearer still,
Woods echo to the strain.
4 Hosanna! on the wings of light,
O'er earth and ocean fly,
Till morn to eve, and noon to night,
And heaven to earth reply.

1149. *The Seasons ordained by God.*
Psalm 147.

1 WITH songs and honors sounding loud,
Address the Lord on high;
Over the heavens he spreads his cloud,
And waters vail the sky.
2 He sends his showers of blessings down
To cheer the plains below;
He makes the grass the mountains crown,
And corn in valleys grow.
3 His steady counsels change the face
Of the declining year;
He bids the sun cut short his race,
And wint'ry days appear.

CORONATION. C. M.

4 His hoary frost, his fleecy snow,
  Descend and clothe the ground;
  The liquid streams forbear to flow,
  In icy fetters bound.

5 He sends his word, and melts the snow,
  The fields no longer mourn;
  He calls the warmer gales to blow,
  And bids the spring return.

6 The changing wind, the flying cloud,
  Obey his mighty word;
  With songs and honors sounding loud,
  Praise ye the sovereign Lord!

379. *The Coronation.*

1 ALL hail, the power of Jesus' name!
  Let angels prostrate fall;
  Bring forth the royal diadem,
  And crown him Lord of all!

2 Crown him, ye martyrs of our God,
  Who from his altar call,
  Extol the stem of Jesse's rod,
  And crown him Lord of all!

3 Ye chosen seed of Israel's race,
  A remnant weak and small,
  Hail him who saves you by his grace,
  And crown him Lord of all!

4 Ye Gentile sinners, ne'er forget
  The wormwood and the gall;
  Go, spread your trophies at his feet,
  And crown him Lord of all!

5 Let every kindred, every tribe,
  On this terrestrial ball,
  To him all majesty ascribe,
  And crown him Lord of all!

6 Oh, that with yonder sacred throng,
  We at his feet may fall!
  We'll join the everlasting song,
  And crown him Lord of all!

971. "*Let the children of Zion be joyful in their King.*"

1 SING, ye redeemed of the Lord,
  Your great Deliverer sing;
  Pilgrims for Zion's city bound,
  Be joyful in your King.

2 His hand divine shall lead you on
  Through all the blissful road,
  Till to the sacred mount you rise,
  And see your smiling God.

3 There garlands of immortal joy
  Shall bloom on every head;
  While sorrow, sighing, and distress,
  Like shadows, all are fled.

4 March on in your Redeemer's strength;
  Pursue his footsteps still;
  And let the prospect cheer your eye,
  While laboring up the hill.

1035. "*Let the wilderness and the cities lift up their voice.*"—Isaiah 42: 10-12.

1 SING to the Lord in joyful strains!
  Let earth his praise resound;
  Ye, too, who on the ocean dwell,
  And fill the isles around!

2 O city of the Lord! begin
  The universal song,
  And let the scattered villages
  Thy joyful notes prolong.

3 Let Kedar's wilderness afar
  Lift up the lonely voice;
  And let the tenants of the rock
  With accent rude rejoice.

4 Oh, from the streams of distant lands,
  Unto Jehovah sing!
  And joyful from the mountain tops
  Shout to the Lord, the King.

5 Let all combined, with one accord,
  Jehovah's glories raise,
  Till in remotest bounds of earth
  The nations sound his praise.

ERNAN. L. M.

66. *Evening Confession.*

1 Great God! to thee my evening song
  With humble gratitude I raise:
 Oh, let thy mercy tune my tongue,
  And fill my heart with lively praise.

2 My days, unclouded as they pass,
  And every gently rolling hour,
 Are monuments of wondrous grace,
  And witness to thy love and power.

3 And yet this thoughtless, wretched heart,
  Too oft regardless of thy love,
 Ungrateful, can from thee depart,
  And, fond of trifles, vainly rove.

4 Seal my forgiveness in the blood
  Of Jesus; his dear name alone
 I plead for pardon, gracious God!
  And kind acceptance at thy throne.

5 Let this blest hope mine eyelids close;
  With sleep refresh my feeble frame;
 Safe in thy care may I repose,
  And wake with praises to thy name!

263. *A Hymn of the Reformation on the Birth of Christ.*

1 All praise to thee, eternal Lord!
  Clothed in a garb of flesh and blood;
 Choosing a manger for thy throne,
  While worlds on worlds are thine alone.

2 Once did the skies before thee bow;
  A virgin's arms contain thee now;
 Angels, who did in thee rejoice,
  Now listen for thine infant voice.

3 A little child, thou art our guest,
  That weary ones in thee may rest;
 Forlorn and lowly is thy birth,
  That we may rise to heaven from earth.

4 Thou comest in the darksome night
  To make us children of the light,—
 To make us, in the realms divine,
  Like thine own angels round thee shine.

5 All this for us thy love hath done
  By this to thee our love is won:
 For this we tune our cheerful lays,
  And shout our thanks in ceaseless praise.

285. *"Behold how He loved him!"* John 11:36.

1 "See how he loved!" exclaimed the Jews,
  As tender tears from Jesus fell;
 My grateful heart the thought pursues,
  And on the theme delights to dwell.

2 See how he loved, who traveled on,
  Teaching the doctrine from the skies!
 Who bade disease and pain begone,
  And called the sleeping dead to rise.

3 See how he loved, who never shrank
  From toil or danger, pain or death!
 Who all the cup of sorrow drank,
  And meekly yielded up his breath.

4 Such love can we, unmoved, survey?
  Oh, may our breasts with ardor glow,
 To tread his steps, his laws obey,
  And thus our warm affections show!

525. *Invitations of Christ.*

1 How sweetly flowed the gospel sound
  From lips of gentleness and grace,
 When listening thousands gathered round,
  And joy and reverence filled the place!

2 From heaven he came, of heaven he spoke,
  To heaven he led his followers' way;
 Dark clouds of gloomy night he broke,
  Unvailing an immortal day.

3 "Come, wanderers, to my Father's home;
  Come, all ye weary ones, and rest;"
 Yes, sacred Teacher, we will come,
  Obey thee, love thee, and be blest.

SEASONS. L. M.

46. *An ancient Psalm of the Morning.*

1 O CHRIST! with each returning morn
Thine image to our heart be borne;
And may we ever clearly see
Our God and Saviour, Lord, in thee!

2 All hallowed be our walk this day;
May meekness form our early ray,
And faithful love our noontide light,
And hope our sunset, calm and bright.

3 May grace each idle thought control,
And sanctify our wayward soul;
May guile depart, and malice cease,
And all within be joy and peace.

4 Our daily course, O Jesus, bless;
Make plain the way of holiness;
From sudden falls our feet defend,
And cheer at last our journey's end.

336. *An ancient Hymn to the Redeemer.*

1 O CHRIST! our King, Creator, Lord!
Saviour of all who trust thy word!
To them who seek thee ever near,
Now to our praises bend thine ear.

2 In thy dear cross a grace is found—
It flows from every streaming wound—
Whose power our inbred sin controls,
Breaks the firm bond, and frees our souls!

3 Thou didst create the stars of night;
Yet thou hast vailed in flesh thy light—
Hast deigned a mortal form to wear,—
A mortal's painful lot to bear.

4 When thou didst hang upon the tree,
The quaking earth acknowledged thee;
When thou didst there yield up thy breath,
The world grew dark as shades of death.

5 Now in the Father's glory high,
Great Conqu'ror, never more to die,
Us by thy mighty power defend,
And reign through ages without end!

605. *Prayer of the penitent Thief.*

1 THOU that didst hang upon the tree,
Our curse and sufferings to remove,
Pity the souls that look to thee,
And save us by thy dying love.

2 Canst thou reject our dying prayer,
Or cast us out who come to thee?
Our sins, ah! wherefore didst thou bear!
Jesus, remember Calvary!

3 For us wast thou not lifted up?
For us a bleeding victim made,
That we, vile sinners, we might hope
Thou hast for all a ransom paid?

4 Oh, might we, with believing eyes,
Thee in thy bloody vesture see!
And cast us on thy sacrifice—
Jesus, my Lord, remember me!

983. *"Dear Lord, to Thee I would return."*

1 AH! wretched, vile, ungrateful heart,
That can from Jesus thus depart;
Thus fond of trifles, vainly rove,
Forgetful of a Saviour's love.

2 Dear Lord! to thee I would return,
And at thy feet repenting mourn;
There let me view thy pardoning love,
And never from thy sight remove.

3 Oh, let thy love, with sweet control,
Bind every passion of my soul,—
Bid every vain desire depart,
And dwell for ever in my heart!

WAYNE. C. M. DOUBLE.

258. *The Love of the Father.*

1 Come, happy souls, approach your God
With new, melodious songs;
Come, render to almighty Grace
The tribute of your tongues.

2 So strange, so boundless was the love
That pitied dying men,
The Father sent his equal Son
To give them life again.

3 Thy hands, dear Jesus, were not armed
With a revenging rod;
No hard commission to perform
The vengeance of a God.

4 But all was mercy, all was mild,
And wrath forsook the throne,
When Christ on the kind errand came,
And brought salvation down.

5 Here, sinners, come and heal your wounds;
Come, wipe your sorrows dry:
Come, trust the mighty Saviour's name,
And you shall never die.

6 See, dearest Lord, our willing souls
Accept thine offered grace;
We bless the great Redeemer's love,
And give the Father praise.

441. *The Name of Jesus.*

1 How sweet the name of Jesus sounds
In a believer's ear!
It soothes his sorrows, heals his wounds,
And drives away his fear.

2 It makes the wounded spirit whole,
And calms the troubled breast;
'T is manna to the hungry soul,
And to the weary, rest.

3 By thee, my prayers acceptance gain,
Although with sin defiled:
Satan accuses me in vain,
And I am owned a child.

4 Jesus! my Shepherd, Guardian, Friend,
My Prophet, Priest, and King;
My Lord, my Life, my Way, my End,
Accept the praise I bring.

5 Weak is the effort of my heart,
And cold my warmest thought;
But when I see thee as thou art,
I'll praise thee as I ought.

6 Till then I would thy love proclaim,
With every fleeting breath;
And may the music of thy name
Refresh my soul in death.

1191. *"Sweet fields, beyond the swelling flood."*

1 There is a land of pure delight,
Where saints immortal reign;
Infinite day excludes the night,
And pleasures banish pain.

2 There everlasting spring abides,
And never-withering flowers:
Death, like a narrow sea, divides
This heavenly land from ours.

3 Sweet fields, beyond the swelling flood,
Stand dressed in living green;
So to the Jews old Canaan stood,
While Jordan rolled between.

4 But timorous mortals start and shrink,
To cross this narrow sea;
And linger, shivering, on the brink,
And fear to launch away.

5 Oh, could we make our doubts remove,
Those gloomy doubts that rise,
And see the Canaan that we love
With unbeclouded eyes!—

6 Could we but climb where Moses stood,
And view the landscape o'er,
Not Jordan's stream, nor death's cold flood
Should fright us from the shore.

178. *"Faithful is He that calleth you."*

1 Begin, my tongue, some heavenly theme,
And speak some boundless thing,

NEW SABBATH HYMN AND TUNE BOOK. 117

MELODY. C. M.

The mighty works, or mightier name,
Of our eternal King.
2 Tell of his wondrous faithfulness,
And sound his power abroad;
Sing the sweet promise of his grace,
And the performing God.
3 His very word of grace is strong,
As that which built the skies;
The voice that rolls the stars along
Speaks all **the promises.**
4 Oh, might I hear thy heavenly tongue
But whisper, "Thou art mine!"
Those gentle words should raise my song
To notes almost divine.

183. *A Song to creating Wisdom.*

1 ETERNAL Wisdom! thee we **praise;**
Thee the creation sings:
With thy loved name, rocks, hills, and seas,
And heaven's high palace rings.
2 Thy hand, how wide it spread the **sky!**
How glorious to behold!
Tinged with a blue of heavenly dye,
And starred with sparkling gold.
3 Infinite strength, and equal skill,
Shine forth the world abroad,
Our souls with vast amazement fill,
And speak the builder, God.
4 But still the wonders of thy grace
Our softer passions move;
Pity divine in Jesus' face
We see, adore, and love.

274. *Object of Christ's Advent.*—Luke 4: 18,19.

1 HARK, the glad sound! the Saviour comes,
The Saviour promised long;
Let every heart prepare a throne,
And every voice a song.
2 He comes, the prisoner to release,
In Satan's bondage held;

The gates of brass before him **burst,**
The iron fetters yield.
3 He comes, from thickest films of vice
To clear the mental ray,
And on the eyes long closed in night
To **pour** celestial day.
4 He comes, the broken heart **to bind,**
The bleeding soul to cure,
And, with the treasures of his grace,
Enrich the humble **poor.**
5 Our glad hosannas, Prince **of Peace,**
Thy welcome shall proclaim,
And heaven's eternal arches ring
With thy beloved name.

309. *The Throne of Love.*

1 COME, let us lift our joyful eyes
Up to the courts above,
And smile to see our Father there,
Upon a throne of love.
2 Come, let us bow before his feet,
And venture near the Lord:
No fiery cherubs guard his seat,
Nor double-flaming sword.
3 The peaceful gates of heavenly **bliss**
Are opened by the Son;
High let us raise our notes of praise,
And reach th' almighty throne.
4 To thee ten thousand thanks we bring,
Great Advocate on high;
And glory to th' eternal King,
Who lays his anger by.

DOXOLOGY.

LET God the Father, and the Son,
And Spirit, be adored,
Where there are works to make him known,
Or saints to love the Lord.

OLNEY. S. M.

446. *Praise to Christ in View of the Fullness of His Glory.*

1 Jesus, the Christ of God,
  The Father's blessèd Son!
The Father's bosom thine abode,
  The Father's love thine own.

2 Jesus, the Lamb of God,
  Who, us from hell to raise,
Hast shed thy reconciling blood,
  We give thee endless praise.

3 God, and yet Man, thou art;
  True God, true Man art thou:
Of man and of man's earth a part,
  One with us thou art now.

4 Great Sacrifice for sin,
  Giver of life for life;
Restorer of the peace within,
  True Ender of the strife.

5 To thee, the Christ of God,
  Thy saints exulting sing—
The bearer of our heavy load,
  Our own anointed King.

503. *"Ask, and ye shall receive."* Matt. 7: 7.

1 "Ask, and ye shall receive,"—
  On this my hope I build;
I ask forgiveness, and believe
  My prayer shall be fulfilled.

2 Seek, and expect to find:
  Wounded to death in soul,
I seek the Saviour of mankind,
  For he can make me whole.

3 Knock, and with patience wait,
  By faith free entrance gain:
I stand, and knock at mercy's gate
  Till I thy grace obtain.

4 Shall I then ask in vain;
  Seek, and not find the Lord?
Knock, and yet no admittance gain,
  And doubt thy holy word?

5 No, Lord, thou 'lt ne'er deceive;
  Thy promises are sure;
In thy good time I shall receive;
  What can I ask for more?

506. *"The Spirit and the Bride say, Come."* Rev. 22: 17.

1 The Spirit, in our hearts,
  Is whispering, "Sinner, come;"
The bride, the church of Christ, proclaims
  To all his children, "Come!"

2 Let him that heareth say
  To all about him, "Come;"
Let him that thirsts for righteousness,
  To Christ, the Fountain, come!

3 Yes, whosoever will,
  Oh, let him freely come,
And freely drink the stream of life;
  'T is Jesus bids him come.

4 Lo! Jesus, who invites,
  Declares, "I quickly come;"
Lord, even so; we wait thine hour;
  O blest Redeemer, come!

507. *"Wait on the Lord."*—Psalm 27.

1 Come, ye with sin distressed,
  And wait upon the Lord:
He will bestow the promised rest,
  And timely aid afford.

2 What though he hide his face,
  And should awhile delay;
He'll grant you fresh supplies of grace,
  For every trying day.

MORNINGTON. S. M.

3 His wisdom, love, and power
Are all engaged for you,
And in affliction's fiery hour
Will bring you safely through.

4 He knows your every pain;
He counts your every tear;
And, while your mourning souls complain,
He lends a pitying ear.

5 Then wait his gracious will
In persevering prayer;
His own blest word will be fulfill,
And make your souls his care.

533. *Give thy Heart.*

1 GIVE to the Lord thine heart;
In him all pleasures meet;
Oh, come and choose the better part,
Low at the Saviour's feet.

2 Hear, and your soul shall live;
His peace shall be your stay—
Peace, which the world can never give,
Can never take away.

3 Go with him to his cross,
Go with him to his tomb;
Your richest gain account but loss,
And tarry till he come.

4 Then, when you hear his voice,
Your faithful Shepherd's call,
Lift up your heads, in him rejoice,
Your God, your Guide, your All!

DOXOLOGY.

THE Father and the Son
And Spirit we adore;
We praise, we bless, we worship thee,
Both now and evermore!

BADEA. S. M.

ALPHEUS. C. M.

307. *"The Lord hath laid on Him the iniquity of us all."*

1 O Christ, our ever blessèd Lord,
　For man's transgression slain,
We thy redeeming love record
　In songs of thankful strain.

2 We upward lift our longing eyes,
　And muse on Calvary;
On thy mysterious sacrifice,
　Thy shame and agony.

3 We all like erring sheep had strayed
　From God the Father's care;
The guilt of all on thee was laid,
　Our burden thou didst bear.

4 O Christ, be thou our present joy,
　Our future great reward;
Our only glory may it be,
　To glory in the Lord!

5 Oh may we through thy cross and pain,
　With all who thee adore,
A blessèd resurrection gain,
　And life for evermore!

370. *"We shall also reign with Him."*
2 Tim. 2: 12.

1 Jesus, our Head, once crowned with thorns,
　Is crowned with glory now;
Heaven's royal diadem adorns
　The mighty victor's brow.

2 Delight of all who dwell above,
　The joy of saints below;
To us still manifest thy love,
　That we its depths may know.

3 To us thy cross, with all its shame,
　With all its grace be given;
Though earth disowns thy lowly name,
　All worship it in heaven.

4 Who suffer with thee, Lord, below,
　Will reign with thee above;

Then let it be our joy to know
　This way of peace and love.

5 To us thy cross is life and health,
　Though shame and death to thee:
On earth, it is our joy and wealth,
　In heaven our crown shall be.

687. *Christ our only Joy.*

1 Jesus! the very thought of thee
　With gladness fills my breast;
But dearer far thy face to see,
　And in thy presence rest.

2 Nor voice can sing, nor heart can frame,
　Nor can the memory find
A sweeter sound than thy blest name,
　O Saviour of mankind!

3 O Hope of every contrite heart,
　O Joy of all the meek!
To those who fall, how kind thou art,
　How good to those who seek!

4 And those who find thee, find a bliss
　Nor tongue nor pen can show:
The love of Jesus—what it is,
　None but his loved ones know.

5 Jesus, our only joy be thou!
　As thou our prize wilt be;
Jesus, be thou our glory now,
　And through eternity!

697. *Sympathy with Christ.*

1 How wondrous was the burning zeal
　Which filled the Master's breast,
When, all his sufferings full in view,
　To Salem's towers he pressed!

2 Dear Lord! no tongue can duly tell
　Thy love's prevailing might;
No thought can comprehend its length,
　And breadth, and depth, and height!

DUNDEE. C. M.

3 Yet grant that we may follow thee
  Through all thine hours of scorn;
And learn with thee to watch and pray,
  With thee to weep and mourn.

4 And still, O blesséd Jesus Christ!
  The more thy cross we see,
The more may each exclaim with joy,
  The Saviour died for me!

706. "*To Thee my inmost spirit cries.*"

1 O Jesus! thou the beauty art
  Of angel-worlds above;
Thy name is music to the heart,
  Enchanting it with love.

2 O Jesus, Saviour! hear the sighs
  Which unto thee I send;
To thee my inmost spirit cries,
  My being's hope and end.

3 Stay with us, Lord, and with thy light
  Illume the soul's abyss;
Scatter the darkness of our night,
  And fill the world with bliss.

4 O Jesus, King of earth and heaven,
  Our life and joy! to thee
Be honor, thanks, and blessings given
  Through all eternity!

791. "*Joint heirs with Christ.*"

1 Blessed be God! for ever blest,
  And glorious be his name:
His Son he gave our souls to save
  From everlasting shame.

2 Th' eternal Life his life laid down—
  Such was the wondrous plan—
And Christ, the Son of God, was made
  A curse, for cursed man!

3 Our flesh he took, our sins he bore,
  Himself for us he gave;

His cross was ours, and we with him
  Were buried in one grave.

4 With him we rose, with him we live,
  With him we sit above;
With him for ever we shall share
  The Father's boundless love.

5 Bless, then, Jehovah's blesséd name;
  And bless our blesséd King!
And songs of glad deliverance
  For ever, ever sing!

809. *An ancient Hymn on Christ as our Model.*

1 O Jesus! King most wonderful,
  Thou Conqueror renowned;
Thou sweetness most ineffable,
  In whom all joys are found!

2 When once thou visitest the heart,
  Then truth begins to shine,
Then earthly vanities depart,
  Then kindles love divine.

3 O Jesus, Light of all below!
  Thou Fount of life and fire!
Surpassing all the joys we know,
  All that we can desire,—

4 May every heart confess thy name,
  And ever thee adore;
And, seeking thee, itself inflame
  To seek thee more and more.

5 Thee may our tongues for ever bless:
  Thee may we love alone;
And ever in our life express
  The image of thine own.

DOXOLOGY.

To Father, Son, and Holy Ghost,
  One God, whom we adore,
Be glory as it was, is now,
  And shall be evermore!

WHYTE. L. M. DOUBLE.

428. *The Star of Bethlehem.*

1 WHEN marshaled on the nightly plain,
  The glittering host bestud the sky;
  One star alone, of all the train,
  Can fix the sinner's wandering eye.
2 Hark! hark! to God the chorus breaks,
  From every host, from every gem;
  But one alone, the Saviour speaks:
  It is the Star of Bethlehem.

3 Once on the raging seas I rode:
  The storm was loud, the night was dark;
  The ocean yawned, and rudely blowed
  The wind that tossed my foundering bark.
4 Deep horror then my vitals froze;
  Death-struck I ceased the tide to stem;
  When suddenly a star arose!
  It was the Star of Bethlehem.

5 It was my guide, my light, my all;
  It bade my dark forebodings cease;
  And thro' the storm, and danger's thrall,
  It led me to the port of peace.
6 Now safely moored, my perils o'er,
  I'll sing, first in night's diadem,
  For ever and for evermore,
  The Star—the Star of Bethlehem!

431. *"His Loving-kindness."*

1 AWAKE, my soul, to joyful lays,
  And sing the great Redeemer's praise;
  He justly claims a song from me:
  His loving-kindness, oh, how free!
2 He saw me ruined in the fall,
  Yet loved me, notwithstanding all;
  He saved me from my lost estate:
  His loving-kindness, oh, how great!

3 Though numerous hosts of mighty foes,
  Though earth and hell my way oppose,
  He safely leads my soul along:
  His loving-kindness, oh, how strong!
4 When trouble, like a gloomy cloud,
  Has gathered thick and thundered loud,
  He near my soul hath always stood:
  His loving-kindness, oh, how good!

5 Soon shall I pass the gloomy vale;
  Soon all my mortal powers must fail;
  Oh, may my last expiring breath
  His loving-kindness sing in death!
6 Then let me mount and soar away
  To the bright world of endless day;
  And sing, with rapture and surprise,
  His loving-kindness in the skies.

YOAKLEY. L. M. 6 LINES.

335. *An ancient Hymn to the Redeemer.*
Thou art the everlasting Son,
O Christ! and, high upon thy throne,
Thou art at the right hand of God,
And hast redeemed us by thy blood ;
And heaven and earth are full of thee,—
The glory of thy Majesty !

When all the sharpness of our death
Was overcome in thy last breath,
Then didst thou open wide heaven's door
To all believers evermore :
O Lamb of God! and thou wilt come,
To be our Judge, and take us home.

In thee we trust : we pray thee, Lord,
Remember thy most precious blood !
In honor may we numbered be
With all the noble company,
Who bow before thy mercy-seat,
And cast their treasures at thy feet.

361. *"We walk by faith, not by sight."*
We did not see thee lifted high,
When men thy sacred body slew,
Nor hear thy meek, imploring cry :
"Forgive, they know not what they do !"
Yet we believe the deed was done,
Which shook the earth and vailed the sun.

We stood not by the empty tomb
Where, Lord, thy sacred body lay,
Nor sat within that upper room,
Nor met thee in the open way ;
But we believe the angels said,
"Why seek the living with the dead ?"

We did not mark the chosen few,
When thou didst through the clouds ascend,
First lift to heaven their wondering view,
Then to the earth all prostrate bend :
Yet we believe that mortal eyes
Beheld that journey to the skies.

4 And now that thou dost reign on high,
And thence thy waiting people bless ;
No ray of glory from the sky
Doth shine upon our wilderness ;
But we believe thy faithful word,
And trust in our redeeming Lord.

467. *An ancient Hymn to the Trinity.*
1 Let glory be to God on high :
Peace be on earth as in the sky ;
Good will to men ! We bow the knee,
We praise, we bless, we worship thee ;
We give thee thanks, thy name we sing,
Almighty Father ! Heavenly King !

2 O Lord, the sole begotten Son,
Who bore the crimes which we had done;
Son of the Father, who wast slain
To take away the sins of men ;
O Lamb of God, whose blood was spilt
For all the world, and all its guilt ;—

3 Have mercy on us, through thy blood ;
Receive our prayer, O Lamb of God !
For thou art holy ; thou alone,
At God's right hand, upon his throne,
In all his glory, art adored,
With thee, O Holy Ghost, One Lord.

511. *"Come unto Me, all ye that labor."*
1 Peace, troubled soul, whose plaintive moan
Hath taught each scene the notes of woe;
Cease thy complaint, suppress thy groan,
And let thy tears forget to flow ;
Behold the precious balm is found,
To lull thy pain, to heal thy wound.

2 Come, freely come, by sin oppressed ;
On Jesus cast thy weighty load ;
In him thy refuge find, thy rest,
Safe in the mercy of thy God :
Thy God's thy Saviour—glorious word !
Oh, hear, believe, and bless the Lord !

ALPHEUS. C. M.

150. *"God is Love."*—1 John 4: 8.

1 Amid the splendors of thy state,
  O God! thy love appears,
Soft as the radiance of the moon
  Among a thousand stars.

2 In all thy doctrines and commands,
  Thy counsels and designs,
In every work thy hands have framed,
  Thy love supremely shines.

3 Sinai, in clouds, and smoke, and fire,
  Thunders thine awful name!
But Zion sings, in melting notes,
  The honors of the Lamb.

4 Angels and men the news proclaim
  Through earth and heaven above;
And all with holy transport, sing
  That God the Lord is love.

322. *"The redemption of their soul is precious."*—Psalm 49.

1 Worlds can not reach the mighty price
  Of one immortal soul:
No: Lord! thy blood and sacrifice
  Alone can make us whole.

2 In thee be our salvation sure;
  No other wealth we seek:
We're rich in thee, however poor,
  And strong, however weak.

365. *"I go to prepare a place for you."*

1 Th' eternal gates lift up their heads,
  The doors are opened wide;
The King of glory is gone up
  Unto his Father's side.

2 Thou art gone in before us, Lord,
  Thou hast prepared a place,
That we may be where now thou art,
  And look upon thy face.

3 And ever on thine earthly path
  A gleam of glory lies;
A light still breaks behind the cloud
  That vails thee from our eyes.

4 Lift up our thoughts, lift up our songs,
  And let thy grace be given,
That, while we linger yet below,
  Our hearts may be in heaven;—

5 That, where thou art at God's right hand
  Our hope, our love may be:
Dwell in us now, that we may dwell
  For evermore in thee.

366. *"Why seek ye the living among the dead?"*

1 Why search ye in the narrow tomb
  For him who lives on high?
Heaven spreads her gates to make him
    room:
His glory fills the sky.

2 Lift up your hearts, and stretch your eyes
  The Saviour is not here
Behold the Conqueror arise,
  To grace a brighter sphere.

3 Angels with loud, exulting songs,
  Welcome their Lord again:
To us the victory belongs;
  For us the Lamb was slain.

4 And shall we, Lord, ascend with thee,
  And see thee as thou art,
From death's terrific power made free,
  And saved from Satan's dart?

5 Saviour, since thou art gone before,
  Oh, grant that we may go
Where sin's dark empire is no more,
  And death a vanquished foe!

MARLOW. C. M.

754. *"Victory through our Lord Jesus Christ."*—1 Cor. 15 : 55.

1 OH for an overcoming faith
To cheer my dying hours !
To triumph o'er the monster, **death,**
And all his frightful powers.

2 Joyful, with all the strength I have,
My quivering lips should sing,
"Where is thy boasted victory, grave?
And where the monster's sting?"

3 If sin be pardoned, I 'm secure ;
Death hath no sting beside :
The law gives sin its damning power,
But Christ, my **ransom,** died.

4 Now to the God of victory
Immortal thanks be paid,
Who makes us conquerors while we die,
Through Christ, our living Head !

1075. *David's Prayer at the Removal of the Ark.*—Psalm 132.

1 ARISE ! O King of grace, arise !
And enter to thy rest ;
Lo ! thy church waits with longing eyes,
Thus to be owned and blest.

2 Enter with all thy glorious **train,**
Thy Spirit and thy word ;
All that the ark did once contain,
Could no such grace afford.

3 Here, mighty God, accept our vows ;
Here let thy praise be spread ;
Bless the provisions of thy house,
And fill thy poor with bread.

4 Here let the Son of David reign ;
Let God's Anointed shine ;
Justice and truth his court maintain,
With love and power divine.

5 Here let him hold a lasting throne,
And as his kingdom grows,

Fresh honors shall adorn his crown,
And shame confound his foes.

1090. *"Sayings of old."*—Psalm 78.

1 LET children hear the mighty deeds,
Which God performed of old,—
Which in our younger years we **saw,**
And which our fathers told.

2 He bids us make his glories known,
His works of power and grace ;
And we 'll convey his wonders down
Through every rising race.

3 Our lips shall tell them to our sons,
And they again to theirs,
That generations yet unborn
May teach them to their heirs.

4 Thus they shall learn, in God alone
Their hope securely stands,
That they may ne'er forget his works,
But practice his commands.

1150. *"Thou crownest the year with thy goodness."*—Psalm 65.

1 'T is by thy strength the mountains stand,
God of eternal power !
The sea grows calm at thy command,
And tempests cease to roar.

2 Thy morning light and evening shade
Successive comforts bring ;
Thy plenteous fruits make harvest glad ;
Thy flowers adorn the **spring.**

3 Seasons and times, and moons and hours,
Heaven, earth, and air are thine ;
When clouds distill in fruitful showers,
The author is divine !

4 Thy showers the thirsty furrows fill ;
And ranks of corn appear ;
Thy ways abound with blessings still—
Thy goodness crowns the year.

ST. NICOLAI. 7s. TWO STANZAS.

228. *"His mercy endureth for ever."*
Psalm 136.

1 Let us with a gladsome mind,
  Praise the Lord, for he is kind:
  For his mercies shall endure,
  Ever faithful, ever sure.

2 He, with all-commanding might,
  Filled the new-made world with light:
  For his mercies shall endure,
  Ever faithful, ever sure.

3 All things living he doth feed;
  His full hand supplies their need:
  For his mercies shall endure,
  Ever faithful, ever sure.

4 He his chosen race did bless,
  In the wasteful wilderness:
  For his mercies shall endure,
  Ever faithful, ever sure.

5 He hath, with a piteous eye,
  Looked upon our misery:
  For his mercies shall endure,
  Ever faithful, ever sure.

6 Let us, then, with gladsome mind,
  Praise the Lord, for he is kind:
  For his mercies shall endure,
  Ever faithful, ever sure.

231. *God's deliverance of his People.*
Psalm 107.

1 Thank and praise Jehovah's name;
  For his mercies, firm and sure,
  From eternity the same,
  To eternity endure.

2 Let the ransomed thus rejoice,
  Gathered out of every land;
  As the people of his choice,
  Plucked from the destroyer's hand.

3 In the wilderness astray,
  Hither, thither, while they roam,
  Hungry, fainting by the way,
  Far from refuge, shelter, home;—

4 Then unto the Lord they cry;
  He inclines a gracious ear,
  Sends deliverance from on high,
  Rescues them from all their fear.

5 To a pleasant land he brings,
  Where the vine and olive grow;
  Where, from flowery hills, the springs
  Through luxuriant valleys flow.

6 Oh that men would praise the Lord,
  For his goodness to their race;
  For the wonders of his word,
  And the riches of his grace!

392. *The Song of Jubilee.*

1 Hark! the song of jubilee;
  Loud as mighty thunders roar,
  Or the fullness of the sea,
  When it breaks upon the shore.

2 Hallelujah! for the Lord
  God omnipotent shall reign:
  Hallelujah! let the word
  Echo round the earth and main.

3 Hallelujah!—hark! the sound,
  From the depths unto the skies,
  Wakes above, beneath, around,
  All creation's harmonies.

4 See Jehovah's banner furled;
  Sheathed his sword: he speaks—'t is done!
  And the kingdoms of the world
  Are the kingdoms of his Son.

WILMOT. 7s.

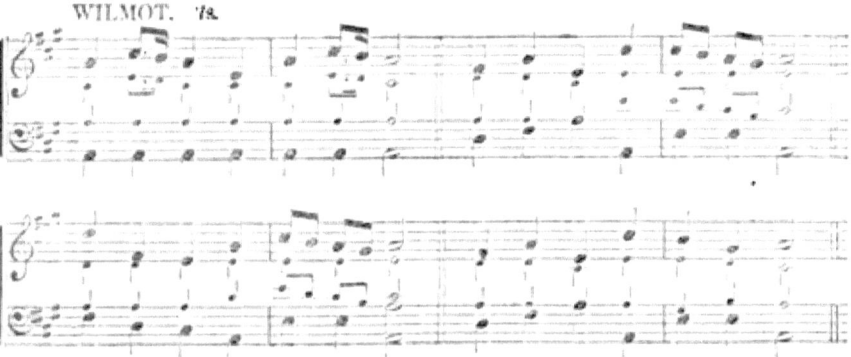

5 He shall reign from pole to pole,
   With supreme, unbounded sway;
  He shall reign when, like a scroll,
   Yonder heavens have passed away.
6 Then the end;—beneath his rod
   Man's last enemy shall fall;
  Hallelujah! Christ in God,
   God in Christ is all in all!

354.   *"Christ, the first-fruits."*

1 Christ, the Lord, is risen to-day!
   Sons of men and angels say:
  Raise your joys and triumphs high;
   Sing, ye heavens! and earth, reply!
2 Love's redeeming work is done,
   Fought the fight, the battle won;
  Lo! our sun's eclipse is o'er;
   Lo! he sets in blood no more.
3 Vain the stone, the watch, the seal—
   Christ hath burst the gates of hell;
  Death in vain forbids his rise,
   Christ hath opened paradise.
4 Lives again our glorious King!
   Where, O Death, is now thy sting?
  Once he died, our souls to save?
   Where's thy vict'ry, boasting Grave?
5 Soar we now where Christ hath led,
   Following our exalted Head;
  Made like him, like him we rise,
   Ours the cross, the grave, the skies!

1142.   *"Lord, Thou hast been favorable unto Thy land."*

1 Praise to God, immortal praise,
   For the love that crowns our days!
  Bounteous source of every joy,
   Let thy praise our tongues employ!

2 For the blessings of the field,
   For the stores the gardens yield,
  For the joy which harvests bring,
   Grateful praises now we sing.
3 Clouds that drop refreshing dews;
   Suns that genial heat diffuse;
  Flocks that whiten all the plain;
   Yellow sheaves of ripened grain;
4 All that Spring, with bounteous hand,
   Scatters o'er the smiling land;
  All that liberal Autumn pours
   From her overflowing stores;
5 These, great God, to thee we owe,
   Source whence all our blessings flow;
  And, for these, our souls shall raise
   Grateful vows, and solemn praise.

1268.   *"The Lord Jesus shall be revealed from heaven."*

1 Hark! that shout of rapturous joy,
   Bursting forth from yonder cloud!
  Jesus comes, and through the sky
   Angels tell their joy aloud!
2 Hark! the trumpet's awful voice
   Sounds abroad, through sea and land;
  Let his people now rejoice!
   Their redemption is at hand.
3 See! the Lord appears in view;
   Heaven and earth before him fly!
  Rise, ye saints, he comes for you—
   Rise to meet him in the sky.
4 Go, and dwell with him above,
   Where no foe can e'er molest;
  Happy in the Saviour's love!
   Ever blessing, ever blest.

BYRD. C. M. DOUBLE.

359. *Looking into the Sepulcher.*

1 YE humble souls that seek the Lord,
   Chase all your fears away;
   And bow, with pleasure, down to see
   The place where Jesus lay.
2 Thus low the Lord of life was brought—
   Such wonders love can do—
   Thus cold in death that bosom lay,
   Which throbbed and bled for you.

3 A moment now indulge your grief:
   Let grateful sorrows rise;
   And wash the crimson stains away
   With torrents from your eyes.
4 Then raise your eyes and tune your songs,
   The Saviour lives again!
   Not all the bolts and bars of death
   The Conqueror could detain.

5 High o'er th' angelic bands he rears
   His once dishonored head;
   And through unnumber'd years he reigns,
   Who dwelt among the dead.
6 With joy like his, shall every saint
   His empty tomb survey;
   Then rise with his ascending Lord,
   Through all his shining way.

610. *"Thou Son of David, have mercy on me."*

1 JESUS, and didst thou condescend,
   When vailed in human clay,
   To heal the sick, the lame, the blind,
   And drive disease away?
2 Didst thou regard the beggar's cry,
   And give the blind to see?
   Jesus, thou Son of David, hear—
   Have mercy, too, on me!

3 And didst thou pity mortal woe,
   And sight and health restore?
   Then pity, Lord! and save my soul,
   Which needs thy mercy more.
4 Didst thou regard thy servant's cry,
   When sinking in the wave?
   I perish, Lord! oh, save my soul!
   For thou alone canst save.

682. *"I know the Lord can save."*

1 AFFLICTION is a stormy deep,
   Where wave resounds to wave;
   Though o'er my head the billows roll,
   I know the Lord can save.
2 The hand that now withholds my joys
   Can soon restore my peace;
   And he who bade the tempest rise
   Can bid that tempest cease.

3 In darkest scenes when sorrows rose
   And pressed on every side,
   The Lord has still sustained my steps,
   And still has been my guide.
4 Here will I rest, and build my hope,
   Nor murmur at his rod!
   He's more than all the world to me—
   My Health, my Life, my God!

705. *Self lost in Christ.*

1 MY God, my God! to thee I cry;
   Thee only would I know:
   Thy purifying blood apply,
   And wash me white as snow.

2 But art thou not already mine?
   Answer, if mine thou art!
   Whisper within, thou Love Divine,
   And cheer my drooping heart.

3 Oh! could I lose myself in thee,
   Thy depth of mercy prove,
   Thou vast, unfathomable sea
   Of unexhausted love!

NAOMI. C. M.

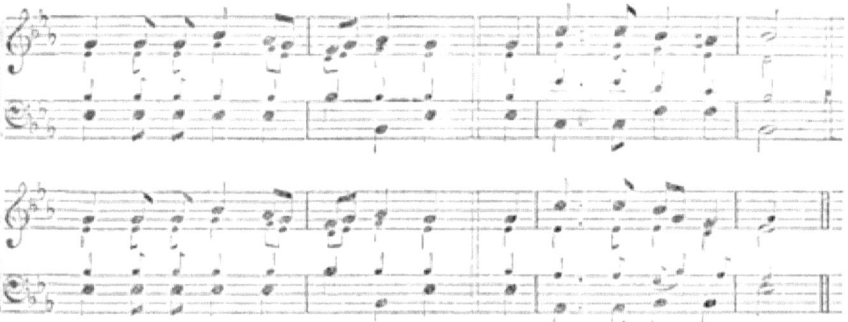

4 My humbled soul, when thou art near,
  In dust and ashes lies!
How shall a sinful worm appear,
  Or meet thy purer eyes!
5 I loathe myself when God I see,
  And into nothing fall;
Content if thou exalted be,
  And Christ be All in All!

761. *Not forsaken.*

1 AND wilt thou now forsake me, Lord?
  I feel it can not be;
No earthly tongue can ever tell
  What thou hast been to me.
2 Through all the changing scenes of life,
  Thy love hath sheltered me;
And wilt thou now forget thy child?
  I feel it can not be.
3 Thy love hath been my heritage
  Through many a weary year;
I've trusted in thy promises,
  And thou hast dried each tear.
4 In life or death, I take my stand
  Where I have ever stood,
Beneath the shelter of thy cross,
  And trusting in thy blood.
5 And then, when youth and health and strength
  And energy have fled,
The shades of evening peacefully
  Shall close around my head.
6 And when in all the helplessness
  Of death I turn to thee,
Thou wilt not then forsake me, Lord!
  I feel it can not be.

917. "*It is good for me that I have been afflicted.*"

1 I CAN not call affliction sweet,
  And yet 'twas good to bear;
Affliction brought me to thy feet,
  And I found comfort there.
2 My weaned soul was all resigned
  To thy most gracious will;
Oh, had I kept that better mind,
  Or been afflicted still.
3 Where are the vows which then I vowed,
  The joys which then I knew?
Those vanished like the morning cloud,
  These, like the early dew.
4 Lord, grant me grace for every day,
  Whate'er my state may be,
Through life, in death, with truth to say,
  My God is all to me!

1163. "*That I may know how frail I am.*"
  Psalm 39.

1 TEACH me the measure of my days,
  Thou Maker of my frame;
I would survey life's narrow space,
  And learn how frail I am.
2 A span is all that we can boast,
  An inch or two of time!
Man is but vanity and dust,
  In all his flower and prime.
3 What should I wish, or wait for, then,
  From creatures, earth and dust?
They make our expectations vain,
  And disappoint our trust.
4 Now I forbid my carnal hope,
  My fond desire recall:
I give my mortal interest up,
  And make my God my all.

DOXOLOGY.

To Father, Son, and Holy Ghost,
  One God, whom we adore,
Be glory as it was, is now,
  And shall be evermore.

SHIRLAND. S. M.

203. *God our Benefactor.*

1 My Maker and my King!
　　To thee my all I owe;
　Thy sovereign bounty is the spring,
　　Whence all my blessings flow.

2 The creature of thy hand,
　　On thee alone I live;
　My God! thy benefits demand
　　More praise than I can give.

3 Lord, what can I impart,
　　When all is thine before?
　Thy love demands a thankful heart:
　　The gift, alas, how poor!

4 Shall I withhold thy due?
　　And shall my passions rove?
　Lord form this wretched heart anew,
　　And fill it with thy love.

299. *The Sacrifice.*

1 Not all the blood of beasts,
　　On Jewish altars slain,
　Could give the guilty conscience peace,
　　Or wash away the stain.

2 But Christ, the heavenly Lamb,
　　Takes all our sins away—
　A sacrifice of nobler name,
　　And richer blood than they.

3 My faith would lay her hand
　　On that dear head of thine,
　While like a penitent I stand,
　　And there confess my sin.

4 My soul looks back to see
　　The burdens thou didst bear
　When hanging on the curséd tree,
　　And hopes her guilt was there.

5 Believing we rejoice
　　To see the curse remove;
　We bless the Lamb with cheerful voice,
　　And sing his bleeding love.

690. *"Whom having not seen ye love."*
　　　　1 Peter 1: 8.

1 Not with our mortal eyes
　　Have we beheld the Lord;
　Yet we rejoice to hear his name,
　　And love him in his word.

2 On earth we want the sight
　　Of our Redeemer's face;
　Yet, Lord, our inmost thoughts delight
　　To dwell upon thy grace.

3 And when we taste thy love,
　　Our joys divinely grow
　Unspeakable, like those above,
　　And heaven begins below.

854. *Boldness in Prayer.*

1 Behold the throne of grace:
　　The promise calls me near;
　There Jesus shows a smiling face,
　　And waits to answer prayer.

2 That rich atoning blood,
　　Which sprinkled round I see,
　Provides for those who come to God
　　An all-prevailing plea.

3 My soul! ask what thou wilt;
　　Thou canst not be too bold:
　Since his own blood for thee he spilt,
　　What else can he withhold?

4 Thine image, Lord, bestow,
　　Thy presence and thy love;
　I ask to serve thee here below,
　　And reign with thee above.

THEON. S. M.

5 Teach me to live by faith;
   Conform my will to thine;
   Let me victorious be in death,
   And then in glory shine.

1225. "*The former things are passed away.*"

1 The people of the Lord
   Are on their way to heaven;
  There they obtain their great reward,
   The prize will there be given.

2 'T is conflict here below;
   'T is triumph there, and peace:
  On earth we wrestle with the foe;
   In heaven our conflicts cease.

3 'T is gloom and darkness here;
   'T is light and joy above:

  There all is pure and all is clear;
   There all is peace and love.

4 There rest shall follow toil,
   And ease succeed to care:
  The victors there divide the spoil;
   They sing and triumph there.

5 Then, let us joyful sing!
   The conflict is not long;
  We hope in heaven to praise our King
   In one eternal song.

DOXOLOGY.

The Father and the Son,
   And Spirit we adore;
We praise, we bless, we worship thee,
   Both now and evermore!

ST. THOMAS. S. M.

ATHENS. C. M. DOUBLE.

279. *Miracles of Christ.*
1 OH, where is he that trod the sea?
  Oh, where is he that spake,
And lepers from their pains are free,
  And slaves their fetters break?
The lame and palsied freely rise,
  With joy the dumb do sing;
And, on the darkened, blinded eyes,
  Glad beams of morning spring!

2 Oh, where is he that trod the sea?
  Oh, where is he that spake,
And demons from their victims flee,
  The dead from slumber wake?
Here, here art thou, almighty Lord!
  Oh, speak to us once more,
And let thy healing, quickening word,
  Our ruined souls restore!

641. " *We love Him, because He first loved us.*"—1 John 4: 19.
1 WE love thee, Lord, because when we
    Had erred and gone astray,
  Thou didst recall our wandering souls
    Into the homeward way;
  When helpless, homeless, we were lost
    In sin and sorrow's night,
  Thou didst send forth a guiding ray
    Of thy benignant light;—

2 Because, when we forsook thy ways,
    Nor kept thy holy will,
  Thou wert not the avenging Judge,
    But gracious Father still;—
  Because, though we 've forgot thee, Lord,
    Thou hast not us forgot,—
  Though we have oft forsaken thee,
    Yet thou forsakest not;—

3 Because, O Lord, thou lovedst us
    With everlasting love;
  Because thou gav'st thy Son to die,
    That we might live above;

Because, when we were heirs of wrath,
  Thou gav'st the hopes of heaven:
We love because we much have sinned,
  And much have been forgiven.

913. *Communion with God in Retirement.*
1 FAR from the world, O Lord, I flee,
    From strife and tumult far;
  From scenes where Satan wages still
    His most successful war.

2 The calm retreat, the silent shade,
    With prayer and praise agree;
  And seem by thy sweet bounty made
    For those who follow thee.

3 There, if thy Spirit touch the soul,
    And grace her mean abode,
  Oh, with what peace, and joy, and love,
    She communes with her God!

4 There, like the nightingale she pours
    Her solitary lays;
  Nor asks a witness of her song,
    Nor thirsts for human praise.

5 Author and Guardian of my life!
    Sweet Source of light divine,
  And—all harmonious names in one—
    My Saviour!—thou art mine!

6 What thanks I owe thee, and what love—
    A boundless, endless store—
  Shall echo through the realms above,
    When time shall be no more.

851. " *He hath put a new song in my mouth.*"
  Psalm 40.
1 I WAITED patient for the Lord:
    He bowed to hear my cry;
  He saw me resting on his word,
    And brought salvation nigh.

2 He raised me from a horrid pit,
    Where, mourning, long I lay,

ORTONVILLE. C. M.

And from my bonds released my feet—
Deep bonds of miry clay.

3 Firm on a rock he made me stand,
And taught my cheerful tongue
To praise the wonders of his hand
In new and thankful song.

4 I'll spread his works of grace abroad;
The saints with joy shall hear,
And sinners learn to make my God
Their only hope and fear.

963. "*The secret place of the Most High.*"
Psalm 91.

1 THERE is a safe and secret place
Beneath the wings divine,
Reserved for all the heirs of grace:
Oh, be that refuge mine!

2 The least and feeblest there may bide,
Uninjured and unawed;
While thousands fall on every side,
He rests secure in God.

3 He feeds in pastures large and fair,
Of love and truth divine;
O child of God, O glory's heir!
How rich a lot is thine!

4 A hand almighty to defend,
An ear for every call,
An honored life, a peaceful end,
And heaven to crown it all!

1103. "*In Thee, the fatherless findeth mercy.*"

1 O GRACIOUS Lord! whose mercies rise
Above our utmost need,
Incline thine ear unto our cry,
And hear the orphan plead.

2 Bereft of all a mother's love,
And all a father's care,
Lord, whither shall we flee for help?
To whom direct our prayer?—

3 To thee we flee, to thee we pray;
Thou shalt our Father be:
More than the fondest parent's care
We find, O Lord, in thee!

4 Already thou hast heard our cry,
And wiped away our tears:
Thy mercy has a refuge found,
To guard our helpless years.

5 Oh, let thy love descend on those
Who pity to us show;
Nor let their children ever taste
The orphan's cup of woe!

1206. "*Sorrow not, even as others which have no hope.*"

1 DEAR as thou wert, and justly dear,
We will not weep for thee;
One thought shall check the starting tear:
It is, that thou art free.

2 And thus shall faith's consoling power
The tears of love restrain:
Oh, who that saw thy parting hour,
Could wish thee back again!

3 Triumphant in thy closing eye
The hope of glory shone;
Joy breathed in thine expiring sigh
To think the fight was won.

4 Gently the passing spirit fled,
Sustained by grace divine;
Oh, may such grace on me be shed,
And make my end like thine!

DOXOLOGY.

To Father, Son, and Holy Ghost,
One God, whom we adore,
Be glory as it was, is now,
And shall be evermore!

GRATITUDE. L. M.

738. *Peace in the Blood of Christ.*

1 Where shall I look for holy calm,
  But in thy blood, thou dying Lamb?
  My only hope of mercy lies
  In thine atoning sacrifice.

2 The world's temptations may assail,
  Its friendships cease, its comforts fail;
  But if thy peace, dear Lord, be mine,
  All else submissive I resign.

3 Oh, let my spirit meekly rest
  In whatso'er thy love sees best;
  Confiding in thy sovereign grace,
  And trusting where I fail to trace.

4 Lord, let thy peace my soul sustain,
  'Mid mingled scenes of joy and pain;
  Till, in the fullness of thy love,
  I reach the Fountain-head above.

768. *"Jesus, remember Calvary."*

1 My sufferings all to thee are known,
  Tempted in every point like me;
  Regard my grief, regard thine own:
  Jesus, remember Calvary!

2 For whom didst thou the cross endure?
  Who nailed thy body to the tree?
  Did not thy death my life procure?
  Oh, let thy mercy answer me!

3 Art thou not touched with human woe?
  Hath pity left the Son of man?
  Dost thou not all my sorrows know,
  And claim a share in all my pain?

4 Thou wilt not break a bruiséd reed,
  Or quench the smallest spark of grace,
  Till through the soul thy power is spread
  Thine all-victorious righteousness.

5 The day of small and feeble things,
  I know thou never wilt despise;
  And soon, with healing in his wings,
  The Sun of righteousness shall rise.

785. *"I will that they be with Me, where I am."*—John 17: 24.

1 Let me be with thee where thou art,
  My Saviour, my eternal Rest;
  Then only will this longing heart
  Be fully and for ever blest.

2 Let me be with thee where thou art,
  Thine unvailed glory to behold;
  Then only will this wandering heart
  Cease to be false to thee and cold.

3 Let me be with thee where thou art,
  Where spotless saints thy name adore;
  Then only will this sinful heart
  Be evil and defiled no more.

4 Let me be with thee where thou art,
  Where none can die, where none remove;
  There neither death nor life will part
  Me from thy presence and thy love.

829. *Living to the Glory of God.*

1 O thou, who hast at thy command
  The hearts of all men in thy hand!
  Our wayward, erring hearts incline
  To know no other will but thine.

2 Our wishes, our desires, control;
  Mold every purpose of the soul;
  O'er all may we victorious be
  That stands between ourselves and thee.

3 Thrice blest will all our blessings prove,
  When through them all we see thy love;
  When each glad heart its tribute pays
  Of humble gratitude and praise.

4 And while we to thy glory live,
  May we to thee all glory give;
  Until the joyful summons come,
  That calls thy willing servants home.

863. *"Forgiving one another."*
Eph. 4: 30–32.

1 The Spirit, like a peaceful dove,
  Flies from the realms of noise and strife;

ERNAN. L. M.

Why should we vex and grieve his love,
  Who seals our souls to heavenly life!
Tender and kind be all our thoughts;
  Through all our lives let mercy run:
So God forgives our numerous faults,
  For the dear sake of Christ, his Son.

554. *Prayer for the Guidance of the Spirit.*

Come, gracious Spirit, heavenly Dove,
  With light and comfort from above;
Be thou our guardian, thou our guide,
  O'er every thought and step preside.

The light of truth to us display,
  And make us know and choose thy way;
Plant holy fear in every heart,
  That we from God may ne'er depart.

Lead us to holiness—the road
  Which we must take to dwell with God;
Lead us to Christ, the living way,
  Nor let us from his pastures stray.

Lead us to God, our final rest,
  To be with him for ever blest;
Lead us to heaven, its bliss to share—
  Fullness of joy for ever there!

563. *" Will He no more to us return?"*

O Lord, and shall our fainting souls
  Thy just displeasure ever mourn?
Thy Spirit grieved, and long withdrawn,
  Will he no more to us return?

Great Source of light and peace! return,
  Nor let us mourn and sigh in vain;
Come, repossess these longing hearts
  With all the graces of thy train.

This temple, hallowed by thine hand,
  Once more be with thy presence blest;

Here be thy grace anew displayed,
  Be this thine everlasting rest!

566. *Repentance at the Cross.*

1 Here, at thy cross, my gracious Lord,
    I lay my soul beneath thy love:
  Oh, cleanse me with atoning blood,
    Nor let me from thy feet remove!

2 Should worlds conspire to drive me thence,
    Moveless and firm this heart should lie;
  Resolved, for that's my last defense,
    If I must perish, there to die.

3 But speak, my Lord, and calm my fear;
    Am I not safe beneath thy shade?
  Thy vengeance will not strike me here,
    Nor Satan dare my soul invade.

4 Yes, I'm secure beneath thy blood,
    And all my foes shall lose their aim:
  Hosanna to my Saviour God!
    And loudest praises to his name.

1067. *" Lord, I am Thine, entirely Thine."*

1 Lord, I am thine, entirely thine,
    Purchased and saved by blood divine;
  With full consent I thine would be,
    And own thy sovereign right in me.

2 Here, O my Lord, my soul, my all,
    I yield to thee beyond recall;
  Accept thine own,—so long withheld,
    Accept what I so freely yield.

3 Grant one poor sinner more a place
    Among the children of thy grace;
  A wretched sinner lost to God,
    But ransomed by Immanuel's blood.

4 The vow is past beyond repeal;
    Now will I set the solemn seal:
  Thine would I live, thine would I die,
    Be thine through all eternity.

SABBATH. 7s. 6 LINES.

55. *The Lord's Day.*

1 SAFELY through another week
   God has brought us on our way;
  Let us now a blessing seek,
   Waiting in his courts to-day:
  Day of all the week the best,
  Emblem of eternal rest.

2 While we pray for pardoning grace,
   Through the dear Redeemer's name,
  Show thy reconciling face;
   Take away our sin and shame:
  From our worldly cares set free,
  May we rest this day in thee.

3 Here we come, thy name to praise;
   Let us feel thy presence near;
  May thy glories meet our eyes,
   While we in thy house appear:
  Here afford us, Lord, a taste
  Of our everlasting feast.

4 May the Gospel's joyful sound
   Conquer sinners, comfort saints;
  Make the fruits of grace abound;
   Bring relief for all complaints:
  Thus let all our Sabbaths prove,
  Till we rest in thee above.

808. *Imitation of Christ in his mild virtues.* Phil. 2: 5.

1 EVER patient, gentle, meek,
   Holy Saviour! was thy mind;
  Vainly in myself I seek
   Likeness to my Lord to find;
  Yet that mind which was in thee,
  May be, must be formed in me.

2 Days of toil, 'mid throngs of men,
   Vexed not, ruffled not thy soul;
  Still collected, calm, serene,
   Thou each feeling couldst control:
  Lord, that mind which was in thee,
  May be, must be formed in me.

3 Though such griefs were thine to bear,
   For each suff'rer thou couldst feel;
  Every mourner's burden share,
   Every wounded spirit heal:
  Saviour! let thy grace in me
  Form that mind which was in thee.

4 When my pain is most intense,
   Let thy cross my lesson prove;
  Let me hear thee, e'en from thence,
   Breathing words of peace and love:
  Saviour! let thy grace in me
  Form that mind which was in thee.

957. *"The precious Sons of Zion."*

1 BLESSÈD are the sons of God!
  They are bought with Jesus' blood;
  They are ransomed from the grave;
  Life eternal they shall have:
  With them numbered may we be,
  Here and in eternity!

2 God did love them in his Son
  Long before the world begun;
  All their sins are washed away;
  They shall stand in God's great day:

ROSEFIELD. 7s. 6 LINES.

With them numbered may we be,
Here and in eternity!

3 They are harmless, meek, and mild,
Holy, humble, undefiled;
They are by the Spirit sealed,
They with love and peace are filled:
With them numbered may we be,
Here, and in eternity!

4 They are lights upon the earth,
Children of a heavenly birth;
One with God, with Jesus one,
Glory is in them begun:
With them numbered may we be,
Here, and in eternity!

475. *Consecration to the Trinity.*

1 Now, O God, thine own I am!
Now I give thee back thine own
Freedom, friends, and health and fame,
Consecrate to thee alone:
Thine I live, thrice happy I!
Happier still, if thine I die.

Take me, Lord, and all my powers;
Take my mind, and heart, and will;
All my goods, and all my hours,
All I know, and all I feel,
All I think, or speak, or do—
Take my soul and make it new!

3 Father, Son, and Holy Ghost,
One in Three, and Three in One,

As by the celestial host,
Let thy will on earth be done:
Praise by all to thee be given,
Glorious Lord of earth and heaven!

909. *The childlike Heart.*

1 QUIET, Lord, my froward heart;
Make me teachable and mild,
Upright, simple, free from art;
Make me as a weaned child,—
From distrust and envy free,
Pleased with all that pleases thee.

2 What thou shalt to-day provide,
Let me as a child receive;
What to-morrow may betide,
Calmly to thy wisdom leave:
'T is enough that thou wilt care;
Why should I the burden bear?

3 As a little child relies
On a care beyond his own,
Knows he's neither strong nor wise,
Fears to stir a step alone;
Let me thus with thee abide,
As my Father, Guard, and Guide.

DOXOLOGY.

BLESSING, honor, glory, might,
And dominion infinite,
To the Father of our Lord,
To the Spirit and the Word:
As it was all worlds before,
Is, and shall be evermore.

STOW. H. M.

176. *God faithful to His Promises.*

1 THE promises I sing,
　Which sovereign love hath spoke;
Nor will th' eternal King
　His words of grace revoke:
They stand secure　| Not Zion's hill
And steadfast still;　| Abides so sure.

2 The mountains melt away,
　When once the judge appears;
And sun and moon decay,
　That measure mortal years:
But still the same,　| The promise shines
In radiant lines,　| Through all the flame.

3 Their harmony shall sound
　Through my attentive ears,
When thunders cleave the ground,
　And dissipate the spheres:
'Mid all the shock　| I stand serene,
Of that dread scene,　| Thy word my rock.

194. *" Looking up."*—Psalm 121.

1 UPWARD I lift mine eyes;
　From God is all my aid;
The God who built the skies,
　And earth and nature made:
God is the tower　| His grace is nigh
To which I fly;　| In every hour.

2 My feet shall never slide,
　And fall in fatal snares,
Since God, my guard and guide,
　Defends me from my fears:
Those wakeful eyes,　| Shall Israel keep
That never sleep,　| When dangers rise.

3 No burning heats by day,
　Nor blasts of evening air,
Shall take my health away,
　If God be with me there:
Thou art my sun,　| To guard my head
And thou my shade,　| By night or noon.

4 Hast thou not given thy word
　To save my soul from death?
And I can trust my Lord
　To keep my mortal breath:
I'll go and come,　| Till from on high
Nor fear to die,　| Thou call me home.

356. *" Thou rising, reigning God."*

1 YES, the Redeemer rose;
　The Saviour left the dead;
And o'er our hellish foes
　High raised his conquering head:
In wild dismay,　| Fall to the ground,
The guards around　| And sink away.

2 Lo! the angelic bands
　In full assembly meet,
To wait his high commands,
　And worship at his feet:
Joyful they come,　| From realms of day
And wing their way,　| To Jesus' tomb.

3 Then back to heaven they fly,
　And the glad tidings bear:
Hark! as they soar on high,
　What music fills the air!
Their anthems say:　| Hath left the dead,
" Jesus who bled　| He rose to-day."

4 Ye mortals, catch the sound,
　Redeemed by him from hell;
And send the echo round
　The globe on which you dwell:
Transported cry:　| Hath left the dead,
" Jesus who bled　| No more to die."

ZEBULON. H. M. 1st.

5 All hail, triumphant Lord,
   Who sav'st us with thy blood!
  Wide be that name adored,
   Thou rising, reigning God!
With thee we rise, | And empires gain
With thee we reign, | Beyond the skies.

900. *"Fight the good fight."*

1 FIGHT the good fight! lay hold
   Upon eternal life;
  Keep but thy shield—be bold!
   Stand through the hottest strife:
With thy great Captain on the field,
Thou canst not fail, unless thou yield.

2 No force of earth or hell,
   Though fiends with men unite,
  Truth's champion can compel,
   However pressed, to flight:
He stands unmoved upon the field;
He can not fall, unless he yield.

3 Trust in thy Saviour's might;
   Yea, till thy latest breath,
  Fight, and like him in fight,
   By dying conquer death:
And, all-victorious in the field,
Then, with thy sword, thy spirit yield.

4 Great words are these, and strong;
   Yet, Lord, I look to thee;
  To whom alone belong
   Valor and victory:
With thee, my Captain, in the field,
I must prevail—I can not yield!

1004. *'By His stripes we are healed."*

1 THY works, not mine, O Christ!
   Speak gladness to this heart;
  They tell me all is done;
   They bid my fear depart:
To whom, save thee | For sin atone,
Who canst alone | Lord! shall I flee?

2 Thy tears, not mine, O Christ,
   Have wept my guilt away;
  And turned this night of mine
   Into a blessèd day:
To whom, save thee | For sin atone,
Who canst alone | Lord! shall I flee?

3 Thy wounds, not mine, O Christ,
   Can heal my bruisèd soul;
  Thy stripes, not mine, contain
   The balm that makes me whole:
To whom, save thee | For sin atone,
Who canst alone | Lord! shall I flee?

4 Thy cross, not mine, O Christ,
   Has borne the awful load
  Of sins that none could bear
   But the incarnate God:
To whom, save thee | For sin atone,
Who canst alone | Lord! shall I flee?

5 Thy death, not mine, O Christ,
   Has paid the ransom due;
  Ten thousand deaths like mine
   Would have been all too few:
To whom, save thee | For sin atone,
Who canst alone | Lord! shall I flee?

6 Thy righteousness alone
   Can clothe and beautify;
  I wrap it round my soul;
   In this I'll live and die:
To whom, save thee | For sin atone,
Who canst alone | Lord! shall I flee?

PETERSBURGH. L. M. 6 LINES.

434. *"Unto you which believe He is precious."*
1 Pet. 2: 7.

1 Oh, speak of Jesus! other names
Have lost for me their interest now;
His is the only one that claims
To be an antidote for woe:
It falls like music on the ear,
When nothing else can soothe or cheer.

2 Oh, speak of Jesus! of his power,
As perfect God, and perfect man,
Which day by day, and hour by hour,
As he wrought out the wondrous plan,
Led him, as God, to save and heal;
As man to sympathize and feel.

3 Oh, speak of Jesus—of his death!
For us he lived, for us he died;
"'Tis finished," with his latest breath,
The Lord, Jehovah-Jesus, cried;
That death of shame and agony
Won life, eternal life for me!

4 Yes, speak of Jesus while mine ear
Can listen to a human voice!
That name my parting soul will cheer,
Will bid me ev'n in death rejoice;
Then prove, when these clay bonds are riven,
My passport at the gates of heaven!

553. *"Here is my heart."*

1 HERE is my heart—I give it thee!
My God, I heard thee call, and say,
"Not to the world, my child—to me!"
I heard thy voice and will obey;
Here is love's offering to my King
Which in glad sacrifice I bring.

2 Here is my heart—the gift tho' poor,
Thou, O my God, wilt not despise;
Long have I sought to make it pure
And fit to meet thy searching eyes:
Corrupted first in Adam's fall,
The stains of sin pollute it all.

3 Here is my heart!—so hard before,
But now by thy rich grace made meet;
Yet bruised and sad it can but pour
Its tears and anguish at thy feet:
It groans beneath the weight of sin,
It sighs salvation's joy to win.

4 Here is my heart!—its longings end
In Christ, as near his cross it draws;
It says, "Thou art my rest, my Friend,
Thy precious blood my ransom was:"
In thee, the Saviour, it has found
That peace and blessedness abound.

694. *"Thine wholly—Thine alone."*

1 JESUS! thy boundless love to me
No thought can reach, no tongue declare;
Oh, knit my thankful heart to thee,
And reign without a rival there!
Thine wholly, thine alone, I live;
Thyself to me, my Saviour, give!

2 O Love! how cheering is thy ray!
All pain before thy presence flies;
Care, anguish, sorrow, melt away,
Where'er thy healing beams arise:
O Jesus! nothing may I see,
Nothing desire, or seek, but thee!

3 What in thy love possess I not?
My star by night, my sun by day,
My spring of life when parched with drought,
My wine to cheer, my bread to stay;
My strength, my shield, my safe abode,
My robe before the throne of God.

ZEPHYR. L. M.

302. *"A Name which is above every name."*
Phil. 2: 9.

1 There is none other name than thine,
Jehovah Jesus! Name divine!
On which to rest for sins forgiven—
For peace with God, for hope of heaven.

2 There is none other name than thine,
When cares, and fears, and griefs are mine,
That, with a gracious power, can heal
Each care, and fear, and grief I feel.

3 There is none other name than thine,
When called my spirit to resign,
To bear me through that latest strife,
And ev'n in death to be my life.

4 Name, above every name! thy praise
Shall fill the remnant of my days;
Jehovah Jesus! Name divine!
Rock of salvation! thou art mine.

750. *"Because I live, ye shall live also."*
John 14: 19.

1 When sins and fears prevailing rise,
And fainting hope almost expires,
Jesus, to thee I lift my eyes,
To thee I breathe my soul's desires.

2 If my immortal Saviour lives,
Then my immortal life is sure;
His word a firm foundation gives;
Here let me build, and rest secure.

3 Here let my faith unshaken dwell;
Immovable the promise stands;
Not all the powers of earth or hell
Can e'er dissolve the sacred bands.

4 Here, O my soul! thy trust repose;
If Jesus is for ever mine,
Not death itself, that list of foes,
Shall break a union so divine.

752. *"We shall also reign with Him."*

1 Weary with sin, I lift mine eyes
To him who toiled and died for me;
My struggling spirit longs to rise
And reign, my Saviour! one with thee.

2 For thee I count all things but loss,
So let me gain thy promised throne;
For me why didst thou bear thy cross,
If not to make me share thy crown?

3 Give, give to me the good I crave;
Cleanse me in thine atoning blood:
Why didst thou love me in thy grave,
If not t' enthrone me near my God?

4 Oh, let my hope, so dear, so bright,
Illumine my dark hour of death!
What if thy glories blind my sight?
Let them allure and cheer my faith.

830. *"Myself I give."*

1 While in the hours of blooming youth,
My God, I've felt and owned thy truth;
Thy mercies, with increasing age,
Shall still my grateful heart engage.

2 No human power shall e'er control
This settled purpose of my soul;
Or urge my constant mind to stray,
But where thy wisdom points the way.

3 To thee, O Lord, myself I give;
'T is to thy glory I would live:
My God! my Strength, my Hope, my Joy,
Thy praise shall all my powers employ.

DOXOLOGY.

Praise God, from whom all blessings flow!
Praise him, all creatures here below!
Praise him above, ye heavenly host!
Praise Father, Son, and Holy Ghost!

MAITLAND. C. M.

240. *Sovereignty of God in His Gift of Grace.*

1 O GIFT of gifts! O Grace of faith!
  My God, how can it be
That thou, who hast discerning love,
  Shouldst give that gift to me!

2 How many hearts thou might'st have had!
  More innocent than mine!
How many souls more worthy far
  Of that pure touch of thine!

3 Ah, Grace! into unlikeliest hearts
  It is thy boast to come;
The glory of thy light to find
  In darkest spots a home.

4 Thy choice, O God of goodness! then
  I lovingly adore;
Oh, give me grace to keep thy grace,
  And grace to long for more!

395. *The Good Shepherd.*

1 To thee, my Shepherd and my Lord,
  A grateful song I'll raise;
Oh, let the feeblest of thy flock
  Attempt to speak thy praise!

2 But how shall mortal tongue express
  A subject so divine?
Do justice to so vast a theme,
  Or praise a love like thine?

3 My life, my joy, my hope, I owe
  To thine amazing love;
Ten thousand, thousand comforts here,
  And nobler bliss above.

4 To thee my trembling spirit flies,
  With sin and grief oppressed;
Thy gentle voice dispels my fears,
  And lulls my cares to rest.

5 Lead on, dear Shepherd!—led by thee,
  No evil shall I fear;

Soon shall I reach thy fold above,
  And praise thee better there.

436. *The Pearl of great Price.*
Matt. 13: 46.

1 YE glittering toys of earth, adieu!
  A nobler choice be mine;
A real prize attracts my view,
  A treasure all divine.

2 Jesus, to multitudes unknown,
  O name divinely sweet!
Jesus, in thee, in thee alone,
  Wealth, honor, pleasure meet.

3 Should earth's vain treasures all depart,
  Of this dear gift possessed;
I'd clasp it to my joyful heart,
  And be for ever blest.

4 Dear Sovereign of my soul's desires,
  Thy love is bliss divine;
Accept the gift that love inspires,
  And bid me call thee mine.

28. *"Pray for the peace of Jerusalem."*
Psalm 122.

1 OH, 't was a joyful sound to hear
  Our tribes devoutly say:
"Up, Israel, to the temple haste,
  And keep your festal day!"

2 At Salem's courts we must appear,
  With our assembled powers,
In strong and beauteous order ranged,
  Like her united towers.

3 Oh, pray we then for Salem's peace!
  For they shall prosperous be,
Thou holy city of our God,
  Who bear true love to thee.

4 May peace within thy sacred walls
  A constant guest be found;
With plenty and prosperity
  Thy palaces be crowned.

LEON. C. M.

585. *"God giveth grace to the humble."*

1 COME, let us to the Lord our God
　With contrite hearts return!
　Our God is gracious, nor will leave
　　The desolate to mourn.

2 His voice commands the tempest forth,
　And stills the stormy wave;
　His arm, though it be strong to smite,
　　Is also strong to save.

3 Our hearts, if God we seek to know,
　Shall know him and rejoice:
　His coming like the morn shall be;
　　Like morning songs his voice.

4 As dew upon the tender herb,
　Diffusing fragrance round;
　As showers that usher in the spring,
　　And cheer the thirsty ground:

5 So shall his presence bless our souls,
　And shed a joyful light;
　That hallowed morn shall chase away
　　The sorrows of the night.

700. *The beloved Name.*

1 BLEST Jesus! when my soaring thoughts
　O'er all thy graces rove,
　How is my soul in transport lost,—
　　In wonder, joy, and love!

2 Not softest strains can charm my ears,
　Like thy belovéd name;
　Nor aught beneath the skies inspire
　　My heart with equal flame.

3 Where'er I look, my wondering eyes
　Unnumbered blessings see;
　But what is life, with all its bliss,
　　If once compared with thee?

4 Hast thou a rival in my breast?
　Search, Lord, for thou canst tell
　If aught can raise my passions thus,
　　Or please my soul so well.

5 No: thou art precious to my heart,
　My portion and my joy;
　For ever let thy boundless grace
　　My sweetest thoughts employ.

814. *"We come unto Thee; for Thou art our God."*

1 I ASK not now for gold to gild
　An aching, weary frame;
　The yearning of the mind is stilled,—
　　I ask not now for fame.

2 But, bowed in lowliness of mind,
　I make my wishes known;
　I only ask a will resigned,
　　O Father, to thine own.

3 In vain I task my aching brain,
　The sage's thoughts to scan;
　I only feel how weak I am,
　　How poor and blind is man.

4 And now my spirit sighs for home,
　And longs for light to see,
　And, like a weary child, would come,
　　O Father! unto thee.

847. *"Is any among you afflicted? Let him pray."*

1 No, never shall my heart despond,
　Long as my lips can pray;
　My latest breath, with effort fond,
　　Shall pass in prayer away.

2 There is a heavenly mercy-seat
　To calm the sinner's fears;
　There is a Saviour at whose feet
　　The mourner dries his tears.

3 When friends depart, and hopes are riven,
　And gathering storms I see,
　My soul is but the sooner driven,
　　Eternal Rock! to thee.

4 Oh for a voice of sweeter sound,
　For every wind to bear,
　To teach the listening world around
　　The blessedness of prayer!

ITALIAN HYMN. 6s & 4s.

63. *"Bless us to-night."*

1 FATHER of love and power,
Guard thou our evening hour,
Shield with thy might:
For all thy care this day
Our grateful thanks we pay,
And to our Father pray,
Bless us to-night.

2 Jesus Immanuel,
Come in thy love to dwell
In hearts contrite:
For many sins we grieve,
But we thy grace receive,
And in thy word believe;
Bless us to-night.

3 Spirit of truth and love,
Life-giving, holy Dove,
Shed forth thy light!
Heal every sinner's smart,
Still every throbbing heart,
And thine own peace impart;
Bless us to-night.

340. *"Worthy is the Lamb."*—Rev. 5.

1 COME, all ye saints of God,
Wide through the earth abroad
Spread Jesus' fame:
Tell what his love hath done;
Trust in his name alone;
Shout to his lofty throne,
"Worthy the Lamb!"

2 Hence, gloomy doubts and fears!
Dry up your mournful tears;
Swell the glad theme:
To Christ, our gracious King,
Strike each melodious string;
Join heart and voice to sing,
"Worthy the Lamb!"

3 Hark! how the choirs above,
Filled with the Saviour's love,
Dwell on his name!
There, too, may we be found,
With light and glory crowned,
While all the heavens resound,
"Worthy the Lamb!"

341. *"The Lamb that was slain."*—Rev. 5.

1 GLORY to God on high!
Let heaven and earth reply,
"Praise ye his name!"
His love and grace adore,
Who all our sorrows bore;
Sing loud for evermore,
"Worthy the Lamb!"

2 While they around the throne
Cheerfully join in one,
Praising his name,—
Ye, who have felt his blood
Sealing your peace with God,
Sound his dear name abroad,
"Worthy the Lamb!"

3 Join, all ye ransomed race,
Our Lord and God to bless:
Praise ye his name!
In him we will rejoice,
And make a joyful noise,
Shouting with heart and voice,
'Worthy the Lamb!"

4 Soon must we change our place,
Yet we will never cease
Praising his name:
To him our songs we bring;
Hail him our gracious King;
And, through all ages sing,
"Worthy the Lamb!"

NORMAN. 6s & 4s.

474. *"To Thee, great One in Three."*

1 Come, thou almighty King,
  Help us thy name to sing,
    Help us to praise!
  Father all glorious,
  O'er all victorious,
  Come, and reign over us,
    Ancient of Days!

2 Jesus, our Lord, descend;
  From all our foes defend,
    Nor let us fall;
  Let thine almighty aid
  Our sure defense be made,
  Our souls on thee be stayed:
    Lord, hear our call!

3 Come, thou incarnate Word,
  Gird on thy mighty sword;
    Our prayer attend:
  Come, and thy people bless,
  And give thy word success:
  Spirit of holiness
    On us descend.

4 Come, holy Comforter,
  Thy sacred witness bear
    In this glad hour:
  Thou, who almighty art,
  Now rule in every heart,
  And ne'er from us depart,
    Spirit of power.

5 To thee, great One in Three,
  The highest praises be,
    Hence evermore!
  Thy sovereign majesty

  May we in glory see,
  And to eternity
    Love and adore!

476. *Prayer to the Trinity for the World's Conversion.*

1 Thou, whose almighty word
  Chaos and darkness heard,
    And took their flight,
  Hear us, we humbly pray,
  And, where the gospel day
  Sheds not its glorious ray,
    "Let there be light."

2 Thou, who didst come to bring,
  On thy redeeming wing,
    Healing and sight,
  Health to the sick in mind,
  Sight to the inly blind,
  Oh, now to all mankind,
    "Let there be light."

3 Spirit of truth and love,
  Life-giving, holy Dove,
    Speed forth thy flight;
  Move on the waters' face,
  Bearing the lamp of grace;
  And in earth's darkest place
    "Let there be light."

DOXOLOGY.

We praise, we worship thee,
Blessèd and holy Three,
  Wisdom, Love, Might!
Boundless as ocean's tide,
Rolling in fullest pride,
O'er the world, far and wide,
  "Let there be light!"

STONEFIELD. L. M.*

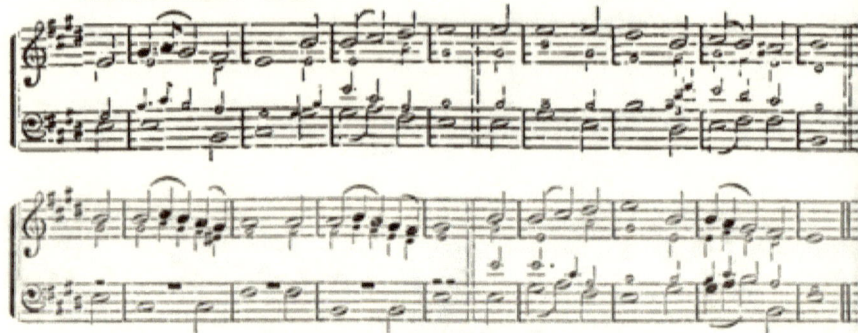

* Or L. M. 6 lines, by repeating the first two lines.

8. *"Surely the Lord is in this place."*

1 Lo, God is here!—let us adore,
And own how dreadful is this place!
Let all within us feel his power,
And silent bow before his face!

2 Lo, God is here!—him, day and night,
United choirs of angels sing:
To him, enthroned above all height,
Let saints their humble worship bring.

3 Lord God of hosts! Oh, may our praise
Thy courts with grateful incense fill!
Still may we stand before thy face,
Still hear and do thy sovereign will!

283. *"Oh, who like Thee!"*

1 How beauteous were the marks divine,
That in thy meekness used to shine,
That lit thy lonely pathway, trod
In wondrous love, O Son of God!

2 Oh, who like thee, so calm, so bright,
So pure, so made to live in light?
Oh, who like thee did ever go,
So patient through a world of woe?

3 Oh, who like thee so humbly bore
The scorn, the scoffs of men, before?
So meek, forgiving, godlike, high,
So glorious in humility?

4 Ev'n death, which sets the prisoner free,
Was pang, and scoff, and scorn to thee;
Yet love through all thy torture glowed,
And mercy with thy life-blood flowed.

5 Oh, in thy light be mine to go,
Illuming all my way of woe!
And give me ever on the road
To trace thy footsteps, Son of God!

289. *His final Entrance into Jerusalem.*
John 12: 12-15.

1 Ride on, ride on in majesty!
In lowly pomp ride on to die:
O Christ! thy triumphs now begin
O'er captive death and conquered sin.

2 Ride on, ride on in majesty!
The wingéd squadrons of the sky
Look down, with sad and wondering eyes,
To see th' approaching sacrifice.

3 Ride on, ride on in majesty!
Thy last and fiercest strife is nigh:
The Father, on his sapphire throne,
Expects his own anointed Son.

4 Ride on, ride on in majesty!
In lowly pomp ride on to die:
Bow thy meek head to mortal pain;
Then take, O God, thy power, and reign!

1267. *"The Lord shall come."*

1 The Lord shall come! the earth shall quake:
The mountains to their center shake;
And, withering from the vault of night,
The stars withdraw their feeble light.

2 The Lord shall come! but not the same
As once in lowly form he came,—
A silent Lamb before his foes,
A weary man, and full of woes.

3 The Lord shall come! a dreadful form,
With wreath of flame, and robe of storm,
On cherub-wings, and wings of wind,
Anointed Judge of human kind!

4 Can this be he, who wont to stray
A pilgrim on the world's highway,
By power oppressed, and mocked by pride,—
The Nazarene, the Crucified?

LYTE. L. M. 6 LINES.

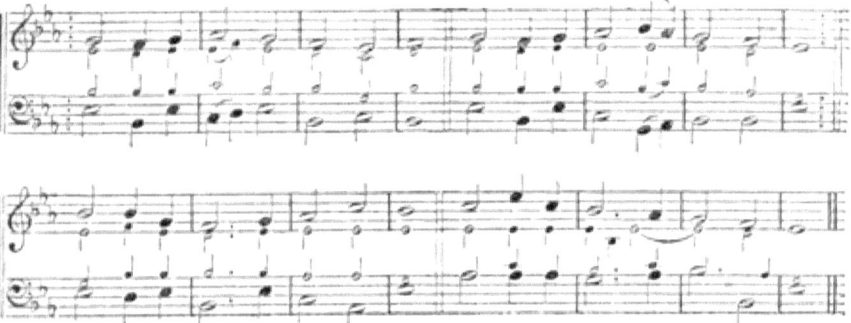

5 While sinners in despair shall call,
"Rocks, hide us! mountains, on us fall!"
The saints, ascending from the tomb,
Shall sing for joy, "The Lord is come!"

10.   *Refuge in the Sanctuary.*

1 FORTH from the dark and stormy sky,
Lord, to thine altar's shade we fly;
Forth from the world, its hope and fear,
Father, we seek thy shelter here;
Weary and weak, thy grace we pray;
Turn not, O Lord! thy guests away.

2 Long have we roamed in want and pain,
Long have we sought thy rest in vain;
Wildered in doubt, in darkness lost,
Long have our souls been tempest-tossed;
Low at thy feet our sins we lay;
Turn not, O Lord! thy guests away.

723.   *"No merits of my own."*

1 FATHER of mercies, God of love!
Oh, hear a humble suppliant's cry!
Bend from thy lofty seat above,
Thy throne of glorious majesty:
Oh, deign to hear my mournful voice,
And bid my drooping heart rejoice!

2 I urge no merits of my own,
No worth, to claim thy gracious smile:
No: when I bow before thy throne,
Dare to converse with God awhile,
Thy name, blest Jesus, is my plea—
Dearest and sweetest name to me!

3 Father of mercies, God of love!
Then hear thy humble suppliant's cry;
Bend from thy lofty seat above,
Thy throne of glorious majesty:
One pardoning word can make me whole,
And soothe the anguish of my soul.

1009.   *"Who is a God like unto thee?"*
            Micah 7:18.

1 GREAT God of wonders! all thy ways
Are worthy of thyself,—divine;
But the bright glories of thy grace,
Beyond thine other wonders shine:
Who is a pardoning God like thee?
Or who has grace so rich and free?

2 Pardon from an offended God:
Pardon for sins of deepest dye;
Pardon bestowed through Jesus' blood;
Pardon that brings the rebel nigh:
Where is the pardoning God like thee?
Or where the grace so rich and free?

3 Oh, may this glorious, matchless love,
This godlike miracle of grace,
Teach mortal tongues, like those above,
To raise this song of lofty praise:
Who is a pardoning God like thee?
Or who has grace so rich and free?

1181.   *"Help me in my hour of need."*

1 WHEN from my sight all fades away,
And when my tongue no more can say,
And when my ears no more can hear,
And when my heart is racked with fear,—
When all my mind is darkened o'er,
And human help can do no more,—

2 Then come, Lord Jesus! come with speed,
And help me in my hour of need;
Then hide my sins, and let my faith
Be brave, and conquer ev'n in death;
Then let me, resting on thy word,
Securely sleep in thee, my Lord.

DOXOLOGY.

PRAISE God, from whom all blessings flow!
Praise him, all creatures here below!
Praise him above, ye heavenly host!
Praise Father, Son, and Holy Ghost!

BROOKLYN. C. M. DOUBLE.

294. *Calvary.*—Luke 23 : 33.

1 There is a dear and hallowed spot
   Oft present to my eye—
By saints it ne'er can be forgot—
   That place is Calvary.
2 Oh, what a scene was there displayed
   Of love and agony,
When our Redeemer bowed his head,
   And died on Calvary!
3 When fainting under guilt's dread load,
   Unto the cross I'll fly;
And trust the merit of that blood
   Which flowed at Calvary.
4 Whene'er I feel temptation's power,
   On Jesus I'll rely;
And, in the sharp, conflicting hour,
   Repair to Calvary.
5 When seated at the feast of love,
   Then will I fix mine eye
On him who intercedes above,
   Who bled on Calvary.
6 When the dark scene of death, the last
   Momentous hour draws nigh,
Then, with my dying eyes, I'll cast
   A look on Calvary.

447. *"Come, Holy Spirit, come!"*

1 Spirit Divine! attend our prayer,
   And make our hearts thy home:
Descend with all thy gracious power:
   Come, Holy Spirit, come!
2 Come as the light; to us reveal
   Our sinfulness and woe;
And lead us in those paths of life
   Where all the righteous go.
3 Come as the fire, and purge our hearts,
   Like sacrificial flame;

Let our whole soul an offering be
   To our Redeemer's name.
4 Come as the dew, and sweetly bless
   This consecrated hour;
May barrenness rejoice to own
   Thy fertilizing power.
5 Come as the wind, with rushing sound,
   With Pentecostal grace;
And make the great salvation known,
   Wide as the human race.
6 Spirit Divine, attend our prayer,
   And make our hearts thy home;
Descend with all thy gracious power;
   Come, Holy Spirit, come!

558. *The Resolve.*—Est. 4: 16.

1 Come, trembling sinner, in whose breast
   A thousand thoughts revolve:
Come, with your guilt and fear oppressed
   And make this last resolve:—
2 "I'll go to Jesus, though my sin
   High as the mountains rose;
I know his courts, I'll enter in,
   Whatever may oppose.
3 "Prostrate I'll lie before his throne,
   And there my guilt confess;
I'll tell him I'm a wretch undone,
   Without his sovereign grace.
4 "I'll to the gracious King approach,
   Whose scepter pardon gives;
Perhaps he may command my touch,
   And then the suppliant lives.
5 "Perhaps he will admit my plea,
   Perhaps will hear my prayer;
But if I perish, I will pray,
   And perish only there.

DOWNS. C. M.

6 "I can but perish if I go;
   I am resolved to try;
   For if I stay away, I know
   I must for ever die."

869. *"Ye are all one in Christ Jesus."*

1 Let saints below in concert sing
   With those to glory gone;
   For all the servants of our King,
   In earth and heaven, are one.

2 One family—we dwell in him—
   One church above, beneath,
   Though now divided by the stream—
   The narrow stream of death;

3 One army of the living God,
   To his command we bow;
   Part of the host have crossed the flood,
   And part are crossing now.

4 Ev'n now to their eternal home
   Some happy spirits fly;
   And we are to the margin come,
   And soon expect to die.

5 Ev'n now, by faith, we join our hands
   With those that went before,
   And greet the ransomed blessèd bands
   Upon th' eternal shore.

6 Lord Jesus! be our constant guide;
   And, when the word is given,
   Bid death's cold flood its waves divide,
   And land us safe in heaven.

660. *Not my will, but Thine.*

1 Author of good! to thee we turn:
   Thine ever-wakeful eye
   Alone can all our wants discern—
   Thy hand alone supply.

2 Oh, let thy love within us dwell,
   Thy fear our footsteps guide;

That love shall vainer loves expel,
   That fear all fears beside.

3 And since, by passion's force subdued,
   Too oft with stubborn will
   We blindly shun the latent good,
   And grasp the specious ill;—

4 Not what we wish, but what we want,
   Let mercy still supply;
   The good we ask not, Father, grant;
   The ill we ask, deny.

665. *Happiness in God only.*

1 In vain I trace creation o'er,
   In search of solid rest;
   The whole creation is too poor,
   Too mean, to make me blest.

2 Let earth and all her charms depart,
   Unworthy of the mind:
   In God alone this restless heart
   Enduring bliss can find.

3 Thy favor, Lord, is all I want;
   Here would my spirit rest:
   Oh, seal the rich, the boundless grant,
   And make me fully blest!

736. *Living by Faith on the Son of God.*

1 Blest Jesus, while in mortal flesh
   I hold my frail abode,
   Still would my spirit rest on thee,
   My Saviour, and my God!

2 On thy dear cross I fix my eyes,
   Then raise them to thy seat;
   Till love dissolves my inmost soul,
   At my Redeemer's feet.

3 Be dead, my heart! to worldly charms,
   Be dead to every sin;
   And tell the boldest foe without,
   That Jesus reigns within.

WINFIELD. 7s.

104. *Third Version of Psalm 117.*

1 All ye nations, praise the Lord!
    All ye lands, your voices raise;
Heaven and earth, with loud accord,
    Praise the Lord—for ever praise!

2 For his truth and mercy stand,
    Past, and present, and to be,
Like the years of his right hand,
    Like his own eternity.

105. *Brief call to praise, from Psalm 150.*

1 Praise, oh, praise the Name divine!
    Praise him at the hallowed shrine;
Let the firmament on high
    To its Maker's praise reply.

2 All who vital breath enjoy,
    In his praise that breath employ;
Heaven and earth the chorus join;
    Praise, oh, praise the Name divine!

537. *"Now is the day of salvation."*

1 Haste, O sinner! now be wise;
    Stay not for the morrow's sun;
Wisdom if you still despise,
    Harder is it to be won.

2 Haste, and mercy now implore;
    Stay not for the morrow's sun,
Lest thy season should be o'er
    Ere the morrow is begun.

3 Haste, O sinner! now return;
    Stay not for the morrow's sun,
Lest thy lamp should cease to burn
    Ere salvation's work is done.

4 Lord! do thou the sinner turn—
    Turn him from his fearful state;
Let him not thy counsel spurn,
    Nor lament his choice too late!

709. *The Test.—John 21 : 16.*

1 Hark, my soul! it is the Lord;
    'T is thy Saviour; hear his word;
Jesus speaks, and speaks to thee:
    "Say, poor sinner, lov'st thou me?"

2 "Mine is an unchanging love,
    Higher than the heights above,
Deeper than the depths beneath,
    Free and faithful, strong as death.

3 "Thou shalt see my glory soon,
    When the work of grace is done;
Partner of my throne shalt be:
    Say, poor sinner, lovest thou me?"

4 Lord! it is my chief complaint
    That my love is cold and faint;
Yet I love thee, and adore:
    Oh for grace to love thee more!

833. *"For to me to live is Christ." Phil. 1 : 21.*

1 Christ, of all my hopes the Ground,
    Christ, the Spring of all my joy,
Still in thee let me be found,
    Still for thee my powers employ.

2 Fountain of o'erflowing grace,
    Freely from thy fullness give;
Till I close my earthly race,
    Be it "Christ for me to live."

3 When I touch the blessèd shore,
    Back the closing waves shall roll;
Death's dark stream shall never more
    Part from thee my ravished soul.

4 Thus, oh, thus an entrance give
    To the land of cloudless sky!
Having known it "Christ to live,"
    Let me know it "gain to die."

NUREMBURG. 7s.

922. *"Who shall dwell in thy holy hill?"*
Psalm 15.

1 Who, O Lord, when life is o'er,
 Shall to heaven's blest mansions soar?
 Who, an ever-welcome guest,
 In thy holy place shall rest?

2 He whose heart thy love has warmed;
 He whose will to thine conformed,
 Bids **his life** unsullied run;
 He whose words and thoughts are one;—

3 He who shuns the **sinner's** road,
 Loving those who love their God:
 Who, with hope and faith unfeigned,
 Treads the path by thee ordained;—

4 He who trusts in Christ alone,
 Not in aught himself hath done;
 He, great God, shall be thy care,
 And thy choicest blessings share.

1264. *"Happy are the faithful dead."*

1 Hark! a voice divides the sky!
 Happy are the faithful dead
 In the Lord who sweetly die!
 They from all their toils are freed.

2 Ready for their glorious crown,
 Sorrows past and sins forgiven,—
 Here they lay their burden down,
 Hallowed and made meet for heaven.

3 Yes! the Christian's course is **run**!
 Ended is the glorious strife;
 Fought the fight, the work is done;
 Death is swallowed up in life!

4 Lo! the prisoner **is released**—
 Lightened of his **heavy load**!
 Where the weary **are at rest**,
 He is gathered **unto God**!

5 When from flesh the spirit freed,
 Hastens homeward to return,
 Mortals cry, "A man is dead!"
 Angels sing, "A child is born!"

ALBON. 7s.

SCOTLAND. 12s.

Hal-le-lu-jah to the Lamb, who hath bought us a par-don! We'll praise him a-gain, when we pass o-ver Jor-dan, We'll praise him a-gain, when we pass o-ver Jor-dan.

521. *"The voice of free Grace."*—Gen. 19: 17.

1 THE voice of free grace cries, "Escape to the mountain,"
For Adam's lost race Christ hath opened a fountain;
For sin and uncleanness, and every transgression,
His blood flows most freely in streams of salvation.
    Hallelujah to the Lamb, who hath bought us a pardon!
    We'll praise him again, when we pass over Jordan.

2 Ye souls that are wounded, oh, flee to the Saviour:
He calls you in mercy—'t is infinite favor;
Your sins are increasing; escape to the mountain:
His blood can remove them, it flows from the fountain.
    Hallelujah to the Lamb, who hath bought us a pardon!
    We'll praise him again, when we pass over Jordan.

3 When Zion we see, having gained the blest shore,
With harps in our hands, we will praise him the more;
We'll range the sweet plains on the banks of the river,
And sing of salvation for ever and ever!
    Hallelujah to the Lamb, who hath bought us a pardon!
    We'll praise him again, when we pass over Jordan.

1109. *"Lord, save us: we perish."*—Matt. 8: 25.

1 WHEN through the torn sail the wild tempest is streaming,
  When o'er the dark wave the red lightning is gleaming,
[For the remaining stanzas see next page.

Nor hope lends a ray, the poor seaman to cherish,
We fly to our Maker: help, Lord, or we perish!

2 O Jesus, once tossed on the breast of the billow,
Aroused by the shriek of despair from thy pillow,
Now seated in glory, the mariner cherish,
Who cries in his danger, "Help, Lord, or we perish!"

3 And, oh! when the whirlwind of passion is raging,
When hell in our hearts its wild warfare is waging,
Arise in thy strength, thy redeeméd to cherish!
Rebuke the destroyer,—help, Lord, or we perish!

1218.* "We will not deplore thee."

1 Thou art gone to the grave! but we will not deplore thee
Though sorrows and darkness encompass the tomb;
The Saviour hath passed through its portals before thee,
And the lamp of his love is thy guide through the gloom.

2 Thou art gone to the grave! we no longer behold thee,
Nor tread the rough paths of the world by thy side;
But the wide arms of mercy are spread to enfold thee,
And sinners may hope, for the Sinless hath died.

3 Thou art gone to the grave! and, its mansions forsaking,
Perchance thy weak spirit in doubt lingered long.
But the sunshine of glory beamed bright on thy waking,
And full on thine ear burst the seraphim's song.

4 Thou art gone to the grave! but we will not deplore thee,
Since God was thy Ransom, thy Guardian, and Guide;
He gave thee, he took thee, and he will restore thee;
And death has no sting, for the Saviour hath died.

* Sing the small note only (half note) in the last measure.

COME, YE DISCONSOLATE. 11s & 10s.

952. "Come, ye disconsolate."

1 Come, ye disconsolate! where'er you languish,
Come to the mercy-seat, fervently kneel:
Here bring your wounded hearts, here tell your anguish;
Earth has no sorrow that heaven can not heal.

2 Joy of the desolate, Light of the straying,
Hope of the penitent; fadeless and pure;—
Here speaks the Comforter, tenderly saying,
Earth has no sorrow that heaven can not cure.

BUTLER. C. M. Double.

685. *Gratitude to Christ.*

1 I love thee, O my God, but not
  For what I hope thereby;
  Nor yet because who love thee not,
  Must die eternally:
  I love thee, O my God, and still
  I ever will love thee,
  Solely because my God thou art
  Who first hast loved me.

2 For me, to lowest depths of woe
  Thou didst thyself abase;
  For me didst bear the cross, the shame,
  And manifold disgrace;
  For me didst suffer pains unknown,
  Blood-sweat and agony,
  Yea, death itself—all, all for me,
  For me, thine enemy.

3 Then shall I not, O Saviour mine!
  Shall I not love thee well?
  Not with the hope of winning heaven,
  Nor of escaping hell;
  Not with the hope of earning aught,
  Nor seeking a reward,
  But freely, fully, as thyself
  Hast loved me, O Lord!

747. *"Of whom I am chief."*

1 I see the crowd in Pilate's hall,
  I mark their wrathful mien;
  Their shouts of "crucify" appall,
  With blasphemy between.

2 And of that shouting multitude
  I feel that I am one;
  And in that din of voices rude,
  I recognize my own.

3 I see the scourges tear his back,
  I see the piercing crown,

  And of that crowd who smite and mock,
  I feel that I am one.

4 Around yon cross, the throng I see,
  Mocking the sufferer's groan;
  Yet still my voice it seems to be,
  As if I mocked alone.

5 'T was I that shed the sacred blood;
  I nailed him to the tree;
  I crucified the Christ of God,
  I joined the mockery!

6 Yet not the less that blood avails
  To cleanse away my sin!
  And not the less that cross prevails
  To give me peace within!

763. *"Casting all your care upon Him."*

1 Lord, it belongs not to my care
  Whether I die or live;
  To love and serve thee is my share,
  And this thy grace must give.

2 If life be long, I will be glad
  That I may long obey;
  If short, yet why should I be sad
  To soar to endless day?

3 Christ leads me through no darker rooms
  Than he went through before;
  No one into his kingdom comes,
  But through his opened door.

4 Come, Lord, when grace has made me meet
  Thy blessed face to see;
  For if thy work on earth be sweet,
  What will thy glory be!

5 Then shall I end my sad complaints,
  And weary, sinful days,
  And join with all triumphant saints
  Who sing Jehovah's praise.

ARLINGTON. C. M.

6 My knowledge of that life is small;
  The eye of faith is dim;
But 't is enough that Christ knows all,
  And I shall be with him.

794. "*I am the Vine, ye are the branches.*"

1 PLANTED in Christ, the living vine,
    This day, with one accord,
  Ourselves, with humble faith and joy,
    We yield to thee, O Lord!

2 Joined in one body may we be:
    One inward life partake;
  One be our heart, one heavenly hope
    In every bosom wake.

3 In prayer, in effort, tears, and toils,
    One wisdom be our guide;
  Taught by one Spirit from above,
    In thee may we abide.

4 Then, when among the saints in light
    Our joyful spirits shine,
  Shall anthems of immortal praise,
    O Lamb of God, be thine!

795. *Union with Christ in Sorrow.*

1 WHO, when beneath affliction's rod,
    Can inward rest attain,
  And bless the chastening love of God
    In some remembered strain?

2 Who, when in pain he lies apart,
    And powers of life decay,
  Can muse with holy joy of heart
    On some familiar lay?

3 He can suffice for these good things
    Whose mind with Christ's is one;
  Who closely in communion clings
    To God's incarnate Son.

4 O Saviour! Fount of wondrous might!
    Let me this gift receive;

Thus, Lord, in sorrow's darkest night
  Thy servant's grief relieve.

5 Let songs of Zion, known of old
    Within the hallowed place,
  My spirit cheer, my faith uphold
    Through thine all-strengthening grace.

800. "*I suffer; nevertheless, I am not ashamed.*"

1 DIDST thou, dear Jesus, suffer shame,
    And bear the cross for me?
  And shall I fear to own thy name,
    Or thy disciple be?

2 Inspire my soul with life divine,
    And make me truly bold;
  Let knowledge, faith, and meekness shine,
    Nor love, nor zeal grow cold.

3 Let mockers scoff, the world defame,
    And treat me with disdain;
  Still may I glory in thy name,
    And count reproach my gain.

4 To thee I cheerfully submit,
    And all my powers resign;
  Let wisdom point out what is fit,
    And I'll no more repine.

943. "*Whom the Lord loveth He chasteneth.*"

1 O THOU whose mercy guides my way,
    Though now it seem severe,
  Forbid my unbelief to say
    There is no mercy here!

2 Oh! may I, Lord, desire the pain
    That comes in kindness down,
  Far more than sweetest earthly gain,
    Succeeded by a frown.

3 Then though thou bend my spirit low,
    Love only shall I see;
  The gracious hand that strikes the blow,
    Was wounded once for me.

URMUND. 8s & 4.

895. *"Our God will fight for us."*

1 Hark! how the gospel trumpet sounds!
Through all the earth the echo bounds!
And Jesus, by redeeming blood,
Is bringing sinners back to God,
And guides them safely by his word
    To endless day.

2 Hail, Jesus! all victorious Lord!
Be thou by all mankind adored!
For us didst thou the fight maintain,
And o'er our foes the vict'ry gain,
That we with thee might ever reign
    In endless day.

3 Fight on, ye conqu'ring souls, fight on!
And when the conquest you have won,
Then palms of vict'ry you shall bear,
And in his kingdom have a share,
And crowns of glory ever wear
    In endless day.

4 There in full chorus shall we join,
With saints and angels all combine
To sing of his redeeming love,
When rolling years shall cease to move;
And this shall be our theme above,
    In endless day.

EFFIELD. 8s & 4s.

466. *The Coming and Office of the Holy Spirit.*—John 16 : 7, 8.

1 Our blest Redeemer, ere he breathed
    His last farewell,
A Guide, a Comforter bequeathed,
    With us to dwell.

2 He came in tongues of living flame
    To teach, subdue;
All-powerful as the wind he came,
    As viewless, too.

3 He comes, his graces to impart,
    A willing guest,
While he can find one humble heart
    Wherein to rest.

4 He breathes that gentle voice we hear,
    As breeze of even;
That checks each fault, that calms each [fear,
    And speaks of heaven.

[For 5th and 6th stanzas see next page.]

WALES. 8s & 4s.

973. *"It is well."*—2 Kings 4 : 26.

1 Through the love of God our Saviour,
　　All will be well:
Free and changeless in his favor;
　　All, all is well:
Precious is the blood that healed us;
Perfect is the grace that sealed us;
Strong the hand stretched out to shield us;
　　All must be well.

2 Though we pass through tribulation,
　　All will be well;
Ours is such a full salvation;
　　All, all is well:
Happy, still in God confiding,
Fruitful, if in Christ abiding,
Holy, through the Spirit's guiding,
　　All must be well.

3 We expect a bright to-morrow;
　　All will be well:
Faith can sing through days of sorrow,
　　All, all is well:

On our Father's love relying,
Jesus every need supplying,
Or in living, or in dying,
　　All must be well.

1175. *"Weep not for me."*

1 When the spark of life is waning,
　　Weep not for me;
When the languid eye is straining,
　　Weep not for me;
When the feeble pulse is ceasing,
Start not at its swift decreasing;
'T is the fettered soul's releasing;
　　Weep not for me.

2 When the pangs of death assail me,
　　Weep not for me;
Christ is mine—he can not fail me;
　　Weep not for me;
Yes, though sin and doubt endeavor
From his love my soul to sever,
Jesus is my strength for ever;
　　Weep not for me.

5 And all the good that we possess,
　　His gift we own;
Yea, every thought of holiness,
　　And victory won.

6 Spirit of purity and grace:
　　Our weakness see;
Oh, make our hearts thy dwelling-place,
　　And worthier thee!

MAITLAND. C. M.

801. *The Cross and the Crown.*

1 MUST Jesus bear the cross alone,
   And all the world go free?
No: there's a cross for every one,
   And there's a cross for me.

2 How happy are the saints above
   Who once went sorrowing here;
But now they taste unmingled love,
   And joy without a tear.

3 The consecrated cross I'll bear,
   Till death shall set me free,
And then go home my crown to wear—
   For there's a crown for me!

805. *Imitation of Christ in Self-denial.*

1 WE tread the path our Master trod;
   We bear the cross he bore;
And every thorn that wounds our feet
   His temples pierced before.

2 Oft do our eyes with joy o'erflow,
   And oft are bathed in tears;
Yet naught but heaven our hopes can raise,
   And naught but sin our fears.

3 We purge our mortal dross away,
   Refining as we run;
And while we die to earth and sense,
   Our heaven is here begun.

859. *"Love as brethren."*

1 How sweet, how heavenly is the sight,
   When those who love the Lord
In one another's peace delight,
   And so fulfill his word!

2 When each can feel his brother's sigh,
   And with him bear a part!
When sorrow flows from eye to eye,
   And joy from heart to heart!

3 When, free from envy, scorn, and pride
   Our wishes all above,
Each can his brother's failings hide,
   And show a brother's love!

4 Let love, in one delightful stream,
   Through every bosom flow,
And union sweet, and dear esteem,
   In every action glow.

5 Love is the golden chain that binds
   The happy souls above;
And he's an heir of heaven who finds
   His bosom glow with love.

903. *"The Cross before the Crown."*

1 ON, speed thee, Christian! on thy way,
   And to thine armor cling;
With girded loins the call obey
   Which grace and mercy bring.

2 There is a battle to be fought,
   An upward race to run,
A crown of glory to be sought,
   A victory to be won.

3 Oh, faint not, Christian! for thy sighs
   Are heard before the throne;
The race must come before the prize,
   The cross before the crown.

979. *"Salvation will God appoint for walls and bulwarks."*

1 ARISE, my soul! my joyful powers,
   And triumph in my God;
Awake, my voice! and loud proclaim
   His glorious grace abroad.

2 The arms of everlasting love
   Beneath my soul be placed,
And on the Rock of Ages set
   My slippery footsteps fast.

BROWN. C. M.

3 The city of my blest abode
  Is walled around with grace;
  Salvation for a bulwark stands,
  To shield the sacred place.

4 Arise, my soul! awake, my voice!
  And tunes of pleasure sing;
  Loud hallelujahs shall address
  My Saviour and my King.

1078. *A Child's Gratitude for Christian Birth.*

1 I THANK the goodness and the grace
  That on my birth have smiled,
  And made me, in these latter days,
  A happy, Christian child.

2 I was not born, as thousands are,
  Where God is never known,
  And taught to say a useless prayer
  To gods of wood and stone.

3 I was not born a little slave,
  To labor in the sun,
  And wish I were but in my grave,
  And all my labor done.

4 My God, I thank thee, who hast planned
  A better lot for me,
  And placed me in this happy land,
  Where I may hear of thee.

1079. *The ransomed Band.*

1 O HAPPY land! O happy land!
  Where saints and angels dwell;
  We long to join that glorious band,
  And all their anthems swell.

2 But every voice in yonder throng
  On earth has breathed a prayer;
  No lips untaught may join that song,
  Or learn the music there.

3 Thou heavenly Friend! thou heavenly Friend!
  Oh, hear us when we pray!
  Now let thy pardoning grace descend,
  And take our sins away.

4 Be all our fresh, our youthful days
  To thy blest service given;
  Then we shall meet to sing thy praise,
  A ransomed band in heaven.

1088. *"Of such is the kingdom of heaven."*

1 AROUND the throne of God in heaven
  Thousands of children stand—
  Children, whose sins are all forgiven,
  A holy, happy band.

2 What brought them to that world above,
  That heaven so bright and fair,
  Where all is peace, and joy, and love?
  How came those children there?

3 Because the Saviour shed his blood
  To wash away their sin;
  Bathed in that pure and precious flood,
  Behold them white and clean.

4 On earth they sought their Saviour's grace,
  On earth they loved his name:
  So now they see his blessed face,
  And stand before the Lamb.

1153. *"The little hills rejoice on every side."*

1 WHEN brighter suns and milder skies
  Proclaim the opening year,
  What various sounds of joy arise!
  What prospects bright appear!

2 Earth and her thousand voices give
  Their thousand notes of praise;
  And all, that by his mercy live,
  To God their offering raise.

3 Thus, like the morning, calm and clear
  That saw the Saviour rise,
  The spring of heaven's eternal year
  Shall dawn on earth and skies.

4 No winter there, no shades of night,
  Obscure those mansions blest,
  Where, in the happy fields of light,
  The weary are at rest.

BONAR. S. M. DOUBLE.

217. *"The Lord is my Shepherd."*
Psalm 23.

1 THE Lord my Shepherd is :
    I shall be well supplied :
  Since he is mine, and I am his,
    What can I want beside?
2 He leads me to the place
    Where heavenly pasture grows ;
  Where living waters gently pass,
    And full salvation flows.

3 If e'er I go astray,
    He doth my soul reclaim :
  And guides me, in his own right way
    For his most holy name.
4 While he affords his aid,
    I can not yield to fear ;
  Though I should walk through death's
      dark shade,
    My Shepherd's with me there.

5 In spite of all my foes,
    Thou dost my table spread ;
  My cup with blessings overflows,
    And joy exalts my head.
6 The bounties of thy love
    Shall crown my future days ;
  Nor from thy house will I remove,
    Nor cease to speak thy praise.

444. *Christ is All.*

1 O EVERLASTING Light !
    Shine graciously within ;
  Brightest of all on earth that's bright,
    Come, shine away my sin !
2 O everlasting Truth !
    Truest of all that's true,
  Sure guide of erring age or youth,
    Lead me and teach me, too.

3 O everlasting Strength !
    Uphold me in the way ;
  Bring me, in spite of foes, at length,
    To joy, and light, and day.
4 O everlasting Love ;
    Well-spring of grace and peace,
  Pour down thy fullness from above ;
    Bid doubt and trouble cease.

5 O everlasting Rest !
    Lift off life's load of care ;
  Relieve, revive this burdened breast,
    And every sorrow bear.
6 Thou art in heaven our all ;
    Our all on earth art thou :
  Upon thy glorious name we call ;
    Lord Jesus bless us now !

675. *"Commit thy way unto the Lord."*
Psalm 37.

1 COMMIT thou all thy griefs
    And ways into his hands ;
  To his sure truth and tender care,
    Who earth and heaven commands—

2 Who points the clouds their course,
    Whom winds and seas obey ;
  He shall direct thy wandering feet,
    He shall prepare thy way.

3 On God alone rely ;
    Then safe shalt thou go on :
  Fix on his work thy steadfast eye ;
    Then shall thy work be done.

4 When he makes bare his arm,
    What shall his aim withstand ?
  When he will save his friends from harm,
    Who, who shall stay his hand ?

5 He hears thy softest prayer,
    He girdeth thee with might ;
  His works the purest blessings are,
    His ways, the purest light.

ST. MICHAEL. S. M.

676. *"Wait thou His time."*—Psalm 30.

1 GIVE to the winds thy fears;
   Hope on, be not dismayed:
God hears thy sighs and counts thy tears;
   God shall lift up thy head.

2 Through waves, and clouds and storms,
   He gently clears thy way;
Wait thou his time: the darkest night
   Shall end in brightest day.

3 Far, far above thy thought
   His counsel shall appear,
When fully he the work hath wrought,
   That caused thy needless fear.

4 What though thou rulest not!
   Yet heaven and earth and hell
Proclaim—God sitteth on the throne,
   And ruleth all things well.

753. *"There is laid up for me a crown."*

1 IF Jesus be my friend,
   And I to him belong,
I care not what my foes intend,
   Though fierce they be, and strong.

2 I rest upon the ground
   Of Jesus and his blood;
For I in him alone have found
   The true, eternal good.

3 He whispers in my breast
   Sweet words of holy cheer,
How all who seek in God their rest
   Shall ever find him near;

4 How God hath built above
   A city fair and new
Where eye and heart shall see and prove
   What faith has counted true.

5 My heart for gladness springs;
   It can not more be sad;

For very joy it smiles and sings,—
   Sees naught but sunshine glad.
6 The sun that lights mine eyes,
   Is Christ, the Lord I love;
I sing for joy of that which lies
   Stored up for me above.

769. *Perfect Peace in Christ.*
Isaiah 26: 3.

1 THOU very present aid
   In suffering and distress,
The soul which still on thee is stayed,
   Is kept in perfect peace.

2 The soul, by faith reclined
   On the Redeemer's breast,
'Mid raging storms exults to find
   An everlasting rest.

3 Sorrow and fear are gone
   Whene'er thy face appears:
It stills the sighing orphan's moan,
   And dries the widow's tears:

4 It hallows every cross;
   It sweetly comforts me;
Makes me forget my every loss,
   And find my all in thee.

5 Jesus, to whom I fly,
   Doth all my wishes fill:
What though created streams are dry,
   I have the fountain still.

6 Stripped of my earthly friends,
   I find them all in One;
And peace and joy that never ends,
   And heaven in Christ begun.

DOXOLOGY.

THE Father and the Son
   And Spirit we adore;
We praise, we bless, we worship thee,
   Both now and evermore!

HORTON. 7s.

534. *Look to Christ.*

1 Weary sinner! keep thine eyes
On the atoning Sacrifice;
View him bleeding on the tree,
Pouring out his life for thee.

2 Surely Christ thy griefs hath borne;
Weeping soul, no longer mourn:
Now by faith the Son embrace,
Plead his promise, trust his grace.

3 Cast thy guilty soul on him;
Find him mighty to redeem:
At his feet thy burden lay;
Look thy doubts and care away.

4 Lord, come thou with power to heal;
Now thy mighty arm reveal:
At thy feet myself I lay;
Take, oh, take my sins away!

941. *"Have mercy upon me, O Lord; for I am weak."*—Psalm 6.

1 Gently, gently lay thy rod
On my sinful head, O God!
Stay thy wrath—in mercy stay,
Lest I sink before its sway!

2 Heal me, for my flesh is weak;
Heal me, for thy grace I seek:
This, my only plea, I make,
Heal me for thy mercy's sake!

3 Who within the silent grave
Shall proclaim thy power to save?
Lord, my trembling soul reprieve;
Speak! and I shall rise and live.

4 Lo! he comes; he heeds my plea;
Lo! he comes; the shadows flee;
Glory round me dawns once more,—
Rise, my spirit, and adore!

994. *"Glorify thyself in me."*

1 Father of eternal grace,
Glorify thyself in me;
Meekly beaming in my face,
May the world thine image see.

2 Happy only in thy love,
Poor, unfriended, or unknown,
Fix my thoughts on things above,
Stay my heart on thee alone.

3 Humble, holy, all resigned
To thy will—thy will be done!
Give me, Lord, the perfect mind
Of thy well-beloved Son.

4 Counting gain and glory loss,
May I tread the path he trod—
Die with Jesus on the cross,
Rise with him to thee, my God.

1007. *"By grace are ye saved, through faith."*

1 Joyful be the hours to-day;
Joyful let the season be;
Let us sing, for well we may;
Jesus! we will sing of thee.

2 Should thy people silent be,
Then the very stones would sing;
What a debt we owe to thee,
Thee, our Saviour, thee our King!

3 Joyful are we now to own,
Rapture thrills us as we trace
All the deeds thy love hath done,
All the riches of thy grace.

4 'Tis thy grace alone can save;
Every blessing comes from thee—
All we have and hope to have,
All we are and hope to be.

5 Thine the Name to sinners dear!
Thine the Name all names before;
Blessèd here and everywhere;
Blessèd now and evermore!

ELDEN. 7s. 6 LINES.

290. *Our Example in Suffering.*

1 Go to dark Gethsemane,
  Ye that feel the tempter's power;
Your Redeemer's conflict see,
  Watch with him one bitter hour:
Turn not from his griefs away,
Learn of Jesus Christ to pray.

2 Follow to the judgment hall,
  View the Lord of life arraigned;
Oh the wormwood and the gall!
  Oh the pang his soul sustain'd!
Shun not suffering, shame, or loss;
Learn of him to bear the cross.

3 Calv'ry's mournful mountain climb;
  There, adoring at his feet,
Mark that miracle of time,
  God's own sacrifice complete:
"It is finished," hear him cry;
Learn of Jesus Christ to die.

4 Early hasten to the tomb
  Where they laid his breathless clay;
All is solitude and gloom;—
  Who hath taken him away?
Christ is risen! he meets our eyes;
Saviour, teach us so to rise.

291. *Gethsemane.*—Luke 22 : 39–44.

1 Many woes had Christ endured,
  Many sore temptations met,
Patient and to pains inured;
  But the sorest trial yet
Was to be sustained in thee,
Gloomy, sad Gethsemane!

2 Came at length the dreadful night;
  Vengeance, with its iron rod,
Stood, and with collected might,
  Bruised the harmless Lamb of God:
See, my soul, thy Saviour see
Prostrate in Gethsemane!

3 There my God bore all my guilt:
  This, through grace, can be believed;
But the horrors which he felt
  Are too vast to be conceived:
None can penetrate through thee,
Doleful, dark Gethsemane!

4 Sins against a holy God,
  Sins against his righteous laws,
Sins against his love, his blood,
  Sins against his name and cause—
Sins immense as is the sea!
Hide me, O Gethsemane!

5 Here's my claim, and here alone:
  None a Saviour more can need;
Deeds of righteousness I've none;
  No; not one good work to plead:
Not a glimpse of hope for me,
Only in Gethsemane.

6 Father, Son, and Holy Ghost,
  One almighty God of love,
Hymned by all the heavenly host,
  In thy shining courts above!
We adore thee, gracious Three—
Bless thee for Gethsemane.

NILO L. M.

541. *"Behold, I stand at the door, and knock."*—Rev. 3 : 20.

1 Behold a Stranger at the door:
He gently knocks, has knocked before;
Has waited long, is waiting still:
You treat no other friend so ill.

2 Oh, lovely attitude! he stands
With melting heart and open hands:
Oh, matchless kindness!—and he shows
This matchless kindness to his foes!

3 Rise, touched with gratitude divine,
Turn out his enemy and thine;
Turn out thy soul-enslaving sin,
And let the heavenly Stranger in.

4 Oh, welcome him, the Prince of Peace!
Now may his gentle reign increase!
Throw wide the door, each willing mind;
And be his empire all mankind.

544. *An Evening Expostulation.*

1 On, do not let the word depart,
And close thine eyes against the light;
Poor sinner, harden not thy heart:
Thou wouldst be saved; why not to-night?

2 To-morrow's sun may never rise
To bless thy long deluded sight;
This is the time; oh, then be wise!
Thou wouldst be saved; why not to-night?

3 Our God in pity lingers still;
And wilt thou thus his love requite?
Renounce at length thy stubborn will;
Thou wouldst be saved; why not to-night?

4 Our blessed Lord refuses none
Who would to him their souls unite;
Then be the work of grace begun:
Thou wouldst be saved; why not to-night?

832. *"Lord, what wilt Thou have me to do?"*

1 My gracious Lord, I own thy right
To every service I can pay,
And call it my supreme delight
To hear thy dictates and obey.

2 What is my being, but for thee,
Its sure support, its noblest end?
Thine ever smiling face to see,
And serve the cause of such a Friend.

3 I would not breathe for worldly joy,
Or to increase my worldly good;
Nor future days nor powers employ
To spread a sounding name abroad.

4 'Tis to my Saviour I would live,
To him who for my ransom died;
Nor could the bowers of Eden give
Such bliss as blossoms at his side.

5 His work my hoary age shall bless,
When youthful vigor is no more;
And my last hour of life confess
His dying love, his saving power.

837. *Joy of Consecration to Christ.*

1 On, sweetly breathe the lyres above,
When angels touch the quivering string,
And wake, to chant Immanuel's love,
Such strains as angel-lips can sing!

2 And sweet, on earth, the choral swell,
From mortal tongues, of gladsome lays;
When pardoned souls their raptures tell,
And, grateful, hymn Immanuel's praise.

3 Jesus, thy name our souls adore;
We own the bond that makes us thine;
And carnal joys, that charmed before,
For thy dear sake we now resign.

4 Our hearts, by dying love subdued,
Accept thine offered grace to-day;
Beneath the cross, with blood bedewed,
We bow and give ourselves away.

5 In thee we trust—on thee rely;
Though we are feeble, thou art strong;
Oh, keep us till our spirits fly
To join the bright, immortal throng!

WARD. L. M.

614. *The Joy unknown in Heaven.*

1 TREMBLING, before thine awful throne,
O Lord, in dust my sins I own.
Justice and mercy for my life
Contend: oh, smile, and heal the strife!

2 The Saviour smiles—upon my soul
New tides of hope tumultuous roll!
His voice proclaims my pardon found;
Seraphic transport wings the sound!

3 Earth has a joy unknown in heaven—
The new-born peace of sins forgiven:
Tears of such pure and deep delight,
Ye angels! never dimmed your sight.

4 Ye know where morn exulting springs,
And evening folds her drooping wings;
Loud is your song: the heavenly plain
Is shaken by your choral strain.

5 But I amid your choir shall shine,
And all your knowledge will be mine;
Ye on your harps must learn to hear
A secret chord which mine will bear!

646. *Blessedness of Love to God.*

1 AH, happy hours! whene'er upsprings
My soul to yon eternal Source,
Whence the glad river downward sings,
Watering with goodness all my course.

2 Can I, with loveless heart, receive
Tokens of love that never cease?
Can I be thankless, Lord, and grieve
Thee, who art all my joy and peace?

3 Forth from thy rich and bounteous store
Life's common blessings daily flow;
More than I dare to ask, far more
Than I deserve, dost thou bestow.

4 Nor here alone; hope pierces far
Through all the shades of earth and time;
Faith mounts beyond the farthest star;
Yon shining heights she fain would climb.

5 Our faith shall rise to sight e'er long;
Soon will that hour of transport come,
When we shall join the angels' song
Of praise to him who brought us home.

1065. *"Oh, happy day, that fixed my choice."*

1 OH, happy day, that fixed my choice
On thee, my Saviour, and my God!
Well may this glowing heart rejoice,
And tell its raptures all abroad.

2 Oh, happy bond, that seals my vows
To him who merits all my love!
Let cheerful anthems fill his house,
While to that sacred shrine I move.

3 'T is done, the great transaction's done;
I am my Lord's, and he is mine;
He drew me, and I followed on,
Charmed to confess the voice divine.

4 Now, rest, my long-divided heart!
Fixed on this blissful center, rest;
With ashes who would grudge to part,
When called on angels' bread to feast.

5 High Heaven, that heard the solemn vow,
That vow renewed shall daily hear;
Till in life's latest hour I bow,
And bless in death a bond so dear.

DOXOLOGY.

PRAISE God, from whom all blessings flow!
Praise him, all creatures here below!
Praise him above, ye heavenly host!
Praise Father, Son, and Holy Ghost!

WILMOT. 7s.

108. *"Let every thing that hath breath praise the Lord."*—Psalm 150.

1 Praise the Lord, his glories show,
Saints within his courts below,
Angels round his throne above,
All that see and share his love!

2 Earth to heaven, and heaven to earth,
Tell his wonders, sing his worth;
Age to age, and shore to shore,
Praise him, praise him, evermore!

3 Praise the Lord, his mercies trace;
Praise his providence and grace—
All that he for man hath done,
All he sends us through his Son.

4 Strings and voices, hands and hearts,
In the concert bear your parts:
All that breathe, your Lord adore;
Praise him, praise him, evermore!

353. *An ancient Hymn of the Resurrection.*

1 Jesus Christ is risen to-day—
Our triumphant holy day—
Who did once, upon the cross,
Suffer to redeem our loss.

2 Hymns of praise then let us sing
Unto Christ, our heavenly King;
Who endured the cross and grave,
Sinners to redeem and save.

3 But the pain which he endured
Our salvation hath procured;
Honor, then, to him, and praise,
Rising on this Day of days!

360. *Morning at the Tomb.*

1 Mourning breaks upon the tomb,
Jesus scatters all its gloom:
Day of triumph through the skies!
See the glorious Saviour rise!

2 Christian! dry your flowing tears;
Chase those unbelieving fears;
Look on his deserted grave;
Doubt no more his power to save.

3 Ye, who are of death afraid,
Triumph in the scattered shade;
Drive your anxious cares away:
See the place where Jesus lay!

4 Lo! the rising sun appears,
Shedding radiance o'er the spheres;
Lo, returning beams of light
Chase the terrors of the night.

380. *A victorious Saviour.*—Rev. 1: 18.

1 Crowns of glory ever bright,
Rest upon the Conqueror's head,
Crowns of glory are his right,—
His, "who liveth and was dead."

2 He subdued the powers of hell;
In the fight he stood alone:
All his foes before him fell,
By his single arm o'erthrown.

3 His the battle, his the toil;
His the honors of the day,
His the glory and the spoil:
Jesus bears them all away.

4 Now proclaim his deeds afar;
Fill the world with his renown:
His alone the victor's car;
His the everlasting crown!

382. *"The King of Zion."*

1 Sons of Zion, raise your songs!
Praise to Zion's King belongs;
His the victor's crown and fame;
Glory to the Saviour's name!

ELTHAM. 7s. DOUBLE.

2 Sore the strife, but rich the prize,
Precious in the Victor's eyes:
Glorious is the work achieved,
Satan vanquished, man relieved!

3 Sing we then the Victor's praise;
Go ye forth and strew the ways;
Bid him welcome to his throne:
He is worthy, he alone!

4 Place the crown upon his brow;
Every knee to him shall bow;
Him the brightest seraph sings;
Heaven proclaims him " King of kings!"

415. *Support in Christ.*

1 EVERLASTING arms of love
Are beneath, around, above:
He who left his throne of light,
And unnumbered angels bright;

2 He who on th' accursèd tree
Gave his precious life for me—
He it is that bears me on,
His the arm **I** lean upon.

3 He who now, enthroned above,
Still retains his heart of love,
Marking still each falling tear
Of his burdened pilgrims here;

4 He who wields creation's rod,
He my Brother, yet my God;
Faithful he, whate'er betide,
Is my everlasting **Guide!**

5 All things hasten to **decay,**
Earth and seas will **pass away;**
Soon will yonder circling sun
Cease his blazing **course to run.**

6 Scenes will vary, friends grow strange,
But the Changeless can not change:
Gladly will I journey on,
With his arm to lean upon.

1130. *" The King of kings, and Lord of lords."*

1 WAKE the song of jubilee!
Let it echo o'er the sea:
Now is come the promised hour;
Jesus reigns with sovereign power.

2 All ye nations! join and sing,
" Christ, of lords and kings, is King!"
Let it sound from shore to shore,
" Jesus reigns for evermore!"

3 Now the desert lands rejoice,
And the islands join their voice:
Joy! the whole creation sings,
" Jesus is the King of kings!"

1143. *" Sing unto the Lord, who prepareth rain for the earth."*

1 PRAISE on thee, in Zion's gates,
Daily, O Jehovah, waits;
Unto thee, O God, belong
Grateful words and holy song.

2 Thou the hope and refuge **art**
Of remotest lands apart;
Distant isles and tribes unknown,
'Mid the ocean waste and lone.

3 Thou dost visit earth, and rain
Blessings **on the** thirsty plain,
From the copious founts on high,
From the rivers of the sky.

4 Thus the clouds thy power confess,
And thy paths drop fruitfulness,
And the voice of song and mirth
Rises from the tribes of earth!

MIGDOL. L. M.

193. *"Who is God, save the Lord?"*
Psalm 18.

1 Just are thy ways, and true thy word,
Great Rock of my secure abode;
Who is a God, beside the Lord?
Or where's a refuge like our God?

2 'T is he that girds me with his might,
Gives me his holy sword to wield;
And while with sin and hell I fight,
Spreads his salvation for my shield.

3 He lives, and blessèd be my Rock;
The God of my salvation lives;
The dark designs of hell he broke:
Sweet is the peace my Father gives.

348. *"I would for ever speak His name."*

1 Oh, the sweet wonders of that cross
Where my Redeemer loved and died!
Her noblest life my spirit draws
From his dear wounds and bleeding side.

2 I would for ever speak his name,
In sounds to mortal ears unknown;
With angels join to praise the Lamb,
And worship at his Father's throne.

453. *Prayer for the Teaching of the Spirit.*

1 Come, blessèd Spirit! Source of light,
Whose power and grace are unconfined,
Dispel the gloomy shades of night,
The thicker darkness of the mind.

2 To mine illumined eyes display
The glorious truths thy word reveals;
Cause me to run the heavenly way;
The book unfold, and loose the seals.

3 Thine inward teachings make me know
The mysteries of redeeming love,
The vanity of things below,
And excellence of things above.

4 While through this dubious maze I stray,
Spread, like the sun, thy beams abroad;
Oh, show the dangers of the way,
And guide my feeble steps to God.

582. *Longing for Freedom from Sin.*

1 Jesus demands this heart of mine,
Demands my love, my joy, my care;
But ah! how dead to things divine,
How cold my best affections are!

2 'T is sin, alas! with dreadful power,
Divides my Saviour from my sight;
Oh, for one happy, cloudless hour
Of sacred freedom, sweet delight!

3 Lord! let thy love shine forth and raise
My captive powers from sin and death,
And fill my heart with life and praise,
And tune my last expiring breath.

743. *"He died for all."*

1 The holy, meek, unspotted Lamb,
Who from the Father's bosom came,
Who died for me, e'en me t' atone,—
Now for my Lord and God I own.

2 Lord, I believe, thy precious blood,
Which, at the mercy-seat of God
For ever doth for sinners plead,
For me, in all my sins, was shed.

3 Lord, I believe were sinners more
Than sands upon the ocean shore,
Thou hast for all a ransom paid,
For all a full atonement made.

4 Thus Abraham, the friend of God,
Thus all heaven's armies, bought with blood,
Saviour of sinners thee proclaim,—
Sinners, the chief of whom I am.

HEBRON. L. M.

5 Jesus! be endless praise to thee,
  Whose boundless mercy hath for me,—
  For me, and all thy hands have made,
  An everlasting ransom paid.

3 Let thronging multitudes around
  Hear from their lips the joyful sound;
  And light thro' distant realms be spread,
  Till Zion rears her drooping head.

828. "*Give me Thyself—I ask no more.*"

1 My dearest Lord, whose changeless love
  To me, nor earth nor hell can part;
  When shall my feet forget to rove?
  Ah! what shall fix this faithless heart?

2 Why do these cares my soul divide,
  If thou indeed hast set me free?
  Why am I thus if thou hast died,
  If thou hast died to ransom me?

3 Great God! thy sovereign aid impart,
  And guard the gifts thyself hast given;
  My portion thou, my treasure art,
  And life, and happiness, and heaven.

4 Would aught with thee my wishes share,
  Though dear as life the idol be,
  That idol from my breast I'll tear,
  Resolved to seek my all from thee.

5 Whate'er I fondly counted mine,
  To thee, my Lord, I here restore;
  I gladly all for thee resign:
  Give me thyself,—I ask no more.

1059. "*Brethren, pray for us.*"

1 Father of mercies, bow thine ear,
  Attentive to our earnest prayer;
  We plead for those who plead for thee;
  Successful pleaders may they be.

2 Clothe thou with energy divine
  Their words, and let those words be thine;
  Teach them immortal souls to gain,
  Nor let them labor, Lord, in vain.

1064. *Welcome to a Pastor.*

1 We bid thee welcome in the name
  Of Jesus, our exalted Head;
  Come as a servant: so he came;
  And we receive thee in his stead.

2 Come as a shepherd; guard and keep
  This fold from hell, and earth, and sin;
  Nourish the lambs, and feed the sheep,
  The wounded heal, the lost bring in.

3 Come as a teacher, sent from God,
  Charged his whole counsel to declare;
  Lift o'er our ranks the prophet's rod,
  While we uphold thy hands with prayer.

4 Come as a messenger of peace,
  Filled with the Spirit, fired with love!
  Live to behold our large increase,
  And die to meet us all above.

1068. *Entering into Covenant with God.*

1 While to thy table I repair,
  And seal the sacred contract there,
  Witness, O Lord! my solemn vow:
  Angels and men! attest it, too.

2 Here at that cross, where flows the blood
  That bought my guilty soul for God,
  Thee, Lord and Master, now I call,
  I consecrate to thee my all.

3 Do thou assist a feeble worm
  The great engagement to perform;
  Thy grace can full assistance lend,
  And on that grace I dare depend.

BUTLER. C. M. DOUBLE.

509. *"Come—without money and without price."*—Isaiah 55: 1, 2.

1 YE wretched, hungry, starving poor,
    Behold a royal feast!
  Where mercy spreads her bounteous store
    For every humble guest.
2 See, Jesus stands with open arms;
    He calls, he bids you come;
  Guilt holds you back, and fear alarms;
    But see, there yet is room—

3 Room in the Saviour's bleeding heart:
    There love and pity meet.
  Nor will he bid the soul depart
    That trembles at his feet.
4 Oh, come, and with his children taste
    The blessings of his love;
  While hope attends the sweet repast
    Of nobler joys above.

5 There, with united heart and voice,
    Before th' eternal throne,
  Ten thousand thousand souls rejoice
    In ecstasies unknown.
6 And yet ten thousand thousand more
    Are welcome still to come;
  Ye longing souls, the grace adore;
    Approach, there yet is room.

565. *"I heard the voice of Jesus."*

1 I HEARD the voice of Jesus say,
    "Come unto me and rest;
  Lay down, thou weary one, lay down
    Thy head upon my breast:"
  I came to Jesus as I was,
    Weary, and worn, and sad;
  I found in him a resting-place
    And he has made me glad.

2 I heard the voice of Jesus say,
    "Behold, I freely give

The living water! thirsty one,
    Stoop down, and drink, and live."
  I came to Jesus, and I drank
    Of that life-giving stream;
  My thirst was quenched, my soul revived,
    And now I live in him.

3 I heard the voice of Jesus say,
    "I am this dark world's light:
  Look unto me; thy morn shall rise,
    And all thy day be bright."
  I looked to Jesus, and I found
    In him my Star, my Sun;
  And in that light of life I 'll walk
    Till all my journey's done.

717. *Mine—Thine.*—1 Cor. 15: 10.

1 ALL that I was, my sin, my guilt,
    My death, was all my own:
  All that I am I owe to thee,
    My gracious God, alone.

2 The evil of my former state
    Was mine, and only mine:
  The good in which I now rejoice
    Is thine, and only thine.

3 The darkness of my former state,
    The bondage—all was mine:
  The light of life in which I walk,
    The liberty—is thine.

4 Thy grace first made me feel my sin,
    And taught me to believe:
  Then, in believing, peace I found,
    And now, I live, I live!

5 All that I am ev'n here on earth,
    All that I hope to be
  When Jesus comes and glory dawns,—
    I owe it, Lord, to thee.

EVAN. C. M.

751. *"The glory which shall be revealed in us."*

1 My thoughts surmount these lower skies,
  And look within the vail;
  There springs of endless pleasures rise—
  The waters never fail.

2 There I behold, with sweet delight,
  The blessèd Three in One;
  And strong affections fix my sight
  On God's incarnate Son.

3 His promise stands **for ever firm**;
  His grace shall ne'er depart;
  He binds my name upon his arm,
  And seals it **on** his heart.

4 Light are the pains that nature brings:
  How short our sorrows are,
  When with eternal future things
  The present we compare!

5 I would not be a stranger still
  To that celestial place,
  Where I for ever hope to **dwell**
  Near **my** Redeemer's face.

875. *"Blessed are the merciful."*

1 BLEST is the man whose **softening heart**
  Feels all another's pain;
  To whom the supplicating eye
  Was never raised in vain :—

2 Whose breast expands with generous warmth,
  A stranger's woe to feel;
  And bleeds in pity o'er the wound
  He wants the power to heal.

3 He spreads his kind, supporting arms
  To every child of grief;
  His secret bounty largely flows,
  And brings unasked relief.

4 To gentle offices of love
  His feet are never slow;
  He views, through mercy's melting eye,
  A brother in a foe.

5 He hears the Saviour's cheering word,
  "My peace to him I give;"
  And when he kneels before the throne,
  His trembling soul shall live.

969. *"My meditation of Him shall be sweet."*

1 WHEN languor and disease invade
  This trembling house of clay,
  'T is sweet to look beyond my pain,
  And long to fly away;

2 Sweet to look inward, and attend
  The whispers of his love;
  Sweet to look upward to the place
  Where Jesus pleads above;

3 Sweet on his faithfulness to rest,
  Whose love can never end;
  Sweet on his covenant of grace
  For all things to depend;

4 Sweet, in the confidence of faith,
  To trust his firm decrees;
  Sweet to lie passive in his hands,
  And know no will but his.

5 If such the sweetness of the streams,
  What must the fountain be
  Where saints and angels draw their bliss
  Direct, O Lord, from thee?

DOXOLOGY.

To Father, Son, and Holy Ghost,
One God, whom we adore,
Be glory as it was, is now,
And shall be evermore!

NETTLETON. 8s & 7s. Double.

92. *"Peace I leave with you."*

1 PEACE be to this sacred dwelling,
  Peace to every soul therein;
Peace, of heavenly joy foretelling,
  Peace, the fruit of conquered sin;
Peace, that speaks its heavenly Giver;
  Peace to worldly minds unknown;
Peace divine, that flows for ever
  From its source, the Lord alone!

2 Prince of peace! for ever near us,
  Fix in all our hearts thy home;
With thy bright appearing cheer us;
  Let thy blessèd kingdom come!
Come, with sweeter consolation,
  Come, and give our souls to prove
All the joys of thy salvation,
  All the joys that spring from love!

101. *Brief Ascription of Praise.*

1 WORSHIP, honor, glory, blessing,
  Lord, we offer to thy name;
Young and old their thanks expressing,
  Join thy goodness to proclaim:
As the hosts of heaven adore thee,
  We, too, bow, before thy throne;
As the angels serve before thee,
  So on earth thy will be done.

964. *"Thou shalt call thy walls salvation."*
Isaiah 60: 18-20.

1 HEAR what God, the Lord, hath spoken:
  O my people, faint and few,
Comfortless, afflicted, broken,
  Fair abodes I build for you;
Scenes of heartfelt tribulation
  Shall no more perplex your ways;
You shall name your walls "Salvation,"
  And your gates shall all be "Praise."

2 Ye no more your suns descending,
  Waning moons no more shall see;
But your griefs for ever ending,
  Find eternal noon in me.
God shall rise, and, shining o'er you,
  Change to day the gloom of night;
He, the Lord, shall be your Glory,
  God your everlasting Light.

966. *"Jesus, I my cross have taken."*

1 JESUS, I my cross have taken,
  All to leave and follow thee;
Naked, poor, despised, forsaken,
  Thou, from hence, my all shalt be:
Perish every fond ambition,
  All I've sought, or hoped, or known;
Yet how rich is my condition!
  God and heaven are still my own.

2 Let the world despise and leave me,
  They have left my Saviour, too;
Human hearts and looks deceive me;
  Thou art not, like them, untrue:
And while thou shalt smile upon me,
  God of wisdom, love, and might,
Foes may hate, and friends may scorn me;
  Show thy face, and all is bright.

3 Man may trouble and distress me,
  'T will but drive me to thy breast;
Life with trials hard may press me,
  Heaven will bring me sweeter rest.
Oh! 'tis not in grief to harm me,
  While thy love is left to me;
Oh! 't were not in joy to charm me,
  Were that joy unmixed with thee.

BARTIMEUS. 8s & 7s.

317. *Glorying in the Cross.*

1 In the cross of Christ I glory,
  Towering o'er the wrecks of time;
All the light of sacred story
  Gathers round its head sublime.

2 When the woes of life o'ertake me,
  Hopes deceive, and fears annoy,
Never shall the cross forsake me:
  Lo! it glows with peace and joy.

3 When the sun of bliss is beaming
  Light and love upon my way,
From the cross the radiance streaming,
  Adds new luster to the day.

4 Bane and blessing, pain and pleasure,
  By the cross are sanctified;
Peace is there, that knows no measure,
  Joys that through all time abide.

5 In the cross of Christ I glory,
  Towering o'er the wrecks of time;
All the light of sacred story
  Gathers round its head sublime.

648. *"Come, thou Fount of every blessing."*

1 Come, thou Fount of every blessing,
  Tune my heart to sing thy grace;
Streams of mercy, never ceasing,
  Call for songs of loudest praise.

2 Teach me some melodious measure,
  Sung by flaming tongues above;
Oh the vast, the boundless treasure
  Of thy free, unchanging love!

3 Jesus sought me when a stranger,
  Wandering from the fold of God;
He, to rescue me from danger,
  Interposed his precious blood.

4 Oh, to grace how great a debtor
  Daily I'm constrained to be!

Let thy goodness, like a fetter,
  Bind my wandering heart to thee.

5 Prone to wander, Lord, I feel it;
  Prone to leave the God I love;
Here's my heart; oh, take, and seal it,—
  Seal it for thy courts above!

990. *"Upward, onward!"*

1 Like the eagle, upward, onward,
  Let my soul in faith be borne;
Calmly gazing, skyward, sunward,
  Let my eye unshrinking turn!

2 Where the cross, God's love revealing,
  Sets the fettered spirit free,
Where it sheds its wondrous healing,
  There, my soul, thy rest shall be!

3 Oh, may I, no longer dreaming,
  Idly waste my golden day,
But, each precious hour redeeming,
  Upward, onward, press my way!

1226. *Rest yonder.*

1 This is not my place of resting,—
  Mine's a city yet to come;
Onward to it I am hasting—
  On to my eternal home.

2 In it all is light and glory;
  O'er it shines a nightless day:
Every trace of sin's sad story,
  All the curse, hath passed away.

3 There the Lamb, our Shepherd, leads us
  By the streams of life along,—
On the freshest pastures feeds us,
  Turns our sighing into song.

4 Soon we pass this desert dreary,
  Soon we bid farewell to pain;
Never more are sad or weary,
  Never, never sin again!

PRESTON. C. M.

313. *"Despised and rejected of men."*
Isaiah 53.

1 REJECTED and despised of men,
 Behold a man of woe!
And grief his close companion still
 Through all his life below!

2 Yet all the griefs he felt were ours,
 Ours were the woes he bore:
Pangs, not his own, his spotless soul
 With bitter anguish tore.

3 We held him as condemned of Heaven,
 An outcast from his God:
While for our sins he groaned, he bled,
 Beneath his Father's rod.

4 His sacred blood hath washed our souls
 From sin's polluting stain;
His stripes have healed us, and his death
 Revived our souls again.

560. *"Against Thee, Thee only, have I sinned."*

1 PROSTRATE, dear Jesus, at thy feet
 A guilty rebel lies;
And upward to thy mercy-seat
 Presumes to lift his eyes.

2 If tears of sorrow would suffice
 To pay the debt I owe,
Tears should from both my weeping eyes
 In ceaseless torrents flow.

3 But no such sacrifice I plead
 To expiate my guilt;
No tears, but those which thou hast shed,
 No blood, but thou hast spilt.

4 Think of thy sorrows, dearest Lord!
 And all my sins forgive;
Justice will well approve the word
 That bids the sinner live.

562. *"Alas! and did my Saviour bleed?"*

1 ALAS! and did my Saviour bleed?
 And did my Sovereign die?
Would he devote that sacred head
 For such a worm as I?

2 Was it for crimes that I had done
 He groaned upon the tree?
Amazing pity! grace unknown!
 And love beyond degree!

3 Well might the sun in darkness hide,
 And shut his glories in,
When God, the mighty Maker, died
 For man the creature's sin.

4 Thus might I hide my blushing face,
 While his dear cross appears;
Dissolve my heart in thankfulness,
 And melt mine eyes to tears.

5 But drops of grief can ne'er repay
 The debt of love I owe:
Here, Lord, I give myself away;
 'T is all that I can do.

568. *'Forgiveness from the Cross.*

1 I SAW One hanging on a tree,
 In agony and blood,
Who fixed his languid eyes on me,
 As near the cross I stood.

2 Sure, never till my latest breath,
 Can I forget that look:
It seemed to charge me with his death,
 Though not a word he spoke.

3 Alas! I knew not what I did,
 But now my tears are vain;
Where shall my trembling soul be hid,
 For I the Lord have slain.

4 A second look he gave, that said,
 "I freely all forgive
This blood is for thy ransom paid
 I die that thou may'st live."

CORINTH. C. M.

Better ending.

583. *Sorrow for Sin, in View of the Cross.*

1 Oh, if my soul were formed for woe,
  How would I vent my sighs!
Repentance should like rivers flow
  From both my streaming eyes.

2 'Twas for my sins my dearest **Lord**
  Hung on the cursèd tree;
And groaned away a dying life
  For thee, **my** soul, for thee!

3 Oh, how I hate those lusts of mine
  That crucified my God— [flesh
Those sins that pierced **and** nailed his
  Fast to the fatal wood!

4 Yes, my Redeemer, they shall die;
  My heart has so decreed;
Nor will I spare the guilty things
  That made **my** Saviour bleed.

5 While with a melting, broken **heart,**
  My murdered Lord I view,
I'll raise revenge against my sins,
  And slay **the** murderers, too.

587. *"Lord, my heart is not haughty."*
Psalm 131.

1 Is there ambition in my heart?
  Search, gracious God, and see;
Or do I act a haughty part?
  Lord, I appeal to thee.

2 I charge my thoughts, be humble still,
  My words and actions mild;
Content, my Father, with thy will,
  And quiet as a child.

3 The patient soul, **the** lowly **mind,**
  Shall have a large reward;
Let saints in sorrow be re-signed,
  And trust a faithful **Lord.**

616. *"How long wilt Thou hide Thy face from me?"*

1 My God!—oh, could I make the claim—
  My Father and my Friend—
And call thee mine by every name
  On which thy saints depend!

2 By every name of power and love,
  I would thy grace entreat,
Nor should my humble hope remove,
  Nor leave thy mercy-seat.

3 Yet, tho' my soul in darkness mourns,
  Thy word is all my **stay;**
Here would I rest till **light returns:**
  Thy presence makes **my** day.

4 Speak, Lord! and bid celestial peace
  Relieve my aching heart;
Oh, smile, and bid my sorrows cease,
  And all the gloom depart!

5 Then shall my drooping spirit rise,
  And bless the healing rays;
And **change** these deep, complaining sighs
  To songs of sacred praise.

658. *"In Him we live, and move, and have our being."*

1 Lord, **what is** man! that child of pride
  That boasts his high degree!
If left one moment to himself,
  He sinks—and where is he?

2 In thee I live, and move, and **am;**
  Thou dealest out my days;
Lord, as thou dost renew my **life,**
  Let me renew thy praise.

3 To thee I come, from thee I am,
  For thee I still would be;
'Tis better for me not to live,
  Than not to live to thee.

4 Thou art my living fountain, Lord;
  On me thy streams still flow;
Myself I render up to thee,
  To whom myself I owe.

DURER. S. M.

2. *"Our Father, which art in Heaven."*
Matt. 6. Luke 11.

1 OUR heavenly Father, hear
  The prayer we offer now:
Thy name be hallowed far and near;
  To thee all nations bow!

2 Thy kingdom come, thy will
  On earth be done in love,
As saints and seraphim fulfill
  Thy perfect law above.

3 Our daily bread supply,
  While by thy word we live;
The guilt of our iniquity
  Forgive, as we forgive.

4 From dark temptation's power,
  From Satan's wiles defend;
Deliver in the evil hour,
  And guide us to the end!

5 Thine, then, for ever be
  Glory and power divine;
The scepter, throne, and majesty
  Of heaven and earth are thine!

162. *"As a father pitieth his children."*
Psalm 103.

1 THE pity of the Lord
  To those that fear his name,
Is such as tender parents feel:
  He knows our feeble frame.

2 He knows we are but dust,
  Scattered with every breath;
His anger, like a rising wind,
  Can send us swift to death.

3 Our days are as the grass,
  Or like the morning flower;
If one sharp blast sweep o'er the field,
  It withers in an hour.

4 But thy compassions, Lord,
  To endless years endure;
And children's children ever find
  Thy words of promise sure.

448. *"Descend in all Thy power."*
Acts 2.

1 LORD God, the Holy Ghost!
  In this accepted hour,
As on the day of Pentecost,
  Descend in all thy power.

2 We meet with one accord
  In our appointed place,
And wait the promise of our Lord,
  The Spirit of all grace.

3 Like mighty rushing wind
  Upon the waves beneath,
Move with one impulse every mind;
  One soul, one feeling breathe.

4 The young, the old, inspire
  With wisdom from above;
And give us hearts and tongues of fire,
  To pray, and praise, and love.

5 Spirit of light, explore
  And chase our gloom away,
With luster shining more and more
  Unto the perfect day.

6 Spirit of truth, be thou,
  In life and death, our guide:
O Spirit of adoption! now
  May we be sanctified.

790. *"I in them, and Thou in me."*

1 DEAR Saviour! we are thine,
  By everlasting bands;
Our hearts, our souls, we would resign
  Entirely to thy hands.

SEIR. S. M.

2 To thee we still would cleave
 With ever-growing zeal;
 If millions tempt us Christ to leave,
 Oh, let them ne'er prevail!

3 Thy Spirit shall unite
 Our souls to thee, our Head;
 Shall form in us thine image bright,
 And teach thy paths to tread.

4 Death may our souls divide
 From these abodes of clay;
 But love shall keep us near thy **side**,
 Through all the gloomy way.

5 Since Christ and we are one,
 Why should we doubt or fear?
 If he in heaven has fixed his throne,
 He'll fix his members there.

1211. *"Let me die the death of the righteous."*
 Num. 23: 10.

1 Oh for the death **of those**
 Who slumber in **the Lord!**
 Oh, be like theirs my last repose,
 Like theirs my last reward!

2 Their bodies in the ground
 In silent hope may lie,
 Till the last trumpet's joyful sound
 Shall call them to the sky.

3 Their ransomed spirits soar,
 On wings of faith and love,
 To meet the Saviour they adore,
 And reign with him above.

4 **With us their names shall live**
 Through long, succeeding years,
 Embalmed with all our hearts can give,
 Our praises and our tears.

5 Oh for the death of those
 Who slumber in the Lord!
 Oh, be like theirs my **last repose**,
 Like theirs my last **reward**!

DOXOLOGY.

THE Father and **the Son**
 And Spirit we adore;
 We praise, we bless, we worship thee,
 Both now and evermore!

BOYLSTON. S. M.

ST. ANN'S. C. M.

230. *"Under the shadow of the Almighty."*
Psalm 34.

1 Through all the changing scenes of life,
  In trouble and in joy,
  The praises of my God shall still
  My heart and tongue employ.
2 Of his deliverance I will boast,
  Till all who are distressed
  From my example comfort take,
  And charm their griefs to rest.

3 Oh, magnify the Lord with me,
  With me exalt his name!
  When in distress to him I called,
  He to my rescue came.
4 The hosts of God encamp around
  The dwellings of the just;
  Deliverance he affords to all
  Who on his succor trust.

5 Oh, make but trial of his love:
  Experience will decide
  How blest are they, and only they,
  Who in his truth confide.
6 Fear him, ye saints, and ye will then
  Have nothing else to fear;
  Make ye his service your delight,
  He'll make your wants his care.

243. *An ancient Hymn of Praise to Christ.*

1 We sing to thee, thou Son of God,
  Thou source of life and grace!
  We praise thee, Son of Man, whose blood
  Redeemed our fallen race!
2 Thee we acknowledge God and Lord,
  The Lamb for sinners slain;
  Who art by heaven and earth adored,
  Worthy o'er both to reign!

3 To thee all angels cry aloud,
  Through heaven's extended coasts;
  Hail, holy, holy, holy Lord
  Of glory and of hosts!
4 The prophets' goodly fellowship,
  In radiant garments dressed,
  Praise thee, thou Son of God, and reap
  The fullness of thy rest.

5 Th' apostles' glorious company
  Thy righteous praise proclaim;
  The martyred army glorify
  Thine everlasting name.
6 Throughout the world thy churches join
  To call on thee, their Head,—
  Brightness of Majesty divine,
  Who every power hast made!

7 Among their number, Lord, we love
  To sing thy precious blood:
  Reign here, and in the worlds above,
  Thou holy Lamb of God!

247. *"Thou shalt call His name Jesus."*

1 Oh, for a thousand tongues to sing
  My dear Redeemer's praise,
  The glories of my God and King,
  The triumphs of his grace!
2 My gracious Master and my God,
  Assist me to proclaim,
  To spread through all the earth abroad
  The honors of thy name.

3 Jesus! the name that calms our fears,
  That bids our sorrows cease—
  'T is music to my ravished ears,
  'T is life, and health, and peace.

CHRISTMAS OLD. C. M. DOUBLE.

4 He breaks the power of reigning sin,
   He sets the prisoner free;
   His blood can make the foulest clean:
   His blood availed for me.

5 He speaks, and, listening to his voice,
   New life the dead receive;
   The mourning, broken hearts rejoice,
   The humble poor believe.

6 Hear him, ye deaf! his praise, ye dumb,
   Your loosened tongues employ!
   Ye blind, behold your Saviour come,
   And leap, ye lame, for joy!

287. *Condescension of Christ.*
Psalm 8.

1 O LORD, our Lord, how wondrous great
   Is thine exalted name!
   The glories of thy heavenly state
   Let men and babes proclaim.

2 When I behold thy works on high,
   The moon that rules the night,
   And stars that well adorn the sky,
   Those moving worlds of light;

3 Lord, what is man, or all his race,
   Who dwells so far below,
   That thou shouldst visit him with grace,
   And love his nature so!

4 That thine eternal Son should bear
   To take a mortal form,
   Made lower than his angels are,
   To save a dying worm!

5 Let him be crowned with majesty,
   Who bowed his head to death;
   And be his honors sounded high,
   By all things that have breath.

6 Jesus, our Lord, how wondrous great,
   Is thine exalted name!
   The glories of thy heavenly state
   Let the whole earth proclaim.

653. *"My soul thirsteth for Thee."*
Psalm 63.

1 OH, who is like the Mighty One,
   Whose throne is in the sky!
   Who compasseth the universe
   With his all-searching eye;
   At whose creative word appeared
   The dry land and the sea;
   My spirit thirsts for thee, O Lord,
   My spirit thirsts for thee!

2 Around him suns and systems swim
   In harmony and light,
   Before him harps angelic hymn
   His praises day and night,
   Yet to the contrite, day and night,
   In mercy turneth he:
   My spirit thirsts for thee, O Lord,
   My spirit thirsts for thee!

3 Yes! though unlimited his works,
   His power upholds them all;
   He clothes the lilies of the field,
   And marks the sparrow's fall:
   Who listens to the raven's cry,
   Will bend his ear to me;
   My spirit thirsts for thee, O Lord,
   My spirit thirsts for thee!

DOXOLOGY.

To Father, Son, and Holy Ghost,
   One God, whom we adore,
   Be glory as it was, is now,
   And shall be evermore!

TULLY. 7s & 6s.

673. "*Fear not, little flock.*"—Luke 12:32.

1 In heavenly love abiding,
  No change my heart shall fear,
And safe is such confiding,
  For nothing changes here:
The storm may roar without me,
  My heart may low be laid,
But God is round about me,
  And can I be dismayed?

2 Wherever he may guide me,
  No want shall turn me back;
My Shepherd is beside me,
  And nothing can I lack:
His wisdom ever waketh,
  His sight is never dim:
He knows the way he taketh,
  And I will walk with him.

3 Green pastures are before me,
  Which yet I have not seen;
Bright skies will soon be o'er me,
  Where darkest clouds have been:
My hope I can not measure;
  My path to life is free;
My Saviour has my treasure,
  And he will walk with me.

842. "*Pray without ceasing.*"

1 Go, when the morning shineth,
  Go, when the noon is bright,
Go, when the eve declineth,
  Go, in the hush of night;
Go, with pure mind and feeling,
  Put earthly thoughts away,
And, in God's presence kneeling,
  Do thou in secret pray.

2 Remember all who love thee,
  All who are loved by thee;
Pray, too, for those who hate thee,
  If any such there be:
Then for thyself, in meekness,
  A blessing humbly claim,
And blend with each petition
  Thy great Redeemer's name.

3 Or, if 'tis e'er denied thee
  In solitude to pray,
Should holy thoughts come o'er thee
  When friends are round thy way,
Ev'n then, the silent breathing
  Thy spirit lifts above,
Will reach his throne of glory,
  Where dwells eternal love.

4 Oh, not a joy or blessing
  With this can we compare—
The grace our Father gives us
  To pour our souls in prayer!
When thou dost pine in sadness,
  On him who saveth call;
And ever in thy gladness,
  Thank him who gave thee all.

GOODWIN. 7s & 6s.

1039. "*All nations shall be blest in Him.*"
Psalm 72.

1 Hail to the Lord's Anointed,
  Great David's greater Son!
Hail, in the time appointed,
  His reign on earth begun!
He comes to break oppression,
  To set the captive free;
To take away transgression,
  And rule in equity.

2 He shall come down like showers
  Upon the fruitful earth;
And love, joy, hope, like flowers,
  Spring in his path to birth:
Before him, on the mountains,
  Shall Peace, the herald, go;
And Righteousness, in fountains,
  From hill to valley flow.

3 Kings shall fall down before him,
  And gold and incense bring;
All nations shall adore him,
  His praise all people sing:
For he shall have dominion
  O'er river, sea, and shore,
Far as the eagle's pinion,
  Or dove's light wing can soar.

4 For him shall prayer unceasing
  And daily vows ascend;
His kingdom still increasing—
  A kingdom without end:
O'er every foe victorious,
  He on his throne shall rest:
From age to age more glorious,
  All blessing and all blest!

1131. "*All the trees of the field shall clap their hands.*"

1 When shall the voice of singing
  Flow joyfully along?
When hill and valley, ringing
  With one triumphant song,
Proclaim the contest ended,
  And him who once was slain,
Again to earth descended,
  In righteousness to reign?

2 Then from the craggy mountains
  The sacred shout shall fly;
And shady vales and fountains
  Shall echo the reply:
High tower and lowly dwelling
  Shall send the hymn around,
All hallelujah swelling,
  In one eternal sound!

SILOAM C. M.

95. *Third Version of the Benediction from Heb. 13 : 20, 21.*

1 THE God of peace, who from the dead
Brought up again our Lord,
And, through the covenant in his blood,
Our souls to peace restored—

2 Confirm our hearts, in each good work,
To do his perfect will;
That, made well pleasing in his sight,
Our course with joy we fill.

3 So shall we, in his heavenly courts,
Hereafter, ever live;
And to his name, through Jesus Christ,
Eternal glory give.

141. *"The Lord searcheth all hearts."*

1 GOD is a Spirit, just and wise;
He sees our inmost mind:
In vain to Heaven we raise our cries,
And leave our hearts behind.

2 Nothing but truth before his throne
With honor can appear;
The painted hypocrites are known
Through the disguise they wear.

3 Their lifted eyes salute the skies;
Their bending knees the ground;
But God abhors the sacrifice,
Where not the heart is found.

4 Lord, search my thoughts, and try my ways,
And make my soul sincere;
Then shall I stand before thy face,
And find acceptance there.

420. *"The unchanging Friend."*
Isaiah 49 : 14, 15.

1 FORGETFUL can a mother be?
Yes: human love is frail;
But thy Redeemer's love to thee,
O Zion! can not fail.

2 No: thy dear name engraven stands,
In characters of love,
On thine atoning Saviour's hands,
And never shall remove.

3 Before his ever watchful eye
Thy mournful state appears,
And every groan, and every sigh,
Divine compassion hears.

4 O Zion! learn to doubt no more;
Be every fear suppressed:
Unchanging truth, and love and power,
Dwell in thy Saviour's breast.

490. *Diverse Influences of the Gospel.*
1 Cor. 1 : 23, 24.

1 CHRIST and his cross are all our theme:
The mysteries that we speak
Are scandal in the Jew's esteem,
And folly to the Greek.

2 But souls enlightened from above
With joy receive the word;
They see what wisdom, power, and love,
Shine in their dying Lord.

3 The vital savor of his name
Restores their fainting breath;
But unbelief perverts the same
To guilt, despair, and death.

4 Till God diffuse his graces down,
Like showers of heavenly rain,
In vain Apollos sows the ground,
And Paul may plant in vain.

552. *"It is God which worketh in you."*

1 NOT all the outward forms on earth,
Nor rites that God has given,
Nor will of man, nor blood, nor birth,
Can raise a soul to heaven.

2 The sovereign will of God alone
Creates us heirs of grace;
Born in the image of his Son,
A new, peculiar race.

PETERBORO'. C. M.

3 The Spirit, like some heavenly wind,
  Blows on the sons of flesh,
  New-models all the carnal mind,
  And forms the man afresh.
4 Our quickened souls awake and rise
  From the long sleep of death;
  On heavenly things we fix our eyes,
  And praise employs our breath.

1053. "*Ten thousand tongues should join the harmony.*"

1 LORD, at thy table I behold
  The wonders of thy grace;
  But most of all admire that I
  Should find a welcome place—
2 I, who am all defiled with sin,
  A rebel to my God!
  I, who have crucified thy Son,
  And trampled on his blood!
3 What strange, surprising grace is this,
  That such a soul has room!
  My Saviour takes me by the hand,
  My Jesus bids me come.
4 Ye saints below, and hosts of heaven!
  In praise join all your powers;
  No theme is like redeeming love!
  No Saviour is like ours!
5 Had I ten thousand hearts, dear Lord!
  I'd give them all to thee;
  Had I ten thousand tongues, they all
  Should join the harmony.

1054. *The Saviour died for me.*

1 PREPARE us, Lord, to view thy cross,
  Who all our griefs hast borne;
  To look on thee, whom we have pierced—
  To look on thee, and mourn.
2 While thus we mourn, we would rejoice,
  And, as thy cross we see,

Let each exclaim in faith and hope—
  "The Saviour died for me!"

1066. "*A good profession before many witnesses.*"—1 Tim. 6: 12.

1 WITNESS, ye men and angels, now
  Before the Lord we speak;
  To him we make our solemn vow
  A vow we dare not break:—
2 That, long as life itself shall last,
  Ourselves to Christ we yield;
  Nor from his cause will we depart
  Or ever quit the field.
3 We trust not in our native strength,
  But on his grace rely,
  That with returning wants the Lord
  Will all our need supply.
4 Oh, guide our doubtful feet aright,
  And keep us in thy ways;
  And, while we turn our vows to prayers,
  Turn thou our prayers to praise!

1091. "*Remember now thy Creator in the days of thy youth.*"—Eccl. 12: 1.

1 REMEMBER thy Creator now,
  In these thy youthful days;
  He will accept thy earliest vow,
  And listen to thy praise.
2 Remember thy Creator now,
  And seek him while he's near;
  For evil days will come, when thou
  Shalt find no comfort near.
3 Remember thy Creator now;
  His willing servant be;
  Then, when thy head in death shall bow,
  He will remember thee.
4 Almighty God! our hearts incline
  Thy heavenly voice to hear;
  Let all our future days be thine,
  Devoted to thy fear.

ERNAN. L. M.

280. *Christ our Example.*

1 My dear Redeemer, and my Lord,
 I read my duty in thy word;
 But in thy life the law appears,
 Drawn out in living characters.

2 Such was thy truth, and such thy zeal,
 Such deference to thy Father's will,
 Such love and meekness so divine,
 I would transcribe and make them mine.

3 Cold mountains and the midnight air
 Witnessed the fervor of thy prayer:
 The desert thy temptations knew,
 Thy conflict, and thy victory, too.

4 Be thou my pattern; make me bear
 More of thy gracious image here:
 Then God, the Judge, shall own my name
 Among the followers of the Lamb.

405. *Strength by the Way.*

1 Jesus, while this rough desert soil
 I tread, be thou my guide and stay:
 Nerve me for conflict and for toil;
 Uphold me on my stranger-way!

2 Jesus, in heaviness and fear,
 Mid cloud, and shade, and gloom, I stray,
 For earth's last night is drawing near;
 Oh, cheer me on my stranger-way!

3 Jesus, in solitude and grief,
 When sun and stars withhold their ray,
 Make haste, make haste to my relief!
 Oh, light me on my stranger-way!

4 Jesus, in weakness of this flesh,
 When Satan grasps me for his prey,
 Oh, give me victory afresh,
 And speed me on my stranger-way!

459. *"He dwelleth with you."*

1 Sure the blest Comforter is nigh;
 'Tis he sustains my fainting heart:
 Else would my hope for ever die,
 And every cheering ray depart.

2 Whene'er to call the Saviour mine,
 With ardent wish my heart aspires,
 Can it be less than power divine,
 That animates these strong desires?

3 And when my cheerful hope can say,
 I love my God, and taste his grace,
 Lord, is it not thy blissful ray
 Which brings this dawn of sacred peace?

4 Let thy kind Spirit in my heart
 For ever dwell, O God of love;
 And light and heavenly peace impart,
 Sweet earnest of the joys above.

504. *"Come, ye heavy laden."*—Matt. 11:28.

1 "Come hither, all ye weary souls;
 Ye heavy-laden sinners, come!
 I'll give you rest from all your toils,
 And raise you to my heavenly home.

2 "They shall find rest who learn of me;
 I'm of a meek and lowly mind;
 But passion rages like the sea,
 And pride is restless as the wind.

3 "Blest is the man whose shoulders take
 My yoke, and bear it with delight:
 My yoke is easy to his neck,
 My grace shall make the burden light."

4 Jesus, we come at thy command;
 With faith, and hope, and humble zeal,
 Resign our spirits to thy hand,
 To mold and guide us at thy will.

NEW SABBATH HYMN AND TUNE BOOK. 185

ZEPHYR. L. M.

652. *"Thou art my God; early will I seek Thee."*

1 O God, thou art my God alone:
  Early to thee my soul shall cry—
A pilgrim in a land unknown,
  A thirsty land, whose springs are dry.

2 O that it were as it hath been,
  When, praying in the holy place,
Thy power and glory I have seen,
  And marked the footsteps of thy grace!

3 Yet, through this rough and thorny maze,
  I follow hard on thee my God:
Thy hand unseen upholds my ways;
  I safely tread where thou hast trod.

4 Thee, in the watches of the night,
  When I remember on my bed,
Thy presence makes the darkness light;
  Thy guardian wings are round my head.

5 Better than life itself thy love,
  Dearer than all beside to me;
For whom have I in heaven above,
  Or what on earth, compared with thee?

664. *Repose in God's Wisdom.*

1 Whither, oh, whither should I fly,
  But to my loving Father's breast!
Secure within thine arms to lie,
  And safe beneath thy wings to rest!

2 In all my ways thy hand I own,
  Thy ruling providence I see;
Assist me still my course to run,
  And still direct my paths to thee.

3 I have no skill the snare to shun;
  But thou, O God, my wisdom art;
I ever into ruin run;
  But thou art greater than my heart.

4 Foolish, and impotent, and blind,
  Lead me a way I have not known;
Bring me where I my heaven may find,
  The heaven of loving thee alone.

678. *"As thy days, so shall thy strength be."*
Deut. 33: 25.

1 While foes are strong, and danger near,
  A voice falls gently on my ear;
My Saviour speaks, he says to me,
  That "as my days, my strength shall be."

2 With such a promise need I fear
  For all that now I hold most dear?
No; I will never anxious be,
  For, "as my days, my strength shall be."

3 When storms of trouble on me fall,
  And when my cup is mixed with gall,
This promise will be sweet to me,
  That "as my days, my strength shall be."

4 And when at last I'm called to die,
  Still on his promise I'll rely;
Yes, Lord, I then will trust in thee,
  That "as my days, my strength shall be."

686. *Delight in Christ.*

1 Jesus, thou Joy of loving hearts!
  Thou Fount of Life! thou Light of men!
From the best bliss that earth imparts,
  We turn unfilled to thee again.

2 Thy truth unchanged hath ever stood;
  Thou savest those that on thee call;
To them that seek thee thou art good,
  To them that find thee—All in All!

3 We taste thee, O thou Living Bread,
  And long to feast upon thee still;
We drink of thee, the Fountain Head,
  And thirst our souls from thee to fill.

4 Our restless spirits yearn for thee,
  Where'er our changeful lot is cast;
Glad, when thy gracious smile we see,
  Blest, when our faith can hold thee fast.

5 O Jesus, ever with us stay,
  Make all our moments calm and bright;
Chase the dark night of sin away,—
  Shed o'er the world thy holy light!

FERRY. C. M.

702. *"Jesus alone deserves my heart."*

1 Ye earthly vanities! depart;
  For ever hence remove;
Jesus alone deserves my heart,
  And every thought of love.

2 His heart, where love and pity dwelt
  In all their softest forms,
Sustained the heavy load of guilt
  For lost, rebellious worms.

3 Can I my bleeding Saviour view,
  And yet ungrateful prove?
And pierce his wounded heart anew,
  And grieve his injured love?

4 Forbid it, Lord! oh, bind this heart,
  This roving heart of mine,
So firm that it may ne'er depart,
  In chains of love divine!

821. *"Giving All to God."*

1 How can I sink with such a prop
  As my eternal God,
Who bears the earth's huge pillars up,
  And spreads the heavens abroad?

2 How can I die while Jesus lives,
  Who rose and left the dead?
Pardon and grace my soul receives
  From my exalted Head.

3 All that I am, and all I have
  Shall be for ever thine;
Whate'er my duty bids me give,
  My cheerful hands resign.

4 Yet, if I might make some reserve,
  And duty did not call,
I love my God with zeal so great,
  That I should give him all.

888. *"It is I; be not afraid."*—Matt. 14: 27.

1 When waves of sorrow round me swell,
  My soul is not dismayed;
I hear a voice I know full well:
  "'T is I; be not afraid."

2 When black the threatening clouds appear,
  And storms my path invade,
That voice shall calm each rising fear:
  "'T is I; be not afraid."

3 There is a gulf that must be crossed:
  Saviour! be near to aid;
Whisper, when my frail bark is tossed,
  "'T is I; be not afraid."

4 There is a dark and fearful vale,—
  Death hides within its shade;
Oh, say, when flesh and heart shall fail,
  "'T is I; be not afraid!"

995. *"Close to Thy bleeding side."*

1 For ever here my rest shall be,
  Close to thy bleeding side;
This all my hope, and all my plea—
  For me the Saviour died.

2 My dying Saviour, and my God,
  Fountain for guilt and sin,
Sprinkle me ever with thy blood,
  And cleanse and keep me clean.

3 Wash me, and make me thus thine own,
  Wash me, and mine thou art;
Wash me, but not my feet alone,—
  My hands, my head, my heart.

4 Th' atonement of thy blood apply,
  Till faith to sight improve;
Till hope in full fruition die,
  And all my soul be love.

996. *"Perfect us in love."*

1 Try us, O God, and search the ground
  Of every sinful heart;

DENFIELD. C. M.

Whate'er of sin in us is found,
Oh, bid it all depart.

2 Help us to help each other, Lord,
Each other's cross to bear;
Let each his friendly aid afford,
And feel his brother's care.

3 Help us to build each other up,
Our heart and life improve;
Increase our faith, confirm our hope,
And perfect us in love.

4 Up into thee, our living Head,
Let us in all things grow,
Till thou hast made us free, indeed,
And spotless here below.

1100. "*For ye have the poor always with you.*"

1 Lord, lead the way the Saviour went,
By lane and cell obscure,
And let our treasures still be spent,
Like his, upon the poor.

2 Like him, through scenes of deep distress,
Who bore the world's sad weight,
We, in their gloomy loneliness,
Would seek the desolate.

3 For thou hast placed us side by side
In this wide world of ill,
And that thy followers may be tried,
The poor are with us still.

4 Small are the offerings we can make;
Yet thou hast taught us, Lord,
If given for the Saviour's sake,
They lose not their reward.

1101. "*Ye have done it unto Me.*"
Matt. 25: 40.

1 Jesus, my Lord, how rich thy grace!
Thy bounties how complete!
How shall I count the matchless sum?
How pay the mighty debt?

2 High on a throne of radiant light
Dost thou exalted shine;
What can my poverty bestow,
When all the worlds are thine?

3 But thou hast brethren here below,
The partners of thy grace;
And wilt confess their humble names
Before thy Father's face.

4 In them thou may'st be clothed and fed,
And visited and cheered;
And, in their accents of distress,
My Saviour's voice is heard.

5 Thy face, with reverence and with love
I, in thy poor, would see;
Oh, rather let me beg my bread,
Than keep it back from thee!

462. "*Come, Holy Spirit, heavenly Dove.*"

1 Come, Holy Spirit, heavenly Dove,
With all thy quickening powers,
Kindle a flame of sacred love
In these cold hearts of ours.

2 Look, how we grovel here below,
Fond of these trifling toys!
Our souls can neither fly nor go
To reach eternal joys.

3 In vain we tune our formal songs;
In vain we strive to rise:
Hosannas languish on our tongues,
And our devotion dies.

4 Dear Lord! and shall we ever live
At this poor, dying rate?
Our love so faint, so cold to thee,
And thine to us so great?

5 Come, Holy Spirit, heavenly Dove,
With all thy quickening powers!
Come, shed abroad a Saviour's love,
And that shall kindle ours.

538.
"Haste thee; escape thither."—Gen. 19: 22.

1 Haste, trav'ler, haste! the night comes on,
 And many a shining hour is gone;
 The storm is gathering in the west,
 And thou art far from home and rest:
  Haste, trav'ler, haste!

2 The rising tempest sweeps the sky;
 The rains descend, the winds are high;
 The waters swell, and death and fear
 Beset thy path; no refuge near:
  Haste, trav'ler, haste!

3 Haste, while a shelter you may gain,—
 A covert from the wind and rain,—
 A hiding-place, a rest, a home,—
 A refuge from the wrath to come:
  Haste, trav'ler, haste!

4 Then linger not in all the plain;
 Flee for thy life—the mountain gain;
 Look not behind; make no delay;
 Oh, speed thee, speed thee on thy way!
  Haste, trav'ler, haste!

1177.
To die is gain."

1 No, no, it is not dying
  To go unto our God;
 This gloomy earth forsaking,
  Our journey homeward taking
  Along the starry road.

2 No, no, it is not dying
  Heaven's citizen to be;
 A crown immortal wearing,
 And rest unbroken sharing,
  From care and conflict free.

[For other stanzas see next page.]

ADNAL. 8s.

1188. *"Having a desire to depart."*

1 To Jesus, the crown of my hope,
   My soul is in haste to be gone;
   Oh, bear me, ye cherubim, up,
   And waft me away to his throne.

2 My Saviour, whom absent I love;
   Whom, not having seen, I adore;
   Whose name is exalted above
   All glory, dominion and power;—

3 Dissolve thou these bands that detain
   My soul from her portion in thee,
   Ah! strike off this adamant chain,
   And make me eternally free.

4 When that happy era begins,
   When arrayed in thy glories I shine,
   Nor grieve any more, by my sins,
   The bosom on which I recline,—

5 Oh, then shall the vail be removed!
   And round me thy brightness be pour'd;
   I shall meet him whom absent I loved,
   I shall see whom unseen I adored.

6 And then, never more shall the fears,
   The trials, temptations, and woes,
   Which darken this valley of tears,
   Intrude on my blissful repose.

1261. *"What must it be to be there!"*

1 WE speak of the realms of the blest,
   That country so bright and so fair,
   And oft are its glories confessed;
   But what must it be to be there!

2 We speak of its pathways of gold,
   Its walls decked with jewels so rare,
   Its wonders and pleasures untold;
   But what must it be to be there!

3 We speak of its freedom from sin,
   From sorrow, temptation, and care,
   From trials without and within:
   But what must it be to be there!

4 We speak of its service of love,
   The robes which the glorified wear,
   The church of the first-born above;
   But what must it be to be there!

5 Do thou, Lord, 'mid sorrow and woe,
   Still for heaven my spirit prepare,
   And shortly I also shall know,
   And feel what it is to be there.

---

3 No, no, it is not dying
   The Shepherd's voice to know;
   His sheep he ever leadeth,
   His peaceful flock he feedeth,
   Where living pastures grow.

4 No, no, it is not dying
   To wear a heavenly crown;

Among God's people dwelling
   The glorious triumph swelling
   Of him whose sway we own.

5 Oh, no! this is not dying,
   Thou Saviour of mankind!
   There streams of love are flowing,
   No hindrance ever knowing;
   Here, only drops we find.

BYRD. C. M. Double.

214. *The God of my Life.*

1 Father of mercies! God of love!
  My Father and my God!
  I'll sing the honors of thy name,
  And spread thy praise abroad.
2 In every period of my life
  Thy thoughts of love appear;
  Thy mercies gild each transient scene,
  And crown each passing year.
3 In all thy mercies, may my soul
  A Father's bounty see;
  Nor let the gifts thy grace bestows
  Estrange my heart from thee.
4 Teach me, in times of deep distress,
  To own thy hand, O God!
  And in submissive silence learn
  The lessons of thy rod.
5 Through every period of my life,
  Each bright, each clouded scene,
  Give me a meek and humble mind,
  Still equal and serene.
6 Then may I close my eyes in death,
  Redeemed from anxious fear,
  For death itself, my God, is life,
  If thou be with me there.

627. *"O for a closer walk with God."*

1 Oh for a closer walk with God,
  A calm and heavenly frame,—
  A light to shine upon the road
  That leads me to the Lamb!
2 Where is the blessedness I knew,
  When first I saw the Lord?
  Where is the soul-refreshing view
  Of Jesus and his word?
3 What peaceful hours I once enjoyed!
  How sweet their memory still!
  But they have left an aching void
  The world can never fill.

4 Return, O holy Dove! return,
  Sweet messenger of rest!
  I hate the sins that made thee mourn,
  And drove thee from my breast.
5 The dearest idol I have known,
  Whate'er that idol be,
  Help me to tear it from thy throne,
  And worship only thee.
6 So shall my walk be close with God,
  Calm and serene my frame;
  So purer light shall mark the road
  That leads me to the Lamb.

1094. *"Brethren, be not weary in well-doing."*

1 Lord, as to thy dear cross we flee,
  And pray to be forgiven,
  So let thy life our pattern be,
  And form our souls for heaven.
2 Help us, through good report and ill,
  Our daily cross to bear;
  Like thee, to do our Father's will,
  Our brother's griefs to share.
3 Let grace our selfishness expel,
  Our earthliness refine;
  And kindness in our bosoms dwell
  As free and true as thine.
4 If joy shall at thy bidding fly,
  And grief's dark day come on,
  We, in our turn, would meekly cry,
  "Father, thy will be done!"
5 Should friends misjudge, or foes defame,
  Or brethren faithless prove,
  Then, like thine own, be all our aim
  To conquer them by love.
6 Kept peaceful in the midst of strife,
  Forgiving and forgiven,
  Oh, may we lead the pilgrim's life,
  And follow thee to heaven!

NAOMI. C. M.

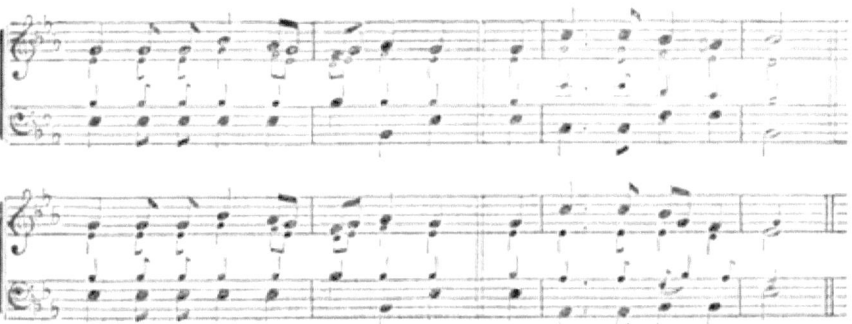

242. *Benevolence of God's Decrees.*

1 SINCE all the varying scenes of time
  God's watchful eye surveys,
Oh, who so wise to choose our lot,
  Or to appoint our ways!

2 Good, when he gives, supremely good;
  Nor less when he denies;
Ev'n crosses from his sovereign hand,
  Are blessings in disguise.

3 Why should we doubt a Father's love,
  So constant and so kind!
To his unerring, gracious will
  Be every wish resigned.

4 In thy fair book of life divine,
  My God, inscribe my name;
There let it fill some humble place
  Beneath my Lord the Lamb!

846. *The safe Retreat.*

1 DEAR Father, to thy mercy-seat
  My soul for shelter flies:
'T is here I find a safe retreat
  When storms and tempests rise.

2 My cheerful hope can never die,
  If thou, my God, art near;
Thy grace can raise my comforts high,
  And banish every fear.

3 My great Protector, and my Lord,
  Thy constant aid impart;
Oh, let thy kind, thy gracious word
  Sustain my trembling heart!

4 Oh, never let my soul remove
  From this divine retreat!
Still let me trust thy power and love,
  And dwell beneath thy feet.

926. *The One Petition.*

1 FATHER! whate'er of earthly bliss
  Thy sovereign hand denies,
Accepted at thy throne of grace,
  Let this petition rise:

2 "Give me a calm, a thankful heart,
  From every murmur free;
The blessings of thy grace impart,
  And make me live to thee.

3 "Let the sweet hope that thou art mine
  My life and death attend;
Thy presence through my journey shine,
  And crown my journey's end."

1001. *"Let me know my Father reigns."*

1 MY God, my Father, blissful name!
  Oh, may I call thee mine?
May I with sweet assurance claim
  A portion so divine?

2 Whate'er thy providence denies
  I calmly would resign;
For thou art good, and just, and wise:
  Oh, bend my will to thine!

3 Whate'er thy sacred will ordains,
  Oh, give me strength to bear!
And let me know my Father reigns,
  And trust his tender care.

4 Thy sovereign ways are all unknown
  To my weak, erring sight;
Yet let my soul adoring own
  That all thy ways are right.

DOXOLOGY.

LET God the Father, and the Son,
  And Spirit, be adored,
Where there are works to make him known,
  Or saints to love the Lord!

JAYNES. 8s & 7s. DOUBLE.

997. *"Ye are the temple of the living God."*

1 Love divine, all love excelling,
   Joy of heaven, to earth come down!
Fix in us thy humble dwelling,
   All thy faithful mercies crown:
Jesus! thou art all compassion;
   Pure, unbounded love thou art:
Visit us with thy salvation;
   Enter every longing heart.

2 Come, Almighty to deliver,
   Let us all thy grace receive;
Hasten thy return, and never,
   Never more thy temples leave!
Dwell in us with thy rich blessing,
   Dwell in us with all thy love;
We will praise thee without ceasing;
   Serve thee as thy hosts above.

3 Finish, Lord, thy new creation;
   Pure and spotless may we be:
Let us see thy great salvation
   Perfectly restored in thee:
Changed from glory into glory,
   Till in heaven we take our place:
Till we cast our crowns before thee,
   Lost in wonder, love, and praise.

421. *The Elder Brother.*

1 Yes, for me, for me he careth
   With a brother's tender care;
Yes, with me, with me he shareth
   Every burden, every fear.

2 Yes, o'er me, o'er me he watcheth,
   Ceaseless watcheth, night and day;
Yes, ev'n me, ev'n me he snatcheth
   From the perils of the way.

3 Yes, for me he standeth pleading,
   At the mercy-seat above;
Ever for me interceding,
   Constant in untiring love.

4 Yes, in me abroad he sheddeth
   Joys unearthly, love and light;
And to cover me he spreadeth
   His paternal wing of might.

5 Yes, in me, in me he dwelleth;
   I in him, and he in me!
And my empty soul he filleth,
   Here and through eternity.

6 Thus I wait for his returning,
   Singing all the way to heaven:
Such the joyful song of morning,
   Such the tranquil song of even.

438. *Our Friend, above all others.*

1 One there is, above all others,
   Well deserves the name of Friend;
His is love beyond a brother's,
   Costly, free, and knows no end.

2 Which of all our friends, to save us,
   Could or would have shed his blood?
But our Jesus died to have us
   Reconciled in him to God.

3 When he lived on earth abased,
   Friend of sinners was his name;
Now, above all glory raised,
   He rejoices in the same.

4 Oh, for grace our hearts to soften!
   Teach us, Lord, at length to love;
We, alas! forget too often
   What a Friend we have above.

KELVIN. 8s & 7s.

419. "*I am with you alway.*"—Matt. 28 : 20.

1 ALWAYS with us, always with us—
  Words of cheer and words of love ;
Thus the risen Saviour whispers,
  From his dwelling-place above.

2 With us when we toil in sadness,
  Sowing much and reaping none ;
Telling us that in the future
  Golden harvests shall be won.

3 With us when the storm is sweeping
  O'er our pathway dark and drear ;
Waking hope within our bosoms,
  Stilling every anxious fear.

4 With us in the lonely valley,
  When we cross the chilling stream ;
Lighting up the steps to glory
  With salvation's radiant beam.

151. "*God is Love.*"—1 John 4 : 8.

1 GOD is love ; his mercy brightens
  All the path in which we rove ;
Bliss he wakes, and woe he lightens :
  God is wisdom, God is love.

2 Chance and change are busy ever ;
  Man decays, and ages move :
But his mercy waneth never ;
  God is wisdom, God is love.

3 Ev'n the hour that darkest seemeth
  Will his changeless goodness prove ;
From the gloom his brightness streameth ;
  God is wisdom, God is love.

4 He with earthly cares entwineth
  Hope and comfort from above :
Every where his glory shineth ;
  God is wisdom, God is love.

249. "*Over all, God blessed for ever.*"

1 CROWN his head with endless blessing,
  Who, in God the Father's name,
With compassions never ceasing,
  Comes salvation to proclaim.

2 Lo ! Jehovah, we adore thee ;
  Thee, our Saviour ; thee, our God !
From his throne his beams of glory
  Shine through all the world abroad.

3 Jesus, thee our Saviour hailing,
  Thee, our God, in praise we own ;
Highest honors, never failing,
  Rise eternal round thy throne.

4 Now, ye saints, his power confessing,
  In your grateful strains adore ;
For his mercy, never ceasing,
  Flows and flows for evermore.

265. "*Being the brightness of His glory.*"

1 BRIGHTNESS of the Father's glory,
  Shall thy praise unuttered lie ?
Break, my tongue, such guilty silence ;
  Sing the Lord who came to die.

2 Did archangels sing thy coming ?
  Did the shepherds learn their lays ?
Shame would cover me, ungrateful,
  Should my tongue refuse to praise.

3 From the highest throne in glory
  To the cross of deepest woe,
All to ransom guilty captives !
  Flow, my praise, for ever flow.

4 Re ascend, immortal Saviour !
  Leave thy footstool, take thy throne ;
Thence return, and reign for ever ;
  Be the kingdom all thine own.

BONAR. S. M. DOUBLE.

551. *Lost, but found.*—1 Pet. 2: 25.

1 I was a wandering sheep,
   I did not love the fold,
I did not love my Shepherd's voice,
   I would not be controlled.

2 I was a wayward child,
   I did not love my home,
I did not love my Father's voice,
   I loved afar to roam.

3 The Shepherd sought his sheep,
   The Father sought his child;
They followed me o'er vale and hill,
   O'er deserts waste and wild.

4 They found me nigh to death,
   Famished, and faint, and lone;
They bound me with the bands of love;
   They saved the wandering one.

5 Jesus my Shepherd is,
   'T was he that loved my soul,
'T was he that washed me in his blood,
   'T was he that made me whole.

6 'T was he that sought the lost,
   That found the wandering sheep,
'T was he that brought me to the fold,
   'T is he that still doth keep.

7 I was a wandering sheep,
   I would not be controlled;
But now I love my Shepherd's voice,
   I love, I love the fold!

8 I was a wayward child;
   I once preferred to roam;
But now I love my Father's voice,—
   I love, I love his home!

857. *Christian Fellowship.*

1 Blest be the tie that binds
   Our hearts in Christian love:
The fellowship of kindred minds
   Is like to that above.

2 Before our Father's throne
   We pour our ardent prayers;
Our fears, our hopes, our aims are one,
   Our comforts and our cares.

3 We share our mutual woes,
   Our mutual burdens bear;
And often for each other flows
   The sympathizing tear.

4 When we asunder part,
   It gives us inward pain;
But we shall still be joined in heart,
   And hope to meet again.

5 This glorious hope revives
   Our courage by the way;
While each in expectation lives,
   And longs to see the day.

6 From sorrow, toil, and pain,
   And sin, we shall be free,
And perfect love and friendship reign
   Through all eternity.

960. "*Say ye to the righteous that it shall be well with him.*"—Isaiah 3: 10.

1 What cheering words are these?
   Their sweetness who can tell?
In time, and to eternal days,
   "'T is with the righteous well."

2 In every state secure,
   Kept as Jehovah's eye,
'T is well with them while life endures,
   And well when called to die;

ELL. S. M.

3 Well, when they see his face,
   Or sink amid the flood;
   Well, in affliction's thorny maze,
   Or on the mount with God.

4 'T is well, when joys arise:
   'T is well, when sorrows flow;
   'T is well, when darkness vails the skies,
   And strong temptations grow.

5 'T is well, when Jesus calls:
   "From earth and sin arise,
   To join the hosts of ransomed souls,
   Made to salvation wise!"

1270. "*How long, O Lord, holy and true?*"

1 The Church has waited long,
   Her absent Lord to see;
   And still in loneliness she waits,
   A friendless stranger she.

2 How long, O Lord our God,
   Holy and true and good,
   Wilt thou not judge thy suffering church,
   Her sighs and tears and blood?

3 Saint after saint on earth
   Has lived, and loved, and died;
   And as they left us one by one,
   We laid them side by side.

4 We laid them down to sleep,
   But not in hope forlorn;
   We laid them but to ripen there,
   Till the last glorious morn.

5 We long to hear thy voice,
   To see thee face to face,
   To share thy crown and glory then,
   As now we share thy grace.

6 Come, Lord! and wipe away
   The curse, the sin, the stain,
   And make this blighted world of ours
   Thine own fair world again.

SHAWMUT. S. M.

WELTON. L. M.

411. *None but Christ.*

1 Thou only Sovereign of my heart,
  My Refuge, my almighty Friend!
And can my soul from thee depart,
  On whom alone my hopes depend?

2 Whither, ah! whither shall I go,
  A wretched wand'rer from my Lord?
Can this dark world of sin and woe
  One glimpse of happiness afford?

3 Eternal life thy words impart;
  On these my fainting spirit lives:
Here sweeter comforts cheer my heart,
  Than all the round of nature gives.

4 Let earth's alluring joys combine;
  While thou art near, in vain they call;
One smile, one blissful smile of thine,
  My dearest Lord! outweighs them all.

5 Thy name my inmost powers adore;
  Thou art my life, my joy, my care:
Depart from thee!—'t is death, 't is more,
  'T is endless ruin—deep despair!

6 Low at thy feet my soul would lie;
  Here safety dwells, and peace divine:
Still let me live beneath thine eye,
  For life, eternal life is thine.

726. *No hope but in Christ.*—Micah 6: 6-8.

1 Wherewith, O God, shall I draw near,
  And bow myself before thy face?
How, in thy purer eyes, appear?
  What shall I bring to gain thy grace?

2 Will gifts delight the Lord our God?
  Can these wash out my guilty stains?
Rivers of oil, and seas of blood—
  Alas! they all must flow in vain.

3 What have I then wherein to trust?
  I nothing have, I nothing am:
Excluded is my every boast,
  My glory swallowed up in shame.

4 Guilty I stand before thy face;
  On me I feel thy wrath abide;
'T is just the sentence should take place,
  'T is just—but oh, thy Son hath died!

5 Jesus, the Lamb of God, hath bled;
  He bore our sins upon his tree;
Beneath our curse he bowed his head;
  'T is finished—he hath died for me!

6 See, where before the throne he stands,
  And pours the all-prevailing prayer;
Points to his side, and lifts his hands,
  And shows that I am graven there!

730. *"Who shall separate us from the love of Christ?"*

1 Lord, didst thou die—but not for me?
  Am I forbid to trust thy blood?
Hast thou not pardons rich and free;
  And grace, an overwhelming flood?

2 Who, then, shall drive my trembling soul
  From thee to regions of despair?
Who has surveyed the sacred roll,
  And found my name not written there?

3 Presumptuous thought, to fix the bound,
  To limit mercy's sovereign reign;
What other happy souls have found
  I'll seek, nor shall I seek in vain.

4 I own my guilt, my sins confess:
  Can men or devils make them more?
Of crimes already numberless,
  Who will attempt to swell the score?

5 Were all my crimes before my sight,
  While I remember thou hast died,
They would but urge my speedier flight
  To seek salvation at thy side.

6 Low at thy feet I'll cast me down,
  To thee reveal my guilt and fear;
And, if thou spurn me from thy throne,
  I'll be the first who perished there.

IOSCO. L. M.

190. *"The voice of the Lord is full of majesty."*

1 ETERNAL God! eternal King!
  Ruler of heaven and earth beneath!
  From thee our hopes, our comforts spring;
  In thee we live, and move, and breathe.

2 Thy word brought forth the flaming sun,
  The changeful moon, the starry host:
  In thine appointed course they run,
  Till in the final **ruin lost**.

3 At thy **command the storm is dumb**;
  And to the sea thy power hath said,
  "No further shalt thou dare to come,
  And here shall thy proud waves be stayed."

4 Thy sway is known below, above,
  And full of majesty thy voice:
  And, as it speaks, in wrath or love,
  The nations tremble or rejoice.

5 The final, awful hour is near,
  Time paces on with ceaseless tread,
  When opening **graves that voice shall hear**,
  And render up **the sleeping dead**.

6 Oh, in **that** great decisive day,
  May we be found in Christ, and stand,
  While flaming worlds shall melt away,
  Accepted, owned, at thy right hand!

699. *"Lovest thou Me more than these?"*

1 LORD, should my path thro' suffering lie,
  Forbid that I should e'er repine:
  Still let me turn **to Calvary**,
  Nor heed my griefs, rememb'ring thine.

2 Oh, let me think how thou didst leave
  Untasted, every pure delight,
  To fast, to faint, to watch, to grieve,
  The toilsome day, the homeless night.

3 To faint, to grieve, to die for me!
  Thou camest not thyself to please:
  And, **dear** as earthly comforts be,
  Shall I not love thee more than these?

4 Yes: I would count them all but loss,
  To gain the notice of thine eye:
  Flesh shrinks and trembles at the cross,
  But thou canst give the victory.

5 Saviour! thy needful grace afford:
  On thee my trembling soul I cast:
  Perfect thy work within me, Lord,
  And own my worthless name at last.

780. *Inconstant Trust.*

1 WHEN darkness long has vailed my mind,
  And smiling day once more appears,
  Then, my Redeemer! then I find
  The folly of my doubts and fears.

2 Straight I upbraid my wandering heart,
  And blush that I should ever be
  Thus prone to act so base a part,
  Or harbor one hard thought of **thee**!

3 Oh, let me then at length be taught
  (What I am still so slow to learn),
  That God is love, and changes not,
  Nor knows the shadow of a turn.

4 Sweet truth, and easy to repeat!
  But when my faith is sharply tried,
  I find myself a learner yet,—
  Unskillful, weak, and apt to slide.

5 But, O my Lord! one look from thee
  Subdues the disobedient will;
  Drives doubt and discontent away,
  And thy rebellious child is still.

6 Thou art as ready to forgive,
  As I am ready to repine;
  Thou, therefore, all the praise receive;
  Be shame and self-abasement mine.

LISCHER. H. M.

329. "*The blood of His Cross.*"—Col. 1: 20.

1 YE saints, your music bring,
　Attuned to sweetest sound;
Strike every trembling string,
　Till earth and heaven resound:
The triumphs of the cross we sing;
Awake, ye saints, each joyful string!

2 The cross, the cross alone,
　Subdued the powers of hell;
Like lightning, from his throne
　The prince of darkness fell:
The triumphs of the cross we sing;
Awake, ye saints, each joyful string!

3 The cross hath power to save
　From all the foes that rise;
The cross hath made the grave
　A passage to the skies:
The triumphs of the cross we sing;
Awake, ye saints, each joyful string!

1033. "*Gird Thy sword upon Thy thigh, O Most Mighty!*"—Psalm 45.

1 GIRD on thy conquering sword!
　Ascend thy shining car,
And march, Almighty Lord!
　To wage the holy war:
Before his wheels,　│Ye valleys, rise,
In glad surprise,　│And sink, ye hills!

2 Before thine awful face
　Millions of foes shall fall,
The captives of thy grace—
　That grace which conquers all:
The world shall　│What wondrous
　know,　　　　│　things
Great King of kings!│Thine arm can do!

3 Here to my willing soul
　Bend thy triumphant way;
Here every foe control,
　And all thy power display:
My heart, thy throne,│Bows low to thee,
Blest Jesus, see,　│To thee alone!

1074. "*Christ is our Corner-stone.*"

1 CHRIST is our Corner-stone;
　On him alone we build;
With his true saints alone
　The courts of heaven are filled:
On his great love　│Of present grace
Our hopes we place,│And joys above.

2 Oh, then, with hymns of praise
　These hallowed courts shall ring!
Our voices we will raise,
　The Three in One to sing;
And thus proclaim　│Both loud and long,
In joyful song,　│That glorious Name.

3 Here, gracious God, do thou
　For evermore draw nigh;
Accept each faithful vow,
　And mark each suppliant sigh:
In copious shower,│Each holy day,
On all who pray,　│Thy blessings pour.

4 Here may we gain from heaven
　The grace which we implore,
And may that grace, once given,
　Be with us evermore,—
Until that day　│To endless rest
When all the blest│Are called away.

LENOX. H. M.

229. *Our Constant Friend.*

1 To God, the mighty Lord,
    Your joyful thanks repeat ;
  To him due praise afford,
    As good as he is great ;
  For God doth prove our constant friend ;
  His boundless love shall never end.

2 He, in our depths of woes,
    On us with favor thought ;
  And from our deadly foes
    In peace and safety brought :
  For God doth prove our constant friend ;
  His boundless love shall never end.

3 He doth the food supply,
    On which all creatures live ;
  To God, who reigns on high,
    Eternal praises give :
  For God doth prove our constant friend ;
  His boundless love shall never end.

523. *The Year of Jubilee.*

1 Blow ye the trumpet, blow,
    The gladly solemn sound !
  Let all the nations know,
    To earth's remotest bound :
  The year of jubilee is come ;
  Return, ye ransomed sinners, home.

2 Jesus, our great High Priest,
    Hath full atonement made ;
  Ye weary spirits, rest ;
    Ye mournful souls, be glad :
  The year of jubilee is come ;
  Return, ye ransomed sinners, home.

3 Exalt the Lamb of God,
    The sin-atoning Lamb ;
  Redemption in his blood
    To all the world proclaim :
  The year of jubilee is come ;
  Return, ye ransomed sinners, home.

4 The gospel trumpet hear—
    The news of heavenly grace ;
  And, saved from earth, appear
    Before your Saviour's face ;
  The year of jubilee is come ;
  Return, ye ransomed sinners, home.

872. *"One Lord, one faith, one baptism."*

1 One sole baptismal sign,
    One Lord, below, above,
  One faith, one hope divine,
    One only watchword—Love :
  From different temples though it rise,
  One song ascendeth to the skies.

2 Our sacrifice is one ;
    One Priest before the throne ;
  The slain, the risen Son,
    Redeemer, Lord alone !
  And sighs from contrite hearts that spring,
  Our chief, our choicest offering.

3 Head of thy church beneath !
    The catholic, the true,
  On all her members breathe ;
    Her broken frame renew !
  Then shall thy perfect will be done
  When Christians love and live as one.

ANTIOCH. C. M.

Observe that in singing the tune "Antioch" the last line of each stanza is sung three times, and also that in the last repetition the first two syllables are also repeated.

256. *"The voice of praise."*

1 Lift up to God the voice of praise,
  Whose breath our souls inspired;
Loud and more loud the anthems raise,
  With grateful ardor fired.

2 Lift up to God the voice of praise,
  Whose goodness, passing thought,
Loads every moment, as it flies,
  With benefits unsought.

3 Lift up to God the voice of praise,
  From whom salvation flows;
Who sent his Son our souls to save
  From everlasting woes.

4 Lift up to God the voice of praise,
  For hope's transporting ray,
Which lights through darkest shades of death
  To realms of endless day.

262. *"Greater love hath no man than this."*

1 Plunged in a gulf of dark despair,
  We wretched sinners lay,
Without one cheerful beam of hope,
  Or spark of glimmering day.

2 With pitying eyes the Prince of Grace
  Beheld our helpless grief;
He saw, and, oh, amazing love!—
  He ran to our relief.

3 Down from the shining seats above,
  With joyful haste he fled,
Entered the grave in mortal flesh,
  And dwelt among the dead.

4 Oh, for this love let rocks and hills
  Their lasting silence break;
And all harmonious human tongues
  The Saviour's praises speak!

5 Angels, assist our mighty joys!
  Strike all your harps of gold!
But when you raise your highest notes,
  His love can ne'er be told.

267. *"Unto us a Child is born."*
  Isaiah 9 : 6, 7.

1 To us a Child of hope is born,
  To us a Son is given;
Him shall the tribes of earth obey,
  Him all the hosts of heaven.

2 His name shall be the Prince of Peace,
  For evermore adored;
The Wonderful, the Counselor,
  The great and mighty Lord!

3 His power, increasing, still shall spread,
  His reign no end shall know;
Justice shall guard his throne above,
  And peace abound below.

4 To us a Child of hope is born,
  To us a Son is given;
The Wonderful, the Counselor,
  The mighty Lord of heaven.

277. *"Joy to the world!"*

1 Joy to the world! the Lord is come!
  Let earth receive her King;
Let every heart prepare him room,
  And heaven and nature sing.

2 Joy to the world! the Saviour reigns!
  Let men their songs employ;
While fields and floods, rocks, hills, and plains
  Repeat the sounding joy.

3 No more let sin and sorrow grow,
  Nor thorns infest the ground;
He comes to make his blessings flow
  Far as the curse is found.

4 He rules the world with truth and grace,
  And makes the nations prove
The glories of his righteousness,
  And wonders of his love.

NEW YORK TUNE. C. M.

337. *The New Song.—Rev. 5.*

1 BEHOLD the glories of the Lamb,
   Amid his Father's throne;
   Prepare new honors for his name,
   And songs before unknown.

2 Let elders worship at his feet,
   The church adore around,
   With vials full of odor sweet,
   And harps of sweeter sound.

3 Those are the prayers of all the saints,
   And these the hymns they raise;
   Jesus is kind to our complaints:
   He loves to hear our praise.

4 Now to the Lamb that once was slain,
   Be endless blessings paid!
   Salvation, glory, joy, remain
   For ever on thy head!

5 Thou hast redeemed our souls with blood,
   Hast set the prisoners free,
   Hast made us kings and priests to God,
   And we shall reign with thee.

363. *"Lift up your heads, O ye gates."*
       Psalm 24.

1 LIFT up your heads, eternal gates!
   Unfold, to entertain
   The King of glory; see! he comes,
   With his celestial train.

2 Who is this King of glory—who?
   The Lord, for strength renowned;
   In battle mighty; o'er his foes
   Eternal Victor crowned.

3 Lift up your heads, ye gates! unfold,
   In state to entertain
   The King of glory; see! he comes,
   With all his shining train.

4 Who is the King of glory—who?
   The Lord of hosts renowned:
   Of glory he alone is King,
   Who is with glory crowned.

387. *"Shout unto God with the voice of triumph."—Psalm 47.*

1 ARISE, ye people, and adore;
   Exulting, strike the chord!
   Let all the earth, from shore to shore,
   Confess th' almighty Lord.

2 Glad shouts aloud, wide echoing round,
   Th' ascending God proclaim;
   Th' angelic choir respond the sound,
   And shake creation's frame.

3 They sing of death and hell o'erthrown
   In that triumphant hour;
   And God exalts his conquering Son
   To his right hand of power.

4 Oh, shout ye people, and adore;
   Exulting strike the chord!
   Let all the earth, from shore to shore,
   Confess th' almighty Lord!

1158. *"Welcome, each closing year."*

1 AWAKE, ye saints! and raise your eyes,
   And lift you voices high;
   Awake, and praise the sovereign love,
   That shows salvation nigh.

2 Swift on the wings of time it flies,
   Each moment brings it near;
   Then welcome, each declining day!
   Welcome each closing year!

3 Not many years their round shall run,
   Not many mornings rise,
   Ere all its glories stand revealed
   To our admiring eyes.

4 Ye wheels of nature, speed your course!
   Ye mortal powers, decay!
   Fast as ye bring the night of death,
   Ye bring eternal day.

ONLAND. 7s.

76. *Close of the Sabbath.*

1 SOFTLY fades the twilight ray
Of the holy Sabbath day;
Gently as life's setting sun,
When the Christian's course is run.

2 Peace is on the world abroad;
'T is the holy peace of God;
Symbol of the peace within,
When the spirit rests from sin.

3 Still the Spirit lingers near,
Where the evening worshiper
Seeks communion with the skies,
Pressing onward to the prize.

4 Saviour, may our Sabbaths be
Days of peace and joy in thee!
Till in heaven our souls repose,
Where the Sabbath ne'er shall close.

206. *Confidence in God's Care.*—Psalm 23.

1 To thy pastures fair and large,
Heavenly Shepherd, lead thy charge;
And my couch, with tenderest care,
'Mid the springing grass prepare.

2 When I faint with summer's heat,
Thou shalt guide my weary feet
To the streams that, still and slow,
Through the verdant meadows flow.

3 Safe the dreary vale I tread,
By the shades of death o'erspread,
With thy rod and staff supplied—
This my guard, and that my guide.

4 Constant to my latest end,
Thou my footsteps shalt attend;
Thou shalt bid thy hallowed dome
Yield me an eternal home.

396. "*I know my sheep, and am known of mine.*"

1 JESUS, Shepherd of the sheep;
Powerful is thine arm to keep
All thy flocks with safest care,
Fed in pastures large and fair.

2 Thee their Guide and Guard they own;
Thee they love, and thee alone:
Thee they follow day by day,
Fearful lest their feet should stray.

3 Lord, thy helpless sheep behold;
Gather all unto thy fold;
Gently lead the wanderers home;
Watch them, lest again they roam.

4 Bring thy sheep, now far astray,
Lost in Satan's evil way;
Then, the fold and shepherd one,
We shall praise thee round the throne.

416. "*Cast thy burden upon the Lord.*" Psalm 55.

1 CAST thy burden on the Lord;
Lean thou only on his word:
Ever will he be thy stay,
Though the heavens shall melt away.

2 Ever in the raging storm,
Thou shalt see his cheering form,
Hear his pledge of coming aid;
"It is I, be not afraid."

3 Cast thy burden at his feet;
Linger near his mercy-seat:
He will lead thee by the hand
Gently to the better land.

4 He will gird thee by his power,
In thy weary, fainting hour;
Lean, then, loving, on his word;
Cast thy burden on the Lord.

SEYMOUR. 7s.

397. *"I lay down my life for the sheep."*

1 Shepherd of the ransomed flock,
   Lead us to the shadowing rock,
   Where the cooling waters flow,
   Where the freshening pastures grow.

2 Grant, O Lord, that we may be
   Ever glad to follow thee;
   And with thankful hearts rejoice,
   When we hear **thy** gracious voice.

3 Saviour, **when** thy loved ones stray
   From the new and living way,
   Gently call thine own by name;
   All our wand'ring steps reclaim.

4 Through the **hours of** darksome **night**
   Keep us in thy watchful sight;
   O'er each deadly foe prevail,
   Let **no harm** thy fold assail.

5 Jesus, who thy life didst give,
   Dying that thy sheep **might live**;
   Let us in thy presence rest,
   With eternal comfort blest.

442. *"Every precious name in **One**."*

1 Sweeter sounds than music knows
   Charm me in Immanuel's name;
   All her hopes my spirit owes
   To his birth, and cross, and shame.

2 When he came, the angels sung,
   "Glory be to God on high:"
   Lord, unloose my stammering tongue;
   Who should louder sing than I?

3 Did the Lord a man become,
   That he might the law fulfill,
   Bleed and suffer in my room,—
   And canst thou, my tongue, be still?

4 No: I must my praises bring,
   Though they worthless are, and weak;

For, should I refuse to sing,
   Sure the very stones would speak.

5 O my Saviour! Shield, and Sun,
   Shepherd, Brother, Lord, and Friend—
   Every precious name in one!
   I will love thee without end.

514. *The Voice of Jesus.*—Matt. 11: 28-30.

1 Come, said Jesus' sacred voice,
   Come, and make my paths your **choice**;
   I will guide you to your home;
   Weary wanderer, hither come!

2 Thou who, homeless and forlorn,
   Long hast borne the proud world's scorn,
   Long hast roamed the barren waste,
   Weary wanderer, hither haste.

3 Ye who, tossed on beds of pain,
   Seek for ease, but seek in vain;
   Ye, by fiercer anguish **torn**,
   In remorse for guilt who **mourn** :—

4 Hither come! for here is found
   Balm that flows for every wound;
   Peace that ever shall endure,
   Rest eternal, sacred, sure.

965. *"The God of my life."*

1 Source and Giver of repose,
   From thee all my comfort flows:
   Peace and happiness are thine;
   Mine they are, if thou art mine.

2 Thee to praise and thee to know,
   Constitute **my** bliss below;
   Thee to see and thee to love
   Constitute **my bliss above.**

3 Lord! it is not life to live,
   If thy presence thou deny:
   Lord! if thou thy presence give,
   'T is no longer death to die.

OLEAN. L. M. 6 LINES.

414. *Christ is mine.*

1 WHY should I fear the darkest hour,
 Or tremble at the tempest's power?
 Jesus vouchsafes to be my tower.
 Though hot the fight, why quit the field?
 Why should I either flee or yield,
 Since Jesus is my mighty Shield?

2 Tho' all the flocks and herds were dead,
 My soul a famine need not dread,
 For Jesus is my living bread.
 I know not what may soon betide,
 Or how my wants shall be supplied;
 But Jesus knows and will provide.

3 Though sin would fill me with distress,
 The throne of grace I dare address,
 For Jesus is my righteousness.
 Against me earth and hell combine,
 But on my side is power divine:
 Jesus is all, and he is mine.

683. *"Loved with an everlasting love."*

1 THOUGH waves and storms go o'er my head,
  Though strength, and health, and friends be gone;
 Though joys be withered all, and dead,
  Though every comfort be withdrawn;
 On this my steadfast soul relies,—
  Father, thy mercy never dies.

2 Fixed on this ground will I remain,
  Though heart may fail, and flesh decay;
 This anchor shall my soul sustain,
  When earth's foundations melt away:
 Mercy's full power I then shall prove,
 Loved with an everlasting love.

868. *The Communion of Saints.*
  Heb. 12: 18-25.

1 NOT to the mount that burned with flame,
  To darkness, tempest, and the sound
 Of trumpets' tone that, startling, came,
  Nor voice of words that rent the ground,
 While Israel heard with trembling awe
 Jehovah thunder forth his law,—

2 But to mount Zion we are come,
  The city of the living God,
 Jerusalem our heavenly home,
  The courts by angel-legions trod;
 Where meet in everlasting love
 The Church of the first-born above;—

3 To God, the Judge of quick and dead,
  The perfect spirits of the just,
 Jesus, our great new-covenant Head,
  The blood of sprinkling,—from the dust,
 That better things than Abel's cries,
 And pleads a Saviour's sacrifice.

4 Oh, hearken to the healing voice,
  That speaks from heaven, in tones so mild!
 To-day, are life and death our choice;
  To-day, through mercy reconciled,
 Our all to God we yet may give:
 Now let us hear his voice, and live.

1145. *"Thou wentest forth for the salvation of Thy people."*

1 LIKE Israel's host to exile driven,
  Across the flood the pilgrims fled;
 Their hands bore up the ark of Heaven,
  And Heaven their trusting footsteps led,
 Till on these savage shores they trod,
 And won the wilderness for God.

2 Then, when their weary ark found rest,
  Another Zion proudly grew;
 In more than Judah's glory dressed,
  With light that Israel never knew;
 From sea to sea her empire spread,
 Her temple heaven, and Christ her Head.

3 Then, let the grateful church, to-day,
  Its ancient rite with gladness keep;
 And still our fathers' God display
  His kindness, though the fathers sleep:
 Oh, bless, as thou hast blest the past,
 While earth, and time, and heaven shall last!

PETERSBURGH. L. M. 6 LINES.

802. *"That we may not be ashamed at His coming."*

1 And art thou, gracious Master, gone,
　A mansion to prepare for me?
Shall I behold thee on thy throne,
　And there for ever sit with thee?
Then let the world approve or blame,
I'll triumph in thy glorious name!

2 Should I, to gain the world's applause,
　Or to escape its harmless frown,
Refuse to love and plead thy cause,
　And make thy people's lot my own,—
What shame would fill me in that day,
When thou thy glory wilt display!

3 No; let the world cast out my name,
　And vile account me, if they will;
If to confess the Lord be shame,
　I purpose to be viler still:
For thee, my God, I all resign,
Content if I can call thee mine.

4 What transport then shall fill my heart,
　When thou my worthless name wilt own;
When I shall see thee as thou art,
　And know as I myself am known!
From sin and fear and sorrow free,
My soul shall find its rest in thee.

823. *"Thee will I love."*

1 Thee will I love, my Strength and Tower,
　Thee will I love, my Joy and Crown,
Thee will I love with all my power,
　In all my works,—and thee alone;
Thee will I love, till that pure fire
Fills my whole soul with strong desire.

2 In darkness willingly I strayed,
　I sought thee, yet from thee I roved;
Far wide my wandering thoughts were spread,
　Thy creatures more than thee I loved:
And now, if more at length I see,
'Tis through thy light, and comes from thee.

3 I thank thee, uncreated Sun,
　That thy bright beams on me have shined;
I thank thee, who hast overthrown

My foes, and healed my wounded mind;
I thank thee, whose enlivening voice
Bids my freed heart in thee rejoice.

4 Thee will I love, my Joy, my Crown;
　Thee will I love, my Lord, my God;
Thee will I love beneath thy frown
　Or smile, thy scepter or thy rod;
What though my heart and flesh decay,
Thee shall I love in endless day.

1152. *"The day is Thine, the night also is Thine."*—Psalm 74.

1 Thou art, O God, the life and light
　Of all this wondrous world we see:
Its glow by day, its smile by night,
　Are but reflections caught from thee;
Where'er we turn, thy glories shine,
And all things fair and bright are thine.

2 When day, with farewell beam, delays
　Among the opening clouds of even,
And we can almost think we gaze
　Through golden vistas into heaven,—
Those hues that mark the sun's decline,
So soft, so radiant, Lord, are thine.

3 When youthful spring around us breathes,
　Thy Spirit warms her fragrant sigh,
And every flower the summer wreathes
　Is born beneath thy kindling eye:
Where'er we turn, thy glories shine,
And all things fair and bright are thine.

1277. *"I know whom I have believed."*

1 My Saviour! can it ever be,
　And wilt thou deign to smile on me?
Yes! thou wilt own me on that day,—
Thou wilt not cast my soul away;
I know in whom I have believed;
I know by whom I am received.

2 'Tis even so, my dying Lord!
Cleansed by thine all-atoning blood,
I venture to believe, that day,
When heaven and earth shall pass away,
Will bring me bliss without alloy,
And consummate and crown my joy.

MANOAH. C. M.

449. *"To Thee for help we cry."*

1 SPIRIT of truth! on this thy day,
  To thee for help we cry,
To guide us through the dreary way
  Of dark mortality.

2 We ask not, Lord, the cloven flame,
  Or tongues of various tone;
But long thy praises to proclaim
  With fervor in our own.

3 No heavenly harpings soothe our ear,
  No mystic dreams we share;
Yet hope to feel thy comfort near,
  And bless thee in our prayer.

4 When tongues shall cease and power decay,
  And knowledge empty prove,
Do thou thy trembling servants stay
  With faith, and hope, and love.

701. *Christ above all else.*

1 COMPARED with Christ, in all beside
  No comeliness I see;
The one thing needful, dearest Lord,
  Is to be one with thee.

2 The sense of thine expiring love
  Into my soul convey;
Thyself bestow! for thee alone,
  My All in All, I pray.

3 Less than thyself will not suffice
  My comfort to restore;
More than thyself I can not crave,
  And thou canst give no more.

4 Whate'er consists not with thy love,
  Oh, teach me to resign!
I'm rich to all th' intents of bliss,
  If thou, O Lord, art mine.

732. *Christ is mine.*

1 WHEN blest with that transporting view,
  That Jesus died for me,
For this sweet hope what praise is due,
  O God of grace, to thee!

2 And may I hope that Christ is mine?
  That source of every bliss,
That noblest gift of love divine?
  What wondrous grace is this!

3 My highest praise, alas, how poor!
  How cold my warmest love!
Dear Saviour, teach me to adore
  As angels do above.

4 Then shall my joyful powers unite
  In more exalted lays,
And join the happy sons of light
  In everlasting praise.

744. *Fullness of Redemption.*

1 IF thou impart thyself to me,
  No other good I need:
If thou, the Son, shalt make me free,
  I shall be free indeed.

2 I can not rest till in thy blood
  I full redemption have;
But thou, through whom I come to God,
  Canst to the utmost save.

3 From sin,—the guilt, the power, the pain,
  Thou wilt redeem my soul;
Lord, I believe—and not in vain;
  My faith shall make me whole.

4 I, too, with thee, shall walk in white;
  With all thy saints shall prove
The length, and breadth, and depth and height
  Of everlasting love.

787. *"Saviour, Thyself reveal."*

1 SAVIOUR, to me thyself reveal,
  While here on earth I rove;
Speak to my heart, and let me feel
  The kindling of thy love.

ARLINGTON. C. M.

2 With thee conversing, I forget
   All time and toil and care;
   Labor is rest, and pain is sweet,
   If thou, my God, art here.

3 Here, then, my God, be pleased to stay,
   And make my heart rejoice;
   My bounding heart shall own thy sway,
   And echo to thy voice.

4 Thou callest me to seek thy face;
   Thy face, O God, I seek,—
   Attend the whisper of thy grace,
   And bear thee inly speak.

5 Let this my every hour employ,
   Till I thy glory see,
   Enter into my Master's joy,
   And find my heaven in thee.

818. *"Now, Lord, I would be Thine alone."*

1 As by the light of opening day
   The stars are all concealed,
   So earthly pleasures fade away
   When Jesus is revealed.

2 These pleasures now no longer please,
   No more content afford;
   Far from my heart be joys like these,
   For I have seen the Lord.

3 Now, Lord! I would be thine alone,
   And wholly live to thee;
   But may I hope that thou wilt own
   A worthless one like me?

4 Yes; though of sinners I'm the worst,
   I can not doubt thy will;
   For if thou hadst not loved me first,
   I had refused thee still.

862. *The Spirit of Peace.*—Psalm 133.

1 Spirit of peace! celestial Dove!
   How excellent thy praise!
   No richer gift than Christian love
   Thy gracious power displays.

2 Sweet as the dew on herb and flower
   That silently distills,
   At evening's soft and balmy hour,
   On Zion's fruitful hills—

3 So, with mild influence from above,
   Shall promised grace descend,
   Till universal peace and love
   O'er all the earth extend!

911. *"I dwell with him that is of a humble spirit."*

1 Thy home is with the humble, Lord!
   The simplest are the best;
   Thy lodging is in child-like hearts;
   Thou makest there thy rest.

2 Dear Comforter! eternal Love!
   If thou wilt stay with me,
   Of lowly thoughts and simple ways
   I'll build a house for thee.

3 Who made this beating heart of mine
   But thou, my heavenly Guest?
   Let no one have it, then, but thee,
   And let it be thy rest!

912. *The Simplicity of Christ.*

1 Oh, see how Jesus trusts himself
   Unto our childish love!
   As though by his free ways with us
   Our earnestness to prove.

2 His sacred name a common word
   On earth he loves to hear;
   There is no majesty in him
   Which love may not come near.

3 The light of love is round his feet,
   His paths are never dim;
   And he comes nigh to us when we
   Dare not come nigh to him.

4 Let us be simple with him, then,
   Not backward, still, nor cold,
   As though our Bethlehem could be
   What Sinai was of old.

MISSIONARY HYMN. 7s & 6s. DOUBLE.

239. *"I have chosen you."*—John 15 : 16.

1 'T is not that I did choose thee,
  For, Lord. that could not be ;
This heart would still refuse thee,
  But thou hast chosen me :
Thou from the sin that stained me
  Hast made me pure and free ;
Of old thou hast ordained me
  That I should live to thee.

2 'T was sovereign mercy called me,
  And taught my opening mind ;
The world had else enthralled me,
  To heavenly glories blind.
My heart owns none above thee ;
  For thy rich grace I thirst ;
This knowing, if I love thee,
  Thou must have loved me first.

894. *"Be strong in the Lord."*

1 O FAINT and feeble-hearted,
  Why thus cast down with fear ?
Fresh aid shall be imparted ;
  Thy God unseen is near.

2 His eye can never slumber,
  He marks thy cruel foes ;
Observes their strength, their number,
  And all thy weakness knows.

3 Though heavy clouds of sorrow
  Make dark thy path to-day,
There may shine forth to-morrow
  Once more a cheering ray.

4 Though doubts and griefs assailing
  Conceal heaven's fair abode ;
Yet now faith's power prevailing
  Should stay thy mind on God.

1051. *An ancient Sacramental Hymn.*

1 O BREAD to pilgrims given,
  O Food that angels eat,
O Manna sent from heaven,
  For heaven-born natures meet !
Give us for thee long pining,
  To eat till richly filled :
Till earth's delights resigning,
  Our every wish is stilled !

2 O Water, life-bestowing,
  From out the Saviour's heart,
A fountain purely flowing,
  A fount of love thou art !
Oh let us, freely tasting,
  Our burning thirst assuage !
Thy sweetness never wasting,
  Avails from age to age.

3 Jesus, this feast receiving,
  We thee unseen adore ;
Thy faithful world believing,
  We take—and doubt no more :
Give us, thou true and loving,
  On earth to live in thee ;
Then death, the vail removing,
  Thy glorious face to see !

ZION. 8s, 7s & 4.

1031. *"Hear, O Israel, I am God, even thy God."*

1 ON the mountain's top appearing,
　Lo! the sacred herald stands,
Welcome news to Zion bearing,
　Zion long in hostile lands:
　　Mourning captive!
　God himself will loose thy bands.

2 Has thy night been long and mournful?
　Have thy friends unfaithful proved?
Have thy foes been proud and scornful,
　By thy sighs and tears unmoved?
　　Cease thy mourning!
　Zion still is well beloved.

3 God, thy God will now restore thee;
　He himself appears thy Friend;
All thy foes shall flee before thee;
　Here their boasts and triumphs end:
　　Great deliverance
　Zion's King vouchsafes to send.

4 Enemies no more shall trouble,—
　All thy wrongs shall be redressed;
For thy shame thou shalt have double,
　In thy Maker's favor blest:
　　All thy conflicts
　End in everlasting rest.

1127. *"Thy kingdom come."*—Matt. 6: 10.

1 O'ER the gloomy hills of darkness
　Look, my soul! be still,—and gaze;
See the promises advancing
　To a glorious day of grace:
　　Blessed jubilee!
　Let thy glorious morning dawn.

2 Let the dark, benighted pagan,
　Let the rude barbarian see
That divine and glorious conquest,
　Once obtained on Calvary:
　　Let the gospel
　Loud resound, from pole to pole!

3 Kingdoms wide that sit in darkness—
　Grant them, Lord, the glorious light;
Now from eastern coast to western
　May the morning chase the night;
　　Let redemption,
　Freely purchased, win the day.

4 Fly abroad, thou mighty gospel!
　Win and conquer,—never cease;
May thy lasting, wide dominions
　Multiply and still increase:
　　Sway thy scepter,
　Saviour! all the world around.

1286. *The Judgment welcomed.*

1 Lo! he cometh—countless trumpets
　Wake to life the slumbering dead;
Mid ten thousand saints and angels,
　See their great, exalted Head:
　　Hallelujah!
　Welcome, welcome, Son of God!

2 Full of joyful expectation,
　Saints behold the Judge appear!
Truth and justice go before him—
　Now the joyful sentence hear:
　　Hallelujah!
　Welcome, welcome, Judge divine!

3 "Come, ye blessed of my Father,
　Enter into life and joy;
Banish all your fears and sorrows;
　Endless praise be your employ:"
　　Hallelujah!
　Welcome, welcome to the skies!

DOXOLOGY.

GREAT Jehovah, we adore thee,
　God the Father, God the Son,
God the Spirit, joined in glory
　On the same eternal throne;
　　Endless praises
　To Jehovah, Three in One!

MAITLAND. C. M.

201. *God a sure Defense.*

1 YE humble souls, approach your God
    With songs of sacred praise;
  For he is good, supremely good,
    And kind are all his ways.
2 All nature owns his guardian care;
    In him we live and move;
  But nobler benefits declare
    The wonders of his love.
3 He gave his well-belovéd Son,
    To save our souls from sin:
  'T is here he makes his goodness known,
    And proves it all divine.
4 To this dear Refuge, Lord, we come,
    And here our hope relies;
  A safe defense, a peaceful home,
    When storms of trouble rise.
5 Thine eye beholds, with kind regard,
    The souls who trust in thee;
  Their humble hope thou wilt reward
    With bliss divinely free.
6 Great God! to thine almighty love
    What honors shall we raise?
  Not all the raptured songs above
    Can render equal praise.

323. *"The Love of Christ constraineth us."*

1 JESUS, in thy transporting name
    What blissful glories rise!
  Jesus—the angels' sweetest theme
    The wonder of the skies!
2 Well might the skies with wonder view
    A love so strange as thine!
  No thought of angels ever knew
    Compassion so divine!
3 Jesus, and didst thou leave the sky
    To bear our sins and woes?

And didst thou bleed, and groan, and die
    For vile, rebellious foes?
4 Is there a heart that will not bend
    To thy divine control?
  Descend, O sovereign Love, descend,
    And melt the stubborn soul!
5 Oh, may our willing hearts confess
    Thy sweet, thy gentle sway!
  Glad captives of resistless grace,
    Thy pleasing rule obey.
6 Come, dearest Lord, extend thy reign,
    Till rebels rise no more;
  Thy praise all nature then shall join,
    And heaven and earth adore.

1134. *"They come, they come—thine exiled bands."*

1 DAUGHTER of Zion! from the dust
    Exalt thy fallen head;
  Again in thy Redeemer trust;
    He calls thee from the dead.
2 Awake, awake! put on thy strength,
    Thy beautiful array;
  The day of freedom dawns at length,
    The Lord's appointed day.
3 Rebuild thy walls, thy bounds enlarge,
    And send thy heralds forth;
  Say to the south, "Give up thy charge,"
    And keep not back, O north!
4 They come, they come!—thine exiled bands,
    Where'er they rest or roam,
  Have heard thy voice in distant lands,
    And hasten to their home.
5 Thus, though the universe shall burn,
    And God his works destroy,
  With songs thy ransomed shall return,
    And everlasting joy.

NEW YORK TUNE. C. M.

870. *Blessedness of the Communion of Saints.*

1 Happy the souls to Jesus joined,
  And saved by grace alone:
 Walking in all his ways, they find
  Their heaven on earth begun.

2 The church triumphant in thy love,—
  Their mighty joys we know:
 They sing the Lamb in hymns above,
  And we, in hymns below.

3 Thee, in thy glorious realm, they praise
  And bow before thy throne:
 We, in the kingdom of thy grace;—
  The kingdoms are but one.

4 The holy to the holiest leads;
  From thence our spirits rise:
 And he that in thy statutes treads
  Shall meet thee in the skies.

871. *"Of one heart and of one soul."*

1 Blest be the dear, uniting love,
  That will not let us part:
 Our bodies may far off remove;
  We still are one in heart.

2 Joined in one spirit to our head,
  Where he appoints we go;
 We still in Jesus' footsteps tread,
  And show his praise below.

3 Oh, may we ever walk in him,
  And nothing know beside!
 Nothing desire, nothing esteem,
  But Jesus crucified!

4 Partakers of the Saviour's grace,
  The same in mind and heart,
 Not joy, nor grief, nor time, nor place,
  Nor life, nor death, can part.

873. *"Sympathy like that of Christ."*
  Luke 10: 30—37.

1 Father of mercies, send thy grace,
  All-powerful from above,
 To form in our obedient souls
  The image of thy love.

2 Oh, may our sympathizing breasts
  That generous pleasure know,
 Kindly to share in others' joy,
  And weep for others' woe!

3 When poor and helpless sons of grief
  In deep distress are laid,
 Soft be our hearts their pains to feel,
  And swift our hands to aid.

4 So Jesus looked on dying men,
  When throned above the skies,
 And in the Father's bosom blest,
  He felt compassion rise.

5 On wings of love the Saviour flew,
  To raise us from the ground,
 And made the richest of his blood
  A balm for every wound!

883. *"They shall be as Mount Zion."*
  Psalm 125.

1 Unshaken as the sacred hill,
  And fixed as mountains be,
 Firm as a rock the soul shall rest,
  That leans, O Lord, on thee!

2 Not walls, nor hills, could guard so well
  Old Salem's happy ground,
 As those eternal arms of love,
  That every saint surround.

3 Deal gently, Lord, with souls sincere,
  And lead them safely on
 To the bright gates of paradise,
  Where Christ, their Lord, is gone.

DOXOLOGY.

To Father, Son, and Holy Ghost,
 One God, whom we adore,
Be glory as it was, is now,
 And shall be evermore!

WARE. L. M.

713. *"Flow fast, my tears!"*—Luke 22: 62.

1 FLOW fast, my tears! the cause is great;
   This tribute claims an injured Friend—
One whom I long pursued with hate,
   And yet he loved me to the end.

2 Fast flow my tears,—yet faster flow!
   Stream copious as yon purple tide:
'T was I that dealt the deadly blow;
   I urged the hand that pierced his side.

3 Fast, and yet faster flow my tears!
   Love breaks the heart, and drowns the eyes;
His visage marred toward heaven he rears,
   And, pleading for his murderers, dies!

783. *Unto Jesus.*

1 SEE a poor sinner, dearest Lord,
   Whose soul, encouraged by thy word,
At mercy's footstool would remain,
   And then would look,—and look again.

2 Ah! bring a wretched wanderer home,
   Now to thy footstool let me come,
And tell thee all my grief and pain,
   And wait and look,—and look again.

3 Take courage, then, my trembling soul;
   One look from Christ will make thee whole:
Trust thou in him, 't is not in vain,
   But wait and look,—and look again.

4 Look to the Lord, his word, his throne;
   Look to his grace, and not your own;
There wait and look, and look again;
   You shall not wait, nor look in vain.

5 Ere long that happy day will come,
   When I shall reach my blissful home;
And when to glory I attain,
   Oh, then I 'll look,—and look again!

984. *"Return unto thy rest, O my soul."* Psalm 116.

1 RETURN, my soul, unto thy rest,
   From vain pursuits and maddening cares,
From lonely woes that wring thy breast,
   The world's alluring, fatal snares.

2 Return unto thy rest, my soul,
   From all the wanderings of thy thought,
From sickness unto death made whole,
   Safe through a thousand perils brought.

3 Then to thy rest, my soul, return,
   From passions every hour at strife:
Sin's works and ways and wages spurn,
   Lay hold upon eternal life.

4 God is thy Rest; with heart inclined
   To keep his word, that word believe:
Christ is thy Rest; with lowly mind,
   His light and easy yoke receive.

1021. *Prayer of the Church in Time of Desertion.*—Psalm 80.

1 GREAT Shepherd of thine Israel,
   Who didst between the cherubs dwell,
And lead the tribes, thy chosen sheep,
   Safe through the desert and the deep!

2 Thy church is in the desert now;
   Shine from on high, and guide us thro';
Turn us to thee, thy love restore:
   We shall be saved, and sigh no more.

3 Hast thou not planted with thy hand
   A lovely vine in this our land?
Did not thy power defend it round,
   And heavenly dew enrich the ground?

4 How did the spreading branches shoot,
   And bless the nations with their fruit?
But now, O Lord, look down and see
   Thy mourning vine, that lovely tree.

5 Return, almighty God, return!
   Nor let thy bleeding vineyard mourn:
Turn us to thee, thy love restore;
   We shall be saved and sigh no more!

HAMBURG. L. M.

497. *No Hope in the Grave.*

1 While life prolongs its precious light,
  Mercy is found, and peace is given;
  But soon, ah! soon, approaching night
  Shall blot out every hope of heaven.

2 While God invites, how blest the day!
  How sweet the gospel's charming sound!
  Come, sinners, haste, oh, **haste away**,
  While yet a pardoning God he's found.

3 Soon, borne on time's most rapid wing,
  Shall death command you to the grave,
  Before his bar your spirits **bring**,
  And none be found to hear **or save**.

4 In that lone land of deep despair
  No Sabbath's heavenly light shall rise;
  No God regard your bitter prayer,
  Nor Saviour call you to the skies.

5 Now **God invites**—how blest the day!
  How sweet the gospel's charming sound!
  Come, sinners, haste, oh, haste away,
  While yet a pardoning God is found.

581. *"Who shall deliver me?"*

1 Oh that my load of sin were gone!
  Oh that I could **at** last submit
  At Jesus' feet to lay it down—
  To lay my soul at Jesus' feet!

2 Rest for **my soul I long to find**:
  Saviour of all, if mine thou art,
  Give me thy meek and lowly mind,
  And stamp thine **image on my heart**.

3 Break off the yoke of inbred sin,
  And fully set my spirit free;
  I can not rest, till pure within—
  Till I am wholly lost in thee.

4 Fain would I learn of thee, my God—
  Thy light and easy burden prove;

  The cross all stained with **hallowed blood**,
  The labor of thy dying **love**.

5 I would—but thou must give the power;
  My heart from every sin release;
  Bring near, bring near the joyful hour,
  And fill me with thy perfect peace!

724. *"All things but loss for Christ."*
Phil. 3: 7, 8.

1 No more, my God, I boast no more
  Of all the duties I have done;
  I quit the hopes I held before,
  To trust the merits of thy Son.

2 Now, for the love I bear his name,
  What was my gain, I count my loss;
  My former pride I call my shame,
  And nail my glory to his cross.

3 Yes; and I must and will esteem
  All things but loss for Jesus' sake;
  Oh, may my soul be found in him,
  And of his righteousness **partake!**

4 The best obedience of my hands
  Dares not appear before thy throne;
  But faith can answer thy demands
  By pleading what my Lord has done.

955. *"He is my defense; I shall not be moved."—Psalm 62.*

1 My spirit looks to God alone;
  My rock and refuge is his throne;
  In all my fears, in all my straits,
  My soul on his salvation **waits**.

2 Trust him, ye saints, in all your ways;
  Pour out your hearts before his face;
  When helpers fail, and foes invade,
  God is our all-sufficient Aid.

DOXOLOGY.

Glory to thee, O God, most high!
Father, we praise thy majesty!
The Son, the Spirit, we adore,
One Godhead, blest for evermore!

OTTO. C. M.

64. *Evening Twilight.*

1 I LOVE to steal, awhile, away
   From every cumbering care,
And spend the hours of settling day
   In humble, grateful prayer.

2 I love, in solitude, to shed
   The penitential tear;
And all his promises to plead,
   Where none but God can hear.

3 I love to think on mercies past,
   And future good implore;
And all my cares and sorrows cast
   On him whom I adore.

4 I love, by faith, to take a view
   Of brighter scenes in heaven;
The prospect doth my strength renew,
   While here by tempests driven.

5 Thus, when life's toilsome day is o'er,
   May its departing ray
Be calm as this impressive hour,
   And lead to endless day!

169. "*Sow in tears—reap in joy.*"
   Psalm 126.

1 WHEN God revealed his gracious name,
   And changed my mournful state,
My rapture seemed a pleasing dream,
   The grace appeared so great.

2 The world beheld the glorious change,
   And did thy hand confess;
My tongue broke out in unknown strains,
   And sung surprising grace.

3 The Lord can clear the darkest skies,
   Can give us day for night;
Make drops of sacred sorrow rise
   To rivers of delight.

4 Let those that sow in sadness wait
   Till the fair harvest come;
They shall confess their sheaves are great,
   And shout the blessings home.

424. "*In all points tempted like as we are.*"

1 WITH joy we meditate the grace
   Of our High Priest above:
His heart is made of tenderness—
   It melts with pitying love.

2 Touched with a sympathy within,
   He knows our feeble frame;
He knows what sore temptations mean,
   For he hath felt the same.

3 He, in the days of feeble flesh,
   Poured out his cries and tears;
And, in his measure, feels afresh
   What every member bears.

4 He'll never quench the smoking flax,
   But raise it to a flame;
The bruised reed he never breaks,
   Nor scorns the meanest name.

5 Then let our humble faith address
   His mercy and his power;
We shall obtain delivering grace
   In the distressing hour.

488. "*Thy Word is a lamp unto my feet.*"

1 How precious is the book divine,
   By inspiration given!
Bright as a lamp its doctrines shine,
   To guide our souls to heaven.

2 It sweetly cheers our drooping hearts,
   In this dark vale of tears;
Life, light, and joy it still imparts,
   And quells our rising fears.

3 This lamp, through all the tedious night
   Of life, shall guide our way;
Till we behold the clearer light
   Of an eternal day.

WOODSTOCK. C. M.

976. *"We are more than conquerors."*
Rom. 8: 35–39.

1 Who, who can part our ransomed souls
From Jesus and his love;
Or break the sacred chain that binds
The earth to heaven above?

2 Let troubles rise, and terrors frown,
And days of darkness fall;—
Through him all dangers we'll defy,
And more than conquer all.

3 Nor death, nor life, nor earth, nor hell,
Nor time's destroying sway,
Can e'er efface us from his heart,
Or make his love decay.

4 Each coming period he will bless,
As he hath blest the past;
He loved us from the first of time,—
He loves us to the last.

1015. *"His grace was not in vain."*

1 Amazing grace! (how sweet the sound!)
That saved a wretch like me:
I once was lost, but now am found,
Was blind, but now I see.

2 'T was grace that taught my heart to fear,
And grace my fears relieved;
How precious did that grace appear,
The hour I first believed!

3 Through many dangers, toils, and snares,
I have already come;
'T is grace has brought me safe thus far,
And grace will lead me home.

1106. *"Neither do I condemn thee."*

1 Oh, if thy brow, serene and calm,
From earthly stain is free,
View not with scorn the erring one,—
He once was pure like thee.

2 Oh, if the smiles of love are thine,
Its joyous ecstasy,
Shun not the poor, forsaken one,—
He once was loved like thee!

3 And still, 'mid shame, and guilt, and woe,
One being loves him still,
Who, blessing thee, hath poured on him
The world's extremest ill.

4 He knows the secret lure which led
Those youthful steps astray;
He knows that they who holiest are
Might fall from him away.

5 Then, with the love of him who said,
"Go thou, and sin no more,"
Save, save the sinner from despair,
And peace and hope restore!

1260. *"In my Father's house are many mansions."*

1 When I can read my title clear
To mansions in the skies,
I bid farewell to every fear,
And wipe my weeping eyes.

2 Should earth against my soul engage,
And hellish darts be hurled,
Then I can smile at Satan's rage,
And face a frowning world.

3 Let cares like a wild deluge come,
And storms of sorrow fall;
May I but safely reach my home,
My God, my heaven, my all,—

4 There shall I bathe my weary soul
In seas of heavenly rest,
And not a wave of trouble roll
Across my peaceful breast.

DOXOLOGY.

To Father, Son, and Holy Ghost,
One God, whom we adore,
Be glory as it was, is now,
And shall be evermore!

YOAKLEY. L. M. 6 LINES.

502. *The constraining Love of Christ.*

1 O LOVE divine, what hast thou done!
   The Lord of life hath died for me!
The Father's coëternal Son
   Bore all my sins upon the tree:
Th' incarnate God for me hath died;
The Lord, my Love, was crucified.

2 Sinners, behold, as ye pass by,
   The bleeding Prince of life and peace,
Come, sinners, see your Saviour die,
   And say, was ever grief like his!
Come, feel with me his blood applied;
The Lord, my Love, was crucified;—

3 Was crucified for you and me,
   To bring us, rebels, back to God;
Salvation now for us is free;
   His church is purchased with his blood:
Pardon and life flow from his side;
The Lord, my Love, is crucified.

4 Then let us sit beneath his cross,
   And gladly catch the healing stream;
All things for him account but dross,
   And give up all our hearts to him:
Of nothing think or speak beside—
The Lord, my Love, was crucified.

631. *The returning Wanderer.*

1 WEARY of wandering from my God,
   And now made willing to return,
I hear, and bow beneath the rod;
   For thee, not without hope, I mourn:
I have an Advocate above,
A Friend before the throne of love.

2 O Jesus, full of truth and grace!
   More full of grace than I of sin;
Yet once again I seek thy face,
   Open thine arms and take me in;
And freely my backslidings heal,
And love the faithless sinner still.

3 Thou know'st the way to bring me back,
   My fallen spirit to restore;
Oh, for thy truth and mercy's sake,
   Forgive, and bid me sin no more!
The ruins of my soul repair,
And make my heart a house of prayer.

704. *Longing to follow Christ.*

1 MORE hard than marble is my heart,
   And foul with sins of deepest stain;
But thou the mighty Saviour art,
   Nor flowed thy cleansing blood in vain:
Ah, soften, melt this rock, and may
Thy blood wash all these stains away!

2 Oh that I, as a little child,
   May follow thee, and never rest,
Till sweetly thou hast breathed thy mild
   And lowly mind into my breast!
May I be one, O Lord, with thee,
And never parted may we be.

3 Still let thy love point out my way;
   How wondrous things that love hath wrought!
Still lead me, lest I go astray;
   Direct my word, inspire my thought:
And if I fall, soon may I hear
Thy voice, and know thy love is near.

4 In suffering be thy love my peace;
   In weakness be thy love my power;
And, when the storms of life shall cease,
   Jesus; in that momentous hour,
In death, as life, be thou my guide,
And save me, who for me hast died!

OLEAN. L. M. 6 LINES.

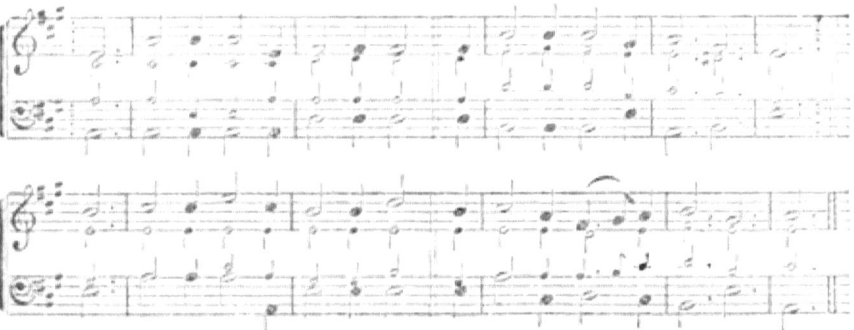

253. *Christ All in All.*

1 Thou hidden Source of calm repose,
　Thou all-sufficient Love Divine,
My help and refuge from my foes,
　Secure I am, if thou art mine!
And lo! from sin, and grief, and shame,
I hide me, Jesus, in thy name.

2 Jesus, my All in All thou art,
　My rest in toil, my ease in pain;
The healing of my broken heart;
　In strife, my peace; in loss my gain;
My smile beneath the tyrant's frown;
In shame, my glory and my crown;—

3 In want, my plentiful supply;
　In weakness, my almighty power;
In bonds, my perfect liberty;
　My light, in Satan's darkest hour;
Thee, in each grief, my joy I call;
My life in death, my All in All!

662. *"Thou hidden Love of God."*

1 Thou hidden Love of God, whose height
　Whose depth unfathomed, no man knows,
I see from far thy beauteous light;
　Inly I sigh for thy repose:
My heart is pained, nor can it be
At rest, till it finds rest in thee!

2 Is there a thing beneath the sun,
　That strives with me my heart to share?
Ah! tear it thence, and reign alone,
　The Lord of every motion there;
Then shall my heart from earth be free,
When it has found repose in thee!

760. *"My soul trusteth in Thee."*

1 Do not I trust in thee, O Lord?
　Do I not rest in thee alone?
Is not the comfort of thy word
　The sweetest cordial I have known?

When vexed with care, bowed down with grief,
　Where else could I obtain relief?

2 And is it not my chief desire
　To feel as if a stranger here?
Do not my hopes and thoughts aspire
　Beyond this transitory sphere?
And art thou not, while here I roam,
My hope, my hiding-place, my home?

3 Oh, yes! these things are ever true;
　Thy promise is for ever sure;
And all I now am passing through,
　And all that I may still endure,
Will but endear thy word to me,
And draw me nearer, Lord, to thee.

4 And now on thee I cast my soul,
　Come life or death, come ease or pain;
Thy presence can each fear control,
　Thy grace can to the end sustain:
Those whom thou lovest, heavenly Friend,
Thou lovest even to the end!

917. *Prayer for Likeness to God.*

1 Now, O my God, thou hast my soul;
　No longer mine but thine I am:
Guard thou thine own, possess the whole;
　Cheer it with hope, with love inflame;
To thee, the Lord of earth and skies,
I come a living sacrifice.

2 Send down thy likeness from above,
　And this let my adorning be:
Clothe me with wisdom, patience, love,
　With lowliness and purity,—
Than gold and pearls more precious far,
And brighter than the morning star.

3 Lord, arm me with thy Spirit's might,
　Since I am called by thy great name.
In thee let all my thoughts unite,
　Of all my works be thou the aim;
Thy love attend me all my days,
And all my pleasure be thy praise!

OVIO. 8s & 7s.

269. *The Song of the Angels.*—Luke 2.

1 HARK! what mean those holy voices,
　　Sweetly sounding through the skies?
Lo! th' angelic host rejoices;
　　Heavenly hallelujahs rise.

2 Hear them tell the wondrous story,
　　Hear them chant in hymns of joy:
"Glory in the highest, glory!
　　Glory be to God most high!

3 "Peace on earth, good-will from **heaven**,
　　Reaching far as man is found;
Souls redeemed, and sins forgiven!
　　Loud our golden harps shall sound.

4 "Christ is born, the great Anointed;
　　Heaven and earth his praises sing!
Oh, **receive whom** God appointed
　　For your **Prophet**, Priest, and King!

5 "Haste, ye mortals, to adore him;
　　Learn his name, and taste his joy:
Till in heaven ye sing before him,
　　'Glory be to God most high!'"

371. *Worship of the living Christ.*

1 JESUS, hail! enthroned in glory,
　　There for ever to abide;
All the heavenly hosts adore thee,
　　Seated **at** thy Father's side.

2 There for sinners thou art pleading,
　　There thou dost our place prepare;
Ever for us interceding,
　　Till in glory we appear.

3 Worship, honor, power and blessing,
　　Thou art worthy to receive;
Loudest praises, without ceasing,
　　Meet it us for is to give.

4 Help, ye bright angelic spirits!
　　Bring your sweetest, noblest lays:
Help to sing our Saviour's merits;
　　Help to chant Immanuel's praise.

649. *"I would love Thee."*

1 I WOULD love thee, God and Father!
　　My Redeemer, and my King!
I would love thee; for, without thee,
　　Life is but **a** bitter thing.

2 I would love thee; **every** blessing
　　Flows to me from **out** thy throne:
I would love thee—he who loves thee
　　Never feels himself alone.

3 I would love thee; look upon **me**,
　　Ever guide me with thine eye:
I would love thee; if not nourished
　　By thy love, my soul would die.

4 I would love thee; may thy brightness
　　Dazzle my rejoicing eyes!
I would love thee; may thy goodness
　　Watch from heaven o'er all I prize.

5 I would love thee, I have vowed it;
　　On thy love my heart is set:
While I love thee, I will never
　　My Redeemer's blood forget.

1102. *"Bring ye all the tithes into the storehouse."*

1 WITH my substance I will honor
　　My Redeemer and my Lord;
Were ten thousand worlds my manor,
　　All were nothing to his word.

WORTHING. 8s & 7s.

2 While the heralds of salvation
   His abounding grace proclaim,
  Let his friends of every station,
   Gladly join to spread his fame.

3 Be his kingdom now promoted,
   Let the earth her Monarch know;
  Be my all to him devoted;
   To my Lord my all I owe.

4 Praise the Saviour, all ye nations!
   Praise him, all ye hosts above!
  Shout, with joyful acclamations,
   His divine, victorious love!

677. *"Under His wings shalt thou trust."*
        Psalm 91.

1 CALL the Lord thy sure salvation,
   Rest beneath th' Almighty's shade;
  In his secret habitation
   Dwell, and never be dismayed!

2 There no tumult can alarm thee,
   Thou shalt dread no hidden snare;
  Guile nor violence can harm thee,
   In eternal safeguard there.

3 Thee, tho' winds and waves are swelling,
   God, thy hope, shall bear through all;
  Plague shall not come nigh thy dwelling,
   Thee no evil shall befall.

4 He shall charge his angel legions
   Watch and ward o'er thee to keep,
  Though thou walk thro' hostile regions,
   Though in desert wilds thou sleep.

5 Since, with firm and pure affection,
   Thou on God hast set thy love,
  With the wings of his protection
   He shall shield thee from above.

1023. *"Zion, city of our God."*

1 GLORIOUS things of thee are spoken,
   Zion, city of our God;
  He whose word can ne'er be broken
   Chose thee for his own abode.

2 Lord, thy church is still thy dwelling,
   Still is precious in thy sight;
  Judah's temple far excelling,
   Beaming with the gospel's light.

3 On the Rock of Ages founded,
   What can shake her sure repose?
  With salvation's wall surrounded,
   She can smile at all her foes.

4 Glorious things of thee are spoken,
   Zion, city of our God;
  He whose word can ne'er be broken
   Chose thee for his own abode.

426. *"And the Light shineth in darkness."*

1 LIGHT of those whose dreary dwelling
   Borders on the shades of death!
  Rise on us, thyself revealing,
   Rise and chase the clouds beneath.

2 Thou, of heaven and earth Creator!
   In our deepest darkness rise;
  Scatter all the night of nature;
   Pour the day upon our eyes.

3 Still we wait for thine appearing;
   Life and joy thy beams impart,
  Chasing all our fears, and cheering
   Every poor, benighted heart.

4 By thine all-sufficient merit,
   Every burdened soul release;
  Every weary, wandering spirit,
   Guide into thy perfect peace.

WAYNE. C. M. DOUBLE.

205. "*I will sing praise to my God while I have my being.*"

1 Yes, I will bless thee, O my God!
  Through all my earthly days;
  And to eternity prolong
  Thy vast, thy boundless praise.
2 In every smiling, happy hour,
  Be this my sweet employ:
  Thy praise refines my earthly bliss,
  And doubles all my joy.
3 When gloomy care, and keen distress
  Afflict my throbbing breast,
  Thy praise shall mingle with my tears,
  And lull each pain to rest.
4 Nor shall my tongue alone proclaim
  The honors of my God;
  My life, with all its active powers,
  Shall spread thy praise abroad.
5 Nor death itself shall stop my song,
  Though it will close my eyes;
  My thoughts shall then to nobler heights,
  And sweeter raptures rise.
6 There shall my lips in endless praise
  Their grateful tribute pay;
  The theme demands an angel's tongue,
  And an eternal day.

698. "*Thou knowest that I love Thee.*" John 21: 15-17.

1 Do not I love thee, O my Lord?
  Behold my heart and see;
  And turn the dearest idol out
  That dares to rival thee.
2 Do not I love thee from my soul?
  Then let me nothing love:
  Dead be my heart to every joy
  When Jesus can not move.
3 Is not thy name melodious still
  To mine attentive ear?
  Doth not each pulse with pleasure bound
  My Saviour's voice to hear?
4 Hast thou a lamb in all thy flock
  I would disdain to feed?
  Hast thou a foe before whose face
  I fear thy cause to plead?
5 Would not my heart pour forth its blood
  In honor of thy name?
  And challenge the cold hand of death
  To damp th' immortal flame?
6 Thou know'st I love thee, dearest Lord;
  But, oh! I long to soar
  Far from the sphere of mortal joys,
  And learn to love thee more.

959. "*All things are yours.*"—1 Cor. 3: 22.

1 If God is mine, then present things
  And things to come are mine;
  Yea, Christ, his word, and Spirit, too,
  And glory all divine.
2 If he is mine, then from his love
  He every trouble sends;
  All things are working for my good,
  And bliss his rod attends.
3 If he is mine, I need not fear
  The rage of earth and hell;
  He will support my feeble power,
  Their utmost force repel.
4 If he is mine, let friends forsake,
  Let wealth and honors flee;
  Sure, he who giveth me himself,
  Is more than these to me.
5 If he is mine, I'll boldly pass
  Through death's dark, lonely vale;
  He is my comfort and my stay,
  When heart and flesh shall fail.
6 Oh, tell me, Lord, that thou art mine;
  What can I wish beside?

HEBER. C. M.

My soul shall at the fountain live,
When all the streams are dried.

272. *"On earth peace."—Luke 2.*

1 CALM, on the listening ear of night,
    Come heaven's melodious strains,
  Where wild Judea stretches far
    Her silver-mantled plains.

2 Celestial choirs, from courts above,
    'Mid sacred glories there;
  And angels, with their sparkling lyres,
    Make music on the air.

3 The answering hills of Palestine
    Send back the glad reply;
  And greet, from all their holy heights,
    The day-spring from on high.

4 O'er the blue depths of Galilee
    There comes a holier calm;
  And Sharon waves, in solemn praise,
    Her silent groves of palm.

5 "Glory to God!" the sounding skies
    Loud with their anthems ring;
  "Peace to the earth—good will to men,
    From heaven's eternal King."

858. *The chief Grace.*

1 HAPPY the heart where graces reign,
    Where love inspires the breast;
  Love is the brightest of the train,
    And strengthens all the rest.

2 Knowledge—alas! 't is all in vain,
    And all in vain our fear;
  Our stubborn sins will fight and reign,
    If love be absent there.

3 This is the grace that lives and sings,
    When faith and hope shall cease;
  'T is this shall strike our joyful strings,
    In realms of endless peace.

4 Before we quite forsake our clay,
    Or leave this dark abode,

The wings of love bear us away,
  To see our smiling God.

905. *"Think gently of the erring."*

1 THINK gently of the erring one!
    And let us not forget,
  However darkly stained by sin,
    He is our brother yet.

2 Heir of the same inheritance,
    Child of the self-same God;
  He hath but stumbled in the path,
    We have in weakness trod.

3 Speak gently to the erring one;
    Thou yet may'st lead him back,
  With holy words, and tones of love,
    From misery's thorny track.

4 Forget not thou hast often sinned,
    And sinful yet must be;
  Deal gently with the erring one,
    As God has dealt with thee.

951. *"I will joy in the God of my salvation."*
    Hab. 3: 17, 18.

1 WHAT though no flowers the fig-tree clothe,
    Though vines their fruit deny,
  The labor of the olive fail,
    And fields no meat supply;

2 Though from the fold, with sad surprise,
    My flock cut off I see;
  Though famine pine in empty stalls,
    Where herds were wont to be;

3 Yet in the Lord will I be glad,
    And glory in his love;
  In him I'll joy, who will the God
    Of my salvation prove.

4 God is the treasure of my soul,
    The source of lasting joy;
  A joy which want shall not impair,
    Nor death itself destroy.

BREMEN. S. M. Double.

784. *"Still with Thee."*—Psalm 139.

1 STILL with thee, O my God,
   I would desire to be;
By day, by night, at home, abroad,
   I would be still with thee:

2 With thee, when dawn comes in,
   And calls me back to care;
Each day returning to begin
   With thee, my God, in prayer:

3 With thee, amid the crowd
   That throngs the busy mart,
To hear thy voice, 'mid clamor loud,
   Speak softly to my heart:

4 With thee, when day is done,
   And evening calms the mind:
The setting as the rising sun
   With thee my heart would find:

5 With thee, when darkness brings
   The signal of repose;
Calm in the shadow of thy wings,
   Mine eyelids I would close:

6 With thee, in thee, by faith
   Abiding I would be;
By day, by night, in life, in death,
   I would be still with thee.

977. *"If God be for us, who can be against us?"*

1 HERE I can firmly rest!
   I dare to boast of this,
That God, the highest and the best,
   My Friend and Father is.

2 In me he ever dwells,
   O'er all my mind he reigns;
All care and sadness he dispels,
   And soothes away my pains.

3 At cost of all I have,—
   At cost of life and limb,

I cling to God, who yet shall save;
   I will not turn from him.

4 The world may fail and flee;
   Thou, God, my Father art;
Not fire, nor sword, nor plague, from thee
   My trusting soul shall part.

5 No joys that angels know;
   No throne nor wide-spread fame,
No love nor loss, nor fear nor woe,
   No grief of heart or shame—

6 Man can not aught conceive,
   Of pleasure or of harm,
That e'er shall tempt my soul to leave
   Her refuge in thine arm.

1263. *"There remaineth therefore a rest."*

1 AND is there, Lord, a rest
   For weary souls designed,
Where not a care shall stir the breast,
   Or sorrow entrance find?

2 Is there a blissful home,
   Where kindred minds shall meet,
And live, and love, nor ever roam
   From that serene retreat?

3 Are there bright, happy fields,
   Where naught that blooms shall die;
Where each new scene fresh pleasure
     yields,
   And healthful breezes sigh?

4 Are there celestial streams
   Where living waters glide,
With murmurs sweet as angel dreams,
   And flowery banks beside?

5 For ever blessèd they,
   Whose joyful feet shall stand,
While endless ages waste away,
   Amid that glorious land!

BOYLSTON. S. M.

6 My soul would thither tend,
  While toilsome years are given;
  Then let me, gracious God, ascend
  To sweet repose in heaven!

1017. *"I love thy kingdom, Lord."*

1 I LOVE thy kingdom, Lord—
  The house of thine abode,
  The church our blest Redeemer **saved**
  With his own **precious** blood.

2 I love thy church, **O God!**
  Her walls before thee **stand**,
  Dear as the apple of thine **eye**,
  And graven on thy hand.

3 For **her** my tears shall fall,
  For her my prayers ascend;
  To her my cares and toils be given,
  Till toils and cares shall end.

4 Beyond my highest joy
  I prize **her** heavenly ways,
  Her sweet communion, solemn **vows**,
  Her hymns **of love** and praise.

5 Jesus, thou Friend divine,
  Our Saviour and our King,
  Thy hand from every snare and **foe**
  Shall great deliverance bring.

6 Sure as thy truth shall last,
  To Zion shall be given
  The brightest glories earth can yield,
  And brighter bliss of heaven.

1002. *"That we should be called the sons of God."*—1 John 3 : 1, 2.

1 BEHOLD, what wondrous grace
  The Father has bestowed
  On sinners of a mortal race,
  To call them sons of God!

2 Nor doth it yet appear
  How great we must be made;
  But **when** we see our Saviour here,
  We shall be like our Head.

3 A hope so much divine
  May trials well endure;
  May purify our souls from **sin**,
  As Christ, the Lord, is pure.

4 If in my Father's love
  I share a filial part,
  Send down thy Spirit, **like a dove**,
  To **rest upon** my heart.

5 We would no longer lie
  Like slaves beneath the throne;
  Our faith shall " Abba, Father," cry,
  And thou the kindred **own**.

773. *Living by Faith only.*

1 IF through unruffled seas
  Toward heaven we calmly sail,
  With grateful hearts, O God, to thee,
  We'll own the fostering gale.

2 But should the surges rise,
  And rest delay to come,
  Blest be the sorrow, kind the storm,
  Which drives us nearer home.

3 Soon shall our doubts and fears
  All yield to thy control;
  Thy tender mercies shall illume
  The midnight of the soul.

4 Teach us, in every state,
  To make thy will our own;
  And, when the joys of sense depart,
  To live by faith alone.

DOXOLOGY.

THE Father and the Son
  And Spirit we adore,
  We praise, we bless, we worship thee,
  Both now and evermore!

OLDEN. L. M.

292. *The Conflict.*

1 'T is midnight, and, on Olive's brow,
  The star is dimmed that lately shone;
  'T is midnight; in the garden now
  The suffering Saviour prays alone.

2 'T is midnight; and, from all removed,
  The Saviour wrestles lone with fears:
  Ev'n that disciple whom he loved,
  Heeds not his Master's grief and tears.

3 'T is midnight; and, for others' guilt,
  The Man of sorrows weeps in blood;
  Yet he, who hath in anguish knelt,
  Is not forsaken by his God.

4 'T is midnight—and from ether-plains
  Is borne the song that angels know
  Unheard by mortals are the strains
  That sweetly soothe the Saviour's woe.

298. *"It is finished."*—John 19 : 30.

1 "'T is finished!"—so the Saviour cried,
  And meekly bowed his head, and died:
  "'T is finished!"—yes, the race is run,
  The battle fought, the victory won.

2 "'T is finished!"—all that heaven foretold
  By prophets in the days of old;
  And truths are opened to our view,
  That kings and prophets never knew.

3 "'T is finished!"—Son of God, thy power
  Hath triumphed in this awful hour;
  And yet, our eyes with sorrow see
  That life to us was death to thee.

4 "'T is finished!"—let the joyful sound
  Be heard through all the nations round;
  "'T is finished!"—let the echo fly
  Thro' heaven and hell, thro' earth and sky.

767. *Fear of denying Christ.*—Matt. 10 : 33.

1 Deny thee? what! deny the way
  That leads to heaven's eternal day?
  Deny the Shepherd who will keep
  Within the fold his wandering sheep?

2 Deny thee, Lord! then who will bear
  My grief, my burden, and my care?
  Thou, thou alone canst calm my breast,
  And bid its weary throbbings rest.

3 In heaven above, on earth below,
  Where, save to thee, Lord, could I go?
  Where fly for strength, 'mid mortal strife?
  Thou hast the words of endless life.

4 My Strength, my Guide vouchsafe to be,
  I can do nothing without thee;
  Save me in every trying hour,
  Thou God of mercy, life, and power!

843. *The blessed Hour.*

1 Blest hour! when mortal man retires
  To hold communion with his God,
  To send to heaven his warm desires,
  And listen to the sacred word.

2 Blest hour! when God himself draws nigh
  Well pleased his people's voice to hear,
  To hush the penitential sigh,
  And wipe away the mourner's tear.

3 Blest hour! for, where the Lord resorts,
  Foretastes of future bliss are given,
  And mortals find his earthly courts
  The house of God—the gate of heaven!

4 Hail, peaceful hour! supremely blest,
  Amid the hours of worldly care;
  The hour that yields the spirit rest,
  That sacred hour—the hour of prayer.

5 And when my hours of prayer are past,
  And this frail tenement decays,
  Then may I spend in heaven at last
  A never-ending hour of praise.

HEBRON. L. M.

531. *"Fear not; I have redeemed thee."*

1 Come, weary souls, with sin distressed,
Come, and accept the promised rest;
The Saviour's gracious call obey,
And cast your gloomy fears away.

2 Oppressed with guilt,—a painful load,—
Oh, come and bow before your God!
Divine compassion, mighty love,
Will all the painful load remove.

3 Here mercy's boundless ocean flows,
To cleanse your guilt and heal your woes;
Pardon, and life, and endless peace—
How rich the gift! how free the grace!

4 Dear Saviour! let thy powerful love
Confirm our faith, our fears remove;
Oh, sweetly reign in every breast,
And guide us to eternal rest.

564. *Giving all to Christ.*

1 My Saviour, how shall I proclaim,
How pay the mighty debt I owe?
Let all I have, and all I am,
Ceaseless to all thy glory show.

2 Too much to thee I can not give;
Too much I can not do for thee;
Let all thy love, and all thy grief
Graven on my heart for ever be.

3 The meek, the still, the lowly mind,
Oh, may I learn from thee, my God!
And love with softest pity joined,
For those that trample on thy blood!

4 Still let thy tears, thy groans, thy sighs,
O'erflow my eyes, and heave my breast;
Till, loose from flesh and earth, I rise,
And ever in thy bosom rest.

822. *"I delight to do thy will, O my God."*

1 O Lord, thy heavenly grace impart,
And fix my frail, inconstant heart;
Henceforth my chief delight shall be
To dedicate myself to thee.

2 Whate'er pursuits my time employ,
One thought shall fill my soul with joy;
That silent, secret thought shall be,
That all my hopes are fixed on thee.

3 Thy glorious eye pervadeth space;
Thy presence, Lord, fills every place;
And, wheresoe'er my lot may be,
Still shall my spirit cleave to thee.

4 Renouncing every worldly thing,
And safe beneath thy sheltering wing,
My sweetest thought henceforth shall be,
That all I want I find in thee.

839. *"Jesus, and can I call Thee mine?"*

1 Lord, when my thoughts delighted rove
Amid the wonders of thy love,
Sweet hope revives my drooping heart,
And bids intruding fears depart.

2 For mortal crimes a sacrifice,
The Lord of life, the Saviour, dies!
What love! what mercy! how divine!
Jesus,—and can I call thee mine?

3 Repentant sorrow fills my heart,
But mingling joy allays the smart;
Oh, may my future life declare
The sorrow and the joy sincere!

4 Be all my heart and all my day
Devoted to my Saviour's praise;
And let my glad obedience prove
How much I owe, how much I love.

CALBRA. 9s & 6s.

367.
"I am He that liveth."

1 Oh, show me not my Saviour dying,
  As on the cross he died;
Nor in the tomb a captive lying,
  For he has left the dead.
Then bid me not that form extended
  For my Redeemer own,
Who, to the highest heavens ascended,
  In glory fills the throne.

2 Weep not for him at Calvary's station,
  Weep only for thy sins;
View where he lay with exultation;
  'T is there our hope begins.
Yet stay not there, thy sorrows feeding,
  Amid the scenes he trod;
Look up and see him interceding
  At the right hand of God.

3 Still in the shameful cross I glory,
  Where his dear blood was spilt:
My soul is melted at the story
  Of him who bore my guilt:
Yet what, 'mid conflict and temptation,
  Shall strength and succor give?
He lives, the Captain of Salvation!
  Therefore his servants live.

4 By death, he death's dark king defeated,
  And overcame the grave;
Rising, the triumph he completed:
  He lives, he reigns to save!
Heaven's happy myriads bow before him;
  He comes, the Judge of men:
These eyes shall see him and adore him;
  Lord Jesus! own me then.

SAVANNAH. 10s.

57. "*Holy Rest.*"

1 Again the day returns of holy rest,
   Which, when he made the world, Jehovah blest;
   When, like his own, he bade our labors cease,
   And all be piety, and all be peace.

2 Let us devote this consecrated day
   To learn his will, and all we learn obey;
   So shall he hear, when fervently we raise
   Our choral harmony in hymns of praise.

3 Father in heaven! in whom our hopes confide,
   Whose power defends us, and whose precepts guide;
   In life our Guardian, and in death our Friend;
   Glory supreme be thine, till time shall end.

314. *Christ our peace.*--Eph. 2:14.

1 I thought upon my sins, and I was sad;
   My soul was troubled sore, and filled with pain;
   But then I thought on Jesus, and was glad—
   My heavy grief was turned to joy again.

2 I thought upon the law, the fiery law,
   Holy, and just, and good in its decree:
   I looked to Jesus, and in him I saw
   That law fulfilled, its curse endured for me.

3 I thought I saw an angry, frowning God,
   Sitting as Judge upon the great white throne:
   My soul was overwhelmed; then Jesus showed
   His gracious face, and all my dread was gone.

4 I saw my sad estate,—condemned to die:
   Then terror seized my heart, and dark despair;
   But when to Calvary I turned my eye,
   I saw the cross, and read forgiveness there.

5 I saw that I was lost, far gone astray;
   No hope of safe return there seemed to be;
   But then I heard that Jesus was the way,
   A new and living way prepared for me.

6 Then in that way, so free, so safe, so sure,
   All sprinkled o'er with reconciling blood,
   Will I abide, and never wander more,
   But walk secure, in fellowship with God.

SWANWICK. C. M.

389. *"Every tongue should confess that Jesus Christ is Lord."*—Phil. 2: 5-11.

1 Jesus! exalted far on high,
  To whom a name is given—
A name surpassing every name
  That's known in earth or heaven!

2 Before thy throne shall every knee
  Bow down with one accord;
Before thy throne shall every tongue
  Confess that thou art Lord.

3 Jesus! thou, in the form of God,
  Didst equal honor claim;
Yet, to redeem our guilty souls,
  Didst stoop to death and shame!

4 Oh, may that mind in us be formed,
  Which shone so bright in thee—
An humble, meek, and lowly mind,
  From pride and envy free!

5 To others we would stoop, and learn
  To emulate thy love;
So shall we bear thine image here,
  And share thy throne above.

487. *"Thy law is my delight."* Psalm 119.

1 Lord, I have made thy word my choice,
  My lasting heritage;
There shall my noblest powers rejoice,
  My warmest thoughts engage.

2 I'll read the histories of thy love,
  And keep thy laws in sight;
While through the promises I rove,
  With ever fresh delight.

3 'T is a broad land, of wealth unknown,
  Where springs of life arise,
Seeds of immortal bliss are sown,
  And hidden glory lies.

4 The best relief that mourners have;
  It makes our sorrows blest;
Our fairest hope beyond the grave,
  And our eternal rest.

626. *Prayer for full Assurance.*

1 Eternal Source of joys divine,
  To thee my soul aspires;
Oh, could I say, "The Lord is mine!"
  'T is all my soul desires.

2 My Hope, my Trust, my Life, my Lord,
  Assure me of thy love;
Oh, speak the kind, transporting word,
  And bid my fears remove!

3 Then shall my thankful powers rejoice,
  And triumph in my God;
Till heavenly rapture tune my voice
  To spread thy praise abroad.

644. *"No joy without God."*—Psalm 73.

1 God, my supporter and my hope,
  My help for ever near,
Thine arm of mercy held me up,
  When sinking in despair.

2 Thy counsels, Lord, shall guide my feet
  Through this dark wilderness;
Thy hand conduct me near thy seat,
  To dwell before thy face.

3 Were I in heaven without my God,
  'T would be no joy to me;
And while this earth is my abode,
  I long for none but thee.

4 What if the springs of life were broke,
  And flesh and heart should faint,
God is my soul's eternal rock,
  The strength of every saint.

5 Then, to draw near to thee, my God,
  Shall be my sweet employ;
My tongue shall sound thy works abroad,
  And tell the world my joy.

DOWNS. C. M.

826. *"Thou art my portion, O Lord!"*
Psalm 119.

1 Thou art my portion, O my **God**;
  Soon as I know thy way,
 My heart makes haste t' obey thy word,
  And suffers no delay.

2 I choose the path of heavenly truth,
  And glory in my choice;
 Not all the riches of the earth
  Could **make** me so rejoice.

3 The testimonies **of** thy grace
  I set before mine eyes;
 Thence I derive my daily strength,
  And there my comfort lies.

4 If once I wander from thy **path**,
  I think upon my ways;
 Then turn my feet to thy **commands**,
  And trust thy pardoning grace.

5 Now I am thine—for ever thine—
  Oh, save thy servant, Lord!
 Thou art my shield, my hiding-place;
  My hope is in thy word.

944. *"Blessed is the man whom thou chastenest."*—Psalm 94.

1 Blest is the man whom thou, **O Lord**,
  In kindness dost chastise,
 And by thy sacred rules to walk,
  Dost lovingly advise.

2 For God will never from his saints
  His favor wholly take;
 His own possession and his lot,
  He will not quite forsake.

3 The world shall then confess thee just
  In all that thou hast done;
 And those who choose thy upright path
  Shall in that path go on.

4 My sure defense is firmly placed
  In thee, the Lord most high;

Thou art my Rock: to thee I may
 For refuge always fly.

1126. *"Let the whole earth be filled with His glory."*

1 Great God! the nations of the earth
  Are by creation thine;
 And in thy works, by all beheld,
  Thy power and glory shine.

2 But, Lord, thy greater love hath sent
  Thy gospel to mankind,
 Unvailing what rich stores of grace
  Are treasured in thy mind.

3 Oh, when shall these glad tidings spread
  The spacious earth around,
 Till every tribe and every soul
  Shall hear the joyful sound?

4 Smile, Lord, on each divine attempt
  To spread the gospel's rays,
 And build on sin's demolished throne
  The temples of thy praise.

1170. *"There is laid up for me a crown of righteousness."*—2 Tim. 4: 6–8, 18.

1 Death may dissolve my body now,
  And bear my spirit home;
 Why do my minutes move so slow,
  Nor my salvation come?

2 God has laid up in heaven for me
  A **crown** which can not fade;
 The **righteous** Judge, at that great day,
  Shall place it on my head.

3 Jesus, the Lord, shall guard me safe
  From every ill design,
 And to his heavenly kingdom take
  This feeble soul of mine.

4 God is my everlasting Aid,
  My Portion and my Friend;
 To him be highest glory paid,
  Through ages without end!

ERNAN. L. M.

358. *"O Death, where is thy sting?"*

1 He dies! the Friend of sinners dies!
   Lo! Salem's daughters weep around:
   A solemn darkness vails the skies;
   A sudden trembling shakes the ground.

2 Here's love and grief beyond degree:
   The Lord of glory dies for men!
   But, lo! what sudden joys we see,
   Jesus, the dead, revives again!

3 The rising God forsakes the tomb;
   Up to his Father's court he flies:
   Cherubic legions guard him home,
   And shout him welcome to the skies.

4 Break off your tears, ye saints, and tell
   How high our great Deliverer reigns;
   Sing how he spoiled the hosts of hell,
   And led the tyrant Death in chains.

5 Say, "Live for ever, glorious King,
   Born to redeem, and strong to save!
   Where now, O Death, where is thy sting?
   And where thy victory, boasting Grave?"

374. *Joy in Christ's Intercession.*

1 He lives,—the great Redeemer lives:
   What joy the blest assurance gives!
   And now, before his father, God,
   Pleads the full merit of his blood.

2 Repeated crimes awake our fears,
   And justice armed with frowns appears;
   But in the Saviour's lovely face
   Sweet mercy smiles, and all is peace.

3 Hence, then, ye black, despairing thoughts;
   Above our fears, above our faults,
   His powerful intercessions rise,
   And guilt recedes, and terror dies.

4 In every dark, distressful hour,
   When sin and Satan join their power,
   Let this dear hope repel the dart,
   That Jesus bears us on his heart.

5 Great Advocate! Almighty Friend!
   On thee our humble hopes depend:
   Our cause can never, never fail,
   For thou dost plead, and must prevail.

375. *"We have an Advocate with the Father."*—1 John 2: 1.

1 Where is my God?—does he retire
   Beyond the reach of humble sighs?
   Are these weak breathings of desire
   Too languid to ascend the skies?

2 Look up, my soul, with cheerful eye!
   See where the great Redeemer stands,
   The glorious Advocate on high,
   With precious incense in his hands.

3 He sweetens every humble groan;
   He recommends each broken prayer;
   Recline thy hope on him alone
   Whose power and love forbid despair.

4 Teach my weak heart, O gracious Lord,
   With stronger faith to call thee mine;
   Bid me pronounce the blissful word,
   My Father—God, with joy divine.

628. *Past Joys remembered.*

1 Oh, where is now that glowing love,
   That marked our union with the Lord?
   Our hearts were fixed on things above,
   Nor could the world a joy afford.

2 Where is the zeal that led us then
   To make our Saviour's glory known?
   That freed us from the fear of men,
   And kept our eye on him alone?

3 Where are the happy seasons spent
   In fellowship with him we loved?
   The sacred joy, the sweet content,
   The blessedness that then we proved?

4 Behold! again we turn to thee;
   Oh, cast us not away, though vile!
   No peace we have, no joy we see,
   O Lord our God! but in thy smile.

WARD. L. M.

233. *"Not that we loved God, but that He loved us."*

1 ERE earth's foundations yet were laid,
  Or heaven's fair roof was spread
      abroad ;
  Ere man a living soul was made,
    Love stirred within the heart of God.

2 Thy loving counsel gave to me
    True life in Christ, thy only Son,
  Whom thou hast made my way to thee,
    From whom all grace flows ever down.

3 O Love, that long ere time began,
    This precious name of child bestowed ;
  That opened heaven on earth to man,
    And called us sinners "sons of God!"

4 I am not worthy, Lord, that thou
    Shouldst such compassion on me show;
  That he who made the world should bow
    To cheer with love a wretch so low.

5 Could I but honor thee aright,
    Noble and sweet my song should be ;
  That earth and heaven should learn thy
      might,
    And what my God hath done for me.

975.   *A good Conscience.*

1 SWEET peace of conscience, heavenly
      guest,
  Come fix thy mansion in my breast ;
  Dispel my doubts, my fears control,
  And heal the anguish of my soul.

2 Come, smiling hope, and joy sincere,
  Come, make your constant dwelling here;
  Still let your presence cheer my heart,
  Nor sin compel you to depart.

3 O God of hope and peace divine,
  Make thou these secret pleasures mine ;
  Forgive my sins, my fears remove,
  And fill my heart with joy and love.

1107. *"They that go down to the sea in ships."*

1 WHILE o'er the deep thy servants sail,
  Send thou, O Lord, the prosperous gale ;
  And on their hearts, where'er they go,
  Oh, let thy heavenly breezes blow !

2 If, on the morning's wings they fly,
  They will not pass beyond thine eye ;
  The wanderer's prayer thou bend'st to hear,
  And faith exults to know thee near.

3 When tempests rock the groaning bark,
  Oh hide them safe in Jesus' ark !
  When in the tempting port they ride,
  Oh, keep them safe at Jesus' side !

4 If life's wide ocean smile or roar,
  Still guide them to the heavenly shore ;
  And grant their dust in Christ may sleep,
  Abroad, at home, or in the deep.

1258.   *"The Lamb is the light thereof."*

1 OH for a sweet, inspiring ray,
    To animate our feeble strains,
  From the bright realms of endless day—
    The blissful realms where Jesus reigns!

2 There, low before his glorious throne,
    Adoring saints and angels fall ;
  And, with delightful worship, own
    His smile their bliss, their heaven,
        their all.

3 Immortal glories crown his head,
    While tuneful hallelujahs rise,
  And love and joy and triumph spread
    Through all the assemblies of the skies.

4 He smiles,—and seraphs tune their songs
    To boundless rapture, while they gaze;
  Ten thousand thousand joyful tongues
    Resound his everlasting praise.

5 There all the followers of the Lamb
    Shall join at last the heavenly choir:
  Oh, may the joy-inspiring theme
    Awake our faith and warm desire !

AVON. C. M.

638. *"A divided Heart."*—Rom. 7.

1 Our hearts, O Lord, with grief are rent,
   O'er vows made all in vain;
   In anguish daily we repent,
   Each day offend again.

2 Now we arise from death to life,
   Then sink from good to ill;
   Here we begin, there leave our strife,
   And work but half thy will.

3 Oh, help us, Lord, amid all pain,
   As warriors true, to stand
   Faithful and firm, and thus to gain
   Thine own, the better land.

4 Thy land—its gates how bright they shine!
   And let no evil in;
   Thy boundless land, and all divine,
   That hath no room for sin.

5 Thy holy land, where none shall stop
   Our souls upon the road,
   And win our weak desires to drop
   From glory and from God.

6 Oh, rich and priceless is the grace
   That we shall there receive!
   Nor once thine image shall deface,
   Nor once thy spirit grieve.

695. *"What shall I render unto the Lord?"*
   Psalm 116.

1 For mercies countless as the sands,
   Which daily I receive
   From Jesus my Redeemer's hands,
   My soul, what canst thou give?

2 Alas! from such a heart as mine,
   What can I bring him forth?
   My best is stained and dyed with sin;
   My all is nothing worth.

3 Yet this acknowledgment I'll make
   For all he has bestowed,
   Salvation's sacred cup I'll take,
   And call upon my God.

4 The best return for one like me,
   So wretched and so poor,
   Is from his gifts to draw a plea,
   And ask him still for more.

5 I can not serve him as I ought;
   No works have I to boast;
   Yet would I glory in the thought,
   That I shall owe him most.

770. *"Haste Thee to help me."*—Psalm 22.

1 Oh, help us, Lord!—each hour of need
   Thy heavenly succor give;
   Help us in thought, and word, and deed,
   Each hour on earth we live.

2 Oh, help us when our spirits bleed,
   With contrite anguish sore;
   And when our hearts are cold and dead,
   Oh, help us, Lord, the more!

3 Oh, help us, through the power of faith,
   More firmly to believe!
   For still the more the servant hath
   The more shall he receive.

4 O, help us, Jesus! from on high
   We know no help but thee;
   Oh, help us so to live and die,
   As thine in heaven to be!

807. *Imitation of Christ in His Humiliation.*

1 A pilgrim through this lonely world,
   The blessèd Saviour passed;
   A mourner all his life was he,
   A dying Lamb at last.

2 That tender heart which felt for all,
   For us his life-blood gave;
   It found on earth no resting-place,
   Save only in the grave!

3 Such was our Lord; and shall we fear
   The cross with all its scorn?
   Or love a faithless, evil world,
   That wreathed his brow with thorn?

DOWNS. C. M.

4 No: facing all its frowns or smiles,
  Like him, obedient still,
  We homeward press, through storm or calm,
  To Zion's blessed hill.

5 Dead to the world, with him who died
  To win our hearts, our love,
  We, risen with our risen Head,
  In spirit dwell above.

6 By faith, his boundless glories there
  Our wondering eyes behold—
  Those glories which eternal years
  Shall never all unfold.

1055. *"Bring in hither the poor and the maimed."—Luke 14: 17–23.*

1 How sweet and awful is the place,
  With Christ within the doors;
  While everlasting love displays
  The choicest of her stores!

2 While all our hearts and all our songs
  Join to admire the feast,
  Each of us cries, with thankful tongue,
  "Lord, why was I a guest?"

3 "Why was I made to hear thy voice,
  And enter while there's room,
  When thousands make a wretched choice,
  And rather starve than come?"

4 'T was the same love that spread the feast,
  That sweetly drew us in;
  Else we had still refused to taste,
  And perished in our sin.

5 Pity the nations, O our God!
  Constrain the earth to come;
  Send thy victorious word abroad,
  And bring the strangers home.

6 We long to see thy churches full,
  That all the chosen race
  May, with one voice, and heart, and soul,
  Sing thy redeeming grace.

1118. *"Turn us again, O Lord God of hosts."*

1 See, gracious God! before thy throne
  Thy mourning people bend;
  'Tis on thy sovereign grace alone
  Our humble hopes depend.

2 Dark, frowning judgments from thy hand
  Thy dreadful power display;
  Yet mercy spares this guilty land,
  And still we live to pray.

3 How changed, alas! are truths divine,
  For error, guilt, and shame!
  What impious numbers, bold in sin,
  Disgrace the Christian name!

4 Oh, turn us, turn us, mighty Lord,
  By thy resistless grace;
  Then shall our hearts obey thy word,
  And humbly seek thy face.

1157. *"On what a slender thread hang everlasting things."*

1 Thee we adore, eternal Name!
  And humbly own to thee
  How feeble is our mortal frame,
  What dying worms are we!

2 The year rolls round, and steals away
  The breath that first it gave;
  Whate'er we do, where'er we be,
  We're traveling to the grave.

3 Great God! on what a slender thread
  Hang everlasting things!
  Th' eternal state of all the dead
  Upon life's feeble strings!

4 Infinite joy, or endless woe
  Attends on every breath;
  And yet, how unconcerned we go
  Upon the brink of death!

5 Waken, O Lord, our drowsy sense,
  To walk this dangerous road!
  And if our souls are hurried hence,
  May they be found with God.

69. *The Evening Blessing.*

1 SAVIOUR, breathe an evening blessing,
　Ere repose our spirits seal:
Sin and want we come confessing;
　Thou canst save, and thou canst heal.

2 Though destruction walk around us,
　Though the arrow near us fly,
Angel-guards from thee surround us;
　We are safe, if thou art nigh.

3 Though the night be dark and dreary,
　Darkness can not hide from thee:
Thou art he who, never weary,
　Watcheth where thy people be.

4 Should swift death this night o'ertake us,
　And our couch become our tomb,
May the morn in heaven awake us,
　Clad in light and deathless bloom.

295.* *"Before the Cross."*

1 SWEET the moments, rich in blessing,
　Which before the cross I spend;
Life, and health, and peace possessing,
　From the sinner's dying Friend.

2 Truly blessèd is this station,
　Low before his cross to lie;
While I see divine compassion
　Beaming in his gracious eye.

3 Here it is I find my heaven,
　While upon the cross I gaze;
Love I much? I've much forgiven;
　I'm a miracle of grace.

4 Love and grief my heart dividing,
　With my tears his feet I'll bathe;
Constant still, in faith abiding,
　Life deriving from his death.

5 Here in tender, grateful sorrow
　With my Saviour will I stay;

* In Hymns 295 and 399 commence with the latter part of the tune for the fifth stanza, when sung to ANLEY.

399.* *"I will feed them upon the mountains."*

1 ISRAEL's Shepherd! guide me, feed me,
　Through my pilgrimage below;
And beside the waters lead me,
　Where thy sheep rejoicing go.

2 Lest I err, thine aid disdaining,
　And forsake thy sheltering fold,
Heedless of thy grace constraining,
　In the strength of nature bold,—

3 Lord, thy guardian presence ever,
　Meekly kneeling, I implore;
Now thy grace hath found me, never
　Would I wander from thee more.

4 Come, my soul, temptation flying,
　Arm thee for the strife within:
Jesus, thy Redeemer, dying,
　Stamps an infamy on sin.

5 Yield, my heart, no longer hardened;
　Rouse thy every latent power:
Cleansed, and washed, and freely pardon'd,
　Go in peace, and sin no more.

759. *Prayer for the Saviour's Guidance.*

1 GENTLY, Lord! oh, gently lead us
　Through this lonely vale of tears;
Through the changes thou'st decreed us,
　Till our last great change appears:
When temptation's darts assail us,
　When in devious paths we stray,
Let thy goodness never fail us;
　Lead us in thy perfect way.

2 In the hour of pain and anguish,
　In the hour when death draws near,
Suffer not our hearts to languish,
　Suffer not our souls to fear:

SICILY. 8s & 7s.

And, when mortal life is ended,
  Bid us on thy bosom rest;
Till, by angel-bands attended,
  We awake among the blest.

586. *Prayer for a lowly Heart.*—Psalm 131.

1 Let thy grace, Lord, make me lowly;
  Humble all my swelling pride;
Fallen, guilty, and unholy,
  Greatness from my eyes I'll hide.

2 I'll forbid my vain aspiring,
  Nor at earthly honors aim;
No ambitious heights desiring,
  Far above my humble claim.

3 Weaned from earth's vexatious pleasures,
  In thy love I'll seek for mine;
Placed in heaven my nobler treasures,
  Earth I quietly resign.

4 Israel, thus the world despising,
  On the Lord alone rely:
Then, from him thy joys arising,
  Like himself, shall never die.

659. *All vain, without God's Blessing.*
       Psalm 127.

1 Vainly through night's weary hours,
  Keep we watch, lest foes alarm;
Vain our bulwarks, and our towers,
  But for God's protecting arm.

2 Vain were all our toil and labor,
  Did not God that labor bless;
Vain, without his grace and favor,
  Every talent we possess.

3 Vainer still the hope of heaven,
  That on human strength relies;
But to him shall help be given,
  Who in humble faith applies.

4 Seek we, then, the Lord's Anointed;
  He shall grant us peace and rest;

Ne'er was suppliant disappointed,
  Who to Christ his prayer addressed.

570.   *Giving the Heart.*

1 Take my heart, O Father, take it!
  Make and keep it all thine own;
Let thy Spirit melt and break it—
  This proud heart of sin and stone.

2 Father, make it pure and lowly,
  Fond of peace, and far from strife;
Turning from the paths unholy
  Of this vain and sinful life.

3 Ever let thy grace surround it;
  Strengthen it with power divine,
Till thy cords of love have bound it:
  Make it to be wholly thine.

4 May the blood of Jesus heal it,
  And its sins be all forgiven;
Holy Spirit, take and seal it,
  Guide it in the path to heaven.

1184. *"Abide with us; for it is toward evening."*

1 Tarry with me, O my Saviour!
  For the day is passing by;
See! the shades of evening gather,
  And the night is drawing nigh.

2 Deeper, deeper grow the shadows,
  Paler now the glowing west;
Swift the night of death advances;
  Shall it be the night of rest?

3 Feeble, trembling, fainting, dying,
  Lord, I cast myself on thee;
Tarry with me through the darkness;
  While I sleep, still watch by me.

4 Tarry with me, O my Saviour!
  Lay my head upon thy breast
Till the morning; then awake me—
  Morning of eternal rest!

MORNINGTON. S. M.

593. *Prayer to Christ for Pardon.*

1 O THOU that wouldst not have
    One wretched sinner die;
Who diedst thyself my soul to save
    From endless misery;
Show me the way to shun
    Thy dreadful wrath severe;
That, when thou comest on thy throne,
    I may with joy appear.

2 Thou art thyself the way;
    Thyself in me reveal:
So shall I spend my life's short day
    Obedient to thy will;
So shall I love my God,
    Because he first loved me,
And praise thee in thy bright abode
    To all eternity.

817. *Peace found only in serving God.*
    Psalm 55.

1 LET sinners take their course,
    And choose the road to death;
But in the worship of my God
    I'll spend my daily breath.

2 My thoughts address his throne,
    When morning brings the light;
I seek his blessing every noon,
    And pay my vows at night.

3 Thou wilt regard my cries,
    O my eternal God!
While sinners perish in surprise,
    Beneath thine angry rod.

4 Because they dwell at ease,
    And no sad changes feel,
They neither fear nor trust thy name,
    Nor learn to do thy will.

5 But I, with all my cares,
    Will lean upon the Lord;
I'll cast my burden on his arm,
    And rest upon his word.

6 His arm shall well sustain
    The children of his love;
The ground on which their safety stands,
    No earthly power can move.

932. *"I opened not my mouth; because Thou didst it."*—Psalm 39.

1 IT is thy hand, my God;
    My sorrows come from thee;
I bow beneath thy chastening rod,
    'T is love that bruises me.

2 I would not murmur, Lord;
    Before thee I am dumb;
Lest I should breathe one murmuring word
    To thee for help I come.

3 My God, thy name is love;
    A Father's hand is thine:
With tearful eyes I look above,
    And cry "Thy will be mine!"

4 I know thy will is right,
    Though it may seem severe;
Thy path is still unsullied light,
    Though dark it oft appear.

5 Jesus for me hath died;
    Thy Son thou didst not spare;
His pierced hands, his bleeding side,
    Thy love for me declare.

6 Here my poor heart can rest;
    My God, it cleaves to thee;
Thy will is love, thine end is best;
    All work for good to me.

555. *"Create in me a clean heart."*

1 Is this the kind return?
    Are these the thanks we owe?
Thus to abuse eternal Love,
    Whence all our blessings flow?

BOYLSTON. S. M.

To what a stubborn frame
  Hath sin reduced our mind!
What strange, rebellious wretches we!
  And God as strangely kind!

3 Turn, turn us, mighty God!
  And mold our souls afresh;
Break, sovereign Grace! these hearts of stone,
  And give us hearts of flesh.

4 Let past ingratitude
  Provoke our weeping eyes,
And hourly, as new mercies fall,
  Let hourly thanks arise.

733. *Faith entreating for Pardon.*

1 O LORD, how vile am I,
  Unholy and unclean!
How can I dare to venture nigh
  With such a load of sin?

2 Myself can hardly bear
  This wretched heart of mine;
How hateful, then, must it appear
  To those pure eyes of thine!

3 And must I then indeed
  Sink in despair and die?
Fain would I hope that thou didst **bleed**
  For such a wretch as I!

4 That blood which thou hast spilt,
  That grace which is thine own,
Can cleanse the vilest sinner's guilt,
  And soften hearts of stone.

5 Low at thy feet I bow;
  Oh, pity and forgive!
Here will I lie and wait **till thou**
  Shalt bid me rise and live.

766. *"Though He slay me, yet will I trust in Him."*

WHEN earthly comforts die,
  And thorns o'erspread the road,

Whither, oh, whither shall I fly,
  But unto thee, my God!

2 When anxious thoughts arise,
  And sorrows compass round,
Amid ten thousand enemies,
  In thee my help is found.

3 Then at thy feet I'll bow,
  And in thy mercy trust;
If I am saved, how good art thou!
  And if I perish, just!

4 Perish!—it can not be,
  Since Jesus shed his blood;
The promise is both rich and free,
  And he will make it good.

778. *"I trust in Thee: let me not be ashamed."*

1 OPPRESSED with sin and woe,
  A burdened heart I bear;
Opposed by many a mighty foe,—
  Yet will I not despair.

2 With this polluted heart,
  I dare to come to thee,
Holy and mighty as thou art,—
  For thou wilt pardon me.

3 I feel that I am weak,
  And prone to every sin;
But thou, who giv'st to those who seek,
  Wilt give me strength within.

4 I need not fear my foes,
  I need not yield to care,
I need not sink beneath my woes
  For thou wilt answer prayer.

5 In my Redeemer's name,
  I give myself to thee;
Through him, unworthy as I am,
  My God will cherish me.

651. *"Filled with all the fullness of God."*

1 O Lord, I would delight in thee,
   And on thy care depend;
   To thee in every trouble flee,
   My best, my only Friend.
2 When all created streams are dried,
   Thy fullness is the same:
   May I with this be satisfied,
   And glory in thy name!
3 No good in creatures can be found,
   But what is found in thee;
   I must have all things and abound
   While God is God to me.
4 Oh that I had a stronger faith,
   To look within the vail,—
   To credit what my Saviour saith,
   Whose word can never fail.
5 He who has made my heaven secure,
   Will here all good provide:
   While Christ is rich, can I be poor?
   What can I want beside?
6 O Lord, I cast my care on thee;
   I triumph and adore:
   Henceforth my great concern shall be
   To love and please thee more.

820. *"What shall I render unto the Lord?"*
     Psalm 116.

1 What shall I render to my God
   For all his kindness shown?
   My feet shall visit thine abode,
   My songs address thy throne.
2 Among the saints that fill thy house,
   My offerings shall be paid;
   There shall my zeal perform the vows
   My soul in anguish made.
3 How much is mercy thy delight,
   Thou ever blessed God!
   How dear thy servants in thy sight!
   How precious is their blood!

4 How happy all thy servants are!
   How great thy grace to me!
   My life, which thou hast made thy care,
   Lord, I devote to thee.
5 Now I am thine, for ever thine,
   Nor shall my purpose move;
   Thy hand hath loosed my bonds of pain,
   And bound me with thy love.
6 Here in thy courts I leave my vow,
   And thy rich grace record;
   Witness, ye saints, who hear me now,
   If I forsake the Lord.

827. *"I will pay my vows unto the Lord."*
     Psalm 116.

1 I love the Lord: he lent an ear
   When I for help implored;
   He rescued me from all my fear;
   Therefore I love the Lord.
2 Return, my soul, unto thy rest;
   From God no longer roam:
   His hand hath bountifully blest;
   His goodness called thee home.
3 What shall I render unto thee,
   My Saviour, in distress,
   For all thy benefits to me,
   So great and numberless?
4 This will I do, for thy love's sake,
   And thus thy power proclaim:
   Salvation's sacred cup I'll take,
   And call upon thy name.
5 Thou God of covenanted grace!
   Hear and record my vow,—
   While in thy courts I seek thy face,
   And at thine altar bow.
6 Henceforth myself to thee I give,
   With single heart and eye,
   To walk before thee while I live,
   And bless thee when I die.

DENFIELD. C. M.

1095. *"Weep with them that weep."*

1 Lord, may our sympathizing breasts
　Thy generous pleasure know,
　Kindly to share in others' joys,
　And weep for others' woe!

2 Where'er the helpless sons of grief
　In low distress are laid,
　Soft be our hearts, their pains to feel,
　And swift our hands to aid.

3 Thus may the sacred law of love
　Through all our actions shine,
　And force a scoffing world to own
　The Christian name divine.

1096. *"Be ye perfect, even as your Father in heaven."*

1 Bright Source of everlasting love,
　To thee our souls we raise;
　And to thy sovereign bounty rear
　A monument of praise.

2 Thy mercy gilds the path of life
　With every cheering ray,
　Kindly restrains the rising tear,
　Or wipes that tear away.

3 To tents of woe, to beds of pain,
　Thy children, Lord, repair;
　And, with the gifts thy hand bestows,
　Relieve the mourners there.

4 The widow's heart shall sing for joy;
　The orphan shall be fed;
　The hungering soul we'll gladly point
　To Christ, the living Bread.

5 Thus what our heavenly Father gave
　Shall we as freely give;
　Thus copy him who lived to save,
　And died that we might live.

1233. *"Earnestly desiring to be clothed upon."*

1 Father! I long, I faint, to see
　The place of thine abode;
　I'd leave thine earthly courts, and flee
　Up to thy seat, my God!

2 There all the heavenly hosts are seen;
　In shining ranks they move;
　And drink immortal vigor in,
　With wonder and with love.

3 Then at thy feet, with awful fear,
　The adoring armies fall;
　With joy they shrink to nothing there,
　Before th' eternal All.

4 The more thy glories strike my eyes,
　The humbler I shall lie;
　Thus while I sink, my joys shall rise
　Immeasurably high.

1239. *Death is Gain.*

1 When musing sorrow weeps the past,
　And mourns the present pain,
　'Tis sweet to think of peace at last,
　And feel that death is gain.

2 'Tis not that murmuring thoughts arise,
　And dread a Father's will;
　'Tis not that meek submission flies,
　And would not suffer still.

3 It is that heaven-born faith surveys
　The path that leads to light,
　And longs her eagle plumes to raise,
　And lose herself in sight.

4 Oh, let me wing my hallowed flight
　From earth-born woe and care,
　And soar above these clouds of night,
　My Saviour's bliss to share!

Doxology.

Let God the Father, and the Son,
　And Spirit, be adored,
Where there are works to make him known,
　Or saints to love the Lord!

WINDHAM. L. M.

134. *The All-seeing God.*—Psalm 139.

1 LORD, thou hast searched and seen me through;
Thine eye commands, with piercing view,
My rising and my resting hours,
My heart and flesh, with all their powers.

2 My thoughts, before they are my own,
Are to my God distinctly known;
He knows the words I mean to speak,
Ere from my opening lips they break.

3 Within thy circling power I stand;
On every side I find thy hand:
Awake, asleep, at home, abroad,
I am surrounded still with God.

4 Amazing knowledge, vast and great!
What large extent! what lofty height!
My soul, with all the powers I boast,
Is in the boundless prospect lost.

5 Oh, may these thoughts possess my breast,
Where'er I rove, where'er I rest!
Nor let my weaker passions dare
Consent to sin, for God is there.

601. *"My soul waiteth for Thee."*
Psalm 130.

1 FROM deep distress and troubl'd thoughts,
To thee, my God, I raise my cries;
If thou severely mark our faults,
No flesh can stand before thine eyes.

2 But thou hast built thy throne of grace,
Free to dispense thy pardons there;
That sinners may approach thy face,
And hope and love, as well as fear.

3 As the benighted pilgrims wait,
And long and wish for breaking day,
So waits my soul before thy gate:
When will my God his face display?

4 My trust is fixed upon thy word,
Nor shall I trust thy word in vain;
Let mourning souls address the Lord,
And find relief from all their pain.

5 Great is his love, and large his grace,
Through the redemption of his Son;
He turns our feet from sinful ways,
And pardons what our hands have done

615. *The Joy of Pardon.*

1 THOU Prince of glory, slain for me,
Breathing forgiveness in thy prayer;
That loving, melting look I see,
That bursting sigh, that tender tear.

2 Can I behold that closing eye,
Still fixed on me, still beaming love!
And can I see my Saviour die,
Nor feel one holy passion move?

3 Let me but hear thy dying voice
Pronounce forgiveness in my breast,
My trembling spirit shall rejoice,
And feel the calm of heavenly rest.

4 Lord, thine atoning blood apply,
And life or death is sweet to me;
In life's last hour, thy presence nigh,
From fear shall set my spirit free.

727. *The only Plea.*

1 JESUS, the sinner's Friend, to thee,
Lost and undone, for aid I flee;
Weary of earth, myself, and sin,
Open thine arms, and take me in.

2 Pity and save my ruined soul;
'T is thou alone canst make me whole;
Dark, till in me thine image shine,
And lost I am till thou art mine.

3 At last I own it can not be
That I should fit myself for thee;
Here, then, to thee I all resign;
Thine is the work, and only thine.

4 What can I say thy grace to move?
Lord, I am sin,—but thou art love:
I give up every plea beside,
Lord, I am lost,—but thou hast died!

HEBRON. L. M.

62. *"Great is thy faithfulness."*

1 My God, how endless is thy love!
  Thy gifts are every evening new;
  And morning mercies, from above,
  Gently distill, like early dew.

2 Thou spread'st the curtains of the night,
  Great Guardian of my sleeping hours!
  Thy sovereign word restores the light,
  And quickens all my drowsy powers.

3 I yield my powers to thy command;
  To thee I consecrate my days:
  Perpetual blessings from thy hand
  Demand perpetual songs of praise.

198. *"The Lord of Hosts is with us."*
Psalm 46.

1 God is our refuge and defense,
  In trouble our unfailing aid;
  Secure in his omnipotence,
  What foe can make our souls afraid?

2 There is a river pure and bright,
  Whose streams make glad the heavenly plains;
  There, in eternity of light,
  The city of our God remains.

3 Not on a seraph's wing of fire,—
  But on the mightier wings of prayer
  We reach that home of pure desire,
  And feel his cloudless presence there.

4 But soon, how soon! our spirits droop,
  Unwont the air of heaven to breathe:
  Yet God, in very deed, will stoop,
  And dwell himself with men beneath.

5 Come to thy living temples, then,
  As in the ancient times appear:
  Let earth be paradise again,
  And man, O God, thine image here!

237. *"How unsearchable are Thy judgments!"*

1 Lord, my weak thought in vain would climb
  To search the starry vault profound;
  In vain would wing her flight sublime,
  To find creation's outmost bound.

2 But weaker yet that thought must prove
  To search thy great eternal plan,—
  Thy sovereign counsels, born of love
  Long ages ere the world began.

3 When my dim reason would demand
  Why that, or this, thou dost ordain,
  By some vast deep I seem to stand,
  Whose secrets I must ask in vain.

4 When doubts disturb my troubled breast,
  And all is dark as night to me,
  Here, as on solid rock, I rest,
  That so it seemeth good to thee.

5 Be this my joy, that evermore
  Thou rulest all things at thy will:
  Thy sovereign wisdom I adore,
  And calmly, sweetly, trust thee still.

806. *Imitation of Christ in Suffering.*

1 Dear Lord, amid the throng that pressed
  Around thee on the cursèd tree,
  Some loyal, loving hearts were there,
  Some pitying eyes that wept for thee.

2 Like them may we rejoice to own
  Our dying Lord, though crowned with thorn;
  Like thee thy blessèd self, endure
  The cross with all its joy or scorn,

3 Thy cross, thy lonely path below,
  Show what thy brethren all should be:
  Pilgrims on earth, disowned by those
  Who see no beauty, Lord, in thee.

KENT. 6s & 4s.

372.
"Plead Thou my cause."

1 PLEAD thou, oh, plead my cause!
  Each self-excusing plea
My trembling soul withdraws,
  And flies to thee.
When justice rears her throne,
Ah! who, save thee alone,
May stand, O spotless One?
  Plead thou my cause!

2 Ah! plead not aught of mine
  Before thine altar throne—
Fragments, when all is thine,
  All, all thine own!
Thou seest what stains they bear,
Oh, since each tear, each prayer,
Hath need of pardon there,
  Plead thou my cause!

3 Plead, when the tempter's art,
  To each fond hope of mine,
Denies this faithless heart
  Can e'er be thine.
If slander whisper, too,
The sin I never knew,
Thou, who couldst urge the true,
  Plead thou my cause!

4 Oh, plead my cause above,
  Plead thine within my breast;
Till there thy peaceful dove
  Shall build her nest.
Thou know'st this will, how frail!
Thou know'st, though language fail,
My soul's mysterious tale;
  Plead thou my cause!

ELAND. 6s & 4s.

427.
"The Light of Life."

1 ON earth was darkness spread—
    One boundless night;
  "Let there be light," God said—
    And there was light!

2 There hung a deeper gloom
    O'er quick and dead,
  But Jesus burst the tomb,
    And darkness fled.

3 God by his word arrayed
    Darkness with light:

God by his Son displayed
    Day without night.

4 'or thee, O man, arose
    Creation's ray!
  For thee, too, brighter glows
    Salvation's day.

5 The beams first poured on earth
    For mortals shone:
  The light of later birth
    Immortals own.

AVA. 6s & 4s.

542.   *"Child of sin and sorrow."*

1 Child of sin and sorrow,
    Filled with dismay,
  Wait not for to-morrow,
    Yield thee to-day;
      Heaven bids thee come,
      While yet there's room;
  Child of sin and sorrow,
    Hear and obey.

2 Child of sin and sorrow,
    Why wilt thou die!
  Come, while thou canst borrow
    Help from on high:
      Grieve not that love,
      Which, from above,
  Child of sin and sorrow,
    Would bring thee nigh.

RYLE. 6s & 5s.

569.   *Yielding Earth for Heaven.*—Heb. 11: 16.

1 My soul, go boldly forth,
    Forsake this sinful earth;
  What hath it been to thee
    But pain and sorrow?
  And think'st thou it will be
    Better to-morrow?

2 Why wilt thou still delay?
    Thou cam'st not here to stay:
  What tak'st thou for thy part
    But heavenly pleasure?
  Where then should be thy heart,
    But where's thy treasure?

3 Thy God, thy Head's above;
    There is the world of love;
  Mansions there purchased are
    By Christ's own merit;
  For these he doth prepare
    Thee, by his Spirit.

4 Lord Jesus, take my spirit;
    I trust thy love and merit:
  Take home thy wandering sheep,
    For thou hast sought it:
  My soul in safety keep,
    For thou hast bought it.

BETHANY. 6s & 4s.

989. *"Nearer, my God, to thee."*

1 NEARER, my God, to thee,
  Nearer to thee:
 Ev'n though it be a cross
  That raiseth me,
 Still all my song shall be,
 |: Nearer, my God, to thee, :|
  Nearer to thee.

2 Though like a wanderer,
  Daylight all gone,
 Darkness be over me,
  My rest a stone,
 Yet in my dreams, I'd be
 |: Nearer, my God, to thee, :|
  Nearer to thee.

3 There let the way appear
  Steps up to heaven;
 All that thou sendest me
  In mercy given,
 Angels to beckon me
 |: Nearer, my God, to thee, :|
  Nearer to thee.

4 Then with my waking thoughts,
  Bright with thy praise,
 Out of my stony griefs,
  Bethel I'll raise;
 So by my woes to be
 |: Nearer, my God, to thee, :|
  Nearer to thee.

5 Or if on joyful wing.
  Cleaving the sky,
 Sun, moon, and stars forgot
  Upward I fly,
 Still all my song shall be,
 |: Nearer, my God, to thee, :|
  Nearer to thee.

1224. *"Strangers and pilgrims on the earth."*

1 I'M but a stranger here,
  Heaven is my home;
 Earth is a desert drear,
  Heaven is my home:
 Danger and sorrow stand
 Round me on every hand;
 Heaven is my fatherland—
  Heaven is my home.

2 What though the tempest rage,
  Heaven is my home;
 Short is my pilgrimage,
  Heaven is my home:
 Time's cold and wint'ry blast
 Soon will be overpast;
 I shall reach home at last—
  Heaven is my home.

3 There, at my Saviour's side,
  Heaven is my home;
 I shall be glorified—
  Heaven is my home:
 There are the good and blest,
 Those I loved most and best,
 And there I, too, shall rest;—
  Heaven is my home!

OAK. 6s & 4s.

1259. *Children's Song of the Happy Land.*

1 THERE is a happy land,
　Far, far away,
Where saints in glory stand,
　Bright, bright as day;
Oh, how they sweetly sing,
Worthy is our Saviour King!
Loud let his praises ring,
　Praise, praise for aye.

2 Come to that happy land—
　Come, come away;
Why will ye doubting stand,
　Why still delay?

Oh! we shall happy be,
When from sin and sorrow free;
Lord, we shall live with thee,
　Blest, blest for aye!

3 Bright, in that happy land,
　Beams every eye;
Kept by a Father's hand,
　Love can not die;
Oh, then to glory run!
Be a crown and kingdom won;
And bright, above the sun,
　We reign for aye!

LYNCH. 6s & 4s.

933. *"O God! be Thou my stay."*

1 FATHER, oh, hear me now!
　Father divine!
Thou, only thou, canst see
The heart's deep agony;
Help me to say to thee
　"Thy will, not mine!"

2 O God! be thou my stay,
　In this dark hour;
Kindly each sorrow hear,

Hush every troubled fear,
Thee let me still revere,
　Still own thy power.

3 In thee alone I trust,
　Thou Holy One!
Humbly to thee I pray
That through each troubled day
Of life, I still may say,
　"Thy will be done!"

HALLE. 7s. 6 LINES.

545. *Pleading with Sinners.*

1 HEART of stone, relent, relent!
  Break, by Jesus' cross subdued;
See his body mangled, rent,
  Covered with his flowing blood:
Sinful soul, what hast thou done!
Crucified th' incarnate Son!

2 Yes: thy sins have done the deed,
  Driven the nails that fixed him there;
Crowned with thorns his sacred head,
  Pierced him with the cruel spear,
Made his soul a sacrifice,
While for sinful man he dies.

3 Wilt thou let him bleed in vain?
  Still to death thy Lord pursue?
Open all his wounds again,
  And the shameful cross renew?
No: with all my sins I'll part;
Break, oh, break, my bleeding heart!

624. *The Hour of Need.*

1 O THOU God who hearest prayer
Every hour and everywhere!
For his sake, whose blood I plead,
Hear me in my hour of need:
Only hide not now thy face,
God of all-sufficient grace!

2 Hear and save me, gracious Lord!
For my trust is in thy word;
Wash me from the stain of sin,
That thy peace may rule within:
May I know myself thy child,
Ransomed, pardoned, reconciled.

3 Dearest Lord! may I so much
As thy garment's hem but touch,
Or but raise my languid eye
To the cross where thou didst die,
It shall make my spirit whole—
It shall heal and save my soul.

4 Leave me not, my Strength, my Trust!
Oh, remember I 'm but dust!
Leave me not again to stray;
Leave me not the tempter's prey.
Fix my heart on things above;
Make me happy in thy love.

632. *Conflict with Sin.*

1 ONCE I thought my mountain strong,
  Firmly fixed, no more to move:
Then my Saviour was my song,
  Then my soul was filled with love:
Those were happy, golden days,
Sweetly spent in prayer and praise.

2 Little then myself I knew,
  Little thought of Satan's power;
Now I feel my sins anew,
  Now I feel the stormy hour:
Sin has put my joys to flight,
Sin has turned my day to night.

3 Saviour! shine, and cheer my soul;
  Bid my dying hopes revive;
Make my wounded spirit whole;
  Far away the tempter drive:
Speak the word and set me free;
Let me live alone to thee.

ROSEFIELD. 7s. 6 LINES.

711. *"Jesus, Saviour, pity me."*

1 Pity Lord! this child of clay,
Who can only weep and pray—
Only on thy love depend:
Thou who art the sinner's Friend,
Thou, the sinner's only plea—
Jesus, Saviour, pity me!

2 From thy flock, a straying lamb,
Tender Shepherd, though I am;
Now, upon the mountain cold,
Lost, I long to gain the fold,
And within thine arms to be:
Jesus, Saviour, pity me!

3 Oh, where stillest streams are poured,
In green pastures lead me, Lord!
Bring me back, where angels sound
Joy to the poor wanderer found
Evermore my Shepherd be:
Jesus, Saviour, pity me!

740. *Prayer for Audience with the God-man.*

1 Saviour, when in dust to thee
Low we bow th' adoring knee;
Pleading all thy pain and woe
Suffered once for man below;
Turn on us a favoring eye,
Hear, oh, hear our humble cry!

2 By thine hour of dire despair,
By thine agony of prayer,
By thy wounds, and pangs, and cries,
By thy perfect sacrifice,—
Bending from thy throne on high,
Hear, oh, hear our humble cry!

3 By thy tomb, whose dark abode
Held in vain the rising God,
Oh, from earth to heaven restored,
Mighty reascended Lord!
On thy seat above the sky,
Hear, oh, hear our humble cry!

741. *Prayer for the manifested Presence of Christ.*—John 14: 21.

1 Son of God! to thee I cry:
By the holy mystery
Of thy dwelling here on earth,
By thy pure and holy birth,
Hear, oh, hear my lowly plea:
Manifest thyself to me!

2 Lamb of God! to thee I cry:
By thy bitter agony,
By thy pangs to us unknown,
By thy spirit's parting groan,
Hear, oh, hear my lowly plea:
Manifest thyself to me!

3 Prince of Life! to thee I cry:
By thy glorious majesty,
By thy triumph o'er the grave,
Meek to suffer, strong to save,
Hear, oh, hear my fervid plea:
Manifest thyself to me!

4 Lord of glory, God most high!
Man exalted to the sky,
With thy love my bosom fill;
Prompt me to perform thy will;
Then thy glory I shall see—
Thou wilt bring me home to thee.

ELLENTHORPE. L. M.

571. *Joy in Heaven over one Penitent.*
Luke 15: 7.

1 Who can describe the joys that rise
Through all the courts of paradise,
To see a prodigal return,
To see an heir of glory born?

2 With joy the Father doth approve
The fruit of his eternal love;
The Son, with joy looks down and sees
The purchase of his agonies.

3 The Spirit takes delight to view
The holy soul he formed anew;
And saints and angels join to sing
The growing empire of their King.

756. *"The faith of joys to come."*

1 'T is by the faith of joys to come
We walk thro' deserts dark as night;
Till we arrive at heaven, our home,
Faith is our guide, and faith our light.

2 The want of sight she well supplies,
She makes the pearly gates appear;
Far into distant worlds she pries,
And brings eternal glories near.

3 Cheerful we tread the desert through,
While faith inspires a heavenly ray;
Though lions roar, and tempests blow,
And rocks and dangers fill the way.

853. *The Worth of Prayer.*

1 What various hindrances we meet
In coming to a mercy-seat!
Yet who that knows the worth of prayer
But wishes to be often there?

2 Prayer makes the darkened clouds withdraw,
Prayer climbs the ladder Jacob saw,
Gives exercise to faith and love,
Brings every blessing from above.

3 Restraining prayer, we cease to fight;
Prayer makes the Christian's armor bright;
And Satan trembles when he sees
The weakest saint upon his knees.

4 Have you no words? ah! think again;
Words flow apace when you complain,
And fill a fellow-creature's ear
With the sad tale of all your care.

5 Were half the breath thus vainly spent
To heaven in supplication sent,
Our cheerful song would oftener be,
"Hear what the Lord hath done for me!"

866. *Nothing without Love.*—1 Cor. 13: 1—3.

1 Had I the tongues of Greeks and Jews,
And nobler speech than angels use,
If love be absent, I am found,
Like tinkling brass, an empty sound.

2 Were I inspired to preach and tell
All that is done in heaven or hell,
Or could my faith the world remove,
Still am I nothing without love.

3 Should I distribute all my store,
To feed the hungry, clothe the poor—
Or give my body to the flame,
To gain a martyr's glorious name—

4 If love to God and love to men
Be absent, all my hopes are vain;
Nor tongues, nor gifts, nor fiery zeal,
The work of love can e'er fulfill.

886. *"When I am weak, then am I strong."*
2 Cor. 12: 7.

1 Let me but hear my Saviour say,
"Strength shall be equal to thy day;"
Then I rejoice in deep distress,
Leaning on all-sufficient grace.

UXBRIDGE. L. M.

2 I can do all things—or can bear
  All suffering, if my Lord be there;
  Sweet pleasures mingle with the pains,
  While he my sinking head sustains.

3 I glory in infirmity,
  That Christ's own power may rest on me;
  When I am weak, then am I strong;
  Grace is my shield, and Christ my song.

1005. "*It is God that justifieth.*"
Rom. 8: 33–37.

1 Who shall the Lord's elect condemn?
  'T is God who justifies their souls;
  And mercy, like a mighty stream,
  O'er all their sins divinely rolls.

2 Who shall adjudge the saints to hell?
  'T is Christ who suffered in their stead;
  And, the salvation to fulfill,
  Behold him rising from the dead!

3 He lives! he lives! and sits above,
  For ever interceding there;
  Who shall divide us from his love,
  Or what should tempt us to despair?

4 Shall persecution, or distress,
  Famine, or sword, or nakedness?
  He who hath loved us bears us through,
  And makes us more than conquerors, too.

5 Not all that men on earth can do,
  Nor powers on high, nor powers below,
  Shall cause his mercy to remove,
  Or wean our hearts from Christ, our love.

1008. "*Not by works of righteousness which we have done.*"

1 Now to the power of God supreme
  Be everlasting honors given;
  He saves from hell—we bless his name—
  He guides our wandering feet to heaven.

2 Not for our duties or deserts,
  But of his own abundant grace,

  He works salvation in our hearts,
  And forms a people for his praise.

3 'T was his own purpose that begun
  To rescue rebels doomed to die;
  He gave us grace in Christ his Son,
  Before he spread the starry sky.

4 Jesus, the Lord, appears at last,
  And makes his Father's counsels known,
  Declares the great transaction past,
  And brings immortal blessings down.

5 He dies,—and, in that dreadful night,
  Did all the powers of hell destroy;
  He rose, and brought our heaven to light,
  And took possession of the joy.

1135. "*Go, preach My Gospel.*"
Mark 16: 15–20.

1 "Go, preach my gospel," saith the Lord;
  "Bid the whole earth my grace receive;
  He shall be saved who trusts my word;
  And they condemned who disbelieve.

2 "I'll make your great commission known,
  And ye shall prove my gospel true
  By all the works that I have done,
  By all the wonders ye shall do.

3 "Teach all the nations my commands;
  I'm with you till the world shall end;
  All power is trusted in my hands;
  I can destroy, and I defend."

4 He spake, and light shone round his head;
  On a bright cloud to heaven he rode;
  They to the farthest nations spread
  The grace of their ascended God.

DOXOLOGY.

To God the Father, God the Son,
And God the Spirit, Three in One,
Be honor, praise, and glory given,
By all on earth, and all in heaven!

NAOMI. C. M.

576. *Prayer for a Sense of Sin.*

1 Oh, for that tenderness of heart
Which bows before the Lord!
Owning how just and good thou art,
And trembling at thy word.

2 Oh, for those humble, contrite tears
Which from repentance flow!
Oh, for that sense of guilt which fears
The long-suspended blow!

3 Saviour, to me in pity give,
For sin, the deep distress—
The pledge thou wilt at last receive;
And bid me die in peace.

4 Oh, fill my soul with faith and love,
And strength to do thy will!
Raise my desires and hopes above;
Thyself to me reveal.

579. *"Oh, wretched man that I am!"*

1 With tears of anguish I lament,
Here, at thy feet, my God,
My passion, pride, and discontent,
And vile ingratitude.

2 Sure, there was ne'er a heart so base,
So false as mine has been;
So faithless to its promises,
So prone to every sin!

3 How long, dear Saviour, shall I feel
These struggles in my breast?
When wilt thou bow my stubborn will,
And give my conscience rest?

4 Break, sovereign Grace, oh, break the charm,
And set the captive free!
Reveal, almighty God, thine arm,
And haste to rescue me.

591. *"O Lord, in wrath remember mercy."*
Psalm 38.

1 Amid thy wrath remember love,
Restore thy servant, Lord;

Nor let a Father's chastening prove
Like an avenger's sword.

2 My sins a heavy load appear,
And o'er my head are gone;
Too heavy they for me to bear,
Too hard for me t' atone.

3 My thoughts are like a troubled sea,
My head still bending down;
And I go mourning all the day,
Beneath my Father's frown.

4 All my desire to thee is known;
Thine eye counts every tear;
And every sigh, and every groan,
Is noticed by thine ear.

5 My God, forgive my follies past,
And be for ever nigh;
Thou God of my salvation, haste,
Before thy servant die.

600. *"There is forgiveness with Thee."*
Psalm 130.

1 Out of the deeps of long distress,
The borders of despair,
I sent my cries to seek thy grace,
My groans to move thine ear.

2 Great God! should thy severer eye,
And thine impartial hand,
Be strict to mark iniquity,
No mortal flesh could stand.

3 But there are pardons with my God,
For crimes of high degree;
Thy Son has bought them with his blood,
To draw us near to thee.

4 I wait for thy salvation, Lord;
With strong desires I wait;
My soul, invited by thy word,
Stands watching at thy gate.

5 In God the Lord let Israel trust;
O sinners, seek his face;
The Lord is good, as well as just,
And plenteous is his grace.

GRAFTON. C. M.

611. *"Turn us, O God of our salvation."*
Psalm 85.

1 LORD! at thy feet we sinners lie,
  And knock at mercy's door:
With heavy heart and downcast eye,
  Thy favor we implore.

2 On us the vast extent display
  Of thy forgiving love;
Take all our heinous guilt away;
  This heavy load remove.

3 'T is mercy—mercy we implore;
  We would thy pity move:
Thy grace is an exhaustless store,
  And thou thyself art love.

4 Oh, for thine own, for Jesus' sake
  Our numerous sins forgive!
Thy grace our rocky hearts can break:
  Heal us, and bid us live.

5 Thus melt us down, thus make us bend,
  And thy dominion own;
Nor let a rival more pretend
  To repossess thy throne.

613. *"I have trusted in Thy mercy."*
Psalm 13.

1 How long wilt thou forget me, Lord?
  Must I for ever mourn?
How long wilt thou withdraw from me;
  Oh! never to return?

2 Hear thou, and to my longing eyes
  Restore thy wonted light,
And suddenly, or I shall sleep
  In everlasting night.

3 Since I have always placed my trust
  Beneath thy mercy's wing,
Thy saving health will come, and then
  My heart with joy shall spring.

4 Then shall I raise glad songs of praise
  To my forgiving Lord;
And thou wilt ever be my Help,
  My Hope, my large Reward.

620. *"Turn Thee unto me, and have mercy upon me."*

1 O THOU, whose tender mercy hears
  Contrition's humble sigh;
Whose hand indulgent wipes the tears
  From sorrow's weeping eye.

2 See, Lord, before thy throne of grace,
  A wretched wanderer mourn:
Hast thou not bid me seek thy face?
  Hast thou not said—"Return?"

3 And shall my guilty fears prevail
  To drive me from thy feet?
Oh, let not this dear refuge fail,
  This only safe retreat!

4 Absent from thee, my Guide! my Light!
  Without one cheering ray,
Through dangers, fears, and gloomy night,
  How desolate my way!

5 Oh, shine on this benighted heart,
  With beams of mercy shine!
And let thy healing voice impart
  A taste of joy divine.

712. *A weeping Saviour.*

1 AND can mine eyes, without a tear,
  A weeping Saviour see?
Shall I not weep his groans to hear
  Who groaned and died for me?

2 Blest Jesus! let those tears of thine
  Subdue each stubborn foe;
Come, fill my heart with love divine,
  And bid my sorrows flow.

DOXOLOGY.

To Father, Son, and Holy Ghost,
  One God, whom we adore,
Be glory as it was, is now,
  And shall be evermore!

PEKIN. S. M.

510. *Gentleness of God's Commands.*
Psalm 55.

1 How gentle God's commands!
  How kind his precepts are!
Come, cast your burdens on the Lord,
  And trust his constant care.

2 Beneath his watchful eye
  His saints securely dwell;
That hand which bears all nature up,
  Shall guard his children well.

3 Why should this anxious load
  Press down your weary mind?
Haste to your heavenly Father's throne,
  And sweet refreshment find.

4 His goodness stands approved,
  Unchanged from day to day:
I'll drop my burden at his feet,
  And bear a song away.

861. *Blessings of Christian Unity.*
Psalm 133.

1 Blest are the sons of peace
  Whose hearts and hopes are one;
Whose kind designs to serve and please
  Through all their actions run.

2 Blest is the pious house
  Where zeal and friendship meet:
Their songs of praise, their mingled vows,
  Make their communion sweet.

3 From those celestial springs
  Such streams of pleasure flow,
As no increase of riches brings,
  Nor honors can bestow.

4 Thus on the heavenly hills
  The saints are blest above;
Where joy, like morning dew, distills,
  And all the air is love!

907. *" My peace I give unto you."*

1 Let not your heart be faint,
  My peace I give to you,—
Such peace as reason never planned,
  Nor sinners ever knew.

2 It tells of joys to come;
  It soothes the troubled breast;
It shines, a star amid the storm—
  The harbinger of rest.

3 Then murmur not, nor mourn,
  My people faint and few;
Though earth to its foundation shake,
  My peace I leave with you.

998. *" The Spirit of God dwelleth in you."*

1 Blest are the pure in heart,
  For they shall see their God.
The secret of the Lord is theirs;
  Their soul is Christ's abode.

2 The Lord, who left the heavens,
  Our life and peace to bring;
To dwell in lowliness with men,
  Their pattern and their King;—

3 He to the lowly soul
  Doth still himself impart,
And for his dwelling, and his throne,
  Chooseth the pure in heart.

4 Lord, we thy presence seek:
  May ours this blessing be;
Oh, give the pure and lowly heart
  A temple meet for thee!

403. *" I will fear no evil, for Thou art with me."*—Psalm 23.

1 While my Redeemer's near,
  My shepherd and my guide,
I bid farewell to anxious fear;
  My wants are all supplied.

GERAR. S. M.

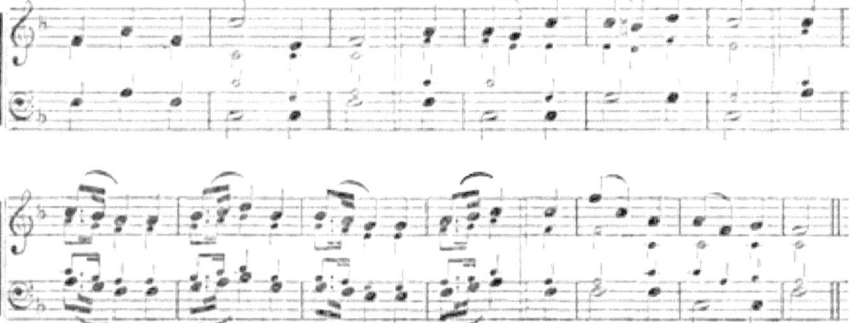

2 To ever fragrant meads,
    Where rich abundance grows,
His gracious hand indulgent leads,
    And guards my sweet repose.

3 Dear Shepherd, if I stray,
    My wandering feet restore;
To thy fair pastures guide my way,
    And let me rove no more.

786.   *Jesus our living Head.*

1 Our heavenly Father calls,
    And Christ invites us near;
With both, our friendship shall be sweet,
    And our communion dear.

2 God pities all our griefs;
    He pardons every day,—
Almighty to protect our souls,
    And wise to guide our way.

3 How large his bounties are!
    What various stores of good,
Diffused from our Redeemer's hand,
    And purchased with his blood!

4 Jesus, our living Head!
    We bless thy faithful care,—
Our Advocate before the throne,
    And our Forerunner there.

5 Here fix, my roving heart;
    Here wait, my warmest love;
Till the communion be complete,
    In nobler scenes above.

DOXOLOGY.

The Father and the Son
    And Spirit we adore;
We praise, we bless, we worship thee,
    Both now and evermore!

DENNIS. S. M.

MALVERN. L. M.

606. *Prayer of the Publican.*
Luke 18: 13.

1 With broken heart and contrite sigh,
A trembling sinner, Lord, I cry;
Thy pardoning grace is rich and free:
O God, be merciful **to me!**

2 I smite upon my **troubled** breast,
With deep and conscious guilt oppressed;
Christ and his cross my only plea:
O **God,** be merciful to me!

3 Far off **I** stand with tearful eyes,
Nor dare uplift them to the skies;
But thou dost all my anguish see:
O God, be merciful to me!

4 Nor alms, nor deeds that **I have done,**
Can for a single sin atone;
To Calvary alone I flee:
O God, be merciful to me!

5 And when redeemed from sin and hell,
With all the ransomed throng I dwell,
My raptured song shall ever be,
God has been **merciful to me!**

633. *Penitence for broken Vows.*

1 When silent steal across **my soul**
Remembrances of broken vows,
And tears, almost beyond control,
Flow, as my guilty spirit bows,—

2 'T is then I've caught the Saviour's eye,
Viewing with looks of injured love,
A soul, for whom he deigned to die,
Inconstant and ungrateful **prove.**

3 Oh! had he not so kindly glanced
(My weeping soul in anguish cries,)
I could have borne that searching look;
But now I yield: my spirit dies.

4 No more on promises I'll rest,
Nor resolutions vainly made;
But leaning on my Saviour's breast,
Implore his Spirit's gracious aid.

1186. *"I have fought a good fight."*
2 Tim. 4: 6-8.

1 The hour of my departure 's come;
I hear the voice that calls me home;
Now, O my God! let trouble cease,
And let thy servant die in peace.

2 The race appointed I have run;
The combat 's o'er, the prize is won;
And now my witness is on high,
And now my record 's in the sky.

3 Not in mine innocence I trust;
I bow before thee in the dust;
And through my Saviour's blood alone
I look for mercy at thy throne.

4 I come, I come, at thy command;
I give my spirit to thy hand;
Stretch forth thine everlasting arms,
And shield me in the last alarms.

1283. *The Day of Wrath.*
(A Hymn of the Thirteenth Century.)

1 That day of wrath! that dreadful day,
When heaven and earth shall pass away!
What power shall be the sinner's stay?
How shall he meet that dreadful day?

2 When, shriveling like a parchéd scroll,
The flaming heavens together roll,
When louder yet, and yet more dread,
Swells the high trump that wakes the dead!—

3 Oh! on that day—that wrathful **day,**
When man **to judgment** wakes from clay,
Be thou the trembling sinner's stay,
Tho' heaven and earth shall pass away!

WINDHAM. L. M.

548. *The narrow Way.*—Matt. 7: 13, 14.
1 BROAD is the road that leads to death,
 And thousands walk together there;
 But wisdom shows a narrow path,
 With here and there a traveler.

2 "Deny thyself, and take thy cross,"
 Is the Redeemer's great command:
 Nature must count her gold but dross,
 If she would gain this heavenly land.

3 The fearful soul that tires and faints,
 And walks the ways of God no more,
 Is but esteemed almost a saint,
 And makes his own destruction sure.

4 Lord! let not all my hopes be vain;
 Create my heart entirely new:
 Which hypocrites could ne'er attain;
 Which false apostates never knew.

1166. *"Whose foundation is in the dust."*
 Job 4: 17–21.
1 SHALL the vile race of flesh and blood
 Contend with their Creator, God?
 Shall mortal worms presume to be
 More holy, wise, or just than he?

2 Behold, he puts his trust in none
 Of all the spirits round his throne;
 Their natures, when compared with his
 Are neither holy, just, nor wise.

3 But how much meaner things are they
 Who spring from dust, and dwell in clay!
 Touched by the finger of thy wrath,
 We faint and vanish like the moth.

4 From night to day, from day to night,
 We die by thousands in thy sight;
 Buried in dust whole nations lie,
 Like a forgotten vanity.

5 Almighty Power! to thee we bow;
 How frail are we! how glorious thou!
 No more the sons of earth shall dare
 With an eternal God compare.

1187. *" Alone with Thee, in that dread strife."*
1 THE moment comes, when strength shall fail,
 When, health, and hope, and courage flown,
 I must go down into the vale
 And shade of death, with thee alone.

2 Alone with thee! in that dread strife
 Uphold me in mine agony;
 And gently be this dying life
 Exchanged for immortality.

3 Then, when th' unbodied spirit lands
 Where flesh and blood hath never trod,
 And in the unvailed presence stands
 Of thee, my Saviour and my God,—

4 Be mine eternal portion this,
 Since thou wert always here with me,
 That I may view thy face in bliss,
 And be for evermore with thee.

1289. *Trembling in Fear of Hell.*
1 FATHER!—if I may call thee so,—
 I tremble with my one desire:
 Lift up this heavy load of woe,
 Nor let me in my sins expire!

2 I tremble, lest the wrath divine,
 Which bruises now my sinful soul,
 Should bruise and break this soul of mine,
 Long as eternal ages roll.

3 Thy wrath I fear, thy wrath alone,
 This endless exile, Lord, from thee!
 Oh, save! oh, give me to thy Son,
 Who trembled, wept, and bled for me!

DOXOLOGY.

GLORY to thee, O God, most high!
Father, we praise thy majesty!
The Son, the Spirit, we adore,
One Godhead, blest for evermore!

MOULTON. S. H. M.

757. *"Faith which worketh by love."*

1 FAITH is the polar star
    That guides the Christian's way,
Directs his wanderings from afar
    To realms of endless day:
It points the course, where'er he roam,
And safely leads the pilgrim home.

2 Faith is the rainbow's form
    Hung on the brow of heaven,
The glory of the passing storm,
    The pledge of mercy given:
It is the bright triumphal arch
Through which the saints to glory march.

3 The faith that works by love,
    And purifies the heart,
A foretaste of the joys above
    To mortals can impart:
It bears us through this earthly strife,
And triumphs in immortal life.

1214. *"Neither shall there be any more pain."*

1 FRIEND after friend departs;
    Who hath not lost a friend?
There is no union here of hearts
    That finds not here an end:
Were this frail world our final rest,
Living or dying, none were blest.

2 Beyond the flight of time,
    Beyond this vale of death,
There surely is some blessèd clime
    Where life is not a breath,—
Nor life's affections transient fire,
Whose sparks fly upward to expire.

3 There is a world above,
    Where parting is unknown,
A whole eternity of love,
    Formed for the good alone;
And faith beholds the dying here
Translated to that happier sphere.

4 Thus star by star declines,
    Till all are passed away,
As morning high and higher shines
    To pure and perfect day:
Nor sink those stars in empty night—
They hide themselves in heaven's own light.

RUNDELL. C. H. M.

[For words (Hymn 937) see opposite page.]

NILE. 8s & 6s.

1112. *"Save Thy people, and bless Thine inheritance."*

1 From foes that would the land devour;
  From guilty pride, and lust of power;
  From wild sedition's lawless hour;
    From yoke of slavery;
  From blinded zeal, by faction led;
  From giddy change, by fancy bred;
  From poisoned error's serpent head,
    Good Lord, preserve us free!

2 Defend, O God, with guardian hand,
  The laws and rulers of our land,
  And grant thy churches grace to stand
    In faith and unity!
  Thy Spirit's help of thee we crave,
  That thy Messiah, sent to save,
  Returning to the world, might have
    A people serving thee!

---

937. *"Sorrowing, yet always rejoicing."*
(Tune Rendell, opposite page.)

1 When I can trust my all with God,
    In trial's fearful hour,
  Bow, all resigned, beneath his rod,
    And bless his sparing power,
  A joy springs up amid distress,—
    A fountain in the wilderness.

  Oh, to be brought to Jesus' feet,
    Though sorrows fix me there,
  Is still a privilege; and sweet

  The energy of prayer,
  Though sighs and tears its language be,
  If Christ be nigh, and smile on me.

3 Then blessèd be the hand that gave;
    Still blessed when it takes;
  Blessed be he who smites to save,
    Who heals the heart he breaks;
  Perfect and true are all his ways,
  Whom heaven adores, and earth obeys.

1144. *"I will praise the name of God with a song."*

1 Let every heart rejoice and sing;
　Let choral anthems rise;
　Ye reverend men, and children, bring
　　To God your sacrifice:
　For he is good,—the Lord is good,
　　And kind are all his ways:
　With songs and honors sounding loud,
　　The Lord Jehovah praise;
　　　While the rocks and the rills,
　　　While the vales and the hills
　　A glorious anthem raise,
　Let each prolong the grateful song,
　　And the God of our fathers praise.

2 He bids the sun to rise and set;
　In heaven his power is known;
　And earth, subdued to him, shall yet
　　Bow low before his throne:
　For he is good,—the Lord is good,
　　And kind are all his ways:
　With songs and honors sounding loud,
　　The Lord Jehovah praise;
　　　While the rocks and the rills,
　　　While the vales and the hills
　　A glorious anthem raise,
　Let each prolong the grateful song,
　　And the God of our fathers praise.

ELLARD. 8s & 6.

945.   *"Blessed are they that mourn."*—Matt. 5:4.

1 I HEARD the voice of love divine,
   Addressing man to trouble born;
 What accents, Saviour, then were thine!
   "Blessèd are they that mourn!"

2 Again it spoke: "Come unto me,
   Thou with distress and labor worn;
 Rest and refreshment are for thee:
   Blessèd are they that mourn!"

3 I heard a voice in truth's pure word,
   A saint who sorrow's yoke had borne:
 "Blest is the man thou chast'nest, Lord!
   Blessèd are they that mourn!"

4 I heard an angel-voice proclaim,
   "Yon victors bright, whom crowns adorn,
 Through tribulation great they came:
   Blessèd are they that mourn!"

5 Why should I then for sufferings grieve,
   Since sorrow leads to joy's bright bourn?
 Let me indeed the words believe:
   "Blessèd are they that mourn!"

NOBLE. 8s & 6.

877.   *Prayer for Christ's aid in Toil.*

1 Lo! the storms of life are breaking;
 Faithless fears our hearts are shaking:
 For our succor undertaking,
   Lord and Saviour, help us!

2 Lo! the world from thee rebelling,
 Round thy church in pride is swelling!
 With thy word their madness quelling,
   Lord and Saviour, help us!

3 On thine own command relying,
 We our onward task are plying;
 Unto thee for safety sighing,
   Lord and Saviour, help us!

4 By thy birth, thy cross, and passion,
 By thy tears of deep compassion,
 By thy mighty intercession,
   Lord and Saviour, help us!

NORWICH. 7s.

450. *Prayer for the Indwelling of the Spirit.*

1 Holy Spirit! Love Divine!
  Let thy light within me shine;
  Breathe thyself into my breast:
  Earnest of immortal rest.

2 Let me never from thee stray,
  Keep me in the narrow way;
  Keep me thine, for ever thine;
  Let thy love and joy be mine.

513. *The Prodigal invited.*

1 Brother, hast thou wandered far
    From thy Father's happy home,
  With thyself and God at war?
    Turn thee, brother; homeward come.

2 Hast thou wasted all the powers
    God for noble uses gave?
  Squandered life's most golden hours?
    Turn thee, brother; God can save.

3 He can heal thy bitterest wound,
    He thy gentlest prayer can hear;
  Seek him, for he may be found;
    Call upon him; he is near.

539. *" Why will ye die?"*—Ezek. 33 : 11.

1 Sinners, turn; why will ye die?
  God, your Maker, asks you why—
  God, who did your being give,
  Made you with himself to live.

2 Sinners, turn! why will ye die?
  God, your Saviour, asks you why—
  He who did your souls retrieve,
  He who died, that ye might live.

3 Will you let him die in vain?
  Crucify your Lord again?
  Why, ye ransomed sinners, why
  Will ye slight his grace, and die?

4 Sinners, turn; why will ye die?
  God, the Spirit, asks you why—
  He who all your lives hath strove,
  Wooed you to embrace his love.

5 Will ye not his grace receive?
  Will ye still refuse to live?
  Oh! ye dying sinners, why
  Will ye grieve your God, and die?

546. *" Where wilt thou appear?"*
1 Pet. 4 : 18.

1 When thy mortal life is fled,
  When the death-shades o'er thee spread,
  When is finished thy career,
  Sinner, where wilt thou appear?

2 When the Judge descends in light,
  Clothed in majesty and might;
  When the wicked quail with fear,
  Where, oh, where wilt thou appear?

3 While the Holy Ghost is nigh,
  Quickly to the Saviour fly:
  Then shall peace thy spirit cheer;
  Then in heaven shalt thou appear.

612. *" Deep regret for follies past."*

1 God of mercy! God of love!
    Hear our sad, repentant song;
  Sorrow dwells on every face,
    Penitence on every tongue.

2 Deep regret for follies past,
    Talents wasted, time misspent;
  Hearts debased by worldly cares,
    Thankless for the blessings lent;

3 Foolish fears and fond desires,
    Vain regrets for things as vain;
  Lips too seldom taught to praise,
    Oft to murmur and complain;

4 These, and every secret fault,
   Filled with grief and shame, we own;
Humbled at thy feet we lie,
   Seeking pardon from thy throne.

5 God of mercy! God of grace!
   Hear our sad, repentant songs;
Oh, restore thy suppliant race,
   Thou to whom all praise belongs!

589.   *"Lovest thou Me?"*

1 Could my heart so hard remain,
   Prayer a task and burden prove,
Every trifle give me pain,
   If I knew a Saviour's love?

2 When I turn my eyes within,
   All is dark, and vain, and wild;
Filled with unbelief and sin,
   Can I deem myself a child?

3 Yet I mourn my stubborn will,
   Find my sin a grief and thrall;
Should I grieve for what I feel,
   If I did not love at all?

4 Lord, decide the doubtful case;
   Thou who art thy people's Sun,
Shine upon thy work of grace,
   If it be, indeed, begun.

5 Let me love thee more and more,
   If I love at all, I pray;
If I have not loved before,
   Help me to begin to-day.

623.   *Confession.*

1 Oh these eyes, how dark and blind!
Oh this foolish, earthly mind!
Oh this froward, selfish will,
Which refuses to be still!

2 Oh these ever roaming eyes,
Upward that refuse to rise!
Oh these wayward feet of mine,
Found in every path but thine!

3 Oh this stubborn, prayerless knee,
Hands so seldom clasped to thee,
Longings of the soul that go,
Like the wild wind, to and fro!

4 To and fro, without an aim,
Turning idly whence they came;
Bringing in no joy, no bliss,
Adding to my weariness.

5 Giver of the heavenly peace,
Bid, oh, bid these tumults cease;
Minister thy holy balm,
Fill me with thy Spirit's calm.

6 Thou, the Life, the Truth, the Way,
Leave me not in sin to stay;
Bearer of the sinner's guilt,
Lead me, lead me, as thou wilt!

838.   *"No more my own, but thine."*
         Luke 23:34.

1 Let me dwell on Golgotha,
Weep and love my life away!
While I see him on the tree
Weep, and bleed, and die for me!

2 Hark! his dying word: "Forgive!
Father, let the sinner live;
Sinner, wipe thy tears away,
I thy ransom freely pay."

3 While I hear this grace revealed,
And obtain a pardon sealed,
All my warm affections move,
Wakened by his dying love.

4 He hath dearly bought my soul;
Lord, accept, and claim the whole!
To thy will I all resign,
Now no more my own, but thine.

SHINING SHORE. 8s & 7s.

1228. *"Thou art to pass over Jordan this day."*

1 My days are gliding swiftly by,
　And I, a pilgrim stranger,
　Would not detain them as they fly,—
　　Those hours of toil and danger:
　For now we stand on Jordan's strand,
　　Our friends are passing over;
　And, just before, the shining shore
　　We may almost discover.

2 Our absent king the watchword gave—
　　"Let every lamp be burning;"
　We look afar, across the wave,
　　Our distant home discerning:
　　　For now, etc.

3 Should coming days be dark and cold,
　　We will not yield to sorrow,
　For hope will sing, with courage bold,
　　"There's glory on the morrow:"
　　　For now, etc.

4 Let storms of woe in whirlwinds rise,
　　Each cord on earth to sever—
　There—bright and joyous in the skies—
　　There is our home for ever;
　For now we stand on Jordan's strand,
　　Our friends are passing over;
　And, just before, the shining shore
　　We may almost discover.

BILLOW. 8s, 7s & 4.

[For words (Hymn 1108) see opposite page.]

LANDER. 11s & 12s.

796. *Soon and for ever with Christ.*

1 Soon—soon and for ever our **union** shall **be**
Made perfect, our glorious Redeemer, in thee;
The sins and the sorrows of time shall be o'er,
Its pangs and its partings remembered no more,
When life can not fail, and when death can not sever,
Then Christians with Christ shall **be—soon** and for ever.

2 Yes, soon and for ever, we'll see as we're seen,
And learn the deep meaning of things that have **been**;
Then droop not in sorrow, despond not in fear,—
A glorious to-morrow is bright'ning and near:
When—blessèd reward of each faithful endeavor!—
True Christians with Christ shall be—soon and for ever!

1108. *The Guiding Star.*

[Tune BILLOW, opposite page.]

1 STAR of peace! to wanderers weary,
  Bright the beams that smile on me;
Cheer the pilot's vision dreary,
  Far, far at sea.

2 Star of hope! gleam on the billow,
  Bless the soul that sighs for thee;
Bless the sailor's lonely pillow,
  Far, far at sea.

3 Star of faith! when winds are mocking
  All his toil, he flies to thee;
Save him, on the billows rocking,
  Far, far at sea.

4 Star divine! oh, safely guide him
  Bring the wanderer home to thee!
Sore temptations long have tried him,
  Far, far at sea.

WILTZ. 6s. DOUBLE.

936. *"My Jesus, as thou wilt."*

1 My Jesus, as thou wilt!
　Oh, may thy will be mine!
Into thy hand of love
　I would my all resign:
Through sorrow, or through joy,
　Conduct me as thine own,
And help me still to say,
　My Lord, thy will be done!

2 My Jesus, as thou wilt!
　Though seen through many a tear,
Let not my star of hope
　Grow dim or disappear:
Since thou on earth hast wept,
　And sorrowed oft alone
If I must weep with thee,
　My Lord, thy will be done!

3 My Jesus, as thou wilt!
　All shall be well for me:
Each changing future scene
　I gladly trust with thee:
Then to my home above
　I travel calmly on,
And sing, in life or death,
　My Lord, thy will be done!

950. *The Discipline of Joy and Sorrow.*

1 My sky was once noon-bright,
　My day was calm the while;
I loved the pleasant light,
　The sunshine's happy smile.

2 I said, "My God, oh! sure
　This love will kindle mine;
Let but this calm endure,
　Then all my heart is thine."

3 Thou trustedst me awhile:
　O Lord! I was deceived;
I reveled in the smile,
　Yet to the dust I cleaved.

4 Then the fierce tempest broke;
　I knew from whom it came;
I read in that sharp stroke
　A Father's hand and name.

5 Must I be smitten, Lord?
　Are gentler measures vain?
Must I be smitten, Lord?
　Can nothing save but pain?

6 I said, "My God! at length
　This stony heart remove;
Deny all other strength,
　But give me strength to love."

987. *More like God.*

1 I DID thee wrong, my God;
　I wronged thy truth and love,
I fretted at the rod,—
　Against thy power I strove.

2 Come nearer, nearer still;
　Let not thy light depart;
Bend, break this stubborn will;
　Dissolve this iron heart!

3 Less wayward let me be,
　More pliable and mild;
In glad simplicity
　More like a trustful child.

4 Less, less of self each day,
　And more, my God, of thee;
Oh, keep me in the way,
　However rough it be.

5 Less of the flesh each day,
　Less of the world and sin:
More of thy Son, I pray,
　More of thyself within.

6 More molded to thy will,
　Lord, let thy servant be;
Higher and higher still,
　More, and still more, like thee!

NILLEN. 6s.

663. *No Rest, but in God.*

1 My soul doth long for thee
   To dwell within my breast;
   Unworthy though I be
   Of so divine a Guest!

2 Of so divine a Guest
   Unworthy though I be,
   Yet hath my heart no rest
   Until it come to thee!

3 Until it come to thee,
   In vain I look around;
   In all that I can see
   No rest is to be found!

4 No rest is to be found,
   But in thy bleeding love:
   Oh, let my wish be crowned,
   And send it from above!

804. *Imitation of Christ in Youth.*

1 I feel within a want
   For ever burning there;
   What I so thirst for, grant,
   O thou who hearest prayer!

2 This is the thing I crave:
   A likeness to thy Son;
   This would I rather have
   Than call the world my own.

3 Like him, now in my youth,
   I long, O God, to be,—
   In tenderness and truth,
   In sweet humility.

4 'T is my most fervent prayer:
   Be it more fervent still—
   Be it my highest care;
   Be it my settled will!

904. *" Be of good cheer; I have overcome the world."*

1 Cheer up, desponding soul!
   Thy longing pleased I see:
   'T is part of that great whole
   Wherewith I longed for thee

   Would count their gain but loss
   To live for ever mine!

925. *Upward!*

1 Go up, go up, my heart!
   Dwell with thy God above;
   For here thou canst not rest,
   Nor here give out thy love.

2 Go up, go up, my heart!
   Be not a trifler here;
   Ascend above these clouds,—
   Dwell in a higher sphere.

3 Let not thy love flow out
   To things so soiled and dim;
   Go up to heaven and God;
   Take up thy love to him.

4 Waste not thy precious stores
   On pleasure here below:
   To God that wealth belongs;
   On him that wealth bestow.

5 Go up, reluctant heart!
   Take up thy rest above;
   Arise, earth-clinging thoughts;
   Ascend, my lingering love!

928. *" Choose Thou for me."*

1 Thy way, not mine, O Lord,
   However dark it be!
   Lead me by thine own hand;
   Choose out the path for me.

2 I dare not choose my lot:
   I would not, if I might;
   Choose thou for me, my God,
   So shall I walk aright.

3 The kingdom that I seek
   Is thine: so let the way
   That leads to it be thine,
   Else I must surely stray.

4 Take thou my cup, and it
   With joy or sorrow fill

PRESTON. C. M.

906. *The inner Calm.*

1 CALM me, my God, and keep me calm:
   Let thine outstretched wing
   Be like the shade of Elim's palm,
   Beside her desert spring.

2 Yes, keep me calm, though loud and rude
   The sounds my ear that greet,—
   Calm in the closet's solitude,
   Calm in the bustling street,—

3 Calm in the hour of buoyant health,
   Calm in the hour of pain,
   Calm in my poverty or wealth,
   Calm in my loss or gain,—

4 Calm in the sufferance of wrong,
   Like him who bore my shame,
   Calm 'mid the threatening, taunting throng,
   Who hate thy holy name.

5 Calm me, my God, and keep me calm,
   Soft resting on thy breast;
   Soothe me with holy hymn and psalm,
   And bid my spirit rest.

914. *"Teach me the way of thy statutes."*
   Psalm 119.

1 OH that the Lord would guide my ways
   To keep his statutes still!
   Oh that my God would grant me grace
   To know and do his will.

2 Oh, send thy Spirit down, to write
   Thy law upon my heart;
   Nor let my tongue indulge deceit,
   Nor act the liar's part.

3 Order my footsteps by thy word,
   And make my heart sincere;
   Let sin have no dominion, Lord,
   But keep my conscience clear.

4 Make me to walk in thy commands,—
   'T is a delightful road;

   Nor let my head, nor heart, nor hands
   Offend against my God.

919. *"Old things are passed away."*

1 WE praise and bless thee, gracious Lord,
   Our Saviour kind and true,
   For all the old things passed away,
   For all thou hast made new.

2 But yet how much must be destroyed,
   How much renewed must be,
   Ere we can fully stand complete
   In likeness, Lord, to thee!

3 Whate'er would tempt the soul to stray,
   Or separate from thee,
   That, Lord, remove, however dear
   To our poor hearts it be!

4 When flesh declines, then strengthen thou
   The spirit from above;
   Make us to feel thy service sweet,
   And light thy yoke of love.

5 So shall we faultless stand at last
   Before thy Father's throne;
   The blessedness for ever ours,
   The glory all thine own!

978. *"Firmly I build my hope on Thee."*

1 I KNOW thy thoughts are peace toward me;
   Safe am I in thy hands;
   Firmly I build my hope on thee,
   For sure thy counsel stands!

2 Whate'er thy word hath promised, all
   Wilt thou full surely give!
   Wherefore, from thee I will not fall;
   Thy word doth make me live.

3 Though mountains crumble into dust,
   Thy covenant standeth fast;
   Who follows thee in pious trust,
   Shall reach the goal at last.

MEDFIELD. C. M.

4 Though strange and winding seems the way,
While yet on earth I dwell,
In heaven my heart shall gladly say,
Thou, God, dost all things well!

1208. *Dust to Dust.*

1 CALM on the bosom of thy God,
Young spirit, rest thee now!
Ev'n while with us thy footsteps trod,
His seal was on thy brow.

2 Dust, to its narrow house beneath!
Soul, to its place on high!
They that have seen thy look in death
No more may fear to die.

3 Lone are the paths, and sad the bowers,
Whence thy meek smile is gone;
But, oh! a brighter home than ours,
In heaven, is now thine own.

1256. *"Lord, I believe a rest remains."*

1 LORD, I believe a rest remains,
To all thy people known;
A rest where pure enjoyment reigns,
And thou art loved alone;—

2 A rest where all our souls' desire
Is fixed on things above;
Where fear and sin and grief expire,
Cast out by perfect love.

3 Oh that I now the rest might know,
Believe and enter in!
Now, Saviour! now the power bestow,
And let me cease from sin.

4 Remove the hardness of my heart,
The unbelief remove;
To me the rest of faith impart—
The Sabbath of thy love.

1257. *Holiness of Heaven.*—1 Cor. 2: 9, 10.

1 NOR eye hath seen, nor ear hath heard,
Nor sense nor reason known,
What joys the Father has prepared
For those that love his Son.

2 But the good Spirit of the Lord
Reveals a heaven to come;
The beams of glory in his word
Allure and guide us home.

3 Pure are the joys above the sky
And all the region peace;
No wanton lips, nor envious eye
Can see or taste the bliss.

4 Those holy gates for ever bar
Pollution, sin, and shame;
None shall obtain admittance there,
But followers of the Lamb.

1265. *"Now they desire a better country."*

1 OH! could our thoughts and wishes fly
Above these gloomy shades,
To those bright worlds beyond the sky
Which sorrow ne'er invades!

2 There joys unseen by mortal eyes,
Or reason's feeble ray,
In ever-blooming prospect rise,
Unconscious of decay.

3 Lord! send a beam of light divine
To guide our upward aim;
With one reviving touch of thine
Our languid hearts inflame.

4 Then shall, on faith's sublimest wing,
Our ardent wishes rise
To those bright scenes, where pleasures spring
Immortal in the skies.

NAUL. 6s & 10s.

737. *"He became obedient unto death."*—Phil. 2 : 8.

1 Thou, who didst stoop below
　To drain the cup of woe,
And wear the form of frail mortality,
　Thy blesséd labors done,
　Thy crown of vict'ry won,
Hast passed from earth—passed to thy
　　home on high.

2 It was no path of flowers,
　Through this dark world of ours,
Belovéd of the Father! thou didst tread;
　And shall we in dismay
　Shrink from the narrow way,
When clouds and darkness are around it
　　spread?

3 O thou who art our Life,
　Be with us through the strife;
Was not thy head by earth's rude tempests
　Raise thou our eyes above　[bowed ?
　To see a Father's love
Beam, like the bow of promise, through
　　the cloud.

4 Ev'n through the awful gloom
　Which hovers o'er the tomb,
That light of love our guiding star shall be;
　Our spirits shall not dread
　The shadowy way to tread,
Friend, Guardian, Saviour! which doth
　　lead to thee.

CAVE. 7s & 3.

(For words, (Hymn 50,) see opposite page.

KNIGHT. 7s, 3 LINES. DOUBLE.

264. The Contrast.

1 Blessèd night, when first that plain
  Echoed with the joyful strain—
  "Peace has come to earth again!"
2 Happy shepherds, on whose ear
  Fell the tidings glad and dear—
  "God to man is drawing near!"

3 Babe of weakness, can it be
  That the earth's great victory
  Is to be achieved by thee?
4 Child of poverty, art thou
  He to whom all heaven shall **bow**,
  And all earth shall pay the **vow**?

5 Heir of pain and toil, whom **none**
  In this evil day will own,
  Art thou the Eternal One?

6 Thou, o'er whom the sword and rod
  Wave, in haste to drink thy blood,
  Art thou very Son of God?

7 We adore thee as our King,
  And to thee our song we sing;
  Our best off'ring to thee bring.
8 Guarded by the shepherds' rod,
  'Mid their flock, thy poor abode;
  Thus **we** own thee, Lamb of God.

9 Lamb of God, thy **lowly** name;
  King of kings, we thee **proclaim**:
  Heaven and earth **shall hear its fame**.
10 Mighty King of righteousness,
  King of glory, King of peace,
  Never shall thy kingdom cease!

50. Christ the Sun of Righteousness.

Tune CAVE, opposite page.

1 Jesus, Sun of righteousness,
  Brightest beam of love divine,
  With the early morning rays
  Do thou on our darkness shine,
  And dispel with purest light
    All our night!

2 Like the sun's reviving ray,
  May thy love, with tender glow,
  All our coldness melt away,
  Warm and cheer us forth to **go**;
  Gladly serve thee and obey
    All the day!

3 Thou our only Life and Guide!
  Never leave us nor forsake:
  In thy light may we abide
  Till th' eternal morning break;
  Moving on to Zion's hill
    Homeward still!

PORTUGUESE HYMN. 11s.

"*How firm a foundation !*"

180. 1 How firm a foundation, ye saints of the Lord,
Is laid for your faith in his excellent word!
What more can he say than to you he hath said,
Who unto the Saviour for refuge have fled :—

2 "Fear not, I am with thee, oh, be not dismayed;
For I am thy God, I will still give thee aid·
I'll strengthen thee, help thee, and cause thee to stand,
Upheld by my righteous, omnipotent hand.

3 "When through the deep waters I call thee to go,
The rivers of sorrow shall not overflow;
For I will be with thee thy troubles to bless,
And sanctify to thee thy deepest distress.

4 "The soul that on Jesus hath leaned for repose,
I will not, I will not desert to his foes:
That soul, though all hell should endeavor to shake,
I'll never—no, never—no, never forsake!"

Looking off.

782. 1 O EYES that are weary, and hearts that are sore!
Look off unto Jesus, now sorrow no more!
The light of his countenance shineth so bright,
That here, as in heaven, there need be no night.

2 While looking to Jesus my heart can not fear;
I tremble no more when I see Jesus near;
I know that his presence my safeguard will be,
For "Why are ye troubled?" he saith unto me.

3 Still looking to Jesus, oh, may I be found,
When Jordan's dark waters encompass me round:
They bear me away in his presence to be:
I see him still nearer whom always I see.

4 Then, then shall I know the full beauty and grace
Of Jesus, my Lord, when I stand face to face;
Shall know how his love went before me each day,
And wonder that ever my eyes turned away.

GOSHEN. 11s.

"Faint, yet pursuing." —Judges 8 : 4.

982.
1 Though faint, yet pursuing, **we go on our way**;
The Lord is our Leader, his **word is our stay**;
Though suffering, and sorrow, and **trial be near**,
The Lord is our refuge, and whom can we **fear?**

2 **He** raiseth the fallen, he cheereth the faint;
The weak, and oppressed—he will hear their **complaint**;
The way may be weary, and thorny the road,
But how can we falter? **our help is in God!**

3 And to his green pastures our footsteps he leads;
His flock in the desert how kindly he feeds!
The lambs in his bosom he tenderly bears,
And brings back the wanderers all safe from **the snares**.

4 Though **clouds** may surround **us**, our God **is our light**;
Though storms rage around **us**, our God **is our might**;
So faint, yet pursuing, **still onward we come**
The Lord is our Leader, **and heaven is our home!**

"He shall be called the Lord our Righteousness." —Jer. 23 : 6.

1006.
1 I once was a stranger to grace and to God;
I knew not my danger, and felt not my load;
Though friends spoke in rapture of Christ on the tree,
Jehovah, my Saviour, seemed **nothing to me.**

2 When free grace awoke me by light from on high,
Then legal fears shook me; I trembled to die;
No refuge, no safety, in self could I see:
Jehovah, thou only my Saviour must be.

3 My terrors all vanished before his sweet name;
My guilty fears banished, with boldness I came
To drink at the fountain so copious and free:
Jehovah, my Saviour, is all things to me.

4 Jehovah, **the Lord**, is my treasure **and boast;**
Jehovah my Saviour,—I ne'er can **be lost:**
In thee I shall conquer, by **flood and by field,**
Jehovah my anchor, Jehovah **my shield!**

5 Ev'n treading the valley, the shadow of death,
This watchword shall rally my faltering breath;
For, while from life's fever my God sets me free,
Jehovah, my Saviour, my death-song shall be.

TWEED. S. M.

452. *Prayer for the sanctifying Influence of the Spirit.*

1 Come, Holy Spirit, come!
  Let thy bright beams arise:
Dispel the sorrow from our minds,
  The darkness from our eyes.

2 Convince us of our sin;
  Then lead to Jesus' blood,
And to our wondering view reveal
  The secret love of God.

3 Revive our drooping faith,
  Our doubts and fears remove,
And kindle in our breasts the flame
  Of never-dying love.

4 'T is thine to cleanse the heart,
  To sanctify the soul,
To pour fresh life in every part,
  And new-create the whole.

5 Dwell, Spirit, in our hearts;
  Our minds from bondage free;
Then shall we know, and praise, and love
  The Father, Son, and Thee.

516. *Now the accepted Time.*—1 Cor. 6: 2.

1 Now is th' accepted time,
  Now is the day of grace;
Now, sinners, come without delay,
  And seek the Saviour's face.

2 Now is th' accepted time,
  The Saviour calls to-day:
To-morrow it may be too late;
  Then why should you delay?

3 Now is th' accepted time,
  The gospel bids you come;
And every promise in his word
  Declares there yet is room.

4 Lord, draw reluctant souls,
  And feast them with thy love:
Then will the angels swiftly fly
  To bear the news above.

915. *"Shall we continue in sin that grace may abound?"*—Rom. 6: 1.

1 Shall we go on to sin
  Because thy grace abounds?
Or crucify the Lord again,
  And open all his wounds?

2 Forbid it, mighty God!
  Nor let it e'er be said
That we, whose sins are crucified,
  Should raise them from the dead.

3 We will be slaves no more,
  Since Christ has made us free,—
Has nailed our tyrants to his cross,
  And bought our liberty.

916. *"Help me to watch and pray."*

1 A charge to keep I have,
  A God to glorify;
A never-dying soul to save,
  And fit it for the sky;

2 To serve the present age,
  My calling to fulfill;—
Oh, may it all my powers engage
  To do my Master's will.

3 Arm me with jealous care,
  As in thy sight to live;
And oh! thy servant, Lord, prepare
  A strict account to give.

4 Help me to watch and pray,
  And on thyself rely;
Assured if I my trust betray
  I shall for ever die.

MORNINGTON. S. M.

918. *Prayer for Likeness to Christ.*
John 14: 6.

1 Thou art, O Christ, the Way:
   Thyself reveal to me;
And let me humbly, day by day,
   Live, move, and walk in thee.

2 Thou art the **Truth divine**:
   Its fullness **may I see**;
Believe, and find the **promise mine**,—
   " The Truth shall **make you free.**"

3 Thou art the Life of God;
   By thee the dying live:
In me diffuse thyself **abroad**,
   And life eternal give.

4 Thus by thyself, the **Way**,
   I to the Father **come**;
Led by the Truth, **I can not stray**;
   The Life and I are **one**.

1147. *Fasting and Prayer for a Revival of Religion.*

1 O Lord, thy work revive,
   In Zion's gloomy hour;
And make her dying graces live
   By thy restoring power.

2 Awake thy chosen few
   To fervent, earnest prayer;
Again their sacred vows renew;
   Thy blessed presence share.

3 Thy Spirit then will speak
   Through lips of feeble clay,
And hearts of adamant will break,
   And rebels will obey.

4 Lord! lend thy gracious **ear**:
   Oh, listen to our cry!
Oh, come and bring salvation here!
   Our hopes on thee rely.

OLMUTZ. S. M.

ST. MARTINS. C. M.

41. *"Give thy heart."*

1 When, as returns this solemn day,
  Man comes to meet his God,
 What rites, what honors shall he pay?
  How spread his praise abroad?

2 From marble domes and gilded spires
  Shall clouds of incense rise?
 And gems, and gold, and garlands deck
  The costly sacrifice?

3 Vain, sinful man!—creation's Lord
  Thine offerings well may spare;
 But give thy heart, and thou shalt find
  Thy God will hear thy prayer.

122. *God, All in All.*

1 Where'er, through all his works, we send
  Our roving eyes abroad,
 The various objects all conspire
  To lead us home to God;—

2 That God, whose word all nature formed,
  Whose eye all nature sees;
 Whose hand all nature rules, sustains,
  Or crushes, as he please;—

3 Before whose high and dazzling throne
  Myriads of angels bow;
 Whose smile is everlasting bliss,
  Whose frown is endless woe.

4 Low at his feet, then, O my soul!
  In prostrate homage fall;
 Make him thy fear, thy love, thy trust,
  Thy joy, thy God, thy all.

135. *"Whither shall I flee from Thy presence?"—Psalm 139.*

1 In all my vast concerns with thee,
  In vain my soul would try

 To shun thy presence, Lord, or flee
  The notice of thine eye.

2 Thine all-surrounding sight surveys
  My rising and my rest;
 My public walks, my private ways,
  The secrets of my breast.

3 My thoughts lie open to the Lord,
  Before they 're formed within;
 And, ere my lips pronounce the word,
  He knows the sense I mean.

4 Oh, wondrous knowledge, deep and high!
  Where can a creature hide?
 Within thy circling arms I lie,
  Beset on every side.

5 So let thy grace surround me still,
  And like a bulwark prove,
 To guard my soul from every ill,
  Secured by sovereign love.

142. *"The living God."*

1 Great God! how infinite art thou!
  What worthless worms are we!
 Let the whole race of creatures bow,
  And pay their praise to thee.

2 Thy throne eternal ages stood,
  Ere seas or stars were made;
 Thou art the ever-living God,
  Were all the nations dead.

3 Eternity, with all its years,
  Stands present in thy view;
 To thee there 's nothing old appears,
  Great God! there 's nothing new.

4 Our lives through various scenes are drawn,
  And vexed with trifling cares;
 While thine eternal thoughts move on
  Thine undisturbed affairs.

WINDSOR. C. M.

5 Great God! how infinite art thou!
    What worthless worms are we!
  Let the whole race of creatures bow,
    And pay their praise to thee.

493. *Man sinful by Nature.*

1 How sad our state by nature is!
    Our sin—how deep it stains!
  And Satan holds our captive minds
    Fast in his slavish chains.

2 But there's a voice of sovereign grace
    Sounds from the sacred word:
  "Ho! ye despairing sinners, come,
    And trust upon the Lord."

3 My soul obeys th' almighty call,
    And runs to this relief;
  I would believe thy promise, Lord:
    Oh, help my unbelief!

4 A guilty, weak, and helpless worm,
    On thy kind arms I fall:
  Be thou my strength and righteousness,
    My Saviour and my All.

549. *Need of Regeneration.*

1 How helpless guilty nature lies,
    Unconscious of her load!
  The heart unchanged can never rise
    To happiness and God.

2 Can aught beneath a power divine
    The stubborn will subdue?
  'Tis thine, almighty Saviour, thine,
    To form the heart anew.

3 'Tis thine the passions to recall,
    And upward bid them rise;
  To make the scales of error fall
    From reason's darkened eyes;—

4 To chase the shades of death away,
    And bid the sinner live:
  A beam of heaven, a vital ray,
    'Tis thine alone to give.

5 Oh, change these wretched hearts of ours,
    And give them life divine!
  Then shall our passions and our powers,
    Almighty Lord, be thine.

557. *Repentance in view of God's patience.*

1 And are we wretches yet alive!
    And do we yet rebel?
  'Tis boundless, 'tis amazing love,
    That bears us up from hell!

2 The burden of our weighty guilt
    Would sink us down to flames;
  And threatening vengeance rolls above,
    To crush our feeble frames.

3 Almighty goodness cries, "Forbear!"
    And straight the thunder stays;
  And dare we now provoke his wrath,
    And weary out his grace?

4 Lord, we have long abused thy love,
    Too long indulged our sin;
  Our aching hearts now bleed to see
    What rebels we have been.

5 No more, ye lusts, shall ye command;
    No more will we obey;
  Stretch out, O God, thy conquering hand,
    And drive thy foes away.

DOXOLOGY.

To Father, Son, and Holy Ghost,
  One God, whom we adore,
Be glory as it was, is now,
  And shall be evermore!

BERRY. L. M.

465. *The power of the Holy Spirit.*

1 Eternal Spirit, we confess
  And sing the wonders of thy grace ;
  Thy power **conveys our blessings down**
  From God the **Father and the Son.**

2 Enlightened by thy heavenly ray,
  Our shades and darkness **turn to day** ;
  Thine inward teachings **make us know**
  Our danger, and our **refuge, too.**

3 Thy power and glory work within,
  And break the chains of reigning sin ;
  All our imperious lusts subdue,
  And form our wretched hearts anew.

4 The troubled conscience knows thy voice
  Thy cheering words awake our joys ;
  Thy words allay the stormy wind,
  And calm the surges of the mind.

946. *"He shall sit as a refiner of silver."*

1 Why should I murmur or repine,
  O Lamb of God, who bled for me?
  What are my griefs compared with thine,
  Thy tears, thy groans, thine agony !

2 If thou the furnace dost **employ,**
  Thou sittest as refiner near,
  To purge away the base alloy,
  Till thine own image bright appear.

3 Though oft thy way is in the sea,
  Thy footsteps in the wingéd storm ;
  Though crested billows threaten **me,—**
  Love slumbers in their frowning **form !**

4 Submissive would I kiss the rod,
  Needful each stroke, I humbly own :
  Help me to trust thee, O my God !
  If now thy wisdom be unknown.

1253. *The Heavenly Rest.*
  (Original Form.)

Lord of the Sabbath hear our vows,
On this thy day, in this thy house;

And own as grateful sacrifice,
The songs which from the desert rise.

2 Thine earthly Sabbaths, Lord, we love,
  But there's a nobler rest above :
  To that our laboring souls aspire,
  With ardent pangs of strong desire.

3 No more fatigue, no more distress,
  Nor sin nor hell shall reach the place ;
  No groans to mingle with the songs
  Which warble from immortal tongues.

4 No rude alarms of raging foes ;
  No cares to break the long repose;
  No midnight shade, no clouded sun,—
  But sacred, high, eternal noon !

5 O long-expected day, begin !
  Dawn on these realms of woe and sin ;
  Fain would we leave this weary road,
  And sleep in death, to rest with God.

1254. *The Heavenly Rest.*
  (Abridged Form.)

1 Thine earthly Sabbaths, Lord, we love,—
  But there's a nobler rest above :
  To that our longing souls aspire,
  With cheerful hope and strong desire.

2 No more fatigue, no more distress,
  Nor sin nor death shall reach the place ;
  No groans shall mingle with the songs
  Which warble from immortal tongues.

3 No rude alarms of raging foes ;
  No cares to break the long repose;
  No midnight shade, no clouded sun,—
  But sacred, high, eternal noon !

4 Thine earthly Sabbaths, Lord, we love,—
  But there's a nobler rest above :
  To that our longing souls aspire,
  With cheerful hope and strong desire.

ALL SAINTS. L. M.

6. *Watchfulness and Prayer.*—Psalm 141.

1 My God, accept my early vows,
  Like morning incense in thy house;
  And let my nightly worship rise
  Sweet as the evening sacrifice.

2 Watch o'er my lips, and guard them,
    Lord,
  From every rash and heedless word;
  Nor let my feet incline to tread
  The guilty path where sinners lead.

3 Oh, may the righteous, when I stray,
  Smite and reprove my wandering way!
  Their gentle words, like ointment shed,
  Shall never bruise, but cheer my head.

4 When I behold them pressed with grief,
  I'll cry to heaven for their relief;
  And, by my warm petitions prove
  How much I prize their faithful love.

921. *"Who shall abide in Thy Tabernacle?"*
  Psalm 15.

1 Who shall ascend thy heavenly place,
  Great God, and dwell before thy face?
  The man who minds religion now,
  And humbly walks with God below:

2 Whose hands are pure, whose heart is
    clean;
  Whose lips still speak the thing they
    mean;
  No slanders dwell upon his tongue;
  He hates to do his neighbor wrong.

3 He loves his enemies, and prays
  For those who curse him to his face;
  And does to all men still the same
  That he would hope or wish from them.

4 Yet when his holiest works are done,
  His soul depends on grace alone:
  This is the man thy face shall see,
  And dwell for ever, Lord, with thee.

948. *"Joy cometh in the morning."*

1 Oh, deem not they are blest alone,
    Whose lives a peaceful tenor keep;
  For God, who pities man, hath shown
    A blessing for the eyes that weep.

2 The light of smiles shall fill again
    The lids that overflow with tears;
  And weary hours of woe and pain
    Are promises of happier years.

3 There is a day of sunny rest
    For every dark and troubled night;
  And grief may bide an evening guest,
    But joy shall come with early light.

4 Nor let the good man's trust depart,
    Though life its common gifts deny;
  Though with a pierced and broken heart,
    And spurned of men, he goes to die.

5 For God has marked each sorrowing day,
    And numbered every secret tear,
  And heaven's long age of bliss shall pay
    For all his children suffer here.

986. *"Ask what thou wilt."*

1 And dost thou say, "Ask what thou wilt?"
    Lord, I would seize the golden hour:
  I pray to be released from guilt,
    And freed from sin and Satan's power.

2 More of thy presence, Lord, impart;
    More of thine image let me bear:
  Erect thy throne within my heart,
    And reign without a rival there.

3 Give me to read my pardon sealed,
    And from thy joy to draw my strength;
  Oh, be thy boundless love revealed,
    In all its height and breadth and length.

4 Grant these requests—I ask no more,
    But to thy care the rest resign:
  Sick, or in health, or rich, or poor,
    All shall be well if thou art mine.

BETHESDA. H. M.

78. *"Ask, and it shall be given you."*
Matt. 7 : 11.

1 O THOU that hearest prayer!
  Attend our humble cry;
And let thy servants share
  Thy blessing from on high:
We plead the promise of thy word;
Grant us thy Holy Spirit, Lord!

2 If earthly parents hear
  Their children when they cry;
If they, with love sincere,
  Their children's wants supply;
Much more wilt thou thy love display,
And answer when thy children pray.

3 Our heavenly Father, thou :
  We, children of thy grace:
Oh, let thy Spirit now
  Descend and fill the place!
That all may feel the heavenly flame,
And all unite to praise thy name.

524. *"Whosoever will."*—Luke 14 : 22.

1 YE dying sons of men,
  Immerged in sin and woe,
The gospel's voice attend,
  While Jesus sends to you:
Ye perishing and guilty, come;
In Jesus' arms there yet is room.

2 No longer now delay,
  Nor vain excuses frame;

He bids you come to-day,
  Though poor, and blind, and lame :
All things are ready; sinner, come;
For every trembling soul there 's room.

3 Drawn by his bleeding love,
  Ye wand'ring sheep draw near;
Christ calls you from above,
  The Shepherd's voice now hear:
Let whosoever will now come;
In Jesus' arms there still is room.

575. *"The sacrifices of God are a broken spirit."*—Psalm 51.

1 A BROKEN heart, O Lord!
  Thou never wilt despise;
'T is written in thy word,
  This is the sacrifice
The sacrifice that thou wilt own—
It is the broken heart alone.

2 Break thou my heart, O Lord;
  The rock within me break:
To tremble at thy word,
  And at thine anger quake :
Let me in deep contrition lie,
And heave the penitential sigh.

3 For mercy dwells with thee;
  Compassion, all divine,
That mercy show to me;
  Be that compassion mine :
For sinners did not Jesus bleed?
And Jesus' blood alone I plead.

ZEBULON. H. M.

942. *Consolation in Christ.*

1 Where is my Saviour now,
   Whose smiles I once possessed?
Till he return, I bow,
   By heaviest grief oppressed:
My days of happiness are gone,
And I am left to weep alone.

2 Where can the mourner go,
   And tell his tale of grief?
Ah! who can soothe his woe,
   And give him sweet relief?
Earth can not heal the wounded breast,
Or give the troubled sinner rest.

3 Jesus! thy smiles impart;
   My dearest Lord return,
And ease my wounded heart,
   And bid me cease to mourn:
Then shall this night of sorrow flee,
And peace and heaven be found in thee.

1204. *"He bringeth down to the grave, and bringeth up."*

1 Father, my spirit owns
   Thy right to mine and me;
Yet pardon human groans
   From human agony;
The eye's desire, the soul's delight,
Thy wisdom hath seen good to blight.

2 Alas! the brittle reed,
   On human life to lean!
A solace frail indeed,
   Vanished as soon as seen!
Then, who shall fill the cheerless void,
Or stay the soul 'mid hopes destroyed?

3 In deep submission, aid
   The broken heart to lie,

Nor, when the stroke is made,
   To murmur or reply;
Great grace for greatest need bestow,
And strong supports for deepest woe.

1203.* *An ancient Burial Hymn.*

1 The pangs of death are near,
   Amid the joys of life;
And when, in guilty fear,
   We end our dying strife,
To whom, most holy Lord,
   Shall we for succor flee?
O thou most mighty God!
   Our help is laid on thee:
Lord Jesus! by thy bloody stains,
Save, save us from hell's bitter pains.

2 The bitter pains of hell
   Awaken our alarm;
We merit only ill
   From thine avenging arm;
Most holy Lord our God,
   To whom but unto thee,
Most merciful and good,
   Can we for refuge flee?
Suffer us not to fall away
From Jesus in our dying day.

3 Our dying day will come,
   And call our crimes to mind;
And when in sorrow dumb,
   No hope on earth we find,
To thee, O Christ, we fly,—
   To thine outflowing blood;
Look with thy pitying eye,
   Spare us, most holy Lord:
Nor let us lose the joys that rise
From thine atoning sacrifice.

* Let the first eight measures of the tune be repeated for this Hymn.

ELIM. C. M. 6 LINES.

138. *"Seeing Him who is invisible."*

1 BEYOND, beyond that boundless sea,
   Above that dome of sky,
Further than thought itself can flee,
   Thy dwelling is on high:
Yet dear the awful thought to me,
   That thou, my God, art nigh:—

2 Art nigh, and yet my laboring mind
   Feels after thee in vain,
Thee in these works of power to find,
   Or to thy seat attain.
Thy messenger, the stormy wind;
   Thy path, the trackless main:

3 These speak of thee with loud acclaim;
   They thunder forth thy praise,
The glorious honor of thy name,
   The wonders of thy ways:
But thou art not in tempest-flame,
   Nor in the noontide blaze.

4 We hear thy voice when thunders roll
   Through the wide fields of air;
The waves obey thy dread control;
   But still, thou art not there:
Where shall I find him, O my soul!
   Who yet is everywhere?

5 Oh! not in circling depth or height,
   But in the conscious breast,
Present to faith, though vailed from sight,
   There doth his Spirit rest:
Oh, come, thou Presence infinite!
   And make thy creature blest.

215. *The Spirit of a little Child.*

1 FATHER, I know that all my life
   Is portioned out for me;
The changes that will surely come,
   I do not fear to see:
I ask thee for a present mind,
   Intent on pleasing thee.

2 I ask thee for a thoughtful love,
   Through constant watching wise,
To meet the glad with joyful smiles,
   And wipe the weeping eyes;
A heart at leisure from itself,
   To soothe and sympathize.

3 I would not have the restless will
   That hurries to and fro,
That seeks for some great thing to do,
   Or secret thing to know:
I would be treated as a child,
   And guided where I go.

4 Wherever in the world I am,
   In whatsoe'er estate,
I have a fellowship with hearts,
   To keep and cultivate;
A work of lowly love to do
   For him on whom I wait.

5 I ask thee for the daily strength,
   To none that ask denied,
A mind to blend with outward life,
   While keeping at thy side;
Content to fill a little space,
   If thou be glorified.

6 And if some things I do not ask,
   Among my blessings be,
I'd have my spirit filled the more
   With grateful love to thee,
More careful—not to serve thee much,
   But please thee perfectly.

305. *" By Thy death we live."*

1 IN vain we seek for peace with God
   By methods of our own;
Blest Saviour! nothing but thy blood
   Can bring us near the throne.

CLARENDON. C. M.

2 The threatenings of thy broken law
   Impress the soul with dread :
   If God his sword of vengeance draw,
   It strikes the spirit dead.

3 But thine atoning sacrifice
   Hath answered all demands ;
   And peace and pardon from the skies
   Are offered by thy hands.

4 'T is by thy death we live, O Lord !
   'T is on thy cross we rest :
   For ever be thy love adored,
   Thy name for ever blest.

478. *All glory to the united Three."*

1 LET them neglect thy glory, Lord.
   Who never knew thy grace ;
   But our loud songs shall still record
   The wonders of thy praise.

2 We raise our shouts, O God, to thee,
   And send them to thy throne ;
   All glory to th' united Three,
   The undivided One !

3 'T was he (and we 'll adore his name)
   That formed us by a word ;
   'T is he restores our ruined frame :
   Salvation to the Lord !

4 Hosanna ! let the earth and skies
   Repeat the joyful sound ;
   Rocks, hills, and vales, reflect the voice
   In one eternal round !

629. *Why so far from God ?*

1 WHY is my heart so far from thee,
   My God, my chief delight ?
   Why are my thoughts no more by day
   With thee, no more by night ?

2 When my forgetful soul renews
   The savor of thy grace,
   My heart presumes I can not lose
   The relish all my days.

3 But, ere one fleeting hour is past,
   The flattering world employs
   Some sensual bait to seize my taste,
   And to pollute my joys.

4 Wretch that I am to wander thus
   In chase of false delight !
   Let me be fastened to thy cross,
   Rather than lose thy sight.

5 Make haste, my days, to reach the goal,
   And bring my heart to rest
   On the dear center of my soul,
   My God, my Saviour's breast !

642. *" God is my portion for ever."*
   Psalm 73.

1 WHOM have we, Lord, in heaven, but thee,
   And whom on earth beside ?
   Where else for succor can we flee,
   Or in whose strength confide ?

2 Thou art our portion here below,
   Our promised bliss above ;
   Ne'er may our souls an object know
   So precious as thy love.

3 When heart and flesh, O Lord, shall fail,
   Thou wilt our spirit cheer,
   Support us through life's thorny vale,
   And calm each anxious fear.

4 Yes, thou shalt be our guide through life,
   And help and strength supply,
   Sustain us in death's fearful strife,
   And welcome us on high.

DOXOLOGY.

LET God the Father, and the Son,
   And Spirit, be adored,
Where there are works to make him
      known,
   Or saints to love the Lord !

IVES. 7s.

1248. *The Song of the Hundred and forty and four thousand.—Rev. 7: 11–17.*

1 WHAT are these in bright array,
   This innumerable throng,
Round the altar night and day,
   Hymning one triumphant song ?—
" Worthy is the Lamb once slain,
   Blessing, honor, glory, power,
Wisdom, riches to obtain,
   New dominion every hour !"

2 These through fiery trials trod ;
   These from great affliction came ;
Now before the throne of God,
   Sealed with his almighty name :
Clad in raiment pure and white,
   Victor-palms in every hand,
Through their dear Redeemer's might,
   More than conquerors they stand.

3 Hunger, thirst, disease unknown,
   On immortal fruits they feed ;
Them the Lamb amid the throne
   Shall to living fountains lead :
Joy and gladness banish sighs ;
   Perfect love dispels all fear ;
And for ever from their eyes
   God shall wipe away the tear.

1249. *"God shall wipe away all tears from their eyes."*

1 HIGH in yonder realms of light,
   Dwell the raptured saints above ;
Far beyond our feeble sight,
   Happy in Immanuel's love :
Pilgrims in this vale of tears,
   Once they knew, like us below,
Gloomy doubts, distressing fears,
   Torturing pain and heavy woe.

2 But these days of weeping o'er,
   Passed this scene of toil and pain,
They shall feel distress no more—
   Never, never weep again :
'Mid the chorus of the skies,
   'Mid th' angelic lyres above,
Hark ! their songs melodious rise,
   Songs of praise to Jesus' love !

3 All is tranquil and serene,
   Calm and undisturbed repose :
There no cloud can intervene,
   There no angry tempest blows :
Every tear is wiped away,
   Sighs no more shall heave the breast,
Night is lost in endless day,
   Sorrow—in eternal rest.

25.* *" All the sons of God shouted for joy."*

1 SONGS of praise the angels sang,
   Heaven with hallelujahs rang,
When Jehovah's work begun,
   When he spake, and it was done.

2 Songs of praise awoke the morn,
   When the Prince of Peace was born :
Songs of praise arose, when he
   Captive led captivity.

3 Heaven and earth must pass away ;
   Songs of praise shall crown that day :
God will make new heavens and earth ;
   Songs of praise shall hail their birth.

4 Saints below, with heart and voice,
   Still in songs of praise rejoice ;
Learning here, by faith and love,
   Songs of praise to sing above.

5 Borne upon their latest breath
   Songs of praise shall conquer death ;
Then, amid eternal joy,
   Songs of praise their powers employ.

* Commence the fifth stanza with the latter part of the tune.

WHITE. 7s. DOUBLE.

896. *Onward go.*

1 OFT in sorrow, oft in woe,
Onward, Christian, onward go!
Fight the fight, maintain the strife,
Strengthened with the bread of life.
2 Onward, Christian, onward go!
Join the war and face the foe;
Will you flee in danger's hour?
Know you not your captain's power?

3 Let your drooping heart be glad;
March, in heavenly armor clad;
Fight! nor think the battle long;
Soon shall vict'ry tune your song.
4 Let not sorrow dim your eye;
Soon shall every tear be dry:
Let not fears your course impede;
Great your strength, if great your need.

5 Onward, then, to battle move!
More than conqu'ror you shall prove;
Though opposed by many a foe,
Christian soldier, onward go!

981. *"Faint not, Christian!"*

1 FAINT not, Christian! though the road,
Leading to thy blest abode,
Darksome be, and dangerous, too:
Christ, thy Guide, will bring thee through.
2 Faint not, Christian! though in rage
Satan would thy soul engage;
Gird on faith's anointed shield,—
Bear it to the battle-field.
3 Faint not, Christian! though the world
Hath its hostile flag unfurled:

Hold the cross of Jesus fast;
Thou shalt overcome at last.
4 Faint not, Christian! though within
There's a heart so prone to sin;
Christ, the Lord, is over all;
He'll not suffer thee to fall.

5 Faint not, Christian! Jesus near
Soon in glory will appear;
And his love will then bestow
Power to conquer every foe.
6 Faint not, Christian! look on high;
See the harpers in the sky:
Patient wait, and thou wilt join—
Chant with them of love divine.

891. *"Let us not sleep, as do others."*

1 SLEEP not, soldier of the Cross!
 Foes are lurking all around;
Look not here to find repose:
 This is but thy battle-ground.
2 Up! and take thy shield and sword;
 Up! it is the call of Heaven:
Shrink not faithless from thy Lord;
 Nobly strive as he hath striven.

3 Break through all the force of ill;
 Tread the might of passion down,
Struggling onward, onward still,
 To the conqu'ring Saviour's crown
4 Through the midst of toil and pain,
 Let this thought ne'er leave thy bre
Every triumph thou dost gain
 Makes more sweet thy coming res

GLYN. 6s & 5s.

418. *Ever Near.*

1 I close my heavy eye,
  Saviour, ever near!
 I lift my soul on high,
  Through the darkness drear:
 Be thou my light, I cry,
  Saviour, ever dear!

2 I feel thine arms around,
  Saviour, ever near!
 With thee if I am found,
  Never can I fear,
 Whatever ills abound;—
  Saviour, ever dear!

3 Thine is the day and night,
  Saviour, ever near!
 Thine is the dark and light,
  Be my covert here:
 Oh, shield me with thy might,
  Saviour, ever dear!

4 And when I come to die,
  Saviour, ever near,
 Receive my parting sigh;
  In the hour of fear,
 Be to my spirit nigh,
  Saviour, ever dear!

MAMRE. 6s & 7s.

1262. *"Everlasting joy shall be upon their heads."*

1 Will that not joyful be,
 When we walk by faith no more,
 When the Lord we loved before,
  As Brother-man we see;
 When he welcomes us above,
 When we share his smile of love,
  Will that not joyful be?

2 Will that not joyful be,
 When to meet us rise and come
 All our buried treasures home,
  A gladsome company!
 When our arms embrace again
 Those we mourned so long in vain,
  Will that not joyful be?

[For 3d and 4th stanzas see next page.]

SEVERN. 6s & 5s.

991. *"I have longed for Thy salvation, O Lord."*

1 PURER yet and purer
  I would be in mind,
  Dearer yet and dearer
  Every duty find;
2 Hoping still and trusting
  God without a fear,
  Patiently believing
  He will make all clear;

3 Calmer yet and calmer
  Trial bear and pain,
  Surer yet and surer
  Peace at last to gain;
4 Suff'ring still and doing,
  To his will resigned,
  And to God subduing
  Heart and will and mind.

5 Higher yet and higher
  Out of clouds and night,
  Nearer yet and nearer
  Rising to the light—
6 Light serene and holy,
  Where my soul may rest,
  Purified and lowly,
  Sanctified and blest.

7 Quicker yet and quicker
  Ever onward press,
  Firmer yet and firmer
  Step as I progress;

8 Oft these earnest longings
  Swell within my breast,
  Yet their inner meaning
  Ne'er can be expressed.

679. *"I am thy God; I will strengthen thee."*

1 OH, let him whose sorrow
  No relief can find,
  Trust in God, and borrow
  Ease for heart and mind!
  Where the mourner, weeping,
  Sheds the sacred tear,
  God his watch is keeping,
  Though none else is near.

2 God will never leave us;
  All our wants he knows;
  Feels the pains that grieve us,
  Sees our cares and woes;
  When in grief we languish,
  He will dry the tear
  Who his children's anguish
  Soothes with succor near.

3 All our woe and sadness
  In this world below,
  Equal not the gladness
  We in heaven shall know,—
  When our gracious Saviour,
  In the realms above,
  Crowns us with his favor,
  Fills us with his love.

---

3 Will that not joyful be,
When we hear what none can tell,
And the ringing chorus swell
  Of angels' melody!
When we join their songs of praise,
Hallelujahs with them raise,
  Will that not joyful be?

4 Yes! that will joyful be;
Let the world her gifts recall;
There is bitterness in all:
  Her joys are vanity!
Courage, dear ones of my heart!
Though it grieves us here to part,
  There we shall joyful be!

BADEA. S. M.

286. *Compassion of Christ.*—Luke 19: 41.

1 DID Christ o'er sinners weep,
  And shall our cheeks be dry?
Let floods of penitential grief
  Burst forth from every eye.

2 The Son of God in tears
  The wondering angels see!
Be thou astonished, O my soul!
  He shed those tears for thee.

3 He wept that we might weep;
  Each sin demands a tear:
In heaven alone no sin is found,
  And weeping is not there.

499. *"How should man be just with God?"*
  Job 9: 2.

1 AH, how shall fallen man
  Be just before his God!
If he contend in righteousness,
  We fall beneath his rod.

2 If he our ways should mark,
  With strict inquiring eyes,
Could we for one of thousand faults
  A just excuse devise?

3 All-seeing, powerful God!
  Who can with thee contend?
Or who that tries th' unequal strife,
  Shall prosper in the end?

4 The mountains, in thy wrath,
  Their ancient seats forsake;
The trembling earth deserts her place,
  Her rooted pillars shake.

5 Ah, how shall guilty man
  Contend with such a God!
None, none can meet him and escape,
  But through the Saviour's blood.

599. *"Out of the depths have I cried unto Thee."*—Psalm 130.

1 OUT of the depths of woe,
  To thee, O Lord! I cry;

Darkness surrounds me, yet I know
  That thou art ever nigh.

2 I cast my hopes on thee;
  Thou canst, thou wilt forgive;
If thou shouldst mark iniquity,
  Who in thy sight could live?

3 I wait for thee; I wait,
  Confessing all my sin:
Lord! I am knocking at thy gate;
  Open, and take me in.

4 Glory to God above!
  The waters soon will cease;
For lo! the swift-returning dove
  Brings home the pledge of peace.

5 Though storms his face obscure,
  And dangers threaten loud,
Jehovah's covenant is sure,
  His bow is in the cloud!

567. *Hope in the Cross.*

1 My former hopes are fled,
  My terror now begins;
I feel, alas! that I am dead
  In trespasses and sins.

2 Ah! whither shall I fly?
  I hear the thunder roar;
The law proclaims destruction nigh,
  And vengeance at the door.

3 When I review my ways,
  I dread impending doom;
But sure a friendly whisper says,
  "Flee from the wrath to come."

4 I see, or think I see,
  A glimmering from afar;
A beam of day that shines for me,
  To save me from despair.

5 Forerunner of the sun,
  It marks the pilgrim's way;
I'll gaze upon it while I run,
  And watch the rising day.

ELL. S. M.

625. *"O Lord, hear me, for I am poor and needy."*

1 My God, my prayer attend;
  Oh, bow thine ear to me—
Without a hope, without a friend,
  Without a help but thee!

2 Oh, guard my soul around,
  Which loves and trusts thy grace;
Nor let the powers of hell confound
  The hopes on thee I place!

3 Thy mercy I entreat:
  Let mercy hear my cries,
While, humbly waiting at thy feet,
  My daily prayers arise.

4 Oh, bid my heart rejoice,
  And every fear control!
Since at thy throne with suppliant voice
  To thee I lift my soul.

848. *Confiding Prayer.*

1 And shall I sit alone,
  Oppressed with grief and fear?
To God, my Father, make my moan,
  And he refuse to hear?

2 If he my Father be,
  His pity he will show;
From cruel bondage set me free,
  And inward peace bestow.

3 If still he silence keep,
  'Tis but my faith to try;
He knows and feels whene'er I weep,
  And softens every sigh.

4 Then will I humbly wait,
  Nor once indulge despair:
My sins are great,—but not so great
  As his compassions are.

Doxology.

To God, the Father, Son,
  And Spirit, glory be,
As was, and is, and shall remain
  Through all eternity!

OLMUTZ. S. M.

RETREAT. L. M.

61. *"Remember the Sabbath day, to keep it holy."*

1 ANOTHER six days' work is done;
Another Sabbath is begun:
Return, my soul, unto thy rest;
Enjoy the day thy God hath blest.
2 Oh that our thoughts and thanks may rise,
As grateful incense to the skies!
And draw from heaven that calm repose,
Which none but he who feels it knows;
3 That heavenly calm within the breast!
It is the pledge of that dear rest
Which for the church of God remains,—
The end of cares, the end of pains.
4 In holy duties let the day,
In holy pleasures, pass away
How sweet a Sabbath thus to spend,
In hope of one that ne'er shall end!

739. *"Is there no Physician there?"*
Jer. 8: 22.

1 WHY droops my soul, with grief oppressed?
Whence these wild tumults in my breast?
Is there no balm to heal my wound?
No kind physician to be found?
2 Raise to the cross thy weeping eyes;
Behold, the Prince of glory dies!
He dies extended on the tree,
Thence sheds a sovereign balm for thee.

3 Dear Saviour! at thy feet I lie,
Here to receive a cure, or die;
But grace forbids that painful fear—
Oh, boundless grace! it triumphs here.
4 Expand, my soul, with holy joy;
Hosannas be thy blest employ,
Salvation thy eternal theme,—
And swell the song with Jesus' name!

816. *"What sinners value, I resign."*
Psalm 17.

1 WHAT sinners value, I resign;
Lord, 't is enough that thou art mine:
I shall behold thy blissful face,
And stand complete in righteousness.
2 This life's a dream, an empty show;
But the bright world to which I go
Hath joys substantial and sincere:
When shall I wake and find me there?
3 Oh, glorious hour! oh, blest abode!
I shall be near and like my God;
And flesh and sin no more control
The sacred pleasures of the soul.
4 My flesh shall slumber in the ground
Till the last trumpet's joyful sound;
Then burst the chains with sweet surprise,
And in my Saviour's image rise!

1168. *"It is even a vapor."*

1 How vain is all beneath the skies!
How transient every earthly bliss!
How slender all the fondest ties,
That bind us to a world like this!
2 The evening cloud, the morning dew,
The withering grass, the fading flower,
Of earthly hopes are emblems true—
The glory of a passing hour!
3 But though earth's fairest blossoms die,
And all beneath the skies is vain,
There is a land, whose confines lie
Beyond the reach of care and pain.
4 Then let the hope of joys to come
Dispel our cares, and chase our fears:
If God be ours, we're traveling home,
Though passing through a vale of tears.

MINTON. L. M.

75. *Sabbath Evening.*

1 Sweet is the light of Sabbath eve,
 And soft the sunbeams lingering there;
 For these blest hours the world I leave,
 Wafted on wings of faith and prayer.

2 Season of rest! the tranquil soul
 Feels the sweet calm, and melts in love;
 And while these sacred moments roll,
 Faith sees a smiling heaven above.

3 Nor will our days of toil be long:
 Our pilgrimage will soon be trod;
 And we shall join the ceaseless song,
 The endless Sabbath of our God.

755. *With Christ in Heaven.*

1 As when the weary traveler gains
 The height of some o'erlooking hill,
 His heart revives, if o'er the plains
 He sees his home, though distant still—

2 So when the Christian pilgrim views,
 By faith, his mansion in the skies,
 The sight his fainting strength renews,
 And wings his speed to reach the prize.

3 "'T is there," he says, "I am to dwell
 With Jesus in the realms of day;
 Then shall I bid my cares farewell
 And he will wipe my tears away."

845. *The Mercy-seat.*

1 From every stormy wind that blows,
 From every swelling tide of woes,
 There is a calm, a sure retreat;
 'T is found beneath the mercy-seat.

2 There is a place where Jesus sheds
 The oil of gladness on our heads,—

A place, than all besides, more sweet;
It is the blood-bought mercy-seat.

3 There is a scene where spirits blend,
 Where friend holds fellowship with friend:
 Though sundered far, by faith they meet
 Around one common mercy-seat!

4 There, there, on eagle wings we soar,
 And sense and sin molest no more,
 And heaven comes down our souls to greet,
 And glory crowns the mercy-seat!

5 Oh! let my hand forget her skill,
 My tongue be silent, cold and still,
 This throbbing heart forget to beat,
 If I forget the mercy-seat.

864. *"How blest the sacred tie!"*

1 How blest the sacred tie that binds,
 In union sweet, according minds!
 How swift the heavenly course they run,
 Whose hearts and faith and hopes are one!

2 To each the soul of each how dear!
 What jealous care, what holy fear!
 How doth the generous flame within,
 Refine from earth and cleanse from sin!

3 Their streaming tears together flow
 For human guilt and human woe;
 Their ardent prayers united rise,
 Like mingling flames in sacrifice.

4 Together oft they seek the place
 Where God reveals his awful face;
 How high, how strong their raptures swell
 There's none but kindred minds can tell.

5 Nor shall the glowing flame expire
 'Mid nature's drooping, sickening fire:
 Soon shall they meet in realms above,
 A heaven of joy, because of love,

CANTERBURY. C. M.

146. *"Our dwelling-place in all generations."*
Psalm 90.

1 Our God, our help in ages past,
  Our hope for years to come,
Our shelter from the stormy blast,
  And our eternal home!

2 Under the shadow of thy throne,
  Thy saints have dwelt secure;
Sufficient is thine arm alone,
  And our defense is sure.

3 Before the hills in order stood,
  Or earth received her frame,
From everlasting thou art God,
  To endless years the same.

4 Thy word commands our flesh to dust:
  "Return, ye sons of men:"
All nations rose from earth at first,
  And turn to earth again.

5 Time, like an ever-rolling stream,
  Bears all its sons away;
They fly, forgotten, as a dream
  Dies at the opening day.

6 Our God, our help in ages past,
  Our hope for years to come,
Be thou our guard while troubles last,
  And our eternal home!

413. *"My Saviour died for me."*

1 Thou art my hiding-place, O Lord!
  In thee I put my trust,
Encouraged by thy holy word—
  A feeble child of dust.

2 I have no argument beside,
  I urge no other plea;
And 'tis enough the Saviour died,
  The Saviour died for me!

3 When storms of fierce temptation beat,
  And furious foes assail,
My refuge is the mercy-seat,
  My hope within the vail.

4 From strife of tongues, and bitter words,
  My spirit flies to thee;
Joy to my heart the thought affords,
  My Saviour died for me!

5 And when thine awful voice commands
  This body to decay,
And life, in its last lingering sands,
  Is ebbing fast away;—

6 Then, though it be in accents weak,
  My voice shall call on thee,
And ask for strength in death to speak,
  "My Saviour died for me."

637. *"Will not Thou deliver my feet from falling?"*

1 Alas, what hourly dangers rise!
  What snares beset my way!
To heaven, oh, let me lift mine eyes,
  And hourly watch and pray.

2 How oft my mournful thoughts complain,
  And melt in flowing tears!
My weak resistance, oh, how vain!
  How strong my foes and fears!

3 O gracious God! in whom I live,
  My feeble efforts aid;
Help me to watch, and pray, and strive,
  Though trembling and afraid.

4 Increase my faith, increase my hope,
  When foes and fears prevail;
And bear my fainting spirit up,
  Or soon my strength will fail.

5 Whene'er temptations fright my heart,
  Or lure my feet aside,
My God, thy powerful aid impart,
  My Guardian and my Guide.

6 Oh, keep me in thy heavenly way,
  And bid the tempter flee!
And let me never, never stray
  From happiness and thee.

WINDSOR. C. M.

1278. *The Judgment-seat of Christ.*

1 THAT awful day will surely come,
   Th' appointed hour makes haste,
  When I must stand before my Judge,
   And pass the solemn test.

2 Thou lovely Chief of all my joys,
   Thou Sovereign of my heart!
  How could I bear to hear thy voice
   Pronounce the sound, "Depart!"

3 Oh, wretched state of deep despair!
   To see my God remove—
  And fix my doleful station where
   I must not taste his love!

4 Jesus, I throw my arms around,
   And hang upon thy breast:
  Without a gracious smile from thee,
   My spirit can not rest.

5 Oh, tell me that my worthless name
   Is graven on thy hands!
  Show me some promise in thy book,
   Where my salvation stands.

6 Give me one kind, assuring word,
   To sink my fears again;
  And cheerfully my soul shall wait
   Her threescore years and ten.

580. *Inconstancy lamented.*

1 LONG have I sat beneath the sound
   Of thy salvation, Lord;
  Yet still how weak my faith is found,
   And knowledge of thy word!

2 How cold and feeble is my love!
   How negligent my fear!
  How low my hope of joys above!
   How few affections there!

3 Great God! thy sovereign power impart
   To give thy word success;
  Write thy salvation in my heart,
   And make me learn thy grace.

4 Show my forgetful feet the way
   That leads to joys on high;
  Where knowledge grows without decay,
   And love shall never die.

1280. *"O, how shall I appear!"*

1 WHEN, rising from the bed of death
   O'erwhelmed with guilt and fear,
  I see my Maker face to face—
   Oh, how shall I appear!

2 If now, while pardon may be found,
   And mercy may be sought,
  My heart with inward horror shrinks,
   And trembles at the thought;—

3 When thou, O Lord! shalt stand disclosed
   In majesty severe,
  And sit in judgment on my soul,
   Oh, how shall I appear!

4 Then, see my sorrows, gracious Lord!
   Let mercy set me free,
  While in the confidence of prayer
   My heart takes hold of thee.

5 For never shall my soul despair
   Thy mercy to procure,
  Since thy beloved Son hath died
   To make that mercy sure.

DOXOLOGY.

LET God the Father, and the Son,
 And Spirit, be adored,
Where there are works to make him
  known,
 Or saints to love the Lord!

42. "*I will that men pray everywhere.*"

1 Jesus, where'er thy people meet,
  There they behold thy mercy-seat;
  Where'er they seek thee, thou art found,
  And every place is hallowed ground.

2 For thou, within no walls confined,
  Inhabitest the humble mind;
  Such ever bring thee where they come,
  And going, take thee to their home.

3 Great Shepherd of thy chosen few!
  Thy former mercies here renew;
  Here to our waiting hearts proclaim
  The sweetness of thy saving name.

89. "*The love of Christ, which passeth knowledge.*"

1 Come, dearest Lord! descend and dwell
  By faith and love in every breast;
  Then shall we know, and taste, and feel
  The joys that can not be expressed.

2 Come, fill our hearts with inward strength,
  Make our enlarged souls possess,
  And learn the height, and breadth, and length,
  Of thine immeasurable grace.

3 Now to the God whose power can do
  More than our thoughts and wishes know,
  Be everlasting honors done
  By all the church, through Christ his Son!

437. "*No other Friend can I desire.*"

1 My precious Lord, for thy dear name
  I bear the cross, despise the shame;
  Nor do I faint while thou art near;
  I lean on thee; how can I fear?

2 No other name but thine is given
  To cheer my soul in earth or heaven;
  No other wealth will I require;
  No other friend can I desire.

3 Yea, into nothing would I fall
  For thee alone, my All in All;
  To feel thy love, my only joy;
  To tell thy love, my sole employ.

988. "*Let Thy presence set me free.*"

1 My soul before thee prostrate lies;
  To thee, her Source, my spirit flies:
  My wants I mourn, my chains I see,—
  Oh, let thy presence set me free!

2 Undone and lost, for aid I cry;
  In thy death, Saviour, let me die;
  Griev'd with thy grief, pain'd with thy pain,
  Ne'er let me live for self again.

3 In life's short day, let me yet more
  Of thine enlivening love implore;
  My mind must deeper sink in thee,
  My foot stand firm, from wandering free.

1200. "*Unvail thy bosom, faithful tomb.*"

1 Unvail thy bosom, faithful tomb;
  Take this new treasure to thy trust,
  And give these sacred relics room
  To slumber in the silent dust.

2 Nor pain, nor grief, nor anxious fear,
  Invade thy bounds; no mortal woes
  Can reach the peaceful sleeper here,
  While angels watch the soft repose.

3 So Jesus slept; God's dying Son
  Passed thro' the grave, and blest the bed:
  Rest here, blest saint, till from his throne
  The morning break, and pierce the shade.

4 Break from his throne, illustrious morn!
  Attend, O earth! his sovereign word;
  Restore thy trust: a glorious form
  Shall then ascend to meet the Lord!

HAMBURG. L. M.

316. *"When I survey the wondrous Cross."*

1 When I survey the wondrous cross
On which the Prince of Glory died,
My richest gain I count but loss,
And pour contempt on all my pride.

2 Forbid it Lord, that I should boast,
Save in the death of Christ my God:
All the vain things that charm me most—
I sacrifice them to his blood.

3 See, from his head, his hands, his feet,
Sorrow and love flow mingled down!
Did e'er such love and sorrow meet,
Or thorns compose so rich a crown?

4 Were the whole realm of nature mine,
That were an offering far too small:
Love so amazing, so divine,
Demands my soul, my life, my all!

501. *Probation in this life only.*
Eccles. 9: 10

1 Life is the time to serve the Lord,
The time t' insure the great reward;
And while the lamp holds out to burn,
The vilest sinner may return.

2 Life is the hour that God has given
T' escape from hell and fly to heaven;
The day of grace,—and mortals may
Secure the blessings of the day.

3 Then what my thoughts design to do,
My hands, with all your might pursue,
Since no device, nor work is found,
Nor faith, nor hope, beneath the ground.

4 There are no acts of pardon passed
In the cold grave to which we haste;
But darkness, death, and long despair
Reign in eternal silence there.

811. *"With my soul have I desired Thee."*

1 My God, permit me not to be
A stranger to myself and thee;
Amid a thousand thoughts I rove,
Forgetful of my highest love.

2 Why should my passions mix with earth,
And thus debase my heavenly birth?
Why should I cling to things below,
And let my God, my Saviour, go?

3 Call me away from flesh and sense;
One sovereign word can draw me thence;
I would obey the voice divine,
And all inferior joys resign.

4 Be earth, with all her scenes, withdrawn;
Let noise and vanity be gone;
In secret silence of the mind
My heaven, and there my God, I find.

923. *"Faith exemplified in the life."*
Tit. 2: 10-13

1 So let our lips and lives express
The holy gospel we profess;
So let our works and virtues shine,
To prove the doctrine all divine.

2 Thus shall we best proclaim abroad
The honors of our Saviour God;
When his salvation reigns within,
And grace subdues the power of sin.

3 Our flesh and sense must be denied,
Passion and envy, lust and pride;
While justice, temperance, truth, and love,
Our inward piety approve.

4 Religion bears our spirits up,
While we expect that blessed hope,
The bright appearance of the Lord,—
And faith stands leaning on his word.

ALVAN. 8s, 7s & 4.

88. *"Keep us, Lord."*

1 Keep us, Lord, oh, keep us **ever!**
Vain our hope, if left by thee;
We are thine; oh, leave us never,
Till thy glorious face we see!
Then to praise thee
Through a bright eternity.

2 Precious is thy word of promise,
Precious to thy people here;
Never take thy presence from us,
Jesus, Saviour, still **be near:**
Living, dying,
May thy name our spirits **cheer.**

297. *The voice from Calvary.*—John 19:30.

1 Hark! the voice of love and mercy
Sounds aloud from Calvary;
See! it rends the rocks asunder,
Shakes the earth, and vails the sky:
"It is finished!"
Hear the dying Saviour cry.

2 "It is finished!"—Oh, what pleasure
Do these charming words afford!
Heavenly blessings, without measure,
Flow to us from Christ, the Lord:
"It is finished!"
Saints, the dying words record.

3 Tune your harps anew, ye seraphs;
Join to sing the pleasing theme:
All on earth and all in heaven,
Join to praise Immanuel's name:
Hallelujah!
Glory to the bleeding Lamb!

536. *Hasten to the Saviour.*

1 Hear, O sinner! mercy hails you;
Now with sweetest voice she calls;
Bids you haste to seek the Saviour,
Ere the hand of justice falls:
Hear, O sinner!
'Tis the voice of mercy **calls.**

2 Haste, O sinner, to the Saviour!
Seek his mercy while you may;
Soon the day of grace is over;
Soon your life will pass away;
Haste, O sinner!
You must perish if you **stay.**

1287. *"The Judgment of the great day."*

1 Day of Judgment—day of wonders!
Hark!—the trumpet's awful sound,
Louder than a thousand thunders,
Shakes the vast creation round!
How the summons
Will the sinner's heart confound!

2 See the Judge our nature **wearing,**
Clothed in majesty divine!
You, who long for his appearing,
Then shall say, "This God is mine!"
Gracious Saviour,
Own me in that day for thine!

3 At his call the dead awaken,
Rise to life from earth and sea;
All the powers of nature, shaken
By his looks, prepare to flee:
Careless sinner,
What will then become of thee?

4 But to those who have confessed,
Loved and served the Lord below,
He will say, "Come near, ye blessed,
See the kingdom I bestow;
You for ever
Shall my love and glory know!"

HAMDEN. 8s, 7s & 4.

772. * *"Draw nigh unto my soul, and redeem it."*

1 When I listen to thy word,
  In thy temple, cold and dead;
  When I can not see thee, Lord,
  All faith's little daylight fled—
    Sun of glory,
  Beam again around **my head.**

2 When thy statutes I forsake;
  When my graces dimly shine;
  When my covenant I break—
  Jesus, then remember thine:
    Check my wanderings
  By a look of love divine.

3 When thy heavenly dew distills,
  And my views, O Lord, are clear—
  Clear and bright from Zion's hills,
  Temper joy with holy fear;
    Keep me watchful,
  Only safe when thou art near.

4 When afflictions cloud my sky,
  When the tide of sorrow flows,
  When thy rod is lifted high,
  Let me on thy love repose:
    Stay the rough wind,
  When thy chilling east wind blows.

5 When the vale of death appears,
  Faint and cold this mortal clay,
  Kind Forerunner! soothe my fears,
  Light me through the darksome way:
    Break the shadows—
  Usher in eternal day!

517. *Free Forgiveness.*

1 Sinners, will you scorn the message
  Sent in mercy from above?

* Observe the tie for this Hymn.

Every sentence, oh, how tender!
  Every line is full of love
    Hear, oh, hear it!
  Every line is full of love.

2 Hear the heralds of the gospel
  News from Zion's King proclaim:
  "To each rebel sinner pardon,
  Free forgiveness in his name:"
    Oh, receive it!
  "Free forgiveness in his name."

3 Now, ye angels, hovering round **us,**
  Waiting spirits, speed your way;
  Haste ye to the court of heaven,
  Tidings bear without delay:
    Rebel sinners
  Glad the message **will obey.**

518. *"Look unto me and be ye saved."*

1 Come, ye sinners, poor and wretched,
  This is your accepted hour;
  Jesus ready stands to save you,
  Full of pity, love, and power:
    He is able,
  He is willing; doubt no more.

2 Agonizing in the garden,
  Lo! the Saviour prostrate lies;
  On the bloody tree behold him!
  Hear him cry, before he dies,
    "It is finished!"
  Sinners, will not this suffice?

3 Lo! th' incarnate God ascended
  Pleads the merit of his blood;
  Venture on him, venture wholly,
  Let no other trust intrude:
    None but Jesus
  Can do helpless sinners good.

CAMBRIDGE. C. M.

257. *"I will declare what He hath done for my soul."*—Psalm 66.

1 O ALL ye lands, rejoice in God !
  Sing praises to his name ;
  Let all the earth, with one accord,
  His wondrous acts proclaim ;

2 And let his faithful servants tell
  How, by redeeming love,
  Their souls are saved from death and hell,
  To share the joys above ;—

3 Tell how the Holy Spirit's grace
  Forbids their feet to slide ;
  And, as they run the Christian race,
  Vouchsafes to be their guide.

4 Oh, then, rejoice, and shout for joy,
  Ye ransomed of the Lord !
  Be grateful praise your sweet employ,
  His presence your reward.

958. *"Happy is the man that findeth wisdom."*—Prov. 3: 13.

1 OH, happy is the man that hears
  Instruction's warning voice ;
  And who celestial wisdom makes
  His early, only choice.

2 For she hath treasures greater far
  Than east and west unfold ;
  And her rewards more precious are
  Than all their stores of gold.

3 She guides the young with innocence,
  In pleasure's paths to tread ;
  A crown of glory she bestows
  Upon the hoary head.

4 According as her labors rise,
  So her rewards increase ;
  Her ways are ways of pleasantness,
  And all her paths are peace.

1234. *"When shall I see my Father's face?"*

1 ON Jordan's stormy banks I stand,
  And cast a wishful eye
  To Canaan's fair and happy land,
  Where my possessions lie.

2 Oh, the transporting, rapturous scene,
  That rises to my sight !
  Sweet fields arrayed in living green,
  And rivers of delight.

3 O'er all those wide extended plains
  Shines one eternal day ;
  There God, the Sun, for ever reigns,
  And scatters night away.

4 No chilling winds, no poisonous breath,
  Can reach that healthful shore ;
  Sickness and sorrow, pain and death,
  Are felt and feared no more.

5 When shall I reach that happy place,
  And be for ever blest ?
  When shall I see my Father's face,
  And in his bosom rest ?

6 Filled with delight, my raptured soul
  Can here no longer stay ;
  Though Jordan's waves around me roll,
  Fearless I'd launch away.

1236. *No Sin in Heaven.*

1 FAR from these narrow scenes of night,
  Unbounded glories rise,
  And realms of infinite delight,
  Unknown to mortal eyes.

2 Fair, distant land ! could mortal eyes
  But half its charms explore,
  How would our spirits long to rise,
  And dwell on earth no more !

BALERMA. C. M.

3 No clouds those blissful regions know—
  Realms ever bright and fair!
  For sin, the source of mortal woe,
  Can never enter there.

4 Oh, may the heavenly prospect **fire**
  Our hearts with ardent love!
  Till wings of faith, and strong desire,
  Bear every thought above.

5 Prepare us, Lord, **by grace divine,**
  For thy bright **courts on high;**
  Then bid our spirits **rise and join**
  The chorus of the sky.

1250. "*He that sitteth on the throne shall dwell among them.*"—Rev. 7: 11-17.

1 How bright these glorious spirits shine!
  Whence all their white array?
  How came they to the blissful seats
  Of everlasting day?

2 Lo! these are they from sufferings great
  Who came to realms of light,
  And in the blood of Christ have washed
  Those robes which shine so bright.

3 Now, with triumphal palms, they **stand**
  Before the throne on high,
  And serve the God they love, amid
  The glories of the sky.

4 His presence fills each heart with joy,
  Tunes every voice to sing;
  By day, by night, the sacred courts
  With glad hosannahs **ring.**

5 The Lamb, that dwells amid the throne,
  Shall o'er them still preside,
  Feed them with nourishment divine,
  And all their footsteps guide.

6 In pastures green he'll lead his flock,
  Where living streams appear;
  And God, the Lord, from every eye
  Shall **wipe off** every tear.

1266. "*I saw a new heaven and a new earth.*"—Rev. 21: 1-5.

1 Lo! what a glorious sight appears
  To our believing eyes!
  The earth and seas are passed away,
  And the old rolling skies.

2 From the third heaven, where God resides,
  That holy, happy place,
  The new Jerusalem comes **down,**
  Adorned with shining grace.

3 Attending angels shout for joy,
  And the bright armies sing:
  "Mortals! behold the sacred seat
  Of your descending King.

4 "The God of glory down to men
  Removes his blest abode,—
  Men, the dear objects of his grace,
  And he, the loving God.

5 "His own soft hands shall wipe the tears
  From every weeping eye;
  And pains, and groans, and griefs, and fears,
  And death itself **shall die.**"

6 How long, dear Saviour! oh, how long
  Shall this bright hour delay?
  Fly swifter round, ye wheels of time,
  And bring the welcome day!

DOXOLOGY.

To Father, **Son,** and Holy Ghost,
  One God, **whom we** adore,
  Be glory as it was, is now,
  And shall be evermore.

ATHOL. S. M.

197. *"The Rock that is higher than I."*
Psalm 61.

1 When overwhelmed with grief,
   My heart within me dies,
Helpless, and far from all relief,
   To heaven I lift mine eyes.

2 Oh, lead me to the Rock
   That's high above my head!
And make the covert of thy wings
   My shelter and my shade.

3 Within thy presence, Lord,
   For ever I'll abide:
Thou art the tower of my defense,
   The refuge where I hide.

4 Thou givest me the lot
   Of those that fear thy name;
If endless life be their reward,
   I shall possess the same.

607. *"My soul, wait thou only upon God."*

1 Thou Lord of all above,
   And all below the sky,
Prostrate before thy feet I fall,
   And for thy mercy cry.

2 Forgive my follies past,
   The crimes which I have done;
Bid a repenting sinner live,
   Through thine incarnate Son.

3 Guilt, like a heavy load,
   Upon my conscience lies;
To thee I make my sorrows known,
   And lift my weeping eyes.

4 The burden which I feel,
   Thou only canst remove;
Do thou display thy pardoning grace,
   And thine unbounded love.

5 One gracious look of thine
   Will ease my troubled breast;

Oh let me know my sins forgiven,
   And I shall then be blest!

634. *"Watch unto Prayer."*

1 O God! my Strength, my Hope,
   On thee I cast my care,
With humble confidence look up,
   And know thou hearest prayer.

2 Oh for a godly fear,
   A quick, discerning eye,
That looks to thee when sin is near,
   And sees the tempter fly!—

3 A spirit still prepared,
   And armed with jealous care,
For ever standing on its guard,
   And watching unto prayer!—

4 A soul inured to pain,
   To hardship, grief, and loss;
Bold to take up, firm to sustain
   My dear Redeemer's cross.

5 Lord, let me still abide,
   Nor from my hope remove,
Till thou my patient spirit guide
   Into thy perfect love.

656. *"My times are in Thy hand."*
Psalm 31.

1 "My times are in thy hand;"
   My God! I wish them there;
My life, my friends, my soul, I leave
   Entirely to thy care.

2 "My times are in thy hand,"
   Whatever they may be;
Pleasing or painful, dark or bright,
   As best may seem to thee.

3 "My times are in thy hand;"
   Why should I doubt or fear?
My Father's hand will never cause
   His child a needless tear.

OLMUTZ. S. M.

4 "My times are in thy hand,"—
  Jesus, the crucified !
The hand my cruel sins had pierced,
  Is now my guard and guide.

5 "My times are in thy hand ;"
  I 'll always trust in thee ;
And, after death, at thy right hand
  I shall for ever be.

671. *"My soul waiteth for the Lord."*
  Psalm 130.

1 FROM lowest depths of woe,
    To God I send my cry ;
  Lord ! hear my supplicating voice,
    And graciously reply.

2 Shouldst thou severely judge,
    Who can the trial bear ?
  But thou forgiv'st, lest we despond,
    And quite renounce thy fear.

3 My soul with patience waits
    For thee, the living Lord ;
  My hopes are on thy promise built,
    Thy never-failing word.

4 My longing eyes look out
    For thine enlivening ray,
  More duly than the morning watch
    To spy the dawning day.

5 Let Israel trust in God ;
    No bounds his mercy knows—
  The plenteous source and spring from
      whence
    Eternal succor flows.

1279. *"Every one of us shall give account
  of himself to God."*

1 THOU Judge of quick and dead,
    Before whose bar severe,
  With holy joy or guilty dread,
    We all shall soon appear !—

2 Our anxious souls prepare
    For that tremendous day ;
  Come, fill us now with watchful care,
    And stir us up to pray ;—

3 To pray, and wait the hour,
    That awful hour unknown,
  When robed in majesty and power,
    Thou shalt from heaven come down !

4 Oh, may we all be found
    Obedient to thy word,—
  Attentive to the trumpet's sound,
    And looking for our Lord !

5 Oh, may we all insure
    A home among the blest ;
  And watch a moment to secure
    An everlasting rest !

1288. *"Knowing the terror of the Lord,
  we persuade men."*

1 AND will the Judge descend,
    And must the dead arise,
  And not a single soul escape
    His all-discerning eyes ?

2 How will my heart endure
    The terrors of that day,
  When earth and heaven before his face
    Astonished shrink away ?

3 But, ere the trumpet shakes
    The mansions of the dead,
  Hark, from the Gospel's cheering sound
    What joyful tidings spread !

4 Ye sinners ! seek his grace
    Whose wrath ye can not bear ;
  Fly to the shelter of his cross,
    And find salvation there.

940.
"Hallow this grief."

1 Father! who in the olive shade,
  When the dark hour came on,
 Didst, with a breath of heavenly aid,
  Strengthen thy Son,—
 Oh, by the anguish of that night,
 Send thou us blest relief;
 Or to the chastened, let thy might
  Hallow this grief!

2 And thou, that, when the starry sky
  Saw the dread strife begun,
 Didst teach adoring faith to cry,
  "Thy will be done!"—
 By thy meek Spirit, thou of all
 That e'er hath mourned the chief—
 Thou Saviour! if the stroke must fall,
  Hallow this grief!

1182.
"I will be with him in trouble."

1 Father, when thy child is dying,
  On the bed of anguish lying,
  Then, my every want supplying,
   To me thy love display!

2 Ere my soul her bonds hath broken,
  Grant some bright and cheering token,
  That for me the words are spoken,
   "Thy sins are washed away!"

3 When the lips are dumb which bless'd me,
  And withdrawn the hand that pressed me,
  Then let sweeter sounds arrest me,
   To call my soul away!

4 Guide me to that world of spirits,
  Where, through thine atoning merits,
  Ev'n thy weakest child inherits
   The joys which ne'er decay.

KITTO. 8s & 5.

407. *"Sing of Jesus."*

1 Sing of Jesus, sing for ever
Of the love that changes never:
Who or what from him can sever
Those he makes his own?

2 With his blood the Lord hath bought them,
When they knew him not, he sought them,
And from all their wand'rings brought
His the praise alone. [them,

3 Through the desert Jesus leads them,
With the bread of heaven he feeds them,
And through all the way he speeds them
To their home above.

4 There they see the Lord who bought them,
Him who came from heaven, and sought them,
Him who by his Spirit taught them:
Him they serve and love.

5 Sing of Jesus, sing for ever,
Sing the love that changes never:
Who or what from him can sever
Those he makes his own?

MEAD. 8s, 6s, 5 & 4.

384. *Hallelujah.*

1 Hallelujah! Hallelujah!
Now is the battle done,
Now is the vict'ry won;
Let us joy, and sing
Hallelujah!

2 Hallelujah, Hallelujah!
Suff'ring death's cruel doom,
Jesus hath hell o'ercome:
Let us praise, and shout
Hallelujah!

3 Hallelujah, Hallelujah!
He rose by his own might
In heavenly love and light:
Let us joy, and sing
Hallelujah!

4 Hallelujah, Hallelujah!
Closed are the gates below,
Heaven's halls are open now:
Let us praise, and shout
Hallelujah!

5 Hallelujah, Hallelujah!
Lord, by thy passion, save
Us from the endless grave:
Let us ever sing
Hallelujah!

ELIM. C. M. Double.

235. "Keep silence, all created things."

1 Keep silence, all created things,
  And wait your Maker's nod!
My soul stands trembling while she sings
  The honors of her God.
2 Life, death, and hell, and worlds unknown,
  Hang on his firm decree;
He sits on no precarious throne,
  Nor borrows leave to be.
3 Before his throne a volume lies,
  With all the fates of men;
With every angel's form and size,
  Drawn by th' eternal pen.
4 His providence unfolds the book,
  And makes his counsels shine;
Each opening leaf, and every stroke,
  Fulfills some deep design.
5 My God, I would not long to see
  My fate with curious eyes;—
What gloomy lines are writ for me,
  Or what bright scenes may rise.
6 In thy fair book of life and grace,
  May I but find my name
Recorded in some humble place,
  Beneath my Lord, the Lamb!

284. "Learning of Thee."

1 O Lord, when we the path retrace
  Which thou on earth hast trod;
To man thy wondrous love and grace,
  Thy faithfulness to God:—
Thy love, by man so sorely tried,
  Proved stronger than the grave;
The very spear that pierced thy side
  Drew forth the blood to save:—

2 Faithful amid unfaithfulness,
  'Mid darkness only light,
Thou didst thy Father's name confess,
  And in his will delight;
Unmoved by Satan's subtle wiles,
  Or, suffering shame and loss;
Thy path, uncheered by earthly smiles,
  Led only to the cross:—

3 O Lord! with sorrow and with shame,
  Before thee we confess
How little we, who bear thy name,
  Thy mind, thy ways express.
Give us thy meek, thy lowly mind:
  We would obedient be;
And all our rest and pleasure find
  In learning, Lord, of thee.

320 "Whom, having not seen, ye love."

1 To Calvary, Lord, in spirit now,
  Our weary souls repair,
To dwell upon thy dying love,
  And taste its sweetness there.
2 Sweet resting-place of every heart
  That feels the plague of sin,
Yet knows the deep, mysterious joy
  Of peace with God within.
3 Dear suffering Lamb! thy bleeding wounds,
  With cords of love divine,
Have drawn our willing hearts to thee,
  And linked our life with thine.
4 Thy sympathies and hopes are ours:
  Dear Lord! we wait to see
Creation, all below, above,
  Redeemed and blest by thee.
5 Our longing eyes would fain behold
  That bright and blessed brow,
Once wrung with bitterest anguish, wear
  Its crown of glory now.

DOWNS. C. M.

6 Why linger, then? Come, Saviour, come,
   Responsive to our call!
   Come, claim thine ancient power, and
      reign
   The heir and Lord of all.

73. "*I lay me down to rest.*"

1 Dread Sovereign, let my evening song
   Like holy incense rise;
   Assist the offering of my tongue
   To reach the lofty skies.

2 Through all the dangers of the day
   Thy hand was still my guard;
   And still to drive my wants away
   Thy mercy stood prepared.

3 Perpetual blessings from above
   Encompass me around;
   But, oh, how few returns of love
   Hath my Redeemer found!

4 What have I done for him who died
   To save my guilty soul?
   How are my follies multiplied,
   Fast as the minutes roll!

5 Lord! with this sinful heart of mine,
   To thy dear cross I flee,
   And to thy grace my soul resign,
   To be renewed by thee.

6 Sprinkled afresh with pardoning blood,
   I lay me down to rest,
   As in the embraces of my God,
   Or on my Saviour's breast.

311. "*His own self bare our sins.*"

1 And did the Holy and the Just,
   The Sovereign of the skies,
   Stoop down to wretchedness and dust
   That guilty man might rise?

2 Yes: the Redeemer left his throne,
   His radiant throne on high—
   Surprising mercy! love unknown!—
   To suffer, bleed, and die.

3 He took the dying traitor's place,
   And suffered in his stead;
   For man—oh, miracle of grace!—
   For man the Saviour bled.

4 Dear Lord, what heavenly wonders dwell
   In thine atoning blood!
   By this are sinners saved from hell,
   And rebels brought to God.

765. *An ancient Hymn of Trust in Christ.*

1 Jesus! our fainting spirits cry,
   When wilt thou show thy face?
   Oh! when our longings satisfy,
   And fill us with thy grace?

2 We, sinners, Lord, with earnest heart,
   With sighs, and prayers, and tears,
   To thee our inmost cares impart,
   Our burdens and our fears.

3 Thy sovereign grace can give relief,
   Thou Source of peace and light!
   Dispel the gloomy cloud of grief,
   And make our darkness bright.

4 Around thy Father's throne on high,
   All heaven the glory sings;
   And earth, for which thou cam'st to die,
   Loud with thy praises rings.

5 Dear Lord! to thee our prayers ascend;
   Our eyes thy face would see.
   Oh! let our weary wanderings end,
   Our spirits rest in thee!

DOXOLOGY.

To Father, Son, and Holy Ghost,
   One God, whom we adore,
Be glory as it was, is now,
   And shall be evermore!

LOUVAN. L. M.

254. *"The Word was God."*—John 1: 4.

1 Ere the blue heavens were stretched abroad,
  From everlasting was the Word:
  With God he was; the Word was God,
  And must divinely be adored.

2 By his own power were all things made;
  By him supported, all things stand:
  He is the whole creation's head,
  And angels fly at his command.

3 But lo! he leaves those heavenly forms:
  The Word descends and dwells in clay,
  That he may hold converse with worms,
  Dressed in such feeble flesh as they.

4 Mortals with joy behold his face,
  Th' eternal Father's only Son;
  How full of truth, how full of grace,
  When thro' his eyes the Godhead shone!

5 Archangels leave their high abode
  To learn new mysteries here, and tell
  The love of our descending God,
  The glories of Immanuel.

417. *"Lord, save us; we perish."*

1 The billows swell, the winds are high;
  Clouds overcast my wintry sky;
  Out of the depths to thee I call;
  My fears are great, my strength is small.

2 O Lord, the pilot's part perform,
  And guide and guard me thro' the storm;
  Defend me from each threatening ill:
  Control the waves; say, "Peace! be still."

3 Amid the roaring of the sea,
  My soul still hangs her hope on thee;
  Thy constant love, thy faithful care,
  Is all that saves me from despair.

4 Tho' tempest-tossed and half a wreck,
  My Saviour through the floods I seek:
  Let neither winds nor stormy main
  Force back my shattered bark again.

749. *The Hiding-place.*

1 Hail, sovereign Love! that formed the plan
  To save rebellious, ruined man;
  Hail! matchless, free, eternal Grace,
  That gave my soul a hiding-place.

2 Against the God who rules the sky
  I fought, with hand uplifted high;
  I madly ran the sinful race,
  Regardless of a hiding-place.

3 Indignant Justice stood in view;
  To Sinai's burning mount I flew:
  But Justice cried, with frowning face,
  "This mountain is no hiding-place."

4 Ere long a heavenly voice I heard;
  A bleeding Saviour then appeared:
  Led by the Spirit of his grace,
  I found in him a hiding-place.

5 On him the weight of vengeance fell,
  That else had sunk a world to hell;
  Then, O my soul! for ever praise
  Thy Saviour God, thy hiding-place!

1129. *"He shall have dominion also from sea to sea."*—Psalm 72.

1 Jesus shall reign where'er the sun
  Does his successive journeys run;
  His kingdom stretch from shore to shore,
  Till moons shall wax and wane no more.

2 People and realms of every tongue
  Dwell on his love with sweetest song;
  And infant voices shall proclaim
  Their early blessings on his name.

3 Blessings abound where'er he reigns;
  The prisoner leaps to loose his chains;
  The weary find eternal rest,
  And all the sons of want are blest.

4 Let every creature rise and bring
  Peculiar honors to our King:
  Angels descend with songs again,
  And earth repeat the loud Amen!

MISSIONARY CHANT. L. M.

962. *Light in Darkness.*—Psalm 112.

1 THAT man is blest, who stands in awe
Of God, and loves his sacred law;
His seed on earth shall be renowned,
And with successive honors crowned.

2 The soul that 's filled with virtue's light
Shines brightest in affliction's night;
His conscience bears his courage up;
He sees in darkness beams of hope.

3 Beset with threatening dangers round,
Unmoved shall he maintain his ground;
The sweet remembrance of the just
Shall flourish when he sleeps in dust.

1121. *The Song of Triumph.*

1 SOON may the last glad song arise
Through all the millions of the skies—
That song of triumph which records
That all the earth is now the Lord's!

2 Let thrones and powers and kingdoms be
Obedient, mighty God, to thee!
And, over land and stream and main,
Wave thou the scepter of thy reign!

3 Oh, let that glorious anthem swell,
Let host to host the triumph tell,
That not one rebel heart remains,
But over all the Saviour reigns!

1136. *"Go ye into all the world."*

1 YE Christian heralds! go proclaim
Salvation through Immanuel's name;
To distant climes the tidings bear,
And plant the rose of Sharon there.

2 He 'll shield you with a wall of fire,
With flaming zeal your breasts inspire,
Bid raging winds their fury cease,
And hush the tempest into peace.

3 And when our labors all are o'er,
Then we shall meet to part no more,—

Meet with the blood-bought throng, to fall,
And crown our Jesus—Lord of all!

1195. *"Asleep in Jesus."*

1 ASLEEP in Jesus! blessed sleep!
From which none ever wake to weep;
A calm and undisturbed repose,
Unbroken by the last of foes.

2 Asleep in Jesus! oh, how sweet
To be for such a slumber meet!
With holy confidence to sing
That death hath lost its venomed sting.

3 Asleep in Jesus! peaceful rest!
Whose waking is supremely blest;
No fear, no woe, shall dim that hour
Which manifests the Saviour's power.

4 Asleep in Jesus! oh, for me
May such a blissful refuge be!
Securely shall my ashes lie,
And wait the summons from on high.

1223. *"Here have we no continuing city."*
Heb. 13: 14.

1 "WE 'VE no abiding city here;"
Sad truth, were this to be our home;
But let this thought our spirits cheer,
"We seek a city yet to come."

2 "We 've no abiding city here;"
We seek a city out of sight:
Zion its name—the Lord is there,
It shines with everlasting light.

3 O sweet abode of peace and love,
Where pilgrims freed from toil are blest!
Had I the pinions of the dove,
I'd fly to thee, and be at rest.

4 But hush, my soul! nor dare repine;
The time my God appoints is best:
While here, to do his will be mine,
And his to fix my time of rest.

NAOMI. C. M.

602. *Pleading the Promise.*

1 Lord, I approach the mercy-seat,
  Where thou dost answer prayer;
  There humbly fall before thy feet,
  For none can perish there.

2 Thy promise is my only plea;
  With this I venture nigh.
  Thou callest burdened souls to thee,
  And such, O Lord, am I.

3 Bowed down beneath a load of sin,
  By Satan sorely pressed,
  By war without, and fear within,
  I come to thee for rest.

4 Be thou my shield and hiding-place,
  That, sheltered near thy side,
  I may my fierce accuser face,
  And tell him thou hast died.

5 Oh, wondrous love!—to bleed and die,
  To bear the cross and shame,
  That guilty sinners, such as I,
  Might plead thy gracious name.

1164. *"Our days on earth are as a shadow."*

1 How short and hasty is our life!
  How vast our soul's affairs!
  Yet senseless mortals vainly strive
  To lavish out their years.

2 Our days run thoughtlessly along,
  Without a moment's stay;
  Just like a story, or a song,
  We pass our lives away.

3 God from on high invites us home,
  But we march heedless on,
  And,'ever hastening to the tomb,
  Stoop downward as we run.

4 How we deserve the deepest hell,
  Who slight the joys above!
  What chains of vengeance should we feel,
  Who break such cords of love!

5 Draw us, O God, with sovereign grace,
  And lift our thoughts on high,
  That we may end this mortal race,
  And see salvation nigh.

1172. *"And after death the judgment."*

1 Stoop down, my thoughts, that used to rise;
  Converse awhile with death;
  Think how a gasping mortal lies,
  And pants away his breath!

2 But, oh! the soul, that never dies!
  At once it leaves the clay;
  Ye thoughts, pursue it where it flies,
  And track its wondrous way.

3 Up to the courts where angels dwell
  It mounts, triumphant there;
  Or plunges guilty down to hell,
  In infinite despair.

4 And must my body faint and die?
  And must this soul remove?
  Oh for some guardian angel nigh,
  To bear it safe above!

5 Jesus! to thy dear, faithful hand
  My naked soul I trust;
  And my flesh waits for thy command
  To drop into my dust.

1205. *"Turn, mortal, turn! thy danger know."*

1 Beneath our feet, and o'er our head,
  Is equal warning given;
  Beneath us lie the countless dead,
  Above us is the heaven!

DUNDEE. C. M.

2 Death rides on every passing breeze;
  He lurks in every flower;
  Each season has its own disease,
  Its peril every hour!

3 Turn, mortal, turn! thy danger **know**;
  Where'er thy foot can tread,
  The earth rings hollow from below,
  And warns thee of her dead!

4 Turn, Christian, turn! thy soul apply
  To truths divinely given;
  The bones that underneath thee lie
  Shall live for **hell or heaven!**

77. *Increase our Faith.*

1 Frequent the day of God returns
  To shed its quickening beams;
  And yet, **how** slow devotion burns!
  How languid are its flames!

2 Accept our faint attempts to **love**;
  Our follies, Lord, forgive:
  We would be like thy saints above,
  And praise thee while we live.

3 Increase, O Lord, our faith and hope,
  And fit us to ascend
  Where the assembly ne'er breaks up,
  And Sabbaths never end :—

4 Where we shall breathe in heavenly air,
  With heavenly luster shine;
  Before the throne of God appear,
  And feast on love divine.

5 There shall we join, **and never tire,**
  To sing immortal lays;
  And, with the bright, seraphic choir,
  Sound forth Immanuel's praise.

136. *"Whither shall I go from Thy Spirit?"*
  Psalm 139.

1 Lord, where shall guilty souls retire,
  Forgotten and unknown!

In hell they meet thy dreadful fire,
  In heaven thy glorious throne.

2 Should I suppress my vital breath,
  T' escape the wrath divine,
  Thy voice would break the bars of death,
  And make the grave resign.

3 If, winged with beams of morning light,
  I fly beyond the west,
  Thy hand which must support my flight,
  Would soon betray my rest.

4 If o'er my sins I think to draw
  The curtains of the night,
  Those flaming eyes that guard thy law
  Would turn the shades to light.

5 The beams of noon, the midnight hour,
  Are **both** alike to thee:
  Oh, may I ne'er provoke that power
  From which I can not flee!

155. *"Thrice Holy Lord."*

1 Holy and reverend is the name
  Of our eternal King;
  "Thrice holy Lord!" the angels cry;
  "Thrice holy!" let us sing.

2 The deepest reverence of the mind,
  Pay, O my soul! to God;
  Lift, with thy hands, a holy heart,
  To his sublime abode.

3 With sacred awe pronounce his name,
  Whom words nor thoughts can reach;
  A broken heart shall please him more
  Than noblest forms of speech.

4 Thou holy God! preserve my soul
  From all pollution free;
  The pure in heart are thy delight,
  And they thy face shall see.

FEDERAL STREET. L. M.

1192. *"Blessed are the dead who die in the Lord."—Rev. 14:13.*

1 How blest the righteous when he **dies!**
  When sinks a weary soul to rest!
  How mildly beam the closing eyes;
  How gently heaves th' expiring breast!

2 So fades a summer cloud away;
  So sinks the gale when storms are **o'er**;
  So gently shuts the eye of day;
  So dies a wave along the shore.

3 A holy quiet reigns around,
  A calm which life nor death destroys;
  And naught disturbs that peace profound,
  Which his unfettered soul enjoys.

4 Farewell, conflicting hopes and fears,
  Where lights and shades alternate dwell;
  How bright th' unchanging morn appears!
  Farewell, inconstant world, farewell!

5 Life's **labor** done, as sinks the clay,
  Light from its load the spirit flies,
  While heaven and earth combine to say,
  "How blest the righteous when he dies!"

1193. *"That they may rest from their labors."*
(Another form of the preceding Hymn.)

1 **Sweet** is the scene when Christians die,
  When holy souls retire to rest;
  How mildly beams the closing eye!
  How gently heaves th' expiring breast!

2 So fades a summer cloud away;
  So sinks the gale when storms are o'er;
  So gently shuts the eye of day;
  So dies a wave along the shore.

3 Triumphant **smiles** the victor's brow,
  Fanned by some guardian angel's wing;
  O Grave! where is thy victory now?
  And where, O Death! where is thy sting?

1194. *"So he giveth His beloved sleep."*

1 **Why** should we start, and fear to die!
  What timorous worms we mortals are!
  Death is the gate of endless joy,
  And yet we dread to enter there.

2 The pains, the groans of dying strife
  Fright our approaching souls away;
  We still shrink back again to life,
  Fond of our prison and our **clay.**

3 Oh, if my Lord would **come and meet**,
  My soul should stretch **her wings in** haste,
  Fly fearless through **death's iron gate,**
  Nor feel the terrors **as she passed!**

4 Jesus can make a dying bed
  Feel soft as downy pillows are,
  While on his breast I lean my head,
  And breathe my life out sweetly there!

1216. *"They are not lost, but gone before."*

1 **Dear** is the spot where Christians sleep,
  And sweet the strains their spirits pour;
  Oh, why should we in anguish **weep?**—
  They are not lost, but gone before.

2 Secure from every mortal care,
  By sin and sorrow vexed no more,
  Eternal happiness they share
  Who are not lost, but gone before.

3 To Zion's peaceful courts above
  In faith triumphant may we soar,
  Embracing, in the arms of love,
  The friends not lost, but gone before.

4 To Jordan's bank whene'er we come,
  And hear the swelling waters roar;
  Jesus! convey us safely home,
  To friends not lost, but gone before.

ALBEC. L. M. 6 LINES.

47. *The morning and evening Light.*

1 When, streaming from the eastern skies,
The morning light salutes mine eyes,
Oh Sun of righteousness divine,
On me with beams of mercy shine!
Oh! chase the clouds of guilt away,
And turn my darkness into day.

2 And when to heaven's all glorious King
My morning sacrifice I bring,
And, mourning o'er my guilt and shame,
Ask mercy in my Saviour's name:
Then, Jesus, cleanse me with thy blood,
And be my Advocate with God.

3 When each day's scenes and labors close,
And wearied nature seeks repose,
With pardoning mercy richly blest,
Guard me, my Saviour, while I rest;
And as each morning sun shall rise,
Oh, lead me onward to the skies!

4 And at my life's last setting sun,
My conflicts o'er, my labors done,
Jesus, thy heavenly radiance shed,
To cheer and bless my dying bed;
And, from death's gloom my spirit raise,
To see thy face, and sing thy praise.

219. *"I will fear no evil."*—Psalm 23.

1 The Lord my pasture shall prepare,
And feed me with a shepherd's care;
His presence my wants supply,
And guard me with a watchful eye:
My noon-day walks he shall attend,
And all my midnight hours defend.

2 When in the sultry glebe I faint,
Or on the thirsty mountain pant,
To fertile vales, and dewy meads,
My weary, wandering steps he leads;
Where peaceful rivers, soft and slow,
Amid the verdant landscape flow.

3 Though in the paths of death I tread,
With gloomy horrors overspread,
My steadfast heart shall fear no ill,
For thou, O Lord, art with me still;
Thy friendly rod shall give me aid,
And guide me through the dreadful shade.

4 Though in a bare and rugged way,
Through devious, lonely wilds I stray,
Thy presence shall my pains beguile:
The barren wilderness shall smile,
With sudden greens and herbage crown'd;
And streams shall murmur all around.

412. *"Jesus wept."*

1 When gathering clouds around I view,
And days are dark, and friends are few,
On him I lean, who not in vain
Experienced every human pain:
He sees my wants, allays my fears,
And counts and treasures up my tears.

2 If aught should tempt my soul to stray
From heavenly wisdom's narrow way,
To fly the good I would pursue,
Or do the ill I would not do;
Still he who felt temptation's power
Will guard me in that dangerous hour.

3 When sorrowing o'er some stone I bend,
Which covers all that was a friend,
And from his hand, his voice, his smile,
Divides me for a little while,
Thou, Saviour, seest the tears I shed,
For thou didst weep o'er Lazarus dead.

4 And, oh! when I have safely passed
Through every conflict but the last,
Still, still unchanging, watch beside
My painful bed, for thou hast died;
Then point to realms of cloudless day,
And wipe the latest tear away!

MOUNT VERNON. 8s & 7s.

1209. *"Weep not: She is not dead, but sleepeth."*

1 Sister, thou wast mild and lovely,
   Gentle as the summer breeze,
Pleasant as the air of evening,
   When it floats among the trees.

2 Peaceful be thy silent slumber—
   Peaceful in the grave so low:
Thou no more wilt join our number:
   Thou no more our songs shalt know.

3 Dearest sister! thou hast left us;
   Here thy loss we deeply feel;
But 't is God that hath bereft us,
   He can all our sorrows heal.

4 Yet again we hope to meet thee,
   When the day of life is fled:
Then in heaven with joy to greet thee,
   Where no farewell tear is shed!

1213. *"And there shall be no more death."*

1 Cease, ye mourners, cease to languish
   O'er the grave of those you love;
Pain and death, and night and anguish,
   Enter not the world above.

2 While our silent steps are straying
   Lonely thro' night's deepening shade,
Glory's brightest beams are playing
   Round the happy Christian's head.

3 Light and peace at once deriving,
   From the hand of God most high,
In his glorious presence living,
   They shall never, never die.

4 Now, ye mourners, cease to languish
   O'er the grave of those you love;
Far removed from pain and anguish,
   They are chanting hymns above.

AMOY. 6s & 4s.

515. *"To-day the Saviour calls."*—Heb 3: 15.

1 To-day the Saviour calls:
   Ye wanderers, come!
Oh, ye benighted souls,
   Why longer roam?

2 To-day the Saviour calls:
   Oh, listen now!
Within these sacred walls
   To Jesus bow.

3 To-day the Saviour calls:
   For refuge fly:
The storm of justice falls,
   And death is nigh.

4 The Spirit calls to-day:
   Yield to his power;
Oh, grieve him not away!
   'T is mercy's hour.

CLAYTON. 6s, 8s & 4.

315. The Name of Names.

1 Father, thy Son hath died
   The sinner's death of woe;
Stooping in love from heaven to earth,
   Our curse to undergo—
   Our curse to undergo,
   Upon the hateful tree:
Give glory to thy Son, O Lord!
Put honor in that Name of names
   By blessing me!

2 Father, thy Son hath poured
   His life-blood on this earth,
To cleanse away our guilt and stains,
   To give us second birth—
   To give us second birth,
   From sin to set us free:
Give glory to thy Son, O Lord!
Put honor in that Name of names
   By cleansing me!

3 Father, thy Son on earth
   No one to own him found;
He passed among the sons of men
   Rejected and disowned—
   Rejected and disowned,
   That we received might be:
Give glory to thy Son, O Lord!
Put honor on that Name of names
   By owning me!

4 Father, thy Son is king:
   Heaven's crown, and earth's is his!
For us, for us he bought the crown,
   For us he earned the bliss—
   For us he earned the bliss:
   Amen, so let it be!
Give glory to thy Son, O Lord!
Put honor on that Name of names
   By crowning me!

CHINA. C. M.

202. *"How are Thy servants blest, O Lord!"*

1 How are thy servants blest, O Lord!
 How sure is their defense!
 Eternal wisdom is their guide,
 Their help, omnipotence.

2 In foreign realms, and lands remote,
 Supported by thy care,
 Through burning climes they pass unhurt,
 And breathe in tainted air.

3 When by the dreadful tempest borne
 High on the broken wave,
 They know thou art not slow to hear,
 Nor impotent to save.

4 The storm is laid, the winds retire,
 Obedient to thy will;
 The sea, that roars at thy command,
 At thy command is still.

5 In midst of dangers, fears, and deaths,
 Thy goodness I'll adore;
 I'll praise thee for thy mercies past,
 And humbly hope for more.

6 My life, while thou preserv'st that life,
 Thy sacrifice shall be;
 And death, when death shall be my lot,
 Shall join my soul to thee.

1210. *"Having a desire to depart, and to be with Christ."*

1 Why do we mourn departing friends,
 Or shake at death's alarms?
 'T is but the voice that Jesus sends
 To call them to his arms.

2 Are we not tending upward, too,
 As fast as time can move?
 Nor would we wish the hours more slow
 To keep us from our love.

3 Why should we tremble to convey
 Their bodies to the tomb?
 There the dear flesh of Jesus lay,
 There hopes unfading bloom.

4 The graves of all his saints he blessed,
 And softened every bed;
 Where should the dying members rest,
 But with the dying Head?

5 Thence he arose, ascending high,
 And showed our feet the way;
 Up to the Lord our souls shall fly,
 At the great rising day.

6 Then let the last loud trumpet sound,
 And bid our kindred rise;
 Awake! ye nations under ground;
 Ye saints! ascend the skies.

1219. *"A name better than of sons and of daughters."*—Isaiah 56: 4, 5.

1 Ye mourning saints, whose streaming tears
 Flow o'er your children dead,
 Say not, in transports of despair,
 That all your hopes are fled.

2 While, cleaving to that darling dust,
 In fond distress ye lie,
 Rise, and with joy and reverence view
 A heavenly parent nigh.

3 Though, your young branches torn away,
 Like withered trunks ye stand;—
 With fairer verdure shall ye bloom,
 Touched by th' Almighty's hand.

4 I'll give the mourner," saith the Lord,
 "In my own house a place;
 No names of daughters and of sons
 Could yield so high a grace.

5 "Transient and vain is every hope
 A rising race can give;
 In endless honor and delight
 My children all shall live."

DUNFERMLINE. C. M.

6 We welcome, Lord, those rising tears,
  Through which thy face we see;
  And bless those wounds which through
    our hearts
  Prepare a way for thee.

1276. "*Behold, I show you a mystery.*"

1 THRO' sorrow's night, and danger's path,
  Amid the deepening gloom,
  We, followers of our suffering Lord,
  Are marching to the tomb.

2 There, when the turmoil is no more,
  And all our powers decay,
  Our cold remains in solitude
  Shall sleep the years away.

3 Our labors done, securely laid
  In this, our last retreat,
  Unheeded, o'er our silent dust,
  The storms of earth shall beat.

4 Yet not thus buried, or extinct,
  The vital spark shall lie,
  For, o'er life's wreck that spark shall rise,
  To seek its kindred sky.

5 These ashes, too, this little dust,
  Our Father's care shall keep,
  Till the last angel rise and break
  The long and dreary sleep.

6 Then love's soft dew o'er every eye
  Shall shed its mildest rays;
  And the long-silent voice awake
  With shouts of endless praise.

220. *Old Scotch Version of the Twenty-third Psalm.*

1 THE Lord's my shepherd, I'll not want:
  He makes me down to lie
  In pastures green; he leadeth me
  The quiet waters by.

2 My soul he doth restore again;
  And me to walk doth make
  Within the paths of righteousness,
  Ev'n for his own name's sake.

3 Yea, though I walk in death's dark vale,
  Yet will I fear no ill;
  For thou art with me, and thy rod
  And staff me comfort still.

4 My table thou hast furnishéd
  In presence of my foes;
  My head thou dost with oil anoint,
  And my cup overflows.

5 Goodness and mercy, all my life,
  Shall surely follow me;
  And in God's house, for evermore
  My dwelling-place shall be.

303. "*My Jesus and my God.*"

1 DEAREST of all the names above,
  My Jesus and my God,
  Who can resist thy heavenly love,
  Or trifle with thy blood?

2 'T is by the merits of thy death
  Thy Father smiles again;
  'T is by thine interceding breath
  The Spirit dwells with men.

3 Till God in human flesh I see,
  My thoughts no comfort find;
  The holy, just, and sacred Three
  Are terror to my mind.

4 But if Immanuel's face appear,
  My hope, my joy, begin;
  His name forbids my slavish fear;
  His grace removes my sin.

5 While Jews on their own law rely,
  And Greeks of wisdom boast,
  I love th' incarnate Mystery,
  And there I fix my trust.

SHERMAN. S. M.

550. *Way of Sin not the Way to Heaven.*

1 Can sinners hope for heaven,
   Who love this world so well?
   Or dream of future happiness,
   While on the road to hell?

2 Shall they hosannahs sing,
   With an unhallowed tongue?
   Shall palms adorn the guilty hand
   Which does its neighbor wrong?

3 Can sin's deceitful way
   Conduct to Zion's hill?
   Or those expect with God to reign
   Who disregard his will?

4 Thy grace, O God, alone,
   Good hope can e'er afford!
   The pardoned and the pure shall see
   The glory of the Lord.

1169. *"Now is our salvation nearer than when we believed."*

1 One sweetly solemn thought
   Comes to me o'er and o'er,
   Nearer my parting hour am I
   Than e'er I was before.

2 Nearer my Father's house,
   Where many mansions be;
   Nearer the throne where Jesus reigns,—
   Nearer the crystal sea;

3 Nearer my going home,
   Laying my burden down,
   Leaving my cross of heavy grief,
   Wearing my starry crown;

4 Nearer that hidden stream,
   Winding through shades of night,
   Rolling its cold, dark waves between
   Me and the world of light.

5 Jesus! to thee I cling:
   Strengthen my arm of faith;
   Stay near me while my way-worn feet
   Press through the stream of death.

1178. *"Whoso believeth in Me shall never die."*

1 It is not death to die—
   To leave this weary road,
   And, 'mid the brotherhood on high,
   To be at home with God.

2 It is not death to close
   The eye long dimmed by tears,
   And wake, in glorious repose,
   To spend eternal years.

3 It is not death to bear
   The wrench that sets us free
   From dungeon chain,—to breathe the air
   Of boundless liberty.

4 It is not death to fling
   Aside this sinful dust,
   And rise, on strong, exulting wing,
   To live among the just.

5 Jesus, thou Prince of life!
   Thy chosen can not die;
   Like thee, they conquer in the strife,
   To reign with thee on high.

1207. *"At midnight there was a cry made."*

1 Servant of God, well done!
   Rest from thy loved employ:
   The battle fought, the victory won,
   Enter thy Master's joy.

2 The voice at midnight came;
   He started up to hear:
   A mortal arrow pierced his frame;
   He fell, but felt no fear.

3 At midnight came the cry,
   "To meet thy God prepare!"
   He woke,—and caught his Captain's eye;
   Then, strong in faith and prayer,

FIELD. S. M.

4 His spirit with a bound
   Left its encumbering clay:
 His tent, at sunrise, on the ground
   A darkened ruin lay.

5 The pains of death are past;
   Labor and sorrow cease;
 And life's long warfare closed at last,
   His soul is found in peace.

6 Soldier of Christ, well done!
   Praise be thy new employ;
 And while eternal ages run,
   Rest in thy Saviour's joy.

1271. "*My flesh also shall rest in hope.*"

1 Rest for the toiling hand,
   Rest for the anxious brow,
 Rest for the weary, way-worn feet,
   Rest from all labor now;—

2 Rest for the fevered brain,
   Rest for the throbbing eye;

Through these parched lips of thine no
   more
 Shall pass the moan or sigh.

3 Soon shall the trump of God
   Give out the welcome sound,
 That shakes thy silent chamber-walls,
   And breaks the turf-sealed ground.

5 Ye dwellers in the dust
   Awake! come forth and sing;
 Sharp has your frost of winter been,
   But bright shall be your spring.

5 'T was sown in weakness here;
   'T will then be raised in power:
 That which was sown an earthly seed,
   Shall rise a heavenly flower!

DOXOLOGY.

The Father and the Son
   And Spirit we adore;
 We praise, we bless, we worship thee,
   Both now and evermore!

BONAR. S. M. DOUBLE.

ELIZABETHTOWN. C. M.

1056. *"Meet and remember Me."*
Luke 22: 19.

1 If human kindness meets return,
  And owns the grateful tie;
  If tender thoughts within us burn,
  To feel a friend is nigh:

2 Oh, shall not warmer accents tell
  The gratitude we owe
  To him who died our fears to quell—
  Our more than orphan's woe?

3 While yet in anguish he surveyed
  Those pangs he would not flee,
  What love his latest words displayed:
  "Meet and remember me!"

4 Remember thee!—thy death, thy shame!
  Our sinful hearts to share!
  O memory! leave no other name
  But his recorded there.

1057. *"Even the death of the cross."*

1 How condescending and how kind
  Was God's eternal Son!
  Our misery reached his heavenly mind,
  And pity brought him down.

2 He sank beneath our heavy woes,
  To raise us to his throne;
  There's ne'er a gift his hand bestows,
  But cost his heart a groan.

3 This was compassion like a God—
  That, when the Saviour knew
  The price of pardon was his blood,
  His pity ne'er withdrew.

4 Now, though he reigns exalted high,
  His love is still as great;
  Well he remembers Calvary,
  Nor let his saints forget.

5 Here let our hearts begin to melt,
  While we his death record,

And, with our joy for pardoned guilt,
  Mourn that we pierced the Lord.

1165. *"As a flower of the field, so he flourisheth."*

1 Let others boast how strong they be,
  Nor death nor danger fear;
  But we confess, O Lord! to thee,
  What feeble things we are.

2 Fresh as the grass our bodies stand,
  And flourish bright and gay:
  A blasting wind sweeps o'er the land,
  And fades the grass away.

3 Our life contains a thousand springs,
  And dies, if one be gone;
  Strange that a harp of thousand strings
  Should keep in tune so long!

4 But 't is our God supports our frame—
  The God who made us first;
  Salvation to th' Almighty Name
  That reared us from the dust!

1171. *"It is appointed unto men once to die."*

1 If I must die, oh! let me die
  With hope in Jesus' blood—
  The blood that saves from sin and guilt,
  And reconciles to God.

2 If I must die, then let me die
  In peace with all mankind,
  And change these fleeting joys below
  For pleasures all refined.

3 If I must die—and die I shall!—
  Let some kind seraph come,
  And bear me on his friendly wing
  To my celestial home.

4 Of Canaan's land, from Pisgah's top,
  May I but have a view,
  Though Jordan should o'erflow its banks,
  I'll boldly venture through.

EVAN. C. M.

1180. *"When blooming youth is snatched away."*

1 When blooming youth is snatched away
By death's resistless hand,
Our hearts the mournful tribute pay
Which pity must demand.

2 While pity prompts the rising sigh,
Oh, may this truth, impressed
With awful power, "I, too, must die,"
Sink deep in every breast!

3 Let this vain world engage no more:
Behold the opening tomb!
It bids us seize the present hour;
To-morrow, death may come.

4 Oh, let us fly—to Jesus fly!
Whose powerful arm can save;
Then shall our hopes ascend on high,
And triumph o'er the grave.

5 Great God! thy sovereign grace impart,
With cleansing, healing power;
This only can prepare the heart
For death's surprising hour.

1196. *"There the weary be at rest."*
Job 3: 17-20.

1 How still and peaceful is the grave!
Where life's vain tumults past,
Th' appointed house, by heaven's decree,
Receives us all at last.

2 The wicked there from troubling cease;
Their passions rage no more;
And there the weary pilgrim rests
From all the toils he bore.

3 There rest the prisoners now released
From slavery's sad abode;
No more they hear th' oppressor's voice,
Or dread the tyrant's rod.

4 There, servants, masters, small and great,
Partake the same repose;

And there, in peace, the ashes mix
Of those who once were foes.

5 All, leveled by the hand of death,
Lie sleeping in the tomb,
Till God in judgment calls them forth
To meet their final doom.

1201. *"What is your life?"*

1 Life is a span—a fleeting hour:
How soon the vapor flies!
Man is a tender, transient flower,
That ev'n in blooming—dies.

2 The once loved form, now cold and dead,
Each mournful thought employs;
And nature weeps her comforts fled,
And withered all her joys.

3 Hope looks beyond the bounds of time,
When what we now deplore
Shall rise in full, immortal prime,
And bloom to fade no more.

4 Cease, then, fond nature, cease thy tears!
Religion points on high;
There everlasting spring appears,
And joys that can not die.

1212. *"And their works do follow them."*
Rev. 14: 13.

1 Hear what the voice from heaven proclaims
For all the pious dead;
Sweet is the savor of their names,
And soft their sleeping bed.

2 They die in Jesus, and are blest!
How kind their slumbers are!
From sufferings and from sin released,
And freed from every snare.

3 Far from this world of toil and strife,
They're present with the Lord;
The labors of their mortal life
End in a large reward.

BERNE. L. M.

471. *Salvation sought from the Trinity.*

1 FATHER of heaven! whose love profound
A ransom for our souls hath found,
Before thy throne we sinners bend:
To us thy pardoning love extend.

2 Almighty Son! incarnate Word!
Our Prophet, Priest, Redeemer, Lord!
Before thy throne we sinners bend:
To us thy saving grace extend.

3 Eternal Spirit! by whose breath
The soul is raised from sin and death,
Before thy throne we sinners bend:
To us thy quickening power extend.

4 Jehovah! Father, Spirit, Son!
Mysterious Godhead! Three in One!
Before thy throne we sinners bend:
Grace, pardon, life, to us extend!

530. *"Come to Me."*—Matt. 11 : 28–30.

1 WITH tearful eyes I look around;
Life seems a dark and stormy sea;
Yet, 'mid the gloom, I hear a sound,
A heavenly whisper, "Come to me."

2 It tells me of a place of rest:
It tells me where my soul may flee:
Oh, to the weary, faint, oppressed,
How sweet the bidding, "Come to me!"

3 "Come, for all else must fail and die;
Earth is no resting-place for thee;
To heaven direct thy weeping eye,
I am thy portion; come to me."

4 O voice of mercy! voice of love!
In conflict, grief, and agony,
Support me, cheer me from above!
And gently whisper, "Come to me."

556. *"God calling yet."*

1 God calling yet!—shall I not hear?
Earth's pleasures shall I still hold dear?
Shall life's swift passing years all fly,
And still my soul in slumbers lie?

2 God calling yet!—shall I not rise?
Can I his loving voice despise,
And basely his kind care repay?
He calls me still: can I delay?

3 God calling yet!—and shall he knock,
And I my heart the closer lock?
He still is waiting to receive,
And shall I dare his Spirit grieve?

4 God calling yet!—and shall I give
No heed, but still in bondage live?
I wait, but he does not forsake;
He calls me still!—my heart awake!

5 God calling yet!—I can not stay;
My heart I yield without delay:
Vain world, farewell! from thee I part;
The voice of God hath reached my heart!

718. *"Ye are not your own."*—1 Cor. 6 : 19.

1 OH, not my own these verdant hills
And fruits and flowers and stream and wood;
But his who all with glory fills,
Who bought me with his precious blood.

2 Oh, not my own this wondrous frame,
Its curious work, its living soul;
But his who for my ransom came:
Slain for my sake, he claims the whole.

3 Oh, not my own the grace that keeps
My feet from fierce temptations free;
Oh, not my own the thought that leaps,
Adoring, blessèd Lord, to thee!

4 "Oh, not my own!" I'll soar and sing,
When life, with all its toils, is o'er,
And thou thy trembling lamb shalt bring
Safe home, to wander never more.

PILESGROVE. L. M.

5. *"Praise waiteth for Thee, O God, in Zion."*
Psalm 65.

1 For thee, O God, our constant praise
In Zion waits, thy chosen seat;
Our promised altars there we'll raise,
And all our zealous vows complete.

2 O thou who to our humble prayer
Didst always bend thy listening ear,
To thee shall all mankind repair,
And at thy gracious throne appear.

3 Our sins, though numberless, in vain,
To stop thy flowing mercy try;
For grace shall cleanse the guilty stain,
And wash away the crimson dye.

4 How blest the man, who, near thee placed,
Within thy heavenly dwelling lives!
While we, at humbler distance, taste
The vast delights thy temple gives.

781. *Trust in Christ at the Hour of Death.*

1 Jesus, in whom but thee above
Can I repose my trust, my love?
And shall an earthly object be
Loved in comparison with thee?

2 How soon, O Lord, will life decay!
How soon this world will pass away!
Ah! what can mortal friends avail,
When heart and strength and life shall fail?

3 Oh, then, be thou, my Saviour, nigh,
And I will triumph while I die;
My strength, my portion, is divine,
And Jesus is for ever mine!

855. *"In whom we have boldness."*

1 Where high the heavenly temple stands,
The house of God not made with hands,

A great High Priest our nature wears,—
The Guardian of mankind appears.

2 Though now ascended up on high,
He bends on earth a brother's eye;
Partaker of the human name,
He knows the frailty of our frame.

3 Our Fellow-sufferer yet retains
A fellow-feeling of our pains;
And still remembers, in the skies,
His tears, his agonies, and cries.

4 In every pang that rends the heart
The Man of sorrows had a part;
He sympathizes in our grief,
And to the sufferer sends relief.

5 With boldness, therefore, at the throne,
Let us make all our sorrows known;
And ask the aid of heavenly power
To help us in the evil hour.

1003. *"Ye have put on Christ."*—Gal. 3: 27.

1 Jesus! thy blood and righteousness
My beauty are, my glorious dress;
'Mid flaming worlds, in these arrayed,
With joy shall I lift up my head.

2 When from the dust of earth I rise
To claim my mansion in the skies,
E'en then shall this be all my plea:
"Jesus hath lived and died for me."

3 This spotless robe the same appears,
When ruined nature sinks in years;
No age can change its glorious hue,—
The robe of Christ is ever new.

4 Oh, let the dead now hear thy voice,
Now bid thy banished ones rejoice;
Their beauty this, their glorious dress—
Jesus! thy blood and righteousness!

MARLOW. C. M.

500. *Conviction by the Law.*—Rom. 7 : 9.

1 Lord, how secure my conscience was,
  And felt no inward dread!
 I was alive without the law,
  And thought my sins were dead.

2 My hopes of heaven were firm and bright,
  But since the precept came
 With such convincing power and light,
  I find how vile I am.

3 My guilt appeared but small before,
  Till I with terror saw
 How perfect, holy, just, and pure
  Is thine eternal law.

4 Then felt my soul the heavy load;
  My sins revived again:
 I had provoked a dreadful God,
  And all my hopes were slain.

5 My God! I cry with every breath,
  For some kind power to save;
 Oh, break the yoke of sin and death,
  And thus redeem the slave.

513. *"He will abundantly pardon."* Isaiah 55 : 7, 8.

1 Sinners, the voice of God regard;
  His mercy speaks to-day:
 He calls you, by his sovereign word,
  From sin's destructive way.

2 Why will you in the crooked ways
  Of sin and folly go?
 In pain you travel all your days,
  To reap eternal woe!

3 But he that turns to God shall live,
  Through his abounding grace;
 His mercy will the guilt forgive
  Of those who seek his face.

4 His love exceeds your highest thoughts;
  He pardons like a God;
 He will forgive your numerous faults
  Through a Redeemer's blood.

939. *"Lord, remember me."*—Luke 23 : 42.

1 O thou, from whom all goodness flows,
  I lift my soul to thee;
 In all my sorrows, conflicts, woes,
  O Lord, remember me!

2 When on my aching, burdened heart,
  My sins lie heavily,
 Thy pardon grant, new peace impart;
  Then, Lord, remember me!

3 When trials sore obstruct my way,
  And ills I can not flee,
 Oh, let my strength be as my day—
  Dear Lord, remember me!

4 When in the solemn hour of death
  I wait thy just decree;
 Be this the prayer of my last breath:
  Now, Lord, remember me!

5 And when before thy throne I stand,
  And lift my soul to thee,
 Then with the saints at thy right hand,
  O Lord, remember me!

954. *"Unto the Lord did I make my supplication."*—Psalm 142.

1 To God I made my sorrows known;
  From God I sought relief;
 In long complaints before his throne
  I poured out all my grief.

2 On every side I cast mine eye,
  And found my helpers gone;
 While friends and strangers passed me by,
  Neglected or unknown.

3 Then did I raise a louder cry,
  And called thy mercy near:
 "Thou art my Portion when I die,
  Be thou my Refuge here!"

HERMON. C. M.

4 Lord! I am brought exceeding low;
  Now let thine ear attend,
  And make my foes, who vex me, know
  I've an almighty Friend.

1173. *"Be not dismayed, for I am thy God."*

1 Thou must go forth alone, my soul!
  Thou must go forth alone,
  To other scenes, to other worlds,
  That mortal hath not known.

2 Thou must go forth alone, my soul,
  To tread the narrow vale;
  But he, whose word is sure, hath said
  His mercy shall not fail.

3 Thou must go forth alone, my soul,
  To meet thy God above;
  But shrink not—he has said, my soul,
  He is a God of love!

4 His rod and staff shall comfort thee
  Across the dreary road,
  Till thou shalt join the blessed ones
  In heaven's serene abode.

1174. *"I must die alone."*

1 That solemn hour will come for me,
  When, though their charms I own,
  All human ties resigned must be;
  For I must die alone.

2 All earthly pleasures will be o'er,
  All earthly labors done,
  And I shall tread th' eternal shore,
  And I must die alone!

3 But, oh, I will not view with dread
  That shadowy vale unknown;
  I see a light within it shed;
  I shall not die alone!

4 One will be with me there, whose voice
  I long have loved and known;

  To die is now my wish, my choice:
  I shall not die alone!

1185. *"Forsake me not when my strength faileth."*

1 When bending o'er the brink of life
  My trembling soul shall stand,
  Waiting to pass death's awful flood,
  Great God! at thy command;

2 O thou great Source of joy supreme!
  Whose arm alone can save,
  Dispel the darkness that surrounds
  The entrance to the grave.

3 Lay thy supporting, gentle hand
  Beneath my sinking head,
  And, with a ray of love divine,
  Illume my dying bed.

1197. *"In Christ shall all be made alive."*

1 When downward to the darksome tomb
  I thoughtful turn my eyes,
  Frail nature trembles at the gloom,
  And anxious fears arise.

2 Why shrinks my soul?—in death's embrace
  Once Jesus captive slept;
  And angels, hovering o'er the place,
  His lowly pillow kept.

3 Thus shall they guard my sleeping dust,
  And, as the Saviour rose,
  The grave again shall yield her trust,
  And end my deep repose.

4 My Lord, before to glory gone,
  Shall bid me come away;
  And calm and bright shall break the dawn
  Of heaven's eternal day.

5 Then let my faith each fear dispel,
  And gild with light the grave;
  To him my loftiest praises swell,
  Who died from death to save.

UNWIN. 8s & 4.

149. *"God is Love."*—1 John 4: 8.

1 I can not always trace the way
  Where thou, almighty One, dost move;
But I can always, always say
  That God is love.

2 When fear her chilling mantle flings
  O'er earth, my soul to heaven above,
As to her native home, upsprings;
  For God is love.

3 When myst'ry clouds my darkened path,
  I'll check my dread, my doubts reprove;
In this my soul sweet comfort hath,
  That God is love.

4 Oh may this truth my heart employ,
  Bid every gloomy thought remove,
And turn all tears, all woes to joy,—
  Thou, God, art Love.

929. *"Thy will be done."*—Matt. 6: 10.

1 My God, my Father, while I stray
  Far from thy home, on life's rough way,
Oh, teach me from my heart to say,
  "Thy will be done!"

2 What though in lonely grief I sigh
  For friends beloved no longer nigh;
Submissive still would I reply,
  "Thy will be done!"

3 If thou shouldst call me to resign
  What most I prize,—it ne'er was mine;
I only yield thee what was thine:
  "Thy will be done!"

4 If but my fainting heart be blest
  With thy sweet Spirit for its guest,
My God, to thee I leave the rest:
  "Thy will be done!"

5 Renew my will from day to day;
  Blend it with thine, and take away
Whate'er now makes it hard to say,
  "Thy will be done!"

6 Then when on earth I breathe no more,
  The prayer oft mixed with tears before,
I'll sing upon a happier shore:
  "Thy will be done!"

1108. *"There is a calm for those who weep."*

1 There is a calm for those who weep,
  A rest for weary pilgrims found;
They softly lie, and sweetly sleep,
  Low in the ground.

2 The storm that racks the wint'ry sky,
  No more disturbs their deep repose
Than summer evening's latest sigh,
  That shuts the rose.

3 I long to lay this painful head
  And aching heart beneath the soil;
To slumber, in that dreamless bed,
  From all my toil.

4 The soul, of origin divine,
  God's glorious image, freed from clay,
In heaven's eternal sphere shall shine,
  A star of day.

5 The sun is but a spark of fire,
  A transient meteor in the sky;
The soul immortal as its Sire,
  Shall never die.

BATES. 5s & 6s. Or 11s.

3. *Third Version of the Lord's Prayer.*

1 Our Father in heaven, We hallow thy name!
  May thy kingdom holy On earth be the same!
  Oh, give to us daily Our portion of bread:
  It is from thy bounty That all must be fed.

2 Forgive our transgressions, And teach us to know
  That humble compassion Which pardons each foe;
  Keep us from temptation, From evil and sin,
  And thine be the glory For ever! Amen!

522. *"Acquaint now thyself with Him."*—Job 22: 21.

1 Acquaint thee, O mortal, acquaint thee with God,
  And joy, like the sunshine, shall beam on thy road;
  And peace, like the dew-drop, shall fall on thy head;
  And sleep, like an angel, shall visit thy bed.

2 Acquaint thee, O mortal, acquaint thee with God,
  And he shall be with thee when fears are abroad;
  Thy safeguard in danger that threatens thy path;
  Thy joy in the valley and shadow of death.

1176.* *"I would not live alway."*—Job 7: 16.

1 I would not live alway: I ask not to stay
  Where storm after storm rises dark o'er the way;
  The few lurid mornings that dawn on us here
  Are enough for life's woes, full enough for its cheer.

2 I would not live alway: no, welcome the tomb!
  Since Jesus hath lain there, I dread not its gloom;
  There sweet be my rest, till he bid me arise
  To hail him in triumph descending the skies.

3 Who, who would live alway, away from his God,
  Away from yon heaven, that blissful abode,
  Where the rivers of pleasure flow o'er the bright plains,
  And the noontide of glory eternally reigns;

4 Where the saints of all ages in harmony meet,
  Their Saviour and brethren transported to greet;
  While the anthems of rapture unceasingly roll,
  And the smile of the Lord is the feast of the soul!

* The small notes will be required in singing this Hymn. See also page 456.

WINCHESTER. L. M.

208. *"Return unto thy rest, O my soul!"*
Psalm 116.

1 RETURN, my soul, and sweetly rest
On thy almighty Father's breast;
The bounties of his grace adore,
And count his wondrous mercies o'er.

2 Thy mercy, Lord, preserved my breath,
And snatched my fainting soul from death;
Removed my sorrows, dried my tears,
And saved me from surrounding snares.

3 What shall I render to the Lord?
Or how his wondrous grace record?
To him my grateful voice I'll raise,
With just thanksgiving to his praise.

4 O Zion! in thy sacred courts,
Where glory dwells, and joy resorts,
To notes divine I'll tune the song,
And praise shall flow from every tongue.

788. *The hidden Life.*

1 OH that I could for ever dwell,
Delighted at the Saviour's feet;
Behold the form I love so well,
And all his tender words repeat!

2 The world shut out from all my soul,
And heaven brought in with all its bliss,
Oh! is there aught, from pole to pole,
One moment to compare with this?

3 This is the hidden life I prize—
A life of penitential love;
When most my follies I despise,
And raise my highest thoughts above;

4 When all I am I clearly see,
And freely own with deepest shame:
When the Redeemer's love to me
Kindles within a deathless flame.

5 Thus would I live till nature fail,
And all my former sins forsake;
Then rise to God within the vail,
And of eternal joys partake.

1215. *"Why should we weep for those who die!"*

1 WHY should we weep for those who die?
Those blessed ones who weep no more?
Jesus hath called them to the sky,
And gladly have they gone before.

2 A few short days they lingered here,
Th' appointed span of trial knew;
Dropped—early dropped the parting tear,
And early now have parted, too.

3 Up, up, in swift ascent, they rise,
Star after star of living light!
Why should we mourn that midnight skies
Become with added glories bright?

4 Far in the distant heavens they shine,
But still with borrowed luster glow:
Saviour, the beams are only thine,
Of saints above, or saints below.

5 For them no bitter tears we shed,—
Their night of pain and grief is o'er,—
But weep our lonely path to tread,
And see the forms we loved, no more.

1244. *"One in our hope of rest above."*

1 STILL one in life and one in death,
One in our hope of rest above;
One in our joy, our trust, our faith,
One in each other's faithful love.

2 Yet must we part, and, parting, weep;
What else has earth for us in store?
Our farewell pangs, how sharp and deep!
Our farewell words, how sad and sore!

ROSEDALE. L. M.

3 Yet shall we meet again in peace,
To sing the song of festal joy,
Where none shall bid our gladness cease,
And none our fellowship destroy.

4 Where none shall beckon us away,
Nor bid our festival be done;
Our meeting-time th' eternal day,
Our meeting-place th' eternal throne.

5 There, hand in hand, firm-linked at last,
And, heart to heart, enfolded all,
We 'll smile upon the troubled past,
And wonder why we wept at all.

691. *"I love the Lord who died for me."*
1 John 4: 19.

1 I LOVE the Lord who died for me;
I love his grace divine and free;
I love his word, for there I read
That he loved me, and for me bled.

2 I love to hear that he was slain;
I love his every grief and pain;
I love to think on him by faith,
And muse upon his cruel death.

3 I love his people and their ways;
I love with them to pray and praise;
I love the Father and the Son;
I love the Spirit he sent down.

4 I love to think the time will come
When I shall be with him at home,—
When I shall love as he loves me,
And praise him through eternity.

1010. *"In my Father's house are many mansions."*—John 14: 2.

1 THY Father's house!—thine own bright home!
And thou hast there a place for me!
Though yet an exile here I roam,
That distant home by faith I see.

2 I see its domes resplendent glow,
Where beams of God's own glory fall;
And trees of life immortal grow,
Whose fruits o'erhang the sapphire wall.

3 I know that thou, who on the tree
Didst deign our mortal guilt to bear,
Wilt bring thine own to dwell with thee,
And waitest to receive me there!

4 Thy love will there array my soul
In thine own robe of spotless hue;
And I shall gaze, while ages roll,
On thee, with raptures ever new!

5 Oh, welcome day! when thou my feet
Shalt bring the shining threshold o'er;
A Father's warm embrace to meet,
And dwell at home for evermore!

1041. *"Jesus, thine own Messiah, reigns."*

1 WHY, on the bending willows hung,
Israel! still sleeps thy tuneful string?—
Still mute remains thy sullen tongue,
And Zion's song denies to sing?

2 Awake! thy sweetest raptures raise;
Let harp and voice unite their strains;
Thy promised King his scepter sways;
Jesus, thine own Messiah, reigns!

3 No taunting foes the song require;
No strangers mock thy captive chain;
But friends provoke the silent lyre,
And brethren ask the holy strain.

4 Nor fear thy Salem's hills to wrong,
If other lands thy triumph share;
A heavenly city claims thy song;
A brighter Salem rises there.

5 By foreign streams no longer roam;
Nor, weeping, think of Jordan's flood;
In every clime behold a home,
In every temple see thy God.

MARLOW. C. M.

856. *What is Prayer?*

1 Prayer is the soul's sincere desire,
 Uttered or unexpressed;
 The motion of a hidden fire
 That trembles in the breast.

2 Prayer is the burden of a sigh,
 The falling of a tear,
 The upward glancing of an eye,
 When none but God is near.

3 Prayer is the simplest form of speech
 That infant lips can try;
 Prayer, the sublimest strains that reach
 The Majesty on high.

4 Prayer is the contrite sinner's voice,
 Returning from his ways;
 While angels in their songs rejoice,
 And cry, "Behold, he prays!"

5 Prayer is the Christian's vital breath,
 The Christian's native air,
 His watchword at the gates of death:
 He enters heaven with prayer.

6 O thou, by whom we come to God,
 The Life, the Truth, the Way!
 The path of prayer thyself hast trod;
 Lord! teach us how to pray.

1013. *"Wherefore do ye spend money for that which is not bread?"*

1 In vain we lavish out our lives
 To gather empty wind;
 The choicest blessings earth can yield
 Will starve a hungry mind.

2 But God can every want supply,
 And fill our hearts with peace;
 He gives by cov'nant, and by oath,
 The riches of his grace.

3 Come, and he'll cleanse our spotted souls,
 And wash away our stains

In that dear fountain which his Son
 Poured from his dying veins.

4 There shall his sacred Spirit dwell,
 And deep engrave his law;
 And every motion of our souls
 To swift obedience draw.

5 Thus will he pour salvation down,
 And we shall render praise,—
 We, the dear people of his love,
 And he, our God of grace.

1097. *"Do it heartily as to the Lord, and not unto men."*

1 Not only when ascends the song,
 And soundeth sweet the word,—
 Not only 'mid the Sabbath throng,
 Our souls would seek the Lord;

2 For, while we every yoke would break,
 And every captive free,
 And every sluggish soul awake,—
 Lord, we are seeking thee!

3 Oh, mean may seem the work we do,
 And vile the name we earn;
 But thou, O Lord, dost search us through,
 Our loyal hearts discern.

4 We lose, we lack, that men may gain,
 We suffer, and we smile:
 But why this joy amid the pain?
 We seek our Lord the while!

5 Oh, everywhere, oh, every day,
 Thy grace is still outpoured;
 We work, we wait, we smile, we pray—
 Behold, we seek thee, Lord!

1190. *"And the city had no need of the sun."*

1 Ye golden lamps of heaven! farewell,
 With all your feeble light;
 Farewell, thou ever-changing moon,
 Pale empress of the night!

BROOKLYN. C. M. DOUBLE.

2 And thou refulgent orb of day,
  In brighter flames arrayed,
  My soul, that springs beyond thy sphere,
  No more demands thine aid.
3 Ye stars are but the shining dust
  Of my divine abode;
  The pavement of those heavenly courts,
  Where I shall reign with God.
4 The Father of eternal light
  Shall there his beams display;
  Nor shall one moment's darkness mix
  With that unvaried day.
5 No more the drops **of piercing grief**
  Shall swell into my **eyes**;
  Nor the meridian sun **decline**
  Amid those brighter skies.
6 There all the millions **of his saints**
  Shall in **one song unite,**
  And each the **bliss of all shall view,**
  With infinite **delight.**

1199. "*He fell asleep.*"

1 BEHOLD the western evening light!
  It melts in evening gloom;
  So calmly Christians sink away,
  Descending to the tomb.
2 The winds breathe low, the withering leaf
  Scarce whispers from the tree;
  So gently flows **the** parting breath,
  When good **men** cease to be.
3 How beautiful on all the hills
  The crimson **light** is shed!
  'T is like the peace the Christian gives
  To mourners round his bed.
4 How mildly on the wandering cloud
  The sunset beam is cast!
  'T is like the memory left behind,
  When loved ones breathe their last.

5 And **now above the dews of night**
  The rising star appears;
  So faith springs in the hearts of those
  Whose eyes are bathed in tears.
6 But soon the morning's happier light
  Its glory shall restore,
  And eyelids that are sealed **in death**
  Shall wake to close no more.

1240. "*Caught up together with them in the clouds.*"

1 HOPE of our hearts! O Lord, appear,
  Thou glorious Star of day!
  Shine forth, and chase **the** dreary night,
  And all our fears away.
2 Strangers on earth we wait **for** thee:
  Oh, leave the Father's throne!
  Come with a shout of victory, Lord,
  And claim us as thine own!
3 Oh, bid the bright archangel then
  The trump of God prepare,
  To call thy saints, the quick, the dead,
  To meet thee in the air!
4 No resting-place we seek on earth,
  No loveliness we see;
  Our eye is on the royal crown
  Prepared for us and thee,
5 But, oh! the thought of sharing, **Lord,**
  Thy glorious throne above,
  What is it to the brighter hope
  Of dwelling in thy love.

DOXOLOGY.

LET God the Father, and the Son,
  And Spirit, be adored,
  Where there are works to make him
    known,
  Or saints to love the Lord!

BOND. C. M. DOUBLE.

597. *"Have mercy upon me, O God!"*
Psalm 51.

1 TURN not thy face away, O **Lord**!
 From them that lowly lie,
Lamenting sore their sinful life
 With tears and bitter cry
Thy mercy-gate **stands** open wide
 To them that mourn their sin;
Shut not that gate against **us**, Lord!
 But let us enter in.

2 Thou knowest, Lord, what things be past
 And all the things that be;
Thou knowest well what is to come;
 There's nothing hid from thee:
So press we to thy mercy-gate,
 Where mercy doth abound,
Imploring pardon for our sin
 To heal our deadly wound.

3 O Lord! we need not to repeat
 What we do beg and crave,
For thou dost know, before we ask,
 The blessing we would have.
Mercy, O Lord! we mercy seek;
 This is the height and sum;
For mercy, Lord, is all our prayer,
 Oh, let thy mercy come!

985. *"Renew my broken vow."*

1 How long the time since Christ **began**
 To call in vain on me!
Deaf to his warning voice, I ran
 Through paths of vanity.
2 He called me when my thoughtless prime
 Was early **ripe** to ill;
I passed from folly on to crime,
 And yet he called me still.
3 He called me in **the time of dread**,
 When death was full in view;

I trembled on my feverish **bed**,
 And rose to sin anew.
4 Yet could I hear him once again,
 As I have heard of old,
Methinks he should not call in vain
 His wanderer to the fold.

5 O thou, who every thought dost know,
 And answerest every prayer!
Try me with sickness, **want**, or woe,
 But snatch me from despair.
6 My struggling will by grace control;
 Renew my broken vow:
What blessed light breaks on my soul!
 My God! I hear thee now.

1012. *"According to His mercy He saved us."*—Titus 3: 5–7.

1 LORD, we confess our numerous faults,
 How great our guilt has been;
Foolish and vain were all our thoughts,
 And all our lives were sin.
2 But, O my soul! for ever praise,
 For ever love his name,
Who turns thy feet from dangerous ways
 Of folly, sin, and shame.
3 'T is not by works of righteousness,
 Which our own hands have done;
But we are saved by sovereign grace,
 Abounding through his Son.
4 'T is from the mercy of our God,
 That all our hopes begin;
'T is by the water, and the blood,
 Our souls are washed from sin.
5 'T is through the purchase of his death
 Who hung upon the tree,
The Spirit is sent down to breathe
 On such dry bones as we.
6 Raised from the dead, we live anew;
 And, justified by grace,
We shall appear in glory, too,
 And see our Father's face.

DOWNS. C. M.

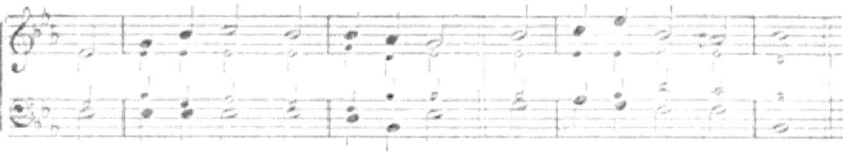

1050. *"This do in remembrance of Me."*
Luke 22: 19.

1 According to thy gracious word,
  In meek humility,
This will I do, my dying Lord!
  I will remember thee.

2 Thy body, broken for my sake,
  My bread from heaven shall be;
Thy testamental cup I take,
  And thus remember thee.

3 Gethsemane can I forget?
  Or there thy conflict see,
Thine agony and bloody sweat—
  And not remember thee?

4 When to the cross I turn my eyes,
  And rest on Calvary,
O Lamb of God! my Sacrifice,
  I must remember thee!

5 Remember thee, and all thy pains,
  And all thy love to me—
Yea, while a breath, a pulse remains
  Will I remember thee!

6 And when these failing lips grow dumb,
  And mind and memory flee,
When thou shalt in thy kingdom come,
  Jesus, remember me!

608. *"I abhor myself, and repent in dust and ashes."*

1 Dear Saviour, when my thoughts recall
  The wonders of thy grace,
Low at thy feet, ashamed I fall,
  And hide this wretched face.

2 Shall love like thine be thus repaid?
  Ah, vile, ungrateful heart!
By earth's low cares so oft betrayed
  From Jesus to depart.

3 But he, for his own mercy's sake,
  My wandering soul restores;

He bids the mourning heart partake
  The pardon it implores.

4 Oh, while I breathe to thee, my Lord,
  The deep, repentant sigh,
Confirm the kind, forgiving word,
  With pity in thine eye!

5 Then shall the mourner at thy feet
  Rejoice to seek thy face;
And, grateful, own how kind, how sweet
  Thy condescending grace!

617. *"Oh, that I were as in months past!"*
Job 29: 2.

1 Sweet was the time when first I felt
  The Saviour's pardoning blood,
Applied to cleanse my soul from guilt,
  And bring me home to God.

2 Soon as the morn the light revealed,
  His praises tuned my tongue;
And, when the evening shade prevailed,
  His love was all my song.

3 In prayer, my soul drew near the Lord,
  And saw his glory shine;
And when I read his holy word,
  I called each promise mine.

4 But now, when evening shade prevails,
  My soul in darkness mourns;
And when the morn the light reveals,
  No light to me returns.

5 Rise, Saviour! help me to prevail,
  And make my soul thy care;
I know thy mercy can not fail;
  Let me that mercy share.

Doxology.

To Father, Son, and Holy Ghost,
  One God, whom we adore,
Be glory as it was, is now,
  And shall be evermore!

SHIRLAND. S. M.

161. *"He hath not dealt with us after our sins."*—Psalm 103.

1 My soul, repeat his praise,
  Whose mercies are so great;
Whose anger is so slow to rise,
  So ready to abate.

2 God will not always chide;
  And when his wrath is felt,
Its strokes are fewer than our crimes,
  And lighter than our guilt.

3 His power subdues our sins,
  And his forgiving love,
Far as the east is from the west
  Doth all our guilt remove.

4 High as the heavens are raised
  Above the ground we tread,
So far the riches of his grace
  Our highest thoughts exceed.

481. *The Bible above Nature.*—Psalm 19.

1 Behold, the morning sun
  Begins his glorious way;
His beams through all the nations run,
  And life and light convey.

2 But where the Gospel comes,
  It spreads diviner light;
It calls dead sinners from their tombs,
  And gives the blind their sight.

3 Thy laws are just and pure,
  Thy truth without deceit;
Thy promises for ever sure,
  And thy rewards are great.

4 My gracious God, how plain
  Are thy directions given!
Oh, may I never read in vain,
  But find the path to heaven!

482. *"The law of the Lord is perfect."* Psalm 19.

1 How perfect is thy word,
  And all thy judgments just;
For ever sure thy promise, Lord,
  And men securely trust.

2 I hear thy word with love,
  And I would fain obey;
Send thy good Spirit from above,
  To guide me, lest I stray.

3 Warn me of every sin;
  Forgive my secret faults;
And cleanse this guilty soul of mine,
  Whose crimes exceed my thoughts.

4 While, with my heart and tongue,
  I spread thy praise abroad;
Accept the worship and the song,
  My Saviour and my God.

535. *"So run that ye may obtain."*

1 My soul, it is thy God
  Who calls thee by his grace;
Now loose thee from each cumbering load,
  And bend thee to the race.

2 Make thy salvation sure;
  All sloth and slumber shun;
Nor dare a moment rest secure,
  Till thou the goal hast won.

3 Thy crown of life hold fast;
  Thy heart with courage stay;
Nor let one trembling glance be cast
  Along the backward way.

4 Thy path ascends the skies,
  With conquering footsteps bright;
And thou shalt win and wear the prize
  In everlasting light.

THATCHER. S. M.

572. *Joy over the returning Prodigal.*
Luke 15 : 7.

1 HARK! through the courts of heaven
　Angelic voices sound :
He that was dead now lives again ;
He that was lost is found.

2 God of unfailing grace,
　Send down thy Spirit **now** ;
Oh, raise the lowly soul **to hope,**
And **make** the lofty bow.

3 In countries far from **home,**
　On earthly husks who **feed,**
Back to their Father's house, O Lord,
Their **wandering** footsteps lead.

4 Then at each soul's **return,**
　The heavenly harps shall sound ;
He that was dead now lives again ;
He that was lost is found !

645. *God All and in All.*

1 My God, my Life, my Love,
　To thee, to thee I call ;
I can not live if thou remove,
For thou art all in all.

2 To thee, and **thee** alone,
　The angels owe their bliss ;
They sit around thy gracious throne
And dwell where Jesus is.

3 Not all the harps above
　Can make a heavenly place,
If God his residence remove,
Or but conceal his face.

4 Nor earth, nor all the sky,
　Can one delight afford—
No, not a drop of real joy—
Without thy presence, Lord.

5 Thou art the sea of love,
　Where all my pleasures roll ;
The circle where my passions move,
And center of my soul.

762. *Having all in Christ.*—Psalm 31.

1 My spirit on thy care,
　Blest Saviour, I recline ;
Thou wilt not leave me to despair,
For thou art love divine.

2 In thee I place my trust ;
　On thee I calmly rest ;
I know thee good, I know thee just,
And count thy choice the best.

3 Whate'er events betide,
　Thy will they all perform ;
Safe in thy breast my head I hide,
Nor fear the coming storm.

4 Let good or ill befall,
　It must be good for me—
Secure of having thee in all,
Of having all in thee.

DOXOLOGY.

THE Father and the Son,
　And Spirit we adore ;
We praise, we bless, we worship thee,
Both now and evermore.

BROOKLYN. C. M. DOUBLE.

304. *"The darkness is past."*—1 John 2: 8.

1 'T is past—the dark and dreary night,
   And, Lord, we hail thee now,
Our Morning Star, without a cloud
   Of sadness on thy brow.
The path on earth, the cross, the grave,
   Thy sorrows all are o'er;
And oh, sweet thought! thy eye shall weep,
   Thy heart shall bleed, no more.

2 Deep were those sorrows—deeper still
   The love that brought thee low;
That bade the streams of life from thee,
   A willing victim, flow.
The soldier, as he pierced thee, proved
   Man's hatred, Lord, to thee;
While in the blood that stained the spear,
   Love, only love, we see.

3 Drawn from thy pierced and bleeding side
   That pure and cleansing flood
Speaks peace to every heart that knows
   The virtues of thy blood.
Yes, 't is not that we know the joy
   Of canceled sin alone,
But, happier far, thy saints are called,
   To share thy glorious throne.

4 So closely are we linked in love,
   So wholly one with thee,
That all thy bliss and glory then
   Our bright reward shall be.
Yes, when the storm of life is calmed,
   The weary desert passed,
Our way-worn hearts shall find in thee
   Their full repose at last.

692. *Memory of Christ's Love precious.*
        John 15: 13

1 My blessèd Saviour, is thy love
   So great, so full, so free!

Behold! I give my love, my heart,
   My life, my all, to thee.
2 I love thee for the glorious worth
   In thy great self I see;
I love thee for that shameful cross
   Thou hast endured for me.

3 No man of greater love can boast
   Than for his friend to die;
But for thy foes, Lord, thou wast slain:
   What love with thine can vie!

4 Though in the very form of God,
   With heavenly glory crowned,
Thou wouldst partake of human flesh
   Beset with troubles round.

5 Thou wouldst, like wretched man, be made
   In every thing but sin;
That we as like thee might become,
   As we unlike have been.

6 O Lord, I'll treasure in my soul
   The memory of thy love;
And thy dear name shall still to me
   A grateful odor prove.

927. *"Make Thy pleasure mine."*

1 O Lord, my best desire fulfill,
   And help me to resign
Life, health, and comfort to thy will,
   And make thy pleasure mine.

2 Why should I shrink at thy command,
   Whose love forbids my fears?
Or tremble at the gracious hand
   That wipes away my tears?

3 No: rather let me freely yield
   What most I prize to thee,
Who never hast a good withheld,
   Or wilt withhold, from me.

LITCHFIELD. C. M.

4 Thy favor, all my journey through
   Thou art engaged to grant;
  What else I want, or think I do,
   'T is better still to want.

5 Wisdom and mercy guide my way;
   Shall I resist them both?
  A poor, blind creature of a day,
   And crushed before the moth!

6 But ah! my inward spirit cries,
   Still bind me to thy sway;
  Else the next cloud that vails my skies
   Drives all these thoughts away.

931. *"I welcome all Thy sovereign will."*

1 My God! the covenant of thy love
   Abides for ever sure;
  And in its matchless grace I feel
   My happiness secure.

2 Since thou, the everlasting God,
   My Father art become,
  Jesus my Guardian and my Friend,
   And heaven my final home,—

3 I welcome all thy sovereign will,
   For all that will is love;
  And when I know not what thou dost,
   I wait the light above.

4 Thy covenant in the darkest gloom
   Shall heavenly rays impart,
  And when my eyelids close in death,
   Sustain my fainting heart.

934. *"The Lord gave and the Lord hath taken away."*—Job 1: 21.

1 It is the Lord,—enthroned in light,
   Whose claims are all divine,
  Who hath an undisputed right
   To govern me and mine.

2 It is the Lord—who gives me all,
   My wealth, my friends, my ease;
  And of his bounties may recall
   Whatever part he please.

3 It is the Lord, my covenant God,—
   Thrice blessed be his name,—
  Whose gracious promise, sealed with blood,
   Must ever be the same.

4 Can I, with hopes so firmly built,
   Be sullen, or repine?
  No: gracious God! take what thou wilt;
   To thee I all resign.

974. *The hidden life of the Christian.*

1 Oh, happy soul, that lives on high,
   While men lie groveling here!
  His hopes are fixed above the sky,
   And faith forbids his fear.

2 His conscience knows no secret stings,
   While peace and joy combine
  To form a life, whose holy springs
   Are hidden and divine.

3 He waits in secret on his God;
   His God in secret sees;
  Let earth be all in arms abroad;
   He dwells in heavenly peace.

4 His pleasures rise from things unseen,
   Beyond this world of time,
  Where neither eyes nor ears have been,
   Nor thoughts of mortals climb.

5 He wants no pomp nor royal throne
   To raise his honor here;
  Content and pleased to live unknown,
   Till Christ his life appear.

BONN. S. M.

661. *"Draw us, and we will run after Thee."*

1 ALONG my earthly way,
   How many clouds are spread!
 Darkness, with scarce one cheerful ray,
   Seems gathering o'er my head.

2 Yet, Father, thou art Love;
   Oh, hide not from my view!
 But when I look, in prayer, above,
   Appear in mercy through!

3 My pathway is not hid;
   Thou knowest all my need;
 And I would do as Israel did,—
   Follow where thou wilt lead.

4 Lead me, and then my feet
   Shall never, never stray;
 But safely I shall reach the seat
   Of happiness and day.

5 And, oh! from that bright throne
   I shall look back, and see,—
 The path I went, and that alone
   Was the right path for me.

893. *"Let this mind be in you, which was also in Christ Jesus."*

1 OH, arm me with the mind,
   Saviour, that was in thee!
 And let my fervid zeal be joined
   With perfect charity.

2 Control my every thought;
   And all my sin remove;
 Let all my works in thee be wrought;
   Let all be wrought in love.

3 Lord, do not let me trust
   In any arm but thine!
 Humble, oh! humble to the dust
   This stubborn soul of mine.

4 Help me to love like thee,
   In all thy footsteps tread;
 Thou hatest all iniquity,
   But nothing thou hast made.

5 Oh, may I learn the art
   With meekness to reprove;
 To hate the sin with all my heart,
   But still the sinner love!

831. *Call to Renewal of Covenant.*

1 COME ye that fear the Lord,
   And love him while ye fear;
 Come, and with heart and hand record
   Your vow and covenant here.

2 Here to his altar brought,
   Your holy vows renew,
 To be, in word, and deed, and thought,
   Faithful to him and true.

3 And true and faithful he
   To you will ever prove,
 Though hills were swept into the sea,
   And mountains should remove.

4 Then be his law our choice,
   The joy of young and old,
 As sheep that hear their shepherd's voice
   And follow to the fold.

5 So shall his staff and rod
   Conduct us and defend:
 God is a covenant-keeping God,
   And loves unto the end.

876. *Doing all things to God's glory.*

1 TEACH me, my God and King,
   In all things thee to see;
 And what I do in any thing,
   To do it as for thee!

ST. MICHAEL. S. M.

2 To scorn the senses' sway,
   While still to thee I tend;
   In all I do, be thou the way,
   In all, be thou the end.

3 All may of thee partake;
   Nothing so small can be
   But draws, when acted for thy sake,
   Greatness and worth from thee.

4 If done beneath thy laws,
   Ev'n servile labors shine;
   Hallowed is toil, if this the cause;
   The meanest work, divine.

1093. *"Good tidings of great joy."*
1 SAVIOUR! what gracious words
   Are ever, ever thine!
   Thy voice is music to the soul,
   And life and peace divine.

2 Good, everlasting good—
   Glad tidings, full of joy,
   Flow from thy lips, the lips of truth,
   And flow without alloy.

3 The broken heart, the poor,
   The bruised, the deaf, the blind,
   The dumb, the dead, the captive wretch,
   In thee compassion find.

4 Lord Jesus! speed the day—
   The promised day of grace
   To all the poor, the dumb, the deaf,
   The dead of Adam's race.

DOXOLOGY.

THE Father and the Son
And Spirit we adore;
We praise, we bless, we worship thee,
Both now and evermore!

BOYLSTON. S. M.

HAMBURG. L. M.

185. *"Who hath known the mind of the Lord?"*—Job 11: 7, 8.

1 WHAT finite power, with ceaseless toil,
   Can fathom the eternal Mind?
   Or who th' almighty Three in One,
   By searching, to perfection find?

2 Angels and men in vain may raise,
   Harmonious, their adoring songs:
   The laboring thought sinks down oppressed,
   And praises die upon their tongues.

3 Yet would I lift my trembling voice,
   A portion of his ways to sing;
   And, mingling with his meanest works,
   My humble, grateful tribute bring.

234. *The Mystery of Providence.*

1 LORD, how mysterious are thy ways!
   How blind are we! how mean our praise!
   Thy steps can mortal eyes explore?
   'T is ours to wonder and adore.

2 Thy deep decrees from our dim sight
   Are hid in shades of awful night;
   Amid the lines, with curious eye,
   Not angel minds presume to pry.

3 Great God! I would not ask to see
   What in my coming life shall be;
   Enough for me if love divine,
   At length, thro' every cloud shall shine.

4 Are darkness and distress my share?
   Then let me trust thy guardian care;
   If light and bliss attend my days,
   Then let my future hours be praise.

5 Yet this my soul desires to know,
   Be this my only wish below,
   That Christ be mine;—this great request
   Grant, bounteous God, and I am blest!

540. *One Thing needful.*

1 WHY will ye waste on trifling cares
   That life which God's compassion spares?
   While, in the various range of thought,
   The one thing needful is forgot?

2 Shall God invite you from above?
   Shall Jesus urge his dying love?
   Shall troubled conscience give you pain?
   And all these pleas unite in vain?

3 Not so your eyes will always view
   Those objects which you now pursue;
   Not so will heaven and hell appear,
   When death's decisive hour is near.

4 Almighty God! thy grace impart;
   Fix deep conviction on each heart;
   Nor let us waste on trifling cares
   That life which thy compassion spares.

619. *The Hiding of God's Countenance.*
   Psalm 13.

1 How long, O Lord, shall I complain,
   Like one who seeks his God in vain?
   Still shall my soul thine absence mourn,
   And still despair of thy return?

2 Hear, Lord! and grant me quick relief,
   Before my death conclude my grief;
   If thou withhold thy heavenly light,
   I sleep in everlasting night.

3 How will the powers of darkness boast,
   If but one praying soul be lost!
   But I have trusted in thy grace,
   And shall again behold thy face.

4 Whate'er my fears or foes suggest,
   Thou art my hope, my joy, my rest;
   My heart shall feel thy love, and raise
   My cheerful voice to songs of praise.

ULM. L. M.

144. *God's Eternity, and Man's Mortality.*
Psalm 90.

1 THROUGH every age, eternal God,
  Thou art our rest, our safe abode:
  High was thy throne ere heaven was
      made,
  Or earth thy humble footstool laid.

2 Long **hadst** thou reigned ere time began,
  Or dust was fashioned into man;
  And long thy kingdom shall endure,
  When earth and time shall be **no** more.

3 But man, weak man, is born **to die**,
  Made up of guilt and vanity;
  Thy dreadful sentence, Lord, **was just**—
  "Return, ye sinners, to your **dust**."

4 Death, like an overflowing stream,
  Sweeps us away; our life's a dream—
  An empty tale—a morning flower,
  Cut down and withered in an hour!

5 Teach us, O Lord, how **frail is man**;
  And kindly lengthen out **our** span,
  Till, by thy grace, we all may be
  Prepared to die and dwell with thee.

310. *Hope through the Sorrows of Christ.*
Psalm 69.

1 DEEP in our hearts let us record
  The deeper sorrows of our Lord;
  Behold the rising billows roll,
  To overwhelm his holy soul!

2 Yet, gracious God, thy power and love
  Have made the curse a blessing prove:
  Those dreadful sufferings of thy Son
  Atoned for crimes which we have done.

3 Oh, for his **sake, our guilt forgive**,
  And let the **mourning sinner live**!
  The Lord will hear us in his name,
  Nor shall our hope be **turned to shame**.

598. *" Cast me not away from Thy presence."*
Psalm 51.

1 OH, turn, great Ruler of the skies!
  Turn from my sin thy searching eyes;
  Nor let th' offenses of my hand
  Within thy book recorded stand.

2 Give me a will to thine subdued,—
  A conscience pure, a soul renewed;
  Nor let me, wrapt in endless gloom,
  An outcast from thy **presence roam**.

3 Oh, let thy Spirit to my heart
  Once more its quickening aid impart;
  My mind from every fear release,
  And soothe **my** troubled thoughts to
      peace.

1162. *"Lord, make me to know the measure
    of my days."*—Psalm 39.

1 ALMIGHTY Maker of my frame,
  Teach me the measure of my days;
  Teach me to know how frail I am,
  And spend the remnant to thy praise.

2 My days are shorter than a span,
  A little point my life appears;
  How frail at best is dying man!
  How vain are all his hopes and fears!

3 Oh, spare me, and my strength restore,
  Ere my few hasty minutes flee!
  And when my days on earth are o'er,
  Let me for ever dwell with thee.

4 Oh, be that noble portion mine!
  My God, I bow before thy throne;
  Earth's fleeting treasures I resign,
  And **fix my** hopes on thee alone.

DOXOLOGY.

PRAISE God, from whom all blessings flow!
Praise him, all creatures here below!
Praise him above, ye heavenly host!
Praise Father, Son, and Holy Ghost!

BARROW. C. M.

232. *"To heaven I lift my waiting eyes."*
Psalm 121.

1 To heaven I lift my waiting eyes:
   There all my hopes are laid:
   The Lord that built the earth and skies
   Is my perpetual aid.

2 Their steadfast feet shall **never fall**
   Whom he designs to keep;
   His ear attends the softest call,
   His eyes can **never sleep**.

3 Israel, rejoice, and rest secure;
   Thy keeper is **the Lord**:
   His wakeful eyes employ his power
   For thine eternal guard.

4 He guards **thy** soul, he keeps thy breath,
   Where **thickest** dangers come;
   Go and return, secure from death,
   Till God commands thee home.

577. *"Oh for a lowly, contrite heart."*

1 Oh for a heart to praise my God!
   A heart **from sin** set free;
   A heart that 's sprinkled with the blood
   So freely shed for me;—

2 A heart resigned, submissive, meek,
   My dear Redeemer's throne;
   Where only Christ is heard to speak,
   Where Jesus reigns alone.

3 Oh for a lowly, contrite heart,
   Believing, true, and clean;
   Which neither life nor death **can part**
   From him that dwells within!

4 Thy nature, gracious Lord, impart;
   Come quickly from above;
   Write thy new name upon my heart,
   Thy new, best name of Love.

689. *Christ loved Unseen.*—1 Peter 1: 8.

1 JESUS, these eyes have never seen
   That radiant form of thine!
   The vail of sense hangs dark **between**
   Thy blessed face and mine!

2 I see thee not, I hear thee not,
   Yet art thou oft with me;
   And earth hath ne'er so dear a spot,
   As where I meet with thee.

3 Like some bright **dream** that comes unsought,
   When slumbers o'er me roll,
   Thine image ever fills my thought,
   And **charms my** ravished soul.

4 Yet though I have not seen, and still
   Must rest in faith alone
   I love thee, dearest Lord!—and will,
   Unseen, but not Unknown.

5 When death these mortal eyes shall seal,
   And still this **throbbing** heart,
   The rending vail shall thee reveal,
   All **glorious** as thou art!

696. *Loving Obedience to Christ.*

1 I WOULD not wish to dwell on earth,
   Though earth were all my own,
   And mortal men should homage yield
   To me, and me alone.

2 I would not **wish** in heaven to dwell,
   And like a seraph shine;
   Though bliss is there, without a tear,
   And all that bliss were mine.

3 But I would dwell where most I may
   Fulfill my Saviour's will;
   My only wish, in life, in death,
   To glorify him still.

4 While action may his praise reveal,
   My cheerful act I'd pay;
   When suffering best may please my Lord,
   By suffering I'd obey.

5 It is not place—above, below—
   My bliss, my heaven can be;

WARWICK. C. M.

To live for him who died for man—
Oh, that is life to me!

432. *"Elect, precious"*

1 Jesus! I love thy charming name;
   'T is music to mine ear;
   Fain would I sound it out so loud,
   That earth and heaven should hear.

2 All that my loftiest powers can wish,
   In thee doth richly meet;
   Not to mine eyes is light so dear,
   Nor friendship half so sweet.

3 Thy grace still dwells upon my heart,
   And sheds its fragrance there—
   The noblest balm of all my wounds,
   The cordial of my care.

4 I'll speak the honors of thy name
   With my last laboring breath;
   Then, speechless, clasp thee in mine arms,
   The Conqueror of death.

707. *Living with Christ.*

1 Oh, could I find, from day to day,
   A nearness to my God!
   Then should my hours glide sweet away,
   While leaning on his word.

2 Lord, I desire with thee to live
   Anew from day to day;
   In joys the world can never give,
   Nor ever take away.

3 Blest Jesus! come and rule my heart,
   And make me wholly thine,
   That I may never more depart,
   Nor grieve thy love divine.

4 Thus, till my last, expiring breath,
   Thy goodness I'll adore;
   And when my frame dissolves in death,
   My soul shall love thee more.

779. *"Lord, I believe; help Thou mine unbelief."*—Mark 9: 24.

1 Lord, I believe; thy power I own,
   Thy word I would obey;
   I wander comfortless and lone,
   When from thy truth I stray.

2 Lord, I believe; but gloomy fears
   Sometimes bedim my sight;
   I look to thee with prayers and tears,
   And cry for strength and light.

3 Lord, I believe; but oft I know,
   My faith is cold and weak;
   My weakness strengthen, and bestow
   The confidence I seek!

4 Yes! I believe; and only thou
   Canst give my soul relief;
   Lord! to thy truth my spirit bow;
   "Help thou mine unbelief!"

1098. *"O Lord, truly I am Thy servant."*

1 Oh, not to fill the mouth of fame
   My longing soul is stirred;
   Oh, give me a diviner name!
   Call me thy servant, Lord!

2 No longer would my soul be known
   As uncontrolled and free;
   Oh, not mine own, oh, not mine own!
   Lord, I belong to thee!

3 Thy servant,—me thy servant choose;
   Naught of thy claim abate!
   The glorious name I would not lose,
   Nor change the sweet estate.

4 In life, in death, on earth, in heaven,
   This is the name for me!
   The same sweet style and title given
   Through all eternity.

INVERNESS. S. M.

72. *"Myself I can not save."*

1 Thou seest my feebleness,
    Jesus, be thou my power,—
  My help and refuge in distress,
    My fortress and my tower.

2 Give me to trust in thee;
    Be thou my sure abode:
  My horn, and rock, and buckler be,
    My Saviour and my God.

3 Myself I can not save,
    Myself I can not keep;
  But strength in thee I surely have,
    Whose eyelids never sleep.

4 My soul to thee alone,
    Now therefore I commend:
  Lord Jesus, love me as thine own,
    And love me to the end.

526. *Rest in God.*—Genesis 8 : 9.

1 Oh, cease, my wandering soul,
    On restless wing to roam;
  All this wide world, to either pole,
    Hath not for thee a home.

2 Behold the ark of God!
    Behold the open door!
  Oh, haste to gain that dear **abode**,
    And rove, my soul, no more.

3 There safe thou shalt abide,
    There sweet shall be thy rest,
  And every longing satisfied,
    With full salvation blest.

563. *"Lord, to whom shall we go?"*
        John 6: 68.

1 Ah! what avails my strife,
    My wandering to and fro?
  Thou hast the words of endless life;
    Ah! whither should I go?

2 Thy condescending grace
    To me did freely move;
  It calls me still to seek thy **face**,
    And stoops to ask my love.

3 My worthless heart to gain,
    The God of all that breathe,
  Was found in fashion as a man,
    And died a curséd death.

4 And can I yet delay
    My little all to give?
  To tear my soul from earth away,
    For Jesus to receive?

5 Ah! no; I all forsake,
    I all to thee resign:
  Gracious Redeemer, take, oh, **take**,
    And seal me ever thine!

496. *"Where shall rest be found?"*

1 Oh, where shall rest be found—
    Rest for the weary soul?
  'T were vain the ocean depths to sound,
    Or pierce to either pole.

2 The world can never give
    The bliss for which we sigh:
  'Tis not the whole of life to live,
    Nor all of death to die.

3 Beyond this vale of tears
    There is a life above,
  Unmeasured by the flight **of years**;
    And all that life is love.

4 There is a death whose pang
    Outlasts the fleeting breath:
  Oh, what eternal horrors hang
    Around the second death!

5 Lord God of truth and grace,
    Teach us that death to shun;
  Lest we be banished from thy face,
    And evermore undone.

AYLESBURY. S. M.

622. *"A broken heart thou wilt not despise."*

1 STILL wilt thou, Lord, be found?
  And may I still draw near?
  Then listen to the plaintive **sound**—
  A sinner's earnest prayer.

2 Jesus, thine aid afford,
  For still the same thou art;
  To thee I **look, to thee, my L**ord,
  Lift up **a helpless heart.**

3 Though late, **I all forsake**;
  My friends, my **life resign**:
  Gracious Redeemer, take, oh, take,
  And seal me **ever thine!**

4 O my offended Lord!
  Restore **my** inward peace:
  I know thou canst—pronounce the **word,**
  And bid the tempest cease.

5 I yield to thy control;
  Thou my Redeemer art:
  Enter and calm my troubled **soul,**
  And soothe my bleeding **heart.**

1160. *"Our days are as an hand-breadth."*

1 MY few revolving years,
  How swift they glide away!
  How short the term of life appears,
  When past—but as a day!—

2 A dark and cloudy day,
  Made up of grief and sin;
  A host of enemies without,
  Of guilty fears within.

3 Lord, through another year,
  If thou permit my stay,
  With watchful care may I pursue
  The true and living way!

DOXOLOGY.

THE Father and the Son
  And Spirit we adore;
We praise, we bless, we worship thee,
  Both now and evermore!

BOYLSTON. S. M.

WOODSTOCK. C. M.

618. *Prayer in extreme Distress.*—Psalm 102.

1 Hear me, O God, nor hide thy face,
    But answer, lest I die!
  Hast thou not built a throne of grace,
    To hear when sinners cry?

2 As on some lonely building's top
    The sparrow tells her moan,
  Far from the tents of joy and hope,
    I sit and grieve alone.

3 But thou for ever art the same,
    O my Eternal God!
  Ages to come shall know thy name,
    And spread thy works abroad.

4 Thou wilt arise, and show thy face,
    Nor will my Lord delay,
  Beyond th' appointed hour of grace,
    That long expected day.

5 He hears his saints, he knows their cry;
    And by mysterious ways
  Redeems the prisoners doomed to die,
    And fills their tongues with praise.

630. *Wanderings from God.*

1 How oft, alas! this wretched heart
    Has wandered from the Lord!
  How oft my roving thoughts depart,
    Forgetful of his word!

2 Yet sovereign mercy calls—"Return!"
    Dear Lord, and may I come?
  My vile ingratitude I mourn:
    Oh, take the wanderer home!

3 And canst thou,—wilt thou yet forgive,
    And bid my crimes remove?
  And shall a pardoned rebel live,
    To speak thy wondrous love?

4 Almighty grace, thy healing power,
    How glorious, how divine!
  That can to life and bliss restore
    A heart so vile as mine.

5 Thy pardoning love, so free, so sweet,
    Dear Saviour, I adore;
  Oh, keep me at thy sacred feet,
    And let me rove no more!

748. *The Shadow of the Cross.*

1 Oppress'd with noon-day's scorching heat,
    To yonder cross I flee;
  Beneath its shelter take my seat:
    No shade like this for me!

2 Beneath that cross clear waters burst—
    A fountain sparkling free;
  And there I quench my desert thirst:
    No spring like this for me!

3 A stranger here, I pitch my tent
    Beneath this spreading tree;
  Here shall my pilgrim life be spent:
    No home like this for me!

4 For burdened ones a resting-place,
    Beside that cross I see;
  I here cast off my weariness:
    No rest like this for me!

774. *"Jesus, I'll turn to Thee."*

1 Jesus, in sickness and in pain,
    Be near to succor me;
  My sinking spirit still sustain:
    To thee I turn, to thee.

2 When cares and sorrows thicken round,
    And nothing bright I see,
  In thee alone can help be found;
    To thee I turn, to thee.

3 Should strong temptations fierce assail,
    And Satan buffet me,
  Then in thy strength will I prevail,
    While still I turn to thee.

4 Through all my pilgrimage below,
    Whate'er my lot may be,
  In joy or sadness, weal or woe,
    Jesus, I'll turn to thee.

MARTYRS. C. M.

621. *Peace restored.*

1 Oh speak that gracious word again,
    And cheer my broken heart!
  No voice but thine can soothe my pain,
    Or bid my fears depart.

2 And canst thou still vouchsafe to own
    A wretch so vile as I;
  And may I still approach thy throne,
    And "Abba, Father," cry?

3 Oh, then, let saints and angels join,
    And help me to proclaim
  The grace that healed a soul like mine,
    And put my foes to shame!

4 My Saviour, by his powerful word,
    Has turned my night to day;
  And his salvation's joy restored,
    Which I had sinned away.

5 Dear Lord, I wonder and adore;
    Thy grace is all divine:
  Oh, keep me, that I sin no more
    Against such love as thine!

655. *"Oh that I knew where I might find Him!"—Job 23: 3, 4.*

1 Oh that I knew the sacred place
    Where I might find my God!
  I'd spread my wants before his face,
    And pour my woes abroad.

2 I'd tell him how my sins arise,
    What sorrows I sustain;
  How grace decays, and comfort dies,
    And leaves my heart in pain.

3 He knows what arguments I'd take
    To wrestle with my God:
  I'd plead for his own mercy's sake—
    I'd plead my Saviour's blood.

4 My God will pity my complaints,
    And drive my foes away;
  He knows the meaning of his saints
    When they in sorrow pray.

5 Arise, my soul! from deep distress,
    And banish every fear;
  He calls thee to his throne of grace,
    To spread thy sorrows there.

667. *"O Lord, save me, and I shall be saved."*

1 Great Source of boundless power and grace!
    Attend my mournful cry;
  In hours of dark and deep distress,
    To thee alone I fly.

2 Thou art my Strength, my Life, my Stay:
    Assist my feeble trust;
  Oh, drive my gloomy fears away,
    And raise me from the dust.

3 Fain would I call thy grace to mind,
    And trust thy glorious name;
  Jehovah, powerful, wise, and kind,
    For ever is the same.

4 Thy presence, Lord, can cheer my heart,
    When earthly comforts die;
  Thy voice can bid my pains depart,
    And raise my pleasures high.

5 Here let me rest—on thee depend,
    My God, my Hope, my All;
  Be thou my everlasting Friend,
    And I shall never fall.

DOXOLOGY.

To Father, Son, and Holy Ghost,
  One God, whom we adore,
Be glory as it was, is now,
  And shall be evermore!

WARD. L. M.

461. *Prayer for the Continuance of the Spirit.*

1 STAY, thou insulted Spirit, stay!
 Though I have done thee such **despite**,
 Cast not a sinner quite away,
 Nor take thine everlasting flight.

2 Though I have **most** unfaithful been
 Of all who e'er **thy** grace received;
 Ten thousand times thy goodness seen,
 Ten thousand times thy **goodness** grieved;

3 Yet, oh, the chief **of** sinners spare,
 In honor of my Great High Priest!
 Nor, in thy righteous anger, swear
 I shall not see thy people's rest.

4 O Lord, my weary soul release,
 Upraise me by thy gracious hand;
 Guide me into thy perfect peace,
 And bring me to the promised land.

492. *"I was shapen in iniquity."* Psalm 51.

1 LORD, I am vile—conceived **in sin**,
 And born unholy and unclean;
 Sprung from the man whose guilty **fall**
 Corrupts the race, and taints us all.

2 Soon as we draw our infant breath,
 The seeds of sin grow up for death;
 Thy law demands a perfect heart;
 But we're defiled in every part.

3 Behold, I fall before thy face;
 My only refuge is thy grace;
 Great God! create my heart anew,
 And form **my** spirit pure and true.

4 No bleeding bird, nor bleeding **beast**,
 Nor hyssop branch, nor sprinkling **priest**,
 Nor running book, nor flood, **nor sea**,
 Can **wash** the dismal stain away.

5 Jesus, my God! thy blood alone
 Hath power sufficient to atone:
 Thy blood can make me white as snow;
 No Jewish types could cleanse me so.

6 While guilt disturbs and breaks my peace,
 Nor flesh nor soul hath rest or ease:
 Lord, let me hear thy pardoning voice,
 And make **my** broken bones rejoice.

498. *"Thou didst set them in slippery places."*—Psalm 73.

1 LORD, what a thoughtless **wretch was I**
 To mourn, and murmur, and repine,
 To see the wicked, **placed on high**,
 In pride and robes of **honor shine!**

2 But oh, their end, their dreadful end!
 Thy sanctuary taught me so:
 On slippery rocks I see them stand,
 And fiery billows **roll below**.

3 Their fancied joys—how fast they flee!
 Just like a dream when man awakes;
 Their songs of softest harmony
 Are but a prelude to their plagues.

4 Now I esteem their mirth and wine
 Too dear to purchase with my blood;
 Lord, 'tis enough that thou art mine,
 My life, my portion, and my God.

584. *"Hide Thy face from my sins."* Psalm 51.

1 HAVE mercy on me, O my God!
 In loving kindness hear my prayer;
 Withdraw the terror of thy rod;
 Lord, in thy tender mercy, spare.

2 Offenses rise where'er I look,
 But I confess their guilt to thee:
 Blot my transgressions from thy book;
 Wash me from all iniquity.

3 Not streaming **blood** nor cleansing fire
 Thy seeming anger can appease;
 Burnt offerings thou dost not require,
 Or gladly I would render these.

WINDHAM. L. M.

4 The **broken** heart in sacrifice,
  Alone, will thine acceptance meet:
My heart, O God, do not despise,
  Abased and contrite at thy feet.

594. *"Show pity, Lord! O Lord, forgive."*
                Psalm 51.
1 Show pity, Lord! O Lord, **forgive**;
  Let a repenting rebel **live**;
  Are not thy mercies large and free?
  May not a **sinner** trust in thee?

2 My crimes are great, but ne'er surpass
  The power and glory of thy grace:
  Great God! thy nature hath no bound,
  So let thy pardoning love be found.

3 Oh, wash my soul from every sin,
  And make my guilty conscience clean!
  Here on my heart the burden lies,
  And past offenses pain mine eyes.

4 My lips with shame my sins confess,
  Against thy law, against thy grace;
  Lord, should thy judgment grow severe,
  I am condemned, but thou art **clear**.

5 Should sudden vengeance seize my breath,
  I must pronounce thee just in death;
  And if my soul were sent to hell,
  Thy righteous law approves it well.

6 Yet save a trembling sinner, Lord!
  Whose hope, still hovering round thy word,
  Would lighton some sweet promise there,
  Some sure support against despair.

595. *" Blot out my transgressions."*
                Psalm 51.
1 O thou that hear'st when sinners cry,
  Though all my crimes before thee lie,
  Behold me not **with** angry look,
  But blot their memory from thy book.

2 Create my nature pure within,
  And form my soul averse to sin;
  Let thy good Spirit ne'er depart,
  Nor hide thy presence from my heart.

3 I can not live without thy light,
  Cast out and banished from thy sight;
  Thy holy joys, my God, restore,
  And guard me that I fall no more.

4 Though I have grieved thy Spirit, Lord,
  His help and comfort still afford;
  And let a sinner seek thy throne,
  To plead the merits of thy Son.

596. *"Restore unto me the joy of Thy salvation."*—Psalm 51.
1 A **broken** heart, my God, my King,
  Is all the sacrifice I bring;
  The God of grace will ne'er despise
  A broken heart for sacrifice.

2 My soul lies humbled in the dust,
  And **owns thy** dreadful sentence just;
  Look down, **O** Lord, with pitying eye,
  And save the soul condemned to die.

3 Then will I teach the world thy ways;
  Sinners shall learn thy sovereign grace:
  I'll lead them to my Saviour's blood,
  And they shall praise a pardoning God.

4 Oh, may thy love inspire my tongue!
  Salvation shall be all my song;
  And all my powers shall join to bless
  The Lord, my Strength and Righteousness.

DOXOLOGY.

To Father, Son, and Holy Ghost,
  The God whom earth and heaven adore,
Be glory as it was of old,
  Is now, and shall be evermore!

TAPPAN. C. M.

464. *"Spirit of Power and Might."*

1 SPIRIT of power and might, behold
    A world by sin destroyed!
Creator Spirit, as of old,
    Move on the formless void.

2 Give thou the word: that healing sound
    Shall quell the deadly strife,
And earth again, like Eden crowned,
    Produce the tree of life.

3 If sang the morning stars for joy
    When nature rose to view,
What strains will angel harps employ
    When thou shalt all renew!

4 And if the sons of God rejoice
    To hear a Saviour's name,
How will the ransomed raise their voice,
    To whom that Saviour came!

5 Lo! every kindred, tongue, and tribe,
    Assembling round the throne,
The new creation shall ascribe
    To sovereign love alone.

999. *"The sons of God."*—Rom. 8 : 19-23.

1 THE whole creation groans and waits
    Till we, who love thee, Lord,
Shall stand within thy temple gates,
    And shine—the sons of God.

2 The sons of God—how bright they shine!
    No mortal eye can see;
We, sinners, shall be made divine!
    We shall be one with thee!

3 One with the Lord and all his saints!
    Thy nature in our own!
Thy crown our rich inheritance!
    Heirs to thy royal throne!

4 Thy throne no joy to us would bring,
    If we from thee were riven;
For all our joy is in our King,
    And thou art all our heaven.

1000. *"My Father, God."*

1 LORD, I address thy heavenly throne;
    Call me a child of thine;
Send down the Spirit of thy Son,
    To form my heart divine.

2 There shed thy choicest love abroad,
    And make my comforts strong;
Then shall I say—"My Father, God,"
    With an unwavering tongue.

1038. *"Mark ye well her bulwarks."*

1 OH, where are kings and empires now,
    Of old that went and came?
But, Lord, thy church is praying yet,
    A thousand years the same.

2 We mark her goodly battlements,
    And her foundations strong;
We hear within the solemn voice
    Of her unending song.

3 For not like kingdoms of the world
    Thy holy church, O God!
Though earthquake shocks are threatening her,
    And tempests are abroad;

4 Unshaken as eternal hills,
    Immovable she stands,
A mountain that shall fill the earth,
    A house not made by hands.

1246. *"He, being dead, yet speaketh."* Heb. 11.

1 RISE, O my soul, pursue the path
    By ancient worthies trod;
Aspiring, view those holy men,
    Who lived and walked with God.

2 Though dead, they speak in reason's ear,
    And in example live;
Their faith, and hope, and mighty deeds
    Still fresh instruction give.

MEAR. C. M.

3 'T was through the Lamb's most precious blood,
  They conquered every foe;
And to his power and matchless grace
  Their crowns of life they owe.

4 Lord! may I ever keep in view
  The patterns thou hast given,
And ne'er forsake the blessed road
  That led them safe to heaven.

1251. "*There the wicked cease from troubling.*"

1 Our sins, alas! how strong they are!
  And, like a raging flood,
They break our duty, Lord, to thee,
  And force us from our God.

2 The waves of trouble—how they rise!
  How loud the tempests roar!
But death shall land our weary souls
  Safe on the heavenly shore.

3 There to fulfill his sweet commands
  Our speedy feet shall move;
No sin shall clog our winged zeal,
  Or cool our burning love.

4 There shall we sit, and sing, and tell
  The wonders of his grace,
Till heavenly raptures fire our hearts,
  And smile in every face.

5 For ever his dear, sacred name
  Shall dwell upon our tongue,
And Jesus and salvation be
  The close of every song.

1273. "*In my flesh shall I see God.*"
       Job 19 : 25, 26.

1 My faith shall triumph o'er the grave,
  And trample on the tomb;
I know that my Redeemer lives,
  And on the clouds shall come.

2 I know that he shall soon appear
  In power and glory meet;

And death, the last of all his foes,
  Lie vanquished at his feet.

3 Then, though the grave my flesh devour,
  And hold me for its prey,
I know my sleeping dust shall rise
  On the last judgment-day.

4 I, in my flesh, shall see my God,
  When he on earth shall stand;
I shall with all his saints ascend
  To dwell at his right hand.

5 Then shall he wipe all tears away,
  And hush the rising groan;
And pains and sighs and griefs and fears
  Shall ever be unknown.

1275. "*Them also which sleep in Jesus.*"
       1 Thess. 4: 14-17.

1 As Jesus died and rose again,
  Victorious, from the dead;
So his disciples rise, and reign
  With their triumphant Head.

2 The time draws nigh, when, from the clouds,
  Christ shall with shouts descend;
And the last trumpet's awful voice
  The heavens and earth shall rend.

3 Then they who live shall changed be,
  And they who sleep shall wake;
The graves shall yield their ancient charge,
  And earth's foundation shake.

4 The saints of God, from death set free,
  With joy shall mount on high;
The heavenly host with praises loud
  Shall meet them in the sky.

5 Together to their Father's house
  With joyful hearts they go;
And dwell for ever with the Lord,
  Beyond the reach of woe.

AITHLONE. C. P. M.

260. *The Mystery of Christ's Love.*
Isaiah 27: 5.

1 O THOU, who hast redeemed of old,
And bidst me of thy strength lay hold,
  And be at peace with thee,
Help me thy benefits to own,
And hear me tell what thou hast done,
  O dying Lamb! for me.

2 Love, only love, thy heart inclined,
And brought thee, Saviour of mankind,
  Down from thy throne above;
Love made my God a Man of grief,
Distressed thee sore for my relief:
  Oh, mystery of Love!

3 As thou hast loved and died for me,
So grant me, Saviour, love to thee,
  And gladly I resign
Whate'er I have, whate'er I am:
My life be all with thine the same,
  And all thy death be mine.

495. *The Two Worlds.*

1 Lo, on a narrow neck of land,
'Twixt two unbounded seas, I stand,
  Secure, insensible!
A point of time, a moment's space,
Removes me to that heavenly place,
  Or shuts me up in hell.

2 O God, my inmost soul convert,
And deeply on my thoughtful heart
  Eternal things impress!
Give me to feel their solemn weight,
And tremble on the brink of fate,
  And wake to righteousness.

3 Before me place in dread array,
The pomp of that tremendous day,
  When thou, with clouds, shalt come
To judge the nations at thy bar;
And tell me, Lord, shall I be there,
  To meet a joyful doom?

4 O Saviour, then my soul receive,
Then bid me in thy presence live,
  And reign with thee above;
Where faith is sweetly lost in sight,
And hope in full, supreme delight,
  And everlasting love.

554. *Surrender to the Love of God.*

1 LORD, thou hast won; at length I yield;
My heart, by mighty grace compelled,
  Surrenders all to thee:
Against thy terrors long I strove,
But who can stand against thy love?
  Love conquers even me.

2 If thou hadst bid thy thunders roll,
And lightnings flash to blast my soul,
  I still had stubborn been:
But mercy has my heart subdued:
A bleeding Saviour I have viewed,
  And now, I hate my sin.

3 Now, Lord, I would be thine alone;
Come, take possession of thine own,
  For thou hast set me free:
Released from Satan's hard command,
See all my powers in waiting stand,
  To be employed by thee.

MERIBAH. C. P. M.

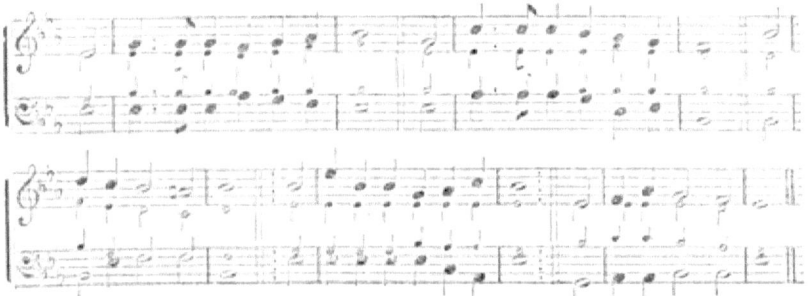

603. *"Remember Thou me."*

1 WHEN thou, my righteous Judge, shalt
    come
  To take thy ransomed people home,
    Shall I among them stand?
  Shall such a worthless worm as I,
  Who sometimes am afraid to die,
    Be found at thy right hand?

2 I love to meet among them now,
  Before thy gracious feet to bow,
    Though vilest of them all;
  But—can I bear the piercing thought?—
  What if my name should be left out,
    When thou for them shalt call!

3 Prevent, prevent it by thy grace;
  Be thou, dear Lord, my hiding-place,
    In this th' accepted day;
  Thy pardoning voice, oh, let me hear,
  To still my unbelieving fear;
    Nor let me fall, I pray!

4 Let me among thy saints be found,
  Whene'er th' archangel's trump shall
    sound,
    To see thy smiling face;
  Then loudest of the throng I'll sing,
  While heaven's resounding mansions
    With shouts of sovereign grace. [ring

725. *"No Refuge of my own."*

1 O THOU, who hear'st the prayer of faith,
  Wilt thou not save a soul from death,
    That casts itself on thee?
  I have no refuge of my own,
  But fly to what my Lord hath done,
    And suffered once for me.

2 Slain in the guilty sinner's stead,
  His spotless righteousness I plead,
    And his availing blood;
  Thy merit, Lord, my robe shall be;
  Thy merit shall atone for me,
    And bring me near to God.

3 Then save me from eternal death,
  The Spirit of adoption breathe,
    His consolations send;
  By him some word of life impart,
  And sweetly whisper to my heart,
    "Thy Maker is thy Friend."

4 The king of terrors then would be
  A welcome messenger to me,
    To bid me come away;
  Unclogged by earth, or earthly things,
  I'd mount, I'd fly with eager wings
    To everlasting day!

DOXOLOGY.

To Father, Son, and Holy Ghost,
The God, whom Heaven's triumphant host
  And saints on earth adore,
Be glory as in ages past,
Is now, and shall for ever last,
  When time shall be no more!

WELT. 5s, 7s, 8 & 6.

573. *"I have found my sheep."*

1 There was joy in heaven!
   There was joy in heaven!
When this goodly world to frame
The Lord of might and mercy came:
Shouts of joy were heard on high,
And the stars sang from the sky—
   "Glory to God in heaven!"

2 There was joy in heaven!
   There was joy in heaven!

When of love the midnight beam
Dawned on the tower of Bethlehem:
And along the echoing hill
Angels sung—"On earth good will,
   Glory to God in heaven!"

3 There is joy in heaven!
   There is joy in heaven!
When the sheep that went astray
Returns in love to virtue's way;
When the soul, by grace subdued,
Sobs its prayer of gratitude,
   Then is there joy in heaven!

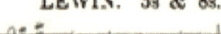
LEWIN. 5s & 8s.

404. *"Jesus, still lead on."*—Luke 5: 11.

1 Jesus, still lead on,
   Till our rest be won:
And although the way be cheerless,
We will follow, calm and fearless;
   Guide us by thy hand
   To our Fatherland!

2 If the way be drear,
   If the foe be near,
Let not faithless fears o'ertake us;
Let not faith and hope forsake us;
   For, through many a foe,
   To our home we go!

3 When we seek relief
   From a long-felt grief;
When temptations come alluring,
Make us patient and enduring,
   Show us that bright shore
   Where we weep no more!

4 Jesus, still lead on,
   Till our rest be won;
Heavenly Leader, still direct us,
Still support, console, protect us,
   Till we safely stand
   In our Fatherland!

ZETA. 7s & 5.

423. *"Touched with the feeling of our infirmities."*

1 When our heads are bowed with woe;
  When our bitter tears o'erflow;
  When we mourn the lost, the dear,
    Gracious Saviour, hear!

2 Thou our feeble flesh hast worn;
  Thou our mortal griefs hast borne;
  Thou hast shed the human tear:
    Gracious Saviour, hear!

3 When the heart is sad within,
  With the thought of all its sin;
  When the spirit shrinks with fear,
    Gracious Saviour, hear!

4 Thou the shame, the grief, hast known;
  Though the sins were not thine own,
  Thou hast deigned their load to bear;
    Gracious Saviour, hear!

5 When our eyes grow dim in death;
  When we heave the parting breath;
  When our solemn doom is near,
    Gracious Saviour, hear!

6 Thou hast bowed the dying head;
  Thou the blood of life hast shed;
  Thou hast filled a mortal bier;
    Gracious Saviour, hear!

443. *Christ our Life.*

1 Lord of mercy and of might,
  Of mankind the life and light,
  Maker, Teacher, Infinite—
    Jesus, hear and save!

2 Strong Creator, Saviour mild,
  Humbled to a little child,
  Captive, beaten, bound, reviled—
    Jesus, hear and save!

3 Borne aloft on angels' wings,
  Throned above celestial things,
  Lord of lords, and King of kings—
    Jesus, hear and save!

4 Soon to come to earth again,
  Judge of angels and of men,
  Hear us now, and hear us then;
    Jesus, hear and save!

456. *"The Comforter, which is the Holy Ghost."*—John 14: 26.

1 Holy Ghost, the Infinite!
  Shine upon our nature's night
  With thy blessed inward light,
    Comforter Divine!

2 We are sinful; cleanse us, Lord;
  We are faint, thy strength afford;
  Lost—until by thee restored,
    Comforter Divine!

3 Like the dew, thy peace distill;
  Guide, subdue our wayward will,
  Things of Christ unfolding still,
    Comforter Divine!

4 In us, for us, intercede,
  And, with voiceless groanings, plead
  Our unutterable need,
    Comforter Divine!

5 In us "Abba, Father," cry—
  Earnest of our bliss on high,
  Seal of immortality—
    Comforter Divine!

6 Search for us the depths of God;
  Bear us up the starry road,
  To the height of thine abode,
    Comforter Divine!

938. *"Saviour, comfort me."*

1 In the dark and cloudy day,
  When earth's riches flee away,
  And the last hope will not stay,
    Saviour, comfort me!

2 When the secret idol's gone
  That my poor heart yearned upon—
  Desolate, bereft, alone,
    Saviour, comfort me!

3 Thou, who wast so sorely tried,
  In the darkness crucified,
  Bid me in thy love confide!
    Saviour, comfort me!

4 Comfort me; I am cast down;
  'Tis my heavenly Father's frown;
  I deserve it all, I own;
    Saviour, comfort me!

5 So it shall be good for me
  Much afflicted now to be,
  If thou wilt but tenderly,
    Saviour, comfort me!

ELLIOT. 8s & 6.

559. *"Just as I am."*

1 Just as I am, without one plea,
But that thy blood was shed for me,
And that thou bid'st me come to thee,
O Lamb of God, I come!

2 Just as I am, and waiting not
To rid my soul of one dark blot,
To thee whose blood can cleanse each spot,
O Lamb of God I come!

3 Just as I am, though tossed about
With many a conflict, many a doubt,
Fightings within, and fears without,
O Lamb of God, I come!

4 Just as I am—poor, wretched, blind;
Sight, riches, healing of the mind,
Yea, all I need, in thee to find,
O Lamb of God, I come!

5 Just as I am—thou wilt receive,
Wilt welcome, pardon, cleanse, relieve,
Because thy promise I believe,
O Lamb of God, I come!

6 Just as I am—thy love unknown
Hath broken every barrier down:
Now, to be thine, yea, thine alone,
O Lamb of God, I come!

572. *"If any man thirst, let him come unto me."*

1 Burdened with guilt, wouldst thou be blest?
Trust not the world; it gives no rest:
I bring relief to hearts oppressed;
O weary sinner, come!

2 Come, leave thy burden at the cross;
Count all thy gains but empty dross;
My grace repays all earthly loss:
O needy sinner, come!

3 Come, hither bring thy boding fears,
Thine aching heart, thy bursting tears;
'T is mercy's voice salutes thine ears:
O trembling sinner, come!

4 "The Spirit and the bride say, Come:"
Rejoicing saints re-echo, Come!
Who faints, who thirsts, who will, may come;
Thy Saviour bids thee come.

373. *Prayer for Christ's Intercession.*

1 O Thou, the contrite sinners' Friend!
Who, loving, lov'st them to the end,
On this alone my hopes depend,
That thou wilt plead for me.

2 When weary in the Christian race,
Far off appears my resting place,
And, fainting, I mistrust thy grace,
Then, Saviour, plead for me.

3 When I have erred and gone astray
Afar from thine and wisdom's way,
And see no glimmering, guiding ray,
Still, Saviour, plead for me.

4 When Satan, by my sins made bold,
Strives from thy cross to loose my hold,
Then with thy pitying arms enfold,
And plead, oh, plead for me!

WISNER. 8s & 6. OR 8s & 4.

5 And when my dying hour draws near,
　Darkened with anguish, guilt, and fear,
　Then to my fainting sight appear,
　　Pleading in heaven for me.

6 When the full light of heavenly day
　Reveals my sins in dread array,
　Say thou hast washed them all away;
　　Oh, say thou plead'st for me!

771. *The unseen Friend.*

1 O HOLY Saviour! Friend unseen,
　Since on thine arm thou bid'st me lean,
　Help me, throughout life's changing scene,
　　By faith to cling to thee!

2 Blest with this fellowship divine,
　Take what thou wilt, I'll not repine;
　For, as the branches to the vine,
　　My soul would cling to thee.

3 Though far from home, fatigued, oppressed,
　Here have I found a place of rest;
　An exile still, yet not unblest,
　　Because I cling to thee.

4 What though the world deceitful prove,
　And earthly friends and hopes remove;
　With patient, uncomplaining love
　　Still would I cling to thee.

5 Though oft I seem to tread alone
　Life's dreary waste, with thorns o'ergrown,
　Thy voice of love, in gentlest tone,
　　Still whispers, "Cling to me!"

6 Though faith and hope are often tried,
　I ask not, need not aught beside;
　So safe, so calm, so satisfied,
　　The soul that clings to thee!

844.* *The Hour of Prayer.*

1 MY God! is any hour so sweet,
　From blush of morn to evening star,
　As that which calls me to thy feet—
　　The hour of prayer?

2 Blest is the tranquil hour of morn,
　And blest that hour of solemn eve,
　When, on the wings of prayer up-borne,
　　The world I leave.

3 Then is my strength by thee renewed;
　Then are my sins by thee forgiven;
　Then dost thou cheer my solitude
　　With hopes of heaven.

4 No words can tell what sweet relief
　There for my every want I find;
　What strength for warfare, balm for grief,
　　What peace of mind!

5 Hushed is each doubt, gone every fear;
　My spirit seems in heaven to stay;
　And ev'n the penitential tear
　　Is wiped away.

6 Lord! till I reach that blissful shore
　No privilege so dear shall be
　As thus my inmost soul to pour
　　In prayer to thee.

　　* Observe the tie for this Hymn.

ITALIAN HYMN. 6s & 4s.

451. *Prayer for the cheering Presence of the Spirit.*

1 Come, Holy Ghost,—in love
  Shed on us from above
    Thine own bright ray!
  Divinely good thou art;
  Thy sacred gifts impart
  To gladden each sad heart:
    Oh, come to-day!

2 Come, tend'rest Friend, and best,
  Our most delightful guest,
    With soothing power
  Rest, which the weary know,
  Shade, 'mid the noontide glow,
  Peace, when deep griefs o'erflow,—
    Cheer us, this hour!

3 Come, Light serene, and still
  Our inmost bosoms fill;
    Dwell in each breast:
  We know no dawn but thine;
  Send forth thy beams divine,
  On our dark souls to shine,
    And make us blest!

4 Exalt our low desires;
  Extinguish passion's fires;
    Heal every wound:
  Our stubborn spirits bend;
  Our icy coldness end;
  Our devious steps attend,
    While heavenward bound.

5 Come, all the faithful bless;
  Let all, who Christ confess,
    His praise employ;
  Give virtue's rich reward;
  Victorious death accord,
  And, with our glorious Lord,
    Eternal joy!

720. *"What have I done for Thee?" Acts 9: 6.*

1 O thou best gift of heaven,
  Thou who thyself hast given,—
    For thou hast died!
  This thou hast done for me:
  |: What have I done for thee, :|
    Thou crucified?

2 I long to serve thee more;
  Reveal an open door,
    Saviour, to me:
  Then, counting all but loss,
  |: I'll glory in thy cross, :|
    And follow thee.

3 Do thou but point the way,
  And give me strength t' obey;
    Thy will be mine:
  Then can I think it joy
  |: To suffer or to die :|
    Since I am thine.

1084. *"He took them up in His arms."*

1 Shepherd of tender youth,
  Guiding in love and truth
    Through devious ways—
  Christ, our triumphant King,
  We come thy name to sing,
  And here our children bring,
    To shout thy praise.

2 Thou art our holy Lord,
  O all-subduing Word,
    Healer of strife:
  Thou didst thyself abase,
  That from sin's deep disgrace
  Thou mightest save our race,
    And give us life.

OLIVET. 6s & 4s.

3 Ever be near our side,
  Our Shepherd and our Guide,
    Our staff and song;
  Jesus, thou Christ of God,
  By thine enduring word
  Lead us where thou hast trod;
    Make our faith strong.

4 So now, and till we die,
  Sound we thy praises high,
    And joyful sing:
  Let all the holy throng,
  Who to thy church belong,
  Unite and swell the song
    To Christ our King!

722. "*My faith looks up to Thee.*"

1 My faith looks up to thee,
  Thou Lamb of Calvary,
    Saviour Divine!
  Now hear me while I pray;
  Take all my guilt away;
  Oh, let me, from this day,
    Be wholly thine!

2 May thy rich grace impart
  Strength to my fainting heart,
    My zeal inspire!
  As thou hast died for me,
  Oh, may my love to thee
  Pure, warm, and changeless be—
    A living fire!

3 While life's dark maze I tread,
  And griefs around me spread,
    Be thou my guide;
  Bid darkness turn to day,
  Wipe sorrow's tears away,

  Nor let me ever stray
    From thee aside.

4 When ends life's transient dream,
  When death's cold, sullen stream
    Shall o'er me roll,
  Blest Saviour! then, in love,
  Fear and distrust remove;
  Oh, bear me safe above—
    A ransomed soul!

1202. "*Forsake me not when my strength faileth.*"

1 LOWLY and solemn be
  Thy children's cry to thee,
    Father divine!
  A hymn of suppliant breath,
  |: Owning that life and death :|
    Alike are thine.

2 O Father! in that hour
  When earth all succoring power
    Shall disavow,
  When spear, and shield, and crown
  |: In faintness are cast down, :|
    Sustain us thou!

3 By him who bowed to take
  The death-cup for our sake,
    The thorn, the rod,—
  From whom the last dismay
  |: Was not to pass away, :|
    Aid us, O God!

4 Trembling beside the grave,
  We call on thee to save,
    Father divine!
  Hear, hear our suppliant breath;
  |: Keep us, in life and death, :|
    Thine, only thine.

CANONBURY. 7s & 6s.

293. "*O sacred Head, now wounded!*"

1 O SACRED Head, now wounded!
   With grief and shame weighed down;
O sacred brow, surrounded
   With thorns, thine only crown!
Once on a throne of glory,
   Adorned with light divine,
Now all despised and gory,
   I joy to call thee mine.

2 On me, as thou art dying,
   Oh, turn thy pitying eye!
To thee for mercy crying,
   Before thy cross I lie.
Thine, thine the bitter passion,
   Thy pain is all for me;
Mine, mine the deep transgression,
   My sins are all on thee.

3 What language can I borrow
   To thank thee, dearest Friend,
For all this dying sorrow,
   Of all my woes the end?
Oh, can I leave thee ever?
   Then do not thou leave me:
Lord, let me never, never
   Outlive my love to thee.

4 Be near when I am dying;
   Then close beside me stand;
Let me, while faint and sighing,
   Lean calmly on thy hand:
These eyes new faith receiving,
   From thine eye shall not move;
For he who dies believing,
   Dies safely in thy love.

DOXOLOGY.

To thee be praise for ever
   Thou glorious King of Kings!
Thy wondrous love and favor
   Each ransomed spirit sings:
We'll celebrate thy glory
   With all thy saints above,
And shout the joyful story
   Of thy redeeming love.

GOODWIN. 7s & 6s.

326. *"The exceeding riches of His grace."*

1 O Lord, thy love's unbounded!
  So full, so sweet, so free!
 Our thoughts are all confounded,
  Whene'er we think on thee;
 For us, thou cam'st from heaven,
  For us to bleed and die;
 That, purchased and forgiven,
  We might ascend on high.

2 Oh, let this love constrain us
  To give our hearts to thee;
 Let nothing henceforth pain us,
  But that which paineth thee!
 Our joy, our one endeavor,
  Through suffering, conflict, shame,
 To serve thee, gracious Saviour,
  And magnify thy name!

1230. *Contrast of Heaven with Earth.*
(An ancient Hymn.)

1 Brief life is here our portion,
  Brief sorrow, short-lived care;
 The life that knows no ending,
  The tearless life is there:
 Reward of grace how wondrous!
  Short toil—eternal rest!
 Oh! miracle of mercy,
  That rebels should be blest!—

2 That we, with sin polluted,
  Should have our home on high!
 That we should dwell in mansions,
  Beyond the starry sky!
 And now we fight the battle,
  And then we wear the crown
 Of full and everlasting,
  And ever bright renown!

3 I know not, oh! I know not
  What social joys are there;
 What pure, unfading glory,
  What light beyond compare:—
 And when I fain would sing them,
  My spirit fails and faints,—
 And vainly strives to image
  Th' assembly of the saints.

4 There is the throne of David,
  And there from toil released,
 The shouts of them that triumph,
  The song of them that feast;
 O Garden free from sorrow!
  O Plains that fear no strife!
 O princely Bowers, all blooming!
  O Realm and Home of life!

HERMON. C. M.

1. *"After this manner, therefore, pray ye."*
Matt. 6. Luke 11.

1 Our Father, God, who art in heaven,
  All hallowed be thy name!
Thy kingdom come: thy will be done,
  In earth and heaven the same!

2 Give us, this day, our daily bread;
  And, as we those forgive
Who sin against us, so may we
  Forgiving grace receive.

3 Into temptation lead us not;
  From evil set us free;
And thine the kingdom, thine the power
  And glory, ever be.

67. *"Thou, Lord, only makest me dwell in safety."*

1 Lord, thou wilt hear me when I pray;
  I am for ever thine;
I fear before thee all the day,
  Nor would I dare to sin.

2 And while I rest my weary head,
  From cares and business free,
'Tis sweet conversing on my bed
  With my own heart and thee.

3 I pay this evening sacrifice;
  And when my work is done,
Great God! my faith and hope relies
  Upon thy grace alone.

4 Thus, with my thoughts composed to peace,
  I give mine eyes to sleep;
Thy hand in safety keeps my days
  And will my slumbers keep.

80. *Blessing in the Sanctuary.*

1 Again our earthly cares we leave,
  And in thy courts appear;
Again with joyful feet we come
  To meet our Saviour here.

2 Within these walls let holy peace,
  And love and concord dwell:
Here give the troubled conscience ease,
  The wounded spirit heal.

3 The feeling heart, the melting eye,
  The humble mind bestow;
And shine upon us from on high,
  To make our graces grow.

4 In faith may we receive thy word,
  In faith present our prayers;
And in the presence of our Lord
  Unbosom all our cares.

5 Show us some token of thy love,
  Our fainting hope to raise;
And pour thy blessings from above,
  That we may render praise.

127. *The Tempest stilled.*

1 Great Ruler of all nature's frame!
  We own thy power divine;
We hear thy breath in every storm,
  For all the winds are thine.

2 Wide as they sweep their sounding way
  They work thy sovereign will;
And, awed by thy majestic voice,
  The tempest shall be still.

3 Thy mercy tempers every blast
  To those who seek thy face;
And mingles with the tempest's roar
  The whispers of thy grace.

4 Those gentle whispers let me hear,
  Till all the tumults cease;
And gales of paradise shall soothe
  My weary soul to peace.

PHUVAH. C. M.

172. *"Herein is Love."*

1 My God, how wonderful thou art,
  Thy majesty how bright!
  How glorious is thy mercy seat,
  In depths of burning light!

2 Yet I may love thee too, O Lord,
  Almighty as thou art;
  For thou hast stooped to ask of me
  The love of my poor heart.

3 No earthly father loves like thee,
  No mother half so mild
  Bears and forbears, as thou hast done
  With me, thy sinful child.

4 My God, how wonderful thou art,
  Thou everlasting Friend!
  On thee I stay my trusting heart,
  Till faith in vision end.

186. *" Thy judgments are a great deep."*

1 Thy way, O Lord, is in the sea;
  Thy paths I can not trace,
  Nor comprehend the mystery
  Of thine unbounded grace.

2 'T is but in part I know thy will;
  I bless thee for the sight:
  When will thy love the rest reveal,
  In glory's clearer light?

3 With rapture shall I then survey
  Thy providence and grace;
  And spend an everlasting day
  In wonder, love, and praise.

213. *"O God, Thou hast taught me from my youth."*—Psalm 71.

1 Almighty Father of mankind!
  On thee my hopes remain;
  And when the day of trouble comes,
  I shall not trust in vain.

2 In early years, thou wast my guide,
  And of my youth, the friend;
  And, as my days began with thee,
  With thee my days shall end.

3 I know the Power in whom I trust,
  The arm on which I lean;
  He will my Saviour ever be,
  Who has my Saviour been.

4 Thou wilt not cast me off when age
  And evil days descend;
  Thou wilt not leave me in despair,
  To mourn my latter end.

5 Therefore, in life I 'll trust in thee;
  In death I will adore;
  And after death will sing thy praise,
  When time shall be no more.

216. *Prayer for Divine Guidance.*

1 O God of Bethel! by whose hand
  Thy people still are fed;
  Who through this weary pilgrimage
  Hast all our fathers led;—

2 Our vows, our prayers, we now present
  Before thy throne of grace;
  God of our fathers! be the God
  Of their succeeding race.

3 Through each perplexing path of life
  Our wandering footsteps guide;
  Give us, each day, our daily bread,
  And raiment fit provide.

4 Oh, spread thy covering wings around,
  Till all our wanderings cease,
  And at our Father's loved abode,
  Our souls arrive in peace.

5 Such blessings from thy gracious hand
  Our humble prayers implore;
  And thou shalt be our chosen God,
  Our portion evermore.

ENEVA. 7s & 6s.

578. *Prayer for a broken heart.*

1 Saviour, Prince, enthroned above,
   Repentance to impart,
 Give me, through thy dying love,
   The humble, contrite heart.
 Give what I have long implored—
   Let me share thy grief unknown:
 Turn and look upon me, Lord,
   And break my heart of stone.

2 See me, Saviour, from above,
   Nor suffer me to die;
 Life, and happiness, and love
   Beam from thy gracious eye:
 Speak the reconciling word,
   All its melting power make known·
 Turn and look upon me, Lord,
   And break my heart of stone.

3 Look, as when thy dying eye
   Was closed, that we might live;
 When thy supplicating cry
   To God was heard, "Forgive:"
 Surely, with that dying word,
   Jesus turns and says, 'tis done:
 Oh, my bleeding, loving Lord,
   This breaks my heart of stone!

728.* *"Thy blood was shed for me."*

1 God of my salvation, hear,
   And help me to believe;
 Simply do I now draw near
   Thy blessing to receive:
 Full of guilt, alas! I am,
   But to thy wounds for refuge flee:
 Friend of sinners, spotless Lamb!
   Thy blood was shed for me.

2 Standing now as newly slain,
   To thee I lift mine eye;
 Balm of all my grief and pain,
   Thy blood is alway nigh:
 Now as yesterday the same
   Thou art, and wilt for ever be:
 Friend of sinners, spotless Lamb!
   Thy blood was shed for me.

3 Saviour! from thy wounded side
   I never will depart:
 Here will I my spirit hide,
   When I am pure in heart:
 Till my place above I claim,
   This only shall be all my plea:
 Friend of sinners, spotless Lamb!
   Thy blood was shed for me.

* Omit the tie for this Hymn.

AMSTERDAM. 7s & 6s.

1049. *" My peace I give unto you."*

1 LAMB of God! whose bleeding love
    We now recall to mind,
Send the answer from above,
    And let us mercy find:
Think on us, who think on thee;
    Every burdened soul release;
Oh, remember Calvary,
    And bid us go in peace!

2 By thine agonizing pain,
    And bloody sweat, we pray—
By thy dying love to man,
    Take all our sins away:
Burst our bonds and set us free,
    From our crime and guilt release;
Oh, remember Calvary,
    And bid **us** go in peace!

3 Through thy blood, by faith applied,
    Do thou our pardon seal;
Speak us freely justified,
    Our wounded spirits heal;
By thy passion on the tree,
    Let our griefs and troubles **cease**;
Oh, remember Calvary,
    And bid **us** go in peace!

1167. *" We all do fade as a leaf."*

1 TIME is winging us away
    To our eternal home;
Life is but a winter's day—
    A journey to the tomb;
Youth and vigor soon will flee,
    Blooming beauty lose its charms;
All that 's mortal soon shall be
    Enclosed in death's cold arms.

2 Time is winging us away
    To our eternal home;
Life is but a winter's day—
    A journey to the tomb;
But the Christian shall enjoy
    Health and beauty, soon, above,
Far beyond the world's alloy,
    Secure in Jesus' **love.**

1238. *" I press toward the mark for the prize."*

1 RISE, my soul! and stretch thy **wings,**
    Thy better portion trace;
Rise, from transitory things,
    Toward heaven, thy native place:
Sun, and moon, and stars decay,
    Time shall soon this earth remove;
Rise, my soul, and haste away
    To seats prepared above!

2 Rivers to the ocean run,
    Nor stay in all their course;
Fire ascending, seeks the sun,—
    Both speed them to their source;
So a soul that 's born of God,
    Pants to view his glorious face,
Upward tends to his abode,
    To rest in his embrace.

3 Cease, ye pilgrims! cease to mourn,—
    Press onward to the prize;
Soon your Saviour will return
    Triumphant in the skies:
Yet a season, and you know
    Happy entrance will be given,
All your sorrows left below,
    And earth exchanged for heaven.

GREENVILLE. 8s & 7s. Double.

742. *Prayer for Deliverance from Evil.*

1 Suff'ring Son of Man, be near me,
  All my suff'rings to sustain,
 By thy sorer griefs to cheer me,
  By thy more than mortal pain;
 By thy fainting in the garden,
  By thy bloody sweat, I pray,
 Write upon my heart the pardon;
  Take my sins and fears away.

2 By the travail of thy spirit,
  By thine outcry on the tree,
 By thine agonizing merit,
  In my pangs, remember me!
 By thy death I now implore thee,
  Lord! my dying soul befriend;
 Make me lovingly adore thee,
  Make me faithful to the end.

745. *" Wash me, and I shall be whiter than snow."*

1 Jesus! who on Calv'ry's mountain
  Poured thy precious blood for me,
 Wash me in its flowing fountain,
  That my soul may spotless be.

2 I have sinned, but, oh, restore me;
  For, unless thou smile on me,
 Dark is all the world before me,
  Darker yet eternity!

3 In thy word I hear thee saying,
  "Come, and I will give you rest;"
 Glad the gracious call obeying,
  See, I hasten to thy breast.

4 Grant, oh, grant thy Spirit's teaching,
  That I may not go astray,
 Till, the gate of heaven reaching,
  Earth and sin are passed away!

1119. *" Remember not against us former iniquities."*

1 Dread Jehovah! God of nations!
  From thy temple in the skies,
 Hear thy people's supplications;
  Now for their deliverance rise.

2 Tho' our sins, our hearts confounding,
  Long and loud for vengeance call,
 Thou hast mercy more abounding:
  Jesus' blood can cleanse them all.

3 Let that love vail our transgression;
  Let that blood our guilt efface;
 Save thy people from oppression;
  Save from spoil thy holy place.

4 Lo! with deep contrition turning,
  Humbly at thy feet we bend;
 Hear us, fasting, praying, mourning,
  Hear us, spare us, and defend!

1281. ** " That great day of wrath and terror."* (A Hymn of the 7th Century.)

1 That great day of wrath and terror,
  That last day of woe and doom,
 Like a thief that comes at midnight,
  On the sons of men shall come;

2 When the King of heavenly glory
  Shall assume his throne on high;
 When the bands of all his angels
  Shall be near him in the sky;

* Commence with the latter part of the tune for the 5th stanza.

JAYNES. 8s & 7s. DOUBLE.

3 When the sun shall turn to sackcloth,
   And the moon be red as blood;
  When the stars shall fall from heaven,
   As the leaves fall in a wood.
4 Therefore, man, while yet thou mayest,
   From the tempter's malice fly!
  Give thy bread to feed the hungry,
   If thou seek'st to win the sky.
5 Let thy loins be straitly girded,
   Life be pure, and heart be right,
  That whene'er the bridegroom cometh,
   Full thy lamp may shine, and bright.

91. *Apostolic Benediction.*

1 MAY the grace of Christ the Saviour,
   And the Father's boundless love,
  With the Holy Spirit's favor,
   Rest upon us from above.
2 Thus may we abide in union
   With each other and the Lord,
  And possess, in sweet communion,
   Joys which earth can not afford.

561. *Penitent Entreaty.*

1 JESUS, full of all compassion,
   Hear thine humble suppliant's cry:
  Let me know thy great salvation;
   See! I languish, faint, and die.
  Guilty, but with heart relenting,
   Overwhelmed with hopeless grief,
  Prostrate at thy feet repenting—
   Send, oh, send me quick relief!
2 Whither should a wretch be flying,
   But to him who comfort gives?
  Whither, from the dread of dying,
   But to him who ever lives?
  While I view thee, wounded, grieving,
   Breathless, on the cursèd tree,
  Fain I'd feel my heart believing
   Thou didst suffer thus for me.

3 In the world of endless ruin,
   Let it never, Lord, be said,
  "Here's a soul that perished, suing
   For the boasted Saviour's aid!"
  Saved!—the deed shall spread new glory
   Through the shining realms above;
  Angels sing the pleasing story,
   All enraptured with thy love.

867.* *"The greatest of these is Charity."* 1 Cor. 13.

1 MEEK and lowly, pure and holy,
   Chief among the blessèd three,
  Turning sadness into gladness,
   Heaven-born art thou, Charity!
2 Pity dwelleth in thy bosom,
   Kindness reigneth o'er thy heart;
  Gentle thoughts alone can sway thee—
   Judgment hath in thee no part.
3 Hoping ever, failing never,
   Though deceived, believing still;
  Long abiding, all confiding
   To thy heavenly Father's will;
4 Never weary of well-doing,
   Never fearful of the end;
  Claiming all mankind as brothers,
   Thou dost all alike befriend.
5 Meek and lowly, pure and holy,
   Chief among the blessèd three,
  Turning sadness into gladness,
   Heaven-born art thou, Charity!

DOXOLOGY.

PRAISE the God of our salvation,
   Praise the Father's boundless love;
  Praise the Lamb, our expiation;
   Praise the Spirit from above;
  Praise the Fountain of salvation,
   Him by whom our spirits live;
  Undivided adoration
   To the one Jehovah give!

* Commence with the latter part of the tune for the 5th stanza.

WOODLAND. C. M.

The third line of each stanza is repeated.

388. *"At the right hand of the Majesty on high."*

1 He who on earth as man was known,
And bore our sins and pains,
Now, seated on th' eternal throne,
The God of glory reigns.

2 His hands the wheels of nature guide
With an unerring skill,
And countless worlds, extended wide,
Obey his sovereign will.

3 While harps unnumbered sound his praise
In yonder world above,
His saints on earth admire his ways,
And glory in his love.

4 When troubles, like the burning sun,
Beat heavy on their head,
To this almighty Rock they run,
And find a pleasing shade.

5 How glorious he! how happy they,
In such a glorious Friend!
Whose love secures them all the way,
And crowns them at the end.

455. *Prayer for the Witness of the Spirit.*

1 Why should the children of a King
Go mourning all their days?
Great Comforter! descend and bring
Some tokens of thy grace.

2 Dost thou not dwell in all thy saints,
And seal them heirs of heaven?
When wilt thou banish my complaints,
And show my sins forgiven?

3 Assure my conscience of her part
In my Redeemer's blood;
And bear thy witness with my heart,
That I am born of God.

4 Thou art the earnest of his love,
The pledge of joys to come;
And thy soft wings, celestial Dove,
Will safe convey me home.

489. *The Bible for the Young.*
Psalm 119.

1 How shall the young secure their hearts,
And guard their lives from sin?
Thy word the choicest rules imparts,
To keep the conscience clean.

2 'Tis like the sun, a heavenly light,
That guides us all the day;
And, through the dangers of the night,
A lamp to lead our way.

3 Thy precepts make me truly wise:
I hate the sinner's road;
I hate my own vain thoughts that rise,
But love thy law, my God.

4 Thy word is everlasting truth,
How pure is every page!
Thy holy book shall guide our youth,
And well support our age.

512. *"Return, O wanderer."*

1 Return, O wanderer, now return,
And seek thy Father's face!
Those new desires, which in thee burn,
Were kindled by his grace.

2 Return, O wanderer, now return!
He hears thy humble sigh;
He sees thy softened spirit mourn,
When no one else is nigh.

3 Return, O wanderer, now return!
Thy Saviour bids thee live;
Go to his bleeding feet, and learn
How freely he'll forgive.

4 Return, O wanderer, now return,
And wipe the falling tear!
Thy Father calls—no longer mourn;
His love invites thee near.

635. *Prayer for a tender Conscience.*

1 Oh for a principle within
Of jealous, godly fear!

MEAR. C. M.

Oh for a tender dread of sin—
 A pain to feel it near!
2 That I from thee no more may part,
 No more thy goodness grieve,
 The filial awe, the fleshly heart,
 The tender conscience, give.

3 Quick as the apple of the eye,
 O God! my conscience make;
 Awake my soul when sin is nigh,
 And keep it still awake.

4 If to the right or left I stray,
 That moment, Lord, reprove;
 And let me weep my life away,
 For having grieved thy love.

5 Oh, may the least omission pain
 My well-instructed soul;
 And drive me to the blood again,
 Which makes the wounded whole!

850. *"Verily, God hath heard me."*
   Psalm 66.
1 Now shall my solemn vows be paid
 To that almighty Power
 That heard the long requests I made
 In my distressful hour.

2 My lips and cheerful heart prepare
 To make his mercies known;
 Come, ye that fear my God, and hear
 The wonders he hath done.

3 When on my head huge sorrows fell,
 I sought his heavenly aid;
 He saved my sinking soul from hell,
 And death's eternal shade.

4 If sin lay covered in my heart
 While prayer employed my tongue,
 The Lord hath shown me no regard,
 Nor I his praises sung.

5 But God—his name be ever blest—
 Hath set my spirit free;

Nor turned from him my poor request,
 Nor turned his heart from me.

865. *The new Commandment.*—John 13 : 34.
1 With love the Saviour's heart o'erflowed;
 Love spoke in every breath;
 Supreme it reigned, throughout his life,
 And triumphed in his death.

2 Behold, this new command he gives
 To those that bear his name,—
 That they shall one another love,
 As he hath lovéd them.

3 In every action, every thought,
 Be this great law fulfilled;
 Forgotten be each selfish aim,
 Each angry passion stilled.

4 Let all who bear the name of Christ,
 While they his sufferings view,
 Think of his words, "Each other love,
 As I have lovéd you."

1217. *"And entered into rest."*
1 Why should our tears in sorrow flow,
 When God recalls his own,
 And bids them leave a world of woe
 For an immortal crown?

2 Is not ev'n death a gain to those
 Whose life to God is given?
 Gladly to earth their eyes they close,
 To open them in heaven.

3 Their toils are past, their work is done,
 And they are fully blest:
 They fought the fight, the victory won,
 And entered into rest.

4 Then let our sorrows cease to flow;
 God has recalled his own:
 And let our hearts, in every woe,
 Still say—"Thy will be done!"

BONAR. S. M. DOUBLE.

1220. *The Pilgrim's Song.*

1 A FEW more years shall roll,
  A few more seasons come;
And we shall be with those that **rest**,
  Asleep within the tomb
Then, O my Lord, prepare
  My soul for that great day;
Oh, wash me in thy precious blood,
  And take my sins away!

2 A few more storms shall beat
  On this wild, rocky shore;
And we shall be where tempests cease,
  And surges swell no more:
Then, O my Lord, prepare
  My soul for that calm day;
Oh, wash me in thy precious blood,
  And take my sins away!

3 A few more struggles here,
  A few more partings o'er,
A few more toils, a few more tears,
  And we shall weep **no more:**
Then, O my Lord, prepare
  My soul for that blest day;
Oh, wash me in thy precious blood,
  And take my sins away!

4 A few more Sabbaths here
  Shall cheer us on our way;
And we shall reach the endless rest,
  Th' eternal Sabbath-day:
Then, O my Lord, prepare
  My soul for that sweet day;
Oh, wash me in thy precious blood,
  And take my sins away!

5 'T is but a little while,
  And he shall come again,

Who died that we might live, who live;
  That we with him may reign:
Then, O my Lord, prepare
  My soul for that glad day;
Oh, wash me in thy precious blood,
  And take my sins away!

1019. *The Church in the Wilderness.*

1 FAR down the ages now,
  Much of her journey done,
The pilgrim church pursues her way,
  Until her crown be won.
2 The story of the past
  Comes up before her view;
How well it seems to suit her still—
  Old, and yet ever new!

3 It is the **oft-told tale**
  Of sin and weariness,
Of grace and love yet flowing down
  To pardon and to bless.
4 No wider is the gate,
  No broader is the way,
No smoother is the ancient path,
  That leads to life and day.

5 No sweeter is the cup,
  Nor less **our** lot of ill:
'T was tribulation ages since,
  'T is tribulation still.
6 No slacker grows the fight,
  No feebler is the foe,
Nor less the need of armor tried,
  Of shield, and spear, and bow.

7 Thus onward still we press,
  Through evil and through good,—
Through pain, and poverty, and want,
  Through peril and through blood.

LISBON. S. M.

3 Still faithful to our God,
And to our Captain true,
We follow where he leads the way,
The kingdom in our view.

527. *Invitation from Heaven to Earth.*

1 Come to the land of peace;
From shadows come away;
Where all the sounds of weeping cease,
And storms no more have sway.

2 Fear hath no dwelling here;
But pure repose and love
Breathe through the bright, celestial air
The spirit of the dove.

3 Come to the bright and blest,
Gathered from every land;
For here thy soul shall find its rest,
Amid the shining band.

4 In this divine abode
Change leaves no saddening trace;

Come, trusting spirit, to thy God,
Thy holy resting-place.

881. *Trustful Activity.*—Eccl. 11: 6.

1 Sow in the morn thy seed,
At eve hold not thy hand;
To doubt and fear give thou no heed;
Broad-cast it o'er the land!

2 Then duly shall appear,
In verdure, beauty, strength,
The tender blade, the stalk, the ear,
And the full corn at length.

3 Thou canst not toil in vain:
Cold, heat, and moist and dry
Shall foster and mature the grain
For garners in the sky.

4 Then, when the glorious end,
The day of God, shall come,
The angel-reapers shall descend,
And heaven sing "Harvest-home!"

STATE STREET. S. M.

BELGRAVE. 7s. DOUBLE.

408. *"Jesus, Lover of my soul."*

1 Jesus, Lover of my soul,
  Let me to thy bosom fly,
While the waters near me roll,
  While the tempest still is high:
Hide me, O my Saviour, hide,
  Till the storm of life is past;
Safe into the haven guide:
  Oh, receive my soul at last!

2 Other refuge have I none:
  Hangs my helpless soul on thee:
Leave, ah! leave me not alone,
  Still support and comfort me:
All my trust on thee is stayed,
  All my help from thee I bring;
Cover my defenseless head
  With the shadow of thy wing.

409. *Christ a sufficient Saviour.*

1 Thou, O Christ, art all I want,
  More than all in thee I find:
Raise the fallen, cheer the faint,
  Heal the sick, and lead the blind.
Just and holy is thy name;
  I am all unrighteousness:
False and full of sin I am;
  Thou art full of truth and grace.

2 Plenteous grace with thee is found,
  Grace to cover all my sin;
Let the healing streams abound,
  Make and keep me pure within.
Thou of life the fountain art,
  Freely let me take of thee;
Spring thou up within my heart;
  Rise to all eternity.

410. *"Looking unto Jesus."*

1 When, along life's thorny road,
  Faints the soul beneath the load,
By its cares and sins oppressed,
  Finds on earth no peace or rest;
When the wily tempter's near,
  Filling us with doubts and fear,
Jesus, to thy feet we flee;
  Jesus, we will look to thee.

2 Thou, our Saviour, from the throne
  List'nest to thy people's moan:
Thou, the living Head, dost share
  Every pang thy members bear;
Full of tenderness thou art,
  Thou wilt heal the broken heart;
Full of power, thine arm shall quell
  All the rage and might of hell.

3 Mighty to redeem and save,
  Thou hast overcome the grave:
Thou the bars of death hast riven,
  Opened wide the gate of heaven:
Soon in glory thou shalt come,
  Taking thy poor pilgrims home:
Jesus, then we all shall be
  Ever, ever, Lord, with thee!

472. *The Thrice Holy One.*

1 Holy, holy, holy Lord
  God of Hosts! when heaven and earth
Out of darkness, at thy word
  Issued into glorious birth,
All thy works before thee stood,
  And thine eye beheld them good;
While they sung with sweet accord,
  Holy, holy, holy Lord.

DALLAS. 7s.

2 Holy, holy, holy! thee,
    One Jehovah evermore,
  Father, Son, and Spirit! we,
    Dust and ashes, would adore:
  Lightly by the world esteemed,
  From that world by thee redeemed,
  Sing we here with glad accord,
  Holy, holy, holy Lord!

3 Holy, holy, holy! all
    Heaven's triumphant choir shall sing,
  While the ransomed nations fall
    At the footstool of their King:
  Then shall saints and seraphim,
  Harps and voices, swell one hymn,
  Blending in sublime accord,
  Holy, holy, holy Lord!

639. *"Whom have I in heaven but Thee?"*

1 LORD of earth! thy forming hand
    Well this beauteous frame hath planned,
  Woods that wave, and hills that tower,
    Ocean rolling in his power:
  Yet, amid this scene so fair,
  Should I cease thy smile to share,
  What were all its joys to me?
  Whom have I on earth but thee?

2 Lord of heaven! beyond our sight
    Shines a world of purer light:
  There, in love's unclouded reign,
    Parted hands shall meet again:
  Oh, that world is passing fair!
  Yet, if thou wert absent there,
  What were all its joys to me?
  Whom have I in heaven but thee?

3 Lord of earth and heaven! my breast
    Seeks in thee its only rest:
  I was lost; thy accents mild
    Homeward lured thy wandering child.
  Oh! should once thy smile divine
  Cease upon my soul to shine,
  What were earth or heaven to me
  Whom have I in each but thee?

874. *The accepted Offering.*

1 LORD, what offering shall we bring,
    At thine altars when be bow?
  Hearts, the pure unsullied spring,
    Whence the kind affections flow;
  Soft compassion's feeling soul,
    By the melting eye expressed;
  Sympathy, at whose control
    Sorrow leaves the wounded breast;

2 Willing hands to lead the blind,
    Bind the wounded, feed the poor;
  Love, embracing all our kind;
    Charity, with liberal store:—
  Teach us, O thou heavenly King,
    Thus to show our grateful mind,
  Thus th' accepted offering bring,
    Love to thee, and all mankind.

1179. *"The valley of the shadow of death."*
        Psalm 23.

1 THOUGH I walk the downward shade,
    Deepening through the vale of death,
  Yet I will not be afraid,
    But, with my departing breath,
  I will glory in my God,
    In my Saviour I will trust,
  Strengthened by his staff and rod,
    While this body falls to dust.

2 Soon on wings, on wings of love,
    My transported soul shall rise,
  Like the home-returning dove,
    Vanishing through boundless skies;
  Then, where death shall be no more,
    Sin nor suffering ne'er molest,
  All my days of mourning o'er,
    In his presence I shall rest.

BYRD. C. M. DOUBLE.

4. *Habitual Devotion.*

1 While thee I seek, protecting Power!
  Be my vain wishes stilled;
  And may this consecrated hour
  With better hopes be filled!
2 Thy love the power of thought bestowed;
  To thee my thoughts would soar:
  Thy mercy o'er my life has flowed;
  That mercy I adore.
3 In each event of life, how **clear**
  Thy ruling hand I see!
  Each blessing to my soul more **dear**,
  Because conferred by thee.
4 In every joy that crowns my days,
  In every pain I bear,
  My heart shall find delight in praise,
  Or seek relief in prayer.
5 When gladness wings my favored hour,
  Thy love my thoughts shall fill;
  Resigned, when storms of sorrow **lower**,
  My soul shall meet thy will.
6 My lifted eye, without a tear,
  The gathering storm shall see;
  My steadfast heart shall know no fear;
  That heart will rest on thee.

211. *"Remembrance of Divine Mercies."*

1 When all thy mercies, O my God,
  My rising soul surveys,
  Transported with the view, I'm lost
  In wonder, love, and praise!
2 Unnumbered comforts on my soul
  Thy tender care bestowed,
  Before my infant heart conceived
  From whom **those** comforts flowed.
3 When, **in the** slippery paths of youth,
  With **heedless** step I ran,
  Thine arm, unseen, conveyed me safe,
  And led me **up to** man.

4 Ten thousand, thousand precious gifts
  My daily thanks employ;
  Nor is the least a cheerful heart,
  That tastes those gifts with joy.
5 Through every period of my life
  Thy goodness I'll pursue;
  And, after death, in distant worlds,
  The glorious theme renew.
6 Through all eternity to thee
  A joyful song I'll raise;
  But, oh! eternity's too short
  To utter all thy praise.

222. *"Your heavenly Father feedeth them."*
  Matt. 6: 25–34.

1 Oh, why despond in life's dark vale?
  Why sink to fears a prey?
  Th' almighty power can never fail,
  His love can ne'er decay.
2 Behold the birds that wing the **air**,
  Nor sow nor reap the grain;
  Yet God, with all a father's care,
  Relieves when they complain.
3 Behold the lilies of the field:
  They toil nor labor know;
  Yet royal robes to theirs must yield,
  In beauty's richest glow.
4 That God who hears the raven's cry,
  Who decks the lily's form,
  Will surely all your wants supply,
  And shield you in the storm.
5 **Seek** first his kingdom's grace to share;
  Its righteousness pursue;
  And all that needs your earthly care
  Will be bestowed on you.
6 Why **then** despond in life's dark vale?
  Why sink to fears a prey?
  Th' almighty power can never fail,
  His love can ne'er decay.

EVAN. C. M.

212. *Divine Providence and Grace.*

1 ALMIGHTY Father! gracious Lord!
  Kind Guardian of my days!
Thy mercies let my heart record
  In songs of grateful praise.

2 In life's first **dawn**, my tender frame
  Was thine indulgent care,
Long ere I could pronounce thy name,
  Or breathe the infant prayer.

3 Each rolling year new favors brought
  From thine exhaustless store;
But, ah! in vain my laboring thought
  Would count thy mercies o'er.

4 Still I adore thee, gracious Lord!
  For favors more divine—
That I have known thy sacred word,
  Where all thy glories shine.

5 Lord, when this mortal frame decays,
  And every weakness dies,
Complete the wonders of thy grace,
  And raise me to the skies.

218. *"Beside the still waters."*—Psalm 23.

1 THE Lord himself, the mighty Lord,
  Vouchsafes to be my guide;
The Shepherd, by whose constant care
  My wants are all supplied.

2 In tender grass he makes me feed,
  And gently there repose;
Then leads me to cool shades, and where
  Refreshing water flows.

3 He does my wandering soul reclaim,
  And, to his endless praise,
Instruct with humble zeal to walk
  In his most righteous ways.

4 I pass the gloomy vale of **death**,
  From fear and danger free;
For there his aiding rod and staff
  Defend and comfort me.

5 Since God doth thus his wondrous love
  Through all my life extend,
That life to him I will devote,
  And in his temple spend.

288. *"And Jesus went before them."*
Mark 10; 32.

1 THE Saviour!—what a noble flame
  Was kindled in his breast,
When, hastening to Jerusalem,
  He marched before the rest!

2 Good will to men, and zeal for God,
  His every thought engross;
He longs to be baptized with blood,
  He pants to reach the cross.

3 With all his sufferings full in view,
  And woes to us unknown,
Forth to the task his spirit flew:
  'T was love that urged him on.

4 Lord, we return thee what we can;
  Our hearts shall sound abroad
Salvation to the dying Man,
  And to the rising God!

5 And while thy bleeding glories here
  Engage our wondering eyes,
We learn our lighter cross to bear,
  And hasten to the skies.

DOXOLOGY.

LET God the Father, and the Son,
  And Spirit, be adored,
Where there are works to make him
    known,
  Or saints to love the Lord!

ROSEFIELD. 7s. 6 LINES.

377. *"Glory to our King."*

1 GLORY, glory to our King!
  Crowns unfading wreathe his head;
  Jesus is the name we sing—
  Jesus risen from the dead;
  Jesus, Conqu'ror o'er the grave;
  Jesus, mighty now to save.

2 Jesus is gone up on high,
  Angels come to meet their King;
  Shouts triumphant rend the sky,
  While the Victor's praise they sing:
  "Open now, ye heavenly gates!
  'Tis the King of glory waits."

3 Now behold him high enthroned,
  Glory beaming from his face!
  By adoring angels owned,
  God of holiness and grace!
  Oh, for hearts and tongues to sing
  "Glory, glory to our King!"

4 Jesus, on thy people shine;
  Warm our hearts and tune our tongues,
  That with angels we may join,
  Share their bliss, and swell their songs;
  Glory, honor, praise, and power,
  Lord, be thine for evermore!

425. *"I am the Light of the World."*

1 CHRIST, whose glory fills the skies,
  Christ, the true, the only light,
  Sun of Righteousness! arise;
  Triumph o'er the shades of night;
  Day-spring from on high, be near;
  Day-star, in my heart appear!

2 Dark and cheerless is the morn,
  If thy light is hid from me;
  Joyless is the day's return,
  Till thy mercy's beams I see—
  Till they inward light impart,
  Glad my eyes, and warm my heart.

3 Visit, then, this soul of mine;
  Pierce the gloom of sin and grief,
  Fill me, radiant Sun divine!
  Scatter all my unbelief:
  More and more thyself display,
  Shining to the perfect day.

106. *"The Praise of all His saints."*

PRAISE to God on high be given!
Praise him, all in earth and heaven;
Praise him at the dawn of light,
Praise him at returning night:
Saints below, and saints above,
Praise, oh, praise the God of love!

DOXOLOGY.

PRAISE the name of God most high;
Praise him, all below the sky;
Praise him, all ye heavenly host—
Father, Son, and Holy Ghost!
As through countless ages past,
Evermore his praise shall last.

HALLE. 7s. 6 LINES.

714. *"How much I owe."*

1 When this passing world is done—
　When has sunk yon glorious sun;
　When we stand with Christ in glory,
　Looking o'er life's finished story;
　Then, Lord, shall I fully know—
　Not till then—how much I owe!

2 When I hear the wicked call
　On the rocks and hills to fall;
　When I see them start and shrink,
　On the fiery deluge brink,
　Then, Lord, shall I fully know—
　Not till then—how much I owe!

3 When I stand before the throne,
　Clothed in beauty not my own;
　When I see thee as thou art,
　Love thee with unsinning heart!
　Then, Lord, shall I fully know—
　Not till then—how much I owe!

4 When the praise of heaven I hear,
　Loud as thunders to the ear,
　Loud as many waters' noise,
　Sweet as harp's melodious voice,
　Then, Lord, shall I fully know—
　Not till then—how much I owe!

715. *Obligation to Christ manifested.*

1 Chosen not for good in me,
　Wakened up from wrath to flee,
　Hidden in the Saviour's side,—
　By the Spirit sanctified—
　Teach me, Lord, on earth to show,
　By my love, how much I owe.

2 Oft I walk beneath the cloud,
　Dark as midnight's gloomy shroud;
　But, when fear is at the height,
　Jesus comes, and all is light;
　Blessed Jesus! bid me show
　Doubting saints how much I owe.

3 Oft the nights of sorrow reign—
　Weeping, sickness, sighing, pain;
　But a night thine anger burns—
　Morning comes, and joy returns:
　God of comforts! bid me show
　To thy **poor** how much I owe.

4 When in flowery paths I tread,
　Oft by sin I'm captive led,
　Oft I fall, **but** still arise—
　Jesus comes—the tempter flies:
　Blessed Jesus! bid me show
　Weary sinners all I owe.

BRIGHTON. S. M.

36. *"Make a joyful noise unto Him with psalms."*—Psalm 95.

1 Come, sound his praise abroad,
  And hymns of glory sing;
Jehovah is the sovereign God,
  The universal King.

2 He formed the deeps unknown;
  He gave the seas their bound;
The watery worlds are all his own,
  And all the solid ground.

3 Come, worship at his throne,
  Come, bow before the Lord:
We are his work and not our own;
  He formed us by his word.

4 To-day attend his voice,
  Nor dare provoke his rod;
Come, like the people of his choice,
  And own your gracious God.

355. *"The Lord is risen indeed."*

1 "The Lord is risen indeed;"
  Now is his work performed;
Now is the mighty Captive freed,
  And death our foe disarmed.

2 "The Lord is risen indeed:"
  The grave has lost his prey,
With him is risen the ransomed seed
  To reign in endless day.

3 "The Lord is risen indeed:"
  He lives, to die no more;
He lives, the sinner's cause to plead,
  Whose curse and shame he bore.

4 "The Lord is risen indeed:"
  Attending angels, hear;
Up to the courts of heaven, with speed,
  The joyful tidings bear.

5 Then take your golden lyres,
  And strike each cheerful chord;
Join all the bright, celestial choirs,
  To sing our risen Lord!

681. *"I stand on Zion's mount."*

1 I stand on Zion's mount,
  And view my starry crown;
No power on earth my hope can shake,
  Nor hell can thrust me down.

2 The lofty hills and towers,
  That lift their heads on high,
Shall all be leveled low in dust—
  Their very names shall die.

3 The vaulted heavens shall fall,
  Built by Jehovah's hands;
But firmer than the heavens, the Rock
  Of my salvation stands.

892. *"So fight I, not as one that beateth the air."*

1 My soul! weigh not thy life
  Against thy heavenly crown,
Nor suffer Satan's deadliest strife
  To beat thy courage down.

2 With prayer and crying strong,
  Hold on the fearful fight;
And let the breaking day prolong
  The wrestling of the night.

3 The battle soon will yield,
  If thou thy part fulfill;
For, strong as is the hostile shield
  Thy sword is stronger still.

4 Thine armor is divine—
  Thy feet with victory shod;
And on thy head shall quickly shine
  The diadem of God!

DOVER. S. M.

898. *"Put on the whole armor of God."*
Eph. 6: 11-14.

1 Soldiers of Christ arise,
  And put your armor on—
 Strong in the strength which **God supplies**
  Through his eternal Son—

2 Strong in the Lord of hosts,
  And in his mighty power;
 Who in the strength of Jesus trusts,
  Is more than conqueror.

3 Stand, then, **in his great might**,
  With all his strength endued;
 But take, to **arm** you for the fight,
  The panoply of God;

4 That, having **all** things done,
  And all your conflicts past
 Ye may o'ercome, through Christ alone,
  And stand entire at last.

1014. *"By the grace of God, I am what I am."*

1 Grace! 'tis a charming sound,
  Harmonious to the ear;
 Heaven with the echo shall resound,
  And all the earth shall hear.

2 Grace first contrived a way
  To save rebellious man;
 And all the steps that grace display,
  Which drew the wondrous plan.

3 Grace taught my wandering feet
  To tread the heavenly road;
 And new supplies each hour I meet,
  While pressing on to God.

4 Grace all the work shall crown,
  Through everlasting days;
 It lays in heaven the topmost stone,
  And well deserves the praise.

DOXOLOGY.

The Father and the Son,
 And Spirit we adore;
We praise, we bless, we worship thee,
 Both now and evermore!

SILVER STREET. S. M.

FEDERAL STREET. L. M.

79. *"Arise, O Lord God, into Thy resting-place."*—2 Chron. 6: 41.

1 God in his temple let us meet;
Low on our knees before him bend;
Here hath he fixed his mercy-seat,
Here, on his Sabbath we attend.

2 Arise into thy resting-place,
Thou, and thy ark of strength, O Lord!
Shine through the vail—we seek thy face;
Speak, for we hearken to thy word.

3 With righteousness thy priests array;
Joyful thy chosen people be;
Let those who teach, and hear, and pray,
Let all be holiness to thee.

82. *Christ present in the Sanctuary.*

1 How sweet to leave the world awhile,
And seek the presence of our Lord!
Dear Saviour, on thy people smile,
And come, according to thy word.

2 From busy scenes we now retreat,
That we may here converse with thee;
Ah, Lord, behold us at thy feet!
Let this the "gate of heaven" be.

3 "Chief of ten thousand!" now appear,
That we by faith may see thy face;
Oh, speak, that we thy voice may hear,
And let thy presence fill this place!

306. *"Neither is there salvation in any other."*

1 How shall the sons of men appear,
Great God! before thine awful bar?
How may the guilty hope to find
Acceptance with th' eternal Mind?

2 Not vows, nor groans, nor broken cries,
Not the most costly sacrifice,
Not infant blood, profusely spilt,
Will expiate a sinner's guilt.

3 Thy blood, dear Jesus, thine alone,
Hath sovereign virtue to atone:
Here will we rest our only plea,
When we approach, great God! to thee.

342. *"Unto the Lamb for ever."* Rev. 5.

1 What equal honors shall we bring
To thee, O Lord our God, the Lamb,
When all the notes that angels sing
Are far inferior to thy name?

2 Worthy is he who once was slain,
The Prince of Peace, who groaned and died;
Worthy to rise, and live and reign
At his almighty Father's side.

3 Blessings for ever on the Lamb,
Who bore the curse for wretched men:
Let angels sound his sacred name,
And every creature say, Amen!

1072. *Solomon's Prayer.*—2 Chron. 6.

1 When in these courts we seek thy face,
And dying sinners pray to live,
Hear thou, in heaven, thy dwelling-place,
And when thou hearest, Lord! forgive.

2 When here thy messengers proclaim
The blessed gospel of thy Son,
Still by the power of his great name
Be mighty signs and wonders done.

3 Hosanna!—to their heavenly King
When children's voices raise that song—
Hosanna!—let their angels sing,
And heaven with earth the strain prolong.

4 But will, indeed, Jehovah deign
Here to abide, no transient guest?
Here will the world's Redeemer reign,
And here the Holy Spirit rest?

ROSEDALE. L. M.

5 That glory never hence depart!
  Yet choose not, Lord, this house alone;
  Thy kingdom come to every heart;
  In every bosom fix thy throne.

949. *"Thou in faithfulness hast afflicted me."*

1 Long unafflicted, **undismayed**,
  In pleasure's path **secure I strayed**;
  Thou mad'st **me feel thy chastening rod**,
  And straight **I turned unto my God**.

2 What though it pierced my fainting heart,
  I blessed thy hand that caused the smart;
  It taught my tears awhile to flow,
  But saved me from eternal woe.

3 Oh! hadst thou left me unchastised,
  Thy precepts I had still despised;
  And still the snare in secret laid
  Had my unwary feet betrayed.

4 I love thee, therefore, O my God!
  And long to reach thy dear abode;
  Where, in thy presence fully blest,
  Thy chosen saints for ever rest.

1124. *"The world shall hear Thy voice."*

1 Sovereign of worlds! display thy power,
  Be this thy Zion's favored hour;
  Bid the bright morning Star arise,
  And point the nations to the skies.

2 Set up thy throne where Satan reigns,—
  On Afric's shore, on India's plains,
  On wilds and continents unknown,—
  And **make** the nations all thine own.

3 **Speak! and the world shall hear thy voice;**
  Speak! and the **deserts shall** rejoice;
  Scatter the gloom of heathen night,
  And bid **all** nations hail **the** light.

1183. *"Why is His chariot so long in coming?"*

1 Gently, my Saviour, let me down,
  To slumber in the arms of death;
  I rest my soul on thee alone,
  Ev'n till my last, expiring breath.

2 Soon will the storm of life be o'er,
  And I shall enter endless rest;
  There I shall live to sin no more,
  And bless thy name, for ever blest.

3 Bid me possess sweet peace within;
  Let childlike patience keep my heart;
  Then shall I feel my heaven begin,
  Before my spirit hence depart.

4 Oh, speed thy chariot, God of love,
  And take me from this world of woe;
  I long to reach those joys above,
  And bid farewell to all below.

5 There **shall** my raptured spirit raise
  Still louder notes than angels sing,—
  High glories to Immanuel's grace,
  My God, my Saviour, and my King!

1227. *"My soul followeth hard after Thee."* Psalm 63.

1 We go **with the** redeemed to **taste**
  Of joy supreme, that never dies;
  Our feet still press the weary waste,
  Our hearts, our home, are in the skies.

2 And, oh! while on to Zion's hill
  The toilsome path of life we tread,
  Around us, loving Father, still
  Thy circling wings of mercy spread.

3 From day to day, **from hour** to hour,
  Oh let our rising spirits prove
  The strength of thine almighty power,
  The sweetness of thy saving love!

MISSIONARY HYMN. 7s & 6s. DOUBLE.

574. *"Renew a right spirit within me."*

1 GREAT Author of my being,
  I am consumed with care,
The ills of thy decreeing,
  Enable me to bear:
The spirit of contrition,
  Oh, may I now receive;
For all my soul's ambition
  Is worthily to grieve.

2 The grief beyond expressing,
  To me, O Lord, impart;
I ask this only blessing—
  An humble, broken heart;
The justice of thy sentence
  With meekest awe to own;
And spend, in deep repentance,
  My last, **expiring** groan.

3 In that decisive hour,
  When pain, with life, shall end,
Then, O thou God of power,
  Thou God of love, attend!
And bear, oh, bear my burden,
  And help my last distress;
And give me back my pardon,
  And bid me die in peace!

972. *"Take no thought for the morrow."*
  Matt. 6: 25–34.

1 IN holy contemplation,
  We sweetly now pursue
The theme of God's salvation,
  And find it ever new:
Set free from present sorrow,
  We cheerfully can say,
"Ev'n let the unknown morrow
  Bring with it what it may."

2 It can bring with it nothing
  But he will bear us through;
Who gives the lilies clothing
  Will clothe his people too:
Beneath the spreading heavens
  No creature but is fed;
And he who feeds the ravens
  Will give his children bread.

1137. *Departure of Missionaries.*

1 ROLL on, thou mighty ocean!
  And, as thy billows flow,
Bear messengers of mercy
  To every land below
Arise, ye gales! and waft them
  Safe to the destined shore;
That man may sit in darkness
  And death's black shade no more.

2 O thou eternal Ruler!
  Who holdest in thine arm
The tempests of the ocean,
  Protect them from all harm!
Thy presence still be with them,
  Wherever they may be;
Though far from us who love them
  Still let them be with thee!

TEMPLE. 7s & 6s.

330. *"To Him that sitteth upon the Throne."*

1 To thee, my God, my Saviour,
 My soul, exulting, **sings**,
 Rejoicing in thy favor,
 Almighty King of kings!
I'll celebrate thy glory,
 With all the saints above,
And tell the joyful story
 Of thy redeeming love.

2 Soon as the morn **with roses**
 Bedecks **the** dewy east,
And when **the** sun reposes
 Upon the ocean's breast,
My voice in supplication,
 My Saviour, thou shalt **hear**;
Oh, grant me thy salvation,
 And to my soul draw near!

3 By thee through life supported,
 I pass the dangerous road,
With heavenly hosts escorted
 Up to their bright abode:
There cast my crown before thee,
 And, all my conflicts o'er,
Unceasingly adore thee—
 What would an angel more?

746. *"He hath borne our griefs, and carried our sorrows."*—Isaiah 53: 4.

1 I LAY my sins on Jesus,
 The spotless Lamb of God;
He bears them all, and frees us
 From the accursèd load:
I bring my guilt to Jesus,
 To wash my crimson stains
White in his blood most precious,
 Till not a stain remains.

2 I lay my wants on Jesus;
 All fullness dwells in him;
He heals all my diseases,
 He doth my soul redeem:
I lay my griefs on Jesus,
 My burdens and my cares;
He from them all releases,
 He all my sorrow shares.

3 I rest my soul on Jesus,
 This weary soul of mine;
His right hand me embraces,
 I on his breast recline.
I love the name of Jesus,
 Immanuel, Christ, the Lord;
Like fragrance on the breezes,
 His name abroad is poured.

4 I long to be like Jesus,
 Meek, loving, lowly, mild;
I long to be like Jesus,
 The Father's holy child;
I long **to** be with Jesus
 Amid the heavenly throng,
To sing with saints his praises,
 To learn the angels' song.

CHIMES. C. M.

94. *"The God of Peace."*—Heb. 13: 20, 21.

1 Now may the God of peace and love,
  Who, from th' imprisoning grave,
  Restored the Shepherd of the sheep,
  Omnipotent to save;

2 Through the rich merits of that blood,
  Which he on Calvary spilt,
  To make th' eternal cov'nant sure,
  On which our hopes are built;

3 Perfect our souls in every grace,
  T' accomplish all his will;
  And all that's pleasing in his sight
  Inspire us to fulfill!

4 For Christ the Mediator's sake
  We every blessing pray;
  With glory let his name be crowned,
  Through heaven's eternal day!

281. *All virtues seen in Christ.*

1 BEHOLD, where, in a mortal form,
  Appears each grace divine;
  The virtues, all in Jesus met,
  With mildest radiance shine.

2 To spread the rays of heavenly light,
  To give the mourner joy,
  To preach glad tidings to the poor,
  Was his divine employ.

3 'Mid keen reproach, and cruel scorn,
  Patient and meek he stood:
  His foes, ungrateful, sought his life;
  He labored for their good.

4 In the last hour of deep distress,
  Before his Father's throne,
  With soul resigned, he bowed, and said,
  "Thy will, not mine, be done!"

5 Be Christ our pattern and our guide;
  His image may we bear;
  Oh, may we tread his holy steps,
  His joy and glory share!

494. *"There is none that doeth good."* Psalm 14.

1 THE Lord, from his celestial throne,
  Looked down on things below,
  To find the man that sought his grace,
  Or did his justice know.

2 By nature all are gone astray,
  Their practice all the same;
  There's none that fears his Maker's hand;
  There's none that loves his name.

3 Their tongues are used to speak deceit,
  Their slanders never cease;
  How swift to mischief are their feet,
  Nor know the paths of peace!

4 Such seeds of sin—that bitter root—
  In every heart are found;
  Nor can they bear diviner fruit
  Till grace refine the ground.

935. *"Blessed be the name of the Lord."* Job 1: 21.

1 NAKED as from the earth we came,
  And entered life at first;
  Naked we to the earth return,
  And mix with kindred dust.

2 Whate'er we fondly call our own
  Belongs to heaven's great Lord;
  The blessings lent us for a day
  Are soon to be restored.

3 'T is God that lifts our comforts high,
  Or sinks them in the grave;
  He gives; and when he takes away,
  He takes but what he gave.

4 Then ever blessed be his name!
  His goodness swelled our store;
  His justice but resumes its own;
  Still we the Lord adore.

PETERBORO'.   C. M.

1061. *"They watch for your souls."*

1 Let Zion's watchmen all awake,
    And take th' alarm they give:
  Now let them from the mouth of God
    Their solemn charge receive.

2 'T is not a cause of small import
    The pastor's care demands;
  But what might fill an angel's heart,
    And filled a Saviour's hands.

3 They watch for souls, for which the Lord
    Did heavenly bliss forego;
  For souls which must for ever live
    In rapture or in woe.

4 May they that Jesus whom they preach,
    Their own Redeemer, see:
  Lord, watch thou daily o'er their souls,
    That they may watch for thee.

1070. *"Come in, thou blessed of the Lord."*
                              Gen. 24 : 31.

1 Come in, thou blessed of the Lord,
    Stranger nor foe art thou:
  We welcome thee with warm accord,
    Our friend, our brother now.

2 The hand of fellowship, the heart
    Of love, we offer thee;
  Leaving the world, thou dost but part
    From lies and vanity.

3 Come with us—we will do thee good,
    As God to us hath done;
  Stand but in him, as those have stood
    Whose faith the victory won.

4 And when, by turns, we pass away,
    And star by star grows dim,
  May each, translated into day,
    Be lost and found in him.

1229. *"Our journey is a thorny maze."*

1 Lord! what a wretched land is this,
    That yields us no supply;
  No cheering fruits, no wholesome trees,
    No streams of living joy!

2 Our journey is a thorny maze,
    But we press upward still—
  Forget these troubles of the ways,
    And march to Zion's hill.

3 There, on a green and flowery mount,
    Our weary souls shall sit;
  And, with transporting joys, recount
    The labors of our feet.

4 Eternal glory to the King
    That brought us safely through!
  Our tongue shall never cease to sing,
    And endless praise renew.

1243. *"I shall go to Him."*

1 Blest hour, when righteous souls shall meet,
    Shall meet to part no more;
  And with celestial welcome greet
    On an immortal shore!

2 The parent finds his long lost child;
    Brothers on brothers gaze:
  The tear of resignation mild,
    Is changed to joy and praise.

3 Each tender tie, dissolved with pain,
    With endless bliss is crowned:
  All that was dead revives again,
    All that was lost is found.

4 Congenial minds, arrayed in light,
    High thoughts shall interchange:
  Nor cease, with ever new delight,
    On wings of love to range.

5 Their Father marks their generous flame,
    And looks complacent down
  The smile that owns their filial claim
    Is their immortal crown.

KANE. S. M. DOUBLE.

680. *"Not far from home."*

1 YOUR harps, ye trembling saints,
　Down from the willows take:
Loud to the praise of love divine
　Bid every string awake.

2 Though in a foreign land,
　We are not far from home;
And nearer to our house above
　We every moment come.

3 His grace will to the end
　Stronger and brighter shine;
Nor present things, nor things to come,
　Shall quench the spark divine.

4 When we in darkness walk,
　Nor feel the heavenly flame,
Then is the time to trust our God,
　And rest upon his name.

5 Soon shall our doubts and fears
　Subside at his control;
His loving kindness shall break through
　The midnight of the soul.

6 Blest is the man, O Lord,
　Who stays himself on thee;
Who waits for thy salvation, Lord,
　Shall thy salvation see.

1237. *"For ever with the Lord."*
　　　　1 Thess. 4: 17.

1 "For ever with the Lord!"
　Amen! so let it be:
Life from the dead is in that word;
　'T is immortality!

2 My Father's house on high,
　Home of my soul! how near,
At times, to faith's aspiring eye,
　Thy golden gates appear!

3 "For ever with the Lord!"
　"Father, if 't is thy will,

The promise of thy gracious word,
　Ev'n here to me fulfill.

4 Be thou at my right hand;
　So shall I never fail:
Uphold thou me and I shall stand;
　Help, and I shall prevail.

5 So, when my latest breath
　Shall rend the vail in twain,
By death I shall escape from death,
　And life eternal gain.

6 Knowing "as I am known,"
　How shall I love that word,
And oft repeat before the throne,
　"For ever with the Lord!"

1269. *"Even so, come, Lord Jesus."*
　　　　Rev. 22: 20.

1 COME, Lord! and tarry not;
　Bring the long-looked-for day;
Oh! why these years of waiting here,
　These ages of delay?

2 Come! for the good are few;
　They lift the voice in vain;
Faith waxes fainter on the earth,
　And love is on the wane.

3 Come, for love waxes cold,
　Its steps are faint and slow;
Faith now is lost in unbelief;
　Hope's lamp burns dim and low.

4 Come! for creation groans,
　Impatient of thy stay,
Worn out with these long years of ill,
　These ages of delay.

5 Come, and make all things new,
　Build up this ruined earth;
Restore our faded Paradise—
　Creation's second birth!

OLMUTZ. S. M.

6 Come, and begin thy reign
    Of everlasting peace ;
  Come, take the kingdom to thyself,
    Great King of righteousness!

1060. *"Watch ye, therefore."*

1 YE servants of the Lord,
    Each in his office wait,
  Observant of his heavenly word,
    And watchful at his gate.

2 Let all our lamps be bright,
    And trim the golden flame ;
  Gird up your loins as in his sight,
    For awful **is his name.**

3 Watch! 't is your Lord's command ;
    And while we speak he's near :"
  Mark the first signal of his hand,
    And ready all appear.

4 Oh, happy servant he
    In such a posture found !
  He shall his Lord with rapture see,
    And be with honor **crowned.**

171. *"What is man, that Thou art mindful of him?"*—Psalm 8.

1 O LORD, our heavenly King,
    Thy name is all divine ;
  Thy glories round the earth are spread,
    And o'er the heavens they shine.

2 When to thy works on high
    I raise my wondering eyes,
  And see the moon, complete in light,
    Adorn the darksome skies ;—

3 When I survey the stars,
    And all their shining forms,
  Lord, what is man, that worthless thing,
    Akin to dust and worms !

4 Lord, what is worthless man,
    That thou shouldst love him so !
  Next to thine angels he is placed,
    And lord of all below.

5 O Lord, our heavenly King,
    Thy name is all divine ;
  Thy glories round the earth are spread,
    And o'er the heavens they shine.

IOWA. S. M.

ST. MARTINS. C. M.

226. *Blessings of God's Presence.*

1 God, in the high and holy place,
    Looks down upon the spheres;
  And in his providence and grace
    To every eye appears.
2 He bows the heavens; the mountains stand
    A highway for our God:
  He walks amid the desert land;
    'T is Eden where he trod.
3 The forests in his strength rejoice;
    Hark! on the evening breeze,
  As once of old, the "Lord God's voice"
    Is heard among the trees.
4 If God hath made this world so fair,
    Where sin and death abound,
  How beautiful beyond compare
    Will Paradise be found!

508. *"Ho! every one that thirsteth."*
    Isaiah 55: 1, 2.

1 Let every mortal ear attend,
    And every heart rejoice;
  The trumpet of the Gospel sounds
    With an inviting voice.
2 Ho! all ye hungry, starving souls,
    That feed upon the wind,
  And vainly strive with earthly toys
    To fill an empty mind:
3 Eternal wisdom has prepared
    A soul-reviving feast,
  And bids your longing appetites
    The rich provision taste.
4 Ho! ye that pant for living streams,
    And pine away and die:
  Here you may quench your raging thirst
    With springs that never dry.
5 Rivers of love and mercy here
    In a rich ocean join;
  Salvation in abundance flows,
    Like floods of milk and wine.
6 The happy gates of gospel-grace
    Stand open night and day:
  Lord, we are come to seek supplies,
    And drive our wants away.

758. *Prayer for strong Faith.*

1 Oh for a faith that will not shrink
    Though pressed by every foe;
  That will not tremble on the brink
    Of any earthly woe!—
2 That will not murmur nor complain
    Beneath the chastening rod,
  But, in the hour of grief or pain,
    Will lean upon its God;—
3 A faith that shines more bright and clear
    When tempests rage without;
  That, when in danger, knows no fear,
    In darkness, feels no doubt;—
4 A faith that keeps the narrow way
    Till life's last hour is fled,
  And with a pure and heavenly ray
    Lights up a dying bed!
5 Lord, give us such a faith as this,
    And then, whate'er may come,
  We'll taste, ev'n here, the hallowed bliss
    Of an eternal home.

992. *"He giveth power to the faint."*
    Isaiah 40: 29-31.

1 Supreme in wisdom as in power,
    The Rock of Ages stands;
  We see him not, yet may we trace
    The working of his hands.
2 He gives the conquest to the weak,
    Supports the fainting heart,
  And courage in the evil hour
    His heavenly aids impart.

TALLIS. C. M.

3 Mere human power shall fast decay,
   And youthful vigor cease;
   But they who wait upon the Lord
   In strength shall still increase.
4 They with unwearied feet shall tread
   The path of life divine;
   With growing ardor onward move,
   With growing brightness shine.
5 On eagles' wings they mount, they soar—
   The wings of faith and love;
   Till, past the cloudy regions here,
   They rise to heaven above.

1032. *The little Flock.*—Luke 12 : 32.

1 CHURCH of the ever-living God,
   The Father's gracious choice,
   Amid the voices of this earth,
   How feeble is thy voice!
2 A little flock!—so calls he thee
   Who bought thee with his blood;
   A little flock, disowned of men,
   But owned and loved of God.
3 Not many rich or noble called,
   Not many great or wise;
   They whom God makes his kings and priests
   Are poor in human eyes.
4 But the chief Shepherd comes at length;
   Their feeble days are o'er,
   No more a handful in the earth,
   A little flock no more.
5 No more a lily among thorns,
   Weary, and faint, and few;
   But countless as the stars of heaven,
   Or as the early dew.
6 Then entering th' eternal halls,
   In robes of victory,
   That mighty multitude shall keep
   The joyous jubilee.

7 Unfading palms they bear aloft;
   Unfaltering songs they sing;
   Unending festival they keep,
   In presence of the King.

1252. *The Eternity of Heaven.*

1 FROM thee, my God, my joys shall rise,
   And run eternal rounds,
   Beyond the limits of the skies,
   And all created bounds.
2 The holy triumphs of my soul
   Shall death itself outbrave,
   Leave dull mortality behind,
   And fly beyond the grave.
3 There, where my blessed Jesus reigns,
   In heaven's unmeasured space,
   I'll spend a long eternity
   In pleasure and in praise.
4 Millions of years my wondering eyes
   Shall o'er thy beauties rove,
   And endless ages I'll adore
   The glories of thy love.
5 My Saviour! every smile of thine
   Shall fresh endearments bring,
   And thousand tastes of new delight
   From all thy graces spring.
6 Haste, my Beloved! raise my soul
   Up to thy blest abode;
   Fly! for my spirit longs to see
   My Saviour and my God!

DOXOLOGY.

LET God the Father, and the Son,
   And Spirit, be adored,
   Where there are works to make him known,
   Or saints to love the Lord!

MORNING. 7s. DOUBLE.

297. *"Truly, my soul waiteth upon God."*

1 FATHER! thy paternal care
  Has my guardian been, my guide;
Every hallowed wish and prayer
  Has thy hand of love supplied:
Thine is every thought of bliss
  Left by hours and days gone by;
Every hope thy offspring is,
  Beaming from futurity.

2 Every sun of splendid ray,
  Every moon that shines serene,
Every morn that welcomes day,
  Every evening's twilight scene,
Every hour which wisdom brings,
  Every incense at thy shrine,—
These, and all life's holiest things,
  And its fairest—all are thine.

3 And for all, my hymns shall rise
  Daily to thy gracious throne:
Thither let my asking eyes
  Turn unwearied, righteous One!
Through life's strange vicissitude,
  There reposing all my care;
Trusting still, through ill and good,
  Fixed, and cheered, and counseled there.

398. *"My sheep hear my voice."*

1 JESUS, seek thy wandering sheep;
  Bring me back, and lead, and keep;
Take on thee my every care,
  Bear me, on thy bosom bear:
Let me know my Shepherd's voice,
  More and more in thee rejoice;
More and more of thee receive;
  Ever in thy spirit live,—

2 Live till all thy life I know,
  Following thee, my Lord, below;
Gladly then from earth remove,
  Gathered to the fold above:
Oh, that I at last may stand
  With the sheep at thy right hand,
Take the crown so freely given,
  Enter in by thee to heaven!

528.* *"Come up hither."—*Rev. 4 : 1.

1 "COME up hither; come away:"
  Thus the ransomed spirits sing;
Here is cloudless, endless day;
  Here is everlasting spring.
2 Come up hither; come and dwell
  With the living hosts above;
Come, and let your bosoms swell
  With their burning songs of love.
3 Come up hither; come and share
  All the sacred joys that rise,
Like an ocean, everywhere
  Through the myriads of the skies.
4 Come up hither; come and shine
  In the robes of spotless white;
Palms, and harps, and crowns are thine;
  Hither, hither wing your flight.
5 Come up hither; hither speed:
  Rest is found in heaven alone;
Here is all the wealth you need;
  Come, and make this wealth your own.

* Commence the fifth stanza with the latter part of the tune.

ASTON. 7s.

24. *"Her saints shall shout aloud for joy."*

1 Sweet the time, exceeding sweet!
   When the saints together meet,
   When the Saviour is the theme,
   When they joy to sing of him.

2 Sing we then eternal love,
   Such as did the Father move:
   He beheld the world undone,
   Loved the world, and gave his Son.

3 Sing the Son's amazing love;
   How he left the realms above,
   Took our nature and our place,
   Lived and died to save our race.

4 Sing we, too, the Spirit's love;
   With our stubborn hearts he strove,
   Filled our minds with grief and fear,
   Brought the precious Saviour near.

5 Sweet the place, exceeding sweet,
   Where the saints in glory meet;
   Where the Saviour's still the theme,
   Where they see and sing of him.

85. *"In Thy light shall we see light."*

1 Stealing from the world away,
   We are come to seek thy face;
   Kindly meet us, Lord, we pray,
   Grant us thy reviving grace.

2 Yonder stars that gild the sky,
   Shine but with a borrowed light;
   We, unless thy light be nigh,
   Wander, wrapt in gloomy night.

3 Sun of righteousness! dispel
   All our darkness, doubts, and fears;
   May thy light within us dwell,
   Till eternal day appears.

4 Warm our hearts in prayer and praise,
   Lift our every thought above;
   Hear the grateful songs we raise,
   Fill us with thy perfect love.

93. *Peace through the Blood of Christ.*
   Heb. 13: 20, 21.

1 Now may he, who from the dead
   Brought the Shepherd of the Sheep,
   Jesus Christ, our King and Head,
   All our souls in safety keep!

2 May he teach us to fulfill
   What is pleasing in his sight;
   Perfect us in all his will,
   And preserve us day and night!

3 Great Redeemer! thee we praise,
   Who the covenant sealed with blood;
   While our hearts and voices raise
   Loud thanksgivings unto God.

1069. *"Thy people shall be my people, and thy God my God."*

1 People of the living God,
   I have sought the world around,
   Paths of sin and sorrow trod,
   Peace and comfort nowhere found.

2 Now to you my spirit turns—
   Turns, a fugitive unblest;
   Brethren! where your altar burns,
   Oh, receive me into rest!

3 Lonely I no longer roam,
   Like the cloud, the wind, the wave:
   Where you dwell shall be my home,
   Where you die shall be my grave.

4 Mine the God whom you adore,
   Your Redeemer shall be mine;
   Earth can fill my soul no more,
   Every idol I resign.

ANVERN. L. M.

9. *"Return, we beseech Thee, O God of Hosts."*

1 Lord, in the temples of thy grace
Thy saints behold thy smiling face;
And oft have seen thy glory shine,
With power and majesty divine.

2 Come, dearest Lord, thy children cry,
Our graces droop, our comforts die;
Return, and let thy glories rise
Again to our admiring eyes:

3 Till filled with light, and joy, and love,
Thy courts below, like those above,
Triumphant hallelujahs raise,
And heaven and earth resound thy praise.

84. *"Kindred in Christ."*

1 Kindred in Christ, for his dear sake,
A hearty welcome here receive;
May we together now partake
The joys which only he can give.

2 May he, by whose kind care we meet,
Send his good Spirit from above,
Make our communications sweet,
And cause our hearts to burn with love.

3 Forgotten be each worldly theme,
When Christians see each other thus;
We only wish to speak of him
Who lived, and died, and reigns for us.

4 We'll talk of all he did and said,
And suffered for us here below;
The path he marked for us to tread;
And what he's doing for us now.

5 Thus, as the moments pass away,
We'll love, and wonder, and adore;
And hasten on the glorious day
When we shall meet to part no more.

140. *God with us everywhere.*

1 O Lord, how full of sweet content
Our years of pilgrimage are spent!
Where'er we dwell, we dwell with thee,
In heaven, in earth, or on the sea.

2 To us remains nor place nor time;
Our country is in every clime:
We can be calm and free from care
On any shore, since God is there.

3 While place we seek, or place we shun,
The soul finds happiness in none;
But with our God to guide our way,
'T is equal joy to go or stay.

4 Could we be cast where thou art not,
That were indeed a dreadful lot;
But regions none remote we call,
Secure of finding God in all.

164. *"I sought the Lord, and He heard me."*
Psalm 34.

1 Lord, I will bless thee all my days;
Thy praise shall dwell upon my tongue;
My soul shall glory in thy grace,
While saints rejoice to hear the song.

2 Come, magnify the Lord with me;
Come, let us all exalt his name;
I sought th' eternal God, and he
Has not exposed my hope to shame.

3 I told him all my secret grief,
My secret groaning reached his ears;
He gave my inward pains relief,
And calmed the tumult of my fears.

4 His holy angels pitch their tents
Around the men who serve the Lord;
Oh, fear and love him, all his saints!
Taste of his grace and trust his word.

FEDERAL STREET. L. M.

51. *"New-born, I bless the waking hour."*

1 In sleep's serene oblivion laid,
  I safely passed the silent night;
  Again I see the breaking shade,
  And drink again the morning light.

2 New-born, I bless the waking hour,
  Once more with awe rejoice to be;
  My conscious soul resumes her power,
  And springs, my guardian God, to thee.

3 Oh, guide me through the various maze
  My doubtful feet are doomed to tread;
  And spread thy shield's protecting blaze
  Where dangers press around my head.

4 A deeper shade will soon impend,
  A deeper sleep mine eyes oppress,
  Yet then thy strength shall still defend,
  Thy goodness still delight to bless.

5 That deeper shade shall break away,
  That deeper sleep shall leave mine eyes;
  Thy light shall give eternal day;
  Thy love, the rapture of the skies.

174. *"He raiseth up the poor out of the dust."*

1 Up to the Lord, who reigns on high,
  And views the nations from afar,
  Let everlasting praises fly,
  And tell how large his bounties are.

2 God, who must stoop to view the skies,
  And bow to see what angels do,—
  Down to our earth he casts his eyes,
  And bends his footsteps downward, too.

3 He overrules all mortal things,
  And manages our mean affairs;
  On humble souls, the King of kings
  Bestows his counsels and his cares.

4 Our sorrows and our tears we pour
  Into the bosom of our God;
  He hears us in the mournful hour,
  And helps to bear the heavy load.

5 Oh could our thankful hearts devise
  A tribute equal to thy grace,
  To the third heaven our song should rise,
  And teach the golden harps thy praise.

810. *Aspiring after God.*

1 Up to the fields where angels lie,
  And living waters gently roll,
  Fain would my thoughts leap out and fly!
  But sin hangs heavy on my soul.

2 Oh! might I once mount up and see
  The glories of th' eternal skies,
  What little things these worlds would be!
  How despicable to my eyes!

3 Had I a glance of thee, my God,
  Kingdoms and men would vanish soon—
  Vanish as though I saw them not,
  As a dim candle dies at noon.

4 Great All in All, eternal King!
  Let me but view thy lovely face,
  And all my powers shall bow and sing
  Thine endless grandeur and thy grace.

849. *Prayer of the Heart and Lips.*

1 O blessed God to thee I raise
  My voice in thankful hymns of praise;
  And when my voice shall silent be,
  My silence shall be praise to thee.

2 For voice and silence doth impart
  The filial homage of my heart;
  And both alike are understood
  By thee, thou Parent of all good—

3 Whose grace is all unsearchable,
  Whose care for me no tongue can tell,
  Who loves my loudest praise to hear,
  And loves to bless my voiceless prayer.

MARTYN. 7s. DOUBLE.

491. *My Bible.*

1 HOLY Bible! book divine!
  Precious treasure! thou art mine:
  Mine to tell me whence I came;
  Mine to tell me what I am;
2 Mine to chide me when I rove;
  Mine to show a Saviour's love;
  Mine thou art to guide and guard;
  Mine to punish or reward;

3 Mine to comfort in distress,
  If the Holy Spirit bless;
  Mine to show, by living faith,
  Man can triumph over death;
4 Mine to tell of joys to come,
  And the rebel sinner's doom:
  O thou holy book divine!
  Precious treasure, thou art mine!

693. *The Three Mountains.*

1 WHEN on Sinai's top I see
  God descend in majesty
  To proclaim his holy law,
  All my spirit sinks with awe.
2 When, in ecstasy sublime,
  Tabor's glorious mount I climb,
  In the too transporting light,
  Darkness rushes o'er my sight.

3 When on Calvary I rest,
  God, in flesh made manifest,
  Shines in my Redeemer's face,
  Full of beauty, truth, and grace.

4 Here I would for ever stay,
  Weep and gaze my soul away;
  Thou art heaven on earth to me,
  Lovely, mournful Calvary!

1159. *"Spared to see another year."*

1 WHILE with ceaseless course the sun
  Hasted through the former year,
  Many souls their race have run,
  Never more to meet us here:
  Fixed in an eternal state,
  They have done with all below;
  We a little longer wait,
  But how little, none can know.

2 As the wingèd arrow flies
  Speedily the mark to find,—
  As the lightning from the skies
  Darts, and leaves no trace behind,—
  Swiftly thus our fleeting days
  Bear us down life's rapid stream;
  Upward, Lord, our spirits raise!
  All below is but a dream.

3 Thanks for mercies past receive,
  Pardon of our sins renew;
  Teach us henceforth how to live,
  With eternity in view;
  Bless thy word to young and old;
  Fill us with a Saviour's love;
  When our life's short tale is told,
  May we dwell with thee above.

MORNING. 7s. DOUBLE.

270.* "*Christ is born in Bethlehem.*"
Luke 2.

1 HARK! the herald angels sing,
"Glory to the new-born King!
Peace on earth, and mercy mild;
God and sinners reconciled."

2 Joyful, all ye nations, rise;
Join the triumphs of the skies;
With th' angelic hosts proclaim,
"Christ is born in Bethlehem."

3 Mild he lays his glory by;
Born that man no more may die;
Born to raise the sons of earth;
Born to give them second birth.

4 Hail, the heaven-born Prince of Peace!
Hail, the Sun of Righteousness!
Light and life to all he brings,
Ris'n with healing in his wings.

5 Let us then with angels sing,
"Glory to the new-born King!—
Peace on earth, and mercy mild;
God and sinners reconciled!"

276. "*Watchman, what of the night?*"
Isaiah 21: 11.

1 WATCHMAN, tell us of the night,
What its signs of promise are.
Traveler, o'er yon mountain's height,
See that glory-beaming star!

2 Watchman, does its beauteous ray
Aught of joy or hope foretell?
Traveler, yes: it brings the day,
Promised day of Israel.

3 Watchman, tell us of the night:
Higher yet that star ascends.
Traveler, blessedness and light,
Peace and truth, its course portends.

4 Watchman, will its beams alone
Gild the spot that gave them birth?
Traveler, ages are its own:
See! it bursts o'er all the earth!

5 Watchman, tell us of the night,
For the morning seems to dawn.

* Commence the fifth stanza with the latter part of the tune.

Traveler, darkness takes its flight,
Doubt and terror are withdrawn.

6 Watchman, let thy wanderings cease;
Hie thee to thy quiet home.
Traveler, lo! the Prince of Peace,
Lo! the Son of God is come!

1042. "*Give place to me that I may dwell.*"—Isaiah 49: 20.

1 "GIVE us room, that we may dwell,"
Zion's children cry aloud;
See their numbers—how they swell!
How they gather like a cloud!

2 Oh, how bright the morning seems!
Brighter from so dark a night:
Zion is like one that dreams,
Filled with wonder and delight.

3 Lo! thy sun goes down no more,
God himself will be thy light;
All that caused thee grief before
Buried lies in endless night.

4 Zion, now arise and shine!
Lo! thy light from heaven is come:
These that crowd from far are thine;
Give thy sons and daughters room.

1114. "*Sing unto Him a new song.*"

1 SWELL the anthem, raise the song;
Praises to our God belong;
Saints and angels! join to sing
Praises to the heavenly King.

2 Blessings from his liberal hand
Flow around this happy land:
Kept by him, no foes annoy;
Peace and freedom we enjoy.

3 Here, beneath a virtuous sway,
May we cheerfully obey;
Never feel oppression's rod,
Ever own and worship God.

4 Hark! the voice of nature sings
Praises of the King of kings;
Let us join the choral song,
And the grateful notes prolong.

HARWELL. 8s & 7s. DOUBLE.

"Hallelujah, Amen," may be added for D. C., or repeat omitted.

386. *Joy in Christ's Reign.*

1 HARK! ten thousand harps and voices
  Sound the note of praise above:
Jesus reigns, and heaven rejoices;
  Jesus reigns, the God of love:
See, he sits on yonder throne;
  Jesus rules the world alone.

2 King of glory, reign for ever!
  Thine an everlasting crown:
Nothing from thy love shall sever
  Those whom thou hast made thine own:
Happy objects of thy grace,
  Destined to behold thy face.

3 Saviour, hasten thine appearing;
  Bring, oh, bring the glorious day,
When the awful summons hearing,
  Heaven and earth shall pass away!
Then, with golden harps we'll sing,
  "Glory, glory to our King!"

70. *Our Guardian.*

1 THROUGH the day thy love has spared us,
  Now we lay us down to rest;
Through the silent watches guard us,
  Let no foe our peace molest:
Jesus, thou our guardian be;
  Sweet it is to trust in thee.

2 Pilgrims here on earth, and strangers,
  Dwelling in the midst of foes,
Us and ours preserve from dangers,
  In thine arms may we repose;
And, when life's short day is past,
Rest with thee in heaven at last.

640. *"Thou knowest that I love Thee."*

1 I WILL love thee, all my treasure;
  I will love thee, all my strength;
I will love thee without measure,
  And without a stain at length:
I will love thee, Light Divine,
Till I die and find thee mine!

2 I will praise thee, Sun of glory!
  For the bliss thy beams have brought;
I will praise thee, will adore thee,
  For the light I long had sought:—
Praise thee that thy words so blest
Soothed my troubled soul to rest!

3 Be my heart more warmly glowing,
  Sweet and calm the tears I shed;
And its love, its ardor, showing,
  Let my spirit onward tread:
Near to thee, and nearer still,
Draw this heart, this mind, this will.

4 I will love in joy or sorrow!
  While I in this body dwell;
I will love to-day, to-morrow,
  With a love no words can tell:
I will love thee, Light Divine,
Till I die, and find thee mine!

980. *"Neither shall any man pluck them out of My hand."—John 10. 28.*

1 CLOUDS and darkness round about thee
  For a season vail thy face;
Still I trust and can not doubt thee,
  Jesus, full of truth and grace:
Resting on thy word I stand:
None shall pluck me from thy hand.

2 Oh, rebuke me not in anger;
  Suffer not my faith to fail;
Let not pain, temptation, languor
  O'er my struggling heart prevail!
Holding fast thy word I stand:
None shall pluck me from thy hand.

3 In my heart thy word I cherish;
  Though unseen, thou still art near;
Since thy sheep shall never perish,
  What have I to do with fear?
Trusting in thy word I stand:
None shall pluck me from thy hand.

MARDEN. 10s & 4s.

1022. *Prayer for Peace to the Church.*

1 O Christ, the leader of that war-worn host,
Who bear thy cross,—now help, or we are lost!
Disperse the foes who long in deadly strife
Have sought our life!

2 Come, Lord, and shield thy children with thine arm;
Restrain the power of him who seeks our harm;
O'er all that would thy members here assail
Do thou prevail!

3 And grant us peace within the church and school,
Peace to the powers that our fair country rule;
To every wounded conscience, aching heart,
Thy peace impart!

4 And heaven and earth eternally shall raise
(Thy goodness and thy boundless love to praise,)
Glad songs to thee, the Guardian of thy flock,
Our sheltering Rock!

MARX. 8s & 7s. 6 LINES.

296. *"It was for us."*

1 Near the cross our station taking,
Earthly cares and joys forsaking,
Meet it is for us to mourn:
'T was for us he came from heaven,
'T was for us his heart was riven;
All his griefs for us were borne.

2 When no eye its pity gave us,
When there was no arm to save us,
He his love and power displayed:
By his stripes our help and healing,
By his death our life revealing,
He for us the ransom paid.

3 Jesus, may thy love constrain us,
That from sin we may refrain us,
In thy griefs may deeply grieve;
Thee our best affections giving,
To thy praise and honor living,
May we in thy glory live!

TYNG. 7s & 6s.

902. *"Stand, therefore, having your loins girt about."*

1 STAND up!—stand up for Jesus!
  Ye soldiers of the cross;
Lift high his royal banner,
  It must not suffer loss:
From vict'ry unto vict'ry
  His army shall he lead,
Till every foe is vanquished,
  And Christ is Lord indeed.

2 Stand up!—stand up for Jesus!
  The trumpet call obey;
Forth to the mighty conflict,
  In this his glorious day:
"Ye that are men, now serve him,"
  Against unnumbered foes;
Your courage rise with danger,
  And strength to strength oppose.

3 Stand up!—stand up for Jesus!
  Stand in his strength alone;
The arm of flesh will fail you—
  Ye dare not trust your own:
Put on the gospel armor,
  And, watching unto prayer,
Where duty calls, or danger,
  Be never wanting there.

4 Stand up!—stand up for Jesus!
  The strife will not be long;
This day the noise of battle,
  The next the victor's song:
To him that overcometh,
  A crown of life shall be;
He with the King of Glory
  Shall reign eternally!

884. *"The Lord is my salvation; whom shall I fear?"*—Psalm 27.

1 GOD is my strong salvation;
  What foe have I to fear?
In darkness and temptation,
  My Light, my Help is near.
2 Though hosts encamp around me,
  Firm in the fight I stand;
What terror can confound me,
  With God at my right hand?

3 Place on the Lord reliance;
  My soul, with courage wait;
His truth be thine affiance,
  When faint and desolate.
4 His might thy heart shall strengthen,
  His love thy joy increase;
Mercy thy days shall lengthen;
  The Lord will give thee peace!

MISSIONARY HYMN. 7s & 6s. DOUBLE.

1132. *"Waft, waft, ye winds, his story."*

1 From Greenland's icy mountains,
　From India's coral strand,
　Where Afric's sunny fountains
　　Roll down their golden sand,—
　From many an ancient river,
　From many a palmy plain,
　They call us to deliver
　　Their land from error's chain.

2 What though the spicy breezes
　　Blow soft o'er Ceylon's isle;
　Though every prospect pleases,
　　And only man is vile;
　In vain with lavish kindness
　　The gifts of God are strown;
　The heathen, in his blindness,
　　Bows down to wood and stone!

3 Shall we, whose souls are lighted
　　With wisdom from on high,—
　Shall we to men benighted
　　The lamp of life deny?
　Salvation, oh, salvation!
　　The joyful sound proclaim,
　Till each remotest nation
　　Has learned Messiah's name.

4 Waft, waft, ye winds, his story,
　　And you, ye waters, roll,
　Till, like a sea of glory,
　　It spreads from pole to pole;
　Till o'er our ransomed nature
　　The Lamb for sinners slain,
　Redeemer, King, Creator,
　　In bliss returns to reign!

1133. *"O that the salvation of Israel were come out of Zion."*—Psalm 14.

1 Oh that the Lord's salvation
　　Were out of Zion come,
　To heal his ancient nation,
　　To lead his outcasts home!
　How long the holy city
　　Shall heathen feet profane?
　Return, O Lord, in pity;
　　Rebuild her walls again.

2 Let fall thy rod of terror;
　　Thy saving grace impart;
　Roll back the vail of error;
　　Release the fettered heart:
　Let Israel, home returning,
　　Their lost Messiah see;
　Give oil of joy for mourning,
　　And bind thy church to thee.

PAUL. 10s, 11 & 12.

993. "*I press toward the mark.*"—Phil. 3: 13, 14.

1 Breast the wave, Christian, when it is strongest;
Watch for day, Christian, when night is longest;
Onward and onward still be thine endeavor;
The rest that remaineth, endureth for ever.

2 Fight the fight, Christian; Jesus is o'er thee;
Run the race, Christian; heaven is before thee;
He who hath promiséd faltereth never;
Oh, trust in the love that endureth for ever.

3 Lift the eye, Christian, just as it closeth;
Raise the heart, Christian, ere it reposeth;
Nothing thy soul from the Saviour shall sever;
Soon shalt thou mount upward to praise him for ever.

LANETON. 10s & 6s.

[For words (Hymn 647) see opposite page.]

COME, LET US ANEW. 11s & 5s.

1161.
"He shall fly away as a dream."

1 Come, let us anew our journey pursue—
    Roll round with the year,
And never stand still till the Master appear;
    His adorable will let us gladly fulfill,
        And our talents improve
    By the patience of hope, and the labor of love.

2 Our life is a dream; our time, as a stream,
        Glides swiftly away,
    And the fugitive moment refuses to stay;
    The arrow is flown; the moment is gone;
        The millennial year
    Rushes on to our view, and eternity's near.

3 Oh that each, in the day of his coming, may say,
    "I have fought my way through;
    I have finished the work thou didst give me to do;"
    Oh that each from his Lord may receive the glad word,
        "Well and faithfully done!
    Enter into my joy, and sit down on my throne!"

647.
"I will love Thee, O Lord, my Strength."
(Tune Langton, opposite page.)

1 I love my God, but with no love of mine,
    For I have none to give;
I love thee, Lord; but all the love is thine,
    For by thy life I live:
I am as nothing, and rejoice to be
Emptied, and lost, and swallowed up in thee.

2 Thou, Lord, alone, art all thy children need,
    And there is none beside;
From thee the streams of blessedness proceed,
    In thee the blest abide,—
Fountain of life and all-abounding grace,
Our Source, our Center, and our Dwelling-place.

BAYTON. C. M.

1077. *Child's Communion with Christ.*

1 Dear Jesus, ever at my side,
  How loving mus' thou be,
To leave thy home in heaven to guard
  A little child like me.

2 I can not feel thee touch my hand,
  With pressure light and mild,
To check me as my mother did,
  When I was but a child;

3 But I have felt thee in my thoughts,
  Rebuking sin for me;
And, when my heart loves God, I know
  The sweetness is from thee.

4 And when, dear Saviour, I kneel down,
  Morning and night, to prayer,
Something there is within my heart
  Which tells me thou art there.

5 Yes! when I pray, thou prayest, too—
  Thy prayer is all for me;
But when I sleep, thou sleepest not,
  But watchest patiently.

6 To God the Father glory be,
  And to his only Son;
The same, O Holy Ghost, to thee,
  While ceaseless ages run!

1080. *Child's Thoughts of God.*

1 How glorious is our heavenly King,
  Who reigns above the sky!
How shall a child presume to sing
  His dreadful majesty?

2 How great his power is, none can tell,
  Nor think how large his grace:
Not men below, nor saints that dwell
  On high before his face.

3 Not angels that stand round the Lord
  Can search his secret will;
But they perform his holy word,
  And sing his praises still.

4 Then let me join this heavenly train,
  And my first offerings bring;
Th' eternal God will not disdain
  To hear an infant sing.

5 My heart resolves, my tongue obeys,
  And angels shall rejoice
To hear their mighty Maker's praise
  Sound from a feeble voice.

1081. *Child's Trust in Christ.*

1 See the kind Shepherd, Jesus, stands,
  And calls his sheep by name;
Gathers the feeble in his arms,
  And feeds each tender lamb.

2 He leads them to the gentle stream,
  Where living water flows;
And guides them to the verdant fields,
  Where sweetest herbage grows.

3 When, wandering from the peaceful fold,
  We leave the narrow way,
Our faithful Shepherd still is near,
  To seek us when we stray.

4 The weakest lamb amid the flock
  Shall be its Shepherd's care;
While folded in our Saviour's arms,
  We're safe from every snare.

1082. *Child's Trust in Christ.*

1 There is a little, lonely fold,
  Whose flock one Shepherd keeps,
Through summer's heat and winter's cold,
  With eye that never sleeps.

2 By evil beast, or burning sky,
  Or damp of midnight air,
Not one in all that flock shall die,
  Beneath that Shepherd's care.

3 For, if unheeding or beguiled
  In danger's path they roam,
His pity follows through the wild,
  And guards them safely home.

EVAN. C. M.

4 O gentle Shepherd, still behold
   Thy helpless charge in me;
   And take a wanderer to thy fold,
   That trembling turns to thee.

1083. *Child's Thoughts of Heaven.*
1 THERE is a glorious world of light
   Above the starry sky,
   Where saints departed, clothed in white,
   Adore the Lord most high.

2 And hark! amid the sacred songs
   Those heavenly voices raise,
   Ten thousand thousand infant tongues
   Unite in perfect praise.

3 Those are the hymns that we shall know,
   If Jesus we obey;
   That is the place where we shall go,
   If found in wisdom's way.

4 Soon will our earthly race be run,
   Our mortal frame decay;
   Parents and children, one by one,
   Must die and pass away.

5 Great God! impress this solemn thought,
   To-day, on every breast;
   That both the teachers and the taught
   May enter to thy rest.

1099. *"How poor a lot was Thine!"*
1 O SAVIOUR! whom this holy morn
   Gave to our world below!
   To mortal want and labor born,
   And more than mortal woe;

2 Incarnate Word! by every grief
   By each temptation tried;
   Who lived to yield our ills relief,
   And to redeem us, died;

3 If richly-clothed, and proudly fed,
   In dangerous wealth we dwell,

Remind us of thy manger bed,
And lowly cottage-cell.

4 If, pressed by poverty severe,
   In envious want we pine,
   Oh, may thy Spirit whisper near,
   How poor a lot was thine!

5 Through fickle fortune's various scene,
   From sin preserve us free:
   Like us, a mourner thou hast been;
   May we rejoice with thee.

1148. *"Is it such a fast that I have chosen?"*
   Isaiah 58: 2-8.
1 Do I delight in sorrow's dress?
   (Saith he who reigns above);
   The hanging head and rueful look—
   Will they attract my love?

2 Let such as feel oppression's load
   Thy tender pity share;
   And let the helpless, homeless poor
   Be thy peculiar care.

3 Go, bid the hungry orphan be
   With thine abundance blest;
   Invite the wanderer to thy gate,
   And spread the couch of rest.

4 Let him who pines with piercing cold
   By thee be warmed and clad;
   Be thine the blissful task to make
   The downcast mourner glad.

5 Then, bright as morning, shall come forth
   In peace and joy thy days;
   And glory from the Lord above
   Shall shine on all thy ways.

DOXOLOGY.
To Father, Son, and Holy Ghost,
One God, whom we adore,
Be glory as it was, is now,
And shall be evermore!

NORMAN. 6s & 4s.

39. *"Let every thing that hath breath praise the Lord."*—Psalm 150.

1 PRAISE ye Jehovah's name,
   Praise through his courts proclaim;
      Rise and adore.
   High o'er the heavens above
   Sound his great acts of love,
   While his rich grace we prove,
      Vast as his power.

2 Now let the trumpet raise
   Sounds of triumphant praise,
      Wide as his fame:
   There let the harp be found;
   Organs, with solemn sound,
   Roll your deep notes around,
      Filled with his name.

3 While his high praise ye sing,
   Strike every sounding string;
      Sweet the accord!
   He vital breath bestows;
   Let every breath that flows,
   His noblest fame disclose:
      Praise ye the Lord.

345. *"At the name of Jesus every knee should bow."*

1 LET us awake our joys;
   Strike up with cheerful voice;
      Each creature sing;
   Angels! begin the song;
   Mortals! the strain prolong,
   In accents sweet and strong,
      "Jesus is King!"

2 Proclaim abroad his name;
   Tell of his matchless fame;
      What wonders done!
   Above, beneath, around,
   Let all the earth resound,
   Till heaven's high arch rebound,
      "Vict'ry is won!"

3 He vanquished sin and hell,
   And our last foe will quell:
      Mourners, rejoice!
   His dying love adore;
   Praise him, now raised in power:
   Praise him for evermore,
      With joyful voice.

4 All hail the glorious day,
   When, through the heavenly way,
      Lo, he shall come!
   While they who pierced him wail,
   His promise shall not fail;
   Saints, see your King prevail;
      Great Saviour, come!

1138. *"Keep not silence."*

1 SOUND, sound the truth abroad!
   Bear ye the word of God
      Through the wide world:
   Tell what our Lord hath done;
   Tell how the day was won,
   And from his lofty throne
      Satan is hurled.

2 Far over sea and land,
   'Tis our Lord's own command,
      Bear ye his name:
   Bear it to every shore;
   Regions unknown explore;
   Enter at every door—
      Silence is shame.

3 Ye, who, forsaking all
   At your loved Master's call,
      Comforts resign;
   Soon will the work be done;
   Soon will the prize be won;
   Brighter than yonder sun.
      Then shall ye shine!

AMERICA. 6s & 4s.

1111. *"God save the State!"*

1 God bless our native land!
 Firm may she ever stand,
  Through storm and night;
 When the wild tempests rave,
 Ruler of winds and wave,
 Do thou our country save
  By thy great might.

2 For her our prayer shall rise
 To God, above the skies;
  On him we wait,
 Thou who art ever nigh,
 Guarding with watchful eye,
 To thee aloud we cry,
  God save the State!

1120. *The Voice of National Joy.*

1 My country, 't is of thee,
 Sweet land of liberty,
  Of thee I sing:
 Land where my fathers died,
 Land of the pilgrim's pride,
 From every mountain side
  Let freedom ring!

2 My native country, thee—
 Land of the noble free—
  Thy name I love:
 I love thy rocks and rills,
 Thy woods and templed hills;
 My heart with rapture thrills
  Like that above.

3 Let music swell the breeze,
 And ring from all the trees
  Sweet freedom's song!
 Let mortal tongues awake;
 Let all that breathe partake;
 Let rocks their silence break—
  The sound prolong!

4 Our fathers' God! to thee,
 Author of liberty,
  To thee we sing:
 Long may our land be bright
 With freedom's holy light;
 Protect us by thy might,
  Great God, our King!

1155. *"The God of harvest praise."*

1 The God of harvest praise;
 In loud thanksgiving raise
  Hand, heart, and voice!
 The valleys laugh and sing;
 Forests and mountains ring;
 The plains their tribute bring;
  The streams rejoice.

2 Yea, bless his holy name,
 And joyous thanks proclaim
  Through all the earth;
 To glory in your lot
 Is comely; but be not
 God's benefits forgot
  Amid your mirth.

3 The God of harvest praise,
 Hands, hearts, and voices raise,
  With sweet accord;
 From field to garner throng,
 Bearing your sheaves along,
 And in your harvest song
  Bless ye the Lord

OTLEY. 7s & 5s.

897. *The Call to Victory.*

1 SAINTS, for whom the Saviour bled,
In your Captain's footsteps tread;
Follow Jesus, and be led
  On to victory!
See your foemen take the ground,
While the signal trumpets sound,
Hear his accents pour around
  Cheering melody!

2 Christian soldier, on with me!
Soon your enemies must flee;
Your reward before you see
  Sparkling from on high!
Boldly take the glorious field;
You may fall—but must not yield;
You shall write upon your shield
  Vict'ry, though you die!

3 By the ransom which he gave,
By his triumph o'er the grave,
Trust his mighty power to save;
  Firm and faithful be:
And when death's dark hour is nigh,
When the tear-drop dims the eye,
You shall, in the parting sigh,
  Grasp the victory.

ROCKVALE. 7s & 5s.

1040. *The Angel of the Lord.*

1 ONWARD speed thy conquering flight,
  Angel, onward speed!
Cast abroad thy radiant light,
  Bid the shades recede;
Tread the idols in the dust,
  Heathen fanes destroy;
Spread the gospel's love and trust,
  Spread the gospel's joy.

2 Onward speed thy conquering flight,
  Angel, onward fly!
Long has been the reign of night;
  Bring the morning nigh;
Unto thee earth's sufferers lift
  Their imploring wail;
Bear them heaven's holy gift,
  Ere their courage fail.

3 Onward speed thy conquering flight,
  Angel, onward speed!
Morning bursts upon our sight,
  Lo! the time decreed:
Now the Lord his kingdom takes,
  Thrones and empires fall;
Now the joyous song awakes,
  "God is All in All!"

MONMOUTH. 8s & 7s.*

* Original form, as composed by LUTHER.

1284. *"Behold the Judge of man appears."*
(A Hymn of the Reformation.)

1 GREAT God! what do I see and hear?—
　The end of things created!
Behold the Judge of man appear,
　On clouds of glory seated!
The trumpet sounds; the graves restore
The dead which they contained before;
　Prepare, my soul, to meet him!

2 The dead in Christ shall first arise,
　At the last trumpet-sounding,—
Caught up to meet him in the skies,
　With joy their Lord surrounding:
No gloomy fears their souls dismay;
His presence sheds eternal day
　On those prepared to meet him.

3 O Jesus! friend to fallen man,
　To me impart thy merit;
Forgive my sin, wash out its stain
　By thine Almighty Spirit:
The trumpet sounds; the Judge is near,
But then my soul, devoid of fear,
　Shall spring with joy to meet him.

200. *A Hymn of the Reformation.*—Psalm 46.

1 GOD is our refuge ever near,
　Our help in tribulation;
Therefore his people shall not fear
　Amid a wrecked creation:
Though mountains from their base be hurled,
And ocean shake the solid world,
　The Lord is our salvation.

2 The stream that flows from Zion's hill,
　Shall yet, serenely gliding,
With joy the holy city fill,
　His presence there abiding:
The Lord, her glory and defense,
Will guard his chosen residence,
　His timely aid providing.

1290.* *Eternity.*

1 ETERNITY—eternity!
O bright, O blest eternity!
Which Jesus hath obtained for those
Who seek in him their sure repose;
A little while they suffer here,
But lo! eternity is near:
Eternity—eternity!

2 Eternity—eternity!
Soon shall these eyes thy wonders see;
Oh, may I now the world despise,
And upward raise my thankful eyes,
And seek the joys that shall abide,
From sin and sorrow purified:
O bright, O blest eternity!

3 Eternity—eternity!
Prepare me for eternity;
Now grant me, Lord, thy humble mind,
To all my Father's will resigned,
Now give me faith that rests on thee
Lord! in thy love remember me
In time and in eternity.

* Omit the ties for this hymn.

MALVERN. L. M.

547. *"My Spirit yearns o'er dying men."*

1 ARISE, my tenderest thoughts, arise;
  To torrents melt my streaming eyes;
  And thou, my heart, with anguish feel
  Those evils which thou canst not heal.

2 See **human** nature sunk in shame;
  See **scandals** poured on Jesus' name;
  The **Father** wounded through the Son:
  The **world** abused, the soul undone.

3 My God, I feel the mournful scene;
  My spirit yearns o'er dying men;
  And fain my pity would reclaim
  And snatch the firebrands from the flame.

4 But feeble my compassion proves,
  And can but weep, where most it loves:
  Thine own all-saving arm employ,
  And turn these drops of grief to joy.

590. *Searching the Heart.*

1 RETURN, my roving heart, **return**,
  And life's vain shadows chase no more;
  Seek out some solitude to mourn,
  And thy forsaken God implore.

2 O thou great God! whose piercing eye
  Distinctly marks each deep retreat,
  In these sequestered hours draw nigh,
  And let me here thy presence meet.

3 Through all the windings of my heart,
  My search let heavenly wisdom guide;
  And still its beams unerring dart,
  Till all be known and purified.

4 Then let the visits of thy love,
  My inmost soul be made to share,
  Till every grace combine to prove
  That God has fixed his dwelling there.

734. *"Hope for the Chief of Sinners."*

1 I LEFT the God of truth and light;
  I left the God who gave me breath,
  To wander in the wilds of night,
  And perish in the snares of death!

2 Sweet was his service, and his yoke
  Was light and easy to be borne:
  Through all his bonds of love I broke;
  I cast away his gifts with scorn!

3 Heart-broken, friendless, poor, cast down,
  Where shall the chief of sinners fly,
  Almighty Vengeance! from thy frown?
  Eternal Justice! from thine eye?

4 Lo! through the gloom of guilty fears,
  My faith discerns a dawn of grace:
  The Sun of Righteousness appears
  In Jesus' reconciling face!

5 Prostrate before the mercy-seat,
  I dare not, if I would, despair;
  None ever perished at thy feet,
  And I will lie for ever there.

777. *Rest for the Weary.*

1 My only Saviour! when I feel
  O'erwhelmed in spirit, faint, oppressed,
  'T is sweet to tell thee, while I kneel
  Low at thy feet, thou art my rest.

2 I'm weary of the strife within:
  Strong powers against my soul contest;
  Oh, let me turn from self and sin
  To thy dear cross, for there is rest!

3 Oh! sweet will be the welcome day,
  When, from her toils and woes released,
  My parting soul in death shall say,
  "Now, Lord! I come to thee for rest."

WARD. L. M.

670. *Looking to God in Trouble.*

1 God of my life! to thee I call;
  Afflicted at thy feet I fall;
  When high the water-floods prevail,
  Leave not my trembling heart to fail.

2 Friend of the friendless and the faint,
  Where should I lodge my deep complaint—
  Where but with thee, whose open door
  Invites the helpless and the poor?

3 Did ever mourner plead with thee,
  And thou refuse that mourner's plea?
  Doth not the word still fixed remain,
  That none shall seek thy face in vain?

4 Poor though I am—despised, forgot,
  Yet God, my God forgets me not;
  And he is safe, and must succeed,
  For whom the Lord vouchsafes to plead.

708. *Sight of the Cross.*

1 I thirst, but not as once I did,
  The vain delights of earth to share;
  Thy wounds, Immanuel, all forbid
  That I should seek my pleasures there.

2 It was the sight of thy dear cross
  First weaned my heart from earthly things,
  And taught me to esteem as dross
  The mirth of fools and pomp of kings.

3 Oh for that grace which springs from thee
  And quickens all things where it flows—
  Which makes a wretched thorn like me
  Bloom as the myrtle or the rose!

4 For sure, of all the plants that share
  The notice of thy Father's eye,
  None proves less grateful to his care,
  Or yields him meaner fruit than I.

1020. *"We wept when we remembered Zion."*
Psalm 137.

1 When we, our wearied limbs to rest,
  Sat down by proud Euphrates' stream,
  We wept, with doleful thoughts oppressed,
  And Zion was our mournful theme.

2 Our harps that, when with joy we sung,
  Were wont their tuneful parts to bear,
  With silent strings neglected hung
  On willow trees that withered there.

3 How shall we tune our voice to sing,
  Or touch our harps with skillful hands?
  Shall hymns of joy, to God our King,
  Be sung by slaves in foreign lands?

4 O Salem! our once happy seat,
  When I of thee forgetful prove,
  Let then my trembling hand forget
  The tuneful strings with art to move.

5 If I to mention thee forbear,
  Eternal silence seize my tongue,—
  Or if I sing one cheerful air,
  Till thy deliverance is my song.

1086. *Prayer for erring Youth.*

1 Dear Saviour, if these lambs should stray
  From thy secure inclosure's bound,
  And, lured by worldly joys away,
  Among the thoughtless crowd be found,

2 Remember still that they are thine,
  That thy dear sacred name they bear;
  Think that the seal of love divine,
  The sign of covenant grace they wear.

3 In all their erring, sinful years,
  Oh, let them ne'er forgotten be!
  Remember all the prayers and tears
  Which made them consecrate to thee.

4 And when these lips no more can pray,
  These eyes can weep for them no more,
  Turn thou their feet from folly's way;
  The wanderers to thy fold restore.

BAVARIA. 8s & 7s. CLOSE.

666. *Joy in the Presence of God.*

1 THOU, O Lord, wilt never leave me,
  Thou wilt never me forsake;
Thou wilt keep, and thou wilt save me,
  While thy word my guide I make:
    Save from evil
  For thy name and mercy's sake!

2 When my soul is dark and clouded,
  Torn with doubt, and worn with care,
Through the vail by which 't is shrouded,
  Light from heaven will soon appear;
    And thy presence
  Banish every doubt and fear.

3 When my sky above is glowing,
  And around me all is bright;
Pleasure, like a river flowing,
  Fills my soul with sweet delight:
    Thou wilt keep me,
  Thou wilt guide my steps aright.

4 When my feeble flame is dying,
  And my soul about to soar
To that land where pain and sighing
  Shall be heard and known no more,
    Thou wilt fill me
  With thy presence evermore.

953. *"His compassions fail not."*

1 EVERY human tie may perish;
    Friend to friend unfaithful prove;
  Mothers cease their own to cherish;
    Heaven and earth at last remove:
      But no changes
    Can avert the Father's love.

2 In the furnace God may prove thee,
    Thence to bring thee forth more bright,
  But can never cease to love thee;
    Thou art precious in his sight:
      God is with thee :—
    God, thine everlasting Light

1048. *Looking to Jesus from his Table.*

1 Now, my soul, thy voice upraising,
    Sing the cross in mournful strain;
  Tell the sorrows all-amazing,
    Tell the wounds and dying pain
      Which our Saviour
    Sinless, bore, for sinners slain.

2 He to freedom hath restored us
    By the very bonds he bare;
  And his flesh and blood afford us
    Each a seal of mercy rare:
      Lo! he draws us
    To the cross, and keeps us there.

3 Jesus! may thy promised blessing
    Comfort to our souls afford,
  May we now thy love possessing,
    And at length our full reward,
      Ever praise thee,
    Thee, our ever-glorious Lord!

1139. *The Missionary's Farewell.*

1 YES, my native land! I love thee;
    All thy scenes, I love them well:
  Home and friends that smile around me,
    Can I bid you all farewell?
      Can I leave you,
    Far in heathen lands to dwell?

2 Scenes of sacred peace and pleasure,
    Holy days and Sabbath bell,
  Richest, brightest, sweetest treasure,
    Can I—can I say "Farewell!"
      Can I leave you,
    Far in heathen lands to dwell?

3 Yes! I hasten from you gladly:
    To the strangers let me tell
  How he died—the blessèd Saviour—
    To redeem a world from hell!
      Let me hasten,
    Far in heathen lands to dwell.

4 Bear me on, thou restless ocean;
    Let the winds my canvas swell:
  Heaves my heart with warm emotion,
    While I go far hence to dwell.
      Glad I bid thee,
    Native land, farewell, farewell!

ALVAN. 8s, 7s & 4.

NOTE.—SICILY may be sung to any of these hymns, by repeating the latter part of the tune.

86. *" Lord, dismiss us with thy blessing."*

1 LORD, dismiss us with thy blessing,
  Fill our hearts with joy and peace ;
Let us each, thy love possessing,
  Triumph in redeeming grace:
    Oh, refresh us,
  Trav'ling through this wilderness!

2 Thanks we give, and adoration,
  For thy Gospel's joyful sound ;
May the fruits of thy salvation
  In our hearts and lives abound ;
    May thy presence
  With us evermore be found.

400. *" He shall feed his flock."*

1 SAVIOUR, like a shepherd lead us ;
  Much we need thy tender care ;
In thy pleasant pastures feed us ;
  For our use thy folds prepare :
    Blessed Jesus !
  Thou hast bought us, thine we are.

2 Thou hast promised to receive us,
  Poor and sinful though we be ;
Thou hast mercy to relieve us,
  Grace to cleanse, and power to free :
    Blessed Jesus !
  Let us early turn to thee.

3 Early let us seek thy favor,
  Early let us learn thy will ;
Do thou, Lord, our only Saviour,
  With thy love our bosoms fill :
    Blessed Jesus !
  Thou hast loved us,—love us still !

1221. *The Pilgrim's Prayer.*

1 GUIDE me, O thou great Jehovah,
  Pilgrim through this barren land ;
I am weak, but thou art mighty ;
  Hold me with thy powerful hand :
    Bread of heaven !
  Feed me till I want no more.

2 Open thou the crystal fountain,
  Whence the healing streams do flow ;
Let the fiery, cloudy pillar
  Lead me all my journey through :
    Strong Deliverer !
  Be thou still my strength and shield.

3 When I tread the verge of Jordan,
  Bid my anxious fears subside ;
Death of death ! and hell's Destruction !
  Land me safe on Canaan's side :
    Songs of praises
  I will ever give to thee.

1222. *The Pilgrim's Prayer.*
(Another form of the preceding Hymn.)

1 SHEPHERD of thine Israel ! lead us,
  Pilgrims o'er this barren sand ;
Thou who hast from bondage freed us,
  Guard us by thine outstretched hand :
    Guide thy chosen
  Safely to the promised land.

2 Feed us with the heavenly manna ;
  Fainting, may we feel thy might ;
Go before us as our banner,
  Cloud by day, and fire by night :
    Great Redeemer,
  Shine around us ;—thou art light.

3 When we come to death's dark river,
  Bid the swelling stream divide ;
Thou who canst our life deliver,
  Bear us through the sundered tide :
    Praises, praises
  Will we sing on Canaan's side.

NORWICH. 7s.

470. *Prayer to the Trinity.*

1 Holy Father, hear my cry;
  Holy Saviour, bend thine ear;
  Holy Spirit, come thou nigh:
  Father, Saviour, Spirit, hear!

2 Father, save me from my sin;
  Saviour, I thy mercy crave;
  Gracious Spirit, make me clean:
  Father, Son, and Spirit, save!

3 Father, let me taste thy love;
  Saviour, fill my soul with peace;
  Spirit, come my heart to move:
  Father, Son, and Spirit, bless!

4 Father, Son, and Spirit—thou
  One Jehovah, shed abroad
  All thy grace within me now;
  Be my Father and my God!

592. *"Humbled in the dust."*

1 Sovereign Ruler, Lord of all!
  Prostrate at thy feet we fall;
  Hear, oh, hear our earnest cry!
  Frown not, lest we faint and die.

2 Vilest of the sons of men,
  Chief of sinners we have been;
  Oft have sinned before thy face;
  Trampled on thy richest grace.

3 Justly might the fatal dart
  Pierce our guilty, broken heart;
  Justly might thy righteous breath
  Doom us to eternal death.

4 Jesus! save our dying soul;
  Make our broken spirit whole:
  Humbled in the dust we lie;
  Saviour! leave us not to die.

604. *"Mercy for the chief of sinners."*

1 Depth of mercy!—can there be
  Mercy still reserved for me?
  Can my God his wrath forbear?
  Me, the chief of sinners, spare?

2 I have scorned the Son of God,
  Trampled on his precious blood,
  Would not hearken to his calls,
  Grieved him by a thousand falls.

3 Lord, incline me to repent;
  Let me now my fall lament—
  Deeply my revolt deplore,
  Weep, believe, and sin no more.

4 Still for me the Saviour stands,
  Shows his wounds, and spreads his hands;
  God is love; I know, I feel;
  Jesus weeps, and loves me still.

908. *A quiet Spirit.*

1 Prince of Peace! control my will;
  Bid this struggling heart be still;
  Bid my fears and doubtings cease,—
  Hush my spirit into peace.

2 Thou hast bought me with thy blood,
  Opened wide the gate to God;
  Peace I ask—but peace must be,
  Lord, in being one with thee.

3 May thy will, not mine, be done;
  May thy will and mine be one:
  Chase these doubtings from my heart;
  Now thy perfect peace impart.

4 Saviour! at thy feet I fall;
  Thou my Life, my God, my All!
  Let thy happy servant be
  One for evermore with thee!

PLEYEL. 7s.

776. *Weary of Self and Sin.*

1 Jesus! full of truth and love,
  We thy kindest word obey;
  Faithful let thy mercies prove;
  Take our load of guilt away.

2 Weary of this war within,
  Weary of this endless strife,
  Weary of ourselves and sin,
  Weary of a wretched life;

3 Burdened with a world of grief,
  Burdened with our sinful load,
  Burdened with this unbelief,
  Burdened with the wrath of God:

4 Lo! we come to thee for ease,
  True and gracious as thou art;
  Now our weary souls release;
  Write forgiveness on each heart.

841. *"A living Sacrifice."*—Psalm 51.

1 Jesus, who upon the tree
  Wast an offering for me,
  Take this throbbing heart of mine,—
  Lay it on thy holy shrine.

2 As thy love accepteth naught
  Save what love itself hath wrought,
  Offer thou my sacrifice,
  Else to heaven it can not rise.

3 Take away my erring will;
  All my wayward passions kill;
  Tear my heart from out my heart,
  Though it cost me bitter smart.

4 Fain were I of self bereft,
  Naught but thee within me left;
  Living sacrifice I am,
  Offered only in thy name.

910. *"Make me like a little child."*

1 Jesus, cast a look on me!
  Give me true simplicity;
  Make me poor, and keep me low,
  Seeking only thee to know.

2 All that feeds my busy pride,
  Cast it evermore aside;
  Bid my will to thine submit;
  Lay me humbly at thy feet.

3 Make me like a little child,
  Simple, teachable, and mild;
  Seeing only in thy light;
  Walking only in thy might!

4 Leaning on thy loving breast,
  Where a weary soul may rest;
  Feeling well the peace of God
  Flowing from thy precious blood!

1044. *"In the name of the Father, the Son, and the Holy Ghost."*—Matt. 25: 19.

1 Heavenly Father! may thy love
  Beam upon us from above;
  Let this infant find a place
  In thy covenant of grace.

2 Son of God! be with us here;
  Listen to our humble prayer;
  Let thy blood, on Calvary spilt,
  Cleanse this child from nature's guilt.

3 Holy Ghost! to thee we cry;
  Thou this infant sanctify;
  Thine almighty power display;
  Seal {him/her} to redemption's day.

4 Great Jehovah!—Father, Son,
  Holy Spirit—Three in One,
  Let the blessing come from thee;
  Thine shall all the glory be!

DENFIELD. C. M.

813. *Prayer for Wisdom.*
1 ALMIGHTY God, in humble prayer,
　To thee our souls we lift:
　Do thou our waiting minds prepare
　　For thy most needful gift.

2 We ask not golden streams of wealth
　Along our path to flow;
　We ask not undecaying health,
　　Nor length of years below;

3 We ask not honors, which an hour
　May bring and take away;
　We ask not pleasure, pomp, and power,—
　　Lest we should go astray:

4 We ask for wisdom: Lord, impart
　The knowledge how to live;
　A wise and understanding heart
　　To all before thee give.

819. *"Thine, wholly Thine, oh, let us be!"*
1 ETERNAL Father, God of love,
　To thee our hearts we raise;
　Thy all-sustaining power we prove,
　　And gladly sing thy praise.

2 Thine, wholly thine, oh, let us be!
　Our sacrifice receive;
　Made and preserved, and saved by thee,
　　To thee ourselves we give.

3 Come, Holy Ghost! the Saviour's love
　Shed in our hearts abroad;
　So shall we ever live and move,
　　And be with Christ, in God.

834. *Giving all for Christ.*—Mark 8: 34.
1 AND must I part with all I have,
　My dearest Lord, for thee?
　It is but right, since thou hast done
　　Much more than this for me.

2 Yes, let it go!—one look from thee
　Will more than make amends
　For all the losses I sustain
　　Of credit, riches, friends.

3 Ten thousand worlds, ten thousand lives,
　How worthless they appear,
　Compared with thee, supremely good,
　　Divinely bright and fair!

4 Saviour of souls! could I from thee
　A single smile obtain,
　The loss of all things I could bear,
　　And glory in my gain.

840. *The New Covenant sealed.*
1 "THE promise of my Father's love
　Shall stand for ever good:"
　He said, and gave his soul to death,
　　And sealed the grace with blood.

2 To this dear covenant of thy word
　I set my worthless name;
　I seal th' engagement to my Lord,
　　And make my humble claim.

3 I call that legacy my own
　Which Jesus did bequeath;
　'T was purchased with a dying groan,
　　And ratified in death.

4 The light and strength, the pardoning grace,
　And glory shall be mine:
　My life and soul, my heart and flesh,
　　And all my powers are thine.

1043. *"Planted together in the likeness of His death."*—Rom. 6: 4, 5.
1 WE long to move and breathe in thee,
　Inspired with thine own breath,
　To live thy life, O Lord, and be
　　Baptized into thy death;—

2 Thy death to sin we die below,
　But we shall rise in love;
　We here are planted in thy woe,
　　But we shall bloom above;—

3 Above we shall thy glory share,
　As we thy cross have borne;
　Ev'n we shall crowns of honor wear,
　　When we the thorns have worn.

DUNDEE. C. M.

4 Thy crown of thorns is all our **boast**,
　While now we fall before
The Father, Son, and Holy Ghost,
　And tremble, love, adore.

1045. *"Suffer them to come unto Me."*
　　　　Matt. 19: 14.

1 SEE, Israel's gentle Shepherd stands
　With all-engaging charms;
Hark, how he calls the tender lambs,
　And folds **them** in his arms!

2 "Permit them **to** approach," **he** cries,
　"Nor scorn their humble name;
For 't was to bless such souls as these,
　The Lord **of** angels came."

3 We bring them, Lord, in thankful hands,
　And yield them up to thee;
Joyful that we ourselves are thine,—
　Thine let our off-spring be.

1046. *"And forbid them not."*
　　　　Matt. 19: 14.

1 OH, wondrous **is** thy mercy, Lord!
　We hear thy word of grace,
"Forbid them not,"—oh, rich **the word**
　That calls our infant race!

2 Our infant race we bring to thee:
　Receive them as thine own!
Now and for ever may they be
　Thine wholly, thine alone.

1047. *"A God unto thee and to thy seed after thee."*—Genesis 17: 7.

1 How large the promise! how divine!
　To Abraham and his seed:
"I'll be a God to thee and thine,
　Supplying all their need."

2 The words of his extensive love
　From age to age endure:
The angel of the covenant proves,
　And seals the blessings sure.

3 Jesus the ancient faith confirms,
　To our great fathers given;

He takes young children to his arms,
　And calls them heirs of heaven.

4 Our God!—how faithful are his ways!
　His love endures the same;
Nor from the promise of his grace
　Blots out the children's name.

1140. *"They are no more twain, but one flesh."*

1 WE join to pray, with wishes kind,
　A blessing, Lord, from thee,
On those who now the bands have twined
　Which ne'er may broken be.

2 We **know** that scenes not always bright
　Must unto them be given;
But over all give thou the light
　Of love, and truth, and heaven.

3 Still hand in hand, their journey through,
　Joint pilgrims may they go;
Mingling their joys as helpers **true**,
　And sharing every **woe**.

4 May each in each still feed the flame
　Of pure and holy love;
In faith and trust and heart the same,
　The same their home above.

1141. *"It is not good that man should be alone."*

1 NOT for the summer hour alone,
　When skies resplendent shine,
And youth and pleasure fill the throne,
　Our hearts and hands we join;

2 But for those stern and wintery days
　Of sorrow, pain, and fear,
When Heaven's wise discipline doth make
　Our earthly journey drear.

3 Not for this span of life alone,
　Which like a blast doth fly,
And, as the transient flowers of grass,
　Just blossom, droop, and die;

4 But for a being without end
　This vow of love we take;
Grant us, O Lord, one home at last,
　For thy great mercy's sake!

VITAL SPARK.

1189. *"O Grave! where is thy victory?"*—1 Cor. 15:55.

1 { Vi - tal spark of heavenly flame! Quit, oh, quit this mor - tal frame;
    Trembling, hop-ing, linger-ing, fly-ing— Oh, the pain.—the bliss of dy - ing! }

2 { Hark! they whisper; an - gels say, "Sis - ter spi - rit, come a - way:"
    What is this ab - sorbs me quite?—Steals my sens - es, shuts my sight, }

Repeat for the Second Stanza.

Cease, fond na - ture, cease thy strife, And let me lan - guish in - to life!
Drowns my spi - rit, draws my breath?—Tell me, my soul, can this be death?

3 The world re - cedes— it dis - ap-pears! Heaven opens on my eyes!—my

ears With sounds se-raph-ic ring! Lend, lend your wings! I mount! I fly! "O Grave, where

is thy vic - to - ry? O Death! where is thy sting? O Death! where is thy sting?

DOXOLOGIES.

1   L. M.

To Father, Son, and holy Ghost,
  The God whom earth and heaven adore,
Be glory as it was of old,
  Is now, and shall be evermore!

2   L. M.

PRAISE God, from whom all blessings
  flow!
Praise him, all creatures here below!
Praise him above, ye heavenly host!
Praise Father, Son, and Holy Ghost!

3   L. M.

To God the Father, God the Son,
And God the Spirit, Three in One,
Be honor, praise, and glory given,
By all on earth, and all in heaven!

4   L. M.

GLORY to thee, O God, most high!
Father, we praise thy majesty!
The Son, the Spirit, we adore,
One Godhead, blest for evermore!

5   L. M. 8l.

ETERNAL Father! throned above,
Thou fountain of redeeming love!
Eternal Word! who left thy throne
For man's rebellion to atone;
Eternal Spirit, who dost give
That grace whereby our spirits live;
Thou God of our salvation, be
Eternal praises paid to thee!

6   C. M.

To Father, Son, and Holy Ghost,
  One God, whom we adore,
Be glory as it was, is now,
  And shall be evermore!

7   C. M.

LET God the Father, and the Son,
  And Spirit, be adored,
Where there are works to make him
  known,
Or saints to love the Lord!

8   S. M.

THE Father and the Son
  And Spirit we adore;
We praise, we bless, we worship thee,
  Both now and evermore!

9   S. M.

To God, the Father, Son,
  And Spirit, glory be,
As was, and is, and shall remain
  Through all eternity!

10   L. P. M.

Now to the great and sacred Three,
The Father, Son, and Spirit, be
Eternal praise and glory given,—
Through all the worlds where God is known,
By all the angels near the throne,
And all the saints in earth and heaven!

11   C. P. M.

To Father, Son, and Holy Ghost,
The God, whom heaven's triumphant host
  And saints on earth adore,
Be glory as in ages past,
Is now, and shall for ever last,
  When time shall be no more!

12   H. M.

To God, the Father, Son,
  And Spirit ever blest,
Eternal Three in One,
  All worship be addressed,
As heretofore
  It was, is now,
And shall be so
  For evermore!

13   H. M.

To God the Father's throne
  Your highest honors raise;
Glory to God the Son,
  To God the Spirit praise:
With all our powers, | Thy name we sing,
Eternal King! | While faith adores.

14 7s.

Sing we to our God above
Praise eternal as his love;
Praise him, all ye heavenly host—
Father, Son, and Holy Ghost!

15 7s.

Praise the name of God most high;
Praise him all below the sky;
Praise him, all ye heavenly host—
Father, Son, and Holy Ghost!
As through countless ages past,
Evermore his praise shall last.

16 7s.

Blessing, honor, glory, might,
And dominion infinite,
To the Father of our Lord,
To the Spirit and the Word:
As it was all worlds before,
Is, and shall be evermore.

17 8s & 7s.

Praise the God of our salvation,
  Praise the Father's boundless love;
Praise the Lamb, our expiation;
  Praise the Spirit from above;
Praise the Fountain of salvation,
  Him by whom our spirits live;
Undivided adoration
  To the one Jehovah give!

18 8s, 7s & 4.

Great Jehovah, we adore thee,
  God the Father, God the Son,
God the Spirit, joined in glory
  On the same eternal throne;
    Endless praises
  To Jehovah, Three in One!

19 7s & 6s. *Iambic.*

To thee be praise for ever
  Thou glorious King of kings!
Thy wondrous love and favor
  Each ransomed spirit sings;
We'll celebrate thy glory
  With all thy saints above,
And shout the joyful story
  Of thy redeeming love.

20 7s & 6s. *Trochaic.*

Father, Son and Holy Ghost,
  One God, whom we adore,
Join we with the heavenly host
  To praise thee evermore:
Live, by heaven and earth adored,
  Three in One, and One in Three,
Holy, holy, holy Lord,
  All glory be to thee!

21 10s.

To Father, Son, and Spirit, ever blest,
Eternal praise and worship be addressed;
From age to age, ye saints, his name adore,
And spread his fame, till time shall be no
  more!

22 11s.

O Father Almighty, to thee be addressed,
With Christ and the Spirit, one God ever
  blest,
All glory and worship, from earth and from
  heaven,
As was, and is now, and shall ever be given!

23 6s & 4s.

To God, the Father, Son,
And Spirit, Three in One,
  All praise be given!
Crown him in every song;
To him your hearts belong
Let all his praise prolong
  On earth, in heaven!

24 *Missionary Doxology.* 6s & 4s.

We praise, we worship thee,
Blessed and holy Three.
  Wisdom, Love, Might!
Boundless as ocean's tide,
Rolling in fullest pride,
O'er the world far and wide,
  "Let there be light!"

SELECTIONS FOR CHANTING.

CHANT. No. I.

Selection, No. 1.

PSALM I.

1 BLESSED is the man that walketh not in the counsel | of the • un- | godly,
   Nor standeth in the way of sinners, nor sitteth in the | seat— | of the | scornful.

2 But his delight is in the | law . of the Lord ;
   And in his law doth he | medi - tate | day and | night.

3 And he shall be like a tree planted by the | rivers • of | water,
   That bringeth forth his | fruit— | in his | season ;

4 His leaf also | shall not | wither;
   And whatso- | ever he | doeth shall | prosper.

5 THE UNGODLY | are not | so :
   But are like the chaff which the | wind— | driveth • a- | way.

6 Therefore the ungodly shall not | stand • in the | judgment,
   Nor sinners in the congre- | gation | of the | righteous :

7 For the Lord knoweth the | way • of the | righteous:
   But the way of the un- | godly | shall— | perish.

Selection, No. 2.

PSALM VIII.

1 O LORD our Lord, how excellent is thy name in | all the | earth !
   Who hast set thy | glory a- | bove the | heavens.

2 Out of the mouth of babes and sucklings hast thou ordained strength be- | cause of • thine | enemies,
   That thou mightest still the | ene - my | and • the a- | venger.

3 When I consider thy heavens, the | work of • thy | fingers,
   The moon and the stars | which thou | hast or- | dained ;

4 What is man, that thou art | mindful • of | him ?
   And the son of man | that thou | visit - est | him ?

5 For thou hast made him a little lower | than the | angels,
   And hast crowned him with | glory | and— | honor.

6 Thou madest him to have dominion over the | works of • thy | hands;
   Thou hast put | all things | under • his | feet :

7 All | sheep and | oxen,
   Yea, and the | beasts— | of the | field ;

8 The fowl of the air, and the | fish • of the | sea,
   And whatsoever passeth through the | paths— | of the | seas.

9 O | Lord our | Lord,
   How excellent is thy | name in | all the | earth !

CHANT. No. II.   PURCELL.

Selection, No. 3.
PSALM XIX.

1 THE HEAVENS declare the | glory • of | God ;
  And the firmament | showeth • his | handy | work.
2 Day unto day uttereth speech, and night unto | night showeth | knowledge.
  There is no speech nor language, where their | voice— | is not | heard.
3 Their line is gone out through | all the | earth,
  And their words to the | end— | of the | world,
4 In them hath he set a tabernacle | for the | sun,
  Which is as a bridegroom coming out of his chamber, and rejoiceth as a strong | man to | run a | race.
5 His going forth is from the end of the heaven, and his circuit unto the | ends— | of it;
  And there is nothing | hid • from the | heat there- | of.
6 THE LAW of the Lord is perfect, con- | verting • the | soul :
  The testimony of the Lord is sure, | making | wise the | simple.
7 The statutes of the Lord are right, re- | joicing the | heart :
  The commandment of the Lord is | pure, en- | lightening • the | eyes.
8 The fear of the Lord is clean, en- | during • for | ever :
  The judgments of the Lord are true and | righteous | alto- | gether.
9 More to be desired are they than gold, yea, than | much fine | gold :
  Sweeter also than honey | and the | honey- | comb.
10 Moreover by them is thy | servant | warned :
   And in keeping of them | there is | great re- | ward.
11 WHO CAN under- | stand his | errors ?
   Cleanse thou | me from | secret | faults.
12 Keep back thy servant also from presumptuous sins ; let them not have do- | minion | over me :
   Then shall I be upright, and I shall be innocent | from the | great trans- | gression.
13 Let the words of my mouth, and the meditation of my heart, be acceptable | in thy | sight,
   O Lord, my | Strength, and | my Re- | deemer.

Selection, No. 4.
PSALM XXIII.

1 THE LORD | is my | shepherd ;
  I | shall— | not— | want.
2 He maketh me to lie down in | green— | pastures ;
  He leadeth me be- | side the | still — | waters.
3 He re- | storeth • my | soul :
  He leadeth me in the paths of righteousness | for his | name's— | sake.
4 Yea, though I walk through the valley of the shadow of death, I will | fear no | evil :
  For thou art with me ; thy rod and thy | staff they | comfort | me.
5 Thou preparest a table before me in the presence | of mine | enemies :
  Thou anointest my head with oil ; my | cup— | runneth | over.
6 Surely goodness and mercy shall follow me all the | days of • my | life ;
  And I will dwell in the | house • of the | Lord for | ever.

27

CHANT. No. III.

Selection, No. 5.   Psalm XXIV.

1 The Earth is the Lord's, and the | fullness . there- | **of**;
  The world, and | they that | dwell there- | in.
2 For he hath founded it up- | on the | seas,
  And established | it up- | on the | floods.
3 Who shall ascend into the | hill . of the | Lord?
  Or who shall stand | in his | holy place?
4 He that hath clean hands, and a | pure — | heart;
  Who hath not lifted up his soul unto vanity, | nor — | sworn de- | ceitfully.
5 He shall receive the blessing | from the | Lord,
  And righteousness from the | God of | his sal- | vation.
6 This is the generation of | them that | seek him,
  That | seek thy | face, O | Jacob.
7 Lift up your heads, O ye gates; and be ye lift up, ye ever- | lasting | doors;
  And the King of | glory | shall come | in.
8 Who is this | King of | glory?
  The Lord, strong and mighty, the | Lord — | mighty . in | battle.
9 Lift up your heads, O ye gates; even lift them up, ye ever- | lasting | doors;
  And the King of | glory | shall come | in.
10 Who is this | King of | glory?
  The Lord of hosts, | he . is the | King of | glory.

Selection, No. 6.   Psalm XXV. 1-14.

1 Unto thee, O Lord, do I lift | up my | soul.
  O my | God, I | trust in | thee :
2 Let me | not . be a- | shamed,
  Let not mine enemies | triumph | over | me.
3 Yea, let none that wait on | thee . be a- | shamed ;
  Let them be ashamed which trans- | gress with- | out — | cause.
4 Show me thy ways, O Lord ; | teach me . thy | paths.
  Lead me in thy | truth, and | teach — | me :
5 For thou art the God of | my sal- | vation ;
  On thee do I | wait — | all the | day.
6 Remember, O Lord, thy tender mercies and thy | loving- | kindnesses ;
  For | they . have been | ever . of | old.
7 Remember not the sins of my youth, nor my | trans-— | gressions ;
  According to thy mercy remember thou me, for thy | goodness' | sake, O | Lord.

CHANT. No. IV. — Dr. Woodward.

8 Good and upright | is the | Lord:
    Therefore will he teach | sinners | in the | way.

9 The meek will he | guide in | judgment:
    And the | meek . will he | teach his | way.

10 All the paths of the Lord are | mercy . and | truth
    Unto such as keep his covenant | and his | testi - mo- | nies.

11 For thy name's sake, O Lord, pardon | mine in- | iquity;
    For | it— | is— | great.

12 What man is he that | feareth . the | Lord?
    Him shall he teach in the | way that | he shall | choose.

13 His soul shall | dwell at | ease:
    And his | seed . shall in- | herit the | earth.

14 The secret of the Lord is with | them that | fear him;
    And he will | shew them | his— | covenant.

Selection, No. 7. From Psalm XXVII.

1 The Lord is my light and my salvation; | whom . shall I | fear?
    The Lord is the strength of my life; of | whom . shall I | be a- | fraid?

2 Though a host should encamp against me, my | heart . shall not | fear;
    Though war should rise against me, in | this will | I be | confident.

3 One thing have I desired of the Lord, that will I | seek — | after:
    That I may dwell in the house of the Lord all the | days of | my — | life,

4 To behold the beauty | of the | Lord,
    And to in- | quire in | his— | temple.

5 For in the time of trouble he shall hide me in | his pa- | vilion:
    In the secret of his tabernacle shall he hide me: he shall set me | up, up- | on a | rock.

6 And now shall mine head be lifted up above mine enemies | round a- | bout me:
    Therefore will I offer in his tabernacle sacrifices of joy; I will sing, yea, I will sing | praises | unto . the | Lord.

7 Hear, O Lord, when I | cry . with my | voice:
    Have mercy also up- | on— | me, and | answer me.

8 When thou saidst, | Seek ye . my | face;
    My heart said unto thee, Thy face, | Lord, will | I— | seek.

9 Hide not thy face | far — | from me;
    Put not thy | servant a- | way in | anger:

10 Thou hast | been my | help:
    Leave me not, neither forsake me, O | God of | my sal - vation.

CHANT. No. V.

Selection, No. 8.   Psalm XXXIII. 1–12.

1 Rejoice in the Lord, | O ye | righteous:
    For praise is | comely | for the | upright.

2 Praise the | Lord with | harp:
    Sing unto him with the psaltery and an | instrument | of ten | **strings**.

3 Sing unto him a | new— | song;
    Play skillfully | with a | loud — | noise.

4 For the word of the | Lord is | right;
    And all his | works are | done in | truth.

5 He loveth | righteousness and | judgment:
    The earth is full of the | goodness | of the | Lord.

6 By the word of the Lord were the | **heavens** — | **made**;
    And all the host of them by the | **breath of** | **his**— |.mouth.

7 He gathered the waters of the sea together | as an | **heap**:
    He layeth up the | depth in | store— | houses.

8 Let all the earth | fear the | Lord:
    Let all the inhabitants of the world | **stand in** | awe of | him.

9 For he spake, and | it was | done;
    He commanded, | and it | stood— | fast.

10 The Lord bringeth the counsel of the | heathen . to | naught:
    He maketh the devices of the | people . of | none ef- | fect.

11 The counsel of the Lord | standeth . for- | ever,
    The thoughts of his heart to | all — | gener- | ations.

12 Blessed is the nation whose | God . is the | Lord;
    And the people whom he hath chosen for his | own in- | her - it- | ance.

Selection, No. 9.   From Psalm XXXIV.

1 I will bless the Lord at | all— | times:
    His praise shall continually | be in | my — | mouth.

2 My soul shall make her | boast . in the | Lord:
    The humble shall | hear there - of, | and be | glad.

3 Oh, magnify the | Lord with | me,
    And let us ex- | alt his | name to- | gether.

CHANT. No. VI.   Rev. W. H. Havergal.

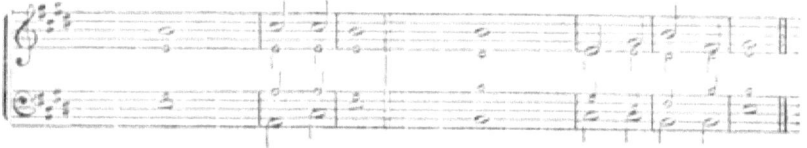

4 I sought the Lord, | and he | heard me,
   And delivered me from | all — | my — | fears.

5 The angel of the Lord encampeth round about | them that | fear him,
   And de- | liver- | eth — | them.

6 Oh, taste and see that the | Lord is | good :
   Blessed is the | man that | trusteth . in | him.

7 Oh, fear the Lord, | ye his | saints :
   For there is no want to | them that | fear — | him.

8 The young lions do lack, and | suffer | hunger :
   But they that seek the Lord shall not | want — | any good | thing.

9 The righteous cry, and the | Lord — | heareth,
   And delivereth them | out of | all their | troubles.

10 The Lord is nigh unto them that are of a | broken | heart ;
    And saveth such as | be of . a | contrite | spirit.

11 Many are the afflictions | of the | righteous :
    But the Lord delivereth him | out of | them — | all.

12 The Lord redeemeth the | soul of . his | servants ;
    And none of them that trust in | him — | shall be | desolate.

Selection, No. 10.   Psalm XXXVI. 5-10.

1 Thy mercy, O Lord, is | in the | heavens :
   And thy faithfulness | reacheth | unto . the | clouds.

2 Thy righteousness is like the great mountains ; thy judgments are a | great — | deep :
   O Lord, thou pre- | servest | man and | beast.

3 How excellent is thy loving- | kindness, . O | God !
   Therefore the children of men put their trust under the | shadow | of thy | wings.

4 They shall be abundantly satisfied with the fatness | of thy | house ;
   And thou shalt make them drink of the | river . of | thy — | pleasures.

5 For with thee is the | fountain . of | life :
   In thy light shall | we — | see — | light.

6 Oh, continue thy loving-kindness unto | them that | know thee ;
   And thy righteousness to the | upright | in — | heart.

CHANT. No. VII. TALLIS.

Selection, No. 11. From Psalms XLII. & XLIII.

1 As the hart panteth after the | water | brooks,
 So panteth my soul after | thee— | O— | God.

2 My soul thirsteth for God, for the | living | God!
 When shall I come and ap- | pear be- | fore— | God?

3 My tears have been my meat | day and | night,
 While they continually say unto me, | where is | thy— | God?

4 When I re- | member . these | things,
 I pour | out my | soul— | in me;

5 For I had gone with the multitude, I went with them to the | house of | God,
 With the voice of joy and praise, with a multitude that | kept— | holy- | day.

6 Why art thou cast down, | O my | soul?
 And why art thou dis- | quiet- | ed in | me?

7 Hope | thou in | God:
 For I shall yet praise him for the | help of | his — | countenance.

8 Oh, send out thy light and thy truth : | let them | lead me;
 Let them bring me unto thy holy hill, and | to thy | taber - na- | cles.

9 Then will I go unto the altar of God, unto God my ex- | ceeding | joy:
 Yea, upon the harp will I praise | thee, O | God, my | God.

10 Why art thou cast down, | O my | soul?
 And why art thou dis- | quiet- | ed with- | in me?

11 Hope | in — | God:
 For I shall yet praise him, who is the health of my | counte - nance, | and my | God.

Selection, No. 12.   Psalm XLVI.

1 God is our | refuge . and | strength,
 A very | present | help in | trouble.

2 Therefore will not we fear, though the | earth . be re- | moved,
 And though the mountains be carried into the | midst— | of the | sea;

3 Though the waters thereof | roar . and be | troubled,
 Though the mountains | shake . with the | swelling . there- | of.

4 There is a river, the streams whereof shall make glad the | city of | God,
 The holy place of the tabernacles | of the | Most — | High.

5 God is in the midst of her; she shall | not be | moved;
 God shall | help her, . and | that right | early.

CHANT. No. VIII.   FARRANT.

6 The heathen raged, the | kingdoms . were | moved:
  He uttered his | voice, the | earth— | melted.

7 The Lord of | hosts is | with us;
  The God of | Jacob | is our | refuge.

8 COME, behold the | works - of the | Lord,
  What desolations he hath | made— | in the | earth.

9 He maketh wars to cease unto the | end . of the | earth;
  He breaketh the bow, and cutteth the spear in sunder; he burneth the | chariot | in the | fire.

10 Be still, and know that | I am | God:
   I will be exalted among the heathen, I will be ex- | alted | in the | earth.

11 The Lord of | hosts is | with us;
   The God of | Jacob | is our | refuge.

Selection, No. 13.   FROM PSALM XLVIII.

1 GREAT IS THE LORD, and greatly to be praised in the city | of our | God,
  In the mountain | of his | holi- | ness.

2 Beautiful for | situ- | ation,
  The joy of the whole | earth, is | Mount — | Zion,

3 On the sides of the north, the city of the | great — | King.
  God is known in her | pala-ces | for a | refuge.

4 WE HAVE thought of thy loving -- | kindness, O | God,
  In the | midst of | thy — | temple.

5 According to thy name, O God, so is thy praise unto the | ends . of the | earth:
  Thy right hand is | full of | righteous- | ness.

6 Let Mount Zion rejoice, let the daughters of | Judah . be | glad,
  Be- | cause of | thy — | judgments.

7 WALK about Zion, and go | round a - bout | her:
  Tell the | towers — | there- — | of.

8 Mark ye well her bulwarks, con- — | sider . her | palaces;
  That ye may tell it to the gener- | ation | follow- | ing.

9 For this God is our God for | ever . and | ever:
  He will be our guide | even | unto | death.

CHANT. No. IX.   Dr. Turner.

Selection, No. 14.   From Psalm LI.

1 Have mercy upon me, O God, according to thy | loving- | kindness:
 According unto the multitude of thy tender mercies | blot out | my trans- | gressions.

2 Wash me thoroughly from | mine in- | iquity,
 And | cleanse me | from my | sin.

3 For I acknowledge | my trans- | gressions:
 And my | sin is | ever . be- | fore me.

4 Hide thy face | from my | sins,
 And blot out | all — | mine in- | iquities.

5 Create in me a clean | heart, O | God;
 And renew a right | spirit . with- | in — | me.

6 Cast me not away | from thy | presence;
 And take not thy | Holy | Spirit | from me.

7 Restore unto me the joy of | thy sal- | vation;
 And uphold me | with thy | free — | Spirit.

9 Then will I teach trans- | gressors . thy | ways;
 And sinners shall be con- | verted | unto | thee.

8 Deliver me from blood-guiltiness, O God, thou God of | my sal- | vation;
 And my tongue shall sing aloud | of thy | righteous- | ness.

10 O Lord, open | thou my | lips:
 And my mouth shall | shew forth | thy — | praise.

11 For thou desirest not sacrifice; | else . would I | give it ·
 Thou delightest | not in | burnt— | offering.

12 The sacrifices of God are a | broken | spirit:
 A broken and a contrite heart, O God, | thou wilt | not de- | spise.

CHANT. No. X.

CHANT. No. XI.

Selection, No. 15.   FROM PSALM LVII.

1 BE thou exalted, O God, a- | bove the | heavens ;
　Let thy glory be a- | bove— | all the | earth.

2 My heart is fixed, O God, my | heart is | fixed ;
　I will | sing and | give— | praise.

3 Awake up, my glory ; awake, | psaltery . and | harp :
　I my- | self . will a- | wake— | early.

4 I will praise thee, O Lord, a- | mong the | people :
　I will sing unto | thee a- | mong the | nations.

5 For thy mercy is great | unto . the | heavens,
　And thy | truth— | unto . the | clouds.

6 Be thou exalted, O God, a- | bove the | heavens ;
　Let thy glory be a- | bove— | all the | earth.

Selection, No. 16.   PSALM LXIII. 1-7.

1 O GOD, | thou art | my God ;
　Early | will I | seek— | thee :

2 My soul thirsteth for thee, my flesh | longeth . for | thee
　In a dry and thirsty land, | where no | water | is ;

3 To see thy power | and thy | glory,
　So as I have seen thee | in the | sanctu- | ary.

4 Because thy loving-kindness is | better . than | life,
　My | lips shall | praise— | thee.

5 Thus will I bless thee | while I | live ;
　I will lift up my | hands in | thy— | name.

6 My soul shall be satisfied as with | marrow . and | fatness ;
　And my mouth shall praise | thee with | joyful | lips :

7 When I remember thee up- | on my | bed,
　And meditate on thee | in the | night— | watches.

8 Because thou hast | been my | help,
　Therefore in the shadow of thy | wings will | I re- | joice.

CHANT. No. XII.   GREGORIAN.

Selection, No. 17.   PSALM LXV.

1 PRAISE waiteth for thee, O | God, in | Zion :
  And unto thee shall the | vow— | be per- | formed.

2 O thou that | hearest | prayer,
  Unto | thee shall | all flesh | come.

3 Iniquities pre- | vail a- | gainst me :
  As for our transgressions, thou shalt | purge— | them a- | way.

4 Blessed is the man | whom thou | choosest,
  And causest to approach unto thee, that he may | dwell in | thy— | courts.

5 We shall be satisfied with the goodness | of thy | house,
  Even | of thy | holy | temple.

6 BY TERRIBLE things in righteousness wilt thou answer us, O God of | our sal- | vation ;
  Who art the confidence of all the ends of the earth, and of them that are afar
      off up- | on the | sea :

7 Which by his strength setteth | fast the | mountains ;
  Being | gird- | ed with | power :

8 Which stilleth the | noise - of the | seas,
  The noise of their waves, and the | tumult | of the | people.

9 They also that dwell in the uttermost parts are a- | fraid at . thy | tokens :
  Thou makest the outgoings of the morning and | evening | to re- | joice.

10 THOU VISITEST the earth, and waterest it : thou greatly enrichest it with the river
      of God, which is | full of | water :
   Thou preparest them corn, when thou hast | so pro- | vided | for it.

11 Thou waterest the ridges thereof abundantly : thou settlest the | furrows . there- | of.
   Thou makest it soft with showers : thou | blessest . the | springing there- | of.

12 Thou crownest the year | with thy | goodness ;
   And thy | paths— | drop— | fatness.

13 They drop upon the pastures | of the | wilderness :
   And the little hills re- | joice on | every | side.

14 The pastures are clothed with flocks ; the valleys also are covered | over . with | corn;
   They shout for | joy, they | also | sing.

Selection, No. 18.   PSALM LXVII.

1 GOD be merciful unto | us, and | bless us ;
  And cause his | face to | shine upon | us.

2 That thy way may be | known up - on | earth,
  Thy saving | health a- | mong all | nations.

CHANT. No. XIII.   TALLIS.

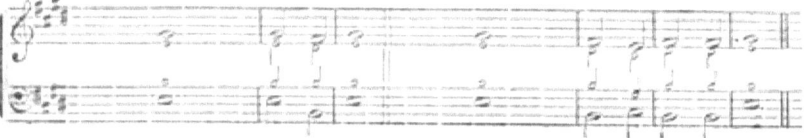

3 LET THE PEOPLE praise | thee, O | God ;
  Let | all the | people | praise thee.

4 Oh let the nations be glad and | sing for | joy :
  For thou shalt judge the people righteously, and govern the | nations | upon | earth.

5 LET THE PEOPLE praise | thee, O | God ;
  Let | all the | people | praise thee.

6 Then shall the earth | yield her | increase
  And God, even | our own | God, shall | bless us.

7 God | shall— | bless us ;
  And all the ends of the | earth shall | fear— | him.

Selection, No. 19.   PSALM LXXXIV.

1 HOW AMIABLE are thy | taber - na- | cles,
  O | Lord— | of— | hosts !

2 My soul longeth, yea, even fainteth for the | courts . of the | Lord :
  My heart and my flesh crieth | out . for the | living | God.

3 Yea, the sparrow hath found an house, and the swallow a nest for herself, where
    she may | lay her | young,
  Even thine altars, O Lord of hosts, my | King, . and | my— | God.

4 Blessed are they that | dwell in * thy | house :
  They will be | still— | praising | thee.

5 Blessed is the man whose | strength * is in | thee ;
  In whose | heart * are the | ways of | them,

6 Who passing through the valley of Baca | make * it a | well ;
  The rain | also | filleth * the | pools.

7 They go from | strength to | strength,
  Every one of them in Zion ap- | peareth * be- | fore— | God.

8 O LORD GOD of hosts, | hear my | prayer :
  Give | ear, O | God of | Jacob.

9 Behold, O | God our | shield,
  And look upon the | face of | thine a- | nointed.

10 For a day in thy courts is better | than a | thousand.
   I had rather be a doorkeeper in the house of my God, than to dwell in the | tents
     of | wicked- | ness.

11 For the Lord God is a | sun and | shield :
   The Lord will give grace and glory : no good thing will he withhold from | them
     that | walk up- | rightly.

12 O | Lord of | hosts,
   Blessed is the | man that | trusteth * in | thee.

CHANT. No. XIV.   PURCELL.

Selection, No. 20.   PSALM LXXXV.

1 LORD, thou hast been favorable | unto * thy | land :
  Thou hast brought back the cap- | tivi- | ty of | Jacob.

2 Thou hast forgiven the iniquity | of thy | people,
  Thou hast | covered | all their | sin.

3 Thou hast taken away | all thy | wrath :
  Thou hast turned thyself from the | fierceness | of thine | anger.

4 TURN US, O God of | our sal- | vation,
  And cause thine | anger * toward | us to | cease.

5 Wilt thou be angry with | us for | ever?
  Wilt thou draw out thine anger to | all— | gener | ations ?

6 Wilt thou not re- | vive us * a- | gain :
  That thy people | may re- | joice in | thee ?

7 Shew us thy | mercy, * O | Lord,
  And | grant us | thy sal- | vation.

8 I WILL HEAR what God the | Lord will | speak :
  For he will speak peace unto his people, and to **his saints: but let them not |**
  turn a- | gain to | folly.

9 Surely his salvation is nigh | them that | fear him ;
  That glory may | dwell— | in our | land.

10 Mercy and truth are | met to- | gether ;
   Righteousness and | peace have | kissed * each | other.

11 Truth shall spring | out * of the | earth ;
   And righteousness shall | look— | down from | heaven.

12 Yea, the Lord shall give | that * which is | good ;
   And our | land shall | yield her | increase.

13 Righteousness shall | go be- | fore him ;
   And shall set us in the | way of | his— | steps.

CHANT. No. XV.   DR. BLOW.

CHANT. No. XVI.

Selection, No. 21.   PSALM LXXXIX. 1-18.

1 I WILL SING of the mercies of the | Lord for | ever
   With my mouth will I make known thy faithfulness to | all — | gener- | ations.

2 For I have said, Mercy shall be built | up for | ever:
   Thy faithfulness shalt thou establish | in the | very | heavens.

3 I have made a covenant | with my | chosen,
   I have sworn unto | David | my — | servant,

4 Thy seed will I es- | tablish . for | ever,
   And build up thy throne to | all — | gener- | ations.

5 And the heavens shall praise thy | wonders, . O | Lord:
   Thy faithfulness also in the congre- | gation | of the | saints.

6 For who in the heaven can be compared | unto . the | Lord?
   Who among the sons of the mighty can be | likened unto . the | Lord?

7 GOD is greatly to be feared in the assembly | of the | saints,
   And to be had in reverence of all | them that | are a- | bout him.

8 O Lord God of hosts, who is a strong Lord | like . unto | thee?
   Or to thy faithfulness | round a- | bout — | thee?

9 Thou rulest the raging | of the | sea:
   When the waves thereof a- | rise, thou | stillest | them.

10 Thou hast broken Rahab in pieces, as | one . that is | slain ; .
   Thou hast scattered thine enemies | with thy | strong — | arm.

11 The heavens are thine, the earth | also . is | thine:
   As for the world and the fullness thereof, | thou hast | founded | them.

12 The north and the south thou hast cre- | ated | them :
   Tabor and Hermon shall re- | joice in | thy — | name.

13 Thou hast a | mighty | arm :
   Strong is thy hand, and | high is | thy right | hand.

14 Justice and judgment are the habitation | of thy | throne :
   Mercy and truth shall | go be- | fore thy | face.

15 Blessed is the people that know the | joyful | sound :
   They shall walk, O Lord, in the | light of | thy — | countenance.

16 In thy name shall they rejoice | all the | day :
   And in thy righteousness | shall they | be ex- | alted.

17 For thou art the glory | of their | strength :
   And in thy favor our | horn shall | be ex- | alted.

18 For the Lord is | our de- | fense ;
   And the Holy One of | Israel | is our | king.

CHANT. No. XVII.

Selection, No. 22.   PSALM XC.

1 LORD, THOU hast been our | dwelling | place
   In | all — | gener- | ations.

2 Before the mountains were brought forth, or ever thou hadst formed the | earth ,
   and the | world,
   Even from everlasting to ever- | lasting, | thou art | God.

3 Thou turnest man | to de- | struction;
   And sayest, Re- | turn, ye | children . of | men.

4 For a thousand years in thy sight are but as yesterday | when . it is | past,
   And as a | watch — | in the | night.

5 Thou carriest them away as with a flood; they are | as a | sleep:
   In the morning they are like | grass which | groweth | up;

6 In the morning it flourisheth, and | groweth | up;
   In the evening it is cut | down and | wither- | eth.

7 For we are consumed | by thine | anger,
   And by thy | wrath — | are we | troubled.

8 Thou hast set our iniquities be- | fore — | thee,
   Our secret sins in the | light of | thy — | countenance.

9 For all our days are passed away | in thy | wrath:
   We spend our years as a | tale — | that is | told.

10 THE DAYS of our years are threescore | years and | ten;
    And if by reason of | strength . they be | fourscore | years,

11 Yet is their strength | labor . and | sorrow;
    For it is soon cut off, | and we | fly a- | way.

12 Who knoweth the power | of thine | anger?
    Even according to thy | fear, so | is thy | wrath.

13 So teach us to | number . our | days,
    That we may apply our | hearts — | unto | wisdom.

14 RETURN, O | Lord, how | long?
    And let it repent thee con- | cerning | thy — | servants.

15 O satisfy us early | with thy | mercy;
    That we may rejoice and be | glad — | all our | days.

16 Make us glad according to the days wherein thou | hast af- | flicted us,
    And the years where- | in we | have seen | evil.

17 Let thy work appear | unto . thy | servants,
    And thy | glory | unto . their | children.

CHANT. No. XVIII.   FARRANT.

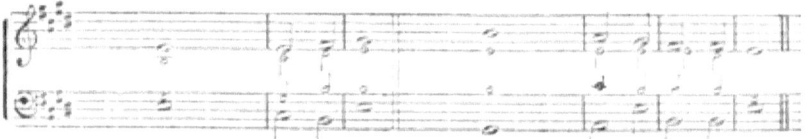

18 And let the beauty of the Lord our God | be up- | on us :
    And establish thou the work of our hands upon us ; yea, the work of our | hands
    es- | tablish . thou | it.

Selection, No. 23.   PSALM XCI. 9-16.

1 BECAUSE thou hast made the Lord which | is my | refuge,
   Even the Most | High, thy | habi- | tation :

2 There shall no | evil . be-) fall thee,
   Neither shall any | plague come | nigh thy | dwelling.

3 For he shall give his angels | charge — | over thee,
   To keep thee in | all — | thy — | ways.

4 They shall bear thee up in their | hands,
   Lest thou dash thy | foot a- | gainst a | stone.

5 Thou shalt tread upon the | lion . and | adder :
   The young lion and the dragon shalt thou | trample | under | feet.

6 BECAUSE he hath set his love upon me, therefore will I de- | liver | him :
   I will set him on high, because | he hath | known my | name.

7 He shall call upon me, and I will | answer | him :
   I will be with him in trouble ; I will deliver | him, and | honor | him.

8 With long life will I | satis · fy | him,
   And | shew him | my sal- | vation.

Selection, No. 24.   PSALM XCIII.

1 THE | LORD — | reigneth,
   He is | clothed . with | majes- | ty ;

2 The Lord is clothed with strength, wherewith he hath | girded . him- | self :
   The world also is established, that it | can not | be — | moved.

3 Thy throne is es- | tablished . of | old :
   Thou | art from | ever- | lasting.

4 The floods have lifted up, O Lord, the floods have lifted | up their | voice ;
   The | floods lift | up their | waves.

5 The Lord on high is mightier than the noise of | many | waters,
   Yea, than the mighty | waves — | of the | sea.

6 Thy testimonies are | very | sure :
   Holiness becometh thine | house, O | Lord, for | ever.

CHANT. No. XIX.

Selection, No. 25.   Psalm XCV.

1 O COME, let us sing un- | to the | Lord:
   Let us make a joyful noise to the | Rock of | our sal- — | vation.

2 Let us come before his presence | with thanks- | giving,
   And make a joyful noise | unto | him with | psalms.

3 For the Lord is a | great — | God,
   And a great | King a- | bove all | gods.

4 In his hand are the deep places | of the | earth ;
   The strength of the | hills is | his — | also.

5 The sea is his, | and he | made . it:
   And his hands | formed | the dry | land.

6 O COME, let us worship and | bow — | down :
   Let us kneel be- | fore the | Lord our | Maker.

7 For he | is our | God ;
   And we are the people of his pasture, and the | sheep of | his — | hand.

8 To-day if ye will hear his voice, harden | not your | heart,
   As in the provocation, and as in the day of temp- | tation | in the | wilderness:

9 When your fathers | tempted | me,
   Proved | me, and | saw my | work. .

10 Forty years long was I grieved with | this . gener - | ation,
   And said, It is a people that do err in their heart, and they | have not | known my | ways:

11 Unto whom I sware | in my | wrath
   That they should not | enter | into . my | rest.

Selection, No. 26.   Psalm XCVI.

1 O SING unto the Lord a | new — | song:
   Sing unto the | Lord, — | all the | earth.

2 Sing unto the Lord, | bless his | name;
   Shew forth his sal- | vation . from | day to | day.

3 Declare his glory a- | mong the | heathen,
   His wonders a- | mong — | all — | people.

4 For the Lord is great, and greatly | to be | praised ;
   He is to be | feared . a- | bove all | gods.

5 For all the gods of the | nations . are | idols:
   But the | Lord — | made the | heavens.

CHANT. No. XX.

6 Honor and majesty | are be - fore | him :
  Strength and beauty are | in his | sanctu- | ary.

7 GIVE unto the Lord, O ye kindreds | of the | people,
  Give unto the Lord | glory | and — | strength.

8 Give unto the Lord the glory due | unto . his | name :
  Bring an offering, and come | into | his — | courts.

9 O worship the Lord in the | beauty . of | holiness ;
  Fear be- | fore him, | all the | earth.

10 Say among the heathen that the | Lord — | reigneth ;
   The world also shall be established, that it shall not be moved : he shall | judge
   the | people | righteously.

11 Let the heavens rejoice, and let the | earth be | glad ;
   Let the sea roar, and the | fullness | there- — | of.

12 Let the field be joyful, and all that | is there- | in :
   Then shall all the trees of the wood re- | joice be- | fore the | Lord :

13 For he cometh, for he cometh to | judge the | earth :
   He shall judge the world with righteousness, and the | people | with his | truth.

Selection, No. 27.   PSALM XCVIII.

1 O SING unto the Lord a new song; for he hath done | marvel - ous | things ;
  His right hand, and his holy arm, hath | gotten | him the | victory.

2 The Lord hath made known | his sal- | vation :
  His righteousness hath he openly shewed in the | sight — | of the | heathen.

3 He hath remembered his mercy and his truth toward the | house of | Israel :
  All the ends of the earth have seen the sal- | vation | of our | God.

4 MAKE a joyful noise unto the Lord, | all the | earth :
  Make a loud noise, and re- | joice, and | sing — | praise.

5 Sing unto the Lord | with the | harp ;
  With the harp, and the | voice — | of a | psalm.

6 With trumpets and | sound of | cornet
  Make a joyful noise be- | fore the | Lord, the | King.

7 Let the sea roar, and the | fullness . there- | of ;
  The world, and | they that | dwell there- | in.

8 Let the floods | clap their | hands :
  Let the hills be joyful to- | gether . be- | fore the | Lord ;

9 For he cometh to | judge the | earth ;
  With righteousness shall he judge the world, and the | people | with— | equity.

28

434 NEW SABBATH HYMN AND TUNE BOOK.

CHANT. No. XXI. Dr. Turner.

Selection, No. 28. Psalm C.

1 Make a joyful noise unto the Lord | all ye | lands.
   Serve the Lord with gladness: come before his | presence | with — | singing.

2 Know ye that the Lord | he is | God:
   It is he that hath made us, and not we ourselves; we are his people, and the | sheep of | his — | pasture.

3 Enter into his gates with thanksgiving, and into his | courts with | praise.
   Be thankful unto him, and | bless — | his — | name.

4 For the Lord is good; his mercy is | ever- | lasting;
   And his truth endureth to | all — | gener- | ations.

Selection, No. 29. Psalm CII. 16–28.

1 When the Lord shall | build up | Zion,
   He shall ap- | pear in | his — | glory.

2 He will regard the prayer | of the | destitute,
   And | not de- | spise their | prayer.

3 This shall be written for the gener- | ation . to | come:
   And the people which shall be cre- | ated . shall | praise the | Lord.

4 For he hath looked down from the height | of his | sanctuary;
   From heaven did the | Lord be- | hold the | earth;

5 To hear the groaning | of the | prisoner, .
   To loose those that are ap- | point- — | ed to | death;

6 To declare the name of the | Lord in | Zion,
   And his praise | in Je- | ru · sa · | lem;

7 When the people are | gathered . to- | gether,
   And the | kingdoms, to | serve the | Lord.

8 He weakened my | strength . in the | way;
   He | shortened | my — | days.

9 I said, O my God, take me not away in the | midst of . my | days.
   Thy years are throughout | all — | gener- | ations.

10 Of old hast thou laid the foundation | of the | earth:
   And the heavens are the | work of | thy — | hands.

11 They shall perish, but | thou . shalt en- | dure:
   Yea, all of them shall wax | old — | like a | garment;

12 As a vesture | shalt thou | change them,
   And they | shall be | chang- — | ed;

13 But thou | art the | same,
   And thy | years shall | have no | end.

14 The children of thy servants | shall con- | tinue.
   And their seed shall be es- | tablish- | ed be- | fore thee.

CHANT. No. XXII.   FITZHERBERT.

Selection, No. 30.
From Psalm CIII.

1 Bless the Lord, | O my | soul :
   And all that is within me, | bless his | holy | name.
2 Bless the Lord, | O my | soul,
   And for- | get not | all his | benefits :
3 Who forgiveth all | thine in- | iquities ;
   Who | healeth . all | thy dis- | eases ;
4 Who redeemeth thy life | from de- | struction ;
   Who crowneth thee with loving | kindness . and | tender | mercies ;
5 Who satisfieth thy mouth with | good — | things ;
   So that thy youth is re- | new - ed | like the | eagle's.
6 The Lord executeth | righteousness . and | judg- | ment
   For | all that | are op- | pressed ;
7 He made known his ways | unto | Moses,
   His acts unto the | children . of | Isra- | el.
8 The Lord is | merciful . and | gracious,
   Slow to anger, and | plenteous | in — | mercy.
9 He will not | always | chide :
   Neither will he | keep his | anger . for | ever.
10 He hath not dealt with us | after . our | sins ;
   Nor rewarded us ac- | cording . to | our in- | iquities.
11 For as the heaven is high a- | bove the | earth,
   So great is his mercy toward | them that | fear — | him.
12 As far as the east is | from the | west,
   So far hath he removed | our trans- | gressions | from us.
13 Like as a father | pitieth his | children,
   So the Lord | pitieth | them that | fear him.
14 For he | knoweth . our | frame ;
   He remembereth that | we — | are — | dust.
15 As for man, his | days . are as | grass ;
   As a flower of the field | so he | flourish- | eth.
16 For the wind passeth over it, | and . it is | gone ;
   And the place there- | of shall | know it . no | more.
17 But the mercy of the Lord is from everlasting to everlasting upon | them that | fear him,
   And his righteousness | unto | children's | children ;
18 To such as | keep his | covenant,
   And to those that remember his com- | mandments to | do — | them.
19 The Lord hath prepared his | throne . in the | heavens ;
   And his kingdom | ruleth | over | all.
20 Bless the Lord, ye his angels, that ex- | cel in | strength,
   That do his commandments, hearkening unto the | voice of | his — | word.
21 Bless ye the Lord, all | ye his | hosts ;
   Ye ministers of | his, that | do his | pleasure.
22 Bless the Lord, all his works, in all places of | his do | minion ;
   Bless the Lord, | O — | my — | soul.

CHANT. No. XXIII.   TALLIS.

Selection, No. 31.   PSALM CXI.

1 PRAISE | ye the | Lord.
    I will praise the Lord with my whole heart, in the assembly of the upright, and | in the | congre- | gation.
2 The works of the | Lord are | great,
    Sought out of all them that have | pleasure | there- — | in.
3 His work is honorable and | glo- — | rious ;
    And his righteousness en- | dureth | for — | ever.
4 He hath made his wonderful works to | be re- | membered :
    The Lord is gracious and | full — | of com- | passion.
5 He hath given meat unto | them that | fear him :
    He will ever be | mindful | of his | covenant.
6 He hath showed his people the | power of . his | works,
    That he may give them the | heri - tage | of the | heathen.
7 The works of his hands are | verity . and | judgment ;
    All his com- | mandments | are — | sure.
8 They stand fast for | ever . and | ever,
    And are done in | truth and | up- — | rightness.
9 He sent redemption unto his people : he hath commanded his | covenant . for | ever :
    Holy and | rever - end | is his | name.
10 The fear of the Lord is the | beginning . of | wisdom :
    A good understanding have all they that do his commandments: his | praise en- | dureth . for | ever.

Selection, No. 32.   FROM PSALM CXV.

1 NOT UNTO us, O Lord | not . unto | us,
    But unto thy name give glory, for thy mercy, and | for thy | truth's — | sake.
2 Wherefore should the heathen say, Where is | now their | God ?
    But our God is in the heavens: he hath done whatso- | ever | he — | pleased.
3 O ISRAEL, trust thou | in the | Lord :
    He is their | help and | their — | shield.
4 O house of Aaron | trust . in the | Lord :
    He is their | help and | their — | shield.
5 Ye that fear the Lord, | trust . in the | Lord :
    He is their | help and | their — | shield.
6 The Lord hath been mindful of us : | he will | bless us ;
    He will bless the house of Israel ; he will | bless the | house of | Aaron.
7 He will bless them that | fear the | Lord,
    Both | small — | and — | great.
8 The Lord shall increase you more and more, | you . and | your | children.
    Ye are blessed of the Lord | which made | heaven and | earth.

CHANT. No. XXIV. DR. TURNER.

9 THE HEAVEN, even the heavens, | are the | Lord's :
    But the earth hath he given | to the | children . of | men.
10 The dead | praise . not the | Lord,
    Neither any that go | down — | into | silence.
11 But we will bless the Lord from this time forth and for } ever- | more.
    Praise | — | the — | Lord.

Selection, No. 33.   FROM PSALM CXVI.

1 I | LOVE the | Lord,
    Because he hath heard my | voice . and my | suppli- | cations.
2 Because he hath inclined his ear | unto | me,
    Therefore will I call upon him as | long as | I — | live.
3 The sorrows of death compassed me, and the pains of hell gat | hold up- | on me :
    I found | trouble | and — | sorrow.
4 Then called I upon the | name of the | Lord ;
    O Lord, I beseech thee, de- | liver | my — | soul.
5 Gracious is the | Lord, and | righteous ;
    Yea, our | God is | merci- | ful.
6 The Lord pre- | serveth . the | simple :
    I was brought low, and | he — | helped | me.
7 Return unto thy rest, | O my | soul ;
    For the Lord hath dealt | bounti- | fully | with thee.
8 For thou hast delivered my | soul from | death,
    Mine eyes from tears, and | my | feet — | from — | falling.
9 WHAT shall I render | unto the | Lord
    For all his | bene - fits | toward — | me?
10 I will take the | cup of . sal- | vation,
    And call upon the |-name — | of the | Lord.
11 I will pay my vows | unto . the | Lord
    Now in the | presence . of | all his | people.
12 Precious in the | sight . of the | Lord
    Is the | death of | his — | saints.
13 O Lord, truly I am thy servant; I am thy servant, and the | son of . thine | handmaid :
    Thou hast | loos - ed | my — | bonds.
14 I will offer to thee the sacrifice of | thanks- — | giving,
    And will call upon the | name — | of the | Lord.
15 I will pay my vows | unto . the | Lord
    Now in the | presence . of | all his | people,
16 In the courts of the Lord's house, in the midst of thee, | O Je- | rusalem,
    Praise | ye — | the — | Lord.

CHANT. No. XXV.

Selection, No. 34.   Psalm CXVIII. 14-29.

1 The Lord is my | strength and | song,
   And is be- | come — | my sal- | vation.

2 The voice of rejoicing and salvation is in the tabernacles | of the | righteous :
   The right hand of the | Lord — | doeth | valiantly.

3 The right hand of the | Lord . is ex- | alted :
   The right hand of the | Lord — | doeth | valiantly.

4 I shall not | die, but | live,
   And declare the | works — | of the | Lord.

5 The Lord hath | chastened . me | sore :
   But he hath not given me | over | unto | death.

6 Open to me the | gates of | righteousness :
   I will go into them, and | I will | praise the | Lord :

7 This | gate . of the | Lord,
   Into | which the | righteous . shall | enter.

8 I will | praise — | thee :
   For thou hast heard me, and art be- | come — | my sal- | vation.

9 The stone which the | builders . re- | fused
   Is become the | head stone | of the | corner.

10 This is the | Lord's — | doing ;
   It is | marvel - ous | in our | eyes.

11 This is the day which the | Lord hath | made ;
   We will rejoice | and be | glad in | it.

12 Save now, I beseech thee, | O — | Lord :
   O Lord, I beseech thee, | send — | now pros- | perity.

13 Blessed be he that cometh in the | name . of the | Lord :
   We have blessed you out of the | house — | of the | Lord.

14 God is the Lord, which hath | shewed . us | light :
   Bind the sacrifice with cords, even unto the | horns — | of the | altar :

15 Thou art my God, and | I will | praise thee :
   Thou art my God, | I — | will ex- | alt thee.

16 O give thanks unto the Lord ; for | he is | good :
   For his | mercy . en- | dureth . for- | ever.

CHANT. No. XXVI. TALLIS.

Selection, No. 35.   PSALM CXXI.

1 I will lift up mine eyes | unto the | hills,
  From | whence — | cometh . my | help.

2 My help cometh | from the | Lord,
  Which | made — | heaven . and | earth.

3 He will not suffer thy | foot . to be | moved;
  He that | keepeth . thee | will not | slumber.

4 Behold, he that keepeth | Isra- | el
  Shall neither | slumber | nor — | sleep.

5 The Lord | is thy | keeper:
  The Lord is thy shade up- | on thy | right — | hand.

6 The sun shall not | smite thee . by | day,
  Nor the | moon — | by — | night.

7 The Lord shall preserve thee from | all — | evil;
  He | shall pre- | serve thy | soul.

8 The Lord shall preserve thy going out and thy | coming | in
  From this time forth, and | even . for | ever- | more.

Selection, No. 36.   PSALM CXXII.

1 I was glad when they said | unto | me,
  Let us go into the | house — | of the | Lord.

2 Our feet shall stand with- | in thy | gates,
  O — | —Je- | rusa- | lem.

3 Jerusalem is builded | as a | city
  That | is com- | pact to- | gether:

4 Whither the tribes go up, the tribes | of the | Lord,
  Unto the testimony of Israel, to give thanks unto the | name — | of the | Lord.

5 For there are set | thrones of | judgment,
  The thrones of the | house — | of — | David.

6 Pray for the peace of Je- | rusa- | lem:
  They shall | prosper . that | love — | thee.

7 Peace be with- | in thy | walls,
  And prosperity with- | in thy | pala- | ces.

8 For my brethren and com- | panions' | sakes,
  I will now say, | Peace— | be with- | in thee.

9 Because of the house of the | Lord our | God
  I will | seek — | thy — | good.

CHANT. No. XXVII.   DR. GREEN.

Selection, No. 37.

PSALM CXXVI.

1 WHEN the Lord turned again the cap- | tivity . of | Zion,
    We were | like — | them that | dream.
2 Then was our mouth | filled . with | laughter,
    And our | tongue — | with — | singing:
3 Then said they a- | mong the | heathen,
    The Lord hath done | great — | things — | for them.
4 The Lord hath done great | things for | us ;
    Where- | of — | we are | glad.
5 TURN AGAIN our captivity, | O — | Lord,
    As the | streams — | in the | south.
6 They that | sow in | tears
    Shall | reap — | in — | joy.
7 He that goeth forth and weepeth, bearing | precious | seed,
    Shall doubtless come again with rejoicing, | bringing . his | sheaves — | with him.

Selection, No. 38.

PSALM CXXX.

1 OUT | of the | depths
    Have I cried | unto | thee, O | Lord.
2 Lord, | hear my | voice:
    Let thine ears be attentive to the | voice of . my | suppli- | cations.
3 If thou, Lord, shouldst | mark in-| iquities,
    O | Lord — | who shall | stand ?
4 But there is for- | giveness . with | thee,
    That thou | mayest | be — | feared.
5 I wait for the Lord, my | soul doth | wait,
    And in his | word do | I — | hope.
6 My soul waiteth for the Lord more than they that | watch . for the | morning :
    I say, more than they that | watch — | for the | morning.
7 Let Israel | hope * in the | Lord :
    For with the Lord there is mercy, and with him is | plen- — | teous re- | demption
8 And he shall redeem | Isra- | el
    From | all — | his in- | iquities.

Selection, No. 39.

FROM PSALM CXXXII.

1 ARISE, O Lord, | into . thy | rest ;
    Thou, and the | ark — | of thy | strength.
2 Let thy priests be clothed with | righteous- | ness ;
    And let thy saints | shout — | for — | joy.

CHANT. No. XXVIII.   DR. TURNER.

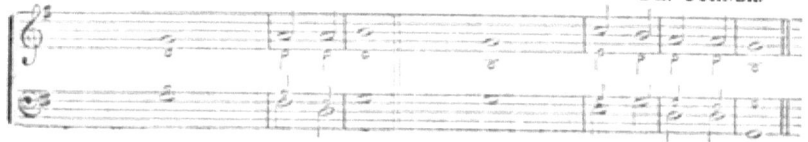

3 For thy servant | David's | sake,
 Turn not away the | face of | thine a- | nointed.

4 FOR THE LORD hath | chosen | Zion;
 He hath desired it | for his | habi- | tation.

5 This is my | rest for | ever:
 Here will I dwell; | for I | have de- | sired it.

6 I will abundantly bless | her pro- | vision:
 I will satisfy her | poor — | with — | bread.

7 I will also clothe her priests | with — | sal- | vation;
 And her saints shall | shout a- | loud for | joy.

Selection, No. 40.   PSALM CXXXVI.

1 OH, GIVE thanks unto the Lord; for | he is | good:
 For his | mercy . en- | dureth . for | ever.

2 Oh, give thanks unto the | God of | gods:
 For his | mercy . en- | dureth . for | ever.

3 Oh, give thanks to the | Lord of | lords:
 For his | mercy . en- | dureth . for | ever.

4 To him who alone | doeth . great | wonders:
 For his | mercy . en- | dureth . for | ever.

5 To him that by wisdom | made the | heavens:
 For his | mercy . en- | dureth . for | ever.

6 To him that stretched out the earth a- | bove the | waters:
 For his | mercy . en- | dureth . for | ever.

7 To him that | made great | lights:
 For his | mercy . en- | dureth . for | ever.

8 The sun to | rule by | day:
 For his | mercy . en- | dureth . for | ever.

9 The moon and stars to | rule by | night:
 For his | mercy . en- | dureth . for | ever.

10 WHO REMEMBERED us in our | low es- | tate:
 For his | mercy . en- | dureth . for | ever:

11 And hath redeemed us | from our | enemies:
 For his | mercy . en- | dureth . for | ever.

12 Who giveth food to | all — | flesh:
 For his | mercy . en- | dureth . for | ever.

13 Oh, give thanks unto the | God of | heaven:
 For his | mercy . en- | dureth . for | ever.

CHANT. No. XXIX. TALLIS.

Selection, No. 41. PSALM CXXXVIII.

1 I WILL praise thee with my | whole — | heart :
    Before the gods will I sing | praise — | unto | thee.
2 I will worship toward thy holy temple, and praise thy name for thy loving-kindness and | for thy | truth :
    For thou hast magnified thy word a- | bove all | thy — | name.
3 In thy day when I cried thou | answer - edst | me,
    And strengthenedst me with | strength — | in my | soul.
4 All the kings of the earth shall praise | thee, O | Lord.
    When they hear the | words of | thy — | mouth.
5 Yea, they shall sing in the | ways . of the | Lord :
    For great is the | glory | of the | Lord.
6 Though the Lord be high, yet hath he respect | unto . the | lowly :
    But the proud he | knoweth . a- | far — | off.
7 Though I walk in the midst of trouble, thou | wilt re- | vive me :
    Thou shalt stretch forth thine hand against the wrath of mine enemies, and | thy right | hand shall | save me.
8 The Lord will perfect that which con- | cerneth | me,
    Thy mercy, O Lord, endureth for ever : forsake not the | works of | thine own | hands.

Selection, No. 42. FROM PSALM CXXXIX.

1 O LORD, thou hast searched me, and | known — | me.
    Thou knowest my downsitting and mine uprising, thou understandest my | thought a- | far — | off.
2 Thou compassest my path and my | lying | down,
    And art acquainted with | all — | my — | ways.
3 For there is not a | word . in my | tongue,
    But lo, O Lord, thou | knowest . it | alto- | gether.
4 Thou hast beset me be- | hind . and be- | fore,
    And | laid thine | hand up- | on me.
5 Such knowledge is too | wonder - ful | for me ;
    It is high, I can not at- | tain — | unto | it.
6 WHITHER shall I go from | thy — | Spirit?
    Or whither shall I | flee from | thy — | presence ?
7 If I ascend up into heaven, | thou art | there :
    If I make my bed in hell, be- | hold,— | thou art | there :
8 If I take the wings of the morning, and dwell in the uttermost | parts . of the | sea,
    Even there shall thy hand lead me, and thy | right hand | shall — | hold me.
9 If I say, Surely the | darkness . shall | cover me ;
    Even the | night . shall be | light a- | bout me.
10 Yea, the darkness hideth not from thee ; but the night shineth | as the | day :
    The darkness and the light are | both a- | like to | thee.
11 SEARCH ME, O God, and | know my | heart :
    Try me, and | know — | my — | thoughts :

CHANT. No. XXX.

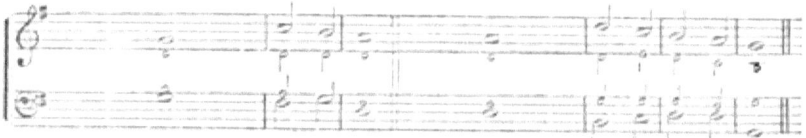

12 And see if there be any | wicked . way | in me,
   And lead me in the | way — | ever- | lasting.

Selection, No. 43.   PSALM CXLV.

1 I WILL extol thee, my | God, O | King ;
   And I will bless thy | name for | ever . and | ever.
2 Every day will I | bless — | thee ;
   And I will praise thy | name for | ever . and | ever.
3 Great is the Lord, **and greatly** | to be | praised ;
   And his | greatness | is un- | searchable.
4 One generation **shall praise thy** | works . to an- | other,
   And shall de- | clare thy | mighty | acts.
5 I will speak of the glorious honor | of thy | majesty,
   And | of thy | wondrous | works.
6 And men shall speak of the might of thy | terrible | acts :
   And | I . will de- | clare thy | greatness.
7 They shall abundantly utter the memory of | thy great | **goodness**,
   And shall | sing of . thy | righteous- | ness.
8 THE LORD is gracious, and | full . of com- | **passion** ;
   Slow to anger, | and of | great — | mercy.
9 The Lord is | good to | all :
   And his tender mercies are | over | all his | **works**.
10 All thy works shall praise | thee, O | **Lord** ;
    And thy | saints shall | bless — | thee.
11 They shall speak of the glory | of **thy** | **kingdom**,
    And | talk of | thy — | power ;
12 To make known to the sons of men his | mighty | acts,
    And the glorious | majes - ty | of his | **kingdom**.
13 **Thy kingdom is an ever-** | **lasting** | **kingdom**,
    And thy dominion endureth throughout | all — | gener- | ations.
14 THE LORD upholdeth | all that | fall,
    And raiseth up all | those that | be bowed | down.
15 The eyes of all | wait up - on | thee ;
    And thou givest them their | meat in | due — | season.
16 Thou | openest . thine | hand,
    And satisfiest the desire of | every | living | thing.
17 The Lord is righteous in | all his | ways,
    And | holy . in | all his | works.
18 The Lord is nigh unto all them that | call **upon** | **him**,
    To all that | call up - on | him in | truth.
19 He will fulfill **the desire** of | them that | fear him :
    He will also **hear their** cry, | and will | save — | them.
20 The Lord preserveth all | them that | love him :
    But all the | **wicked** . will | he de- | stroy.
21 My mouth shall speak the | praise . of the | Lord :
    And let all flesh bless his holy | name for | ever and | ever.

CHANT. No. XXXI.

Selection, No. 44.   PSALM CXLVI.

1 PRAISE | ye the | Lord.
  Praise the Lord | O — | my — | soul.
2 While I live will I | praise the | Lord :
  I will sing praises unto my God | while I | have any | being.
3 Put not your | trust in | princes,
  Nor in the son of man, in | whom there | is no | help.
4 His breath goeth forth, he returneth | to his | earth ;
  In that very | day his | thoughts— | perish.
5 HAPPY is he that hath the God of Jacob | for his | help.
  Whose hope is | in the | Lord his | God :
6 Which made heaven, and earth, the sea, and all that | therein | is :
  Which | keepeth | truth for | ever :
7 Which executeth judgment | for the . op- | pressed :
  Which giveth | food — | to the | hungry.
8 The Lord | looseth . the | prisoners :
  The Lord openeth the | eyes — | of the | blind :
9 The Lord raiseth them that are | bow - ed | down :
  The Lord | loveth | the — | righteous :
10 The Lord preserveth the strangers ; he relieveth the | fatherless * and | widow :
  But the way of the wicked he | turneth | upside | down.
11 The **Lord shall reign for** ever, even thy God, O Zion, unto | all * gener- | ations.
  Praise | ye — | the — | Lord.

Selection, No. 45.   PSALM CXLVII. 12-20.

1 PRAISE the Lord, O Je- | rusa- | lem ;
  Praise thy | God,— | O — | Zion.
2 For he hath strengthened the | bars of . thy | gates ;
  He hath blessed thy | children | with- — | in thee.
3 He maketh peace | in thy | borders,
  And filleth thee with the | finest | of the | wheat.
4 He sendeth forth his commandment | upon | earth :
  His word | runneth | very | swiftly.
5 He giveth | snow like | wool :
  He scattereth the | hoar-frost | like — | ashes.
6 He casteth forth his | ice like | morsels ;
  Who can | stand be- | fore his | cold ?
7 He sendeth out his | word, and | melteth them :
  He causeth his wind to blow, | and the | waters | flow.
8 He showeth his word | unto | Jacob,
  His statutes and his judgments | unto | Isra- | el.
9 He hath not dealt so with any nation : and as for his judgments, they | have not |
    known them.
  Praise | ye — | the — | Lord.

CHANT. No. XXXII.

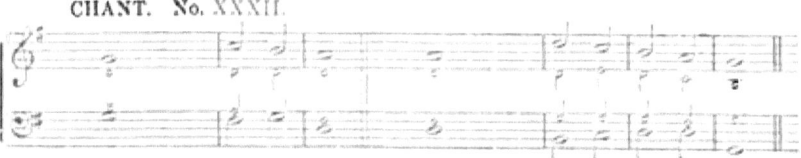

Selection, No. 46.   Psalm CXLVIII.

1 Praise | ye the | Lord.
　Praise ye the Lord from the heavens : | **praise him** | in the | heights.
2 Praise ye him, | all his | angels :
　Praise ye | him, all | his — | hosts.
3 Praise ye him, | sun and | moon :
　Praise him, | all ye | stars of | light.
4 Praise him, ye | heavens of | heavens,
　And ye waters that | be a- | bove the | heavens.
5 Let them praise the name | of the | Lord :
　For he commanded, | and they | were cre- | ated.
6 He hath also established them for | ever . and | ever.
　He hath made a de- | cree which | shall not | pass.
7 Praise the Lord from the earth, ye dragons, and | all — | deeps :
　Fire, and hail ; snow, and vapors ; stormy | wind ful- | filling . his | word :
8 Mountains, and all hills ; fruitful trees, and | all — | cedars :
　Beasts, and all cattle ; creeping | things, and | flying | fowl :
9 Kings of the earth, and | all — | people ;
　Princes, and all | judges | of the | earth :
10 Both young men, and maidens ; | old . men, and | **children** :
　Let them praise the | name — | of the | Lord :
11 For his name a- | **lone is** | excellent ;
　His glory is a- | bove the | earth and | heaven.
12 He also exalteth the | horn of　his | **people,**
　The | praise of | all his | saints ;
13 Even of the children of Israel, a people | near . unto | him.
　Praise | ye — | the — | Lord.

Selection, No. 47.   Psalm CL.

1 Praise | ye the | Lord.
　Praise God in his sanctuary : praise him in the | firma - ment | of his | power.
2 Praise him for his | mighty | acts
　Praise him according to his | excel- lent | great- — | ness.
3 Praise him with the | sound . of the | trumpet :
　Praise him with the | psalter- | y and | harp.
4 Praise him with the | timbrel . and | dance :
　Praise him with **stringed** | in - stru- | ments and | organs.
5 Praise him upon the | loud — | cymbals ;
　Praise him upon the | high — | sounding | cymbals.
6 Let every thing that hath breath | praise the | Lord.
　Praise | ye — | the — | Lord.

CHANT. No. XXXIII.   Rev. W. H. Havergal.

Selection, No. 48.   1 Chron. XXIX. 10-13.

1 Blessed be thou, Lord God of | Israel . our | father,
  For | ev - er | and — | ever.

2 Thine, O Lord, is the greatness, | and the | power,
  And the glory, and the | victo - ry, | and the | majesty.

3 For all that is | in the | heaven
  And | in the | earth is | thine;

4 Thine is the | kingdom, . O | Lord,
  And thou art exalted as | head a- | bove — | all.

5 Both riches and honor | come of | thee,
  And thou | reignest | over | all:

6 And in thine hand is | power . and | might;
  And in thine hand it is to make great, and to give | strength — | unto | all.

7 Now, therefore, our God, we | thank — | thee,
  And | praise thy | glorious | name.

Selection, No. 49.   From Isaiah XII.

1 O Lord, | I will | praise thee :
  Though thou wast angry with me, thine anger is turned away, | and thou | com- fortedst | me.

2 Behold, God is | my sal- | vation ;
  I will | trust and | not . be a - | fraid :

3 For the Lord JEHOVAH is my strength | and my | song :
  He also is be- | come — | my sal- | vation.

4 Therefore with joy shall ye | draw — | water
  Out of the | wells — | of sal- | vation.

5 And in that day | shall ye | say,
  Praise the Lord, | call up- | on his | name,

6 Declare his doings a- | mong the | people,
  Make mention that his | name — | is ex- | alted.

7 Sing unto the Lord ; for he hath done | excellent | things :
  This is | known in | all the | earth.

8 Cry out and shout, thou in- | habitant . of | Zion :
  For great is the Holy One of Israel | in the | midst of | thee.

CHANT. No. XXXIV.

Selection, No. 50. ISAIAH LII. 7–9.

1 How BEAUTIFUL up- | on the | mountains
   Are the feet of him that bringeth good | tidings, . that | publish - eth | peace;
2 That bringeth good tidings of good, that publisheth | sal — | vation ;
   That saith unto | Zion, Thy | God — | reigneth !
3 Thy watchmen shall lift | up the | voice ;
   With the voice to- | gether | shall they | sing:
4 For they shall see | eye to | eye,
   When the Lord shall | bring a- | gain — | Zion.
5 BREAK | forth into | joy,
   Sing together, ye waste places | of Je- | rusa- | lem:
6 For the Lord hath | comforted . his | people,
   He hath re- | deem - ed . Je- | rusa- | lem.
7 The Lord hath made bare his holy arm in the eyes of | all the | nations;
   And all the ends of the earth shall see the sal- | vation | of our | God.

Selection, No. 51. FROM ISAIAH LIII.

1 HE IS despised and re- | jected . of | men ;
   A man of sorrows, | and ac- | quainted . with | grief:
2 And we hid as it were our | faces | from him ;
   He was despised, and | we es- | teemed . him | not.
3 Surely he hath borne our griefs, and | carried . our | sorrows ;
   Yet we did esteem him stricken, | smitten . of | God, . and af- | flicted.
4 BUT HE was wounded for | our trans- | gressions,
   He was | bruised . for | our in- | iquities ;
5 The chastisement of our peace | was up- | on him,
   And with | his stripes | we are | healed.
6 All we like sheep have | gone a- | stray ;
   We have turned every | one to | his own | way ;
7 And the Lord hath | laid on | him
   The in- | iqui-ty | of us | all.
8 WHEN THOU shalt make his soul an | offering . for | sin,
   He shall see his seed, he | shall pro- | long his | days,
9 And the pleasure of the Lord shall prosper | in his | hand,
   He shall see of the travail of his soul, and | shall be | satis- | fied.

CHANT. No. XXXV.

Selection, No. 52.   LUKE I. 68-75.

1 BLESSED be the Lord | God of | Israel ;
   For he hath visited and re- | deem-ed | his — | people,
2 And hath raised up an horn of sal- | vation | for us
   In the | house . of his | servant | David ;
3 As he spake by the mouth of his | holy | prophets,
   Which have been | since the | world be- | gan :
4 That we should be saved | from our | enemies,
   And from the hand of | all that | hate — | us ;
5 To perform the mercy promised to our fathers, and to remember his | holy | covenant ;
   The oath which he sware to our | father | Abra- | ham,
6 That he would grant unto us, that we, being delivered out of the | hand of . our |
      enemies,
   Might serve | him with- | out — | fear.
7 In holiness and righteousness be- | fore— | him,
   All the | days of | our — | life.

Selection, No. 53.   FROM REVELATION IV. & V.

1 HOLY, holy, holy, Lord | God al- | mighty,
   Which was, and | is, and | is to | come.
2 THOU art worthy, O Lord, to receive glory, and | honor . and | power ;
   For thou hast created all things, and for thy pleasure they | are and | were cre- | ated.
3 WORTHY is the Lamb | that was | slain,
   To receive power, and riches, and wisdom, and strength, and | honor, . and | glory, . and | blessing.
4 BLESSING, and honor, and | glory, . and | power,
   Be unto him that sitteth upon the throne, and unto the | Lamb for | ever . and | ever.

Selection, No. 54.   TE DEUM LAUDAMUS.*

1 WE praise | thee, O | God :
   We acknowledge | thee to | be the | Lord.
2 All the earth doth | worship | thee,
   The | Father | ever- | lasting.
3 To thee all angels | cry a- | loud,
   The heavens, and | all the | powers there- | in.

* This hymn is said to have been written by Ambrose of Milan, at the baptism of Augustine, about A. D. 373.

CHANT. No. XXXVI.

4 To thee | cherubim, . and | seraphim,
   Con- | tinu - al- | ly do | cry,

5 Holy, | holy, | holy,
   Lord | God of | Saba- | oth ;

6 Heaven and | earth are | full
   Of the | majes - ty | of thy | glory.

7 The glorious company of the apostles | praise — | thee.
   The goodly fellowship of the | prophets | praise — | thee.

8 The noble army of martyrs | praise — | thee.
   The holy church throughout all the world | doth ac- | knowledge | thee,

9 The Father, of an | infi - nite | majesty ;
   Thine adorable, | true and | only | Son ;

10 Also the | Holy | Ghost,
   The | Com- — | fort- — | er.

11 Thou art the King of | glory, O | Christ,
   Thou art the everlasting | Son . of the | Fa- — | ther.

12 When thou tookest upon thee to de- | liver | man,
   Thou didst humble thyself to be | born — | of a | virgin.

13 When thou hadst overcome the | sharpness . of | death,
   Thou didst open the kingdom of | heaven to | all be- | lievers.

14 Thou sittest at the right hand of God, in the glory | of the | Father.
   We believe that thou shalt | come to | be our | judge.

15 We therefore pray thee, | help thy | servants,
   Whom thou hast redeemed | with thy | precious | blood.

16 Make them to be numbered | with thy | saints,
   In | glory | ever- | lasting.

17 O Lord, save thy people, and | bless thine | heritage ;
   Govern them and | lift them | up for | ever.

18 Day by day we | magni - fy | thee ;
   And we worship thy name ever, | world with- | out — | end.

19 Vouensafe, O Lord, to keep us this day | without | sin ;
   O Lord, have mercy upon us, have | mer - cy up- | on — | us,

20 O Lord, let thy mercy be up- | on — | us,
   As our | trust — | is in | thee.

21 O Lord, in thee | have I | trusted ;
   Let me | never | be con- | founded.

29

CHANT. No. XXXVII.

CHANT. No. XXXVIII. (*For 5th, 6th, 7th, and 8th verses.*)

Selection, No. 55. Gloria in Excelsis.*

1 Glory be to | God on | high,
  And on earth | peace, good | will towards | men.
2 We praise thee, we bless thee, we | worship | thee,
  We glorify thee, we give thanks to | thee, for | thy great | glory,
3 O Lord God, | heavenly | King,
  God the | Father | Al — | mighty.
4 O Lord, the only begotten Son, | Jesus | Christ,
  O Lord God, Lamb of God, | Son — | of the | Father,
5 That takest away the | sins . of the | world,
  Have | mer · cy up· | on — | us.
6 Thou that takest away the | sins . of the | world,
  Have | mer· cy up· | on — | us.
7 Thou that takest away the | sins . of the | world,
  Re- | ceive — | our — | prayer.
8 Thou that sittest at the right hand of | God the | Father,
  Have | mer· cy up· | on — | us.
9 For thou | only art | holy ;
  Thou ! only | art the | Lord ;
10 Thou only, O Christ, with the | Holy | Ghost,
  Art most high in the glory of God the | Father. | A — | men.

Selection, No. 56. Gloria Patri.

1 Glory be to the Father, and | to the | Son,
  And | to the | Holy | Ghost ;
2 As it was in the beginning, is now, and | ever . shall | be,
  World | without | end. A- | men.

* Ascribed to Telesphorus, Bishop of Rome, A. D. 128-139.

CHANT. No. XXXIX. TALLIS.

Selection, No. 57.   BAPTISMAL HYMN.

Before the Administration.
Psalm 103: 17, 18.

1 THE mercy of the Lord is from everlasting to everlasting upon | them that | fear him,
   And his righteousness | unto | children's | children.
2 To such as | keep his | covenant ;
   And to those that remember his com- | mandments to | do — | them.

Mark 10: 14

3 Suffer little children to come unto me, and for- | bid them | not ;
   For of | such . is the | kingdom . of | heaven.

After the Administration.
Ez. 36: 25, 26.

1 THEN will I sprinkle clean | water . up- | on you,
   And | ye shall | be — | clean :
2 A new heart also | will I | give you,
   And a new spirit | will I | put with- | in you,
3 And I will take away the stony heart | out of . your | flesh,
   And I will | give . you a | heart of | flesh.

Is. 44: 3, 4.

4 I will pour my Spirit up- | on thy | seed,
   And my | blessing . up- | on thine | offspring :
5 And they shall spring up as a- | mong the | grass,
   As | willows . by the | water | courses.

Acts 2: 39.

6 For the promise is unto you, and | to your | children ;
   And to all that are afar off, even as many as the | Lord our | God shall | call.

Selection, No. 58.   THE LORD'S PRAYER.

Matt. 6: 9-13.

1 OUR FATHER who | art in | heaven,
   Hallowed | be — | thy — | name ;
2 Thy | kingdom | come.
   Thy will be done on earth | as it | is in | heaven.
3 Give us this day our | daily | bread ;
   And forgive us our debts, as | we for- | give our | debtors ;
4 And lead us not | into | temp- | tation,
   But de- | liv - er | us from | evil :
5 For thine is the kingdom, and the | power, and the | glory,
   For | ever. | A — | men.

APPENDIX.

4. *Habitual Devotion.*

1 WHILE thee I seek, protecting **Power!**
  Be my vain wishes still'd;
  And may this consecrated hour
  With better hopes be filled!
2 Thy love the power of thought bestowed;
  To thee my thoughts would soar:
  Thy mercy o'er my life has flowed;
  That mercy I adore.
3 In each event of life, how clear
  Thy ruling hand I see!
  Each blessing to my soul more dear,
  Because conferred by thee.

4 In every joy that crowns my days,
  In every pain I bear,
  My heart shall find delight in **praise**,
  Or seek relief in prayer.
5 When gladness wings my favored hour,
  Thy love my thoughts shall fill;
  Resigned, when storms of sorrow lower,
  My soul shall meet thy will.
6 My lifted eye, without a tear,
  The gathering storm shall see;
  My steadfast heart shall know no fear;
  That heart will rest on thee.

119. *"The hand that made us is Divine."*

1 The spacious firmament on high,
  With all the blue ethereal sky,
  And spangled heavens, a shining frame,
  Their great Original proclaim.

2 Th' unwearied sun, from day to day,
  Does his Creator's power display,
  And publishes to every land
  The work of an Almighty hand.

3 Soon as the evening shades prevail,
  The moon takes up the wondrous tale,
  And nightly to the listening earth
  Repeats the story of her birth;

4 While all the stars that round her burn,
  And all the planets in their turn,
  Confirm the tidings as they roll,
  And spread the truth from pole to pole.

5 What though, in solemn silence all
  Move round this dark, terrestrial ball?
  What though no real voice nor sound
  Amid their radiant orbs be found?

6 In reason's ear they all rejoice,
  And utter forth a glorious voice;
  For ever singing as they shine,
  "The hand that made us is Divine."

LOVING-KINDNESS. L. M.

431. *"His Loving-kindness."*

1 Awake, my soul, to joyful lays,
And sing the great Redeemer's praise;
He justly claims a song from me:
His loving-kindness, oh, **how free!**

2 He saw me ruined in **the** fall,
Yet loved me, notwithstanding all;
He saved me from my lost estate;
His loving-kindness, oh, how great!

3 Though numerous hosts of mighty foes,
Though earth and hell **my** way oppose,
He safely leads my soul **along:**
His loving-kindness, oh, **how strong!**

4 When trouble, like a gloomy cloud,
Has gathered thick and thundered loud,
He near my soul hath always **stood**;
His loving-kindness, oh, how good!

5 Soon shall I pass the gloomy vale;
Soon all my mortal powers must fail;
Oh, may my last expiring breath
His loving-kindness sing in death!

6 Then let me mount and soar away
To the bright world of endless day;
And sing, with rapture and surprise,
His loving-kindness in the skies!

PALESTINE. L. M. 6 LINES.

511. *"Come unto Me, all ye that labor."*

1 PEACE, troubled soul, whose plaintive moan
  Hath taught each scene the notes of woe;
  Cease thy complaint, suppress thy groan,
  And let thy tears forget to flow
  Behold the precious balm is found,
  To lull thy pain, to heal thy wound.

2 Come, freely come, by sin oppressed;
  On Jesus cast thy weighty load,
  In him thy refuge find, thy rest,
  Safe in the mercy of thy God;
  Thy God's thy Saviour — glorious word!
  Oh, hear, believe, and bless the Lord!

REO. C. M.

424. *"In all points tempted like as we are."*

2 Touched with a sympathy within,
  He knows our feeble frame;
  He knows what sore temptations mean,
  For he hath felt the same.

3 He, in the days of feeble flesh,
  Poured out his cries and tears;
  And, in his measure, feels afresh
  What every member bears.

4 He'll never quench the smoking flax,
  But raise it to a flame,
  The bruiséd reed he never breaks,
  Nor scorns the meanest name.

5 Then let our humble faith address
  His mercy and his power;
  We shall obtain delivering grace
  In the distressing hour.

FREDERICK. 11s.

1176. "*I would not live alway.*"—Job 7 : 16.

1 I WOULD not live alway: I ask not to stay
  Where storm after storm rises dark o'er the way;
  The few lurid mornings that dawn on us here
  Are enough for life's woes, full enough for its cheer.

2 I would not live alway: no, welcome the tomb!
  Since Jesus hath lain there, I dread not its gloom;
  There sweet be my rest, till he bid me arise
  To hail him in triumph descending the skies.

3 Who, who would live alway, away from his God,
  Away from yon heaven, that blissful abode,
  Where the rivers of pleasure flow o'er the bright plains,
  And the noontide of glory eternally reigns;

4 Where the saints of all ages in harmony meet,
  Their Saviour and brethren transported to greet;
  While the anthems of rapture unceasingly roll,
  And the smile of the Lord is the feast of the soul!

BENEVENTO. 7s. DOUBLE.

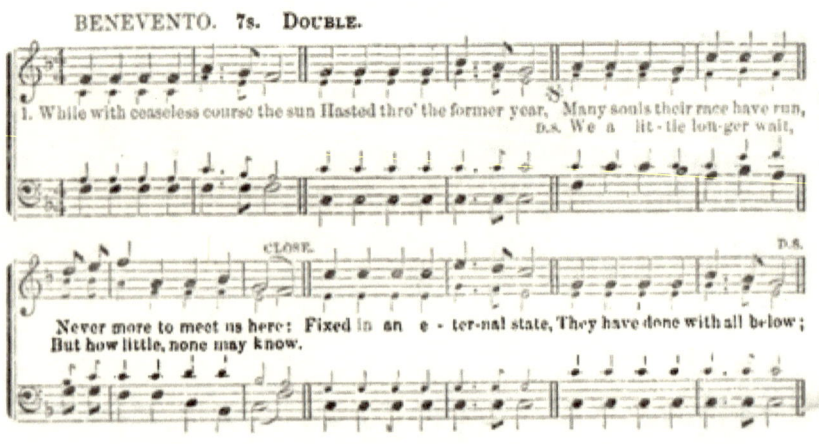

1159. *"Spared to see another year."*

1 WHILE with ceaseless course the sun
  Hasted through the former year,
Many souls their race have run,
  Never more to meet us here;
Fixed in an eternal state,
  They have done with all below;
We a little longer wait,
  But how little, **none can know**.

2 As the wingèd arrow flies
  Speedily the mark to find,—
As the lightning from the skies
  Darts, and leaves no trace behind,—
Swiftly thus our fleeting days
  Bear us down life's rapid stream:
Upward, Lord, our spirits raise!
  All below is but a dream.

3 Thanks for mercies past receive,
  Pardon of our sins renew;
Teach us henceforth how to live,
  With eternity in view;
Bless thy word to young and old;
  Fill us with a Saviour's love;
When our life's short tale is told,
  May we dwell with thee above.

MORNING STAR. 7s. DOUBLE.

1. Watchman, tell us of the night, What its signs of promise are. Traveler, o'er yon mountain's height, See that glory-beaming star! 2. Watchman, does its beauteous ray Aught of joy or hope foretell? Traveler, yes: it brings the day, Promised day of Is-ra-el.

276. *"Watchman, what of the night!"*—Isaiah 21:11.

1 WATCHMAN, tell us of the night,
  What its signs of promise are.
Traveler, o'er yon mountain's height,
  See that glory-beaming star!

2 Watchman, does its beauteous ray
  Aught of joy or hope foretell?
Traveler, yes: it brings the day,
  Promised day of Israel.

3 Watchman, tell us of the night;
  Higher yet that star ascends.
Traveler, blessedness and light,
  Peace and truth, its course portends.

4 Watchman, will its beams alone
  Gild the spot that gave them birth?
Traveler, ages are its own;
  See! it bursts o'er all the earth!

5 Watchman, tell us of the night,
  For the morning seems to dawn.
Traveler, darkness takes its flight,
  Doubt and terror are withdrawn.

6 Watchman, let thy wanderings cease;
  Hie thee to thy quiet home.
Traveler, lo! the Prince of Peace,
  Lo! the Son of God is come!

CANAAN. C. M.

1. Around the throne of God in heaven Thousands of children stand—Children, whose sins are all forgiven, A holy, happy band, Singing glory, glory, Glory be to God on high.

1088. *"Of such is the kingdom of heaven."*

1 Around the throne of God in heaven
  Thousands of children stand—
  Children, whose sins are all forgiven,
  A holy, happy band.
    Singing glory, &c.

2 What brought them to that world above,
  That heaven so bright and fair,
  Where all is peace, and joy, and love?
  How came those children there?
    Singing glory, &c.

3 Because the Saviour shed his blood
  To wash away their sin;
  Bathed in that pure and precious flood,
  Behold them white and clean.
    Singing glory, &c.

4 On earth they sought their Saviour's grace,
  On earth they loved his name;
  So now they see his blessèd face,
  And stand before the Lamb.
    Singing glory, &c.

SELVIN. S. M.

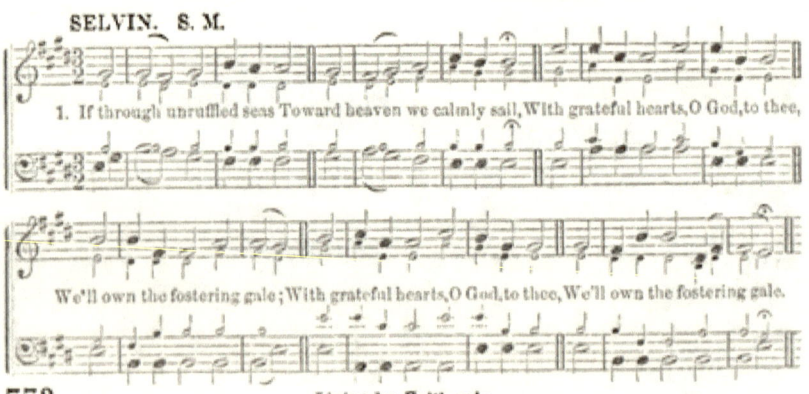

1. If through unruffled seas Toward heaven we calmly sail, With grateful hearts, O God, to thee, We'll own the fostering gale; With grateful hearts, O God, to thee, We'll own the fostering gale.

773. *Living by Faith only.*

2 But should the surges rise,
  And rest delay to come,
  Blest be the sorrow, kind the storm,
  Which drives us nearer home.

3 Soon shall our doubts and fears
  All yield to thy control;

  Thy tender mercies shall illume
  The midnight of the soul.

4 Teach us, in every state,
  To make thy will our own;
  And, when the joys of sense depart,
  To live by faith alone.

INDEX OF FIRST LINES OF HYMNS.

(The figures on the left hand designate the numbers of the Hymns, those on the right the pages.)

HYMN		PAGE	HYMN		PAGE
706	A broken heart, my God, my King	345	503	Ask, and ye shall receive	138
575	A broken heart, O Lord	278	1195	Asleep in Jesus! blessed sleep!	365
916	A charge to keep I have	272	660	Author of good! to thee we turn	149
1220	A few more years shall roll	365	331	Awake, and sing the song	196
483	A glory gilds the sacred page	34	48	Awake, my soul, and with the sun	43
807	A pilgrim through this lonely world	232	901	Awake, my soul! lift up thine eyes	74
1050	According to thy gracious word	320	880	Awake, my soul! stretch every nerve	55
522	Acquaint thee, O mortal, acquaint thee	323	431	Awake, my soul, to joyful lays	122, 454
682	Affliction is a stormy deep	128	182	Awake, my tongue, thy tribute bring	75
80	Again our earthly cares we leave	355	890	Awake, our souls! away, our fears	74
57	Again the day returns of holy rest	227	1158	Awake, ye saints! and raise your eyes	201
60	Again the Lord of life and light	34	58	Awake, ye saints, awake!	24
646	Ah, happy hours! whene'er upsprings	165			
409	Ah! how shall fallen man	287	35	Be joyful in God, all ye lands of	79
563	Ah! what avails my strife	340	100	Be thou exalted, O my God	36
983	Ah! wretched, vile, ungrateful heart	115	33	Before Jehovah's awful throne	53
562	Alas! and did my Saviour bleed?	174	729	Before thy cross, my dying Lord	192
637	Alas! what hourly dangers rise!	290	731	Before thy throne with tearful eyes	102
379	All hail the power of Jesus' name!	113	110	Begin, my soul, th' exalted lay	47
81	All people that on earth do dwell	17	178	Begin, my tongue, some heavenly	116
263	All praise to thee, eternal Lord!	114	541	Behold a Stranger at the door	164
717	All that I was, my sin, my guilt	170	337	Behold the glories of the Lamb	205
104	All ye nations, praise the Lord!	150	481	Behold, the morning sun	230
212	Almighty Father! gracious Lord!	371	854	Behold the throne of grace!	150
213	Almighty Father of mankind!	359	1199	Behold the western evening light!	327
813	Almighty God, in humble prayer	410	1002	Behold, what wondrous grace	223
1162	Almighty Maker of my frame	357	281	Behold, where, in a mortal form	250
661	Along my earthly way	334	1205	Beneath our feet and o'er our head	50
419	Always with us, always with us	193	135	Beyond, beyond that boundless sea	28
885	Am I a soldier of the cross?	27	150	Bless, O my soul! the living God	71
1015	Amazing grace! (how sweet the sound!)	215	957	Blessed are the sons of God!	138
150	Amid the splendors of thy state	124	791	Blessed be God! for ever blest	121
501	Amid thy wrath remember love	250	264	Blessed night, when first that plain	209
557	And are we wretches yet alive!	275	648	Blessed Saviour! thee I love	130
842	And art thou, gracious Master, gone?	205	993	Blest are the pure in heart	252
712	And can mine eyes, without a tear	251	861	Blest are the sons of peace	252
811	And did the Holy and the Just	303	871	Blest be the dear, uniting love	211
986	And dost thou say, "Ask what	277	857	Blest be the tie that binds	194
1263	And is there, Lord, a rest	223	1071	Blest be thou, O God of Israel	85
834	And must I part with all I have	410	843	Blest hour! when mortal man retires	234
1274	And must this body die?	93	1343	Blest hour! when righteous souls	582
848	And shall I sit alone	287	944	Blest is the man whom thou, O Lord	229
1288	And will the Judge descend	299	875	Blest is the man whose softening heart	177
761	And wilt thou now forsake me, Lord	129	700	Blest Jesus! when my soaring thoughts	113
114	Angels, assist to sing	24	736	Blest Jesus! while in mortal flesh	189
61	Another six days' work is done	288	59	Blest morning! whose young dawning	41
970	Arise, my soul, my joyful powers	158	523	Blow ye the trumpet, blow	159
547	Arise, my tend'rest thoughts, arise	405	1052	Bread of heaven! on thee I feed	199
1075	Arise! O King of grace, arise!	125	993	Breast the wave, Christian	895
387	Arise, ye people, and adore	291	1220	Brief life is here our portion	352
893	Arise, ye saints, arise!	165	248	Bright King of glory! dreadful God?	82
1054	Around the throne of God in heaven	19, 458	1093	Bright source of everlasting love	523
618	As by the light of opening day	207	266	Brightest and best of the sons	70
1275	As Jesus died and rose again	347	265	Brightness of the Father's glory	193
654	As pants the hart for cooling streams	95	548	Broad is the road that leads to death	255
755	As when the weary traveler gains	259	513	Brother, hast thou wandered far	260

INDEX OF FIRST LINES OF HYMNS.

HYMN		PAGE
532	Burdened with guilt, wouldst thou	352
1089	By cool Siloam's shady rill	104
677	Call the Lord thy sure salvation	219
906	Calm me, my God, and keep me calm	266
1203	Calm on the bosom of thy God	207
272	Calm, on the listening ear of night	221
550	Can sinners hope for heaven	314
416	Cast thy burden on the Lord	202
1213	Cease, ye mourners, cease to languish	310
904	Cheer up, desponding soul!	265
542	Child of sin and sorrow	243
715	Chosen, not for good in me	373
490	Christ and his cross are all our theme	182
1074	Christ is our Corner-stone	198
883	Christ, of all my hopes the Ground	150
354	Christ, the Lord, is risen to-day!	127
425	Christ, whose glory fills the skies	372
1032	Church of the ever-living God	355
980	Clouds and darkness round about thee	392
240	Come, all ye saints of God	144
453	Come, blessed Spirit! Source of light	163
89	Come, dearest Lord! descend and dwell	292
332	Come, every pious heart	40
454	Come, gracious Spirit, heavenly Dove	135
258	Come, happy souls, approach your God	116
435	Come, heavenly Love! inspire my song	95
504	Come hither, all ye weary souls	184
451	Come, Holy Ghost—in love	354
452	Come, Holy Spirit, come!	272
463	Come, Holy Spirit, heavenly Dove	187
970	Come, humble souls, ye mourners, come	104
1070	Come in, thou blessed of the Lord	381
109	Come, let our voices join to raise	48
1161	Come, let us anew our journey pursue	397
339	Come, let us join our cheerful songs	112
303	Come, let us lift our joyful eyes	117
330	Come, let us sing the song of songs	74
585	Come, let us to the Lord our God	143
1269	Come, Lord! and tarry not	382
129	Come, O my soul! in sacred lays	30
514	Come, said Jesus' sacred voice	203
36	Come, sound his praise abroad	374
474	Come, thou almighty King	145
648	Come, thou Fount of every blessing	173
394	Come, thou long-expected Jesus	84
529	Come to the ark, come to the ark	39
527	Come to the land of peace	367
55	Come, trembling sinner, in whose breast	148
505	Come unto me, all ye who mourn	108
528	Come up hither; come away	386
968	Come, we who love the Lord	33
531	Come, weary souls, with sin distressed	225
952	Come, ye disconsolate! where'er	153
518	Come, ye sinners, poor and wretched	295
831	Come, ye that fear the Lord	334
507	Come, ye with sin distressed	118
675	Commit thou all thy griefs	160
791	Compared with Christ, in all beside	206
559	Could my heart so hard remain	261
249	Crown his head with endless blessing	193
380	Crowns of glory ever bright	166
1030	Daughter of Zion! awake from thy	79
1154	Daughter of Zion! from the dust	210
1257	Day of judgment—day of wonders	294
1206	Dear as thou wert, and justly dear	133
646	Dear Father, to thy mercy-seat	191

HYMN		PAGE
1216	Dear is the spot where Christians sleep	398
1077	Dear Jesus, ever at my side	398
846	Dear Lord, amid the throng that pressed	241
729	Dear Lord, and will thy pardoning love	44
668	Dear Refuge of my weary soul	55
1086	Dear Saviour, if these lambs	405
790	Dear Saviour! we are thine	176
603	Dear Saviour, when my thoughts recall	329
303	Dearest of all the names above	313
1170	Death may dissolve my body now	229
310	Deep in our hearts let us record	387
767	Deny thee? what! deny the way	224
604	Depth of mercy!—can there be	408
1235	Descend from heaven, immortal Dove!	21
321	Despised is the Man of grief	102
286	Did Christ o'er sinners weep	286
800	Didst thou, dear Jesus, suffer shame	155
87	Dismiss us with thy blessing, Lord	49
1148	Do I delight in sorrow's dress?	399
698	Do not I love thee, O my Lord?	220
760	Do not I trust in thee, O Lord?	217
1119	Dread Jehovah! God of nations!	302
73	Dread Sovereign! let my evening song	303
44	Early, my God! without delay	54
233	Ere earth's foundations yet were laid	231
254	Ere the blue heavens were stretched	304
819	Eternal Father, God of love	410
190	Eternal God I eternal King!	197
158	Eternal Power! almighty God!	69
719	Eternal Rock! to thee I flee	93
626	Eternal Source of joys divine	228
465	Eternal Spirit, we confess	276
183	Eternal Wisdom! thee we praise	117
1290	Eternity—eternity!	403
808	Ever patient, gentle, meek	136
415	Everlasting arms of love	167
953	Every human tie may perish	406
981	Faint not, Christian! though the road	283
757	Faith is the polar star	256
19	Far as thy name is known	50
1019	Far down the ages now	366
1222	Far from my heavenly home	99
21	Far from my thoughts, vain world	42
913	Far from the world, O Lord, I flee	132
1236	Far from these narrow scenes of night	296
850	Father, how wide thy glory shines!	81
215	Father, I know that all my life	280
1283	Father, I long, I faint to see	239
1289	Father!—if I may call thee so	255
1204	Father, my spirit owns	279
933	Father, oh, hear me now!	245
994	Father of eternal grace	162
471	Father of heaven, whose love profound	315
63	Father of love and power	144
1069	Father of mercies, bow thine ear	163
214	Father of mercies, God of love!	190
722	Father of mercies, God of love! Oh, hear	147
485	Father of mercies, in thy word	49
873	Father of mercies, send thy grace	211
207	Father, thy paternal care	386
315	Father, thy Son hath died	311
926	Father, whate'er of earthly bliss	121
1182	Father, when thy child is dying	300
940	Father, who in the olive shade	300
899	Fear not, O little flock, the foe	47
900	Fight the good fight! lay hold	133

INDEX OF FIRST LINES OF HYMNS.

HYMN		PAGE	HYMN		PAGE
882	Firm as the earth thy Gospel stands..	45	15	Great God! attend, while Zion sings..	52
713	Flow fast, my tears! the cause is great	212	142	Great God! how infinite art thou!	274
1147	For all thy saints, O God..	99	45	Great God! indulge my humble claim.	42
635	For mercies countless as the sands....	232	204	Great God! let all my tuneful powers.	92
5	For thee, O God, our constant praise..	319	1009	Great God of wonders! all thy ways	147
506	For ever here my rest shall be.......	186	1126	Great God! the nations of the earth..	229
1237	For ever with the Lord!............	382	66	Great God! to thee my evening song.	114
420	Forgetful can a mother be?...........	183	1156	Great God! we sing that mighty hand.	31
19	Forth from the dark and stormy sky..	147	1284	Great God! what do I see and hear?..	403
1146	Fount of everlasting love!...........	29	1123	Great God! whose universal sway.....	70
77	Frequent the day of God returns......	307	1025	Great is the Lord our God...........	23
1214	Friend after friend departs..	253	128	Great is the Lord! what tongue.......	65
163	From all that dwell below the skies....	30	473	Great One in Three, great Three in One	82
691	From deep distress and troubled tho'ts	240	127	Great Ruler of all nature's frame!...	558
845	From every stormy wind that blows...	289	1021	Great Shepherd of thine Israel!......	213
1112	From foes that would the land devour.	257	667	Great Source of boundless power.....	543
1132	From Greenland's icy mountains......	395	1221	Guide me, O thou great Jehovah!....	407
671	From lowest depths of woe...........	299			
520	From the cross uplifted high.........	100	866	Had I the tongues of Greeks and Jews.	244
1252	From thee, my God, my joys shall rise	385	1011	Hail, my ever blessed Jesus!..........	85
1092	From yon delusive scene..............	110	749	Hail, sovereign Love! that formed....	304
			273	Hail the night! all hail the morn!.....	29
941	Gently, gently lay thy rod...........	162	1039	Hail to the Lord's Anointed!........	181
759	Gently, Lord, oh, gently lead us......	234	381	Hail to the Prince of life and peace!..	87
1183	Gently, my Saviour, let me down.....	377	384	Hallelujah! hallelujah!..............	301
1033	Gird on thy conquering sword!......	198	173	Hallelujah! raise, oh, raise..........	28
1245	Give me the wings of faith to rise....	97	1029	Happy the church, thou sacred place!.	61
154	Give thanks to God; he reigns above..	48	858	Happy the heart where graces reign ..	221
168	Give thanks to God most high........	40	1087	Happy the home, when God is there..	39
166	Give to our God immortal praise.....	64	870	Happy the souls to Jesus joined......	211
513	Give to the Lord thine heart..........	119	1264	Hark! a voice divides the sky!.......	151
123	Give to the Lord, ye sons of fame.....	86	273	Hark! hark! the notes of joy.........	62
675	Give to the winds thy fears..........	161	895	Hark! how the gospel trumpet sounds!	156
1041	Give us room, that we may dwell.....	391	709	Hark! my soul! it is the Lord.......	159
29	Glad was my heart to hear...........	32	366	Hark! ten thousand harps and voices..	292
1043	Glorious things of thee are spoken...	219	1268	Hark! that shout of rapturous joy.....	127
377	Glory, glory to our King.............	372	274	Hark! the glad sound! the Saviour...	117
341	Glory to God on high!..............	144	270	Hark! the herald angels sing........	391
1076	Glory to the Father give.............	29	392	Hark! the song of Jubilee..	126
65	Glory to thee, my God, this night....	49	297	Hark! the voice of love and mercy....	294
875	Go, labor on; spend and be spent....	57	512	Hark! through the courts of heaven..	351
876	Go, labor on; your hands are weak...	57	271	Hark! what celestial sounds..........	111
1135	Go, preach my gospel, saith the Lord..	249	269	Hark! what mean these holy voices...	213
290	Go to dark Gethsemane.............	163	537	Haste, O sinner! now be wise.......	159
925	Go up, go up, my heart!.............	265	538	Haste, traveler, haste! the night comes	198
842	Go, when the morning shineth.......	180	1105	Hasten, O Lord, that happy time.....	83
251	Go, worship at Immanuel's feet.......	87	584	Have mercy on me, O my God!......	341
1111	God bless our native land!..........	401	358	He dies! the Friend of sinners dies...	230
596	God calling yet!—shall I not hear?....	318	374	He lives! the great Redeemer lives!..	230
79	God in his temple let us meet........	376	1285	He reigns! the Lord, the Saviour reigns	70
226	God, in the high and holy place......	384	383	He who on earth as man was known...	364
141	God is a Spirit, just and wise........	183	618	Hear me, O God! nor hide thy face...	342
151	God is love; his mercy brightens.....	193	536	Hear, O sinner! mercy hails you......	294
854	God is my strong salvation..........	394	964	Hear what God, the Lord, hath spoken	172
198	God is our refuge and defense.......	241	1212	Hear what the voice from heaven.....	357
196	God is our refuge and our strength....	18	545	Hearts of stone, relent, relent!.......	45
200	God is our refuge ever near..........	403	1044	Heavenly Father! may thy love......	400
192	God is the refuge of his saints........	90	566	Here, at thy cross, my gracious Lord..	135
236	God moves in a mysterious way.....	80	977	Here I can firmly rest...............	223
644	God, my supporter and my hope.....	228	553	Here is my heart—I give it thee!.....	144
137	God of almighty power..............	51	157	High in the heavens, eternal God!...	43
612	God of mercy! God of love!.........	260	1249	High in yonder realms of light......	282
961	God of my life! through all my days..	43	165	Holy and reverend is the name......	307
670	God of my life! to thee I call........	405	491	Holy Bible! book divine!..	299
728	God of my salvation, hear...........	360	470	Holy Father! hear my cry	405
368	God's holy law, transgressed.........	98	456	Holy Ghost, the Infinite!...........	251
1014	Grace! 't is a charming sound.......	375	458	Holy Ghost, thou Source of light!....	67
574	Great Author of my being...........	373	457	Holy Ghost! with light divine........	66

INDEX OF FIRST LINES OF HYMNS.

HYMN		PAGE
7	Holy, holy, holy Lord! Be thy......	66
472	Holy, holy, holy Lord God of hosts!..	308
98	Holy, holy, holy Lord! In the highest, Lord......	66
710	Holy Lamb, who thee receive.........	66
450	Holy Spirit! Love Divine!..........	260
1240	Hope of our hearts! O Lord appear...	327
390	Hosanna! be our cheerful song......	112
202	How are thy servants blest, O Lord!..	312
1062	How beauteous are their feet........	50
283	How beauteous were the marks divine.	146
1192	How blest the righteous when he dies!	308
864	How blest the sacred tie that binds....	280
1250	How bright these glorious spirits shine	297
621	How can I sink with such a prop......	186
22	How charming is the place............	23
1057	How condescending and how kind.....	316
27	How did my heart rejoice to hear.....	22
180	How firm a foundation, ye saints......	270
510	How gentle God's commands!.........	252
1080	How glorious is our heavenly King....	308
312	How heavy is the night...............	98
549	How helpless guilty nature lies.......	275
1028	How honored is the sacred place......	35
1047	How large the promise, how divine!..	411
619	How long, O Lord, shall I complain...	336
985	How long the time since Christ began.	328
613	How long wilt thou forget me, Lord?..	251
13	How lovely are thy dwellings fair.....	18
630	How oft, alas! this wretched heart....	342
482	How perfect is thy word.............	330
14	How pleasant, how divinely fair......	52
860	How pleasant 't is to see.............	46
26	How pleased and blest was I.........	46
485	How precious is the book divine......	214
493	How sad our state by nature is.......	275
306	How shall the sons of men appear.....	376
459	How shall the young secure their hearts	164
1164	How short and hasty is our life!......	306
1196	How still and peaceful is the grave!...	317
1055	How sweet and awful is the place......	233
850	How sweet, how heavenly is the sight.	153
441	How sweet the name of Jesus sounds..	116
82	How sweet to leave the world awhile .	376
525	How sweetly flowed the gospel sound..	114
1168	How vain is all beneath the skies!....	283
184	How wondrous great, how glorious....	80
697	How wondrous was the burning zeal..	120
814	I ask not now for gold to gild........	143
149	I can not always trace the way........	322
947	I can not call affliction sweet.........	322
418	I close my heavy eye................	284
987	I did thee wrong, my God............	264
804	I feel within a want..................	265
477	I give immortal praise...............	63
565	I heard the voice of Jesus say........	170
945	I heard the voice of love divine	259
368	I know that my Redeemer lives, And..	94
369	I know that my Redeemer lives; He..	73
978	I know thy thoughts are peace........	266
746	I lay my sins on Jesus................	379
734	I left the God of truth and light.......	404
152	I'll bless the Lord, I'll bless the Lord	72
221	I'll praise my Maker with my breath..	83
647	I love my God, but with no love of mine	397
670	I love the Lord; he heard my cries...	77
827	I love the Lord; he lent an ear.......	238
691	I love the Lord who died for me......	325

HYMN		PAGE
464	I love the volume of thy word........	88
685	I love thee, O my God, but not.......	154
1017	I love thy kingdom, Lord.............	223
64	I love to steal awhile away...........	214
1224	I'm but a stranger here.............	244
797	I'm not ashamed to own my Lord.....	55
1006	I once was a stranger to grace........	271
568	I saw One hanging on a tree.........	174
747	I see the crowd in Pilate's hall.......	154
815	I send the joys of earth away.........	69
117	I sing of God—the world he made.....	36
118	I sing th' almighty power of God.....	26
681	I stand on Zion's mount..............	374
1078	I thank the goodness and the grace...	150
708	I thirst, but not as once I did........	405
314	I thought upon my sins, and I was sad	227
429	I've found the pearl of greatest price.	95
851	I waited patient for the Lord........	132
551	I was a wandering sheep............	194
640	I will love thee, all my treasure......	392
649	I would love thee, God and Father..	218
1176	I would not live alway; I ask not..	323, 456
696	I would not wish to dwell on earth.....	388
959	If God is mine, then present things....	220
1056	If human kindness meets return......	316
1171	If I must die, oh! let me die.........	316
753	If Jesus be my friend................	161
744	If thou impart thyself to me	206
773	If through unruffled seas..........223, 458	
135	In all my vast concerns with thee.....	274
673	In heavenly love abiding.............	180
972	In holy contemplation...............	378
51	In sleep's serene oblivion laid........	389
317	In the cross of Christ I glory........	173
938	In the dark and cloudy day...........	351
665	In vain I trace creation o'er.........	149
1013	In vain we lavish out our lives........	216
305	In vain we seek for peace with God....	280
1122	Indulgent sovereign of the skies.......	103
499	Infinite excellence is thine...........	94
587	Is there ambition in my heart?.......	175
555	Is this the kind return?..............	236
399	Israel's Shepherd! guide me, feed me.	254
1178	It is not death to die................	314
934	It is the Lord! enthroned in light.....	333
932	It is thy hand, my God...............	236

139	Jehovah, God! thy gracious power....	68
145	Jehovah reigns; he dwells in light....	31
189	Jehovah reigns; his throne is high....	83
156	Jehovah reigns; let all the earth.....	70
1221	Jerusalem! my happy home.........	97
326	Jesus, all-atoning Lamb.............	67
610	Jesus, and didst thou condescend......	122
798	Jesus, and shall it ever be............	56
910	Jesus, cast a look on me!............	409
353	Jesus Christ is risen to-day..........	166
582	Jesus demands this heart of mine.....	108
389	Jesus exalted far on high............	228
561	Jesus, full of all compassion.........	363
776	Jesus, full of truth and love..........	409
371	Jesus, hail! enthroned in glory......	218
244	Jesus, hail! thou great I AM.........	100
318	Jesus,—harmonious name!..........	62
432	Jesus, I love thy charming name......	239
906	Jesus, I my cross have taken........	177
714	Jesus, in sickness and in pain	342
325	Jesus, in thy transporting name.......	213

INDEX OF FIRST LINES OF HYMNS.

HYMN		PAGE
781	Jesus, in whom but thee, above	319
408	Jesus, Lover of my soul	368
7.5	Jesus, my All, to heaven is gone	60
1101	Jesus, my Lord, how rich thy grace!	187
765	Jesus, our fainting spirits cry	303
370	Jesus, our Head, once crowned	120
398	Jesus, seek thy wandering sheep	386
1129	Jesus shall reign where'er the sun	304
396	Jesus, Shepherd of the sheep	292
404	Jesus, still lead on	350
50	Jesus, Sun of righteousness	269
835	Jesus, take me for thine own	67
446	Jesus, the Christ of God	118
727	Jesus, the sinner's Friend, to thee	240
687	Jesus, the very thought of thee	120
689	Jesus, these eyes have never seen	338
385	Jesus, thou everlasting King!	93
686	Jesus, thou Joy of loving hearts!	185
1085	Jesus, thou Shepherd of the sheep	71
1003	Jesus, thy blood and righteousness	319
694	Jesus, thy boundless love to me	140
42	Jesus, where'er thy people meet	292
405	Jesus, while this rough desert soil	184
745	Jesus, who on Calv'ry's mountain	362
841	Jesus, who upon the tree	470
716	Jesus, whom angel hosts adore	93
440	Join all the glorious names	25
277	Joy to the world! the Lord is come!	200
1097	Joyful be the hours to-day	162
193	Just are thy ways, and true thy word	168
559	Just as I am, without one plea	352
235	Keep silence, all created things	302
88	Keep us, Lord, oh, keep us ever!	294
84	Kindred in Christ, for his dear sake	388
187	Kingdoms and thrones to God belong	70
967	Know, my soul, thy full salvation	64
1049	Lamb of God, whose bleeding love	361
107	Let all the earth their voices raise	88
177	Let all the just to God with joy	73
40	Let all the lands, with shouts of joy	26
1090	Let children bear the mighty deeds	125
1144	Let every heart rejoice and sing	208
508	Let every mortal ear attend	384
467	Let glory be to God on high	123
785	Let me be with thee where thou art	134
886	Let me but hear my Saviour say	245
838	Let me dwell on Golgotha	261
907	Let not your heart be faint	252
1165	Let others boast how strong they be	316
860	Let saints below in concert sing	149
817	Let sinners take their course	236
1125	Let the seventh angel sound on high	82
478	Let them neglect thy glory, Lord	281
686	Let thy grace, Lord, make me lowly	235
345	Let us awake our joys	400
228	Let us with a gladsome mind	126
1034	Let Zion and her sons rejoice	72
1061	Let Zion's watchmen all awake	381
1201	Life is a span—a fleeting hour	317
501	Life is the time to serve the Lord	293
256	Lift up to God the voice of praise	200
363	Lift up your heads, eternal gates!	201
364	Lift up your heads, ye gates! and wide	65
426	Light of those whose dreary dwelling	219
990	Like the eagle, upward, onward	173
1145	Like Israel's host to exile driven	204

HYMN		PAGE
352	Like sheep we went astray	98
8	Lo, God is here!—let us adore	116
1286	Lo! he cometh—countless trumpets	390
495	Lo! on a narrow neck of land	315
877	Lo! the storms of life are breaking	259
1026	Lo! what a glorious corner-stone	65
1266	Lo! what a glorious sight appears	207
825	Long as I live, I'll bless thy name	45
580	Long have I sat beneath the sound	294
949	Long unafflicted, undismayed	377
460	Lord, am I precious in thy sight?	108
1094	Lord, as to thy dear cross we flee	190
611	Lord, at thy feet we sinners lie	251
1053	Lord, at thy table I behold	183
730	Lord, didst thou die—but not for me?	126
86	Lord, dismiss us with thy blessing	407
448	Lord God, the Holy Ghost!	176
234	Lord, how mysterious are thy ways!	336
500	Lord, how secure my conscience was	320
1000	Lord, I address thy heavenly throne	346
1067	Lord, I am thine, entirely thine	135
492	Lord, I am vile—conceived in sin	344
602	Lord, I approach the mercy-seat	306
1256	Lord, I believe a rest remains	267
779	Lord, I believe; thy power I own	359
487	Lord, I have made thy word my choice	228
104	Lord, I will bless thee all my days	388
43	Lord, in the morning thou shalt hear	38
9	Lord, in the temples of thy grace	388
763	Lord, it belongs not to my care	354
789	Lord Jesus, are we one with thee?	195
1100	Lord, lead the way the Saviour went	187
1045	Lord, may our sympathizing breasts	289
237	Lord, my weak thought	241
639	Lord of earth, thy forming hand	369
443	Lord of mercy and of might	351
1253	Lord of the Sabbath, hear our vows	276
16	Lord of the worlds above	111
699	Lord, should my path through suffering	197
134	Lord, thou hast searched and seen me	240
554	Lord, thou hast won; at length I yield	348
67	Lord, thou wilt hear me when I pray	355
1012	Lord, we confess our numerous faults	328
498	Lord, what a thoughtless wretch was I	344
1229	Lord, what a wretched land is this	381
658	Lord, what is man! that child of pride	175
874	Lord, what off'ring shall we bring	369
839	Lord, when my thoughts delighted rove	229
1104	Lord, when thine ancient people cried	82
136	Lord, where shall guilty souls retire	307
112	Loud hallelujahs to the Lord	65
957	Love divine, all love excelling	193
1202	Lowly and solemn be	355
329	Majestic sweetness sits enthroned	105
291	Many woes had Christ endured	105
239	May not the sovereign Lord on high	103
91	May the grace of Christ the Saviour	361
867	Meek and lowly, pure and holy	263
74	Millions within thy courts have met	20
775	Mine eyes and my desire	98
704	More hard than marble is my heart	216
360	Morning breaks upon the tomb	166
801	Must Jesus bear the cross alone	173
692	My blessed Saviour, is thy love	332
1120	My country, 't is of thee	401
1228	My days are gliding swiftly by	363
780	My dear Redeemer, and my Lord	184

464   INDEX OF FIRST LINES OF HYMNS.

HYMN		PAGE	HYMN		PAGE
828	My dearest Lord, whose changeless....	169	90	Now may the Lord, our Shepherd, lead	82
722	My faith looks up to thee............	355	1048	Now, my soul, thy voice upraising..	406
1273	My faith shall triumph o'er the grave.	347	475	Now, O God, thine own I am.........	137
1160	My few revolving years..............	341	917	Now, O my God, thou hast my soul...	217
567	My former hopes are fled............	286	850	Now shall my solemn vows be paid....	365
6	My God, accept my early vows........	277	165	Now to the Lord a noble song........	75
62	My God, how endless is thy love!....	241	325	Now to the Lord, who makes us know.	87
172	My God, how wonderful thou art!.....	350	1008	Now to the power of God supreme...	249
844	My God, is any hour so sweet........	353			
1001	My God, my Father, blissful name!...	191	257	O all ye lands, rejoice in God!........	296
929	My God, my Father, while I stray....	322	803	Oh, arm me with the mind...........	334
705	My God, my God, to thee I cry.......	128	224	Oh, bless, the Lord, my soul! His....	32
824	My God, my King, thy various praise.	86	223	Oh, bless the Lord my soul! Let all...	32
645	My God, my Life, my Love...........	331	849	Oh blessed God! to thee I raise......	389
643	My God, my Portion, and my Love...	69	1051	O Bread to pilgrims given...........	208
625	My God, my prayer attend............	287	526	Oh, cease, my wandering soul.......	340
616	My God—oh! could I make the claim.	175	307	O Christ, our ever blessed Lord......	120
811	My God, permit me not to be.........	293	356	O Christ, our King, Creator, Lord!...	115
931	My God, the cov'nant of thy love.....	333	1022	O Christ, the Leader of that war-worn.	302
684	My God, the spring of all my joys....	96	46	O Christ, with each returning morn...	115
832	My gracious Lord, I own thy right....	164	83	Oh, come, loud anthems let us sing...	70
936	My Jesus, as thou wilt..............	264	707	Oh, could I find, from day to day....	339
103	My Maker, and my King..............	130	433	Oh, could I speak the matchless worth	37
777	My only Saviour! when I feel........	434	1265	Oh, could our thoughts and wishes fly.	267
437	My precious Lord, for thy dear name..	292	949	Oh, deem not they are blest alone....	277
1277	My Saviour, can it ever be...........	205	544	Oh, do not let the word depart.......	164
564	My Saviour, how shall I proclaim....	225	444	O everlasting Light!.................	160
609	My Saviour, let me hear thy voice....	54	783	O eyes that are weary, and hearts....	270
324	My Saviour, my almighty Friend!....	104	894	O faint and feeble-hearted..........	208
950	My sky was once noon-bright........	264	627	Oh for a closer walk with God.......	190
636	My soul, be on thy guard.............	167	758	Oh for a faith that will not shrink....	384
988	My soul before thee prostrate lies.....	232	577	Oh for a heart to praise my God......	338
663	My soul doth long for thee...........	265	635	Oh for a principle within............	364
560	My soul, go boldly forth.............	243	153	Oh for a shout of joy................	62
160	My soul, inspired with sacred love....	49	375	Oh for a shout of sacred joy.........	27
535	My soul, it is thy God...............	330	1258	Oh for a sweet, inspiring ray........	231
161	My soul, repeat his praise...........	330	247	Oh for a thousand tongues to sing....	178
892	My soul, weigh not thy life..........	374	754	Oh for an overcoming faith..........	125
935	My spirit looks to God alone........	213	576	Oh for that tenderness of heart......	259
762	My spirit on thy care...............	331	1211	Oh for the death of those...........	177
768	My suff'rings all to thee are known....	134	240	Oh gift of gifts! oh, grace of faith!...	142
751	My thoughts surmount these lower....	171	1115	O God, beneath thy guiding hand....	31
656	My times are in thy hand............	298	52	O God, my heart is fully bent........	19
			190	O God, my Refuge, hear my cries....	76
935	Naked as from the earth we came....	380	634	O God, my Strength, my Hope.......	298
296	Near the cross our station taking......	393	216	O God of Bethel, by whose hand.....	359
989	Nearer, my God, to thee.............	244	17	O God of hosts, the mighty Lord!....	68
660	No change of time shall ever shock....	77	652	O God, thou art my God alone.......	185
724	No more, my God, I boast no more....	213	1103	O gracious Lord, whose mercies rise...	133
847	No, never shall my heart despond....	143	30	Oh hallowed is the land, and blest.....	53
1177	No, no, it is not dying...............	188	1065	Oh, happy day, that fixed my choice...	165
1251	Nor eye hath seen, nor ear hath heard.	267	958	Oh, happy is the man who hears......	296
299	Not all the blood of beasts...........	130	1079	Oh, happy land! oh, happy land!.....	159
552	Not all the outward-forms on earth....	182	974	Oh, happy soul, that lives on high....	383
1141	Not for the summer hour alone.......	411	770	Oh, help us, Lord!—each hour of need,	232
1097	Not only when ascends the song.....	326	97	O holy, holy Lord...................	41
275	Not to condemn the sons of men.....	91	771	O holy Saviour, Friend unseen.......	353
868	Not to the mount that burned with...	204	486	Oh, how I love thy holy law!........	19
690	Not with our mortal eyes............	130	583	Oh, if my soul were formed for woe..	175
252	Now be my heart inspired to sing.....	92	1106	Oh, if thy brow, serene and calm.....	215
261	Now begin the heavenly theme.......	28	869	O Jesus! King most wonderful.......	121
351	Now for a tune of lofty praise........	60	706	O Jesus! thou the beauty art.........	121
490	Now, in a song of grateful praise.....	56	679	Oh, let him whose sorrow...........	285
516	Now is th' accepted time............	272	463	O Lord, and shall our fainting souls...	135
346	Now joyful strains we lift on high.....	27	140	O Lord, how full of sweet content.....	388
1242	Now let our souls on wings sublime...	93	269	O Lord, how infinite thy love!........	44
93	Now may he, who from the dead......	387	733	O Lord, how vile am I...............	237
94	Now may the God of peace and love...	380	651	O Lord, I would delight in thee.......	253

INDEX OF FIRST LINES OF HYMNS. 465

HYMN		PAGE
927	O Lord, my best desire fulfill	332
929	O Lord, our carnal mind control	103
1116	O Lord, our fathers oft have told	45
1128	O Lord, our God, arise	51
171	O Lord, our heavenly King	283
247	O Lord, our Lord, how wondrous great	179
822	O Lord, thy heavenly grace impart	225
326	O Lord, thy love's unbounded!	357
1147	O Lord, thy work revive	273
284	O Lord, when we the path retrace	303
703	O Love divine, how sweet thou art!	36
502	O Love divine, what hast thou done!	216
792	Oh, mean may seem this house of clay	109
718	Oh, not my own, these verdant hills	318
1038	Oh, not to fill the mouth of fame	339
167	Oh, praise the Lord, for he is good	19
181	Oh, render thanks to God above	86
295	O sacred Head, now wounded!	336
1009	O Saviour, whom this holy morn	399
912	Oh, see how Jesus trusts himself	207
367	Oh, show me not my Saviour dying	226
434	Oh, speak of Jesus! other names	140
621	O, speak that gracious word again	343
903	Oh, speed thee, Christian, on thy way	158
837	Oh, sweetly breathe the lyres above	164
788	O that I could for ever dwell	324
655	Oh that I knew the secret place	343
581	Oh that my load of sin were gone!	213
914	Oh that the Lord would guide my ways	266
1133	Oh that the Lord's salvation	395
348	Oh, the sweet wonders of that cross	168
623	Oh, these eyes, how dark and blind!	261
720	O thou best gift of heaven!	554
939	O thou, from whom all goodness flows	320
624	O thou God who hearest prayer	246
73	O thou that hearest prayer	278
505	O thou that hear'st when sinners cry	345
593	O thou that wouldst not have	236
373	O thou, the contrite sinner's Friend	352
170	O thou, to whom all creatures bow	44
402	O thou, to whose all-searching sight	102
334	O thou, who art enrobed with light	54
829	O thou who hast at thy command	134
260	O thou who hast redeemed of old	348
725	O thou who hear'st the prayer of faith	349
943	O thou whose mercy guides my way	155
1073	O thou whose own vast temple stands	45
620	O thou whose tender mercy hears	251
598	Oh, turn, great Ruler of the skies	337
28	Oh, 't was a joyful sound to hear	142
1038	Oh, where are kings and empires now	346
279	Oh, where is he that trod the sea?	182
628	Oh, where is now that glowing **love**	230
436	Oh, where shall rest be found	340
653	Oh, who is like the Mighty One	179
222	Oh, why despond in life's dark vale	370
1046	Oh, wondrous is thy mercy, Lord!	411
115	Oh, worship the King, all-glorious	58
1127	O'er the gloomy hills of darkness	209
896	Oft in sorrow, oft in woe	283
427	On earth was darkness spread	242
1234	On Jordan's stormy banks I stand	296
1031	On the mountain's top appearing	209
1117	On thee, O Lord our God, we call	103
632	**Once** I thought my **mountain strong**	246
873	**One sole** baptismal sign	199
1169	**One** sweetly solemn thought	314
435	One there is, above all others	192

HYMN		PAGE
1040	**Onward** speed thy conquering flight	402
748	Oppressed with noon-day's scorching	342
779	Oppressed with sin and woe	237
466	Our blest Redeemer, ere he breathed	156
1	Our Father, God, who art in heaven	358
3	Our Father in heaven	323
146	Our God, our help in ages past	290
638	Our hearts, O Lord, with grief are rent	232
780	Our heavenly Father calls	253
2	Our heavenly Father, hear	176
1151	Our helper, God, we bless thy name	43
362	Our Lord is risen from the dead	64
794	Our sins, alas! how strong they are!	347
600	Out of the deeps of long distress	259
599	Out of the depths of woe	286
92	**Peace** be **to** this sacred dwelling	172
511	**Peace**, troubled soul, whose plaintive	123,454
1063	People of the living God	387
711	Pity, Lord, the child of clay	247
794	Planted in Christ, the living vine	155
872	Plead thou, oh, plead my cause!	242
262	Plunged in a gulf of dark despair	200
1058	Pour out thy Spirit from on high	71
179	Praise, everlasting praise, be paid	65
105	Praise, oh, praise the Name divine!	150
1143	Praise on thee, in Zion's gates	167
103	Praise the Lord, his glories show	166
1142	**Praise to** God, immortal praise	127
106	**Praise to** God on high be given!	872
99	**Praise to** thee, thou great Creator!	84
83	Praise ye Jehovah's name	400
1019	Praise ye the Lord; exalt his name	61
111	Praise ye the Lord; my heart shall join	48
469	Praises to him who built the hills	21
856	Prayer is the soul's sincere desire	326
1054	Prepare us, Lord, to view thy cross	183
903	Prince of Peace, control my will	408
560	Prostrate, dear Jesus, at thy feet	174
991	**Purer** yet and **purer**	285
903	**Quiet, Lord,** my froward **heart**	137
255	Raise your triumphant songs	106
313	Rejected and despised of men	174
391	Rejoice! the Lord is king	63
422	Rejoice! ye saints, rejoice and praise	55
1001	Remember thy Creator now	183
1271	Rest for the toiling hand	315
590	Return, my roving heart, return	404
203	Return, my soul, and sweetly rest	324
984	Return my soul, unto thy rest	212
512	Return, O wanderer, now return	364
289	Ride on, ride on in majesty!	179
393	Rise, crowned with light; great Salem	57
1238	Rise, my soul, and stretch thy wings	361
1246	Rise, O my soul, pursue the path	346
721	Rock of ages! cleft for me	101
1137	Roll on, thou mighty ocean!	375
55	Safely through another week	136
897	Saints for whom the Saviour bled	402
1016	Salvation! oh, the joyful sound!	35
61	Saviour, breathe an evening blessing	284
754	Saviour, happy would I be	141
480	Saviour, like a shepherd lead us	407
518	Saviour, Prince, enthroned above	360
757	Saviour, to me thyself reveal	200

INDEX OF FIRST LINES OF HYMNS.

HYMN		PAGE
1093	Saviour, what gracious words	335
740	Saviour, when in dust to thee	247
783	See a poor sinner, dearest Lord	212
1118	See, gracious God, before thy throne	233
285	See how he loved! exclaimed the Jews	114
1045	See Israel's gentle Shepherd stand	411
1081	See the kind Shepherd, Jesus, stands	399
1027	See what a living stone	50
1207	Servant of God, well done!	314
343	Shall hymns of grateful love	40
1166	Shall the vile race of flesh and blood	255
915	Shall we go on to sin	272
1034	Shepherd of tender youth	354
397	Shepherd of the ransomed flock	203
1222	Shepherd of thine Israel! lead us	407
524	Show pity, Lord! O Lord, forgive	345
242	Since all the varying scenes of time	191
407	Sing of Jesus, sing for ever	301
1035	Sing to the Lord in joyful strains	113
38	Sing to the Lord Jehovah's name	72
971	Sing, ye redeemed of the Lord	113
543	Sinners, the voice of God regard	390
539	Sinners, turn; why will ye die?	260
517	Sinners, will you scorn the message	295
1209	Sister, thou wast mild and lovely	310
891	Sleep not, soldier of the Cross!	283
923	So let our lips and lives express	293
76	Softly fades the twilight ray	202
898	Soldiers of Christ! arise	375
741	Son of God, to thee I cry	247
25	Songs of praise the angels sang	283
382	Sons of Zion, raise your songs!	166
674	Soon as I heard my Father say	55
1121	Soon may the last glad song arise	305
796	Soon—soon and for ever	263
1138	Sound, sound the truth abroad	400
965	Source and Giver of repose	203
1124	Sovereign of worlds! display thy power	377
592	Sovereign Ruler, Lord of all!	408
657	Sovereign Ruler of the skies	66
881	Sow in the morn thy seed	367
447	Spirit Divine! attend our prayer	149
862	Spirit of peace, celestial Dove!	207
464	Spirit of power and might! behold	346
449	Spirit of truth! on this thy day	206
113	Stand up, and bless the Lord	107
889	Stand up, my soul, shake off thy fears	74
902	Stand up!—stand up for Jesus!	394
1103	Star of peace, to wanderers weary	263
461	Stay, thou insulted Spirit, stay!	344
85	Stealing from the world away	387
1244	Still one in life and one in death	324
622	Still wilt thou, Lord, be found?	341
784	Still with thee, O my God	223
1172	Stoop down, my thoughts	206
742	Suff'ring Son of Man, be near me	362
68	Sun of my soul! thou Saviour dear	42
992	Supreme in wisdom as in power	381
450	Sure the blest Comforter is nigh	184
75	Sweet is the light of Sabbath eve	289
147	Sweet is the mem'ry of thy grace	69
1193	Sweet is the scene when Christians die	308
11	Sweet is the work, my God, my King	20
12	Sweet is the work, O Lord	22
975	Sweet peace of conscience	231
295	Sweet the moments, rich in blessing	244
24	Sweet the time, exceeding sweet!	387
617	Sweet was the time when first I felt	329

HYMN		PAGE
442	Sweeter sounds than music knows	203
1114	Swell the anthem, raise the song	391
570	Take my heart, O Father, take it!	255
1184	Tarry with me, O my Saviour!	255
876	Teach me, my God and King	334
1163	Teach me the measure of my days	129
231	Thank and praise Jehovah's name	126
1278	That awful day will surely come	291
1283	That day of wrath! that dreadful day	254
1281	That great day of wrath and terror	362
962	That man is blest who stands in awe	305
1174	That solemn hour will come for me	321
376	Th' atoning work is done	63
417	The billows swell, the winds are high	304
1270	The Church has waited long	195
365	Th' eternal gates lift up their heads	124
56	The festal morn, my God, has come	36
116	The God of Abrah'm praise	59
1155	The God of harvest praise	401
95	The God of peace, who from the dead	182
344	The goodly land I see	50
357	The happy morn is come	110
479	The heavens declare thy glory, Lord	91
743	The holy, meek, unspotted Lamb	168
1186	The hour of my departure's come	254
1282	The last loud trumpet's wondrous sound	89
124	The Lord descended from above	80
494	The Lord, from his celestial throne	389
218	The Lord himself, the mighty Lord	371
163	The Lord! how wondrous are his ways!	43
141	The Lord is great! ye hosts of heaven	78
125	The Lord is King! lift up thy voice	57
355	The Lord is risen indeed	374
121	The Lord Jehovah reigns, And royal	46
188	The Lord Jehovah reigns, His throne	41
219	The Lord my pasture shall prepare	300
217	The Lord my Shepherd is	100
20	The Lord of glory is my light	38
130	The Lord our God is full of might	76
131	The Lord our God is Lord of all	76
1267	The Lord shall come! the earth	146
220	The Lord's my shepherd, I'll not want	313
133	The Lord, the God of glory, reigns	84
210	The mercies of my God and King	94
1187	The moment comes, when strug	255
1203	The pangs of death are near	279
1225	The people of the Lord	131
16	The pity of the Lord	170
1036	The praise of Zion waits for the	61
840	The promise of my Father's love	430
176	The promises I sing	153
288	The Saviour!—what a noble flame	374
119	The spacious firmament on high	90, 453
506	The Spirit, in our hearts	113
863	The Spirit, like a peaceful dove	151
489	The starry firmament on high	92
541	The voice of free grace cries	152
909	The whole creation groans and wails	346
96	Thee we adore, eternal Lord!	39
1157	Thee we adore! eternal name!	231
823	Thee will I love, my Strength	205
205	Thee will I love, O God, and own	52
672	Their hearts shall not be moved	119
1198	There is a calm for those who weep	333
294	There is a dear and hallowed spot	148
300	There is a fountain filled with blood	96
301	There is a fountain filled with blood	96

INDEX OF FIRST LINES OF HYMNS

HYMN		PAGE
1083	There is a glorious world of light	399
1250	There is a happy land	245
1191	There is a land of pure delight	116
1082	There is a little lonely fold	288
963	There is a safe and secret place	133
852	There is an eye that never sleeps	105
1255	There is an hour of peaceful rest	55
309	There is none other name than thine	141
573	There was joy in heaven!	359
1241	These are the crowns that we shall wear	97
1254	Thine earthly Sabbaths, Lord, we love	276
905	Think gently of the erring one	221
1272	Think, mighty God, on feeble man	89
1226	This is not my place of resting	173
23	This is the day the Lord hath made	34
1218	Thou art gone to the grave	153
413	Thou art my hiding place, O Lord	290
826	Thou art my portion, O my God	223
918	Thou art, O Christ, the Way	273
1152	Thou art, O God, the life and light	265
335	Thou art the everlasting Son	123
445	Thou art the way; to thee alone	38
333	Thou dear Redeemer, dying Lamb	54
662	Thou hidden Love of God, whose height	217
253	Thou hidden Source of calm repose	217
1279	Thou Judge of quick and dead	290
607	Thou Lord of all above	293
1178	Thou must go forth alone, my soul!	321
400	Thou, O Christ, art all I want	368
666	Thou, O Lord, wilt never leave me	406
411	Thou only Sovereign of my heart	196
615	Thou Prince of Glory, slain for me	240
72	Thou seest my feebleness	84
605	Thou that didst hang upon the tree	115
793	Thou to our woe who down didst come	100
760	Thou very present aid	161
737	Thou who didst stoop below	208
227	Thou who dwell'st enthroned above	28
476	Thou whose almighty word	145
982	Though faint, yet pursuing, we go on	271
1179	Though I walk the downward shade	369
1037	Though now the nations sit beneath	61
683	Though waves and storms go o'er	204
230	Through all the changing scenes	173
143	Through endless years thou art the same	76
144	Through every age, eternal God	337
1276	Through sorrow's night, and danger's	313
70	Through the day thy love has spared us	393
973	Through the love of God our Saviour	157
71	Thus far the Lord hath led me on	43
1010	Thy Father's house! thine own	325
1110	Thy footsteps, Lord, with joy we trace	83
148	Thy goodness, Lord, our souls confess	73
911	Thy home is with the humble, Lord!	207
1154	Thy mighty working, mighty God!	37
102	Thy name, almighty Lord	33
928	Thy way, not mine, O Lord	265
186	Thy way, O Lord, is in the sea	359
1004	Thy works, not mine, O Christ!	139
1167	Time is winging us away	361
756	'T is by the faith of joys to come	248
1150	'T is by thy strength the mountains	125
298	"'T is finished!"—so the Saviour cried	224
292	'T is midnight, and, on Olive's brow	224
239	'T is not that I did choose thee	203
304	'T is past—the dark and dreary night	332
320	To Calv'ry, Lord, in spirit now	302
515	To-day the Saviour calls	310

HYMN		PAGE
463	To God be glory, peace on earth	81
954	To God I made my sorrows known	320
229	To God, the mighty Lord	190
216	To God, the only wise	34
232	To heaven I lift my waiting eyes	339
245	To him who loved the souls of men	87
1488	To Jesus, the crown of my hope	189
337	To our Redeemer's glorious name	25
401	To praise our Shepherd's care	23
339	To thee, my God, my Saviour	373
395	To thee, my Shepherd, and my Lord	143
812	To thee, O God, my prayer ascends	190
206	To thy pastures fair and large	292
81	To thy temple I repair	28
267	To us a Child of hope is born	290
614	Trembling, before thine awful throne	165
883	Triumphant, Christ ascends on high	94
1024	Triumphant Zion! lift thy head	56
993	Try us, O God, and search the ground	186
5.7	Turn not thy face away, O Lord!	328
883	Unshaken as the sacred hill	211
37	Unto the Lord, unto the Lord	53
1209	Unvail thy bosom, faithful tomb	292
810	Up to the fields where angels lie	339
195	Up to the hills I lift mine eyes. There	63
125	Up to the hills I lift mine eyes. Th'	91
174	Up to the Lord, who reigns on high	289
194	Upward I lift mine eyes	138
650	Vainly! through night's weary hours	235
1189	Vital spark of heavenly flame!	412
241	Wait, O my soul, thy Maker's will!	103
1130	Wake the song of Jubilee!	167
954	Walk in the light! so shalt thou know	30
276	Watchman, tell us of the night	391, 457
1064	We bid thee welcome in the name	169
361	We did not see thee lifted high	123
1227	We go with the redeemed to taste	377
1140	We join to pray, with wishes kind	4.1
40	We lift our hearts to thee	22
4.6	We'll sing the power of him who died	105
1043	We long to move and breathe in thee	419
641	We love thee, Lord, because when we	135
919	We praise and bless thee, gracious Lord	206
319	We sing the praise of him who died	93
243	We sing to thee, thou Son of God	173
1261	We speak of the realms of the blest	189
805	We tread the path our Master trod	158
1223	We've no abiding city here	395
631	Weary of wandering from my God	213
534	Weary sinner, keep thine eyes	162
752	Weary with sin, I lift mine eyes	141
54	Welcome, delightful morn	24
53	Welcome, sweet day of rest	22
930	Welcome to me the darkest night	71
1248	What are these in bright array?	283
960	What cheering words are these?	194
342	What equal honors shall we bring	376
185	What finite power, with ceaseless toil	336
282	What grace, O Lord, and beauty shone	108
175	What secret place, what distant star	31
820	What shall I render to my God	235
816	What sinners value, I resign	288
951	What though no flowers the fig-tree	221
853	What various hindrances we meet	244
211	When all thy mercies, O my God	370

INDEX OF FIRST LINES OF HYMNS.

HYMN		PAGE
410	When along life's thorny road	363
41	When, as returns this solemn day	274
1185	When bending o'er the brink of life	321
732	When blest with that transporting view	206
1190	When blooming youth is snatched away	317
1153	When brighter suns and milder skies	151
780	When darkness long has vailed	197
1197	When downward to the darksome tomb	321
766	When earthly comforts die	237
1181	When from my sight all fades away	147
412	When gathering clouds around I view	209
169	When God revealed his gracious name	214
1260	When I can read my title clear	215
987	When I can trust my all with God	257
772	When I listen to thy word	275
216	When I survey the wondrous cross	293
1072	When in these courts we seek thy face	376
1113	When Israel, of the Lord beloved	71
960	When languor and disease invade	171
428	When marshaled on the nightly plain	122
1239	When musing sorrow weeps the past	129
588	When, my Saviour, shall I be	67
693	When on Sinai's top I see	390
423	When our heads are bowed with woe	351
197	When, overwhelmed with grief	203
1290	When, rising from the bed of death	201
1131	When shall the voice of singing	181
633	When silent steal across my soul	254
750	When sins and fears prevailing rise	141
47	When streaming from the eastern skies	309
1175	When the spark of life is waning	157
714	When this passing world is done	373
603	When thou my righteous Judge	349
1109	When through the torn sail	152
546	When thy mortal life is fled	260
888	When waves of sorrow round me swell	186
1020	When we our wearied limbs to rest	405
887	Whence do our mournful thoughts	77
555	Where high the heavenly temple stands	319
375	Where is my God?—does he retire	230
943	Where is my Saviour now	279
738	Where shall I look for holy calm	134
122	Where'er, through all his works	274
726	Wherewith, O God, shall I draw near	196
679	While foes are strong, and danger near	185
830	While in the hours of blooming youth	141
437	While life prolongs its precious light	213
493	While my Redeemer 's near	253
1107	While o'er the deep thy servants sail	221
263	While shepherds watched their flocks	112
4	While thee I seek, protecting Power	370,452
1063	While to thy table I repair	169
1159	While with ceaseless course the sun	390,456
664	Whither, oh, whither should I fly	185
571	Who can describe the joys that rise	248
923	Who, O Lord, when life is o'er	151
921	Who shall ascend thy heavenly place	277
1005	Who shall the Lord's elect condemn?	241
795	Who, when beneath affliction's rod	155
976	Who—who can part our ransomed	215
642	Whom have we, Lord, in heaven	281
1210	Why do we mourn departing friends	312
739	Why droops my soul, with grief	288
629	Why is my heart so far from thee	281
1041	Why, on the bending willows hung	325
366	Why search ye in the narrow tomb	124
414	Why should I fear the darkest hour	204
946	Why should I murmur or repine	276
1217	Why should our tears in sorrow flow	365
455	Why should the children of a King	364
1194	Why should we start and fear to die?	308
1215	Why should we weep for those	394
540	Why will ye waste on trifling cares	336
1263	Will that not joyful be	284
956	With all my powers of heart and tongue	75
6	With broken heart and contrite sigh	254
1063	With heavenly power, O Lord, defend	82
18	With joy we hail the sacred day	38
424	With joy we meditate the grace	214, 455
865	With love the Saviour's heart	365
1102	With my substance I will honor	218
32	With one consent, let all the earth	17
132	With reverence let the saints appear	18
1149	With songs and honors sounding loud	112
530	With tearful eyes I look around	319
579	With tears of anguish I lament	250
250	With transport, Lord, our souls	83
1006	Witness, ye men and angels, now	183
322	Worlds can not reach the mighty price	124
101	Worship, honor, glory, blessing	172
347	Worthy the Lamb of boundless sway	83
1136	Ye Christian heralds! go proclaim	305
524	Ye dying sons of men	278
702	Ye earthly vanities! depart	185
436	Ye glittering toys of earth, adieu!	142
1190	Ye golden lamps of heaven, farewell!	326
126	Ye hosts of heaven, ye mighty ones	19
201	Ye humble souls, approach your God	210
359	Ye humble souls that seek the Lord	128
1219	Ye mourning saints, whose streaming	312
34	Ye nations round the earth, rejoice	17
379	Ye saints, your music bring	193
349	Ye servants of God	58
1060	Ye servants of the Lord	383
190	Ye tribes of Adam, join	25
519	Ye who in these courts are found	101
509	Ye wretched, hungry, starving poor	170
491	Yes, for me, for me he careth	192
205	Yes, I will bless thee, O my God!	220
1153	Yes, my native land! I love thee	406
356	Yes, the Redeemer rose	133
980	Your harps ye trembling saints	382

SELECTIONS FOR CHANTING.

		PAGE
Arise, O Lord,	....Psalm CXXXII......	440
As the hart panteth,	" XLII, XLIII.	422
Because thou hast,	" XCI, 9-16.....	431
Be thou exalted, O,	" LVII.........	425
Blessed be the Lord,	.Luke I, 68-75.......	448
Blessed be thou,	....1 Chr. XXIX, 10-13...	446
Blessed is the man,	..Psalm I............	416
Bless the Lord, O,	" CIII.........	435
Glory be to God,	...Gloria in Excelsis....	450
Glory be to the,	....Gloria Patri......	450
God be merciful,	....Psalm LXVII........	426
God is our refuge,	" XLVI.........	422
Great is the Lord,	" XLVIII.......	423
Have mercy upon,	" LI..........	424
He is despised and	..Isaiah LIII..........	447
Holy, holy, holy,	...Rev. IV and V......	448
How amiable are,	..Psalm LXXXIV.....	427
How beautiful upon,	.Isaiah LII, 7-9......	447
I love the Lord,	....Psalm CXVI.......	437
I was glad when,	" CXXII.........	439
I will bless the,	" XXXIV.......	420
I will extol thee,	" CXLV.........	443
I will lift up mine,	" CXXI.........	439
I will praise thee,	" CXXXVIII....	442
I will sing of the,	" LXXXIX, 1-18	429
Lord, thou hast,	" LXXXV......	428
Lord, thou hast been,	" XC...........	430
Make a joyful noise,	" C.............	434
Not unto us, O,	" CXV.........	436

		PAGE
O come, let us,	.....Psalm XCV.........	432
O God, thou art,	" LXIII, 1-7....	425
O Lord, I will,	......Isaiah XII	446
O Lord, our Lord,	..Psalm VIII.........	416
O Lord, thou hast,	" CXXXIX......	442
O sing unto the,	" XCVI.........	432
O sing unto the Lord,	" XCVIII........	433
Oh, give thanks,	" CXXXVI......	441
Our Father, who,	...The Lord's Prayer...	451
Out of the depths,	..Psalm CXXX........	440
Praise waiteth for,	" LXV..........	426
Praise ye the Lord,	" CXI..........	436
Praise ye the, (from	" CXLVIII......	445
Praise ye the, (in	" CL...........	445
Praise ye the, (O	" CXLVII, 12-20	444
Praise the Lord, O,	" CXLVI........	444
Rejoice in the Lord,	" XXXIII, 1-12..	420
The earth is the,	" XXIV.........	418
The heavens declare,	" XIX...........	417
The Lord is my,	" XXVII.........	419
The Lord is my,	" XXIII.........	417
The Lord is my,	" CXVIII, 14-29.	438
The Lord reigneth	" XCIII.........	431
The mercy of the,	...Baptismal Hymn....	451
Thy mercy, O Lord,	..Psalm XXXVI, 5-10..	421
We praise thee, O,	..Te Deum Laudamus.	448
When the Lord shall,	.Psalm CII, 16-28.....	434
When the Lord,	" CXXVI........	440
Unto thee, O Lord,	" XXV, 1-14.....	418

ALPHABETICAL INDEX OF TUNES.

*The Asterisk (*) is affixed to such tunes as **have been compiled** or arranged from the source indicated.*
Tunes by living American authors are inserted by special permission.

	PAGE
ABRIDGE. *Isaac Smith*, 1800.	69
ABVILLE	188
ACTON	300
ADNAL	189
AITHLONE... *German Tune*.	348
ALBEC	309
ALBION	151
ALL SAINTS.... *W. Knapp*	277
ALPHEUS.... **M Eberwein.* 8s, 124,	124
ALVAN..........294,	407
AMERICA........*English.*	401
AMOY...... *Dr. L. Mason.*	310
AMSTERDAM.........*Nares.*	361
ANLEY	234
ANTIOCH*	200
ANVERN ....*Dr. L. Mason.*	388
ARIEL....*Dr. L. Mason.*	37
ARLINGTON. ...*Arne.*.15},	2
ASTON	387
ATHENS ....*Giardini.*	132
ATHOL.....*R. Harrison.*	298
AVA.......*Dr. Hastings.*	243
AVON.............80,	252
AYLESBURY..*Dr. M Greene.*	341
BADEA..*German.*51, 99, 119,	286
BAIRD.. **French Tune,*	102
BALERMA..... *H. Wilson.*	297
BARBY ... *Wm. Tansur*	95
BARROW . .	338
BARTIMEUS...*Am. Melody.*	173
BARTOW	97
BATES .....*Dr. L. Mason.*	323
BAVARIA........ ..	406
BAYTON	398
BELGRAVE	368
BENEVENTO ......*Webbe.*	456
BERNE.	318
BERRY	276
BETHANY...*Dr. L. Mason.*	244
BETHESDA.....*Dr. Green.*	278
BILLOW ....*Dr. L. Mason.*	262
BONAR.......*Dr. L. Mason.* 160, 194, 315,	366
BOND...............	328
BONN.....	334
BOYLSTON...*Dr. L. Mason,* 177, 224, 237, 325,	341
BRADFORD ....*Handel.*	94
BRATTLE STREET.... *Pleyel.*	452
BREMEN.............82,	222

	PAGE
BRIGHTON...*Dr. L. Mason.*	374
BROOKLYN. 148, 327,	382
BROWN.. *Wm. B. Bradbury.*	159
BUTLER...............154,	170
BYRD............128, 190, 238,	370
CALISA.................	226
CAMBRIDGE......*Randall.*	296
CANAAN... *H. E. Mathews.*	458
CANONBURY............	356
CANTERBURY. *From Playford's Psalms,* 1671. .	294
CAVE..................	268
CEPHAS......*Dr. L. Mason.*	458
CHIMES.....*Dr. L. Mason.*	380
CHINA...............*Swan.*	312
CHRISTMAS.* *Old En. Carol.* 18, 112,	179
CHRISTMAS......*Handel.* 19,	35
CLARENDON ....*Tucker.*	281
CLAYTON	311
COME LET US ANEW. *Webbe.*	397
COME YE DISCONSOLATE....	158
CORINTH....*Dr. L. Mason.*	175
CORONATION .....*O. Holden.*	113
COWPER ....*Dr. L. Mason*	96
DALLAS.*........ ...261,	369
DALSTON .....*A. Williams*	46
DEDHAM...*Wm. Gardiner.*	39
DENFIELD.*......*Gliser.* 169, 187, 239,	410
DENNIS....**H. G. Nageli.*	253
DOVER.........*Unknown.*	375
DOWNS......*Dr. L. Mason.* 149, 229, 233, 363,	329
DUANE STREET.........	60
DUKE STREET..*J. Hatton.* 53,	83
DUNDEE ....*S. Psalter.* 76, 121, 307,	411
DUNFERMLINE... ...*Scotch Psalter.*	313
DURER	176
EFFIELD	156
EFFINGHAM............	92
ELAND	242
ELDEN	163
ELIM..*Dr. L. Mason.* 280,	302
ELIZABETHTOWN....*Greatorex.*............	316
ELL.............195,	287
ELLARD...............	259
ELLENTHORPE......*Linley.*	248

	PAGE
ELLIOT. ..*Dr. L. Mason.*	352
ELTHAM....*Dr. L. Mason.*	167
ELTON...............	188
ENEVA. ....*Dr. L. Mason.*	300
ERFURT. *Martin Luther.*	75
ERNAN....*Dr. L. Mason.* 114, 135, 184,	230
EVAN.......171, 317, 371,	399
FEDERAL STREET....*H. K. Oliver.*......308, 356,	389
FERRY............*Webbe.*	186
FIELD...............22,	315
FLEET STREET.........41,	62
FOLSOM.........**Mozart.*	79
FREDERICK.....*Kingsley.*	456
GANGES.....**Old Melody.*	47
GERAR......*Dr. L. Mason.*	253
GLYN............... 37,	284
GOLDEN HILL..*Amer. Mel.*	51
GOODWIN.*Geo J. Webb.*181,	357
GOSHEN ......*Old German,*	271
GRAFTON. ..*Dr. L. Mason.*	251
GRATITUDE ......*Bost*	134
GRETNA...............	86
GROVE..............20, 64,	90
GREENVILLE. *Rousseau.*85,	362
HADDAM....*Dr. L. Mason.*	49
HALLE .*Dr. Hastings.*.246,	373
HAMBURG....*Arr. Dr. L. Mason.*......213, 293,	336
HAMPDEN...**Dr.** *L. Mason.*	295
HARDY	55
HARWELL.*Dr. L. Mason.* 84,	392
HAVERHILL..*Dr. L. Mason.*	98
HEBER....*George Kingsley.*	221
HEBRON.....*Dr. L. Mason.* 42, 169, 225,	241
HENDON........*Dr. Malan.*	28
HERMON.*Dr. L. Mason.* 321,	358
HOLBEIN....*Wm. Mason.*	68
HORTON... *Von Wartensee.*	162
HOWARD....*Mrs. Cuthbert.*	84
HOXTON...............	300
HULL..............71,	78
INVERNESS..*Dr. L. Mason.*	340
IOSCO........*John Huss.*103,	197
IOWA......*American Tune.*	383
ITALIAN HYMN ...*Giardini*.144,	354
IVES. ....*E. Ives*	282
JAYNE.............192,	368

ALPHABETICAL INDEX OF TUNES. 471

	PAGE
KAME	59, 382
KELVIN	193
KENT	242
KITTO	394
KNIGHT	269
LABAN *Dr. L. Mason*	24, 107
LANDER	263
LANESBORO *Eu. Tune*	54
LANETON	396
LANSING	26, 72
LENOX *Edson*	25, 193
LEON *Dr. L. Mason*	143
LEWIN	390
LISBON *D. Read*	367
LISCHER *Dr. L. Mason*	198
LITCHFIELD *Dr. L. Mason*	333
LORAINE	191
LOUVAN *V. C. Taylor*	304
LOVING-KINDNESS	454
LYNCH	245
LYONS *Joseph Haydn*	58
LYTE	147, 292
MAITLAND *Amer. Tune.* 142, 158, 210	
MALVERN *Dr. L. Mason* 43, 254, 404	
MAMRE	234
MANOAH *Greatorex Coll.*	296
MARDEN	393
MAEX	393
MARLOW *Eng.* 125, 326, 326	
MARTYN *S. B. Marsh*	390
MARTYRS *Scotch Psalter*	343
MEAD	391
MEAR *Unknown*	347, 365
MEDFIELD *Wm. Mather*	267
MELODY *American Tune*	117
MENDON *Ger. Melody* 56, 61	
MERIBAH *Dr. L. Mason*	349
MIGNOL *Dr. L. Mason* 48, 168	
MINTON	289
MISSIONARY CHANT *C. Zenner*	305
MISSIONARY HYMN *Dr. L. Mason* 268, 378, 395	
MONMOUTH *Martin Luther, Original form*	403
MORNING *Spanish* 384, 391	
MORNING STAR *Dr. L. Mason*	457
MORNINGTON *Mornington* 119, 256, 273	
MOULTON *Dr. L. Mason*	256
MOUNT VERNON *Dr. L. Mason*	316
MURRAY *Dr. L. Mason*	24
NAOMI *Dr. L. Mason* 129, 191, 250, 306	
NASHVILLE *Old Ch. Mel.*	88
NAUL	268
NETTLETON	172
NEWCOURT *H. Bond*	59
NEW YORK TUNE *Scotch Tune* 73, 201, 211	
NILE	257
NILLEN	265

	PAGE
NILO	164
NOBLE	229
NOEL	59
NORMAN	145, 400
NORWICH *Dr. L. Mason* 264, 408	
NUREMBURG *Able,* 1673, 29, 151	
OAK *Dr. L. Mason*	245
OLDEN	224
OLD HUNDREDTH *Wm. Franc, Geneva Ps.,* 1545 17, 30, 82	
OLEAN	24, 217
OLIVET *Dr. L. Mason*	335
OLMUTZ *From Gregorian Chant,* 78, 273, 287, 299, 383	
OLNEY *Dr. L. Mason*	118
ONLAND	262
ORD	78
ORION	258
ORTONVILLE *Hastings,* 105, 133	
OTLEY	462
OTTO	214
OVIO *Dr. L. Mason*	218
PALESTINE *Muzzinghi.*	454
PALMER	44
PARK STREET *Vennet,* 52, 74	
PAUL	396
PEKIN *Wm. Mason*	252
PETERBORO *Webb* 183, 384	
PETERSBURGH *Russian,* 140, 205	
PHUVAH *Melchior Vulpius*	81, 359
PILESGROVE *N. Mitchell*	319
PLEYEL *J. Pleyel*	409
PORTUGUESE HYMN *Romish Melody*	273
PRESTON	108, 174, 266
RAYFORD	164
RANNER	196
REO *Dr. L. Mason*	455
RETREAT *Dr. T. Hastings*	288
ROCKINGHAM *Dr. L. Mason* 21, 65, 71	
ROCKVALE	402
ROSEDALE *G. F. Root,* 325, 377	
ROSEFIELD *From Dr. C. Melin,* 67, 187, 247, 372	
ROTHWELL *Wm. Tansur,* 57	
RUNDELL	256
RYLE	243
SABBATH *Dr. L. Mason*	136
SAVANNAH *Pleyel*	227
SCOTLAND *Dr. J. Clarke*	152
SEASONS *Pleyel*	115
SEIR *Dr. L. Mason*	177
SELVIN *Dr. L. Mason*	458
SEVEEN	285
SEYMOUR *Greatorex Coll.*	203
SHAWMUT *Dr. L. Mason*	195
SHERMAN *Amer. Tune.*	314
SHINING SHORE *G. F. Root*	262
SHIELAND *Stanley,* 194, 324	
SICILY *Italian*	285
SILOAM *Woodbury*	182
SILVER STREET *I. Smith*	375
SIVAN	75

	PAGE
STATE STREET *J. C. Woodman*	367
STEPHENS *W. Jones,* 1780, 27	
STONEFIELD *Stanley*	146
STOW *Dr. L. Mason*	138
ST. ANN'S *Dr. Wm. Croft*	175
ST. MARTINS *Tansur,* 1735, 45, 274, 384	
ST. MICHAEL *Day's Ps,* 164, 325	
ST. NICOLAI *Rosenmuller,*	126
ST. THOMAS *Williams,* 53, 181	
SWAINE	111
SWANWICK *Lucca,* 228	
TALLIS *Thos. Tallis,* 77, 385	
TALLIS' EVENING HYMN *Tallis*	49
TAPPAN *Kingsley*	346
TEMPLE	379
THATCHER *Handel's Sosarme*	331
THE OLD HUNDREDTH *W. Franc, Geneva Ps,* 1545 17, 30, 82	
THEON	131
TOPLADY *Dr. T. Hastings*	100
TULLY	180
TWEED *English,*	272
TYNG	394
ULM *Dr. L. Mason.*	337
UNWIN	322
URMUND *Dr. L. Mason.*	156
UXBRIDGE *Dr. L. Mason,* 86, 91, 249	
VITAL SPARK	412
WALES	157
WARD *Scotch,* 165, 231, 344, 405	
WARE	212
WARWICK *S. Stanley*	339
WATCHMAN *Leach.*	107
WAYNE	116, 220
WELLS *J. Holdroyd.*	93
WELT	350
WELTON *German.*	196
WHITE	283
WHYTE	122
WIMBORNE *Greatorex Coll.*	87
WINCHESTER *Dr. Croft.*	324
WINDHAM *D. Read,* 249, 255, 345	
WINDSOR *Scotch Ps,* 275, 291	
WINFIELD 66, 150	
WILMOT *Carl Von Weber,* 127, 166	
WILTZ	264
WISNER	353
WOODLAND *N. D. Gould*	364
WOODSTOCK *Geo. Dutton,* 215, 342	
WORTHING *Schultz,*	219
YOAKLEY *Yoakley,* 123, 216	
ZEBULON *Dr. L. Mason,* 63, 110, 139, 279	
ZEPHYR *Wm. B. Bradbury,* 141, 185	
ZETA	351
ZION *Dr. T. Hastings*	209

METRICAL INDEX OF TUNES.

L. M.

	PAGE
Albec, (6 lines)	309
All Saints	277
Anvern	388
Baird	102
Berne	318
Berry	276
Cephas, (8 lines)	433
Duane St.	64
Duke Street	53, 83
Effingham	92
Ellenthorpe	248
Erfurt	75
Ernan	114, 135, 184, 230
Federal Street	308, 376, 389
Gratitude	134
Grove, (8 lines)	20, 64, 99
Hamburg	213, 293, 336
Herron	42, 169, 225, 241
Hull	81, 70
Iosco	103, 197
Louvan	394
Loving Kindness	454
Lyte, (6 lines)	147, 292
Malvern	42, 254, 404
Mendon	56, 61
Migdol	48, 168
Minton	289
Missionary Chant	305
Nilo	161
Olden	224
Old Hundredth	17, 30, 82
Olean, (6 lines)	204, 217
Palestine, (6 lines)	454
Park Street	52, 74
Petersburgh, (6 lines)	140, 205
Pilesgrove	319
Retreat	258
Rockingham	21, 65, 71
Rosedale	325, 377
Rothwell	57
Seasons	115
Stonefield	146
Tallis' Evening Hymn	49
The Old Hundredth	17, 30, 82
Ulm	337
Uxbridge	86, 91, 249
Ward	165, 231, 344, 405
Ware	212
Wells	93
Welton	196
Whyte, (8 lines)	122
Wimborne	57
Winchester	324
Windham	240, 255, 345
Yoakley, (6 lines)	123, 216
Zephyr	141, 185

C. M.

	PAGE
Abridge	69
Alpheus	88, 120, 124
Antioch	260
Arlington	155, 207
Athens, (3 lines)	182
Avon	80, 292
Balerma	297
Barby	95
Barrow	338
Bartow	97
Bayton	398
Bond, (8 lines)	328
Bradford	94
Brattle Street, (8 lines)	452
Brooklyn, (8 lines)	148, 327, 332
Brown	159
Butler, (8 lines)	154, 170
Byrd, (8 lines)	128, 190, 238, 370
Cambridge	296
Canaan	458
Canterbury	290
Chimes	380
China	312
Christmas, (Handel's)	19, 85
Christmas, (old, 8 lines)	18, 112, 179
Clarendon	281
Corinth	175
Coronation	113
Cowper	96
Dedham	39
Denfield	109, 187, 239, 410
Downs	149, 229, 283, 303, 329
Dundee	76, 121, 307, 411
Dunfermline	313
Elim	280, 362
Elizabethtown	316
Evan	171, 317, 371, 399
Ferry	186
Grafton	251
Hardy	55
Heber	221
Hermon	321, 358
Holbein	68
Lanesboro'	54
Lansing, (8 lines)	26, 72
Leon	143
Litchfield	333
Maitland	142, 158, 219
Manoah	206
Marlow	125, 320, 326
Martyrs	343
Mear	347, 365
Medfield	267
Melody	117
Naomi	129, 191, 250, 306
New York Tune	73, 201, 211
Ortonville	105, 133
Otto	214
Palmer	44
Petersboro'	183, 381
Pinvah	81, 359
Preston	106, 174, 266
Rayford, (8 lines)	104
Reo	435
Siloam	1-2
Stephens	27
St. Ann's	178
St. Martin's	45, 274, 354
Swanwick	228
Tallis	77, 285
Tappan	346
Warwick	339
Wayne, (8 lines)	116, 220
Windsor	275, 291
Woodland	364
Woodstock	215, 342

S. M.

	PAGE
Athol	298
Aylesbury	341
Badea	51, 90, 119, 286
Bonar, (8 lines)	160, 194, 315, 366
Bonn	334
Boylston	177, 223, 237, 335, 341
Bremen, (8 lines)	32, 222
Brighton	374
Dennis	253
Dover	375
Durer	176
Ell	195, 287
Field	22, 315
Gerar	253
Golden Hill	51
Haverhill	98
Inverness	340
Iowa	383
Kane, (8 lines)	50, 383
Laban	23, 107
Lisbon	367
Mornington	119, 236, 273
Olmutz	28, 273, 287, 299, 383
Olney	118
Pekin	252
Rayner, (8 lines)	106
Seir	177
Selvin	458
Shawmut	195
Sherman	314
Shirland	133, 224
Silver Street	375
State Street	367
St. Michael	161, 338

	PAGE
St. Thomas	38, 131
Thatcher	331
Tilden	131
Tweed	272
Watchman	107

P. M.
Vital Spark	412

H. M.
Bethesda	278
Fleet Street	41, 62
Haddam	40
Lenox	25, 139
Lischer	128
Murray	34
Stow	138
Swaine	111
Zebulon	63, 110, 189, 279

L. P. M.
Nashville	88
Newcourt	59

C. P. M.
Athalone	348
Ariel	37
Ganges	47
Geetna	36
Meribah	349

C. H. M.
Rundell	256

S. P. M.
Dalston	46

S. H. M.
Moulton	256

5s & 8s.
Lewin	350

5s, 7s, 8 & 6.
Welt	350

5s & 6s, or 11s.
Bates	323

6s.
Nillen	265
Wiltz, (8 lines)	264

6s & 4s.
America	401
Amoy	310
Ava	243
Bethany	244
Eland	242
Italian Hymn	144, 354
Kent	242
Lynch	245
Norman	145, 400
Oak	245
Olivet	355

6s & 5s.
Glyn	284
Hale	243
Severn	285

6s & 7s.
Mamre	284

6s, 8s & 4s.
Clayton	311
Noel	59

	PAGE
6s & 10s.	
Naul	268
7s.	
Albon	151
Aston	387
Belgrave, (8 lines)	368
Benevento, (8 lines)	456
Dallas	261, 369
Elden, (6 lines)	163
Eltham, (8 lines)	167
Halle, (6 lines)	246, 373
Hendon	28
Horton	162
Ives, (8 lines)	282
Knight, (8 lines Double)	269
Loraine, (6 lines)	101
Martyn, (8 lines)	390
Morning, (8 lines)	386, 391
Morning Star, (8 lines)	457
Norwich	260, 408
Nuremburg	29, 151
Onland	202
Pleyel	409
Rosefield, (6 lines)	67, 187, 247, 372
Sabbath, (6 lines)	186
St. Nicolai, (8 lines)	126
Seymour	203
Toplady, (6 lines)	180
White, (8 lines)	283
Winfield	66, 150
Wilmot	127, 166

7s & 3.
Cave	268

7s & 5s.
Otley	402
Rockvale	402
Zeta	351

7s & 6s.
Abville	188
Amsterdam	364
Canonbury	356
Eneva	360
Goodwin	181, 357
Missionary Hymn, 2s, 373	95
Temple	379
Tully	180
Tyng	394

8s.
Adnal	189

8s & 4.
Effield	156
Elton	188
Unwin	322
Urmund	156
Wales	157

8s & 5s.
Kitto	301

8s & 6s.
Acton	260
Ellard	259
Elliot	322
Nile	257
Noble	259
Orion	258
Wisner	353

	PAGE
8s, 6s & 4s.	
Hoxton	300
8s, 6s, 5 & 4.	
Mead	301
8s & 6, or 8s & 4.	
Wisner	353
8s & 7s.	
Anley, (8 lines)	234
Bartimeus	173
Greenville, (8 lines)	85, 362
Harwell, (8 lines)	84, 392
Jaynes, (8 lines)	192, 361
Kelvin	193
Marx, (6 lines)	393
Monmouth	403
Mount Vernon	310
Nettleton, (8 lines)	172
Ovid	218
Shining Shore	262
Sicily	235
Worthing	219

8s, 7s & 4.
Alvan	294, 407
Billow, (Peculiar)	262
Bavaria	406
Hamden	295
Zion	209

9s & 6s.
Calbha	226

10s.
Savannah	227

10s & 4.
Marden	393

10s, 5, 6 & 12s.
Come let us anew	397

10s & 6s.
Laneton	396

10s & 11s, or 5s & 6s.
Lyons	58

10s, 11 & 12.
Paul	396

11s.
Goshen	271
Portuguese Hymn	270
Frederick	456

11s & 8s.
Ord	78
Sivan	78

11s & 10s.
Come ye Disconsolate	153
Folsom	79

11s & 12s.
Lander	263

12s.
Scotland	152

INDEX

FOR THE IMMEDIATE FINDING OF ANY HYMN BY ITS NUMBER.

This Index does away with the necessity for the Minister's stating the page of the Hymn and Tune Book.

Hymn	Page	Hymn	Page	Hymn	Page	Hymn	Page	Hymn	Page	Hymn	Page	Hymn	Page
1	358	41	274	81	28	121	46	161	330	201	210	241	103
2	176	42	292	82	376	122	274	162	176	202	312	242	191
3	323	43	38	83	70	123	86	163	43	203	130	243	178
4	370	44	54	84	388	124	80	164	388	204	92	244	100
5	319	45	42	85	387	125	57	165	75	205	220	245	81
6	277	46	115	86	407	126	19	166	64	206	202	246	33
7	66	47	309	87	49	127	358	167	19	207	386	247	178
8	146	48	49	88	294	128	65	168	40	208	324	248	87
9	388	49	22	89	292	129	30	169	214	209	52	249	193
10	147	50	269	90	82	130	76	170	44	210	94	250	83
11	20	51	389	91	363	131	76	171	383	211	370	251	87
12	22	52	19	92	172	132	18	172	359	212	371	252	92
13	18	53	22	93	387	133	86	173	28	213	359	253	217
14	52	54	24	94	380	134	240	174	389	214	190	254	304
15	52	55	136	95	182	135	274	175	31	215	280	255	106
16	111	56	36	96	30	136	307	176	138	216	359	256	200
17	68	57	227	97	41	137	51	177	73	217	160	257	296
18	38	58	24	98	66	138	280	178	116	218	371	258	116
19	50	59	44	99	84	139	68	179	65	219	309	259	44
20	38	60	34	100	30	140	388	180	270	220	313	260	348
21	42	61	288	101	172	141	182	181	86	221	88	261	28
22	22	62	241	102	33	142	274	182	75	222	370	262	200
23	34	63	144	103	30	143	76	183	117	223	32	263	114
24	387	64	214	104	150	144	337	184	80	224	32	264	269
25	282	65	49	105	150	145	31	185	336	225	91	265	193
26	46	66	114	106	372	146	290	186	359	226	384	266	79
27	26	67	358	107	88	147	69	187	70	227	28	267	200
28	142	68	42	108	166	148	73	188	41	228	126	268	112
29	32	69	234	109	48	149	322	189	83	229	199	269	218
30	53	70	392	110	47	150	124	190	197	230	178	270	391
31	17	71	42	111	48	151	193	191	78	231	126	271	111
32	17	72	340	112	65	152	72	192	90	232	338	272	221
33	53	73	303	113	107	153	62	193	168	233	231	273	62
34	17	74	20	114	24	154	48	194	138	234	336	274	117
35	78	75	289	115	58	155	307	195	68	235	302	275	91
36	374	76	202	116	59	156	76	196	18	236	80	276	391
37	53	77	307	117	36	157	48	197	298	237	241	277	200
38	72	78	278	118	26	158	69	198	241	238	103	278	29
39	400	79	376	119	90	159	75	199	76	239	208	279	132
40	26	80	358	120	25	160	49	200	403	240	142	280	184

INDEX TO HYMNS AND PAGES.

Hymn	Page	Hymn	Page	Hymn	Page	Hymn	Page	Hymn	Page	Hymn	Page	Hymn	Page
281	380	334	54	387	201	440	25	493	275	546	260	599	286
282	108	335	123	388	364	441	116	494	380	547	404	600	250
283	146	336	115	389	228	442	203	495	348	548	255	601	240
284	302	337	201	390	112	443	351	496	340	549	275	602	306
285	114	338	112	391	63	444	160	497	213	550	314	603	349
286	286	339	74	392	126	445	38	498	344	551	194	604	408
287	179	340	144	393	57	446	118	499	286	552	182	605	115
288	371	341	144	394	84	447	148	500	320	553	140	606	254
289	146	342	376	395	142	448	176	501	293	554	348	607	298
290	163	343	40	396	202	449	206	502	216	555	236	608	329
291	163	344	59	397	203	450	260	503	118	556	318	609	54
292	224	345	400	398	386	451	354	504	184	557	275	610	128
293	356	346	27	399	234	452	272	505	108	558	148	611	251
294	148	347	82	400	407	453	168	506	118	559	352	612	260
295	234	348	168	401	23	454	135	507	118	560	174	613	251
296	393	349	58	402	102	455	364	508	384	561	363	614	165
297	294	350	81	403	252	456	351	509	170	562	174	615	240
298	224	351	60	404	350	457	66	510	252	563	340	616	175
299	130	352	98	405	184	458	67	511	123	564	225	617	329
300	96	353	166	406	105	459	184	512	364	565	170	618	342
301	96	354	127	407	301	460	108	513	260	566	135	619	336
302	141	355	374	408	368	461	344	514	203	567	286	620	251
303	313	356	138	409	368	462	187	515	310	568	174	621	343
304	332	357	110	410	368	463	135	516	272	569	243	622	341
305	280	358	230	411	196	464	346	517	295	570	235	623	261
306	376	359	128	412	309	465	276	518	295	571	248	624	246
307	120	360	166	413	290	466	156	519	100	572	331	625	287
308	98	361	123	414	204	467	123	520	100	573	350	626	228
309	117	362	64	415	167	468	81	521	152	574	378	627	190
310	337	363	201	416	202	469	21	522	323	575	278	628	230
311	303	364	65	417	304	470	408	523	199	576	250	629	281
312	98	365	124	418	284	471	318	524	278	577	338	630	342
313	174	366	124	419	193	472	368	525	114	578	360	631	216
314	227	367	226	420	182	473	82	526	340	579	250	632	246
315	311	368	94	421	192	474	145	527	367	580	291	633	254
316	293	369	73	422	56	475	137	528	386	581	213	634	298
317	173	370	120	423	351	476	145	529	39	582	168	635	364
318	62	371	218	424	214	477	63	530	318	583	175	636	107
319	93	372	242	425	372	478	281	531	225	584	344	637	290
320	302	373	352	426	219	479	91	532	352	585	143	638	232
321	102	374	230	427	242	480	92	533	119	586	235	639	369
322	124	375	230	428	122	481	330	534	162	587	175	640	392
323	210	376	63	429	94	482	330	535	330	588	67	641	132
324	104	377	372	430	56	483	34	536	294	589	261	642	281
325	87	378	27	431	122	484	88	537	150	590	404	643	69
326	357	379	113	432	339	485	68	538	188	591	250	644	228
327	34	380	166	433	37	486	19	539	260	592	408	645	231
328	105	381	87	434	140	487	228	540	336	593	230	646	165
329	198	382	166	435	95	488	214	541	164	594	345	647	397
330	379	383	94	436	142	489	364	542	243	595	345	648	173
331	106	384	301	437	292	490	182	543	320	596	345	649	218
332	40	385	92	438	192	491	390	544	164	597	328	650	77
333	54	386	392	439	95	492	344	545	246	598	337	651	238

INDEX TO HYMNS AND PAGES.

Hymn	Page	Hymn	Page	Hymn	Page	Hymn	Page	Hymn	Page	Hymn	Page	Hymn	Page
652	185	705	128	758	384	811	293	864	289	917	217	970	104
653	179	706	121	759	234	812	109	865	365	918	273	971	113
654	95	707	339	760	217	813	410	866	248	919	266	972	378
655	343	708	405	761	129	814	143	867	363	920	109	973	157
656	298	709	150	762	331	815	60	868	204	921	277	974	333
657	66	710	66	763	154	816	288	869	149	922	151	975	231
658	175	711	247	764	101	817	236	870	211	923	293	976	215
659	235	712	251	765	303	818	207	871	211	924	39	977	222
660	149	713	212	766	237	819	410	872	199	925	265	978	266
661	334	714	373	767	224	820	238	873	211	926	191	979	158
662	217	715	373	768	134	821	186	874	369	927	332	980	392
663	265	716	93	769	161	822	225	875	171	928	255	981	283
664	185	717	170	770	232	823	205	876	334	929	322	982	271
665	149	718	318	771	353	824	86	877	259	930	71	983	115
666	406	719	93	772	295	825	45	878	57	931	353	984	212
667	343	720	354	773	223	826	229	879	57	932	236	985	328
668	55	721	101	774	342	827	238	880	35	933	245	986	277
669	77	722	355	775	98	828	169	881	367	934	333	987	264
670	405	723	147	776	409	829	134	882	45	935	380	988	292
671	299	724	213	777	404	830	141	883	211	936	264	989	244
672	110	725	349	778	237	831	334	884	394	937	257	990	173
673	180	726	196	779	339	832	164	885	27	938	351	991	285
674	55	727	240	780	197	833	150	886	248	939	320	992	384
675	160	728	360	781	319	834	410	887	77	940	300	993	396
676	161	729	102	782	270	835	67	888	186	941	162	994	162
677	219	730	196	783	212	836	67	889	74	942	279	995	186
678	185	731	102	784	222	837	164	890	74	943	155	996	186
679	285	732	206	785	134	838	261	891	283	944	229	997	192
680	382	733	237	786	253	839	225	892	374	945	259	998	252
681	374	734	404	787	206	840	410	893	106	946	276	999	346
682	128	735	60	788	324	841	409	894	208	947	129	1000	346
683	204	736	149	789	108	842	180	895	156	948	277	1001	191
684	96	737	268	790	176	843	224	896	283	949	377	1002	223
685	154	738	134	791	121	844	353	897	402	950	264	1003	319
686	185	739	288	792	109	845	289	898	375	951	221	1004	139
687	120	740	247	793	109	846	191	899	47	952	153	1005	249
688	100	741	247	794	155	847	143	900	139	953	406	1006	271
689	338	742	362	795	155	848	287	901	74	954	320	1007	162
690	130	743	168	796	263	849	349	902	394	955	213	1008	249
691	325	744	206	797	35	850	365	903	158	956	75	1009	147
692	332	745	362	798	56	851	132	904	265	957	136	1010	325
693	390	746	379	799	44	852	105	905	221	958	296	1011	85
694	140	747	154	800	155	853	248	906	266	959	220	1012	328
695	232	748	342	801	158	854	130	907	252	960	194	1013	326
696	338	749	304	802	205	855	319	908	408	961	43	1014	375
697	120	750	141	803	334	856	326	909	137	962	305	1015	215
698	220	751	171	804	265	857	194	910	409	963	133	1016	35
699	197	752	141	805	158	858	221	911	207	964	172	1017	223
700	143	753	161	806	241	859	158	912	207	965	203	1018	61
701	206	754	125	807	232	860	46	913	132	966	172	1019	366
702	186	755	289	808	136	861	252	914	266	967	84	1020	405
703	36	756	248	809	121	862	207	915	272	968	33	1021	212
704	216	757	256	810	389	863	134	916	272	969	171	1022	393

INDEX TO HYMNS AND PAGES.

Hymn	Page	Hymn	Page	Hymn	Page	Hymn	Page	Hymn	Page	Hymn	Page	Hymn	Page	Hymn	Page
1023	239	1062	50	1101	187	1139	405	1177	188	1215	324	1253	276
1024	56	1063	82	1102	218	1140	411	1178	314	1216	308	1254	276
1025	23	1064	169	1103	133	1141	411	1179	369	1217	365	1255	55
1026	61	1065	165	1104	82	1142	127	1180	317	1218	153	1256	267
1027	54	1066	18	1105	83	1143	167	1181	147	1219	312	1257	267
1028	35	1067	135	1106	215	1144	258	1182	300	1220	366	1258	231
1029	61	1068	169	1107	231	1145	204	1183	377	1221	407	1259	245
1030	79	1069	387	1108	253	1146	29	1184	235	1222	407	1260	215
1031	239	1070	381	1109	152	1147	273	1185	321	1223	305	1261	189
1032	385	1071	85	1110	83	1148	399	1186	254	1224	244	1262	284
1033	198	1072	376	1111	401	1149	112	1187	255	1225	131	1263	222
1034	72	1073	45	1112	257	1150	125	1188	189	1226	173	1264	151
1035	115	1074	198	1113	71	1151	43	1189	412	1227	377	1265	267
1036	61	1075	125	1114	391	1152	205	1190	326	1228	262	1266	297
1037	61	1076	29	1115	31	1153	159	1191	116	1229	381	1267	146
1038	346	1077	398	1116	45	1154	37	1192	308	1230	357	1268	127
1039	181	1078	159	1117	103	1155	401	1193	308	1231	97	1269	382
1040	402	1079	159	1118	233	1156	31	1194	308	1232	99	1270	195
1041	325	1080	398	1119	362	1157	233	1195	305	1233	239	1271	315
1042	391	1081	398	1120	401	1158	201	1196	317	1234	296	1272	89
1043	410	1082	398	1121	303	1159	390	1197	321	1235	21	1273	347
1044	409	1083	399	1122	103	1160	341	1198	322	1236	296	1274	99
1045	411	1084	354	1123	70	1161	397	1199	327	1237	382	1275	347
1046	411	1085	71	1124	377	1162	357	1200	292	1238	361	1276	313
1047	411	1086	405	1125	82	1163	129	1201	317	1239	239	1277	205
1048	406	1087	39	1126	229	1164	306	1202	355	1240	327	1278	291
1049	361	1088	159	1127	209	1165	316	1203	279	1241	97	1279	299
1050	329	1089	104	1128	51	1166	255	1204	279	1242	93	1280	291
1051	203	1090	125	1129	304	1167	361	1205	306	1243	381	1281	362
1052	101	1091	183	1130	167	1168	288	1206	133	1244	324	1282	89
1053	183	1092	110	1131	161	1169	314	1207	314	1245	97	1283	254
1054	183	1093	335	1132	395	1170	229	1208	267	1246	346	1284	403
1055	233	1094	190	1133	395	1171	316	1209	310	1247	99	1285	70
1056	316	1095	239	1134	210	1172	306	1210	312	1248	282	1286	209
1057	316	1096	239	1135	249	1173	321	1211	177	1249	282	1287	294
1058	71	1097	326	1136	305	1174	321	1212	317	1250	297	1288	299
1059	169	1098	339	1137	378	1175	157	1213	310	1251	347	1289	255
1060	383	1099	399	1138	400	1176	323	1214	256	1252	385	1290	403
1061	381	1100	187											

The SABBATH HYMN BOOK is printed in two sizes; first, the small quarto edition, bound in three styles, in cloth, in sheep, and in morocco; second, the 16mo. edition, in large type, and bound in five styles, in sheep, in morocco, in morocco gilt edge, in Turkey morocco, and in Turkey morocco antique. The SABBATH HYMN AND TUNE BOOK is printed in two sizes: first, the 16mo. edition, bound in four styles, in cloth, in morocco, in morocco gilt edge, and in Turkey morocco; second, the octavo edition, in large type, bound in four styles, in cloth, in morocco, in morocco gilt edge, and in Turkey morocco. The SABBATH TUNE BOOK, containing the tunes alone of the above work, in cloth binding. The NEW SABBATH HYMN AND TUNE BOOK is printed in two sizes: first, the 16mo. edition, bound in four styles, in cloth, in morocco, in morocco gilt edge, and in Turkey morocco; second, the octavo edition, bound in four styles, in cloth, in morocco, in morocco gilt edges, and in Turkey morocco. Editions of all of the above, prepared for the use of Baptist Churches by Dr. Wayland, are also published.

www.ingramcontent.com/pod-product-compliance
Lightning Source LLC
Chambersburg PA
CBHW051856300426
44117CB00006B/422